LYNDON

Also by Merle Miller

LYNDON

AN ORAL BIOGRAPHY

MERLE MILLER

G. P. PUTNAM'S SONS
NEW YORK

The author gratefully acknowledges permission from the following to reprint material in
this book:

Afro-American Life and History, Inc., for material from an article "Lyndon Johnson and
Blacks: The Early Years," by Monroe Billington, which appeared in the January 1977
issue of *The Journal of Negro History*, copyright © 1977 by Afro-American Life and
History, Inc.

Alkatraz Corner Music, BMI, for lines from "I Feel Like I'm Fixin' to Die Rag," by Joe
McDonald, © 1965 by Joe McDonald.

Horace Busby for "LBJ Toward the End: Getting Things in Order," copyright © 1973 by
Horace Busby. L. A. Times, publishers.

Bill Davidson for "Lyndon Johnson: Can a Southerner Be Elected President?" copyright
© 1959 by Bill Davidson. *Look* Magazine article; published by Cowles Broadcasting,
Inc.

Doubleday & Company, Inc., for material from *Education of a Public Man* by Hubert
Humphrey, copyright © 1976 by Hubert H. Humphrey.

Foreign Affairs for "One Thing We Learned," by Bill D. Moyers, copyright © 1968 by
Council on Foreign Relations, Inc.

Harper's Magazine Company for "LBJ's Rambunctious Retirement," by Mary Hardesty.
Reprinted from the January 24, 1975, issue of *Harper's Weekly*, copyright © 1975 by
Harper's Magazine Company.

Harper & Row, Publishers, for material from *The Mission* by Martin Caidin and Edward
Hymoff, published by J. B. Lippincott Company, copyright © 1964 by Martin Caidin
and Edward Hymoff.

Holt, Rinehart & Winston for material from *A White House Diary* by Lady Bird
Johnson, copyright © 1970 by Claudia T. Johnson.

Holt, Rinehart & Winston for material from *The Vantage Point* by Lyndon Baines
Johnson, copyright © 1971 by HEC Public Affairs Foundation.

Leo Janos for "The Last Days of the President," copyright © 1973 by Leo Janos,
published by The Atlantic Monthly.

The New York Times for an article by Tom Wicker, copyright © 1965 by The New York
    Times Company.
The Saturday Evening Post for "Lyndon Johnson: How Does He Do It?" by Stewart
    Alsop, copyright © 1959 by The Curtis Publishing Company.
Texas Monthly for "Farewell to LBJ: A Hill Country Valediction" by Bill Porterfield,
    copyright © 1973 by Mediatex Communications Corp.
Time, Inc., for "One More Call to Reason Together" by Hugh Sidey, *Life* copyright ©
    1972 by Time, Inc.
United Artists Music Co., Inc., for lines from "Lyndon Johnson Told the Nation" by
    Tom Paxton, © 1965, 1968 by United Artists Music Co., Inc.
Waco Tribune-Herald for material by Harry Provence, "Thousands Fill Capitol to Bid
    Lyndon Farewell," © 1973 by Waco Tribune-Herald.
The Wall Street Journal for "The Johnson Wealth" by Louis Kohlmeier, copyright ©
    1964 by Dow Jones & Company, Inc.
The Washington Post for "The Real LBJ" by Haynes Johnson, copyright © 1973 by The
    Washington Post; and for "Recollections" by Haynes Johnson. Reprinted from January
    24, 1973, *Washington Post*, copyright © 1973 by The Washington Post.
The Washington Star for an article by Isabelle Shelton in September, 1972, copyright ©
    1972 by The Washington Star Co.

Library of Congress Cataloging in Publication Data

Miller, Merle, date.
    Lyndon, an oral biography.

    Bibliography: p.
    Includes index.
    1. Johnson, Lyndon Baines, Pres. U.S., 1908-
1973. 2. Presidents—United States—Biography.
I. Title.
E847.M54   1980   973.923′092′4 [B]
ISBN 0-399-12357-1   80-273
ISBN 0-399-12497-7 boxed

PRINTED IN THE UNITED STATES OF AMERICA

For my friends David and Carol

Contents

5 The Creek Is Rising

6 The Winter of LBJ

LYNDON

INTRODUCTION

Oral History is a relatively new way of dealing with the men and women and the events of the recent past. It's a particularly good way of dealing with someone like Lyndon Johnson, who almost never stopped talking himself, and about whom an extraordinary number of people had a great deal to say. I first heard of Oral History thirty years ago when a group of scholars at Columbia University, chief among them the historian Allan Nevins, decided that a collection of taped interviews with people who had memories of that past and of the people who shaped it would be a valuable addition to the historical record.

I did not read an Oral biography until 1969 when I first encountered T. Harry Williams' biography of a man much admired by Lyndon Johnson, Huey Long, the Louisiana governor and senator. Long's motto was, "Every man a king," and President Franklin Roosevelt was afraid of him and of his possible strength in the 1936 presidential election in which Long said he would be a candidate. But he was shot and fatally wounded in Baton Rouge, Louisiana, in September 1935. Dr. Williams, a professor of history at Louisiana State University in Baton Rouge, wrote that witnesses remembered Long's last words as being, "God, don't let me die. I have so much to do." How like Lyndon Johnson.

In the Preface of *Huey Long*, Dr. Williams stated, "I believe that some men, men of power, can influence the course of history. They appear in response to conditions, but they may alter conditions, may give a new direction to history. In the process they may do great good or evil or both, but whatever the case they leave a different kind of world behind them. Their accomplishment should be recognized. I believe that Huey Long was this kind of man."

Dr. Williams thought that Lyndon Johnson was "this kind of man," and at the time of his death in 1978 he was working on an Oral History of Johnson. We talked to many of the same people.

Another pioneer in the field of Oral History was the esteemed, certainly by me, Studs Terkel of Chicago, whose Oral History, *Division Street: America* was published in 1967.

In it seventy people talked not only about Chicago but about American life everywhere. In 1970 Terkel published the immensely popular *Hard Times, An Oral History of the Great Depression*, and more recently there was *Working, People Talk About What They Do All Day and How They Feel About What They Do.*

One reason I have felt a particular affinity for Studs is that, like me, he appears to have no mechanical aptitude, none, and when his tape recorder broke down, as tape recorders not infrequently do, he swore at it and, like me, on occasion kicked it. Also like me, Terkel has never been able to drive a car, ride a bicycle, roller-skate, swim or dance.

Reluctant tape recorders are not the only problem with Oral History. There is the interview itself and the preparation for it. Some Oral Historians at the Lyndon Baines Johnson Library in Austin say that the proper preparation for an interview takes a minimum of three days. One has to know as much as possible about the subject involved and about the interviewee's relation to it and, in this case, to Lyndon Johnson. And one has to ask the right questions, listen carefully to the answer and, equally important, *hear* the answer. Hearing is not always easy because the interviewer is at the same time phrasing in his mind the next question—and, of course, keeping the capricious tape recorder in order.

There is an Oral History story, no doubt apocryphal, about an Oral Historian interviewing Alice Roosevelt Longworth. Mrs. Longworth was saying, "And, of course, on Tuesday afternoon we all had to leave the White House while my father entertained his mistress."

Oral Historian: "Mrs. Longworth, we were discussing the Panama Canal. I wonder if you could clear up your father's views on the building of locks on the canal."

I tell you, you've got to hear.

This book was more than five years in the making. It involved thirty-nine trips to Washington, D.C., trips to New York, Chicago, and numerous cities and towns in Texas, Georgia, and California. There were 180 personal interviews; researchers conducted several more; two Texas historians, Ted Gittinger and Gary Gallagher, were particularly useful. I interviewed many people several times. With David W. Elliott's assistance, some 276 Oral Histories at the Lyndon Baines Johnson Library were consulted as well as nine others in an Interior Department Oral History Project at Johnson City; eighty-nine at the John F. Kennedy Library, and several (see bibliography) at other presidential libraries. Material at the Franklin D. Roosevelt Library in Hyde Park, N.Y., was especially helpful.

Lady Bird Johnson proved enormously helpful in opening a great many doors that previously had been closed; she opened many of them without mentioning it to me and never once asked to see any part of my work.

It was a long journey, exploring the history of Lyndon Johnson; it was like exploring a continent, maybe two continents and a couple of ocean beds as well.

He was—is—without doubt one of the most complex, fascinating, difficult, colorful personages in American history. There may have been other Presidents like Johnson in American history. Andrew Jackson comes readily to mind, but he was a simple man by comparison. I don't think we've ever seen the likes of Lyndon Johnson before, and I doubt we will ever again.

PROLOGUE

Harry McPherson: "Lyndon Johnson was a true sophisticate. I know that's what most people think he wasn't, but they are wrong. He was an enormously sophisticated man about life, about what makes things happen, what causes people to do what they do."

Wilber J. Cohen: "Psychiatrists would say that your personality is always internally consistent, but I found Lyndon Johnson was a man of such tremendously different kinds of characteristics that it's difficult, perhaps impossible, to grasp all of his personalities.

"I went down to the Ranch with John Gardner—this was in 1966 or 1967—and after we finished our business we went out and rode around the Ranch. He started to tell us in the most vulgar kind of language about the breeding of cattle, referring to all sorts of sexual characteristics of the animals and of people. How you bred cattle, and so on. I knew nothing about cattle, so I just listened. But it was vulgar.

"About an hour later as the sun went down, we reached a hill and he stopped the car. We watched the sunset over the mountains, and he started talking what was really pure poetry—about the land, about the Hill Country, about the sun, about the seasons, about his hopes and aspirations for people. Pure poetry.

"Now, there within one hour was a man being three different things. First, he dealt with our business problems, the president of the United States dealing with matters of momentous national policy on an executive planning basis. Then he was a small-time cattle breeder in the way any two-bit farmer is who wants to get better cows or calves. And then, a half hour later, the same man was talking in the most emotional terms about the earth and the world and the incomprehensibilities of life. He was like a combination of Boccaccio and Machiavelli and John Keats.

"When I went away I said to myself, 'This man is larger than life.' He simply does not fit into any pattern. You can see a man being *one* of those things, two of those things even, but to see within an hour one man being *three* of them, you know you're in the presence of a great diversity, great flexibility, great competence, because of the range of his sensibilities. I think Johnson, as he experienced these different things, realized that he was an actor on a big stage. I have that feeling. The reason I feel that way is that while he was doing it, all of a sudden he would take that role as if in the way when you're eating something you really like, you smack your lips and say it's great. Or a wine you truly enjoy. I felt he understood that nature had given him this element of being able to do what he did and that he had maximized it in his role as president, which few people have the opportunity to do. But he did it brilliantly."

John B. Connally: "There is no adjective in the dictionary to describe him. He was cruel and kind, generous and greedy, sensitive and insensitive, crafty and naïve, ruthless and thoughtful, simple in many ways yet extremely complex, caring and totally not caring; he could overwhelm people with kindness and turn around and be cruel and petty towards those same people; he knew how to use people in politics in the way nobody else could that I know of. As a matter of fact it would take *every* adjective in the dictionary to describe him."

Adrian Spears: "When my daughter was in college she worked in Senator Johnson's office one summer. And she was just amazed at the work these people did for him, the hours they kept, the dedication they had to him, the loyalty. And I know that a lot of senators were going around shaking their heads saying, 'How in the world does he do it? They work for him for half of what I have to pay and he gets the same amount of money allocated to him.' But he could just get more people to do the work for him for less pay."

Willie Day Taylor: "When he said, 'Go,' it didn't matter when it was; you went."

J. Russell Wiggins: "Johnson was an expert on the art of the possible. He sensed more quickly than anyone else what could be done and, without losing sight of the ultimate objective, was interested in making some progress. Whenever he did this, he got a deluge of abuse from ideologues who wanted to get everything, heaven before breakfast, and Johnson was too practical to be for heaven before breakfast."

Richard Neustadt: "Mr. Johnson had a fine eye for the human vulnerabilities of people he was working with and looked for that soft spot and then turned the knife in it as a means of attaching people more securely. There may have been also a streak of cruelty in him like the Roosevelt streak, of just liking to pull the wings off flies."

Hubert H. Humphrey: "It is true that Johnson could be very rough. He didn't spend a lot of time trying to figure out whether he was going to hurt your feelings, but after he got you all bruised up, he put his arms around you and gave you a bear hug and told you that you were the greatest man that ever lived. And he'd get you almost to believe it for half an hour or so.

"Just keep in mind that he had all the weaknesses and strengths of a big man. He loved women; he loved to take a drink; he loved a good earthy story; he understood politics and power. He was a patriarch of absolutely unbelievable dimensions. He wanted to do good. He was a soft-hearted guy with all the big veneer.

"He really was interested in poor people, truly interested. And he never was able to project that as sincerely as I knew it to be. He never did forget those days when he taught school to those Mexican-American kids. He never forgot about it. He romanticized it a lot, that I know. And people thought he just used that, but that wasn't true.

"He was an All-American president. He was really the history of this country, with all of the turmoil, the bombast, the sentiments, the passions. It was all there. All in one man.

"Now of course you have to understand that above all he was a man steeped in politics. Politics was not an avocation with him. It was it. It was *the* vocation. It was his life, it was his religion, it was his family, it was his social and economic life; it was his totality. And he gave himself to it, absorbed it. He was a phenomenon. And if you liked politics, it was like being at the feet of a giant. Because it just poured out of him. Every time you saw him it wasn't like seeing a man; it was like seeing an institution, a whole system that just encompassed you. Johnson thought he could pick up the globe and walk off with it."

George W. Ball: "He was a strong, strong man with a great intellectual capacity. The thing about Johnson that always impressed me most was that in the quiet times he would lean back and really talk about his vision for the United States.

"This was a man who had been a poor boy and who felt he hadn't had the education he should have had. He was going to have a United States that would let everybody have a chance at an education, and not know the poverty he had known."

Harrison Salisbury: "I suppose everyone has his own theory as to why Lyndon was so persuasive so much of the time. My theory comes from my experiences in Russia. If you've ever been to the theater in Russia, you find that every actor is bigger than life. He shouts louder than you expect him to; his gestures are more broad; everything is that much bigger.

"At first I couldn't understand it because Russians are good actors. And then suddenly I realized that everything in Russia is like that. The ordinary Russian shouts more than we do. He uses stronger language. He makes a drama out of a little street scene—an argument with a policeman or something like that. So if you're going to have a drama on stage it has to go up another several decibels.

"Now I think Lyndon was a little like that, a little like the Russians, making a drama out of small street scenes. He was an actor, and everything was a little larger than life to him because he was larger than life, and not just physically. A lot of what he was may have to do with his being a Texan. In general they seem to come on a little stronger than anyone else. But Lyndon was stronger than most Texans, and I imagine that is one of the reasons he was so effective."

Bill Moyers: "Johnson had an uncanny ability to see himself as if he were an actor and a spectator at the same time. And he had this double layer—bifocal vision in a sense. He could be acting and yet, while he was performing, he was existentially involved in the moment—he always was outside the process looking at himself. This was a flaw at times, and I think helped to bring him down.

"Since Johnson studied too much his effect on the audience of which he was artificially a member, he was on stage, he was in the act; he was in the drama and he worried too much about how he was appearing."

George E. Reedy: "Every time I think of Johnson, the first thought that springs into my head is Pirandello. Pirandello is a playwright who would leave you with the most baffled wonderment as to whether the whole thing was a figment of somebody's imagination; whether this man really was a king, or whether he was just a demented lunatic that was surrounded by some others. Johnson would leave you like that."

Elizabeth Goldschmidt: "With the physique he had plus his acting ability he could be a terrible bully. He would shake his hand under your nose, stride up and down, raise his arms. He knew exactly what he was doing.

"And he also had a tremendous capacity for concentration. Everyone was amazed at how much Johnson knew, say, about the details of the federal budget. He could just reel off statistics and facts that he had absorbed and all those controversial laws that he dealt with. He knew backward and forward not only what was in them but what the issues were, who was on what side. He had an encyclopedic memory, like an elephant."

Sam Houston Johnson: "A lot of people never knew Lyndon had a sense of humor, but he did. He was always telling stories, and the stories always had a point.

"Our father was a good imitator and storyteller, just like Lyndon. Maybe that's where he got it from. Lyndon could screw up his mouth and sound just like Eisenhower and even Dean Acheson. You wouldn't think that was possible, Acheson being a fancy-panter from way back, but they were friends, and Lyndon could imitate him till you couldn't tell them apart. He could even imitate Acheson saying the word *fuck*, and I tell you that wasn't easy.

"He could mimic old Eisenhower; he liked Eisenhower, but a lot of the time he didn't think Ike'd done his homework when he was president. He could even imitate Roosevelt, making his voice sound just like Franklin's. But of course he never made fun of Roosevelt. Not to my knowledge."

Marianne Means: "He was always on, always manipulating, never happy without some kind of human exchange or confrontation. It was more than a performance, because you felt that he was reliving an experience. I mean, that he was involved in it. He wasn't just repeating something.

"But he was primarily an actor, and a good one, with all the requisite body gestures and facial expressions, and he gave a real performance, especially with his stories about the Hill Country people and about his childhood. He was reliving it, and sometimes his imagination heightened and exaggerated his stories—that was how he got this reputation of lying."

Hugh Sidey: "My whole experience as a journalist was that Johnson was outrageous in some of the devices he used. He would lie, beg, cheat, steal a little, threaten, intimidate, but he never lost sight of that ultimate goal, and he never violated the law, to the best of my knowledge, to achieve it. He would never have clapped reporters in jail or do the things Nixon did in his White House. He'd go up to the edge, but he respected the system. In his personal maneuvering—goddamn, he was a wild man."

Tom Johnson: "All of the people who came in contact with Lyndon Johnson—his family, his friends, his political associates, the members of the White House staff—each of them has his or her slice of Lyndon Johnson. Now some of the slices are larger than others. Bill Moyers's slice is a very large slice. Mrs. Johnson's slice is surely the largest.

"But nobody has ever put all of the slices together. The things that have been written about him, all of them are very limited, taking in a very small slice. What has to be done is to put all the slices of the pie together. If it can be done."

1

Young Lyndon

A STORMY ARRIVAL

Aunt Jessie Hatcher: "The night that Lyndon came, why, we had the biggest storm we ever had, and couldn't get a doctor. And that was the beginning."

Lyndon was born in the west room of the farmhouse by the Pedernales (pronounced Purd'n Alice) in the Texas Hill Country at, or so his mother Rebekah recorded later,[1] the auspicious hour of daybreak. Rebekah liked such omens of divine approval. The baby, Rebekah also recorded, was a "large, perfectly formed child" weighing, in an age of considerable guesswork in that regard, eleven pounds.

Rebekah's mother was there to help, as was Aunt Kate on the father's side. The father himself, Sam Ealy, Jr., was—no one bothered to record where. Perhaps in the east room. In any case it was the grandfather, Sam Ealy, Sr., "Big Sam" as he was called, who went for the midwife. As Aunt Jessie later described it:

"The doctor was twenty miles away, and he couldn't get across the river anyhow. The Pedernales was on the biggest rise it ever had been.[2] My father had to go up a half mile above the crossing in order to get through at the crossing, across the river. He went and got this Mrs. Lindig, one of the nicest women in the whole county. She was really a good woman. As a midwife, she brought lots of children. And it just tickled my father nearly to death to think that he could do that, especially when we couldn't get a doctor.

"Doctor just laughed about it when they told him; said, 'Why, she's just as well off. Mrs. Lindig's just as fine a doctor as I am.'

"I was fixing to say, I don't think Rebekah would have ever wanted anybody to say that Lyndon came with a midwife instead of a real doctor. I don't think she would've ever wanted that said. But still it was one of those accident things that happen."

Aunt Jessie was right; Rebekah hoped that aspect of Lyndon's birth would be lost to history. Rebekah always was, as Lyndon was to become, concerned with keeping up appearances. Life was hard in the harsh Texas Hill Country in those days, and often appearances were just about all you had.

Ralph Yarborough: "Johnson comes from hardscrabble country where you have a drought every three years, and unless you get a good crop, you nearly starve. These people are in the same position as Scarlett O'Hara was in *Gone With the Wind* when she picked up that last turnip. They are always picking up that last turnip.

"The first Anglo-Americans that went out there tried to farm. They weren't basically ranchers. But as a result of the Spaniards and others, there were a million head of wild cattle. So you went out and rounded up some wild cattle.

"Johnson's grandfather was one of the great trail drivers of Texas."

Lyndon: "My grandfather and his brother came here to the Hill Country in the early 1850s; they were orphan boys. They started driving cattle up the trail to Abilene, Kansas—the old Chisholm Trail. And the two Johnson brothers had a cattle concentration point at what is now Johnson City.

"They would assemble them there and drive them up the trail. And that's where they put down their stakes, and that's where they've all stayed since. And those that are living live in this general area; those that are dead are buried in the little family graveyard near the ranch house."

The Hill Country, in spite of its harshness, had its own beauty, and its spell was considerable. According to John Graves: "A friend of mine from Houston said, 'This is where everybody would like to come from. There isn't a soul in Texas that wouldn't have been born here in these hills if he could have managed it.'"[3]

Lyndon loved the Hill Country, and loved Hill Country lore, savored it, trotted it forth whenever occasion demanded and often when it didn't.

"My daddy . . ." he would begin, "or my grandaddy . . ." and a typical Hill Country story would follow. Rebekah Baines Johnson may have thought she married beneath herself—both she and *her* daddy, Joseph Wilson Baines, were college graduates—but there is no indication that Lyndon ever thought she had. He grew up on the Johnson ranch, later in Johnson City, petted and prodded by his parents as well as the Johnson grandparents; the Baineses, those that were left, were shadowy and somewhat colorless by comparison.

When Lyndon's grandaddy, Sam Ealy, Sr., and his brother Tom settled in the Pedernales Valley they joined forces with three Johnson nephews—Jesse, James, and John. All five were bachelors. They built a log cabin with a loopholed rock barn for defense against Indian raids; this was the embryo of Johnson City. The family partnership was, they stipulated, strictly male; if a member married, he checked out, appropriated his share, and went it alone. But they were, while they were all there together, the largest trail-driving operation in the Hill Country. They drove cattle eastward to Kansas and as far north as Wyoming and Montana.

The first intrusion came with the Civil War.

Joe Payne: "My grandfather and Sam Johnson were in the Confederate army together. My grandfather got shot, I think in the right shoulder, and Grandpa Johnson got his horse shot from under him."

The second intrusion was the arrival in the Hill Country of Eliza Bunton from Kentucky.

Lyndon: "Grandpa came in '53; then grandmother came. I can remember my grandparents talking about the ranch, how they had wanted to settle here."

So the rangy Texas cattle driver and his black-eyed young wife, Eliza, set up housekeeping in a log cabin on a corner of the ranch. There was nobody else there then—except the Indians.

Lyndon: "The last Indian fight up here was in 1873, and from the time my people came in 1853—that twenty-year period was pretty heavy going. There are a good many stories about grandmother hiding the children in the basement and the Indians coming in and ransacking the house. Shooting the horses in the pen.

"Plenty of times she hid down there. She'd get in the flour barrel and cover herself up whenever she heard the war whoops."

Finally Eliza decided that the Hill Country, or at least Sam Ealy's corner of it, was not a healthy place for babies, and she persuaded Sam to move to the more settled prairie country around Buda, Texas. There, after four successive daughters, Eliza at last, on October 11, 1877, bore a son—named, predictably, for his father.

By the time the last child had arrived, Big Sam now the father of nine, began to yearn for the old ranch and the carefree, trail-driving life it represented. The Indian threat was past, so, Big Sam asked his wife, why not return to the Hill Country? Eliza conceded; not only that, she sold her most prized possession—the silver-mounted carriage with its matched span of horses that Sam's brother Tom had given her[4] for a sum large enough to meet the down payment on a farm on the Pedernales.[5] The farm, midway between Johnson City and Fredericksburg and not far from the original Johnson ranch, was where Sam Ealy, Jr. grew up.

There was, however, nothing carefree about farming in the Hill Country, as both Big Sam and young Sam Ealy soon discovered.

Rebekah: "Sam's services on the farm were needed, and it required sacrifice on the part of his parents much of the time to send him to school at nearby Johnson City. Once his father gave him some cattle, saying, 'This is all I can do on your schooling this year.' . . . [He] slaughtered and cut up a steer and sold steaks and soupbones to tide him over until next 'butchering day.'

"Later on, he bought a barber's chair and tools from the town barber who had become ill and . . . soon Sam was a full-fledged barber on Saturdays. . . ."[6]

Sam was, at that time, trying his hand at whatever came along, with varied success. According to Sam Houston Johnson, Lyndon's brother, their father was "a teacher for a little while down near Sandy at the White Oak school. He always wanted to be a lawyer, but he never did become one. He'd have been a good one, too."

But to go from teaching to law required at least a modicum of money and drive. and Sam Ealy Johnson, Jr., had not quite enough of either. When he tired of teaching, he returned to the ranch. He served for a while as justice of the peace, but it was politics that really interested him. The little cabin he occupied on the farm was, many nights, the scene of animated political discussion, lasting often well into the morning.

At one such session he learned that the seat in the legislature for the Eighty-ninth (soon to be renumbered Eighty-seventh) District, then occupied by one Joseph Wilson Baines of Blanco, would next year, under the tricounty rotation system, fall to Gillespie County. Why shouldn't Sam run for it?

Sam did, and at age twenty-seven Sam Ealy Johnson, Jr. was elected to the Texas state legislature. Not long afterward he received a request for an interview from a reporter on the *Blanco County Gazette*. His interviewer, to his surprise, turned out to be a young woman; not only that, she was the daughter of that same Joseph Wilson Baines, his predecessor.

Her name, he soon learned, was Rebekah.

Rebekah's lineage, a term she often used, was quite different from Sam's. Her grandfather, George Washington Baines, had been a Baptist minister, much revered. During the Civil War and afterward he presided over Baylor College, one of the earliest seats of higher learning in the state. Her father, Joseph Wilson Baines, was a student at Baylor when Sam Ealy Johnson, Sr., was traveling the Chisholm Trail. The Civil War, while it temporarily interrupted his studies, apparently did not afford him cause for such excitement as it had Big Sam. After the war he took a teaching position in the town of Rowlett, Texas. Joseph Wilson was a handsome young man, slender, with the droopy mustache popular at the time. Among his pupils was pretty Ruth Huffman, blond and blue-eyed, and not yet fifteen when they married.

Faced with providing for a wife and, one always assumed, a close succession of offspring, Joseph Wilson decided to study law. He also edited a local paper; neither was a great success, but he was accepted by the bar, and he did become secretary of state for Governor John Ireland.

After their first child, Rebekah, was born, the family moved to Blanco, also a Hill Country town. Joseph Wilson added cattle raising and farming to his law and editing endeavors, but none was very lucrative or pursued with much enthusiasm. Reading was his passion—by nature he was a scholar, and Texas in the 1880s was hardly the time or place for that. His law practice dwindled over the years. Several years of drought made further farming impossible. The farm was sold in 1903, not an uncommon occurrence in the Hill Country.

Joseph Wilson, much chastened and much poorer, moved his family to Fredericksburg and was elected to the legislature. Just why he chose that course is uncertain, perhaps he did not know what else to do. Only in his mid-fifties, he was a broken man, and neither psychologically nor economically did he ever recover. He served out his two-year term and, just before he died, turned over his seat in the Eighty-ninth District to that promising young man from neighboring Gillespie County—Sam Ealy Johnson, Jr.

When Rebekah interviewed the new young legislator, she asked him, among other matters, his views on the controversial U.S. Senator, Joseph Weldon Bailey. They were negative, and that interested the young reporter even more. Opposition to Senator Bailey was not yet a popular course to take. Sam Ealy, in his turn, was equally interested; reporting for newspapers was not the usual occupation of young women in 1906. Miss

Baines, he learned, had just graduated from Baylor; she was obviously a person of intelligence and determination. Besides, she was beautiful.

In her *Album* Rebekah describes "frequent visits from a dashing and dynamic young legislator,"[7] which in short order became a whirlwind courtship. There is no mention of church suppers, country dances, river strolls, the conventional pursuits of a young Hill Country couple in love at the time. Instead she describes a "Confederate Reunion where we enjoyed the oratory"[8] and writes of hearing "William Jennings Bryan, whom we both admired extravagantly, address the Legislature."[9] Sam was delighted to find a girl who really liked politics.

There was no mention of love either, but then that wasn't much talked of in those days. When Joseph Wilson Baines died, Rebekah, who had adored him, sought comfort. He had been, as she later expressed it, "the dominant force in my life."[10] She had to adjust herself to life without her "most interesting companion."[11] and she did this by marrying Sam Ealy Johnson, Jr.

"We were married August 20, 1907, and moved out to the farm on the Pedernales River in Gillespie County."[12] There, on August 27, 1908, Lyndon was born.

There was, almost immediately, the quandary of what to name their son. Apparently the happy parents had not thought to decide it beforehand, and three months were to pass before it was resolved. Rebekah described how, baby in one arm, she would

> copy long lists of names and submit them for his father's approval. None ever quite suited the exacting father . . . His being un-named sorely irked his mother, so one cold November morning she decided upon a plan to remedy that situation. . . .
>
> Sam called to me from his place in front of the roaring fire in the fireplace in our room: "Everything is nice and warm now, Rebekah, get up and cook breakfast." I had taken the *baby* from his bassinet by my bed and lay there thinking that my beautiful boy must have a name all his own that very day and hour; so I nonchalantly replied, "No, Sam, I am not cooking breakfast until this baby is named. . . ."
>
> Sam studied a moment, then looked up from tying his shoe to say, "How would you like Clarence?" "Not in the least," came my prompt reply. Then he asked, "What would you think of Dayton?" "That is much better but still not quite the name for this boy," I said.
>
> He thought of the third of his three lawyer friends and said, "Would you call him Linden?" There was a long pause, and I said, "Yes, if I may spell it as I please, for L-y-n-d-o-n Johnson would be far more euphonious than L-i-n-d-e-n Johnson." "Spell it as you please," said Sam. "I am naming him for a good and smart man, a true friend, and how you spell it doesn't matter. We will call the baby for him and for your father." "All right," I responded. "He is named Lyndon Baines Johnson."
>
> I got up and made the biscuits.[13]

Now that he was named, and to everyone's satisfaction, baby Lyndon proved more captivating than ever.

Rebekah: "Lyndon's earliest . . . one of his earliest public appearances was the spring of 1909 when his parents took him to a general picnic near Stonewall. As Sam entered the grounds carrying the baby, he was constantly greeting friends and neighbors. Lyndon gave each his happy smile and usually extended his arms in an attempt to go from his father's arms to the friend's. Eddie Hahn, a general leading citizen of the community, exclaimed, 'Sam, you've got a politician there. I've never afore seen such a friendly baby. He's a chip off the old block. I can see him running for office twenty years from now.'" [14]

Lyndon: "My first memory. I remember standing in front of the pump near the house I was born in. And my mother was crying. My daddy was buying cotton at the gin, and he hadn't come home; he stayed there until the last cotton was ginned, usually about midnight. And here she was with two tiny children and alone. [15]

"She went out to pump some water. It was dark; we didn't have lights then, and I could hold the lamp while she pumped the water. I remember she was crying, and she said she was frightened. I told her I'd take care of her."

Well, that's how Lyndon remembered it later. In any case, he was clearly a precocious child.

Rebekah: "Lyndon learned readily and knew his alphabet and the Mother Goose rhymes, many juvenile poems from Tennyson and Longfellow, and brief speeches when he was only two. He read quite early and at three could spell words ranging from *cat* to *grandpa*. His little cousins, Ava and Margaret, attended the little country schoolhouse, Junction, in sight of his home, so at recess Lyndon would run over to see them." [16]

Kathryn Deadrich Loney: "I was hired for teaching at the little school up there. Lyndon and his family lived nearby, and he would run away from home and attend the school, day in and day out. He didn't care about playing with the children; he just kind of hung on to my skirt and hung around when I was teaching. So I told his mother that if we could get the board's permission, I would take him—he wanted to come to school so badly. And they said 'Okay.'

"I taught all eight grades in the same room, one little room. I had about thirty-five children. That's the only way we had in those days."

Rebekah: "Lyndon from his earliest days possessed a highly inquisitive mind. He was never content long to play quietly in the yard. He must take his toys apart to see what made them go, or he must set out to conquer that new unexplored world beyond the gate or up the lane." [17]

Lyndon: "I remember that when I was a boy, that I walked through the sand, hot sand, up to see my grandfather. A child of five or six—I would cross the dusty field and walk along the banks of the river.

"My granddaddy would ask me questions. He would say, 'How many ponies do you have? How many chickens do you have? How many cows are down there at your place? Tell me about the state of the crops—when are you going to start picking your cotton?'

"I would stand there and wiggle my toes in the sand with my finger in my mouth. And if I knew the answers and answered all his questions correctly, grandpa would take me in and open a black mahogany desk he had and reach in and get an apple. And I would walk satisfied and quite proudly back across the fields along the bank of the river. If I failed, the walk seemed endless—if I hadn't known the answers.

"And those hills and those fields and that river were the only real world that I really had in those years. So I did not know much about how much more beautiful it was than that of many other boys, for I could imagine nothing else from sky to sky. Yet the sight and the feel of that country somehow or other burned itself into my mind."[18]

REBEKAH

Rebekah: "The first year of my marriage . . . I was confronted not only by the problem of adjustment to a completely opposite personality, but also to a strange and new way of life, a way far removed from that I had known in Blanco and Fredericksburg. . . . However, I was determined to overcome circumstances instead of letting them overwhelm me. At last I realized that life is real and earnest and not the charming fairy tale of which I had so long dreamed."[1]

There was little of the fairy tale romance in life on the farm by the Pedernales. Sam Ealy Johnson, Jr., in his dusty boots and battered Stetson, bore little resemblance to Prince Charming; moreover, it must have been very early apparent to Rebekah that he would never replace her father in intellectual companionship as she had hoped. Sam Ealy's mind was, as Lyndon's would be, essentially pragmatic, not philosophical.

The farmhouse, too, was no castle, not even a rose-covered cottage; it was quite unlike her girlhood home, which Rebekah remembered as "a two-story rock house with a fruitful orchard of perfectly spaced trees, terraced flower beds, broad walks, purple plumed wisteria climbing to the room, fragrant honeysuckle at the dining room windows whose broad sills were seats for us children."

There were other differences. Her own parents were childless the first twelve years of their marriage; Rebekah became pregnant almost immediately and seemed always to be so in the decade that followed. Lyndon Baines, born 1908, was followed by Rebekah Luruth in 1910, Josefa Hermine in 1912, Sam Houston in 1914, and Lucia Huffman in 1916. After which the bearing ended, and the bearing up began.

Aunt Jessie: "Rebekah wasn't used to the rough ranch life like I was. She never had done much of anything except schoolwork. And it was hard on her. I used to go down and help her all the time. I'd go in and help her wash the dishes, help her sweep the floor, help her bathe the babies. I'd just do anything that was to be done. Now that was all there was to it."

Rebekah alludes to the vagaries of the great iron stove and the chickens as her greatest trials, but Lyndon, who had a very early memory of his mother crying at the pump, focused on water.

Lady Bird: "A lot of the way he felt about water came from seeing his mother have to draw the water from the well and not having a washing machine and having to scrub the floor on her hands and knees."

Virginia Foster Durr: "Bird had this luncheon for Mrs. Maury Maverick, and Bird's mother-in-law was out from Texas, Lyndon's mother. She was an extremely beautiful woman; she had a very aristocratic, if you want to call it that, a very beautiful bone structure. I sat by her at the luncheon table, and she had rather large, swollen and very red hands. As she began to eat lunch, she said to me in sort of a whisper, 'You know, I'm always so embarrassed and ashamed about my hands. Where we lived at down in the country when I was young, I had to do so much hard work, and my hands never recovered. Even as a little boy Lyndon used to say to me, "Oh, mamma, when I get big I'm going to see that you don't have to do any of this hard work so you can have pretty white hands."' She remembered that even as a little boy, you know, he was worried about it. I really think this is one of the reasons that Lyndon had this passion against poverty and this passion for electricity. He did remember his mother doing all this hard, heavy work, and it did hurt him, and he did want to see her life made easier and he wanted to see the life of women like her made easier."

Kathryn Deadrich Loney: "Nearly every day after school I went by to see Miss Rebekah. She was older than I, so sweet and so patient. She was always ready to help you if you wanted advice. To me she was just precious.

"I don't think she was strict with Lyndon. She would appeal to him to do things. I don't think she ever scolded him. I never heard her scold her children. She would just talk to them in a little gentle voice, and they seemed to understand that that was right."

There is no doubt, though, that the pivot of Rebekah's life was her eldest child.

History is full of examples of firstborn children pushed into prominence by ambitious parents; Rebekah seemed to consider it the normal course of things. Of her childhood she wrote, "I was fortunate in being the firstborn of my parents, a happy circumstance of superior advantage."[2]

Rose McKee: "His mother said that as a child she was timid, but her own father taught her confidence by saying: 'My little girl can do anything she wants to do.' When her own children came along, she said, 'The only thing I knew about bringing them up was what my father had told me.'"[3]

Rebekah (much later, on hearing rumors that her son might become president): "I'm not surprised. 'Course it's a mother talking, but from the first time I looked into his eyes, none of his accomplishments have surprised me."[4]

John Skuce: "I can't see anything of what I know of the family, stories that I've been told, that makes me think that Mama Johnson cared about any other child but him. She was just overwhelmed with Lyndon."

Horace Busby: "Members of the Johnson family, including brothers and sisters, quietly dispute his portrayal of the family home life; before her death in 1957 his mother, Rebekah, became greatly distressed about the inaccuracy of Lyndon's memory. Former contemporaries who knew him in his Johnson City youth insist he was disabled not by parental deprivation but by parental indulgence which left him 'spoiled rotten.' Success, he thought, denied him the sympathy that comes with failure and the affection accorded the ineffectual. To compensate, he constructed for himself a past which he believed would transform him into a weak, even pitiable figure. Surely the young, the intellectuals, the writers—all those put off by his power and success—would be moved to compassion if only they understood he was disadvantaged by his birthplace, deprived by his schooling, and demeaned by his lack of hereditary graces and manner."[5]

Sam Houston Johnson: "They say, some people say, Lyndon was a mama's boy, but I don't think that's so, not that I'm sure I know what a mama's boy is. More often than not our mother was doing Lyndon's bidding, rather than the other way around."

The geographic sphere of Rebekah's experience was limited to central Texas, and there is little doubt that within her world of Blanco, Waco, Fredericksburg, and Johnson City, the most rural, seemingly the least civilized was Johnson City, where Sam Ealy Johnson, Jr., moved his little family when Lyndon was six.

Stella Glidden: "When I first came to Johnson City—well, I came from Fredericksburg, a town where you could almost eat off the streets. In Johnson City there was very little except just living from day to day and being grateful."

Emmette Redford: "All of us lived in circumstances that don't compare at all with the way we live today. Not many people had indoor plumbing; virtually nobody had electric lights. Whatever we now regard as the normal standard of living just didn't exist in Johnson City at that time. So that if you had a home and food and clothes, you were a middle-class family."

Glidden: "When I came to Johnson City at that time, I thought I had come to the end of the world. Mr. Sam came down that afternoon, and I was sitting on the porch of the hotel all by myself, and he asked me how I was liking it. I said, 'Well, for one thing, I'm not going to sleep up here!' He said, 'Well, where are you going to sleep?' I said, 'I'm going to go down to the print shop and sleep on that pile of paper and cover up with my coat.' (It was March.) So he went off, and he came back directly, and he said, 'Rebekah wants you to come up to the house.' So that's how I spent my first night in that house. I slept in the east room with little Rebekah, Josefa, and Lucia, who was then just a very little child. I never did know how the two west rooms looked, because in those days we didn't go all over people's houses. And that was Mr. Sam's and Miz Rebekah's room, and a room for the boys. It was one of the best houses in Johnson City.

"I wondered just why people would like a town like Johnson City, but it wasn't long before I, too, liked it, because I found the people so warm and so friendly. It seemed after a period of about three months that I had lived in this little town all my life."

But even the best house in Johnson City would have commanded only a portion of Rebekah's attention. And Sam Johnson understood, possibly even admired, that in her.

Liz Carpenter: "Sam Johnson always indulged his wife's independence. One day he appeared with two presents for her—a Victrola and a newspaper, the *Record-Courier*, a weekly newspaper in Johnson City. The owner of both had to go west for his health and he persuaded Sam Johnson to buy them.

"The newspaper gave Mrs. Johnson an opportunity to do what she had always loved—write. Despite the fact that she had five little children under eight years of age, she wrote out—on yellow tablet paper—every line of copy that went into the weekly paper for a year.

"And during this time she also was correspondent for the *Dallas News*, the *Austin American*, and the *San Antonio Express*, signing her stories RBJ."[6]

Rebekah was always one for keeping up appearances. Johnson City may not have been her choice, but it was her lot in life. It was certainly better than the farm, and she would make the best of it.

Aunt Jessie: "She dressed them little children—oh, they looked just like little angels, her little children did. Of course, this kid like Sam and like I was, we came up hamper-scamper, you know. Anything that mama put on us was all right. But Rebekah's children were always dressed."

Simon Burg: "We'd go visit on a Sunday afternoon, and Mrs. Johnson would call the children up on the porch and each of them would recite a declamation or an extemporaneous speech. She was the type of person who wanted to teach the children how to meet a problem and how to speak on it."

But Rebekah did not limit her concern for proper speech to her own children. She was generous with her time and her talents in public speaking; it was her great love, that and dramatics.

Lyndon: "There is hardly a boy or girl that ever went to Johnson City school district that she didn't prepare for the declamation contest up at the little theater. She was the dramatics teacher, public-speaking teacher. She could teach anything."

Ben Crider: "She coached her high school people in literary events; she taught them how to debate, how to stand, taught girls how to sit down properly, and helped in every way without any pay. We didn't have any money to pay with. She did this of her own free will without any cost. She was a brilliant woman—graduated from Baylor—and we had very few college graduates in our country at that time."

But whatever her other activities, and they were many, nothing in Rebekah's life superseded the welfare of her eldest child. She coached him first, everybody else second.

When Lyndon was thirteen Rebekah sent him to summer school at an academy in San Marcos. No letters between them from this early a period have survived, but beginning with his college years we have much of their correspondence,[7] mostly undated, and a bit fulsome on both sides, but apparently they were comfortable with that.

Dearest Mother,

Have all of my books arranged before me in preparation for a long evening of study. You can't realize the difference in the atmosphere after one of your sweet letters. I know of nothing so stimulating and inspiring to me as one of your encouraging, beautifully-written letters . . . Mother, I love you so. Don't neglect me . . .

My dear Mother,
   The end of another busy day brought me a letter from you. Your letters always give me more strength, renewed courage, and that bull dog tenacity so essential to the success of any man . . .[8]

During at least some periods of his life, Rebekah wrote Lyndon every day. The sheer volume of what survives is staggering. Newsy, chatty letters for the most part, but always with the extra line or two (or ten) of superlatives:

                                                                                —1934

Dearest Lyndon,
   Was greatly disappointed in not hearing from you . . . I never see you alone any more. I never could talk freely or naturally before outsiders. Often I think with pleasure of the long confidential talks we used to have when you would come in from San Marcos and sit on the bed and tell me all your hopes, disappointments and dreams. You were always so close to my heart and my life, darling . . . With dearest love to my dear, dear, splendid son,

                                                                                Mama

He was her "dearest love," her "splendid sweet son," but Rebekah could hardly be called possessive; she expected Lyndon to take his place in the larger world, and she never objected to his leaving home as long as his plans coincided with her own expectations. Neither did she, as far as anyone ever heard, protest his rapid-fire courtship and near elopement with Lady Bird, and if she worried a little at its precipitousness and because Bird was an Episcopalian, it was a pretty normal worry.
   Lady Bird: "She regarded me, when she first saw me, with great concern and I won't say hostility, but with just a sort of wondering what on earth kind of person I was and what I would mean in the life of her son and his relation to his family. But she was also a person to whom marriage was a mighty important institution, a very good member of the Baptist church. So once we were married, she was going to make *the* loving best of it.
   "And she did."

                                                                                —1939

My precious Boy,
   . . . You know how I feel in regard to Bird. She is one of the nicest people in the world to live with and that is saying a great deal . . . I think my daughter-in-law is second to none. I am indeed thankful for your sake, as well as for my own, that you made such a wise and fortunate choice . . .

Lady Bird: "She was the sort of person that I truly enjoyed being with. If I had an extra hour in Austin before I had to catch a plane or train to Washington, I would think of all the friends I could call, but I usually decided I would rather go and see Mrs. Johnson. We would sit together and talk about books, about household decorating, about family.

We were very good friends, and that is probably much better than loving one's in-laws."

Durr: "I think Lyndon was accustomed to two adoring women all his life, his mother and his wife."

Rebekah never really cared for the farm, or for Johnson City,[9] and when her husband died (shortly before Lyndon's first election to Congress), Lyndon found a house for her just outside Austin, and she made periodic visits to Washington. With her scene thus set, she could act her preferred roles, the intellectual, the proud mother of the increasingly famous son, the Texas grandlady.

Charles Boatner: "Whenever I would go to Austin on a story or some detail regarding the paper, why I always would call Mrs. Johnson and take her to the Driskill to dinner. Because I was—I had the feeling—I didn't know Mr. Johnson would ever become president, but I thought he was going to be a great man in the United States government, and I wanted to learn as much as I could about him, and I thought she was the best source, as she was.

"She was such a gracious lady, too, that—well, you'd walk into the Driskill with her on your arm, and they had an old white-haired maître d' in the dining room. And when he saw her, his head just swept the floor. That old white head went all the way to the floor. And, selfishly, you always got a better meal when she was there.

"She had good political instincts. I think he inherited his from both of them. I've watched her at political rallies when he was running, and she didn't go out of her way to shake hands with people. It seemed like people wanted to come up and shake her hand. She never failed to give them a nice smile, and they went away feeling like they had received an accolade. She just had that presence."

The 1956 convention was what Lady Bird once described as Rebekah's "last hurrah." It was there in Chicago that for the first time she admitted she had, and had had for some time, "nodules" on her arms, and that they were more numerous than before. The doctor's prognosis—on lymphosarcoma—was not favorable, but then as Lady Bird said, getting her to a doctor had in itself been a major project.

She did not live to see her son's ultimate triumph, although perhaps, depending on how you view it, since she saw him majority leader, she did just that and was spared the rest. She died September 12, 1958, age seventy-eight, and was buried next to Sam Ealy Johnson, Jr., in the family graveyard.

Lyndon: "She was a great moral influence over me. A Christian lady that was brought up with a Bible in her hand and a preacher in the front room."

Willie Day Taylor: "They were so fond of each other; they understood each other much better than parents and children frequently understand each other. He always felt that he could talk with her about everything, and she always had complete confidence in him. He could just do anything; I'm sure she knew he was going to be president."

RUNNING, RUNNING, RUNNING

Joe Payne: "First time I knew him was in '17. He was about nine. He had on a pair of blue overalls, high-top shoes, had them old buckles on the side that you wrapped the string in. Straw hat—looked like the goats had been eating on it."

Lyndon's childhood was divided between Johnson City and the farm in Stonewall, which, in any case, were only about thirteen miles apart. The family moved back to the farm after the deaths of Grandpa Sam and Grandma Eliza; the real estate business in town had not exactly prospered; the farm at least offered sustenance of a sort. Aside from being more isolated, life on the farm was not that different; there was no electricity or running water in either place. The wood stove on the farm was not dissimilar to the one in town, and as far as Lyndon was concerned both places had school, friends, and roughly the same amount of chores.

Sam Houston Johnson: "You know, if you live on a farm, there are always a lot of chores to do, and of course there were eventually five of us, but somehow Lyndon did fewer chores than the rest of us. He was like the foreman, you might say—the boss—and he got me and my sisters Rebekah and Lucia and Josefa to do the work like slopping the pigs and getting the wood in the wood box and gathering the eggs. I used to think it was because he was older. I now think it was because—well, to put it one way, he was smarter."

Rebekah: "Certain chores were assigned Lyndon, among them was bringing in the wood for the cookstove and the two fireplaces before sundown. Lyndon's usual method of discharging this duty was to arrive hurriedly just before six with several playmates. With a hearty 'Otis, you take Cecil and Clarence and I'll race you with Tom and Willie. Come on, boys, let's see who can stack the biggest pile the quickest.' In vain were the protests of his mother that she desired wood only for the next day's usage. The back porch in a few minutes would have two huge piles of wood. Lyndon would applaud the willing workers, pass out the cookies to all as he bade them good night, would wash his perspiring face and grimy hands for supper and greet his father at the front door with 'Daddy, all the wood was in before six and I've just been waiting for you to come in.'"[1]

Benno Eckert: "Sometimes he rode a donkey to school. It was about four miles. His legs were so long, they drug the ground mostly. Some more of the kids rode donkeys, too; they just tied them up during classes. In those days they didn't have a nice schoolground; just kind of a little pasture. They had a fence around it.

"We had about sixty or seventy kids in the school. They taught up through the tenth grade.[2] Not many of us made the tenth grade. They had two rooms, and they had three teachers. Sometimes we only had two. One teacher had half the grades, and the other teacher had the others."

Kittie Clyde Leonard: "Of course, there wasn't very much ready cash, so boys had to make their spending money. They did it in various ways. They went varmint hunting, and then sold the furs—foxes, raccoons, ringtails, skunks. We didn't like the boys to come to school after they'd killed a skunk."

Truman Fawcett: "In those days you weren't in society unless you was a cotton picker. You picked cotton, got together with all the young people and had a good time that way. Once I picked in the same patch as Lyndon. I don't believe either one of us was expert cotton pickers."

Simon Burg: "In the summer months I would go out and pick cotton—a dollar a hundred pounds, and I could pick about a hundred a day. So I was working for a dollar a day."

Aunt Jessie: "Didn't matter where he was, he was always running, running, running. He even had a business of his own at one time, a shoe-shine outfit. That was five cents a shine. And he even had an ad in the paper, 'Lyndon Johnson Shoe Shine Shop.' I don't think his daddy liked it much and made him take it out."

Leonard: "Lyndon shined shoes in a barbershop. There he sat around and listened to the men talk politics. He was listening, learning, and enjoying it. And he worked on ranches and farms, just any kind of odd jobs.

"There were about two hundred people in Johnson City then. We knew everyone all around the area. We'd have parties. As smaller children we'd gather at someone's home and play on Sunday afternoon, or late in the evenings we'd play games, baseball. If it was moonlight, we'd even play baseball in the street, kick-the-can, hide-and-seek."

Payne: "We'd play marbles. Lyndon was fair; he could shoot pretty good. He didn't like to be beat at nothin'. Even as a kid when he went into something, he put his heart and soul into it. But getting beat in a marble game or something like that apparently never worried him none; anyway, he'd beat *him* next time."

Sam Houston: "We were all talkers, and we shouted at each other, and we teased each other and fought, and Lyndon took advantage of me as often as he could get away with it, but I always thought that's what older brothers did."

Stella Glidden: "Lyndon and his brother would have fights, and often the fights would get so bad that Mrs. Johnson, when Mr. Johnson was gone, would often call in a neighbor and try to get him to make them behave. There was often paddlings by neighbors instead of by Mrs. Johnson. Nobody minded it at that time."

Ava Johnson Cox: "One of the things we did, we had cob fights in the barn in Johnson City. We'd take the white cobs and the red cobs and we'd choose sides. Lyndon would always have to be the leader. Didn't make any difference whose side he was on or what color cob he had, he was going to be the leader. So, one time he was our leader, and we had the white cobs, and the Redford boy and James Ealy had the others. Well, all of us got killed, and we had to throw down some hay out of the barn, in fact we knocked it down was what happened, and we hollered to Lyndon to jump, and to jump on that hay and run around the other side of the barn.

"So Lyndon was always pretty awkward and clumsy about things, and when he started to jump out of that barn, for some reason he didn't jump, he just more or less fell out of it. And broke his leg. And he screamed and he cried out 'Oh, I'm killed, I'm killed!' and he screamed bloody murder, and boy every kid just scattered! I mean from one end to the other! And the oldest Redford boy started running—he was real tall—he's Dr. Emmette Redford today, at the University of Texas. He ran to town and got Dr. Barnwell.

"Old Doc Barnwell, when he come up, he said, 'How bad are you hurt, Lyndon?' Lyndon said, 'Oh, I'm killed, I'm killed.'

"So he said, 'Well, Lyndon, you do have a broken leg all right, but we'll get that fixed up.' And Aunt Rebekah came out there, and she just knew that he was going to die! And she was in about as bad a shape as he was, and taking on, and so the doctor told her that he'd give Lyndon a shot and he would get over it. And Lord, when he said, 'give him a shot,' old Lyndon come up from there and he said, 'Oh, please, doctor, don't shoot me—I want to live awhile longer!'

"And the doctor carried him into the house, and he set the leg right there. He didn't carry him into town. And there wasn't any hospital. And he set that leg on a table, a long table, and put him out back there on that back porch.

"Then in two or three days they moved him and I never will forget, Miz Baines[3] had a wooden bed. Now the rest of their beds were iron, and he decided he wanted to sleep on her bed. So he did. And some of the kids came up to see him, and Margaret and I came by from school to give him his lessons, and he wanted to play.

"He said, 'Hand me my knife.' He had one of those little knives with a tin handle on it. He said, 'We're going to play mumblety-peg.' I said, 'Lyndon, there's no place to play mumblety-peg in here.' And he said, 'That's what you think.' and he turned around in that bed with that leg in that cast, and stuck that knife in the headboard of that wooden bed.

"And I said, 'Lyndon, my daddy would just blister me good if he catched me doing something like that!' And he said, 'Well, they're not going to catch *me*.' And sure enough they didn't."

SAM EALY

Sam Houston: "He was away a lot, our daddy, when Lyndon was a boy. He worked on the farm, and that wasn't an easy way to make a living in those days. And of course he served in the state legislature at five dollars a day and two dollars a day for their special sessions. Couldn't get rich doing that."

At heart Sam Ealy Johnson was a Texas politician, and probably never had a hankering for anything higher. His legislative career came in two parts: the first when he was courting Rebekah and in their early marriage, and the second, a decade later, after all five children had been born.

He was first elected in 1904, and when his two years were up, he should by tradition have passed the seat along to Llano County, but he could not bear to relinquish it. A senseless custom anyway, he said. After two years one was just getting warmed up. So he announced for reelection, and staked his two years of experience and his enthusiasm against local custom. He won, and the rotation system was not heard from again.

Now that Sam had been elected for his person rather than his geographical habitation, he began to flap his wings a little, give freer rein to his always independent spirit. His vote was frequently with the minority. He thought of himself as a people's man, a direct descendant of James Stephen Hogg, governor during the previous decade, who had championed the small farmer and attacked all the giants—insurance companies, railroads, out-of-state road companies, the gold standard. Not that Sam Ealy had frequent occasion to deal with such large issues; the legislation he sponsored was chiefly matters of the Alamo purchase bill (his picture hangs inside the mission), Confederate veterans' pensions, and a bill to provide a home for Confederate widows.

It was during this session, too, that Sam Ealy formed a lasting friendship with the newly elected representative from the district, another Sam, young Sam Rayburn of Bonham.

Sam Ealy debated running for a third term in 1908, but that was the year Lyndon was born, and five dollars a day was not much to support a family on. Rebekah's interest in politics had been superseded by a greater interest, the family's livelihood. So Sam gave up the legislature and returned to farming.

Otto Lindig: "People planted about 20 percent of their cultivated land in corn and other seed crops and the rest in cotton. Cotton was the only cash crop we had.

"I believe there were about a hundred acres on the Johnson farm in cultivation and about four hundred acres of pasture land. They had maybe forty to fifty head of cows on the place."

Simon Burg: "Lyndon's father was farming on the place where Lyndon was born, and his daddy used to trade with my grandfather, who had a general merchandise store. I can remember his daddy coming up and buying groceries and Lyndon coming along. His daddy had to buy his things on credit until he got his cotton crop. He'd sell his cotton and pay his grocery bill. And he wasn't the only one—there were a lot of them that way. Ninety-five percent of the merchandising business was a credit business in those days."

Benno Eckert: "They had a nice piece of property down there, but Lyndon's daddy, when they moved from here, he owed my daddy two hundred dollars for ginning at the cotton gin. He couldn't pay it. Year after year he'd renew that note. And after Lyndon got to working in Washington, one day he came up to dad and he said, 'Mr. Eckert, I can't pay all of dad's bills, but if you'd accept half of the face of that note, I'll pay that.' And he did, and dad took it.

"I always thought that was real nice of Lyndon—he didn't have to pay that if he didn't want to. Sam always paid the interest on it."

No one remembers Sam Ealy caring much for farming. After five years of it the family moved into Johnson City and Sam took up real estate, but no one remembers him liking that much either. Politics was always his real love. He was always a member of that largely unrecognized group of Texas rebels, far fewer now than in his day, who were more concerned with the welfare of a dispossessed constituent's farm than with that of the rich and mighty. It is not that there are fewer dispossessed now; it is that the rich are mightier and getting elected to political office depends more on their largesse.

Sam Houston: "Our daddy liked to talk about Sam Rayburn and Wright Patman and Jim Ferguson. Especially old Ferguson. He was in his forties when he first ran for the governorship, and he was in the banking business, but you never would have known it to hear him talk, because he talked like a farmer, and he dressed like one as well. He spit tobacco with the best of them, and the politicians, the regulars, thought he didn't have a chance."

There was a lot about Jim Ferguson's brand of populism that Sam Ealy might have found difficult to champion. His gubernatorial practices included vetoing the appropriation for the University of Texas (in his words, a nesting place for sinners and profligates), transferring a school fund of more than $100,000 into his own bank and then loaning the money to himself, and accepting a $165,000 "gift" from Texas brewers; naturally he was against Prohibition. He was impeached and—in spite of his bravura, "I am governor of Texas. I don't have to give reasons"—removed from office in the middle of his second term and banned from ever holding state office again. Which did not, however, silence him politically.

Sam Houston: "In a special election [1924] they followed old Jim's advice and voted in his wife, Miriam Amanda ('Ma') Ferguson, as governor, electing her again in 1932. To no one's surprise, Ma allowed her husband to give her a hand now and then—like every hour on the hour—providing him with an office next door so it wouldn't be too inconvenient.

"Whatever his detractors may say or write about him, Jim Ferguson gave the poor a better shake in Texas and thus influenced a lot of young people like my brother Lyndon."[1]

William W. Heath: "After he was president, one of Johnson's ways of sort of teasing some of his staff at the White House when they were getting a little high and mighty was to say, 'Why, he doesn't even know who Jim Ferguson is!'"

Sam Ealy reentered the Texas House in an undisputed special election early in 1918.

Wright Patman: "I didn't know Sam Ealy Johnson until January 1921 when I was a member of the legislature from Cass County, and we were assigned to the same desk, right at the back of the hall. The second or third day that the legislature was in session, Lyndon came in. He was six feet tall and twelve years old. I've known him ever since.

"I'll tell you this. As a member of the legislature, when Sam Ealy Johnson said something, it was that way. No mealymouth business, no ifs, ands, or buts.

"I never did know him to vote the way anybody told him to or wanted him to. He voted the way he felt. He was a contrary man, and he was an honest man, and you can take my word for that."

Robert Phinney: "One of the interesting things about Lyndon Johnson's father was that he made a speech one day to the House of Representatives against the Ku Klux Klan. At that time I would say the body was made up about 65 to 70 percent of people who were favorable to the Klan, and I would say it was really an unpopular time to make this speech. But he had a mind of his own, and he never hesitated about speaking on those issues. Following him, another member of the House of Representatives named Wright Patman made a speech also.

"I would say that Sam Ealy Johnson's attack on the Klan was the opening edge of the fight that ultimately destroyed them."

Lyndon: "My father fought the Klan many long years ago in Texas and I have fought them all my life because I believe them to threaten every community where they exist. I shall continue to fight them because I know their loyalty is not to the United States of America, but instead to a hooded society of bigots."

Sam Houston: "My daddy called them 'Kukluxsonofabitch.' I had heard him use that phrase way back in my childhood, during those early-morning breakfast chats when I was only four or five years old. 'Kukluxsonofabitch.' I never realized that 'sonofabitch' was a separate word standing all by itself, until I got to high school . . .

"Of course, my daddy had good reason to tie those words together. . . . The Ku Klux Klan had threatened to kill him on numerous occasions after he had made a widely publicized speech on racial tolerance before the state legislature. His words were quoted in newspapers all over the state, mostly in articles and editorials that condemned his stand, and almost immediately he started receiving anonymous phone calls and unsigned letters that threatened his entire family.

"Then, one night, when we had a visit from his brothers George and Tom, my daddy got another one of those anonymous calls.

"'Now, listen here, you Kukluxsonofabitch,' he shouted into the receiver, 'if you and your goddamned gang think you're man enough to shoot me, you come on ahead. My brothers and I will be waiting for you out on the front porch. Just come on ahead, you yellow bastards.'

"Without hardly saying a word, the three men motioned the women into the cellar and got some shotguns from the hall closet. My uncles stationed themselves at either end of the wide porch and my father stood on the middle stoop, his eyes scanning the darkness as if to spot a rattlesnake. . . .

"They waited there until dawn, and the Kukluxsonofabitches never showed up. But after that my daddy carried a gun wherever he went, even as he sat in the House of Representatives in Austin."[2]

Lyndon: "The Ku Klux Klan was at its height when my father was in the Texas legislature. They'd elected a couple of senators and they had power and position around. They threatened him. Those campaigns used to get pretty hot. Men were called upon and told they'd be tarred and feathered, and a good many of them, friends of ours, were. I was only a fifteen-year-old boy in the middle of all this, and I was fearful that my daddy would be taken out and tarred and feathered."

Patman: "Of course there were times—well, I remember at least twice he didn't vote on bills that had to do with the black people voting. But about the Ku Klux he never wavered."[3]

Blanco County Record, October 15, 1920: "Hon. S.E. Johnson announced in this issue of *The Record* as a candidate of the 87th District.

"The farmers of West Texas will recall with gratification the aid Johnson rendered in his passage of the bill appropriating over $2,000,000 for the drouth [*sic*] stricken to obtain seed and feed to produce crops during the dry years, . . . aid for the rural schools of this district, enabling all to have seven months free school, . . . his strenuous labor for good roads and his unfailing devotion to his people, influence us to feel confident that the people of Blanco County will at the polls give him the large and well merited majority he has always received from the people who know him best."[4]

Blanco County Record, November 15, 1920: "Sam E. Johnson was elected over all three of his opponents by a majority of between 1,000 and 1,500 votes."[5]

Truman Fawcett: "Lyndon's father had debates in the towns around us. The Johnson family seemed to know more about politics than the rest of us. Sam was in politics and ran for office and was interested in his friends being elected. The children took part, too."

Stella Glidden: "Sam Ealy would line up the children in front of the fireplace and would say, 'Now, let's have a debate.' And of course Lyndon was the oldest, and he always won, which was very disheartening to the younger ones."

Ava Johnson Cox: "Uncle Sam was a driver. He really believed in drill. He expected you to think, and think right fast, and he didn't wait for an answer. And that rubbed off on Lyndon. Whenever he asked anything, he wanted you to be able to answer him right now—he didn't want to wait a second for it.

"Uncle Sam was a fellow who thought a child should read the newspaper, keep up with the current events. And he would drill you on what was happening. Once he asked me about the Socialist Party, asked me what it was, and I said, 'Well, I don't know,' and he said, 'Well, tomorrow evening, you know!' And he gave me a *Pathfinder* magazine, and he said, 'Here it is, and I want you to read it.' It was an article on Eugene B. Debs— how he organized it, and what he stood for. And he was running for president. And sure enough, the next day when he asked, I knew.

"Aunt Rebekah was great for elocution, public speaking, and plays; but when it come right down to making you get it, Uncle Sam's the guy that stood there and saw that you had it done."

It was difficult to find anybody who didn't like Sam Ealy, and most people who knew him, loved him. He was six feet tall, had big ears; Lyndon later said that he and his father looked a lot alike, but that his father was handsome. He was a shouter and a waver-of-arms like his son, he was a great believer in nose-to-nose contact when he wanted to persuade you of something. He was a good-natured man, not without humor. He named all the good horses on the farm after Democratic presidents and all the plodders after Republicans. He drank too much and too often, and he knew failure, too. People who observed him weren't sure which came first.

Mary Rather: "When things went really bad, he did start drinking too much. He didn't do that always, but when things got too bad, you know, when the depression was at its worst, and the cattle market and the cotton market was really gone, his means of livelihood just vanished. And he had a wife and five children. Then he did get depressed, but other times he was an energetic, vital kind of man, like Lyndon."

Lyndon: "I wanted to copy my father always, emulate him. Do what he did. He loved the outdoors, and I grew to love the outdoors. He loved the political life, and I followed him."

Virginia Foster Durr: "I think all this crazy stuff about his mother being the dominating influence in his life is so exaggerated. He had a great respect for his father. And I think he had that sort of respectful attitude toward older men. As I say, when we saw him and Alvin Wirtz together, Lyndon would always call him 'Yes, sir' and 'No, sir.' The same way with Sam Rayburn. It was the junior to the senior—a father-son type of thing."

Ben Crider: "He was very proud of his daddy's record as a member of the Texas House of Representatives. I have heard him speak of it a lot. I wasn't a bit surprised when he decided to run for Congress."

During Lyndon's first session as congressman, Sam Ealy suffered a major heart attack (his second), and was hospitalized at Temple, Texas, 150 miles north of Johnson City. But on his son's return at the end of the session, he persuaded Lyndon to take him home.

Lyndon: "My father was dying in a Temple hospital. I wanted him to stay there, because the medical care available in that hospital was vastly superior to anything in Johnson City, but he said no. "He said, 'Lyndon, I am going to put on my britches, and I am going to get out of here. I want you to take me home.'

"Well, I argued with him for a while, but he said, 'No, I want to be in the part of the world I love best, where people know when you are sick, care when you die, and love you when you live.' So I took him home."

Austin Sunday American, October 24, 1937, . . . Former Rep. Sam E. Johnson of Johnson City, 60, member of a family prominent in Texas public affairs from the founding of the republic, died Saturday at 3:40 P.M. at the home of his son, Cong. Lyndon Johnson.

Russell Morton Brown: "Lyndon had to bury the old man. It was a great embarrassment to Lyndon. The old man had bills all over the place, and Lyndon had to pay them.

"I remember a day or so after the funeral he was sitting in his office, and it was half dark in there. He was rubbing his forehead, and he said, 'My God, Russ, I'm in debt five thousand dollars and all I make is three thousand a year. But I'm in debt five thousand dollars, what with the funeral and all. I'll never get all my debts paid.'

"And I told him he would, and of course he did. But it wasn't easy. I remember there were tears running down his cheeks, and after I said we'd make it, he said, 'We'd better, buddy. We'd better.'"

THREE CHURCHES AND A COURTHOUSE

Kittie Clyde Leonard: "Life in Johnson City then was so different from life in Johnson City now that it's hard to make people understand how different it was. The families were closely knit. Everyone helped other people."

Ava Johnson Cox: "We had Christmas parties—that was regular, and we had house parties, and every week or two we'd have candy breakers, box suppers. We made our own entertainment. Sometimes we had picture shows.

"The opera house was what is now the bank building. It was upstairs. Uncle Sam owned that for a while, and we would put on plays in there, and charge for them, and use the money to buy things for the church. It didn't particularly have to be the Methodist church or the Baptist church or the Christian church—if they needed window shades, why, we took the money and bought them. And everybody took part."

Hilmer Eckert: "I went to school with him in Stonewall. I was a grade ahead of him. He was about a foot taller than the rest of the kids, and his arms were that much longer than anyone else's.

"I boxed with him every night after school. And we'd play baseball. Lyndon, he was a pretty good first baseman. He could reach out there—he could stretch half a mile, by God.

"He never took a book home, but he got straight A's on his report card. That old bugger—he was smart."

Ben Crider: "We lived on a ranch three miles from Johnson City, and when Lyndon lived in town we visited quite often. Lyndon took a liking to me. I went to school with him. He was in a lower grade. I was much older; I am seven years older than he is.

"One thing about Lyndon—he wouldn't run with anyone his own age. He wanted to run with older people, usually about five to ten years older. He was a very brilliant young man, and the boys his age just wasn't in his class mentally. He always went with older girls, too."

Emmette Redford: "This was a community in which—well, the only things that were there that would attract anybody's attention were the three churches and the courthouse. And the courthouse did attract a great deal of attention. Those were periods when district court would be held, trials would be set, and all the other things that occur around a county courthouse. Lyndon had an interest in all those things.

"There was an occasion on which Lyndon thought that Mr. Klett, who was the civics teacher and also the superintendent, ought to adjourn the civics class and let them go to a trial that was occurring at the courthouse. Mr. Klett at first demurred, but Lyndon was so persistent that in the end they were allowed to attend.

"In Johnson City, political interest was always high. So Lyndon developed his interest in politics quite naturally. Of course, he had the interest of his relatives, particularly his father. Somebody in the community got the *Congressional Record*, and this was passed around among the students. I know that Lyndon and my brother Cecil constantly looked at the *Congressional Record* when they were in ninth, tenth, or eleventh grades."

Rebekah: "Lyndon entered a public-speaking contest in the Interscholastic League when he was thirteen. Coached by his mother, he made a creditable appearance and confidently expected to win out in the contest at Fredericksburg.

"However, his mother, believing any child ambitious enough to enter a contest deserved training, had also trained the son of the neighboring German Lutheran minister. The boy, a manly little fellow much smaller in size than Lyndon tho' very little younger, had a pronounced accent. After the coaching lessons were over, Lyndon could be heard continuing his mother's instructions with 'Say it like I do, Walter. Not "I am an Americ*an*" but "I am an A*meri*can."' To his mother's dismay the judges were not, as in later interscholastic contests, qualified teachers of public speaking, but German-speaking citizens selected by the Fredericksburg manager of the contest. The boy's father was a popular, well-known pastor, and his son was known personally to all the judges. They awarded the palm to Walter."[1]

Speaking of that loss to Stewart Alsop in 1965, Lyndon said, "I was so disappointed I went right into the bathroom and was sick."

Alsop added, "There was not a flicker of a smile on his face."[2]

A great deal has been made of the fact that Lyndon, who came from an awesome line of Baptists, including his illustrious great-grandfather Baines, at fifteen joined the Christian church. The official version is that while spending the summer at his Uncle Tom Johnson's place in Johnson City, he accompanied his cousins, Ava and Margaret, to several revival meetings of the Christian sect, and on one particularly feverish evening when the evangelist asked the simplistic question "Do you believe that Jesus is the Christ, son of God?," Lyndon shouted that he did and was immediately led along with several other converts to a pool near a grove of pecan trees not far from the Pedernales and dunked.

Charles Boatner: "His mother told me that an evangelist for the Christian church held a meeting and Mr. Johnson was quite smitten with a young lady there in town and she happened to be a member of that church. And he escorted her to revival every night. So the last night of the revival when they were really working for converts, he joined the Christian church."

Kitty Clyde Leonard: "The dating wasn't like it is now. The dating was more in groups. A group would get together and go someplace. On Friday nights some parent would have a party for the youngsters at their home, or maybe it would be Saturday night.

"Lyndon had several girl friends. I went with him some. There was no such thing as going steady in those days; we didn't go steady, but we did go around together for a while. He was just with me as much as possible at school and other places, and that's one of the things we just took for granted.

"We were talking about that not long ago when we were together. He and Lady Bird invited us to the Ranch, and we were talking about it, and he said, 'You know, Kittie Clyde, I just can't even remember. Things aren't like they were when we went together, are they? I don't even remember ever kissing you!'

"Lyndon was president of the graduating class. There were only six of us—four girls and two boys.

"We always felt that with his ability and personality, he would go far. All of us liked Lyndon. He always said that he never would have graduated if it hadn't been for the girls in the class, but that isn't true. He was just being flattering, that's all. His parents saw to it that he didn't come to school unprepared.

"Boys then wore all kinds of clothing—overalls and blue jeans and khakis. Lyndon always liked to wear a necktie. Many times he would come to school with a white shirt and necktie. I don't know why—he just liked to.

"He had a real persuasive way about him. We always felt that he would be involved in government some way."

In May 1924, at fifteen, Lyndon graduated from the Johnson City high school; class motto was "Give the world the best you have and the best will come back to you." He delivered the class poem and prophecy, and was said to be the youngest graduate in the history of the high school; he was six feet three, and the prediction the class had for him was that he would one day be governor of Texas.

The graduation, which, with all those honors, should have been a day of reflected glory for Rebekah, wasn't; the evening ended with a lively family disagreement. Lyndon told his mother that he never planned to go to school again, any school of any kind, for the rest of his life.

Rebekah repeated words Grandmother Johnson had often thrown out: "You're going to end up in the penitentiary—just mark my words."

Lyndon, then a crusader against strong drink, nevertheless went out with the Crider brothers and got sloshed, mildly so.

Lyndon: "I don't mean things always went just right when I was a kid and that we never had any quarrels in our family. But in what family don't they? I bet even the Lincolns and Jeffersons and I've been told by historians that the Washingtons exchanged a word or two now and again.

"But the fact that I always kept coming back here must mean it wasn't too unhappy a place. I've known kids who left their home place and never came back."

SAN MARCOS

Lyndon: "People who didn't know the depression just don't know about what being poor means. When I finished high school in 1924 there wasn't anything going, no work at all in Johnson City, nowhere around here. My father finally got me kind of a job—not that I wasn't grateful for it—down in Robstown, Texas, which is south of Houston. It was a clerical job and didn't pay much and wasn't in any way the kind of job I had in mind, sitting behind a desk all day.

"I don't think I stayed there more than a few weeks and then I quit or got fired maybe. I don't remember.

"Then I came back here and decided to follow old Horace Greeley's advice. Going west made sense to me. Couldn't go alone, of course. Didn't have a cent to my name to speak of.

"Five or six of us pooled our resources that ranged from twenty to thirty dollars apiece in cash that we made from odd jobs. We had acquired a T-Model Ford without a top or a windshield. It was kind of a pickup, that Model T, and we loaded it up with groceries and things that our mothers gave us and started out to seek our fortunes."[1]

Sam Houston Johnson: "A lot of damfool things have been written about that trip. I told you, people saying that he never broke off from his mother's apron strings, that kind of thing. Well, it was our daddy who raised holy hell about it. He did everything he could think of to stop him, but it didn't work. All mama did, after Lyndon took off, she called Aunt Josefa in Fredericksburg to tell her that Lyndon hadn't taken a pillow and would Aunt Josefa lend him one of hers if she could flag down the car when it passed.

"It was a damn good thing Aunt Josefa never saw the car; Lyndon never would have lived that one down."

O.B. Summy: "We started to California on the third of July in 1925. Lyndon, Otto, Tom Crider, Payne Roundtree, and myself. We lived entirely on fatback and bacon, cornbread and homemade molasses. We only got one flat tire and that was when we got to San Bernardino where Lyndon left us."

Lyndon: "It took us perhaps eight to ten days to make that long trip. When we got there, I had several jobs but didn't hold any of them for long. I washed a few cars. I hashed in a café. I'd say, 'Shipwreck, two, please.' That means scramble two eggs.

"Finally, I worked as an elevator operator in the Platt Building in San Bernardino, California."

Lady Bird: "His cousin, Thomas Martin, a lawyer, finally got Lyndon a job in the same office where he was, which was a considerable step up the ladder from running the elevator. He was only the office boy, carried suitcases and took papers around."

Lyndon's later memories of California, publicly anyway, were all straight John Steinbeck; he was forever a Joad out of *The Grapes of Wrath*, the only movie through which he was known to have stayed awake. As always, he liked to remember the hard times, such as hitchhiking home, half starved, thinner than he had ever been. Actually, he was driven home by Clarence Martin, from whose widow, Aunt Frank, Lyndon and Lady Bird many years later bought the Ranch. Clarence had a good deal to do with Lyndon's early political career, and it is doubtful if he allowed young Lyndon to become hungry along the way. Still, the hitchhiking and hunger make a good story, and as Sam Houston once put it: "Lyndon often remembered things as being worse than they were."

Lyndon: "I was homesick in California, but it was probably a good thing for me to get away from home. I was too young to go to college and at that time I wasn't interested. A lot of people thought I was grown up because I was tall, but I wasn't grown up. Not that I'd have admitted it at the time."

When Lyndon got back to Johnson City he got a job driving a gravel truck on a road across the river, and his father daily gave him a hard time.

"He said I'd never be more than a day laborer and that if I had the brains of the rest of the family I'd be making something of myself. I used to resent the hell out of it and it wasn't until much, much later that I realized he was only trying to get me out of a rut.

"Mother kept urging me to go to school, and finally one Sunday she came in and asked me one more time if I wouldn't go down and find out about enrolling at Southwest Texas State Teachers College in the spring semester in 1927.

"I'd just gone through January on the road gang, and it was cold weather, very cold. At that moment the prospect of going to school in the spring had some appeal to me.

"I said I'd do it.

"It took her about two minutes to get the president of San Marcos, Dr. Cecil Evans, on the phone, and the first thing I knew I was on my way. I don't think my mother was ever much happier than she was that night."[2]

He hitchhiked to the San Marcos campus, and later he remembered, sometimes with a slight tremolo in his voice, that he carried all he owned, all he took anyway, in a cardboard suitcase. The cardboard suitcase, according to Sam Houston, is an invention; the suitcase was either leather or what appeared to be leather.

Lyndon arrived on the campus on what he described as a "dark day in February in 1927," but then, as he later said, "The first winter down there always seemed to be dark, and it always seemed to be cold in those days, too."

Sam Houston: "Hell, if the sun shone, Lyndon would have remembered the day as the day it snowed eight feet, not that it ever snowed eight feet."

Lyndon had whatever he had saved from the road gang—sometimes he remembered a salary of a dollar a day, sometimes two—plus seventy-five dollars that he had borrowed from the banker Percy Brigham of Blanco, fourteen miles from Johnson City. He got the loan on his own signature, although he was underage, largely because Brigham was a great admirer of Grandfather Joseph W. Baines and of Rebekah.

Wilbur J. Cohen: "He had to borrow money to go to college. I think borrowing money to go to college influenced him in all that he did about financial aid for higher education. He wanted to make it easier for people to borrow or get scholarships to go to college. That was a very important experience for him."

All five Johnson children attended Southwest Texas State Teachers College, in print SWTTC, colloquially referred to as just "San Marcos"—pronounced "Marcus" as in Nieman-Marcus. This in spite of the fact that the University of Texas at Austin was equidistant, and that Rebekah was a proud alumnus of Baylor College, of which her grandfather had been president. But with Lyndon having deferred his college entrance, there were never less than two, and often three, Johnson children attending college at the same time. Tuition at San Marcos was seventeen dollars a term, books included, and in that part of Texas at that time San Marcos was where almost everybody who didn't have much money went.

The student body was heavily "Anglo" (white native American) with some immigrant children (German, Polish, Czech) detectable by their accents, a very occasional Mexican-American, and of course no blacks. Three girls for every boy.

In 1927 there were fifty-six faculty members, and the library had twenty-one thousand volumes. The buildings were then and are now without beauty, but the college owned a strip of land along the San Marcos River near the campus, where the water was crystal clear and seventy degrees all year round.[3] For a few the charm of that area somewhat made up for the lack of ivied halls.

San Marcos was administered at that time by a liberal southerner, Dr. Cecil E. Evans. He was a moderate in politics, for which he had a spectatorial passion, and was not inconsiderably embarrassed by the fact that his brother Hiram was Imperial Wizard of the Klan,[4] a fact generally known but never commented upon by him.

Lyndon was in for what he later described as "one of the greatest shocks of my life, and I was scared, too; I thought sure it was back to the road gang for me."

He found he was ineligible to enter. The high school at Johnson City had only eleven grades instead of the usual twelve and, therefore, was not accredited. He could, however, attend a six-week subcollege on the campus and try to "prove" his high school credits; among the doubtful credits were English, always a difficult subject for him, and plane geometry. He enrolled in the subcollege. Several days before the exams Rebekah came over from Johnson City to help prepare him. He was particularly worried about plane geometry.

Lyndon: "My mother sat up all night at a house on North Astor trying to get me to memorize enough plane geometry to get me admitted to college. I made seventy, and seventy was passing, and I never had another damned bit of use for plane geometry before and I never have since.

"They told me I had to have plane geometry because it was logical and orderly and trained the mind and so forth. Now there may be something to that, but what good would it have done if I'd had to drop out and go home, and there have been a lot of college dropouts because of things like that.".

Alfred B. Johnson—"Boody": "Those stories that Lyndon helped pay his way by sweeping floors, waiting on tables, and laying concrete sidewalks are exaggerated.

"Our first campus job was in the maintenance department, and we were picking up trash on the campus. But Lyndon didn't go for that kind of work; he didn't go for physical labor of any kind—and it didn't pay much either.

"He once said to me, 'Boody, the way you get ahead in this world, you get close to those that are the heads of things. Like President Evans, for example.'

"And before long he was working as a clerk in Prexy's office. I got promoted to inspector of buildings at thirty-five dollars a month. Lyndon later claimed he got that job for me, but I already had it lined up. Lyndon liked to have credit for things."

Boody, who was to become captain of the football team, was a sophomore on the campus when Lyndon arrived and was already considered a figure of importance. The two quickly became known as "Johnson and Johnson" and "The Johnson Boys," though they were not related. For two years they were roommates in a room over Dr. Evans's garage.

Boody: "We made fair money for college boys at our side jobs, but Lyndon liked to run up to Austin and watch the legislature at work, and talk to politicians, and that always took money.

"And when we were short, Lyndon would talk Prexy into letting us paint the garage. We painted that garage three times in two years, and Prexy once said that it might not be the best-painted garage in San Marcos, but it was the most painted garage there."

Professor H.M. Greene, who taught government and debate, was Lyndon's favorite teacher, and Greene once stated what was the essence of Lyndon's philosophy all through his life, including in the presidency. Greene maintained that "Democracy is of necessity a compromise. It is made of strong-minded men who cannot all prevail as individuals. Therefore, their concerted action must be a compromise."[5]

Professor Greene was the kind of iconoclast of whom there is always one on every campus. He challenged authority, including that of Dr. Evans, although never too outrageously; he challenged whatever sacred cows were grazing about, though never unforgivably; he taught classes wearing khaki shirts and patched trousers, and, to be sure, was immensely popular with the students.

Dean A.H. Nolle: "Lyndon literally sat at the feet of Professor Greene. Though not a profound scholar, Professor Greene had a remarkable understanding of political trends and events, and this evidently fascinated his student. They were unusually close."

Greene retired in 1957, but in January 1965 when his former student was inaugurated as president, he attended as a special guest.

Lyndon and Greene had other things in common besides an interest in politics. As has been observed, Greene was not a particularly scholarly man; like Lyndon he was seldom seen to read a book, but again like Lyndon, he devoured newspapers. Both seemed able to pluck ideas out of the air and out of other men's minds. Both were dedicated askers of questions.

Greene, like Lyndon, was fond of stories that shocked the faint of heart; his humor, too, was largely oriented to the barnyard. He was also the debate coach, and when he and his two star debaters, Lyndon and Elmer Graham, who was to become a Baptist minister in San Antonio, were on their way to another college for a debate, the earthy exchanges between them shocked young Graham.

Graham was also less than enthusiastic over the fact that he and usually he alone had to do the meticulous research necessary in preparing a debate, and he always opened the debate. Lyndon, uninhibited by preparation, listened to Elmer and then to their first opponent, jotting down the opponent's weaknesses, then coming on so aggressively that the other team was often reduced to mindlessness. "Ruthless" was the way Graham described Johnson's technique.

True, it was successful; they won all their debates, but Graham was not one of Lyndon's idolators on campus.

Willard Deason: "The year Lyndon and I were both seniors during the first term the president of the class was an athlete, a very popular fellow by the name of Dick Spinn.

"Everybody thought Spinn was sure to be reelected, but Lyndon thought I ought to run, and my name was put up. We all worked hard, especially Lyndon, but the night before the election we started counting noses, counting who had the vote. It wasn't too difficult; there weren't but about two hundred seniors.

"It soon got to be pretty clear that I couldn't win, that I was at least fifteen to twenty votes behind.

"Most of us were ready to throw in the towel, but Lyndon said no. He said, 'This is a challenge, and a challenge is an opportunity. You're not going to give up when you're that close.'

"That was about midnight. Now there were those who supported the Black Stars on the campus, and the people who supported us,[6] and there was a group of about twenty or so that they called the YMCA group, and Dick Spinn was a member of the YMCA, and those were the ones Lyndon went after.

"As I say, it was about midnight when we started, and he went around to the various dormitories and talked to people in the YMCA group. I don't know how he did it, but between midnight and two in the morning he did.

"By the next morning—we voted early—at ten o'clock the election was over, and I had won by eight votes.

"It's the kind of thing I guess Lyndon did later in the Senate when he was majority leader. Until the last vote was committed, you couldn't get him to stop."

One of Lyndon's major campus activities was the *College Star*, the weekly newspaper, on which he served in various capacities and as editor in chief at least twice. Files of the newspaper offer many editorials under his name, written in the best Lyndon style of the time, and the style, alas, seldom improved much.

From the February 1, 1928, issue:

> Behind all constructive work is a vision, a dream, a plan. Without this the work would lack spirit, organization and power. It is the great compelling force that puts forth the first effort of the worker, that sustains him in discouragement and cheers him in consummation of the task. It starts the ball to rolling and keeps it going in every-day practice. Vision is the soul of work.

The *Star*'s editorship paid about seventy-five dollars a month, and offered Lyndon the vehicle he desired to express his ideas. It also opened the door to other activities.

Most students at San Marcos were either uninterested or unaware that in the early summer of 1928 the Democrats were to hold their national convention at Sam Houston Hall in Houston. Lyndon had no intention of missing it.

Professor Tom Nichols of the School of Business Administration: "For many weeks before the convention the *College Star* carried big headlines and long stories about the forthcoming meeting. I wondered about the undue emphasis on politics in a student newspaper, but we had always given the editor a rather free hand, and I did not interfere.[7]

"Later I learned that Lyndon carried a bundle of those papers to Houston, spread out all the big headlines before the proper officials, and got himself accredited as a correspondent.

"He also persuaded someone to drive him to Houston, and he got him into the convention, too."

Deason: "Lyndon was always into several things at once. He was working for a living, and at the same time he was into campus politics in a big way, on the debating team, and president of the journalism club. He was never popular with his fellow students, though. They thought he was arrogant. They may have been jealous of him because he had so much energy and could accomplish so much."

Lyndon: "In my senior year I've never worked so hard. I carried seven courses. Generally you carried five. And they wouldn't let anybody take but six courses, but I hid one, and I carried a seven-course load. I was halfway into it before they caught on, and I made them give me credit for it.

"And I taught two courses in freshman government and was secretary to the college president. When I wound up, I had about a thousand dollars in the bank. I had a date every night, too—never got more than three or four hours' sleep."

But before that senior year and state of wealth, Lyndon, in financial difficulties, took nine months off. By the summer of 1928, he had completed the five required education courses that earned him a "two-year certificate" and eligibility to teach at the grade-school level, and he got a job in Cotulla, Texas, as teacher and principal of a small school in which all the students were Mexican-Americans, as they were then called.

"To lead inquiring and impressionable minds into the great treasure house of knowledge that the world has accumulated is of itself a priceless privilege," he wrote for the *College Star*. "To be of service to humanity is recompense for struggling years and patient study."

And so young Lochinvar went off to Cotulla. The experience was to remain with him for the rest of his life.

HOW DO YOU DO, MR. JOHNSON?

Lyndon, speaking before Congress on March 15, 1965: "My first job after college was as a teacher in Cotulla, Texas, in a small Mexican-American school.[1] Few of them could speak English, and I couldn't speak much Spanish. My students were poor and they often came to class without breakfast, hungry. They knew even in their youth the pain of prejudice. They never seemed to know why people disliked them. But they knew it was so, because I saw it in their eyes. I often walked home late in the afternoon, after the classes were finished, wishing there was more that I could do. But all I knew was to teach them the little that I knew, hoping that it might help them against the hardships that lay ahead.

"Somehow you never forget what poverty and hatred can do when you see its scars on the hopeful face of a young child."

Wilbur J. Cohen: "Again and again in talking to me he would go back to that year he spent teaching those Mexican children in Cotulla. He would talk about how that experience motivated him to come out of a narrow, rural, opinionated, conservative atmosphere into a large, throbbing idealism under Roosevelt. I think his conception of the presidency always was: 'If only I can do the same thing for my time that Roosevelt did for his.'

"I feel that experience of his teaching those Mexican kids was a very important aspect of his whole life. It motivated him on the education bills, on his nondiscrimination, on civil rights, and a great many basic ideas that were developed during his presidency. I think when he saw those hungry children digging into garbage, it was the first time he had really seen grinding poverty.

"Now nobody had much, if any, money when he was growing up but this was poverty of a different sort, and it really shocked him. He had these experiences in his youth, and they were very meaningful to him. He was not an intellectual in the typical meaning of that word, being able to develop a theory or concept just by spinning it out as a professor would. It all grew out of his own relationship with reality. Now if you call that corny or sentimental, that's the way he was. And I see nothing wrong with it. It's in the best pragmatic tradition of all great political leaders. I think it was true of Theodore Roosevelt and Franklin Roosevelt.

"The experience of Cotulla was basic."

Cotulla, halfway between San Antonio and Laredo, is not near anything of the slightest importance, and it is not a place anyone would go if he had anyplace else to go. Lyndon arrived the first week in September 1928. The weather was still hot—it often goes above 110 degrees in the summer—and the streets were crowded with cowboys or with men who dressed like cowboys. The land, called the Neuces Plains, is flat and treeless, suitable only for raising cattle.

Dorothy Nichols: "There were only about three thousand people in town, so everybody knew everybody else.

"He taught in the Mexican school; it was a new school that had just been open a couple of years, called the Welhausen School in the Mexican part of town. He was the principal and taught the sixth and seventh grades; I believe those were the grades. There were five other teachers all together, and he was in charge of them.

"The children all spoke Spanish at home, but at school he made them speak English; they couldn't get into high school unless they could speak and read English.

"I remember one of the things he did; he found out that the janitor, who was an old man, couldn't read or write. He bought a primer and started teaching that man. I think it took most of the year he was there, but he did it.

"There was one boy—I don't remember his name[2]—who couldn't pass the English test to get into the high school, so Lyndon took him home and he and his mother tutored him. I understand he did pass the test."

[Cotulla, undated]

Dearest Mother,

I rec'd your sweet letter yesterday when I needed it so much. I sometimes get so homesick when Sunday comes around.

Went to church last night at the Baptist church. Wish you could have been there.

I want 200 pkg. of toothpaste. We soon will have over 250 in school. They are all rather small and I think they would appreciate it very much. . . .

Dan Garcia, one of Lyndon's pupils, later a successful Cotulla businessman and member of the town council: "We used to come in there—the three grades—there used to be about thirty of them in the class—and all of them would sit down and wait for him to come in after the bell rang. He would come in and stand in front of the desk and he would ask us to stand up for the regular singing—the regular morning class singing—and we used to sing: 'How do you do, Mr. Johnson.

> 'How do you do, Mr. Johnson,
> 'How do you do?
> 'Is there anything that we can do for you?
> 'We will do it if we can,
> 'We'll stand by you to a man.
> 'How do you do, Mr. Johnson,
> 'How do you do, do, do?'[3]

"He would come and sit at his desk and I believe he was teaching us Texas history and arithmetic problems—1, 2, 3, 4, 5, 6, 7, 8, 9 multiplied by 1, 2, 3, 4, 5, 6, 7, 8, 9—and he would put this on the blackboard and give us so much time to see who would finish first and with the right answers and he would get all kinds of answers, you know, for such a long multiplication table. And then of course he would ask questions about Texas history of us and he would mention the fact that this country is a great big country of great liberties and opportunities for everybody, and that any individual by studying hard and working hard would possibly be able to become president of the United States."

Lyndon speaking before the National Conference on Educational Legislation, March 1, 1965:
"The Johnson administration's continuing concern is for improved educational opportunity for all children in this land. . . .
"Now you can keep your blood pressure down if you want to. You can sit in your rocking chair and talk about the days that have gone by if you choose. But as far as I am concerned, I am going to use every rostrum and every forum and every searchlight that I can to tell the people of this country and their elected representatives that we can no longer afford overcrowded classrooms and half-day sessions. We just must not, we just cannot afford the great waste that comes from the neglect of a single child."[4]
In his postpresidency years Lyndon, addressing the students at San Marcos, said: "I left here as a sophomore, and I became the principal of a six-teacher school in Cotulla. It was mostly, in fact I guess entirely, Mexican-American students who were there then, and they didn't have anything to do during recess except fight each other, which they did, and the teachers all went to the bathrooms and smoked.
"I tried to get some organized play activity started, but the teachers said those Mexican kids didn't want to do anything but fight. They wouldn't have anything to do with it; and when I started some softball and had some dancing and musical instruments to entertain the kids during recess—those poor people that lived down there on the border of Texas, I never understood it, but they and the Mexican people in Texas have been voting for me ever since. They knew what I was doing.
"But the teachers went out on strike on me; they said they weren't supervising any recesses with *those* kids; and they were some of the best-connected people in town, the

daughter of a banker was one I remember, and another was a sister of the mayor and another the sister of the postmaster. You can see how things worked in those days in Cotulla.

"Well, I went to a woman in town who was on the school board and who was a graduate of Randolph Macon College and told her what happened, and she just said, 'If those teachers have resigned or struck on you, just accept their resignations and go back to San Marcos and get replacements for them, replacements that will come here and supervise during recess.'

"They had a school board meeting, and this woman made a motion to the effect of what she said, and the board voted with me. After that the original teachers came back and said they would stay and they would supervise.

"So we taught these children to play games, and we taught them to sing, and we organized a band and had a debating team."

Lyndon also organized a volleyball team, that we know, and a basketball and a baseball team, all at no extra salary. He organized a literary society, which for a nonreader was surprising, and he volunteered to coach the debate team, which for a man who considered most of life to be one long debate is not surprising.

Since there were no buses to take Mexican children anywhere in those days, Lyndon found out which parents owned cars and persuaded them to drive the debaters to out-of-town debates. In Cotulla as in Washington it was nearly impossible to say no to Lyndon.

In addition, he found time to fall in love, and he took and passed correspondence courses from Southwest Texas State Teachers giving him an additional twelve hours of credit.

It was a busy year, but then, which one was not?

Lyndon: "Another thing about that year. I was very much in love with a pretty girl. And she got a job that paid her a hundred and fifty dollars a month. Very much to my humiliation. She could make more than I could.[5]

"Every Friday night I would go up to see her. She lived thirty-five miles away. And I'd write her lesson plans for her for all the next week.

"She was teaching civics and American history. She didn't know a thing about either. Never had heard of a county judge even, but was an expert in Spanish. I needed the Spanish, and she needed the civics and history. She tried to teach me to say 'buenas tardes, amigos' or something, and I would try to tell her the difference between a governor and a president.

"And then we'd transact a little other business like going to the movies or something like that.

"They offered me another contract, but I wanted to finish my college work, and in June of '29 I went back to San Marcos and continued right straight through until August of 1930 when I got a bachelor of science degree.

"Well, of course, I was young, and those years always seem to people in later life to have been the best. But in those years I was involved directly with *education*. You see,

I've always been interested in education. There are those who say I've never had much myself, and they may be right. But that doesn't mean I don't care about it. I do.

"I remember when I was at San Marcos and was given a test by this history professor or political science professor, I forget which. The question he put on the blackboard was this, 'Discuss fully what the federal Constitution has to say about education.' So I did, and, hell, it must have gone on for ten pages or so.

"Well, I got that paper back with a big red *F* across it. And the professor wrote on the paper, 'The Constitution doesn't mention education.'

"Well, I decided right then and there that if there wasn't anything in the Constitution on the subject of education, there ought to have been. And I decided I was going to do something about it, and if you look back on the bills that were passed during my administration, I think you might say that I have."

SPEAKING FOR PAT NEFF

When Lyndon was handed his degree in August 1930, it could, as was said at the time, with a nickel buy a cup of coffee.

There were many more degrees than jobs.

Rebekah had said that the only three things a Texas boy could do to fulfill himself were to teach, to preach, or to go into politics. Lyndon wasn't ready for the latter, or vice versa. To become a preacher he would need another kind of degree, which was, of course, impossible. So he decided to return to teaching. First, he had his highly successful experience at Cotulla to recommend him. Second, he had Uncle George Desha Johnson, who taught history at Houston's Sam Houston High School.

It was true that teachers with years of experience were being laid off and, after their meager savings had disappeared, were going on relief, of which there was little.

Uncle George, however, was earning $2,800 a year, or so Lyndon remembered, and George had often said that he hoped the day would come when he and Lyndon could teach at the same school. There were not, however, any immediate openings, and Lyndon accepted a job as principal of a high school in Pearsall, Texas, at $165 a month.[1] About a month later a job as a public speaking teacher opened up at Sam Houston at $160 a month,[2] and Lyndon took it.

The morning he arrived at Sam Houston, Lyndon asked for and got an appointment with the principal. The new debate coach was shocked, he said, to see that Sam Houston had lost to San Jacinto High four years in a row. Well, Lyndon Johnson had no intention of losing in the city, in the district, in the state.

Luther E. Jones, Jr.,: "I was a senior when he was there. I was part of his debating team.

"Then, as now, he was characterized by enormous physical energy. In fact, all the qualities that people associate with him as president were manifested at this early period. I mean the human dynamo, the intense dedication to a particular problem at hand, unlimited enthusiasm. I never will forget—the principal of the school was W.J. Moyes, and I can recall two or three discussions where I was present and heard rather vigorous arguments by Mr. Johnson. He'd be asking for money, for example, to take the debaters on trips, and he would be informed that it had never been done. Mr. Johnson would say, 'Yes, but you've never had a teacher like me.'

Gene Latimer, one of his star debaters: "Let's say it is an October day in 1930 at Sam Houston High School as I enter my speech class. A few things become quickly apparent. If I am to continue on the debate team, my outside activities will be confined to after-school practice and visits to the city library in the search of arcane references to the jury system, which is the subject selected for this year's high school debates.[3] For the 'Chief,' as I and others came to call him, has already decided he will make state champions of us."

Lyndon: "I felt about my students very much like I feel about my staff. If they would take one side of a question, I would take the other, and I would just try to run them underground, just almost stomp them. But always made it clear that I loved them, so they never ran completely off. But I'd humiliate them and embarrass them, and I would make fun of them and everything until they got to where they could take care of themselves, which they did. And I developed several better speakers—much better than I was.

"I used to have pep rallies before debating contests. I'd have people get up and sing songs, and I'd have people hurrah for Jones and Latimer, just like you would at a football game. And we had them running out of seats at the final debate and you couldn't get in. Every place was taken in the balcony, every one on the floor, and they were sitting in the windows to hear the debate.

"We had sixty-seven debates and lost one, and we lost that, the state championship of Texas, three to two. And it was on the question—Resolved, that the jury system should be abolished. We had no trouble when we debated on the side that it shouldn't be abolished. But when we had the affirmative we always had trouble.

"I just almost cried when we drew the affirmative, and we lost by just one vote—three to two."[4]

The defeat did not, however, diminish the enthusiasm of the citizens of Houston for the debate team and its coach. The school board, which that year had cut the salaries of a great many teachers, voted to give him a hundred-dollar-a-year raise.

That summer Lyndon delivered his first political speech and managed his first, and successful, campaign.

Welly K. Hopkins: "In 1930, I was a candidate for the state senate inasmuch as Alvin Wirtz had voluntarily retired. I had announced my candidacy, and Wirtz had put me in touch with his supporters around the district, and among these was Lyndon's father. I saw him from time to time in the early phases of the campaign, but I had no occasion to run into Lyndon until I went up to a political gathering.

"It was a typical occasion. There was a speaking platform consisting of just a country delivery wagon with the tailgate let down. I heard the master of ceremonies call the name of Pat Neff, and he called two or three times and nobody responded. Neff was a former governor of Texas and up for reelection to the state railroad commission.

"The master of ceremonies called again on Pat Neff or somebody to speak for him. He was about to pass on to the next one when—I remember it very well—I saw coming through the crowd a young fellow, kind of waving his arms about, calling out, 'By God, I'll make a speech for Pat Neff.' Whereupon he climbed up on the tailgate and in the next ten minutes or so made a stemwinding, arm-swinging speech in behalf of Neff.

"He had been introduced, as I recall, as 'Lyndon Johnson, Sam Johnson's son.' Everybody in the countryside knew Sam Johnson.

"Later I asked him why he had made this speech, and his reply I've never forgotten. It was in substance: 'Governor Neff once gave my daddy a job when he needed it, so I couldn't let him go by default.'

"Lyndon and I became friendly within a very short time. I asked him if he would try to help me in my campaign. He readily consented. So I kind of turned my campaign over to him in the sense of Blanco and Hays Counties, and he did a magnificent job."

Then, the following fall, after Lyndon had returned to Sam Houston High, Congressman Harry M. Wurzbach died in a hospital in San Antonio. Among the candidates who announced to succeed him—ten at the beginning, eight at the end—was an amiable man in his early forties named Richard Kleberg, whose father, Robert J. Kleberg, was one of the owners of the King Ranch, the largest in the world, a million acres more or less, larger, as Lyndon used to say, than the entire state of Connecticut.

Kleberg won, and as Hopkins remembered it, "I felt that Dick coming up as a new congressman would do well to have a young fellow like Lyndon with him. Dick had never met Lyndon, but Roy Miller, his campaign manager, agreed to recommend Lyndon."

Helen Weinberg, a history teacher at Sam Houston High School, was in the administrative office when the long-distance call came for Johnson: "He was so excited he didn't know what to say. He said that he would consult with his uncle and call back in a few minutes. When he hung up, he turned to me and said with great excitement, 'Mr. Kleberg wants me to be his private secretary. I'll have to go up and tell Uncle George.'"[5]

Jones: "Lyndon would use Uncle George as a sounding board. There was a lot of respect for Uncle George, and I have a feeling that Uncle George played maybe a pretty important part in Lyndon's life at that stage, for good advice. Lyndon was an impetuous sort of fellow, and I'm sure it didn't hurt him to have an older man cautioning him once in a while about the quicksands." Lyndon left Sam Houston High with some reluctance; teaching was a calling that had always been close to his heart, one to which, in his last days in the presidency, he would have dreams of returning in retirement. Still . . ."

Lyndon: "I was never *dis*interested in politics. But I did think about teaching. Dr. Evans, president of the college when I was there, and my Uncle George both had the same idea, that teaching was a wonderful profession and gave a man a satisfaction that he could never get out of just making money, but it did have one drawback. This is what they said, both of them. The teacher was a law unto himself in the classroom, and it wasn't the competitive operation that either the law or politics would bring out. They bring out more of what is in you than teaching, because if you are in a courtroom talking to a jury, or if you are out stumping, debating a man, or if you are in a legislative hall trying to present a pro and someone presents a con—you have to prepare and develop and react and be alert to an extent that is not required if you are in a classroom with thirty young boys and girls and you know it all and they don't.

"Over all, I wouldn't say I had any serious regrets at finally choosing politics as a career. But I could give you a very long list of people who wish I had gone into some other line of work."

MISTER DICK

When "Mister Dick," as the newly elected congressman liked to be called, arrived in Washington with Lyndon—it had been the latter's first train trip outside of Texas—the weather was bleak and cold.

Lyndon also liked to remember that he looked outside Union Station, and the Capitol dome seemed only a few steps away. That, he remembered thinking, was a place he had every intention of being one day as "a congressman in my own right." The Texas legislature in Austin might be good enough for Sam Ealy, but his elder son had greater dreams of glory.

"I would not say I was without ambition, ever. You just had to look around, and it was very exciting to me to realize that the people, many of them that you were passing, were probably congressmen at least, maybe senators, members of the cabinet. And there was the *smell* of power. It's got an odor, you know, power I mean." [1]

Mister Dick hailed a taxi to take them to the Mayflower, by far the grandest hotel Lyndon had ever seen. The first few nights in Washington he was Mister Dick's guest there, and he described it in a bantering letter to his close friend and college classmate Jesse Kellam back in Texas: "They got red carpeting all over the place, and you know what that means where we come from . . . Of course, my mind is *all* business at this stage of the game."

Mister Dick's, however, wasn't. Winning the election had been pleasant enough; he liked winning things, especially when it didn't take too much effort, but serving his constituents, some of whose jobs were to serve him at the King Ranch, was a bore. After all, the front gate of the ranch was twenty miles from the front door of the house, and as a boy whenever he traveled it was in a private railroad car. He was not a bad man; he was a lazy man, though, and his imagination was limited. He was more interested in breeding fast horses, which he sometimes raced himself, bird dogs, and fighting cocks. Whenever young Lyndon brought up the subject of what he liked to refer to as the congressman's obligations to his constituents, the congressman rushed off for a day of golf at the Burning Tree Course in Maryland.

When they had been in Washington less than a week Lyndon wrote his mother on Mayflower stationery:

Dearest Mother:

I don't know when I've been so tired as I am tonight. . . .

To start to tell you how I've worked since I came here would require more time and effort than I feel like expending. I get up at 6 o'clock and go to the office by 7:30, take off 30 minutes sometime during the day for lunch and leave the office about six or seven depending on the correspondence. I *run* the office *force*. Mr. Kleberg doesn't spend an hour a day there and then only signing letters. Frequently I go back at night to finish so I won't get behind. Am learning fast and doing a good job of my work. The only expressions that Mister Dick has made regarding my work go like this: "Great—Good—That's what I want etc." I work for one of the ablest men in Washington and I'm confident the best. He treats me like his brother. Eat, sleep, and work with him. He spares no expense for my comfort, sacrifices everything for my desire. I'm going to move from here before the holidays. Don't know where I'll go but am going to find a nice place.

Am afraid I can't come home Xmas. You don't know how I want to. Am 2,087 miles from S.A. over 1,000 from St. Louis. He may let me go tho'.

Must go. Mr. Kleberg has just come in. I'm placing a call now for him to Mrs. Kleberg in Corpus Christi.

Love to all. Please write. Lyndon Baines.

Lyndon realized from the beginning that he not only had to *run* the office *force*; he had to run the congressman as well, and on those rare occasions when he saw Mister Dick he did. For instance, very early on he took Mister Dick to the offices of both Texas senators, Tom Connally and Morris Sheppard, which, although Kleberg didn't realize it, was a brash act for a freshman congressman.

Except for the fact that he was one of the Klebergs of the King Ranch, Mister Dick didn't make much of an impression on the senators, but Lyndon Johnson did, which was what he had in mind.

Arthur Perry, who was Connally's secretary, remembered later that Lyndon did most of the talking, but that was no surprise to Perry. He and Lyndon were already friends and fellow tenants with Robert Jackson, then a clerk in the office of Congressman R. E. Thomason, also from Texas, in subbasement rooms of the dowdy Dodge Hotel, which was within easy walking distance of the Capitol and the Senate and House office buildings. Subsequent tenants included Gene Latimer, Luther Jones, and Carroll Keach, whom Lyndon recruited from Texas to join Kleberg's office staff.

Gene Latimer: "The Dodge Hotel was an extremely respectable place, almost totally inhabited by elderly widows, but the basement was used for impecunious persons such as ourselves. It was here that many of the secretaries of members of the House and Senate resided. I can recall that when work was finished on many occasions the Chief, Bob Jackson, and Arthur Perry and I walked together from the Capitol complex over to the Dodge. After washing up we usually went together to some place to eat.

"Our financial situation was such that this turned out to be, in most instances, Childs Restaurant, a place close to the Union Station. When I think of Childs, I think of a little discussed side of the Chief, and that is that prior to his marriage to Lady Bird, he had an eye for girls with pretty faces and figures and did not regard too much what was behind those faces. One of the beauteous young ladies at Childs succumbed almost instantly, at least after two or three nights, and I was not to see the Chief until the early hours of the morning.

"As for the Dodge itself, during the winter the pipes hammered from steam, but it was a place that we all used together for animated discussions always led by Lyndon Johnson."

Luther E. Jones, Jr.: "John Connally was down there for a while. He came later. You know what I remember about John? The way he loved his hair.

"Bear in mind this is a very young man. He devoted much more time than you would imagine to combing his hair, brushing his hair. You know, he'd look at his hair, and he'd brush it, and he'd brush it. If we'd kid him about it, he'd say, 'Well, this will guarantee that it will never come out; it will never be thin. I'm going to keep it like this all my life.'"

Congressional staffs were smaller and less influential then than they are now, but the members knew all about everybody and were willing, even anxious to share their knowledge—which congressmen drank too much, which were misbehaving in other ways, which were most sexual, and which had power. It was the latter who interested Lyndon most.

Russell Morton Brown, for whom Lyndon first got a job writing letters in Kleberg's office: "He'd say, 'But how did he do it? (whatever it was.) Did he *know* somebody? Is he a nice guy? What's his secret of getting ahead?' I'd say, 'I don't know as he has any special secret,' and Lyndon would say, and this is what I remember, 'Well, I tell you one thing, it isn't any accident.' I'd say, 'Maybe he's just lucky,' and he'd say, 'I don't believe in luck. You look into it and you'll find it's always a lot more than just luck.'"

While he was working for Dick Kleberg, Lyndon considered dinner simply another opportunity to discuss politics; after he learned all that Bob Jackson and Arthur Perry knew on the subject, and it didn't take long, then he would argue with them, often taking positions he didn't really support just to see how they would react. He was an eternal debater.

After dinner, Lyndon, at least, would often go back to work.

Robert M. Jackson: "He would frequently go back up to Congressman Kleberg's office and work until ten or eleven o'clock at night and come back to the hotel and wake me up and we would sit around and talk for hours. His energy is almost impossible to exaggerate."

Brown: "It need be no secret that Lyndon was in effect the real congressman at that time, because Congressman Kleberg left everything to Lyndon. The congressman would ordinarily come to the office about 10:00 A.M. three or four days a week, especially when there were important visitors from Texas, would greet them effusively and call one of the staff to bring in the whiskey, 'so we can strike a blow for liberty.' This was Garner's slogan of protest against the Eighteenth Amendment.

"It was customary for Congressman Kleberg to answer 'the call of the House,' meaning the roll call at the convening of the House, daily at twelve noon. He would then call the office, and one of the staff would meet him at the back door of the House Office Building for any last-minute messages, requests, or information. The congressman then proceeded directly to the Burning Tree Country Club."

Members of Congress had, at that time, so-called patronage jobs at their disposal—jobs like elevator operator, post office employee, doorkeeper for the House gallery—which they doled out to relatives or sons of close friends. As the system generally worked, after the day's work was over, the employee was on his own time. Lyndon, however, improved on the system. He needed more help in the office to handle the voluminous amounts of mail he felt were necessary to Kleberg's political security back home, so whoever held one of Kleberg's patronage jobs was expected to report to Lyndon immediately after that day's work was done, at which point the serious work of the day began.

Jones: "At first Lyndon Johnson was a hard man to work for because he insisted on perfection. Everything had to look just right, and it had to be the way *he* wanted it.

"At the beginning he dictated a lot, but ultimately no dictation was required. I mean, he'd have a pile of letters and he'd just make a few comments: 'Say "yes," say "no," "put him off," "butter him up."' In due time I knew what he wanted. But at first I wrote literally hundreds of letters over. And he had no compunction at all about making you write them over, even if you had to stay till midnight. You handed him fifty, sixty letters at five o'clock, and he might mark out every one of them.

"It's fantastic how absorbed he was in that job, even to the extent of writing personal letters to Dick Kleberg's mother.

"Most people wouldn't believe the way we worked. Johnson would wake up at five, five thirty, very early, and he'd see that we got out of bed. We'd have breakfast by the time the dining room opened, and we'd be working by seven or seven thirty and not get home till midnight many nights.

"But you know, nobody minded. I mean, the atmosphere was full of challenge, and this guy's enthusiasm was just absolutely contagious. Even in those days we were all speculating: 'This guy's going to be either president or the equivalent—he's going to be a man of destiny.' We all had that feeling."

Sam Fore: "When he was Kleberg's secretary, he made a number of trips back to our county—Wilson County—and he'd have those farmers and ranchers meet him at the courthouse and give him their troubles. He'd take them in his car even to Houston to try to save their farms through the Federal Land Bank. Then he'd come back and go to the RFC in San Antonio—the Reconstruction Finance Corporation—to finish up the job.

"I think he stayed about two or three weeks one time just on jobs like that, doing things for people in distress."

Ben Crider: "He wanted to do something for the people. And when the depression was at its worst, he was working the farmers just like some gray-headed man. He was out there in his early twenties talking to them, patting them on the back, and the appraisers, the district appraisers, told me, isn't it a miracle he can handle those old folks like he can?

"They were losing their farms, and he was furious. He was trying to get Congress to liberalize those appraisals. They were too tight. They weren't allowing enough evaluation on the property, and he was trying to get them to raise that, and they finally did."

Jackson: "Very quickly after I met him, the campaign of 1932 started, and he was just terribly stirred up about the Roosevelt campaign and Franklin Roosevelt. Radios were not very common then. Car radios were especially unusual, but Arthur Perry had a little Chevy coupe with a radio in it. Every time Roosevelt talked, and it was broadcast, we would get in this little coupe and drive around. We would get the reception better down around Haines Point. We would drive around and around there, listening to the speech."

Franklin D. Roosevelt was inaugurated for the first time on March 4, 1933, and after assuring the nation that "the only thing we have to fear is fear itself," he immediately started terrifying a substantial minority of the voters by launching what to a man like Dick Kleberg seemed radical and possibly even communistic programs such as the Agricultural Adjustment Act. Lyndon, on the other hand, supported the New Deal totally.

Brown: "When the AAA was proposed, the idea was to reduce production of some crops because there was too much, and to diversify production, because it was necessary for the welfare of the farming communities. For example, there were more areas that were producing cotton without regard to the market need for cotton. Or there were areas that were producing corn and hogs, without reference to how much the market could absorb. And so the AAA was set up with the purpose of having the agricultural community diversify.

"Kleberg, who was a big-business man essentially, with a multimillion-dollar background, was against it. And of course all the lobbyists were against it—'You're going to bankrupt the country! Giving people money not to plant crops! Giving money to people to kill little pigs!'

"Kleberg and Lyndon had a conference, and Lyndon tried to persuade him to support the legislation. And Kleberg said, 'I can't do it, Lyndon, and I'm not going to do it. I don't believe it's good for the country. And I'm off to Burning Tree.' And he went.

"Well, he seldom came back to the office at the end of the day, but that particular day for some reason he came back to sign some mail, if I understand it. And Lyndon was cleaning out his desk and packing the stuff in boxes. And Kleberg says, 'What's going on?'

"Lyndon says, 'Mister Dick, I'm going home.' Kleberg looked at him, and he said, 'What do you mean, Lyndon, you're going home?' He said, 'I'm resigning. My resignation is on your desk.'

"'Oh, now, Lyndon, what's going on here?' Lyndon said, 'Well, Mister Dick, if you throw down the president on this bill all the folks at home who elected you, who sent you up here to represent them, are going to be thrown down at the same time. They *want* us to vote for this legislation.'

"He said, 'They *need* this legislation. With some of those families down there, it's a matter of keeping bread on the table. If you throw them down, I can't go home and face them. I'm here with you—they're going to hold me as responsible as they hold you. If you vote against this legislation, you're throwing down the president of the United States, who's head of our party—the party that elected you. I just can't stay, because I feel that I'd be betraying the folks at home just as much as you are.'

"Now Kleberg's kinda breathless, thinking what he's going to do without Lyndon. And Lyndon said, 'Not only that, Mister Dick, but the bill is going to pass. I've polled the House, and it's going to pass with a big margin.'

"He had checked with every administrative assistant on the Hill. Kleberg said, 'You mean that bill is a cinch to pass, Lyndon?' Lyndon said, 'Not only is it a cinch to pass, but you're going to stand out like a traitor to the country if you're one of the few Democrats who vote against the president, and against this legislation.'

"So Dick Kleberg voted in favor of the agriculture act."

"IT WAS ANNOUNCED TODAY"

Hubert H. Humphrey: "You must never underestimate the importance of Sam Rayburn in Johnson's career. During their long years of association, beginning with the Kleberg days, very few days passed when they did not confer. Of course Rayburn was very much Johnson's senior. He had been in Congress since 1913, and, as you know, that was the year Woodrow Wilson became president. A very long time.

"Their relationship was usually described as a father-son relationship."

Robert H. Fleming: "When Lyndon was working for Congressman Kleberg, he was living in the basement of the Dodge Hotel, and one day he got so sick he just couldn't go in, and for Lyndon that meant that he was very sick. He just stayed in bed that day, and late in the afternoon or early in the evening he woke up and saw Mr. Rayburn asleep in a chair by his bed, cigarette ashes falling all down the front of his suit.

"In a little while Rayburn woke up, and Lyndon said, 'What are you doing here?' And Mr. Rayburn said, 'When I was at Kleberg's office today they said young Lyndon was sick.' I said, 'Is that Sam Johnson's boy?' They said it was, and it struck me that maybe Sam Johnson's boy didn't have anybody who cared whether he was sick or not. So I want to know how you are.' It turned out Lyndon had pneumonia."

Lyndon: "We got to be the best of friends when I was still working for Dick Kleberg. I'd drop in to see him, and he'd be all alone. Many days he just was there at home reading. He'd be there to midnight reading. That's really when we got to be best friends. And after many years, after he'd tested me from every angle and found out that it was all right, he'd come out to the house three or four times a week, have dinner with us, just like a member of the family. I think sometimes he was lonesome."

That most members of Congress were lawyers was a fact not lost upon Lyndon, and in the fall of 1934 he started night classes at Georgetown Law School.

Luther E. Jones, Jr.: "Wirtz kept telling him, 'If you'll get a law degree and get a license and come to Texas, either join me or I'll set us up some way. You can make a ton of money and be a very powerful man.' In other words, the law was another option. I know Wirtz was stimulating him to go to law school. Wirtz kept telling him, 'You can better yourself, I mean tremendously, if you'll become a lawyer.'

"He didn't have much of a career in law school, though. It just didn't hit him right. He was not a stranger to tedious work. Maybe it was because he was preoccupied with other things. I think he was in the throes of being in love and wanting to get married, and I suppose that would cloud any man's vision. Bird was much nicer than any law school."

Gene Latimer: "In the fall of 1934 the Chief met Lady Bird Taylor in Austin, immediately decided she should be his wife, and told her so. Apparently she was impressed but not stampeded, and I have often wondered what must have gone through her mind as he pursued her relentlessly. He had to return to Washington shortly after their first meeting, and his proposal had not been accepted."

Lyndon: "I was on a mission from my congressman in my district, and an old friend, Gene Boehringer, told me about Lady Bird. We arranged to meet later on in the afternoon in Gene's office. We went out together and had a cup of coffee in the middle of the afternoon. And we met again the next day."

Lady Bird: "He was tall and gangling, and he talked quite incessantly. At first I thought he was quite a repulsive young man. Then I realized he was handsome and charming and extremely bright.

"It would be hard to say what I thought. I was just astonished, amazed. It was just like finding yourself in the middle of a whirlwind. I just had not met up with that kind of vitality before. I wanted to stay off on the edges of it. I wasn't sure I wanted to get caught up in it as a matter of self-preservation.

"But I do remember with warmth and pride my father's evaluation, after I brought Lyndon home the first time. He said, 'Well, honey, you've brought home a lot of boys, but this time I think you've brought home a man.'"

Latimer: "After he returned from Austin, the first thing he did upon arrival was go into Mister Dick's office, there to continue his courtship via the U.S. mails. Lady Bird was a journalism major while at the University of Texas, and he dedicated to these daily letters the same meticulous detail he gave to every top-drawer project. He would frequently read a sentence and ask me whether a comma or a semicolon was called for, or check the spelling of a word.

"In November he went back to Texas and returned with Lady Bird, now Mrs. Lyndon Baines Johnson. I don't think Lady Bird ever had a chance once he set eyes on her."

Dan Quill: "This is what happened. He called me here in San Antonio on Saturday morning. He had been visiting Lady Bird at her home in Karnack about 350 miles from here.

"He said, 'Lady Bird and I want to be married tonight at the Episcopal church—St. Mark's Episcopal Church—and we haven't done anything, and I wish you'd make the arrangements and we'll see you about six o'clock at the Plaza Hotel.'

"In those days when we used to have something pretty difficult to do, we'd say, 'Put this down,' then say, 'Much obliged,' and just hang up the phone and stay away from the phone the rest of the time until the things were done. That's exactly what he did to me. He said, 'Fix everything up,' and hung up the phone."

Henry Hirschberg: "The first thing I knew about the impending marriage was a message from Dan Quill, who told me that my wife and I would be needed that evening, that he had received a telegram from Lyndon stating in substance, 'Get Henry, a preacher, a license, and'—I think it was—'two hundred dollars.'

"We broke an engagement in order to appear at St. Mark's Episcopal Church sufficiently in advance of the time that Lyndon and his bride-to-be were expected. I'd never even heard of her; I met her for the first time that evening.

"As I recall it, there weren't over seven or eight, maybe at the most ten of us, standing around waiting—awaiting the pleasure of Lyndon and the lady and also awaiting the pleasure of Mr. McKinstry, the rector, who was getting a little bit impatient.

"In any event, Lyndon and Lady Bird and her bridesmaid did arrive, and we went into the church. It was around seven or seven thirty on Saturday evening. The service was brief. I don't recall now whether it was Dan Quill who pushed me or Mr. McKinstry who pulled me forward to stand in place where the best man would normally be standing, but that's where I stood, and we signed the register more or less that way."

The date was November 17, with no member of either family present. In the meantime, Lyndon's Washington family waited their turn, and the morning after their arrival there in early December, Gene and Luther E. and Carroll and the others came trooping up—the newlyweds had temporarily engaged an upstairs room at the Dodge—to be introduced. The verdict was favorable, from both sides.

Kleberg had raised his secretary's salary to $325 a month; Lyndon kept out $100 to cover his lunches on the Hill, the installment payments on his car, and insurance. From the remaining Lady Bird paid the rent ($42.50 for their first one-bedroom apartment at 1910 Kalorama Road), purchased the food, bought what few items of furniture and clothing were considered necessary, paid for once-a-week cleaning help, and still had enough left over for a monthly savings bond—and for the entertaining that Lyndon sometimes embarked upon.

Russell Morton Brown: "He used to entertain the press. He'd call Bird—I used to hear him—and say, 'Get the furniture insured. I'm having the newspapermen out to the house on Friday night!' He'd get several cases of whiskey, and everybody would get crazy with booze.

"But at the office it was all work. Lyndon always ran the show, and even then he got his name in the papers. I mean he'd find out about a new CCC[1] camp for such and such an area in Texas, and Lyndon would announce it from his office.

"'It was announced today by Lyndon B. Johnson, secretary to Congressman Kleberg, that a new CCC camp will be opened at . . .'"

William S. White: "Senator Tom Connally used to get very put out because he would have got something for Kleberg's district, and before he could announce it, it would be in the papers as coming from Kleberg's office.

"Connally went steaming in there one day and said, 'Dick, I want to know how in the hell it is that this gets back to the Fourteenth Congressional District before my message does.'

"Kleberg turned to Lyndon and said, 'Now tell me how that happens.' Lyndon said, 'The first people I got well acquainted with when I came to Washington were the Western Union boys, and I find out a lot of things first.'"

Kleberg himself had no objection to what his secretary was doing; to the contrary, he felt it made the voters back home feel he was attending to the job for which he was elected. But Mrs. Kleberg, or Miz Mamie, as she insisted on being called back on the ranch and in the office, was less than pleased. She had had ideas of dominating Washington society in the way she had dominated that of Corpus Christi, but to Washingtonians she was just a farmer's wife with a funny accent. So what if the farm had a million acres? Also it was soon apparent that her husband was never going to be much of a power on the Hill. After a while Miz Mamie got peevish, and she often demonstrated her discontent with the young upstart who was running her husband's office and, for all one knew, might even have visions of running for his congressional seat as well.[2]

Brown: "She always wanted to be the one who gave the orders, and Lyndon wouldn't stand for it. For example, she'd say, 'I want somebody to bring the congressman's car out for me.' They were living at the Shoreham Hotel at the time, and Lyndon would say, 'Miz Mamie, I can't send anybody out with that car. We're using all the cars for business purposes.'"

Lady Bird: "It was a difficult position for Lyndon to be in, because Mr. Kleberg asked him to pay the bills, to take the money that he had and pay them, family bills. And there was never enough, because his family lived very well and liked beautiful things, beautiful clothes, beautiful furniture, beautiful everything. Lyndon had to be the one, unhappily, to say to the merchants, 'We'll pay you part of it this month and part next,' and to say to the family, 'We've just got to hold down on X, Y, or Z.'

"Of course that was never well received. On the other hand, the money came from the member of the family who was much tougher, Mr. Bob Kleberg. Mister Dick was gentle and kindly and happy-go-lucky. Mr. Bob Kleberg was by all odds much tougher, very able, autocratic. He ran the ranch until the day he died."

In any case, during the three and a half years he worked for Dick Kleberg, Lyndon managed to put up with the embarrassments over money and the frequent tantrums of Miz Mamie because he was clearly building a bright future for himself. In 1932 he managed Kleberg's successful reelection campaign. It was a momentous year for elections. Besides Roosevelt's victory, Huey P. Long, already governor of Louisiana, was elected senator as well, and migrated to Washington.

Lyndon had three heroes in those early Washington days, three men that he revered then and throughout his life—Franklin Roosevelt, Maury Maverick, and Huey Long.

Lady Bird: "It is quite true; he admired them all. He admired, certainly to my thinking, Roosevelt far and away the most. For one thing he was an Olympian character. Maury—he just knew him darn well, all the good things and all the bad things and on balance it came out affection and admiration, but he did know the warts and all."

Maury Maverick was elected to Congress in 1935. He was third generation of a famous Texas pioneer family;[3] short, bulllike in shape and manner, dogmatic, impatient, and possibly the only first-term congressman who had only to pick up the phone to reach Roosevelt himself.

Jones: "When Maury came to Washington, he lived in the Dodge Hotel for a while down on the bottom floor. We saw him every day. He was quite a character—unusual, unorthodox. He'd go out to supper with a bunch of us younger men and regale us with his unorthodox opinions. He was very liberal, of course. I think he enjoyed shocking people. If you were easy to shock, why, Maury could shock you."

Huey Long was something else again.

Lady Bird: "Huey was something of a mystery to Lyndon, like he was to a lot of people. But Lyndon was very well aware and often quoted the fact of how many schools Huey had built in Louisiana, how many school books he had distributed, and also the people that he had done battle against to achieve all of those things, because I think a good deal of the tax money came from resources, manufacturing, oil production, such as that. At any rate, Huey had gained—earned is the right word, I guess—the undying hostility of a lot of powerful business factions."

Brown: "Huey Long had a program which he called 'Every Man a King,' and he published it as a book. He was proposing gigantic giveaways, you know. And he prided himself on the fact that when he became governor of Louisiana, for the first time children could go to school without having money to buy school books. And he talked about his tangle with the oil companies, and making them pay for a lot of benefits by virtue of his tax policies."

Jones: "I remember that Mr. Johnson got hold of 'Every Man a King,' and he and Bob Jackson read it and discussed it at great length. Back in those days Mr. Johnson wasn't as favorable to spending; he thought you should have more efficiency in government as distinguished from the excessive expenditures. See, Huey wanted to spend great quantities of money, and Johnson was critical. His position was you should be more efficient, not waste the money."

Sam Houston Johnson: "Huey was way ahead of Roosevelt in every way. And he was the most against poverty of anybody I've ever known about in public life, except maybe Lyndon.

"Many people thought Lyndon, when he spoke of doing things for 'the folks,' was talking pure hogwash, but it was a direct pickup from Huey's language."

Lyndon: "Huey thought that every man had a right to a job, and that was before the Full Employment Act. He thought that every boy and girl ought to have all the education he could take, and that was before the GI Bill of Rights. He thought that old folks ought to have social security and old-age pensions. I remember when he scared the dickens out of Mr. Roosevelt and went on nationwide radio talking for old folks' pensions. And out of that came our social security system.

"He hated poverty with all his soul and spoke against it until his voice was hoarse."

In the 1930s congressional secretaries had a club called Little Congress.

Brown: "When Lyndon first came to Washington, it was sort of dull, and the membership had fallen. It had originally started with the idea of getting congressmen and senators to come and talk and make friends and meet everybody on the Hill.

"Arthur Perry, who was then in Tom Connally's office, told him, 'This has to be a wonderful vehicle to get to know everybody. But we'd have to go to work and build it up and get the people who are running it to make it interesting and exciting.' So Arthur Perry and Lyndon decided that Lyndon should be speaker."

Robert M. Jackson: "This was quite unheard of. The organization was somewhat like the regular Congress. They were heavy on seniority. And they had the idea that here was some young whippersnapper that had only attended two meetings—if I'm not mistaken, he was elected speaker on the very second meeting."

Carroll Keach: "It was quite an occasion. It was held in the Democratic caucus room or the main caucus room in the old House Office Building. It was packed to the rafters, and people even standing around the walls.

"They had all the news media of the day there, klieg lights all over the place, taking pictures. . . ."

As a result of his victory Lyndon got his first significant publicity in Washington—a two-column story in the *Washington Evening Star* under the headline "Little Congress Upset—Progressives Put Over New Slate in Election."

Brown: "When Lyndon became speaker, he began to map out a program of inviting the leading congressmen of the day, chairmen of committees, to come and speak.

"He invited Huey Long. At that time Huey Long was threatening to run for president against Roosevelt. And at the time it was a lot of talk, but every once in a while there'd be a story in the paper that somebody'd sent him a bomb. We'd all laugh about it.

"I think it was '35, February or March. You know in those days we didn't have any television, but we did have newsreels. Well, the word got out that Huey was going to speak to Little Congress. There must have been twenty newsreel cameras lined up there along the sides of the room.

"Huey came in with some men who I thought at the time were his office people. But they were bodyguards. And he got up in front to speak, and he had apparently made some kind of arrangement with the press and with the photographers so that when he raised his hand in a certain way they would take his picture. Because he had apparently been told that he looked best in that pose. And I noticed that he would deliberately assume certain poses, and that when he did, the flashbulbs went off.

"Huey stood in front of the table facing everybody, maybe two or three hundred people. Possibly more. Because it was jammed. All of a sudden one of the photographers took his picture, and his flashbulb exploded. It went off, *Bang!* Well, I thought Huey was going to jump over the table. He turned white—terrified! Then he realized, and then he kind of smiled.[4]

"This is the speech he gave, essentially. He said, 'I'm here to talk to you young people. You've got it so much better than I had it when I was going to school.'

"He said, 'You know, I was the youngest of eleven or twelve children, and I grew up on a farm down in Louisiana. I saw my older brothers couldn't go to school because we couldn't afford to pay for school books. I saw them hitched up and pulling a plow like an animal. I saw that. I saw them marry and father children who have no better future than their fathers had. I vowed it wasn't going to happen to me. I made up my mind—I was going to get some schooling.'

"He said, 'Now we live in a great country. Believe me, we've got a marvelous, wonderful country with a great future. Stop and think. If we went to a church party with a lot of food spread out on the tables, enough for everybody to eat, and there's a hundred people there, and fifteen people go take 85 percent of the food and run off with it. What are we going to do about it? Are we going to let them go? No, sir!

"'We're goin' to go get 'em by the neck and say, "Come back with that grub you ain't got no business with!"'

"He said, 'Now in this country today, 15 percent of the people own 85 percent of the wealth. But that's not true in Louisiana anymore. 'Cause the state of Louisiana has declared itself a partner! We've got beautiful roads. We've got public schools where poor kids can go to school whether they can buy books or not. Education—education is the boast of modern times.'

"He didn't mention Lyndon that I remember, but I remember seeing him later with his arm around Lyndon. And Lyndon put his arm around him."

Lyndon's triumphs in the Little Congress did not enhance his popularity with Mamie Kleberg. There are those who claim that Miz Mamie came into the office and said to Mister Dick, "Either he goes or I go." And there are some who say that Mister Dick hesitated.

Brown, however, who was in the office at the time, insists that Lyndon quit, and with no hard feelings at all. Indeed, after Lyndon himself was elected to Congress, his office and Kleberg's were adjacent, and they sometimes borrowed pencils, typewriters, and on occasion personnel from each other. Lyndon even suggested to Mister Dick that he hire Sam Houston as his successor, which he did, and if Lyndon felt any bitterness when he left Kleberg's office in 1935, it was never voiced. Besides, it was clearly time to move on.

LADY BIRD

Antonio Taylor: "We were all born in Karnack, Texas, the three children of Thomas Jefferson Taylor and Minnie Lee Patillo Taylor. The eldest was Thomas Taylor, Jr.; I was three years younger, and Claudia—Lady Bird—was about eight years younger than I.

"Lady Bird was born three days before Christmas in 1912. She got the name Lady Bird . . . well, we're not all in agreement on the timing, but I think Alice Tittle, this colored woman, when she first saw her . . . maybe a day or two after her birth . . . said that she was just as pretty as a little ladybird. There are some who say it came about much later, but I don't think so."

Lady Bird: "Our house was in very deep East Texas, about fifteen miles from the Louisiana border, which is totally part of the Old South in terms of the look of the land—pine trees, rolling hills—and the economy, which was cotton, principally. And little subsistence farms and many, many blacks."

The Taylor and the Patillo families had been neighbors in Alabama; the Patillos were aristocrats, tracing their lineage back to early Spanish settlers, and the Taylors were what in those days one euphemistically referred to as "hardy yeoman stock." Emma Louise Bates Taylor Bishop, Lady Bird's grandmother, was married four times. Three husbands died. She had a total of thirteen children. Husband number three was Lady Bird's grandfather, Thomas Jefferson Taylor. They had five children, the last of which, a son, was named for his father.

Thomas Jefferson, Jr., was big, broad-shouldered, handsome, but of small means. That last, however, was of little concern to Minnie Lee Patillo on her large neighboring plantation. She rebelled against virtually all the constraints of her narrow Alabama society; Thomas J. was only one of her points of departure. After she married him, much against her family's wishes, they migrated to Texas and she continued her idiosyncratic behavior by compiling a considerable library, advocating women's suffrage, becoming a vegetarian, and concerning herself with the well-being of the many poor blacks in the vicinity of Karnack. She "went east" to Chicago—which is, of course, twice as much north as it is east but even she could not admit to going north—for the opera season every winter, and she sent her two sons "east" to New York boarding schools. Then when Lady Bird was five, Minnie Lee died of complications resulting from a bad fall in an over-forty pregnancy, and Lady Bird was left the primary object of affection of an adoring father.

Thomas Jefferson Taylor was still tall and broad-shouldered, but his means were no longer small. He owned, by this time, much of Harrison County, including cotton gins and a country store, later two, over which hung the sign "T. J. Taylor, Dealer in Everything."

Antonio Taylor: "My father was a country merchant, landowner, cotton farmer, engaged in a type of operation that is practically known as 'advancing.' He 'advanced' the land and the equipment to farm it and the seeds and the sustenance of the tenants, and . the reckoning came in the fall. The tenant could pay in cash if he wished, sell his crop elsewhere if he wished. The common practice was, of course, that he would turn his crop over to the landlord, and the landlord would return what was due the tenant."

Minnie Patillo Taylor left her small daughter, along with a considerable sum of money and extensive tracts of Alabama farmland, a host of adoring uncles and aunts, most important of whom were her brother, Claude, for whom Lady Bird had been named Claudia Alta, and her younger sister, Effie.

Cousin Elaine Fischesser: "When her mother died she came to Billingsley, Alabama, a small town, to live with her Aunt Effie in my home. I will never forget the moment she arrived with a big French bonnet on. She was a beautiful child and a very interesting child, good company for anyone. Aunt Effie was an invalid at the time. Lady Bird would come back and forth to Texas during vacation and would spend a part of every summer with us wherever we were.

"She liked to play and would tolerate playmates. But it was very evident that it was a tolerance in most cases. I can picture her stretched out in a chair or a swing with a book in her hand and either dried figs or dried peaches or dried apricots over on the side, munching them. That was very characteristic."

Lady Bird: "Aunt Effie was the gentlest person you just about ever saw. She had really genuinely poor health, I think; also, I'm sure that some of it must have been psychosomatic. She was completely mild and unaggressive, and yet she had a great joy of life and read to me as long as her eyes held out. And then later on, I read to her. She encouraged me and opened up the world of reading to me—the myths of the Greeks and the Romans and the Germans and all those, and adventure books like Zane Grey and James Oliver Curwood—and she also stirred and stimulated my interest in the world of nature. On the other hand, there was also a contra influence, because I saw how inhibiting it was to her life to be so weak and full of illnesses, and so I set my sights on being more like my father, who was one of the most physically strong people I have ever known."

So she grew up in the protective enclaves of her father's house and the houses of her various Alabama relatives which she visited in the summers rather like a small princess making her annual *chevauchée*. Around strangers she was shy.

She was shy at first, too, at the University of Texas in Austin, but she always made friends easily, perhaps because she always went out of her way to be considerate.

D. B. Hardeman: "I knew Lady Bird at the University of Texas. I was going with a little French girl who lived in a boardinghouse right off the campus. And Lady Bird lived there, only she wasn't called Lady Bird then—she was called Claudia.

"The thing I remembered most about Claudia—I didn't know her at all well—was how much the other girls in the boardinghouse liked her. She was tremendously popular."

Lady Bird enjoyed her years at college, but then there is no period of her life that, according to her, she did not enjoy. She was always a good student; she dressed well, lived in one of the best boardinghouses, and drove her own Buick—this in the height of the depression. That she did none of those things ostentatiously is attested to by her popularity in spite of them.

And she considered her future—seriously, but with no undue concern.

Lady Bird: "When I went to the University of Texas, I had no *firm* intention of being *anything*. I got a teacher's certificate—not that I was interested in teaching in the village next door or even the city next door. I thought I might actually be interested in Hawaii or Alaska. I also learned typing and shorthand because I might want to get a secretarial job—not that I would want to do *that* for long. But I had the feeling, which was certainly bolstered up by later experience, that if you were really bright and knew and could use good English and got to be a secretary, you could probably advance to most any place in the business from running the business to marrying the boss. And I still think that's quite possible.

"And then third I took journalism because by that time, through a friend, I had come to know a number of newspaper people. I thought they were interesting and always seemed to be in the place and with the people where things were happening. It was a lively life.

"What I wanted to do was get several tools or skills so that I could make a living in an interesting fashion, and then I would just see what happened."

Her graduation gift from her father was a trip to Washington, and her good girl friend, Gene Boehringer, who knew Lyndon, gave her his number, but Lady Bird was too shy to call. But in Austin at the end of the summer when she dropped by one day to see Gene, Lyndon was there.

Lady Bird: "We wound up spending practically the entire next day together. We rode around and talked, and he was extremely direct. He told me all sorts of things about his job, what he liked about it, his family, his ambitions. I was just sort of listening wide-eyed and not really knowing what I felt.

"My recollection is that he asked me to marry him on the first or second date. Let us say, the second date. I just thought it was sheer lunacy. And I really didn't think he meant it. But after a while I realized that he really did mean it.

"It must have been the next morning he told me he wanted me to go to San Marcos to meet his mother and father and then drive on down to Corpus and meet his boss.

"I remember his father was already old and the touch of the years was on him. His mother was sweet and charming, but I could feel her kind of backing off, looking at me."

She survived the experience, however, with outward equanimity, and from San Marcos they went to Corpus Christi so that Lyndon could introduce Lady Bird to his boss—in fact to the whole Kleberg family. It might have seemed a bit much for one day, but Lyndon did most of the talking, and Lady Bird was too much the southern gentlewoman, even at twenty-one, to be disconcerted by *families*.

Then, before Lyndon returned to Washington, Lady Bird took him to Karnack.

Lady Bird: "Daddy and Lyndon did a good bit of talking, both with me present and with me not present, and I could sense that Lyndon was impressed with my daddy—it was easy to be impressed with daddy—and that daddy was impressed and respectful of him and liked him.

"Not much later, when I was saying that Lyndon wanted to marry me, he did not go up in smoke and say how unwise that was; he said something like, 'Hmmm, some of the best trades I ever made I made in a hurry.' *Trading* was quite a word in the vocabulary of a businessman, a merchant, and a farmer in those days."

Another matter weighed heavily on Lady Bird's mind. She had not yet told Aunt Effie of Lyndon, and she knew, somehow, that she would not approve.

Lady Bird: "Lyndon was very concerned about Aunt Effie, because he thought Aunt Effie would somehow prevent us from getting married, or she would be afraid for me because I was the only real tie to life that she had. She was an invalid and had been for so long, and I was really all she had.

"She was scared to death for me. I look back now, and I hurt for her and I did then. But my daddy was determined that I not make all of my decisions based on what was best for *her*. He told me so, and bluntly. She never, never would have done anything without thinking it was for my best interest. And it did seem kind of whacky. You know, some man comes in and wants to marry you, and you've only known him two months or whatever. So she certainly had a side to it.

"Well, I thought about it a great deal from then until the day I married him. There were very many ups and downs—some when I thought I would and some when I was sure I wouldn't. Sometimes in the course of the indecision I would get out the prayer book and look at the marriage service, which is actually a contract, you know, and read it and decide, 'My gosh, I have changed so much in the five years I've been having dates— what if I had married one of those boys? That would have been disaster. I can't promise to love somebody forever; I might change.' Well, finally I decided that although one did change, one made the decision and went forward with hope."

"ON THE WAY"

Franklin Roosevelt set up the National Youth Administration, an ambitious program designed to help young people continue their education, in 1935.

Thomas G. Corcoran: "In 1935 there were still millions of kids out of work. It didn't take the Old Man long to see that those who wanted to continue school or training of some kind ought to have a chance to do it, and that's how the NYA started."

The president chose as its head Aubrey Williams, an often embarrassingly outspoken man from Alabama who was tall and dark and whom everyone described as looking like Lincoln. Among most Republicans on the Hill, Williams was almost as hated as Roosevelt himself, or Harry Hopkins, who lived in the White House and was Williams's boss on the Works Progress Administration, another organization for those who, many said, could easily find work if they looked.

Lyndon's friend Malcolm Bardwell of San Antonio was secretary to Congressman Maury Maverick.

Bardwell: "Mr. Maverick had told me that Aubrey Williams wanted somebody to head up the NYA in Texas. And Lyndon said, 'I'd like that job.' So we got busy and we got hold of Arthur Perry who was secretary to Tom Connally, and then we got in touch with the secretary of Senator Sheppherd. And we met at Maury's office."

Without mentioning it to Lyndon, Maverick had also spoken to Roosevelt about the appointment; the president thought a *boy* not yet quite twenty-seven was too young to head the NYA in the largest state in the union, but said he'd think it over.

In the meantime Lyndon had persuaded Sam Rayburn to see Senator Tom Connally just to be sure of his support. Connally was generally wary of the New Deal and its "alphabet soup" agencies, but he told Rayburn that he would support Johnson's getting the job. Roosevelt, who needed Connally's blessing for a lot of new "alphabet soup" agencies that were being dreamed up daily, then agreed.

Naturally, since he was boss, Williams had also to agree, and Lyndon went to see him. They got along at once, two populists, and Lyndon was hired. Their friendship was to continue throughout their lifetimes.

Elizabeth Goldschmidt, then employed by the Works Progress Administration of which the NYA was a subsidiary: "Lyndon was very much of a hero-worshiper, and in those days Aubrey was certainly very much one of his heroes. Aubrey was a poor boy from Alabama; I think his father was a sharecropper,[1] and he was very radical in his beliefs, home-grown radicalism, populism really, and Lyndon was that way, too. I always thought he was very much a populist.

"Anyway, I think he very much liked Aubrey, revered him even then."

After his interview with Williams, Lyndon called Lady Bird. Later he would be able to anticipate how she would react to almost everything, but at that time they had been married for less than nine months. He wasn't sure.

Lady Bird: "I can remember it well. I had gone home to Karnack to visit my daddy. When I had been home for a few days or a week or so, I got a call from Lyndon. I can still remember that light, ebullient voice on the other end saying, 'How would you like to live in Austin?'

"It was almost like he had said, 'How would you like to go to heaven?'"

Aubrey Williams announced Johnson's appointment on July 26, 1935, and a few days later Lyndon flew to Austin.

Lady Bird: "The NYA was the natural next step up, and it suited him like a glove on a hand. That was a wonderful period. I loved it, and Lyndon loved it. Not many things have ever meant so much to us as the NYA, brief though it was."

Lyndon's first appointment when he got back was to see the young governor, James V. Allred, who was a New Dealer and, many observers feel, the most liberal Texas governor of this century. Allred gave Johnson and the NYA his full backing, after which Lyndon flew around the state meeting various mayors and telling them about the NYA, asking for their support.

What mayor could be against additional federal funds for his community, especially to help the young? Lyndon got his picture in local newspapers all over Texas, and it was invariably mentioned that at twenty-seven he was the youngest state director in the country. In those days he was always the youngest in everything.

Lyndon started recruiting his staff before he left Washington, and the first name that came to mind was that of his old college chum, Willard Deason. True, Deason already had a good job, which was rare enough in those days; moreover, it was permanent, guaranteed by the rules of the civil service, which was rarer still. No matter.

Willard Deason: "God knows what arguments he used on me! I don't even remember them all; I just know that he called me from Washington in July of '35. Said, 'Have you had your vacation?' I said, 'No.' 'Get it next week and come up and meet me in Austin. I want you to help me.' 'What are you talking about?' 'I've got a new job. You can help me get started.' 'Tell me about it.' 'I'll tell you when I get down there. We're talking long distance. This is costing money. You just meet me there Monday morning in Austin, in the Littlefield Building.'

"I met him up in Austin. He said, 'I want you to help me get this organization set up.' After working two weeks he said, 'Now you go back to your job in Houston and see if you can get a six-month leave of absence. We don't have this thing on the way yet. I've still got to have you here.'

"So I went back and explained to the personnel office again. I got a six-month leave of absence. And some forty years later I'm still on it."

Several other old friends were similarly recruited within the week: Ben Crider and Sherman Birdwell from Johnson City days, and his college classmate Jesse Kellam. Crider gave up a job in the Land Bank—the best job, he said, he'd ever had in his life. Kellam was working for the state education department; Lyndon wrangled an indefinite leave of absence for him and hired him as assistant director of the NYA. His major personnel needs satisfied, he got right into his job, as usual.

Mary Rather: "He organized his office overnight, and was operating all over the state of Texas within the briefest time imaginable."

Ray Roberts, later congressman from Texas, was working in the WPA office in Dallas when he was "borrowed" by the NYA office to be assistant director. Two months later he heard from Lyndon in Austin.

Ray Roberts: "I got a call from him, and he said, 'I know you're too young and can't handle the job, but I've got nobody else. You ought to try to be district director. I've got to make five districts in Texas instead of four.' I said, 'Yes, sir, I'd like to try.'

"He was a man who could challenge you to do things beyond your ability and your capacity. He understood my limitations, but still challenged me, and I understood what he was trying to do.

"He inspired us to work so hard that we didn't know it was work. We worked six days and drove to Austin and back on Sunday. We had a staff meeting every Sunday. And some of us were two, three hundred miles away. We'd work in the district until nine o'clock Saturday night. Then we drove to Austin and had a meeting all day Sunday and were back on the job the next morning."

Fenner Roth: "One time Aubrey Williams came to Texas. Lyndon was taking him on a tour of the projects. It got around one or two o'clock and Aubrey said, 'I'm hungry.' And Lyndon just wheeled into a hamburger joint and said, 'Give him a hamburger. We're in a hurry.'"

On August 20, even before Lyndon really had his staff organized, he was called back to Washington for a meeting with Aubrey Williams and the other state directors of the NYA. He managed to get most of the publicity, the youngest director, the largest state, and to be sure, the biggest talker. His job, he told newspapermen, was to work himself out of a job. It was to "get the young people in school and get them to work. Once that is done, I will no longer be necessary."

Williams was delighted with him and got him a few extra thousand to use teaching trade skills to youngsters not in regular schools.

After the Washington meeting Lyndon returned to Austin, and by November he announced, "The NYA will have twenty thousand Texas boys and girls either in schools or in part-time jobs soon. The work in Texas is well under way, and there is not a high school or county which cannot have some of its young people in school or at work."

What he did not announce in the press, in November or later, was that among those young people would be a great many—in the language of the times—Negro and Mexican-American children.

Instead, he quietly called a meeting of local Negro leaders in the basement of the Austin Negro Methodist church and announced that he would, of course, be including Negro youths in his job program. With their help he formed a Negro Advisory Committee separate from its white counterpart. He regularly consulted with the presidents of Texas Negro colleges—there weren't many—on how their students might best participate, and when he established his Freshman College Center Program throughout the state, fifteen of the centers were in Negro colleges.[2]

What Lyndon did *not* do—and there were Negroes, Mary McLeod Bethune, national director of the NYA's division of Negro activities, among them, who complained—was to hire Negroes for staff positions. Not that he wouldn't have liked to, he assured his superiors in a special report to Washington, but there had been for "the past one hundred years in Texas . . . a definite system of customs," and "so long as these customs are observed, there is peace and harmony between the races in Texas."

But the Negro kids in their own colleges—he'd do everything in the world for them. Which in Texas, 1936, wasn't a small thing.

Deason: "He never asked what *color* people were. If we had the money, we hired the kids. It was as simple as that."

Robert C. Weaver: "Frank Horne—he was Lena Horne's uncle—was working for the NYA at that time—as a matter of fact, I had recruited him for the job—and he kept talking about this guy in Texas who was really something. His name was Lyndon Johnson, and Horne said Johnson didn't think the NYA was for middle-class people, the way a lot of congressmen did; he thought it was for poor people, including Mexican-Americans and Negroes.

"That's when I first heard about Lyndon Johnson. As far as most federal agencies were concerned, the Negroes weren't even considered, but this guy in Texas was giving them and the Mexican-Americans a fair break. That made quite an impression on me."

Lady Bird: "Lyndon had the most extraordinary streak, sort of like he was born yesterday. I can hardly think of any prejudices that he had. And then also there was the fact that he grew up in a community that did not have blacks. He often told how the first black came there working on a highway contract when he was a young man. So he did not grow up absorbing the attitudes of his parents and neighbors toward blacks. I really think that one of his first acquaintances with this was during the NYA, which was a very formative period of his life when he worked closely and with more success than most of his clients in trying to get jobs or education for black youngsters."

O. H. Eliot, bursar of what was then called Samuel Huston College, a Negro college: "We couldn't have paid our faculty except for Mr. Johnson. He'd send us our quota of money. Then, off the record, he'd say, 'I've got a little extra change here. Can you find a place for it?' We could always find a place."[3]

Meanwhile, as godmother to the NYA, Eleanor Roosevelt made several trips to Texas to see for herself the miracles Aubrey Williams had told her Lyndon was achieving. And wherever she went Lyndon managed to find the time to be at her side. He was a *most* ingratiating young man; she often spoke to Franklin of how he impressed her.

And then, on February 22, 1937, Texas Congressman James P. Buchanan, age seventy, suffered a fatal heart attack in Washington.

Buchanan's death caused no great mourning at the White House. While Buck, who had first been elected to Congress in 1913, the same year as Sam Rayburn, had gone along with a good many New Deal measures, he had done so reluctantly. He was by nature a fiscal conservative and by no means the aggressive, free-spending chairman of the House Appropriations Committee that Roosevelt wanted.

Thomas G. Corcoran (better known to posterity as Tommy the Cork) remembered that the first name that came to mind to succeed Buchanan was that of R.H. Montgomery, the colorful iconoclast of the department of economics at the University of Texas. Lyndon, who knew, loved and admired him, called him "the bomb thrower." Dr. Montgomery was, as he often said, a 101 percent New Dealer; he was a great orator and was often called on to speak at meetings all over the country to explain what he felt the Roosevelt administration was all about. But Montgomery, although he was tempted, eventually decided not to run.

Another name mentioned was that of the young director of the Texas NYA.

Corcoran: "When Aubrey Williams heard about it, he practically went out of his mind. He called me, and he said I had to have Roosevelt stop Johnson from running. He said his whole NYA program in Texas would go to hell if Johnson quit. So I talked to Roosevelt, and he said, all right, tell him not to run. I had a hell of a time getting hold of Johnson, and when I did, it was too late. He'd already quit and announced he was going to run."

Lyndon: "I was frequently in Houston and stayed with my Uncle George.[4] I was with him the night Mr. Buchanan died. Uncle George said he had four or five hundred dollars in the bank up at Johnson City that he would give to me if I would run for Congress.

"That put the idea pretty firmly in my mind."

Rather: "The very moment that Congressman Buchanan died, Senator Wirtz was saying, 'Get Lyndon for me.' And he immediately went into a huddle with him and said, 'You must run for this office.'"

Goldschmidt: "I would say that in his early period, Alvin Wirtz was his first political mentor. Alvin was much older. He really had a frontiersman's view of political organization, and I think it was in part he that instilled that same populist tradition or belief in Johnson."

Rather: "Senator Wirtz was not a state senator anymore, but he was called senator to the day he died because he had been a very prominent state senator, and somehow the title just fit him. Anywhere in Mr. Johnson's files as congressman and senator, when you read letters and somebody says, 'The senator said so-and-so,' they are talking about Senator Wirtz. You didn't even have to say Wirtz; you just said 'senator,' and everybody knew who it was."

Of course, Lyndon had to make sure of Bird's approval. Bird must have sighed, but her sighs were never, then or later, voluble. If Lyndon had already made up his mind to run, she, of course, would go along with the decision.

Not only did Bird go along, she went to Wirtz and asked how much he thought the campaign would cost. He said ten thousand dollars at the very least. Lady Bird nodded, and on the Sunday following Buchanan's death she called her father and asked if he would advance her ten thousand on her inheritance from her mother. Without hesitation he said yes, although she and Lyndon would have to wait until Monday morning when he could get to a bank.

Deason: "I was stationed in San Antonio for the NYA at the time Buchanan died, and Lyndon called and said, 'Have you heard?' I said that I had. And he said, as ⊥ remember it, 'There's talk of my running for the office, and we're meeting this afternoon at Jesse Kellam's. Could you be there?' I said, 'I'll be there.'

"That was a Saturday morning, I think. We met Saturday afternoon."

Dan Quill came up from San Antonio, too; Sam Fore, publisher of the Floresville *Journal*, and Ray E. Lee, an Austin newspaperman, were also present.

Dan Quill: "We didn't have any money. Everybody was broke. We started the meeting about one and didn't get out until five. I had to go back to San Antonio—I had a date. I had to make this date. So I said, 'I'll tell you something, Lyndon, the only way you can win her is to run for her.' And he said, 'Well, I'll just run.'

"Then I remember Senator Wirtz was there. He represented the Magnolia Petroleum Company, and I think he phoned and somebody said they'd put five hundred dollars in the pot to start things rolling."

Alvin Wirtz said that Lyndon must make clear that he supported Franklin Roosevelt totally, including Roosevelt's controversial proposal to enlarge the U.S. Supreme Court.

That, said Lyndon, would be no problem.

Roosevelt had won the 1936 presidential election with 523 electoral votes; his Republican opponent, Alfred M. Landon, governor of Kansas, had 8. Roosevelt's plurality was eleven million votes. There had been nothing like it before in American history, and there was nothing like it again until 1964.

Even so, Roosevelt's plan to expand the Supreme Court caused an immediate and nationwide furor. Those who had accused him of ambitions to be a dictator now said that their predictions had been justified. Practically every newspaper in the country was against Roosevelt's plan, including the *New York Times*. Constitutional lawyers were against it; so were most state legislators, including the state senate of Texas, and an impressive number of congressmen and senators.

Even Sam Rayburn, then floor leader of the House, had been heard to say that he had doubts that the bill could get through the House and, with difficulty, helped convince Roosevelt that it should be considered by the Senate first. Roosevelt was told again and again that the Court plan would be defeated. But he refused to withdraw it or water it down.

Why, then, did Senator Alvin Wirtz urge Lyndon to support such an apparently unpopular proposal? For one thing, Wirtz said, most of the other candidates in the congressional race would either be wishy-washy or against the plan. For another, nobody except a few intellectuals gave a damn about the Court business one way or another. For a third, Johnson's support would not go unnoticed by the then beleaguered president. For a fourth, 100 percent support of Roosevelt was what Lyndon must campaign on. After all, Roosevelt had had 85 percent of the votes in Texas in 1936, and there was no evidence anywhere that the enthusiasm for him had diminished. Texans, like the majority of southerners in those days, considered themselves more "liberal" than "conservative."[5]

Lyndon, as he usually did, took Wirtz's advice, and the senator, also as usual, was proved right.

Lady Bird: "San Marcos was exactly the right place to launch the campaign. I sat on the stage behind Lyndon, and I remember his mother and sisters were up there. One of the most reassuring things I saw was the governor of the state, James Allred, a young, handsome governor, a most remarkable man, sitting there close to the front.

"There was a little story that Lyndon told about when he first went in to see the governor. He had on a new style young man's hat with a sort of narrow brim. I guess maybe it was one of those flip-down-in-the-front hats. The governor looked at it and said, 'You will never win in Texas with that kind of hat. I'm going to give you one.' And he gave him a regular Western hat, a Stetson, which Lyndon wore for the rest of the campaign."

D.B. Hardeman: "Jimmy Allred was in his thirties when he was elected, and he was a man of great vigor and total honesty.

"So he indirectly recommended Lyndon Johnson in that first race for Congress. He called attention to him a couple of times. He said something like, 'Well, you know he's among the candidates, and he's done a fine job with the NYA,' something like that, indirect but still an endorsement."

Johnson told his listeners in San Marcos that "If the people of this district are for bettering the lot of the common man, if the people of this district want to run their government rather than have a dollar man run it for them, if the people of this district want to support Roosevelt on this vital issue,[6] I want to be your congressman."

The first problem was to choose a campaign manager; Claude C. Wild, who had headed Governor Jimmy Allred's campaign, was persuaded to take the position. Gene Latimer and Luther Jones came to help, and Carroll Keach resigned from the NYA to offer his services.

One immediate problem in the campaign was that Lyndon felt his 1934 Ford wasn't up to it; on the other hand, Ray Roberts, his colleague in the NYA, had a brand-new 1938 Oldsmobile.

Roberts: "So he made the race in my automobile, which I had bought on credit. He just said he had to have it; so, of course, I turned it over to him. That's the type of fellow he was. He just looked at you, and you belonged to him."

Carroll Keach: "I did all the driving. If he had close friends in the town, they would put us up for the night. He had a lot of connections that he had made through his NYA program. He had built quite a base there of friendships with the public officials, school people from the college level on down, business leaders, civic leaders at all levels.

"We had a sound truck, you know, an automobile with a record player in it. I'd get in this car and play these records and make the announcements: 'Come hear Lyndon Johnson speak at the courthouse square, such-and-such a time.'

"While he was speaking, I'd go around town putting placards in drugstores and tacking up placards and handing out stickers. His speeches were all extemporaneous. He carried all of his stuff in his head. He very rarely used notes, unless it was a radio broadcast, and of course this irritated him a whole lot because they demanded prepared scripts in advance in those days, a lot of radio stations did.

"And Mrs. Johnson kept the home fires burning. Laundry was a problem. I mean, we'd run by and grab a few clean shirts and a couple of suits and toss the laundry bag in and say, 'Good-bye. We're going somewhere. See you later.'"

All the other candidates were older than Lyndon. Most of them were more experienced and better known than he, and five were also supporting Roosevelt's Court plan. No matter, said Lyndon, brushing the matter aside. They were not as *enthusiastic* in their support as he. "They offer a one-sentence declaration of support. But there is one candidate—Lyndon Johnson—who declared from the first that he supported the president wholeheartedly, including the controversial Supreme Court issue.

"I didn't have to hold back. I support Franklin Roosevelt the full way, all the way, every day. That's what I intend to do when elected as your representative in Congress, and that includes enlarging the Supreme Court of the United States. When that comes up, I'm not going to be out in the woodshed practicing ways to duck."

Wirtz saw to it that speeches like that were not solely for the voters of the Tenth Congressional District; he frequently air-mailed copies to Washington where they found their way to the desk of Tommy the Cork, and Corcoran saw to it that they got the attention of Roosevelt.

Robert C. Eckhardt: "I'm not sure that Johnson had any great *philosophical* feelings about what was called the Court-packing plan, either during the campaign or later. Maury Maverick, who was in Congress at the time and for the plan, said that if Roosevelt hadn't floated the Court-packing plan, he would never have broken the court logjam with the New Deal.

"In other words, while the plan was never passed,[7] it in effect permitted all the New Deal legislation to move.

"It was a very pragmatic position that Roosevelt took, as he often did, and it was that kind of Rooseveltian pragmatism that Johnson copied most of his life. Including in the presidency. Sometimes it worked, and sometimes it didn't, but I think it's fair to say that Roosevelt was just as pragmatic as Johnson."

Claude C. Wild: "In 1937 we had ten counties in this congressional district, and there was no runoff in a special election. So high man took the deal. And we had about ten candidates from the different counties around here. And I hit on the strategy of having Johnson speak out against a different one everywhere. We'd pick a fight with the one at Burnet or another one down here somewhere.

"We were going on the theory that some of the vote would go for anybody that was sympathetic to Roosevelt. That's the role we wanted; we figured that would win for Johnson and let the others split up. That was the philosophy of the campaign, and it worked.

"Mrs. Johnson thought what I was doing to these people was mud-slinging. And she came and told me that she was helping finance this campaign herself and that she wanted her husband to be a gentleman. She didn't want him to be doing that.

"I remember my comment was, 'Mrs. Johnson, you're going to have to make up your mind whether you want your husband to be a congressman or a gentleman.'"

Sherman Birdwell: "His campaign was on a person-to-person basis. He was energetic; he had long legs; he'd cover lots of territory. He went all over every town, every community, and every hamlet, shaking hands. 'I'm Lyndon Johnson. I want to be your congressman.' He'd look them in the eye. He liked to 'press the flesh,' as he said, and 'look them in the eye.' This was the reason for his tremendous success."

Sam Fore: "He always told me, never take NO for an answer. I've been riding with him in his old Ford car, and he'd stop in the fields there and with his long legs would crawl over that barbwire fence, and he'd stop a farmer—he'd wait until he came in out of the plowing, you know, and then he'd stop him—and he'd take about two minutes, and he'd sold him."

The election was on Saturday, April 10, and on Thursday evening Lyndon was to speak at a meeting at the courthouse.

Ray E. Lee: "Thursday afternoon Mr. Johnson was drooping about his apartment in Austin, saying he didn't feel good. We didn't attach any importance to it.

"I got back to his house about a quarter to seven and he was in the bathroom. He said that he was in pain and that he had taken purgatives but couldn't get any relief.

"After a few minutes we got in the car and went down to the courthouse. He shook hands all around the room there with friends and people, and he got up in front to speak. He was going along pretty good, but all of a sudden he sort of folded over in the middle and pulled his arms up to his belly. Then he sat down.

"No doctor was in the audience, so he sat there for five minutes. Then he was able to straighten up and say to the people, 'Well, I'm really sorry, but I've had this bad pain. You'll excuse me if I don't complete my speech, but I want to shake hands with all of you and thank you for coming and urge you to be sure to vote Saturday and to get some other people to vote for me, too.'

"He shook hands around. I got him out to the car and took him home; he was having more pains. He telephoned his cousin, Dr. Claude Martin, and said, 'I'm sick.' And Claude said, 'I'll be right over.'

"Dr. Martin came, and I left because I had to go to the newspaper. I got back to the apartment around ten o'clock and found that Johnson had gone to Seton Hospital. He was being operated on by Dr. Martin by the time I got there. They took out his appendix. I think it was not ruptured, but it was kind of close. He was in pretty bad shape.

"Claude Wild came to the hospital. We held a little council and agreed that the best thing to do was to get the best news publicity we could on the true facts.

"I got back down to the newspaper and found that they were closing their midnight central Texas edition. This is the edition that would go to Georgetown, Lockhart, San Marcos, Johnson City, and all the towns in the district. So I told Mr. Fulcher what had happened, and he said he couldn't get it in the central Texas edition, but he remade the front page for the home edition and put a top line over the *Austin American* masthead— the top line over that—saying that Johnson had had a midnight appendix operation, and was apparently doing well.

"The news was well circulated in Austin, and of course it was telephoned to various people around the various counties. I remember that a doctor down in Lockhart, who had been supporting someone else, called up Dr. Beverly and wanted to know if this was really on the level that Lyndon had appendicitis. Dr. Beverly, being a man of great conscience, chewed out the other doctor over the phone and said, 'You know damn well it is so or I wouldn't have said so!'"

Luther E. Jones: "I think the operation was good for his campaign. One reason for that, Wild made the speech that he was going to make on that last day. And Wild was a better speaker than Lyndon Johnson. He had just the right touch. 'The man has been stricken, but he's doing fine, and he'll be up in a couple of days. So sorry he couldn't be here, but he sends everybody good wishes.' You know, the real baloney stuff, but it was very effective."

Quill: "Lyndon was in the hospital on election day. I remember that I was going to Washington on election day, and Sam Fore had promised me that he'd send a telegram about the election to Muskegee, Oklahoma, when I got there at eleven o'clock that night. I think the trains crossed there. And I got off the train, and there was a Western Union messenger, and he had a telegram there that said Lyndon Johnson had been elected to Congress."

The eyes of the nation certainly had not been on the Tenth Congressional District in Texas the night Lyndon spoke at San Marcos, but on Sunday morning, April 11, the eyes of the White House almost certainly were. Lyndon's victory made the front page of the *New York Times*:

> Austin, April 10, 1937—Youthful Lyndon B. Johnson, who shouted his advocacy of President Roosevelt's Court reorganization all over the Tenth Texas District, was elected today to the seat in Congress which the late James P. Buchanan held for twenty-four years.
>
> At a hospital, where he was operated on for appendicitis two days ago, he happily received reports of an emphatic victory over seven opponents and said he considered the result a vote of confidence in Mr. Roosevelt and his program.

If Roosevelt had read on, he would have seen that five of the losers had also been for the plan, but Franklin, like Lyndon, was not interested in losers.

By happy coincidence, beginning May 1 Roosevelt was to begin a ten-day fishing trip in the Gulf of Mexico, and White House headquarters were to be in Galveston. While there, why not express his gratitude and give his blessing to young Lochinvar, young Lyndon?

Governor Allred and Johnson flew to Galveston on May 11 and Roosevelt, tanned and pleased with his success at catching tarpon, congratulated Lyndon on his victory. Lyndon, in turn, congratulated Roosevelt on the seventy-seven-pound tarpon the president was said to have caught, and confessed that he, too, had long been fond of fishing, which would have surprised those who knew him.

Knowing that both Franklin and his Uncle Teddy had a passion for the navy, Lyndon said something else that would have astonished his friends. He said that he had since childhood had a consuming interest in the U.S. Navy and that that interest had been inspired by the two Roosevelts.[8]

Roosevelt, who never had any difficulty accepting praise as his due, was delighted with the young congressman and invited him to be his guest on the presidential train as far as Fort Worth. (Lyndon did not, as has been reported by some biographers, go all the way to Washington.) The two didn't have much time to talk on the way. Roosevelt was too busy waving to crowds.

Just before the train got to Fort Worth—by then it was late in the day—Roosevelt gave Lyndon Tommy Corcoran's telephone number and told him to call Tommy once he got to Washington. Tommy would take care of him.

Although Lyndon seldom disputed the notion that he had gone all the way to Washington with Roosevelt, one man who knew that he did not was Walter Trohan, Washington correspondent of the *Chicago Tribune*, who was also on the train. The conductor had asked Lyndon to pay the fare to Fort Worth, he told Trohan, and it had taken all his available cash.

"I paid the conductor," said Lyndon, "but I want to know if I did right. After all the president invited me aboard."

"You did," said Trohan. "And let this be a profitable lesson to you. The president is very generous with everybody's money but his own, and don't you forget it."[9]

Lady Bird remembers Lyndon kissing his ailing father good-bye at the railroad station in Austin early on the morning of May 11. Lyndon left for Washington; he arrived in time to be sworn in on May 13. Sherman Birdwell and Carroll Keach, who would serve on his staff, were to follow.

Robert M. Jackson: "The night he came to Washington, my wife and I met him at Union Station and brought him to our apartment.

"We lived in an apartment house, now torn down, on the side of the New Senate Office Building. We walked there from the Union Station, and he kept us up practically all night telling us about his campaign. He gave us a blow-by-blow account of the whole thing. My wife, she had never met him before; she was just amazed by him. She said, 'That man is going to be president of the United States,' and that was the first time I ever recall anybody who knew him say that in all seriousness.

"I remember it because I argued with my wife that nobody from Texas could ever be president of the United States."

Birdwell: "Mr. Johnson had gone to Washington and had taken the oath of office a day or two before Carroll Keach and I arrived. We arrived late in the afternoon, and we were driving over to the House Office Building. We had not even gone to try to find a place to stay. As we arrived, we saw Mr. Johnson walking by the side of the Old House Office Building. He said, 'I've got an office,' and he gave us the number. I remember it was on the first floor.

"We went to the office, and there were thirteen bags of mail waiting to be opened. After his election on April tenth no one had been there for some five or six weeks, and Mr. Johnson had delayed his actual going to Washington until after the opportunity to meet President Roosevelt. All the mail asking for jobs from postmaster general down to janitor of the Federal Building in Austin were there waiting for us—thirteen bags of mail—and Carroll Keach and I started on them that night, opening them up and sorting them, till way after midnight."

REMAKING AMERICA

Late in life Lyndon used to say that he couldn't decide whether he preferred Washington in the days when he was a freshman congressman when anything seemed possible and often was, or those later years when he was the most powerful man in town. Both were intoxicating.

Washington had once been considered sleepy and dull, but by 1937 when Lyndon returned, Roosevelt and his New Deal had changed all that. Suddenly *everybody* wanted to come to Washington. First of all, almost everybody needed a job, and second, where else could one better find a job that paid a living wage and offered one all that satisfying idealism?

Lady Bird: "When we first got to Washington we would go out to Aubrey Williams's house, which was, as I recall, a big, rambling frame house. They would be likely to have a very lively bunch of people out there. Good conversation was in abundant quantity in Washington in those days—exciting conversation. The phrase about 'Roll up your sleeves and remake America'—we sought out or gravitated to the people who were figuring on doing that. Lyndon soon knew all or many of the characters on the stage: Tom Corcoran, Ben Cohen, Abe Fortas. And, of course, the Goldschmidts, Tex and Wicky, and Cliff and Virginia Durr.

"Conversations always got back to politics, but they all had a social-economic bent. There was always a goal to achieve, some sort of improvement in agriculture or welfare or building dams or education. Reform and improvement were considered highly possible, and they were the people who were going to do it.

"I think Roosevelt had a lot to do with it. He set the tenor of the time."

The newly elected congressman from the Tenth District of Texas was known on arrival as a total New Dealer, a new brand of southern politician, a Texan with admirable radical instincts, and he *knew* Roosevelt. In fact, he was on a first-name basis with him. Anyway, the president was on a first-name basis with Lyndon; true, on first meeting,

Roosevelt called *everybody* by his first name in what many people considered a patronizing manner. But Lyndon had the telephone number of Tommy the Cork, and he used it frequently.

Tommy the Cork had first come to Washington in 1926 as secretary to Justice Oliver Wendell Holmes, who was said to have observed, "Corcoran is quite noisy, quite satisfactory, and quite noisy."

Corcoran: "Roosevelt was getting the shit kicked out of him over that Court plan which, if he'd listened to me, would never have happened. I told him it wasn't a good plan, but he went right ahead. It made him angry that so many people were against it, especially Texans, and along comes this young guy who's backing him. Naturally he's impressed. And when he got back from that trip to Texas, he told me to take care of this boy and put him on the Naval Affairs Committee. There were others who'd been around for a while and were in line, but I called Carl Vinson[1] and naturally Lyndon got the appointment."

Lady Bird: "When we first came to Congress—I can't really remember when we began to go to Speaker Rayburn's, but it was early, and it was one of the most exciting things we did. He had an apartment—it was right off Connecticut Avenue, named the Anchorage, as I recall—a modest but comfortable place. Believe me, it was the site of good meals, good conversation, warm evenings. He really was a great host—and the food was good. I think he had it sent over from the café across the street. It always just appeared, certainly with no great effort on his part."

Paul A Porter: "In the early days in Washington we used to meet in Mister Sam's office. I felt, as everybody did, very close to Mister Sam, and I was frequently invited to so-called board of education meetings. It was a controversial group, and I sometimes said that we could look at the same clock and not agree on the time of day. But it *was* a very exciting period and Lyndon was a very meaningful part.

"I'll tell you this. Lyndon was *never* anonymous."

Virginia Foster Durr: "The first thing that impressed me about the Johnsons when I met them was that they looked so extremely young. Lyndon was very tall and thin, and he had a boyish look. Bird was a sweet-looking, dark-haired, dark-eyed girl who seemed to adore her husband and let him have the floor. And he did hold the floor, and he held it very well.

"The thing about the New Deal in those days was that there was a great intertwining of both personal and governmental relationships. Now Washington has gotten so enormous, and there are so many people here, it's very difficult to realize that this small group knew each other so well. And then, of course, we were all united in this really passionate admiration of Franklin D. Roosevelt and Mrs. Roosevelt."[2]

But it would probably not have occurred to the Durrs or to people like them to combine the governmental with the social in quite the manner Lyndon did.

James H. Rowe: "He busted in my office one day and said, 'You know, Rayburn is having a birthday next Monday,' or whatever the day was. And he suggested trying to involve the president in a little surprise party.

"Remember that Lyndon was a very junior congressman, and my feeling then was, and probably still is, that there is more of a hierarchy in Texas than most states in terms of age and seniority and so forth. So I said, 'Well, maybe it is a good idea.'

"And he said, 'You write the memorandum to the Boss.' He said, 'You write better than I do.' I don't know what his theory was, that maybe if I wrote it, it would seem more impartial. I sent the president a memo, and Johnson also talked to Grace Tully. He was never a man to rely on any one person. And I think Grace and I both talked to the president, and he thought it was a great idea.

"It was supposed to be a surprise party. The interesting thing about it was that Johnson made up the guest list. And it was a careful list. He had the right chairmen. He invited them and told them it was a secret. And then the day of the party Roosevelt sent word to Rayburn that he had to have him immediately.

"Johnson had the whole dialogue worked out. Rayburn came rushing up, and everybody was hiding off somewhere. Rayburn came in, and Roosevelt said, 'Sam, you are in real trouble, and I am the fellow to tell you.' Scared the daylights out of him.

"Then Roosevelt said, 'You are the age of such and such,' and everybody came in singing 'Happy Birthday.'

"The thing I noticed when they started taking pictures was that there was Roosevelt, and there was Rayburn, and the fellow in the middle behind them was Lyndon Johnson. I began to think I had really met an operator. Johnson had even bought a Texas Stetson for Roosevelt and gave it to him.

"The point is—Lyndon did it *all*, down to the last detail. He always paid terrific attention to detail. The thing that amazed me most about Johnson through the years was how he did everything himself. He never trusted anybody else to do anything."

Another person who retained vivid memories of Lyndon as a freshman congressman was Grace Tully, Roosevelt's secretary, who later told the following story to Ernest Goldstein:

Goldstein: "She said that about six weeks after Johnson came to Washington as a congressman, he called the White House and asked for an appointment with Roosevelt and indicated that it was a matter of emergency.

"According to Miss Grace, the people in President Roosevelt's staff were somewhat amused at the thought that a freshman of six weeks in Washington would have something so urgent that it required the ear of the president of the United States. Nevertheless, they did tell President Roosevelt about the request, and with his good humor he suggested that he might as well have the young congressman in and see what was bothering him.

"So Congressman Johnson came to see President Roosevelt. His problem was with Milo Perkins, who was then head of the AAA [Agricultural Adjustment Administration] and high among the angels if not the saints of minorities according to then standards. And this was a rather shocking thing, that there would be a complaint against Milo Perkins. Well, it seemed that back in the Tenth Congressional District of Texas, Negroes were not receiving any of the benefits of the operation of the AAA.[3]

"Miss Grace said that President Roosevelt's first automatic instinct was, 'Now, this is a smart politician.' And then he pulled himself up short and realized that this was the day of the lily-white primary in Texas, and that contrary to the idea of adding votes or aiding the political career of Congressman Johnson, this might even backfire on him. But he was impressed with principle being the controlling factor in what seemed to be the right thing."

Anna Rosenberg Hoffman: "My greatest contact with Lyndon was on legislation that President Roosevelt was interested in, social legislation, and he would say, 'Go up and talk to the men on the Hill,' and so on. He was there awhile when President Roosevelt said to me, 'I want you to work with that young congressman from Texas, Lyndon Johnson. He's a comer, and he's a real liberal.'"

Lady Bird: "In those days, every year there was at least one reception at which the lowliest congressional member and his wife were invited to the White House. It was a white-tie reception at nine o'clock in the evening.

"So Lyndon at my request would rent a white tie and tails and a top hat, a silk hat which you wore there very much to your wife's admiration, and then you took it off and checked it at the entrance so it was really a sort of foolish indulgence. But it was the custom of the time. We would stand in line, and there would be fully a thousand people there: 335 plus 96 and their wives, and they would have a few extras, maybe cabinet. I remember getting a very nice note saying that they had heard that Lyndon's mother was visiting us and to bring her, too. After meeting the president and Mrs. Roosevelt, we would go to the dining room and have some light refreshments and drinks and visit with all the other congressmen. Lyndon would make a beeline to whomever he had to do business with, and I would sort of stand around in awe. I remember distinctly meeting the president, and although I had read it in the papers and intellectually knew it, somehow, face to face I didn't know it, that he was crippled. I dare say there were millions of people who felt the same way. It came as ever so slight a shock to me.

"I forgot what he was leaning on, but he was leaning on something, and you could tell he was being supported. We shook hands, and it was really the briefest encounter. However, Lyndon saw a great deal more of him, and he would come back and tell me about it. For instance, I remember one of the things he mentioned was that he had lunch with him in one of the upstairs rooms one time, on something that he described as a bridge table—a small, little table. Maybe it was in the Yellow Sitting Room.

"Once he saw Roosevelt when he was in bed, and he had on a navy cape, sort of a dark blue cape around his shoulders. Of course, one only went at the president's request, but at any rate he did go several times in that fashion, because he would always tell me about it."

Lyndon, when he returned to the Tenth District after his first session, carried some very respectable accomplishments with him. He had managed to get a considerable sum in emergency loans for the crop farmers among his constituents. Three PWA (Public Works Administration) grants had been awarded to the Tenth District on his urging— one for a city hall and fire station in Austin, another for a new federal building in the town of Elgin, and a third for a school in, yes, Johnson City. And the town of Lockhart would have postal delivery, which it had never had before. Nothing major, but a not inconsiderable record for a freshman congressman who had only arrived in May.

The 1938 session was even more productive. Lyndon conferred at length with the Agriculture Department and managed to get them to increase Texas feed acreage quotas by about one-third. He also got Agriculture to back his plan to use WPA funds to buy surplus cotton. By late September he was able to announce that the Pedernales Cooperative (an electric power cooperative) had been approved, and that the government had allotted $1.3 million to construct 1,718 miles of power lines, and the next month he was pushing rural co-op refrigerators run by LCRA power.

These, of course, were Texas matters. Nationally, Lyndon voted with the Roosevelt Democrats, always. But concerning Texas, he had, sometimes, to be careful.

Russell Morton Brown: "Not too long after he got elected to Congress, I would say this was in '38, he was talking to Senator Wirtz about how he had voted with the New Dealers to shut off debate on one of the civil rights bills and close it up for a vote.

"The southern Democrats were filibustering and trying to keep it from coming to a vote, but Lyndon had voted the other way. And Senator Tom Connally called Lyndon in and said to him—I'm paraphrasing, but this is the way I remember being told it—'Now, Lyndon, you're here as a Texan. And don't ever forget that as a Texan, you're a southerner. If you throw down the South and forget your origins, you're going to foreclose your progress. Because the only people that will stand with you are the people from the South. The people from the North are never going to have any respect for you.'

"And Lyndon said to Senator Wirtz, 'I did what I did, voted the way I did, because I was representing the interests of my constituents rather than their opinions of the moment.'

"Senator Wirtz said to him, 'Well, Lyndon, it'll be all very well voting for your constituents' interests as against their opinions, but suppose they don't recognize and appreciate what you've done and don't reelect you?'"

Rowe: "Once, I was pushing him for something liberal, and he said, 'I just can't do that.' He said, 'Just remember our old friend Maury Maverick isn't here anymore. Maury got too far ahead of his people, and I'm not going to do that.'[4] Johnson saw Maverick go down, and he made a little note of that: 'Don't get too far away from those Texans.'"

But Lyndon joined Maury in one liberal-oriented legislative venture in the spring of 1938.

The minimum wage bill—the first of its kind in the United States—had passed the Senate but was bottled up in the House Rules Committee. In an attempt to free it, a petition circulated among the Democrats in the House to caucus and bring the Senate bill to the floor. When that tactic worked, the bill was brought to a vote and passed 314–97.

The bill, which provided for the base wage of twenty-five cents an hour, was not popular in Texas. "What? Pay that lazy Mexican twenty-five cents an hour? Not on your . . ." So when the petition circulated, only six of the twenty-one Texas congressmen—Lyndon, Maury, and Sam Rayburn among them—would sign it. And when the Texas primary rolled around that summer, two of those six—Maury Maverick and D.W. McFarlans—were defeated, although quite possibly for other reasons.

Lyndon himself had no opposition in 1938. But he generally ignored that fact when he told the story in later years. "We were all threatened with political oblivion and defeat," he would say, and then to make it more dramatic he often omitted three of his fellow congressmen from the tale altogether and said that only three Texans had signed it, and he was the only survivor. He did not, of coure, tell the story that way when Sam Rayburn was around.

Rowe: "Johnson always knew just how far he could go, and that's how far he went. He recognized that to be an effective politician you have to survive, and he was often much more liberal than he voted. I remember he once said, 'There's nothing in the world more useless than a dead liberal.'

"As a congressman from the Tenth District, Johnson was an excellent New Dealer. For good reasons. He wanted water; he wanted dams; he wanted all the rural electrification he could get. He wanted all the things he fought for in that country, especially for the farmers."

Sim Gideon: "Floods on the Colorado River had been causing damages in the millions of dollars, and people lost their lives due to drowning. Sometimes the Colorado River would practically dry up, and other times there would be one or two floods in one year and people would drown and millions of dollars worth of property would be lost.

"Senator Wirtz and Congressman Johnson were both very interested in these problems. I recall a speech Mr. Johnson made in a little schoolhouse when he was running for reelection as a congressman. He told the people that if they would reelect him to Congress, he would see that they would get electric lights, and I thought at that time just how far would a man go in order to get a vote because I just didn't think they'd bring lights out ten or fifteen miles. But sure enough, the congressman talked to President Roosevelt and got a gigantic REA[5] loan.

"In those days if you built a line out to a rural place, all the man wanted was a drop light in the house. That's all he ever expected from electricity. Nobody at that time ever thought about air conditioning and feed mills and milking and washing clothes and radios and television and so many other things."

Virginia Foster Durr: "Lyndon and Alvin Wirtz wanted to start a TVA on the lower Colorado River. They got a bill through the Texas legislature authorizing the setting up of the Lower Colorado River Authority. The Pedernales River was a part of this system.

"Lyndon was so involved in the LCRA. When Lyndon got into anything, you know, he absolutely concentrated on it. Oh, I got so tired hearing about it! Every time we'd go out to dinner, Lyndon would set forth on the Lower Colorado River.

"The thing that made Lyndon different from other people, I suppose, was that when he started doing something, he poured every ounce of his energy into it, and it became the great overriding thing of his life. He didn't hold back anything. He just pounded and pounded on it. And then, of course, he cultivated everybody that could be of any help to him at all."

Lyndon: "I had visions of damming the Colorado and Pedernales rivers, of building a simple, rural electrical line out to the farmers that lived in my Hill Country, of providing flood control, irrigation, cheap power, of conserving the land and putting in new grasses that would hold the soil and prevent excessive wash-off. And I knew it was electricity that could do all this.

"But the power companies wouldn't let me do it. I didn't know I needed their permission, but I found out that I did. I met with the president of the most powerful power company in the state, and he had one word—'cooperation.' He looked a good deal like a Methodist bishop; he had long gray hair. He would say, 'I want to cooperate. I want to cooperate.' And he just cooperated me out of every meeting I got in. The negotiations went on and on and on.

"And when I went to Washington, my proposals were rejected several times. I failed every step of the way—had a complete strike-out every pitch I made.

"Finally, in desperation I went in to see President Roosevelt.

"I went to ask him to use his influence and get me a loan for the Pedernales electric cooperative. I started talking to him, and President Roosevelt said, 'Did you ever see a Russian woman naked?' And I said, 'No, but then I never have been in Russia.' And then he started telling me what Harry Hopkins, who had just been to Russia, had told him—how their physique was so different from the American woman because they do the heavy work, you know, and as a consequence it had its effect on their muscles. He was very interested.

"Well, before I knew it my fifteen minutes was gone, and old Pa Watson[6] was tugging at the end of my coattails, and I found myself in the West Lobby without ever having made my proposition. So I had to go back and make that damn appointment all over again. I went over and consulted with Ben Cohen, Tommy Corcoran, Jim Rowe, Harold Ickes, and all the various close friends of Roosevelt.

"And Tommy the Cork said, 'Roosevelt likes pictures, the bigger the better. That's where you made your mistake. You should have gotten a picture of some dam and pictures of your transmission lines and of the big cities, Houston and Dallas and San Antonio. That would have gotten his attention.' So I went over and got pictures of the Buchanan Dam and of transmission lines they were building that led into Austin and on to Houston and Dallas, and I ordered up thirty-six-inch photographs. Then I went to see Roosevelt again.

"I pulled out this big picture map and showed it to him, and I showed him these transmission lines and charts of power consumption, and I had a picture of one of those little old tenant farmer's houses, you know, under these transmission lines.

"I said, 'Here we have the largest multiple arch dam we just built and here's that big transmission line just wheeling with power. But it's all those city big shots that belong to Houston Power and Light and Texas Power and Light that are getting the power. And the poor people living right under the line, shadowed by it, they can't get any.

"So Roosevelt got John Carmody on the phone. John was as arrogant as he could be; he'd already turned me down flat, had thrown me out a dozen times, see, telling me I didn't meet the standards, that he wasn't going to lend any money down there where there were only one and a half customers per mile.

"Roosevelt said, 'John, what about these dams on the Colorado River, this REA allotment for the Pedernales Electric Cooperative? I have a young congressman in here, Lyndon Johnson.'

"John said that yes, he knew me, and said that population density was holding it back. He gave Roosevelt this big propaganda talk about density, and Roosevelt listened to him, and when he got through he said, 'John, I know you've got to have guidelines and rules and I don't want to upset them, but you just go along with me—just go ahead and approve this loan and charge it to my account. I'll gamble on those folks because I've been down in that country and those folks—they'll catch up to that density problem because they breed pretty fast.'

"And he made old John give me that first loan, which resulted in the Pedernales Electric Cooperative. I walked out of there with a million-dollar loan. That was about one of the happiest moments of my life."

The next year Roosevelt politely offered Lyndon the post of administrator of the REA, which Lyndon politely refused, explaining he wanted to remain the congressman from the Tenth District of Texas. Tommy the Cork told Lyndon that it had only been a gesture on the president's part anyway. He said that Roosevelt had never expected Lyndon to leave Congress to take a job like that, but that he, Roosevelt, thought the publicity would help Lyndon.

Making electric power available to the common man remained one of the passions of Lyndon's life. Long after the problem had been solved in Texas, the importance of it dominated Lyndon's mind. It would provide a common ground for discussion with underdeveloped countries after he became vice-president, and it would even assume major importance in his impractical dreams for the Mekong Delta after he became president.

ROOSEVELT'S BOY

John Kenneth Galbraith: "I first went to Washington in 1940 to work with Leon Henderson in the Office of Price Administration, and then joined Chester Davis on the National Defense Advisory Committee. And at that time and in the ensuing years, Johnson was one of the very rare specimens of the young, liberal, New Deal congressman. Particularly from the South, of course. Some of the other names would be surprising—John Sparkman, for instance. Not on civil rights, but then there were no civil rights. Albert Gore was another. And this was the group of young New Dealers that I was automatically to know."

Harry McPherson: "Lyndon loved to say that when he came up here in the thirties as a congressional secretary and later as a congressman, that all his friends were Bolsheviks. And I don't know that that was an overstatement. He knew a number of people who were considered to be far to the left in the late thirties and early forties.

"He began to trim his sails very sharply in the middle forties because he figured he had to do that to get elected to the Senate from Texas, and he was probably right, but he did like to go back to those radical beginnings and find himself there."

Mike Monroney: "I was very fond of Lyndon Johnson when I came into the Congress. You know, to a newcomer, a two-year-old veteran is very important. He was very cordial, very interested, naturally, in Oklahoma because just the Red River separates the two—and it's dry half the time so you can't tell just where the lines divide. We've gone to war a few times against Texas on oil royalties and things of that kind as the river changed courses.

"My early impression was that Lyndon was probably a little overenthusiastic about what he was trying to do, and a little overemphatic on his projects, not too much a team player with the freshmen. He didn't spend as much time with freshmen as he did with senior members, and he recognized the points of power even at two or three years in the Congress, and had a standing that very few men of that number of years experience possessed."

Thomas G. Corcoran: "Lyndon very quickly got to be friends with all the young New Dealers, who weren't all that many in those days. And they did favors for him. He'd say what he wanted for his district, and he always knew what he wanted and who could get it for him. And he got more for his district than anybody else."

Lyndon had grown up knowing rural poverty, but it was only after his election to Congress that he saw firsthand how the urban poor lived. In December 1937 he went through the slums of Austin for the first time, and he was as shocked as he had been back in Cotulla when he saw those hungry Mexican-American children scrambling for orange peels.

The next month he made a radio broadcast in Austin asking for slum clearance and public housing for the area. The speech was titled "Tarnish on the Violet Crown"—O. Henry, who lived there, had once referred to Austin as "the city of the Violet Crown"— and included a rather vivid description of the city's slum population. He said, "Recently a man said to me, 'Lyndon, I am against this program because I am told it is government in competition with private business.' He asked me if this was true, and I said, 'Yes, sir, it is true. The government is competing with shacks and hovels and hog sties and all the other holes in which the underprivileged have to live. The government is attempting to wipe out those wretched excuses for American homes. If you object to that kind of government competition, then I'm disappointed in you.'"

Leon H. Keyserling: "When he was a freshman congressman, I was deputy administrator and general counsel of the U.S. Housing Authority. And around the end of '37 or early '38 we were awarding our first aid to the cities for low-rent projects. We were going to start with three cities. One of them was New York; one of them was New Orleans, which requires no explanation; the third one was Austin, Texas. Now it was sensible to have one of the first three projects in a small southern city, but how did it happen to be Austin?

"Because there was this first-term congressman who was so on his toes and so active and so overwhelming that he was up and down our corridors all the time, and I became friendly with him. It was his go-getterness that got the first project for Austin. That's how

I first got to know him. Then he called up, and he said, 'Lady Bird and I want you to have cocktails with us.' I said, 'How's that?' He said, 'Well, we want Austin to be announced first.' I said, 'Why first? Mayor La Guardia of New York City might not like that.' He said, 'Well, it's first in the alphabet, isn't it?' We announced all three simultaneously."

D.B. Hardeman: "He was very proud of that project and bragged about it all the time and in places where it couldn't have done him the slightest good, only the opposite."

But whatever his interest in the welfare of black people and Mexican-Americans, Lyndon knew that in Texas you did not translate that interest into legislation. You might wish you could, but if you tried it, you just wouldn't be there next time around. So whenever a federal antilynching law came up, Lyndon voted against it, and whenever an antidiscrimination rider appeared on any bill, he voted against that. And every time it came up, he voted against federal legislation to end state poll taxes.[1]

Virginia Foster Durr: "The fight over the poll tax went on for years and years and years. The point is that Lyndon didn't take any active part in it. In fact, he voted against it each time it came up in the House. I would always reproach him very bitterly when I saw him about it, you know, and Lyndon would put his arm around me and say, 'Honey . . .' What was it he would say?"

Clifford Durr: "'You're dead right! I'm all for you, but we ain't got the votes. Let's wait till we get the votes.'"

Leonard Baker: "In those years it was standard during any civil rights discussion for a southern member to rant about the Negro's being responsible for more crime, more illegitimate babies, more welfare, and on and on. On Capitol Hill it was known as 'talking Nigra.' Every southerner at one time or another was expected to 'talk Nigra.' No one was considered exempt from the practice. . . .

"Lyndon Johnson, however, never 'talked Nigra.' Never in his twelve years in the House did he even discuss the issue on the floor of the House; never did he insert an anti-civil-rights diatribe in the *Congressional Record*. Except for his nay votes, the issue might not have existed for him. He was the perfect politician for his congressional district. He did as he wanted to do—secured the dams and the public works projects to give the residents of his district the moderately comfortable life they sought, worked in the Congress to make America strong militarily, did nothing to aggravate the racial situation for his white constituents—and he was consistently returned to Congress."[2]

The young congressman was, of course, constantly on the lookout for able staff members. Among the new recruits in 1939 was a young fellow Texan named John B. Connally.

Connally: "There were two reasons why I went. First, at that time we were all looking for jobs, and they weren't at all plentiful for young lawyers. And though I had a chance to become assistant attorney general under Gerald C. Mann, Mr. Johnson offered me a job to come to Washington as his top administrative aide—they called them secretaries—and I thought, I'd never been to Washington, and I thought it would be a highly interesting and exciting experience. So I decided to go to Washington instead."

Another person who went to work for Lyndon in 1939 was Walter Jenkins. Like the average depression college graduate, Jenkins had never been outside Texas. He and Connally rode to Washington together and took up residence in, of course, the basement of the Dodge Hotel.

Jenkins: "In those days patronage was considered as a supplement—a congressman could have a little more money to run his office staff. Mr. Johnson asked me if I'd like to go on the police force. I was on from 3:45 P.M. till 11:45 at night. A newly elected congressman got an elevator man. If he'd been there a year or two, he'd graduate and get a policeman. Then if he'd been there five years, he might get a doorkeeper. That was the nicest job, because there'd be weeks and weeks and weeks when you could work in the office full time and still get paid for being a doorkeeper. I'd work in the office from eight thirty till three thirty and then take my typewriter and stuff down to the guard's desk and work down there.

"I guess it's not absolutely 100 percent true that every letter was answered the day it arrived. But it's 99 percent true. That was the rule, and if we got caught and there was one carried over, then we were in trouble. If we didn't have an answer, we wrote them a letter and told them we were getting the answer. He had a fetish about it. It was one of the things he thought got you reelected, and I think he was right.

"He also believed in the use of the franking privilege. And he took full advantage of all the things that you could send out to constituents from what to do with babies to stuff from the Agriculture Department about crops. Whatever was appropriate he sent out."

Leslie Carpenter: "No request from a constituent was too big or too small to be given the most vigorous attention. The men and women back home who made up the Tenth Congressional District were a little dizzy with the service they were getting out of Washington.

"One man in Bastrup, Texas, said, 'I wrote Lyndon Johnson about a claim I had at the Veterans' Administration which had been lying around there for more than five years. I had a letter back immediately telling me he had received my letter and was at work on the problem. The next day I had another letter saying he was still working on it and hoped to have results quickly. I had another letter saying my case was looking good. The next day I had a letter saying my claim had been granted. I never saw anything like it. Why, I'd vote for that fellow for president."[3]

James H. Rowe Jr.: "Generally, Lyndon went along with Sam Rayburn in those early days. Rayburn often said—and it's a defensible idea in politics—'To get along, go along.' Johnson usually did, but then there was the incident involving John Nance Garner, for example."

In 1932 John Nance Garner, who was known as an enemy of Herbert Hoover though not necessarily a friend of progressive government, had decided he was ready to become president. Sam Rayburn, with little enthusiasm and almost no hope for success, had managed his campaign; he did it because he, like Garner, was a Texan but more because Garner was then Speaker of the House, a job that Rayburn coveted.

At that year's convention in Chicago a hasty marriage of convenience was arranged. Roosevelt for president, Garner for vice-president. Garner could never have won the nomination, but after three ballots it looked very much as if Roosevelt could lose. The marriage was a bad one from the start. Garner consistently made it clear that he was opposed to Roosevelt and almost all that the New Deal represented; he said so publicly and privately. Roosevelt saw him only when it was necessary, and what he said about him privately was unprintable, certainly unprinted. In those far-off days before investigative reporting such matters were not considered news.[4]

By 1939 Roosevelt had not, at least said he had not, made up his mind whether or not to take that unprecedented step and run for a third term.

Garner, on the other hand, although he was then seventy-one, made it clear that he wanted Roosevelt's job.

Then in July 1939 John L. Lewis, head of the CIO as well as the United Mine Workers and still a Roosevelt loyalist, called the vice-president "a labor-baiting, whiskey-drinking, poker-playing evil old man." Garner was upset, although most of his friends and supporters told him that any denunciation by Lewis should be considered a compliment and would win him votes.

Nevertheless, Garner called Mister Sam, then majority leader of the House, and told him that he must get the Texas delegation together—there were twenty-three members— and pass a resolution saying that *none* of the things Lewis had said were true. Rayburn sighed and said he would do his best; Texans defend other Texans.

Rayburn did not know that the youngest Texas congressman, Lyndon, would receive a number of calls suggesting that Roosevelt did *not* want any such resolution passed.

Corcoran: "*Everybody* called him. I called him. Ickes called him. I think Hopkins called him. Maybe even Bill Douglas called him. There wasn't any doubt about what the Old Man wanted."

Later in his *Secret Diary*, Harold Ickes told the story of what happened as Roosevelt had told it to him and as, no doubt, Lyndon had told it to Roosevelt:

> The only voice [in the Texas delegation] raised in opposition was that of Congressman Lyndon B. Johnson, of Austin. Johnson said that he couldn't subscribe to any such language and that the delegation would look foolish if such a statement were issued because everybody knew that Garner was a heavy drinker and that he was bitterly opposed to labor. The argument went on for some two hours with Johnson maintaining his ground. Then Sam Rayburn suggested that he take Johnson into his office and talk to him. Of course everyone thought that Rayburn would administer a spanking. However, Johnson still continued to hold his ground, and the crestfallen Rayburn led him back to the caucus where he said that he hadn't been able to do anything with him. It was agreed that unless every member signed the resolutions there was no point in issuing them. So the task was given to Johnson to draft such resolutions as he would be willing to sign.[5]

Wright Patman: "When Lyndon said that he couldn't and wouldn't sign any such thing, Mister Sam said, 'Lyndon, I'm looking you right in the eye.'

"And Lyndon said, 'And I'm looking you right back in the eye.'

"I think they sent Lyndon out to write something that would be satisfactory to him, but I don't believe he ever came back with anything. So it all just died."

When Garner formally announced his candidacy for the presidency, Roosevelt proved to be not unmindful of the whole incident. He said, "I see that the vice-president has thrown his bottle—I mean his hat—into the ring."

In the congressional elections of 1938 and 1940 Lyndon ran unopposed, what Lady Bird called "a free ride," but in the fall of 1940 he suddenly found himself immersed in the election battles of a number of his fellow Democratic House members.

Ray Roberts: "I went to Washington with Mr. Rayburn, so I got to observe Mr. Johnson in his day-to-day operations in the Congress. He made lots of enemies, by the way. He was brash, he was eager, he was a comer, and everybody knew it, and he wanted people to move out of the way. I think the thing that really gave him his power was becoming chairman of the congressional campaign committee.

"In 1940 it appeared that the Democrats were on the downgrade, and they were going to lose the House. No one wanted to risk his political future by being congressional campaign manager for the House. So after talking to two or three other people and finding nobody available, I don't know how it came up, but Mr. Rayburn went to the White House and said, 'Mr. President, I can't get anybody to run this, and I want you to give it to Lyndon Johnson.' The president just threw up his hands and said, 'The idea of giving it to a man who is only up here on his second term—making him chairman! Why do you recommend him?' Rayburn said, 'Because he can do the job.' Well, they beat it around, it must have been a week or ten days before the White House could say, 'There is just nobody else available, and we have got to put somebody out there.' It's typical of the way things worked."

Jenkins: "Lyndon left our House office around about the first of October as I recall and opened an office in downtown Washington. It was all done in a great hurry; I think he found an office, rented it, furnished it, and had opened up for business all in a matter of a few hours.

"He got in touch with every Democratic candidate to find out what he needed or wanted—Roosevelt to come speak, Ickes to speak—whatever was needed, including money; we tried and for the most part succeeded in getting what we wanted.

Rowe: "People running for Congress in those days never had much money; it had been that way for years, but Lyndon decided to do something about it; he got in it with both feet, the way he did everything, and he raised a hell of a lot of money. Of course, he was really trying to build a power base as a new congressman.

"I was in the White House at the time, and I worked with him. I think he got most of the money out of Texas, and then he got some from New York. I remember he went to New York several times and spoke to people, largely Jewish groups, I believe."

Robert S. Allen: "In the early fall I suddenly discovered that Lyndon Johnson was holed up in a little one-room office on E Street. He didn't tell me this, but I got the information from various sources that he had come up with a campaign fund of a hundred or more thousand dollars. He was contacting Democratic candidates for the House, incumbents who were in trouble and needed money.[6]

"His money undoubtedly came from oil sources. When I caught up with him, he made it clear that it was all very confidential, and that's the way I kept it until after the election. He was being a one-man national committee and was financing a lot of desperate House fights."

Jenkins: "I remember election night. He went out to Jim Rowe's house, and I was in the office. Around nine he called me. He said, 'I can't handle this. You come out here.' And he was getting reports on Jim Rowe's phone from all over the country. It was expected that the Democrats would lose seats in the House.

"About midnight Roosevelt called to see how things were going. He was at Hyde Park. I didn't have anything but numbers written on little slips of paper in Jim Rowe's bedroom, but we were able to tell Roosevelt that we didn't think we were going to lose any seats, that we might even gain some, and that pleased him very much."[7]

Roberts: "Instead of losing the House, we picked up seats, and from that day forward, there were some thirty or forty people that figured they owed their seat in the House to Lyndon Johnson. Whenever he called on them, he could count on this group being for whatever he wanted."

The election of 1940 was a battle not only for congressional seats but for the presidency itself. Roosevelt had deprecated his opponents in '32 and '36, but in '40 he was running scared. Not only was there the unprecedented third term issue, but also Wendell Willkie was a very appealing man. Their positions on national defense and aid to Britain (then undergoing the blitz) were virtually the same, and Willkie had a large personal following. Not large enough, as it happened, but Roosevelt was worried. He preferred to leave no stone unturned, and one of his stones, a real boulder, was Ambassador Joseph P. Kennedy.

Hugh Sidey: "Of course my relationship with Lyndon didn't really begin until 1958 when he was majority leader, but we'd have long conversations about when he was a young congressman and about how he'd see Roosevelt. I remember he claimed he was with Roosevelt when Roosevelt fired Joe Kennedy as ambassador to England.

"It was a typical Johnson story in which he said, 'You know, that poor old man was down there in the White House all by himself. Eleanor was out with the niggers someplace, and Elliott was sacked out with somebody. Roosevelt was sitting there all by himself, dying.'

"Johnson said, 'I used to go down sometimes and have a meal with him. He'd call me up.' Johnson said, 'I was there one time when the phone rang, and a lady came in and said, "It's Ambassador Kennedy. He's fought his way back from England, and he's in New York. He wants to talk to you."

"'Kennedy was in trouble; this was before the war, but he was supporting the Nazis and had been asked to come back. Roosevelt turned to me and said, "Oh, boy, this is a real problem, and I've got to handle it."

"'He got him on the phone, and he said, and you know Roosevelt talked loud on the phone, he said, "*JOE, HOW ARE YA?* Been sittin' here with Lyndon just thinkin' about you and I want to talk to you, my son. I can't wait. When do you think you can come down? We'll make it a meal. Make it tonight. Well, make it tomorrow, but you hurry down here because I've got a lot to talk to you about." He put the phone down, turned to me and said, "I'm going to fire the sonofabitch," and that was the end of ole Joe's diplomatic career.'"

Horace Busby: "Recollections can be untrustworthy. I'm convinced that Johnson was that way about Roosevelt. I think he put himself into many many imaginary situations. As a young man he identified with him, and he put himself in there talking to Roosevelt, and thirty years later he believed the fiction."

According to Roosevelt's appointment book, Lyndon was in his office that day, October 27, 1940, when Ambassador Kennedy's plane arrived in New York from London via Lisbon. But the image of a neglected, ill old man that Sidey reports Lyndon giving is hard to reconcile with a president actively caught up in the last throes of a bitterly fought election campaign while at the same time running the country almost single-handedly.

In any case, whatever Lyndon's memories, he had performed spectacularly for his party and for his president. Roosevelt was very pleased with the young Texas congressman from the Tenth District that fall.

Corcoran: "Johnson could get things done, and that is what impressed Roosevelt. He was never much impressed with theory or theoreticians. He always wanted to know what you could do and had you done it and was there someone else who could have done it better. Roosevelt, contrary to some, was a very down-to-earth politician, and so was Lyndon, and that's why they got along.

"The fact, of course, is that the biggest component in Johnson's life—in the beginning anyway—was Roosevelt laying his hand on him and saying, 'This is my boy.'

"And in 1941 when Lyndon wanted to run for the Senate, why, Roosevelt wanted him to do it. Because he knew that Johnson was a man he could count on for support."

THE DEFEAT

> Wirtz thinks that Johnson has a chance to win the race, and everyone seems to agree that the fight is between O'Daniel and Johnson. I am afraid the hillbilly vote will put over the pious faker O'Daniel, but Johnson will still be in the House, and the defeat of Dies, who seems to be running well toward the rear, will be the balm of Gilead so far as I am concerned.
> —Harold L. Ickes, *Secret Diary*[1]

In spite of the fact that Lyndon lost—the first and only time for that—the 1941 campaign for the Senate was Mrs. Johnson's favorite. And no wonder. It was a dazzling combination of circus and carnival the like of which had never before happened in Texas or probably anywhere else.

There were twenty-nine candidates on the ballot. One early candidate who later dropped out was Hal Collins, who promised to give away "a real nice $29.50 mattress" to the largest family in each audience that had paid the poll tax.

Another candidate who dropped out was Dr. John Brinkley, a gland surgeon who owned a powerful radio station in Del Rio, Texas, over which he advertised a goat-gland preparation guaranteed to keep the user eternally young.

But consider those who stayed in the race—a graduate of Annapolis who wanted an immediate declaration of war against Japan, another who advocated a five-ocean navy, two men with beards who claimed that the beards alone qualified them for the Senate. Plus Edwin Waller III, who for twenty years had announced his candidacy for whatever state or local position fell vacant, and campaigned from his rocking chair in San Marcos. He received twenty-eight votes. Another candidate was Arlon B. ("Cyclone") Davis, who was for 100 percent preparedness in case of invasion of the United States. It was, he said, the "height of folly to follow a lot of scarecrows and warmongers headlong into a war in Europe without a gun, a bagpipe, or a bayonet." Cyclone got 174 votes.

The winner was as odd as any of the losers. His name was Wilbert L. O'Daniel, a flour salesman from Kansas. Originally, he called himself Wilbert O'Daniel, but in Texas he shortened Wilbert to an initial and lengthened L. to Lee. O'Daniel said that a Yankee uncle who had been wounded in the War between the States had been so well treated by southerners that out of sheer gratitude W. Lee's mother had named him after the Confederate general.[2]

In Forth Worth O'Daniel continued selling flour, first for other people, then for himself. On each bag was printed a poem of O'Daniel's own composition, just under a picture of a billy goat:

> Hillbilly music on the air,
> Hillbilly flour everywhere;
> It tickles your feet—It tickles your tongue,
> Wherever you go, its praises are sung.

Under that, in black capitals, was the word GUARANTEED. What the flour was guaranteed to do or not to do was never stated. At the bottom of the bag in red letters was the slogan, "Please pass the biscuits, Pappy."

Naturally, O'Daniel soon became known throughout Texas as "Pass the Biscuits, Pappy" or, more often, just "Pappy."

He had begun his Texas flour crusade in the early 1930s, appearing on station WMOL in Forth Worth with a hillbilly band. Although he did not himself play a musical instrument, he announced each number and in many cases had written the words and music for the songs himself. These included such favorites as "The Boy Who Never Gets Too Big to Comb His Mother's Hair," "Sons of the Alamo," "The Orphan Newsboy," and "Marvelous Mother."[3]

Pappy also on occasion hummed or whistled along with the band. He spoke of God and how He could be counted on in a pinch; he launched a campaign to educate children to walk on the left side of the street, so as to face oncoming traffic. And he urged husbands and wives who did not have children of their own to adopt an orphan or two, a crusade so popular that most orphanages in Texas were stripped of their charges.

Pappy spoke of the virtues of hillbilly flour and of his own three attractive children, who had started appearing on the program. His daughter Molly played the accordion, Pat, the banjo, and Mike, the fiddle.

Their theme song, composed naturally by Pappy, ran:

> I like mountain music,
> Good old mountain music,
> Played by the hillbilly band
> I like bread and biscuits,
> Big white fluffy biscuits—
> Hillbilly flour makes 'em grand

There are today, nearly forty years later, many Texans who, if one is not very careful, will after a few drinks sing Pappy's hillbilly flour song not once but several times.

As Lady Bird said, "It's a wonder Lyndon survived at all in times like those."

Jesse Kellam recalled that in the spring of 1938 Pappy's contract on Station KFJZ was about to be renegotiated. "On Palm Sunday when Pappy went into the office of the station manager, Hal Hough, Hough said, 'Pappy, I'm not sure I'm going to renegotiate. You do the same old thing day after day, week after week. You've got the same band; you strike up the same old chord; you play the same old tunes. Why don't you do something different?'

"Pappy said, 'Like what?' Hough said, 'Well, why don't you see if your audience, if you've got an audience, would like you to run for governor? We've got a dozen or so entered already. One more won't make any difference.'

"So Pappy went into the studio; the band played a tune, and he said, 'There's been a lot of folks who've asked me why I don't run for governor. I'm not a professional politician. But I want all you folks to tell me what you think.'

"The next day he made two such announcements and the next day two more. Sunday, Monday, and Tuesday. And on Friday he claimed he had fifty-four thousand letters telling him to run."

And so Pappy's political career began. For a professional politician, what to do about a political program might have been a problem, but not for the Great Flour Salesman. His platform, he said, was the Ten Commandments. Later he announced that he was also for the Golden Rule and that he was for thirty-dollar-a-month old-age pensions. He bought a bus with "O'Daniel for Governor" painted on the side and a platform and microphone on top, and he, the Hillbillies, Texas Rose, a singer from the radio program, and Pat and Mike and Molly started to barnstorm the state; at every stop Pappy's latest composition, "Them Hillbillies Are Politicians Now," was featured.

Tens of thousands of people waited along the highways for hours for the arrival of Pappy and his flour barrels. The barrels were small wooden kegs with money slots on top; on the side of each were the words "Flour, Not Pork," and when Pappy's children and other members of the band passed through the audience, the barrels were quickly filled with nickels and dimes and dollars.

At the end of the campaign Pappy donated eight hundred dollars to the Red Cross; that, he said, was the amount "the people donated above my expenses in the race for governor."

Pappy was elected by a vote almost thirty-two thousand larger than the vote of all the other candidates combined. And in 1940, although he had not provided the old-age pensions or much of anything else he had promised (he said the legislature was to blame), he was reelected by an even greater majority.

Kellam remembered that during Pappy's second campaign he (Kellam) said to a relative, "'Who are you going to vote for?' And he said, 'Pappy.' I said, 'Pappy O'Daniel? You can't mean that. What the hell has he done?' And he said, 'Hasn't done a damn thing, and we need more of it.'"

While he was governor, Pappy asked the legislature to pass a law encouraging outside industries to move into Texas; he said that the industries could pay workers whatever they liked, and if there were any objections, the objecting workers would be rounded up, arrested, and put to picking cotton in gangs.

His general popularity did not seem to diminish, though. The big question was where he would go after his second term as governor or, as it turned out, *during* his second term as governor.

Senator Morris Sheppard of Texas died on April 4, 1941; he was sixty-five years old. On April 19 Governor O'Daniel announced that a special election would be held on June 28 to choose a successor to Senator Sheppard.[4] Then he appointed an interim senator, who, despite his name, would give the governor the minimum amount of trouble should he decide to enter the race himself.

That was Andrew Jackson Houston, the only surviving son of Sam Houston, who had also been a U.S. senator. A.J. Houston was in his late eighties in mind and body, although O'Daniel claimed that when he was told of the appointment, he smiled. Apparently, the smile exhausted the old man because he rested for a month, then got on a train and went to Washington where he was sworn in by Vice-President Wallace just ninety-five years after his father had been sworn in.

Walter Jenkins: "I happened to have been the first one to tell Mr. Johnson that there was a vacancy in the Senate. I was on the police desk at the front door of the New House Office Building, and early that morning someone came in and said that Morris Sheppard had just died.

"I picked up the phone on the desk and called Mr. Johnson. He said 'Well, I won't be in this morning.' I'm sure he started calling Alvin Wirtz and others—he must have decided immediately that he *wanted* to run, but it took a while to decide that he *would*. He was a very careful studier, deciding whether he had a chance or not."

Mary Rather: "Senator Wirtz was in Washington as undersecretary of the interior. I was working as his secretary. I walked in that morning and hung up my coat and walked on back to the undersecretary's office. I opened the door, and there he was at his desk. He looked up, and he said, 'Are you thinking what I'm thinking?' I said, 'I knew what you were thinking. I got here as early as I could.' It wasn't but a little while later that Congressman Johnson and Senator Wirtz were discussing his candidacy."

Indeed, when later that month Lyndon went to Austin to address the joint houses of the legislature on San Jacinto Day,[5] he delivered a speech that was said to have been written in the White House. It dwelt on the fact that the United States must prepare for war. "We don't know in days, hours, weeks, or months when this hurricane may come to us." He warned labor against strikes when the country was in peril. And he warned farmers that when the government called on them, they must be ready for sacrifice. "The government of the whole country is above that of any single group—labor, capital, or farmer."

He got a standing ovation from the legislators, after which he went to see the governor. Was Pappy thinking of running for Morris Sheppard's seat? Pappy assured Lyndon that he was not even considering it. What would a Texas country boy like himself do in Washington? No, no, no—there was still too much to be accomplished as governor.

And Lyndon believed him.[6]

Late that night Lyndon flew back to Washington. Arriving in the early morning hours, he took a taxi from the airport, and went directly to the White House. First, he told the president the happy news about Pappy. The president was delighted. Next Lyndon showed him the draft of a statement he had written on the plane announcing his own candidacy for the Senate. The President suggested that Lyndon read the statement on the White House steps, and a few minutes later he did.

In the beginning of the campaign it looked as if the race would be primarily between Lyndon, Congressman Martin Dies, and the state's attorney general, Gerald C. Mann. All three men were oversized, physically imposing. Dies was nationally known and loved or hated because of his position as chairman of the House Committee on Un-American Activities. He had neither the imagination nor the evil flair of the great red hunter Joseph R. McCarthy, who was to take over in the fifties, and he lacked the doggedness and easy adaptability to change of Richard M. Nixon. But he did his best and stressed the vast importance of his surveillance work against an alien "army" inside the country larger than the U.S. Army itself that was infiltrating aircraft factories and munitions plants and was, he said, answerable to Hitler or Stalin alternatively.

In spite of the drama of his subject, though, Dies, was apt, when he spoke, to put his audiences to sleep.

Gerald C. Mann was young like Lyndon, and a much admired former all-southwestern quarterback from Southern Methodist. Deeply religious, he had helped work his way through Harvard Law School by preaching in a Congregational church in a suburb of Gloucester, Massachusetts. He was considered a man of honor and had been an unusually effective attorney general, but, like Dies, he was dull. He carried a Bible wherever he went and while speaking thumped it on occasion, a gesture aimed, it was said, to appeal to O'Daniel supporters; he advocated a larger FBI—a sop, it was claimed, to the Dies folks—and he insisted that he was as enthusiastic a supporter of Roosevelt as was Johnson.

As he had in 1937, Lyndon opened this campaign in San Marcos. The streets were crowded with buses from all over the state; "Franklin D. and Lyndon B." the signs said. The Austin High School band played, and in the parade to the auditorium Lyndon turned up the brim of his hat the way Roosevelt did.

In his speech Lyndon announced that the slogan of his campaign would be "Roosevelt and unity." He took his stand domestically for full parity prices for farmers, federal old-age pensions from age sixty on, and state control over conservation of natural resources, especially oil. As for the impending war, he said, as he was to repeat many times, it was his show-stopper in 1941, "If the day ever comes when my vote must be cast to send your boy to the trenches, that day Lyndon Johnson will leave his Senate seat and go with him."

Lyndon of course received considerable support from the White House, although Roosevelt did not intervene directly in the campaign. In a syndicated column that everybody felt was planted by the White House, Robert Kintner and Joseph Alsop wrote that Franklin personally had persuaded Lyndon to run, though Lyndon had said he had infected tonsils and no money.

Robert Kintner: "You might say the White House had something to do with inspiring that column, but I don't think there was anyone in Washington with any political knowledge who didn't know that Roosevelt wanted Johnson to win. And he was doing all he could to make that happen, which in those days was a lot."

Pappy was the last of the major candidates to announce and he waited until the sixth week of the campaign to do so. He said that nothing in the world would have induced him to leave the good folks of Texas, but fate—or God, if you prefer—had stepped in and told him that his job as governor had been accomplished and that by going to Washington he would "be able to perform a more useful service for our great people."

At each stop on the tour that followed the band played O'Daniel's newest song, "I'll Be With You When I'm Gone."

Malcolm Bardwell: "Pappy O'Daniel was a freak in public office. Everybody would drop a dime in the flour barrel, and when they'd put a dime in, everybody would go vote for him."

Kellam: "You couldn't find anybody who was going to vote for Pappy in 1941; at least you couldn't find anybody who was going to admit planning to vote for him. But once somebody put that damn dime in, although none of us realized it at the time, there was no way whoever it was *wasn't* going to vote for him."

Lady Bird: "We finally decided if you couldn't beat 'em, you might as well join 'em; so we got ourselves a band and we had ourselves a starlet."

Actually, in that campaign Lyndon had *two* bands, the expected hillbilly musicians and a jazz band, *two* singers, a hefty lady who was always introduced as "the Kate Smith of the South," and sang "God Bless America" with the voters joining in on the chorus. Then came a thinner, somewhat younger singer who stepped forward with her rendition of something like "San Antonio Rose." After which the portly singer returned to give the voters "Dixie" and "The Eyes of Texas Are Upon You."

Then came a kind of dramatization and/or pageant of the history of the United States from the depression on. With appropriate background music a narrator explained how the United States had been saved from collapse, planned by persons from Wall Street and by Republicans (Herbert Hoover chief among them), by the happy arrival in Washington of Franklin D. Roosevelt. Now, the narrator went on, the Republic was threatened by another menace—Adolf Hitler. And, he added, as the menace crept closer to the United States, Franklin Roosevelt needed "a man who loves his country, who loves the people. . . . This man is Lyndon Johnson."

A ruffle of drums, and then Lyndon appeared, wearing a white Stetson with the brim rolled up and a grin that a few friends said reminded them of Franklin D.

Willard Deason: "Congressman Johnson's problem was that he was known only in the Tenth District. He had to meet as many people as he could as fast as he could, and he would travel five or six hundred miles a day. He had to make up in energy what he lacked in exposure."

Lyndon not only moved around a lot, he talked a lot. His speeches were, as always, lengthy; sometimes the first would last an hour. Here he differed from Harry Truman, who said, "You can't win many votes if people are asleep or walking out on you"—a lesson Lyndon never learned.

In 1941, as always, Lyndon would speak of polls. The first Joe Belden poll[7] had showed Pappy, who hadn't yet even announced his candidacy, with 32.8 percent of the vote, Gerald Mann with 28.2, Martin Dies with 27.9, and Lyndon with 9.3.

"You know, I don't know much about polls," Lyndon would say. "I know they made me feel mighty bad when my mother and my wife told me I was the last man in the race. I know that my throat got bad on me, and I had to spend a few days in the hospital."

John B. Connally: "He got sick out at Happy Hollow Lane. Dr. Arthur Scott ministered to him and he had pneumonia, as I remember, but he didn't want anything said about it. I said, 'You can't do that, for God's sake, you've got a week's schedule of speaking engagements.' He said, 'Well, get Everett Looney to take them. He can do it.' I said, 'Yeah, but how are we going go explain Everett Looney speaking? And you being incommunicado for several days or a week? There's no way you can do this.'

"Gordon Fulcher and I were out at his house, and we had a confrontation about it. He just threw a fit, went into a tirade, ordered us out of the house, said he never wanted to talk to us again. So we left.

"He got to feeling much better, but he'd been quite abusive to us. He got mad—we got mad. We went for about a week. Then one day I just got on the phone again."

Lyndon was, as always, sure that his hospitalization had knocked him out of the campaign. Instead his popularity doubled, largely because while his opponents had waited for the usual drenching spring rains to end, Lyndon had his stand-ins speaking for him. Besides, that was the week that Rudolph Hess flew from the German Reich to Scotland and dominated the Western press, Texas included. Then, too, either Wirtz or Connally, or both, probably with the president's connivance, had spread the rumor that Franklin D. was coming to Texas to speak for Lyndon B.

Thomas G. Corcoran: "I never heard it denied in the White House; as I recall, the question was evaded, but the trip didn't happen."

Mrs. Johnson's "home movies" of the campaign show that at the campaign's end Lyndon had developed a skin rash caused by nervous tension and looked ten years older than he did at the beginning. But that could be because he hardly ever slept, never relaxed, never stopped fretting, seldom ate, and was convinced of defeat.

In his basic 1941 speech, he would say: "We must stop the beast of Berlin before he reaches America. Now if you want your senator to go up there to Washington to snoop and sneak and snipe at your commander in chief, don't vote for Lyndon Johnson. Because he'll always support your commander in chief and the elected Democratic leaders of this great Republic of ours."

Then in a hushed voice he would continue: "Over yonder in that Senate chamber there's a vacant seat. It was filled by a young congressman some thirty years ago. You promoted him from the House to the Senate. He was one of Roosevelt's strong right arms. Morris Sheppard, chairman of the Military Affairs Committee.

"He worked himself to death. He was trying to build the greatest army that any nation ever knew. You must fill that seat. When you elect Lyndon Johnson to fill that seat, your commander in chief can look at that seat and say, 'There sits the boy from Johnson City that can't be bought!'

"You know, folks, they don't get to be twenty-one up in my country if they're not honest."

Then Lyndon would ostentatiously throw aside his prepared speech and say, "Now let's get down to my country-boy style of talking." Applause, cheers. And then there would be at least half an hour, more likely an hour of stories, first about Sam Ealy—"My daddy always said, 'Lyndon, take care of the people and the election will take care of itself.'"

After that would come some stories about the Crider boys in Johnson City and several devastating and accurate imitations of his political opponents. Next came the lottery, and those with the lucky numbers won up to $715 worth of defense bonds.

All together, it made for a late evening, but there wasn't much else to stay up for.

The telegram held an important place in Lyndon's campaign psychology. There was still a sense of the magic about it—most people in Texas had never received one—and it had the distinct advantage that it could be pulled dramatically from a vest pocket and waved before an audience.

The president saw to it that Lyndon had plenty to wave. He assigned an assistant White House press secretary to draft a continuous succession of telegrams to be signed by cabinet members and other well-known administration figures saying that Lyndon was needed in the Senate. The candidate seemed to have a new one at almost every rally.

Then toward the end of the campaign, Wirtz began to worry that maybe there was such a thing as being too pro-Roosevelt. So Lyndon for the first time stressed his opposition to federal control of oil production, although the administration backed it, and, with an eye to the future, he defended the 27½ percent oil-depletion allowance, although it too was hardly in line with New Deal philosophy.[8] Meanwhile, Mann and Dies began to reiterate more strongly their own support of the president, and even O'Daniel, who only a few weeks before had equated the New Deal with "Communistic labor unions," found areas of agreement with his chief executive, whom he referred to as "that boy."

On election day Lyndon voted in Johnson City, then went to the Stephen F. Austin

Hotel in Austin where he had his headquarters, took a sleeping pill, and woke up in time for the early returns.

They were promising. When Lyndon finally retired for the night, he was ahead by three thousand votes, and when he woke up the next morning, his lead was nearly five thousand. Newspapers all over the state were saying that he had been elected. So were all of his major campaign workers save three—Alvin Wirtz, John B. Connally, and Mayor Tom Miller of Austin. They were well aware that there were more elements affecting the outcome than just the voters and the candidates.

Two days before, Miller, a longtime friend of Lyndon's, had sent a telegram to Senator Claude Pepper, who had in turn sent it to Grace Tully for the president, saying that the polls showed the Lyndon was twenty-five thousand votes ahead of the governor. But Miller added, "Only doubt is that gambling, horse-racing, and whiskey-beer combination will throw behind O'Daniel to get him out of state. Stevenson may become governor and stop Prohibition drive which O'Daniel started last week."

A few days before the election "Pa" Ferguson, the former governor, pointed out in a series of ads that in voting for O'Daniel for the Senate the voters would get Lt. Governor Coke Stevenson for governor. Although Ferguson did not say so, Stevenson, like himself, was not a Prohibitionist and was close to the liquor interests. Pa later explained that a dry senator in Washington wouldn't bother the liquor interests much, but a governor like Pappy, who could make a dried up desert of Texas in wartime, was a real threat.

Thus, as soon as the first returns were counted, showing Lyndon ahead, fifteen state senators, who for various and no doubt valid reasons hated O'Daniel, met with representatives of the liquor companies and drew up plans to do whatever was necessary to get Pappy out of Austin.

The Johnson forces continued to roll happily ahead.

Jenkins: "Mr. Johnson was anxious for the headlines to say he'd won. So in the counties where we had strong leads we urged them to get their votes in as quickly as they possibly could.

"As I remember, when there were forty thousand votes left to count, Mr. Johnson was five thousand votes ahead. With four major candidates, that was almost a cinch to be a victory. The lead began to dwindle as the outlying counties' votes came in. But I wasn't concerned, because I thought we were so far ahead that we couldn't possibly lose."

New York Times. Dallas, Texas, June 30. W. Lee O'Daniel slashed Rep. Lyndon Johnson's lead to 77 votes and threatened to overtake the New Deal congressman in tonight's 11:30 unofficial tabulation in the special election.

It was the first time that Mr. O'Daniel has come within 100 votes of the lead which Mr. Johnson took on Saturday night. Late reporting boxes with heavy O'Daniel strength steadily ground down the margin.

Some 2,000 to 3,500 are not counted. Most of them are from rural areas.

Gordon Fulcher: "Johnson was leading until the vote counting dragged on and on and on. It was then, and it still is, my opinion that a sufficient number of votes was switched or, to just put it baldly, stolen in a number of counties in deep east Texas to defeat Johnson and to put O'Daniel in the Senate."

New York Times. Dallas, Texas, July 1. Gov. W. Lee O'Daniel has been elected to the United States Senate on the basis of complete unofficial returns of the State Election Bureau.

Governor O'Daniel, whose strength was in the country districts, where he had carried on a homespun campaign, forged ahead of Representative Johnson early today and increased his margin hourly until he had a lead of 1,095 votes in the final count.

Jenkins: "Most of those late-arriving votes for O'Daniel came from parts of Texas where former Governor Ferguson was still active and where a lot of Dies's votes suddenly turned up for O'Daniel. That's what they say happened anyway, and that's what won the election for O'Daniel.[9]

"We wanted, a lot of us did, to have him contest the election, but he never would. He said if you contest an election, even if you win the contest, you go into office under a cloud, and you haven't won anything.

"And he was right. It never would have changed. A contest would have satisfied us, but it wouldn't have helped him."

James Blundell: "There's no question about it in my mind. It wasn't O'Daniel that beat Johnson. It was Coke Stevenson and the fact that a lot of people wanted him to be governor that had the greatest force on the election.

"I know that our lead dwindled·every day during the week after the election. Now I don't know if the Stevenson people'had been withholding their votes or just waiting to see how many votes they needed. I do know that on Saturday night the Stevenson supporters met in the Driskill Hotel, across the street from the Stephen F. Austin, which was where we were. And after that meeting they scattered all over the state, but especially to east Texas.

"I don't know what they did, but whatever it was, apparently it was effective."

The defeat caused considerable comment, notably from Drew Pearson and Walter Winchell. In his Sunday night broadcast that week Winchell said that the FBI was going to look into the whole matter of the Texas senatorial election. Two congressional committees said that they were, too, and so did at least two committees of the Texas legislature, one of which wanted to look not only into the election but into Drew Pearson.

For many reasons no investigation of any kind ever happened. As the days passed, election officials in various counties who had taken the ballot boxes home with them or locked them up or mislaid them, started opening them; it was discovered that Lyndon in those instances had little or no support or that the fools who had voted for him had not understood how to mark their ballots, and that said ballots were thus invalid. Other election officials discovered that they had made errors in giving Lyndon too many votes, and they hurriedly sent in their "corrected" totals. Most of the "corrections" were in Pappy's favor.

On July 14 the state canvassing board came up with its official computations. Of 575,879 votes cast in the election, W. Lee O'Daniel received 175,590, winning by a plurality of 1,311 over Lyndon Johnson. Johnson's defeat was a decided shock to those who had believed that Roosevelt's word, even if only implied, was all powerful in Texas.

O'Daniel's career did not flourish in Washington. He made the mistake of continuing his campaign rhetoric on the Senate floor. Walter Hall remembers Sam Rayburn telling him: "'What you say about the Senate when you're out in the hustings campaigning, out speechmaking, doesn't matter. But you don't get up in the United States Senate and denounce the United States Senate.'"

The only significant legislative effort of Pappy's career was an attempt to get the Senate to repeal Roosevelt's Fair Labor Standards Act, which required employers to pay time and a half for those who worked more than forty hours a week; he failed. In Texas it was said of him that his aim, always, was to save the soul of a poor man and the wealth of a rich man.

James H. Rowe, Jr.: "When Johnson got back to Washington, Roosevelt gave him a hard time over that loss. Roosevelt told him, 'Lyndon, apparently you Texans haven't learned one of the first things we learned up in New York State, and that is that when the election is over, you have to sit on the ballot boxes.'"

Corcoran: "In that 1941 race we gave him everything we could, everything; we wanted him to win over that O'Daniel. He didn't win, though, and I'll never forget what he said to me afterwards. He said, 'Well, Tommy, in the political business if you're counted out, you're never a crybaby in public about it.'

"And then he said, 'It's strange how few people in public life there are in your generation, and you get to know them all. Did you ever see a shooting gallery with its circular, rotating discs with lots of pipes and rabbits on the circuit? Well, when you miss one the first time, you get a second chance. And the sonofabitch who trimmed you will always come up again. And then you can get him.'"

PEARL HARBOR—BEFORE AND AFTER

Lady Bird: "I'll never forget the way he looked when he took the plane back to Washington after losing that election in 1941—jaunty, unbowed. Sometimes one thinks that fate may guide us at times. Because when the draft was continued in August, just a little more than a month later, it was by a margin of one vote.

"So it was really all right that he lost the 1941 race. Sometimes you are in the right place and at the right time."

In October 1940, nine hundred thousand young men had been drafted for a year of service "unless Congress declares that the national security is imperiled."

True, in the spring of 1941 Roosevelt had declared a national emergency, but that declaration was not binding on Congress, and the country was by no means united behind Roosevelt's increasing "meddling in the affairs of Europe," which was what Colonel Charles A. Lindbergh called it.

Many if not most of the nine hundred thousand draftees had no intention, or so they said, of serving beyond October. They said they did not know why they were in the army anyway. It looked as if Hitler had more than he could handle, now that he had invaded Russia, and the Japanese seemed to be totally bogged down in China.

Besides, it looked like playing soldier more than soldiering itself. Many draftees were drilling not with guns but with broomsticks, and trucks were unsuccessfully masquerading as tanks. Maneuvers in the early summer of 1941 had been a fiasco everywhere. And organizations of mothers were demanding that their boys be sent home in October. On the walls of training camps all over the United States the initials *O.H.I.O.* were scrawled, meaning "Over the Hill in October"; they would depart come October no matter what the law said. Secretary of War Henry L. Stimson, as Waspish and Ivy League as a man could comfortably be, who thought there could be no greater destiny than dying for one's country, wanted the draft extended for an indefinite period. Sam Rayburn knew that was impossible and suggested that it be extended for another thirteen months, which meant for those already in a total of thirty months service—"servitude," most draftees called it.

Four days before the vote on extending the draft, which came on August 12, Lyndon made his first major speech on the floor of Congress.[1] He said:

> Texas boys come from a race of men who fought for their freedom at the Alamo and Goliad and San Jacinto. . . . Texas boys prefer service now to slavery later.
>
> The question still is freedom or slavery. There is no way to escape it. Some cry out for appeasement, but there is a 100 percent record of destruction and death in every attempt toward appeasement of the Axis powers.
>
> The world is in war to decide freedom or slavery. We are in that world. That war may wash nearer our shores any time. Darker days may lie ahead of us, but perhaps they are nearer than we think.

Carl Vinson: "During the debate of this issue by the House he knew that the vote would be close. It may be that this was when he started arm-twisting.

"Anyway, I recall that he worked very hard for the enactment of this bill. The extension of the public draft period was carried by only one vote, and Lyndon Johnson had as much to do with winning that victory as any man in the Congress of the United States at that time."

William S. White: "At that time Roosevelt was making a great deal of private use of Lyndon Johnson. By that I mean Lyndon was not then in the leadership of the House. Nevertheless, Mr. Roosevelt often leaned on him, particularly for inside information about the estimates of what the House would really do, and he did so in this case.

"He called Lyndon to the White House and asked his advice abuot how he, Mr. Roosevelt, could best move to have the draft continued.

"Lyndon told him, as he later told me, that he thought the wisest thing was to have the final appeal made to the House not by the secretary of the army but rather by Cordell Hull, the secretary of state. That seemed a little odd to the president, and he said, 'Why would you do that, Lyndon?' He said, 'Because, Mr. President, this is really a gut matter, and although Cordell Hull is not secretary of the army, he's a former member of Congress, and he has enormous goodwill there and enormous private respect. And it would come better from him.'[2]

"In fact, Mr. Roosevelt did ask Mr. Hull to make the final appeal. And it may well have been the thing that put it over."

Lyndon: "I went to Mr. Rayburn's house that morning for breakfast, and we tried to get a nose count, and it didn't look too good. It was August, before Pearl Harbor.

"We canvassed a good many members. And I finally suggested to the Speaker, midmorning, that we should try to get Secretary of State Cordell Hull to write a letter urging the Congress to extend the draft.

"Mr. Rayburn was a very deliberate man and rather cautious, and he didn't know about the wisdom of asking the secretary of state to be sending a letter with the debate in the House at the last moment. But after some reflection he agreed to it. And the letter was delivered about ten minutes before the debate closed.[3]

"Mr. Rayburn went to the well of the House, and with some doubts, I think, about the wisdom of the suggestion I had made, he read the letter from Cordell Hull.

"And it brought great applause.

"Then Mr. Rayburn took the gavel and the Speaker's chair, and we were several votes behind as the roll call was ended. But then a few members changed their votes, and finally we got one vote ahead."

Ray Roberts: "It was one of the first days I was permitted the floor privilege—you know, not many folks are on the floor except members. I was there counting on my fingers whether we were leading or behind. We got up to the tail end of the vote, and we were two votes behind, I guess, and only three votes out. And two of those were Republican. And we got all three of them, and won it 203 to 202."

Lyndon: "Mr. Rayburn banged down the gavel and announced the vote. And our army was not sent home in August before Pearl Harbor."

Rayburn was accused, and with considerable justice, of parliamentary shenanigans in this instance. When the voting ended with that of Orville Zimmerman of Missouri, Rayburn said, "On this vote 203 members have voted aye, 202 members have voted no, and the bill is passed."

Those who were opposed to the bill asked that the vote be reopened so that additions and alterations could be made, which was a House custom. Rayburn ruled against them. He did agree to a recapitulation of the actual voting. When that was completed, without as much as a second's delay, Rayburn said, "No correction in the vote; the vote stands, and the motion to reconsider is laid on the table."

Congressman Dewey Short, an isolationist from Missouri, said that he had heard no motion to reconsider. Rayburn gaveled him into silence. The bill was passed, and the mothers in the galleries moaned and booed and wept.

On Saturday, December 6, 1941, Marvin McIntyre, Franklin Roosevelt's liaison with Capitol Hill, sent the president a memo saying, "Have a request from Congressman Lyndon Johnson who wants to see you next week."

That same day Lyndon called Edwin M. ("Pa") Watson, the presidential secretary in charge of appointments, saying he wanted to see the president to discuss (1) the youth of the country—Lyndon was proposing a bill that would combine the CCC and the NYA; (2) a judgeship in Texas; (3) his own future as to where he could best serve the president; (4) the congressional elections in Texas.

Watson noted, "He hopes to go to Texas next Friday and would like very much to see the president before that time."

The appointment was, of course, never made.

Lady Bird: "I was in Billingsley, Alabama, on December seventh. My Uncle Claude had died with a sizable estate to be settled, and he had been handling some of my property which my mother had left me. I heard the news and tried to reach Lyndon, but the phones were pandemonium. When I finally reached him, he told me of the extensive damage and how Pearl Harbor had been wiped out. He was very excited, very angry, and very determined to volunteer for active duty."

Rebekah, when she heard about Pearl Harbor, was at the home in Austin that Lyndon had secured for her after Sam Ealy died. "I am wondering what you will do," she wrote Lyndon. "I know your ideas about this differ from mine. I hope you will *not* get into a branch of service on the sea. Your training would not fit you for that. Some administrative work is more in your line." She signed it, typically, "my heart is with my precious boy, so inexpressibly dear to me, my dearest love, Mother."

Lyndon's response five days later was also typical. "You know that the last thing in the world I want to do is give you a moment of anxiety, but . . ."

At 12:23 on December 8, before the assembled members of both houses of Congress, the cabinet, and the members of the United States Supreme Court, Speaker Sam Rayburn rapped his gavel for silence and said, "The president of the United States!"

There was a moment of silence, and then, after a tumultuous ovation, Franklin Roosevelt spoke for six and a half minutes. December 7, 1941, was, he said, "a date which will live in infamy." He asked that Congress declare that a state of war existed between the United States and the Japanese Empire. That, of course, was done. There was only one vote in either House against such a declaration, that of the congresswoman from Montana, Jeannette Rankin.

Also on December 8, whether before or after the president's speech is not certain, Lyndon drafted the following letter to Roosevelt: "My dear Mr. President, As a member of the Naval Reserve of the United States Navy, I hereby urgently request my commander in chief to assign me immediately to active duty with the Fleet. Sincerely, Lyndon B. Johnson."

Rebekah would not have been pleased.

Lyndon turned his office over to Lady Bird on December 10, and on the eleventh he and all the other members of the House except Miss Rankin agreed to Roosevelt's request for the United States to declare war against Germany and Italy. Miss Rankin voted "present." Almost immediately thereafter Lyndon rose and said, "Mr. Speaker, I ask unanimous consent for an indefinite leave of absence."

Rayburn: "Is there objection to the request of the gentleman from Texas?"

There was none.

Rayburn: "So be it."

A few minutes later Lyndon picked up the papers on his desk, stuffed them in a briefcase, and left the floor of the House. Three days later—he was already a lieutenant commander in the U.S. Naval Reserve—he became the first member of the House to be in uniform.

When Lyndon told the story, it ended there; his friend and fellow congressman Warren Magnuson of Washington, however, remembers it somewhat differently.

Magnuson: "When Pearl Harbor was attacked, Lyndon and I immediately went down. We had become acquainted in the Naval Affairs Committee with Admiral Chester Nimitz, who is from Texas, too—from Fredericksburg. So Lyndon and I went down together and said, 'We want to go to war.' We got our papers to the point where all Nimitz had to do was sign them. And we went down there, and he looked up and said, 'Oh, you two here again?'

"But he signed the papers. We didn't resign from Congress; we just went."

In any case, the Texas press was duly informed, at least about Lyndon. After all, a scant six months had passed since he had been proclaiming throughout the state, "If the day ever comes when my vote must be cast to send your boy to the trenches, that day will Lyndon Johnson leave his Senate seat and go with him!" Well, the seat was, unfortunately, still in the House, but the promise held.

Right after Christmas, Lyndon reported to Headquarters, Twelfth Naval District, San Francisco. It was there that Roosevelt wrote him on December 30 to thank him for the "wonderful turkey"—one of the famous Texas turkeys that Lyndon was fond of dispensing on appropriate holidays—and to express his pleasure that Lyndon was "getting a firsthand picture of things." Enclosing good wishes for the New Year, Roosevelt concluded, "Do run in and see me when you get back."

Lyndon made sure that he got back quickly. In San Francisco he reported to the Office of the Chief, United States–New Zealand Naval Command, an assignment he was sure he would hate. It was, he later said, "a paper-shifting job, placating the navy and placating the New Zealanders; it was nothing. I had given up my seat in Congress for nothing."

Only a few days after his arrival in San Francisco he asked for and was given permission to return to Washington "to settle a personal problem." Back in the capital he immediately asked for and got an appointment with the president—on January 23—and although no record of what they talked about is available, a few days later he was assigned to the office of the undersecretary of the navy, James V. Forrestal.

John B. Connally: "Lyndon was in the office of Undersecretary of the Navy, James Forrestal, and was working with a Dr. Barker of Columbia, who was engaged in civilian manpower training. He and I spent about five months there in 1942, going up and down the West Coast primarily, helping to set up training programs for the tremendous number of people who would obviously be coming in with the new shipbuilding program. We worked with the navy, and we worked with private ship builders like Henry J. Kaiser who started the Kaiser shipyards, all the way up and down the coast—San Diego, Los Angeles, San Francisco, Portland, Seattle."

Lady Bird: "I went with Lyndon to the West Coast taking a typewriter and trying to be his secretary. I believe Bill Deason was with us, and John Connally. Lyndon was working on James Forrestal's program, seeing how efficient the naval yards were in their training programs to take on an enormous amount of personnel.

"Then I went back to Washington about the middle of January to work in the office with Nellie Connally. For a while I stayed in our apartment and then moved in with Nellie. Lyndon did make a trip or two back to Washington. I remember going to Union Station to see him off with Speaker Rayburn and Nellie. It was a dramatic moment when the train pulled out."

Lyndon, however, wanted an overseas assignment.

He finally saw Roosevelt on April 26, and a few days later was on his way to Australia where General Douglas MacArthur had recently arrived after a defeat in the Philippines that had been humiliating both to the Allies and to him, although MacArthur would himself probably have reversed that order. MacArthur was not pleased with the news that his command, the Southwest Pacific Area, was not to receive top priority so far as men or supplies were concerned; that priority was to be Europe.

The general was demonstrably and volubly unhappy, and Roosevelt felt that his reports were unreliable. Would Lyndon look into that? There have through the years been recurrent rumors that the president was also curious about MacArthur's political plans, if any, but there is no evidence that he asked Lyndon to look into that too.

While reports from the Southwest Pacific Area were contradictory, it was rumored that MacArthur was treating even high-ranking officers of the air corps with disdain. Lyndon might want to find out about that. While Lyndon was not expected to solve any of these problems. a report on them, Lyndon's own observation of them, would be appreciated, and good luck.

Lyndon gave up his congressional salary of ten thousand dollars a year while he was on active duty, accepting a lieutenant commander's pay of three thousand a year. Mrs. Johnson served without salary.

Lady Bird: "Running the office while Lyndon was in the navy was a very good building part of my life for two reasons. One, it made me understand Lyndon a lot better. It made me know why he was tired or tense or frustrated when he got home at night, because dealing with a great variety of problems from the ten counties and the three hundred thousand people takes a lot out of you.

"Second, it gave me a sense of, sort of reassurance about myself because I finally emerged thinking that—well, I *could* make a living for myself. Maybe not a very good one, but I did know how to do some of those things, and I could learn more.

"Now Lyndon always had a marvelous staff, close-knit and able, but there's nobody who cares quite as much about your business as yourself and, next to yourself, your wife. I decided to serve because I cared that extra little bit. To put it bluntly, I also realized that I could probably get into a few offices and see a few people that the staff members couldn't.

"And this was important to Lyndon's constituents. I believed that the people of his district would feel a closer bond to their congressman if his wife served as a kind of liaison."

Jake Pickle: "Mrs. Johnson wasn't the only congressman's wife who took over the office when her husband was gone, but she was the only one who considered it a full-time job and did it."

At the end of April, Lyndon and Lady Bird had a few days in Washington together. Then just before midnight on the first of May, or just after on the second, versions differ, Lyndon left for the Pacific.

PACIFIC JOURNEY

When Lyndon was president and about to embark on a seventeen-day, twenty-five-thousand-mile Asian-Pacific trip to Australia, New Zealand, the Philippines, Thailand, Malaysia, and South Korea, he entertained his travel party with a showing of the films he himself had taken twenty-four years before on his wartime Pacific journey. There might be noticed, he said, a slight resemblance to a more famous movie of the same subject, *South Pacific*, except that in his production "the cameraman, director, producer, and sometimes the performer are all one and the same, and as will shortly be very apparent, he was a rank amateur at making movies.

"Like a lot of young men in a hurry to be where the action is," he said, "I was saying my good-byes when my wife thrust a sixteen-millimeter camera into my hand and said, 'Send pictures.' I always followed orders from her.

"It is at best a very small piece of history that probably isn't important to anyone but me because it brings back a flood of memories of some very vivid, challenging, exciting—sometimes frightening—days in 1942 when I saw a small part of World War II at a very rough hour."

The journey was undertaken while Lyndon was working as deputy to Secretary of the Navy Forrestal. Among the problems that poured over their desks was the "major one of knowing what we were really up against in the Pacific. We were taking real losses. Our equipment was not of the best—second-, sometimes third-rate, against the superb Japanese planes and hardware. Everything seemed pretty disorganized and uncertain. Communications were most unsatisfactory, and President Roosevelt was having trouble getting the facts."

Lyndon was part of the three-man survey team Roosevelt decided to send. "We were directed to get below the top brass," Lyndon said, "below General MacArthur's command headquarters in Australia, to the men in combat and see for ourselves what they were facing. President Roosevelt wanted his own eyes and ears in the field. I was the navy officer picked to go.

"By spring our team of three was literally hitchhiking its way by whatever was flying, and that wasn't much, to the South Pacific."

What Lyndon did not tell his audience that night was that he also kept a diary during that Pacific journey, the only diary, as far as we know, that he ever did keep.

Lyndon's South Pacific odyssey started with fever and night sweats in Palmyra (due south of Hawaii) and ended with pneumonia in a Fiji Island hospital. As such it was not untypical, although briefer than most tours at that time.

From Palmyra he flew to Canton, Suva in the Fiji Islands, Nouméa, the capital of New Caledonia, and Auckland, New Zealand. There he tallied up the number of American battleships, cruisers, destroyers, carriers, and submarines as compared to the Japanese. They had more of almost everything. Admiral Chester A. Nimitz traveled with Lyndon at this juncture. From Auckland they flew to Sydney, Australia, and from Sydney to Brisbane. At each stop Lyndon recorded what was needed, which was practically everything—more equipment, better communications, and some way to give the men a sense of what they were fighting for. He deplored the fact that the American and Australian forces spent so much time squabbling, that the headquarters was a good three thousand miles from the front, that there seemed to be no top young men barking orders, that delay, indecision, and procrastination reigned.

Aside from that, Lyndon liked Australia. "Country hilly," he wrote in his diary, "few streams, rare houses, occasional roads—looks like good cattle and sheep country—like Johnson City country. Hills and draws." He thought a good deal, he said, about Miss Jesus, the appellation he had inexplicably assigned to Lady Bird. And everywhere he jotted down names and addresses of Texans, officers and enlisted men alike.

At this stage of his trip he was accompanied by two lieutenant colonels of the general staff in Washington, both out there, as was he, to find out what was happening in SWPA (the Southwest Pacific Area). They had become good friends; Lieutenant Colonel Francis Stevens was "Steve," Lieutenant Colonel Samuel Anderson, "Andy," and Lyndon, for the first and only time in his life, "Johnny."

Johnny? Rebekah would not have approved.

On Tuesday, June 9, Lyndon saw combat duty for the first and only time, an experience only two of the three friends survived. As Lyndon described the day in his diary:

> Got up at 2 AM. Left for airport at 2:30 after having tea and toast. Got in air at 3:15. Generals Marquart, Royce, Colonel Anderson, Stevens. Arrived Moresby. 7 of 8 pursuit on 1st mission says Wagner. Almost froze for 3 hours. Stood up beat my legs, stomped my feet, put on windbreak sweater, fur coat, etc.—to no avail. Hit——immediately left on mission to attack Lae. Andy with Prell. Marquart with Hatch, Steve with Lt. Bench and me with Greer.[1] After we were

off field with Prell and Greer leading, Greer's generator went out: crew begged him to go on. For next 30 minutes we flew on one generator. Due to drop bombs at 10:10 having supposedly sucked zeroes up to 17,000 and 12,000 by B17 and B25 respectively. Plan did not work. At 9:55 we turned. At 9:58 Zeroes intercepted—Andy leader got 3 and probably another. B-25 got 2 more and fighters (p39) got 4. Total 9 zeroes. One B-26 shot down. I lost my friend Steve— One fighter down. Another P-39 lands with wind and only 2 gallons gas. Devine brings B-26 down on belly wonderful—Boys unshaven, breath smells, they haven't bathed but Crockett, Bowie, Bonham and Travis had nothing on them in guts. Buzz Wagner takes me to 3——field in jeep. He should design our new fighters. He knows what it takes. To bed at 8:30 after bath and shave and scotch. Couldn't get my mind off Steve, Lt. Bench and other fine boys.

This terse account of the dramatic events of Tuesday, June 9, is a capsulated version of how Lyndon experienced it. It is of necessity incomplete and occasionally inaccurate. Some twenty-odd years later Martin Caidin and Edward Hymoff investigated the events of that day, interviewed many of the participants who were still alive, including Japanese, and published their findings in a book called *The Mission.*[2] Much of the information and many of the quotations which follow come from this source.

Lyndon and Lieutenant Colonels Anderson and Stevens had spent the night before in Townsville, Australia. At dinner Major General William Marquat emphatically pointed out to Lyndon that losses on such missions as the one he proposed to join over Lae had been as high as 15 to 25 percent; it was foolhardy to go, Marquat said, and if he had the authority, he would forbid it. Lyndon said that he had come to the Southwest Pacific on orders from the president to "see personally . . . just what conditions were like, and I cannot find out what they *are* like if I don't go along on this mission."[3]

End of argument.

The commander at the Seven-Mile Drome was Brigadier General Martin F. Scanlon, who had been notified that a planeload of VIPs was arriving; the message from MacArthur's headquarters added that one of the VIPs was an "important congressman." That had been done without Lyndon's knowledge or approval.

Scanlon: "He was an affable, nice person in the uniform of a lieutenant commander, who was doing a job and making very little fuss about it. He was the first congressman who ever showed up at Moresby, where we were getting plenty of attention from the Japanese, who used to bomb us at least two or three nights a week, plus day raids and strafing attacks by Zeros that would shoot anything that moved at our base."[4]

The Twenty-second Bomb Group at the Seven-Mile Drome had twelve B26 medium bombers—Marauders. Lyndon had been assigned to one called the "Wabash Cannonball." He was introduced to the crew, got on the plane, then for reasons that were never made clear got off for a few minutes. When he got back on, Colonel Stevens was sitting in his seat. Stevens smiled and said he was not about to give up the seat: Lyndon would just have to find himself another plane. So Lyndon flew on another Marauder, called the "Heckling Hare"; the pilot was Lieutenant Walter H. Greer, "Arkie."[5]

About an hour after the mission took off the "Wabash Cannonball" was shot down by Saburo Sakai, who was to become Japan's most famous ace. The Marauder hit the water and disintegrated immediately. There were, of course, no survivors.

No one on the "Heckling Hare" knew that Lyndon was an "important congressman" or that he was on a special mission for the president of the United States.

Corporal Harry G. Baren, the tail gunner, remembered that they hadn't paid much attention to Johnson at first.

"We started to kibitz around. The moment you started talking with him, you liked the guy. There wasn't any mistaking his interest; you get a sixth sense about that. Then we started kidding him. I said to him, 'Commander, what are you doing here anyway? We don't need the navy to help us out.'

"He laughed at me and explained he was on an inspection mission to see just what conditions were like in the area. One thing led to another and we began to talk about the mission we were about to fly. It suddenly dawned on me that this guy was really coming along to Lae with us.

"He must have been crazy; I told him that. . . . Lae especially was suicide."[6]

According to Sergeant Claude A. McCredie, a member of the crew, Baren tried to dissuade Lyndon from going. "Commander, let me give you some advice," he began. "This ain't no milk run, believe me! You don't need to come along and get shot up to find out about conditions here, or the things we need; we'll *tell* you that.

"He said to me that the only way a man could ever know what things were like was to go out and see it with his own eyes, and to experience it for himself. He sure didn't go much for secondhand information; he was absolutely determined to get on that mission with us."[7]

McCredie said that when Lyndon asked them what specifically they needed, Harry Baren answered, "Get us some fighters out here. It would be a pleasure for those Zeros to have somebody to worry about, instead of our worrying about them. Fighters—that's what we need. Fighters that can go all the way with us over the target, and let us really get those bombs in where they belong.

"I told Johnson," Baren related, "that we couldn't have cared less about what the papers were saying about MacArthur back in the States. Out here, where the chips were down, he was probably the most unpopular man we knew of.

"I said then—and I stand on what I said—that we felt a lot of our people were being killed without any real reason.

"All we ever knew about MacArthur were his fancy press pictures and his statements about the war. We'd read official communiqués[8] that went back to the States about smashing air attacks and how many Zeros were shot down and so forth. Well, if we ever shot down as many planes as his headquarters used to say, we'd have wiped out the Jap air force in two months."[9]

As Lyndon observed in his diary, the "Heckling Hare" lost the use of its right generator. While "the loss of a generator under normal flight conditions was not critical, Greer and his crew were not even remotely close to a 'normal flight' situation. They were loaded to almost their maximum gross weight, with a full crew, guns, and ammunition, a heavy fuel load, and a maximum load of bombs—every pound was critical. The airplane was at fourteen thousand feet when the generator went out and caused a sudden loss of power. The early B-26 model that Greer flew was, under these weight conditions, almost at its maximum altitude and needed all the power it could get from its engines to hold its present altitude and speed. . . .

"Abruptly the 'Heckling Hare' fell back out of the formation, its speed cut drastically. The pilots [10] looked at one another grimly; they both knew that this was the mission from which they might not return. For they were now a sitting duck for the Zeros." [11]

At normal speed a Zero could maneuver 100 miles an hour faster than a Marauder.

Among the Zero pilots watching all this was Saburo Sakai: "The bomber was weaving and skidding desperately; whoever was at the controls of that airplane flew like he was in the cockpit of a fighter. I had shot down many of the enemy Marauders and Mitchells, but never had I seen a B-26 flown like this. The bomber was literally being kicked and pushed wildly through the air. Even as it dove and picked up speed, it kept up its skidding and weaving maneuvers. Never for a second was it still. I snapped out several more bursts. Again I saw my cannon shells and bullets striking the body and wings of the Marauder; and again there seemed to be no effect!

"By now seven other Zeros had caught up to me, and they came in in a wild rush, the pilots snapping bursts in a steady fashion against the airplane." [12]

Corporal Lillis Walker, the radio machine gunner on the "Heckling Hare," remembered that "It sure was rough up there. We were really getting shot up pretty bad. The Zeros stayed with us, working us over, like they were having a field day with target practice, a long-running fight while they kept whacking away at us.

"When I went forward I had to crawl through the bomb bay to get to the radio. And there was this passenger of ours, just as calm as if we were on a sight-seeing tour. I mean that; he was really taking the whole thing as though nothing was wrong. Bullets were singing through the plane all about us and we were being hit by those cannon shells and he was—well, just calm, and watching everything.

"He was standing on the stool in the compartment; from up there that's a sight to scare the living daylights out of you. A couple of Zeros were in front of us and coming in, firing everything they had, and you're looking straight into the face of death when *that* happens.

"He had to get off the stool so I could get to the radio. He stepped down and turned to me and said, 'Boy! It's rough up here, isn't it!'

"I just nodded at him.

"Then he asked me, 'You get kind of scared, don't you?'

"Now, that's one question I can answer very easily. I looked him right in the eyes and I said, 'Yeah, I'm *always* scared up here.'

"He burst out laughing at me—I'm sure he felt exactly the way I did, but he just didn't show it. He didn't show it a bit." [13]

The day after the mission to Lae, Lyndon, now accompanied only by Andy, continued his fact-finding tour, and flew to Longreach and then on to Melbourne.

Lyndon had, at this point, been in the South Pacific for more than a month. He had talked, as the lingo went, to umpty-ump rank from generals on down and heaven only knows how many enlisted men; he had inspected numerous barracks, mess halls, and whatever passed for a hospital; he had seen combat at its most frightening; and he had observed, although not experienced, the inactivity, the boredom, the ennui of war in the Pacific theater. He had heard the requests, an endless refrain, for better food, mail service, equipment, more leaves, cigarettes, planes—above all more planes. "Give us planes and we'll be home for Christmas," they kept telling him.

That was in June of 1942.

Lyndon and Anderson had planned to start home on the eighteenth, but about 7:00 A.M. that morning they received a call that General MacArthur wanted to see them at 10:30. Lyndon recorded the meeting in his diary:

> Thursday, June 18: Saw MacArthur at 11:45 A.M. Very sad. Head down. Low voice—"Glad to see you two fellows here where three were last. It was a mistake of the head to go on combat mission but it did justice to your heart. It was just what I would have done. I'm giving you the Silver Star. Gave Stevens DSC because he was your leader and gave his life—such is war."

In later years as Lyndon rose politically, MacArthur, no mean politician himself, said that had he but known he would have given him an even higher award, what was then called the Congressional Medal of Honor, for example.

When he returned home, Lyndon was apparently of two minds about the decoration. He drafted a letter to the Adjutant General, War Department, Washington, in which he played down his own action and questioned whether or not he actually deserved the award:

> . . . While appreciative of the award tendered, I cannot in good conscience receive this decoration and wear the coveted medal. My service with the gallant officers and men in this theatre of operation make me most mindful of their sacrifices and all the more aware that I cannot accept a gallantry decoration or citation of recognition for the inconsequential part I played in learning and facing with them the problem which they are encountering from time to time. . . .

The letter, apparently a sincere expression of Lyndon's feelings at the time was probably never sent. Most likely the political advantage of wearing the Silver Star overcame his doubts as to whether it was deserved. He wore it almost daily for the rest of his life.

On Friday June 19, the day after their meeting with MacArthur, Lyndon and Anderson flew to Sydney where Lyndon promptly came down with the flu. Two days later when he arrived in Nouméa, he was seriously ill and had a high fever. The next morning, he insisted on flying to Suva, though by the time the plane landed, he had to be taken off, heavily wrapped in blankets. Within the hour he was delirious, and a doctor who examined him said he was seriously, perhaps critically, ill with pneumonia and removed him to the hospital.

Lyndon finally reached Pearl Harbor on Sunday, June 26, and remained there for treatment at the navy hospital until July 7. By July 10 he was back in Washington.

On July 1 Roosevelt had ordered all congressmen in uniform to return to their legislative duties; they would be of more value to their country in Congress, the president said. On July 16 Lyndon took off his uniform and resumed his congressional seat. He had already made a four-hour personal report to the president on what he had observed in the Pacific, and a few days later he made a speech in the House.

He spoke of the need to rid the armed forces of "the indecisive, stupid, selfish, and incompetent among our generals, admirals, and others in high military positions"—he did not name names—and of coordinating "dive bombers and domestic politics." He spoke of the "dead wood" at home, of "men who have become entrenched in power," men whose "notions" were "dangerously outmoded." Again he named no names.

Lyndon's gloom about what he had seen in the Pacific was repeated so often in the next months that not a few of his colleagues tended to avoid him. They had heard it all before, many times. One afternoon after he had been particularly doleful about our military inadequacies in the Pacific, Sam Rayburn said that Lyndon reminded him of a letter he claimed recently to have received from a constituent.

"He wrote," Rayburn said, "that one of his bald-faced heifers had broken her back and died, that some hunters had set fire to his oatfield stubble, that a tornado had blown down his windmill, that storms had killed all his chickens, that the rain had soaked his oats so they couldn't be stored. And he ended his letter by saying, 'Hope you are the same, I am truly yours . . .'".

THE HOME FRONT

While Lyndon was in the Pacific, more or less incommunicado for almost two months, various efforts on his behalf were taking place on the home front. Bird was, of course, managing his congressional office. The Texas primaries were coming up, but no one in the Tenth District felt that challenging an incumbent wearing a navy uniform and currently serving the country in the perilous South Pacific would be worth his while, so Lyndon was safe in that regard. However, there was still the senatorial election.

John B. Connally: "When Lyndon left to go to the South Pacific, he left two completed forms with me; one, the application to be filed to seek his congressional seat in the 1942 election, and two, a set of papers which he had executed and signed seeking the office of the United States senator. He said, 'You talk to Lady Bird and talk to Senator Wirtz and talk to Jimmy Allred, and you decide which office to file for.'"

"Jimmy Allred was a federal judge and a former attorney general and then governor of Texas. He was extremely interested in running, had all but announced, but he felt he required the assurances of Lyndon Johnson that *he* wasn't going to run. They were extremely good friends, very close friends. And Jimmy Allred wanted to run.

"We labored over it a long, long time. I felt at that time that the war had just started; Mr. Johnson had just gone overseas. We did not know how long he would be overseas, how long the war would last. I felt he had a right to ask to be reelected to his congressional seat without question. But our ability to run an effective campaign for the United States Senate against an incumbent while Lyndon was overseas—well, I thought it was the better part of wisdom just to file for reelection, for which I already knew he'd have no opposition.

"At that point I had no idea he'd be called out of the service and be back by the end of the year.

"In the end it was a tight race; O'Daniel beat Jimmy Allred in a very close election."

Lyndon, of course, did not know whether he was part of that Senate race until it was nearly over. In a letter to Rebekah dated June 14, Lady Bird comments on an AP story that Congressman Johnson, interviewed at "some Allied Nations base in the Southwest Pacific Ocean . . . did not even know whether his name was on the ticket for reelection, whether he had an opponent, etc.! That means he did not get a couple of cablegrams John and I sent him around and after the filing date."

Back on Capitol Hill Lyndon completed his report to his commander in chief, followed it up with an explosive personal chat over breakfast, and then proceeded to repeat his denunciations of wartime bureaucracy and incompetence to Sam Rayburn, Lady Bird, and no doubt any other captive audience he could muster. He looked longingly at Harry Truman's Senate watchdog committee by means of which the Missourian was overseeing war production, and hinted that a similar committee in the House with himself as head might not be amiss, but Mr. Sam informed him that others had already had such designs and been refused, that the job could perfectly well be handled by the House Military and Naval Affairs committees. Of which he, Lyndon, was already a member. [1]

There can be little question but that Lyndon repeated his personal war experiences as well, and often, but then everyone did that, and in the fall of 1942 not enough servicemen had returned yet for anyone to be very bored. As with everyone, the experience grew a bit larger in proportion to the interest of the listeners, and Lyndon was known to speak of "plowing through the jungles of New Guinea," a story which might have surprised his Pacific companions. He had his films developed and invited friends over to watch. Drew Pearson said, "Whenever there was a fellow from Texas, he would point to him, and say 'There's so and so from Austin, or so and so from Beaumont.' Finally Ben Cohen said, 'Lyndon, now why don't you just tell us the fellows that aren't from Texas? It would save you some time.'"

Heroism, however, is not confined to the battlefield; it can be practiced almost anywhere, including on the floor of Congress, and Lyndon's vote against the oil interests in 1943 could quite fairly be classified as an act of unusual bravery.

Paul A. Porter: "The oil industry was clamoring for a price increase of a minimum of twenty-five cents a barrel on crude oil. Harold Ickes, who was the fuels administrator, was advocating such an increase.

"Chester Bowles, director of the federal Office of Price Administration, took the position that rationing and mandatory controls should be used so as not to have the inflationary impact that such an increase would produce. Fred Vinson, of course, was in the middle, and he had to resolve these differences and make this determination. He assigned me the task of making the inquiry.

"Vinson, who later became chief justice and had been a member of Congress, was a great friend—crony—of Sam Rayburn's, and he called the speaker and told him of my recommendation to deny the price increase. Rayburn was disappointed and said he was going to support legislation to increase the price of crude oil.

"The bill came up on the floor of the House, and the Speaker, Mr. Rayburn, left the speaker's rostrum, got in the well of the House, and made a personal appeal, stating that we were going to be short of fuel supplies unless the oil industry was given this incentive to increase production. Well, we had found exactly to the contrary. And when the matter came to a vote, there were two young freshmen congressmen from the Southwest that voted against the oil-price increase. One was Mike Monroney from Oklahoma, the other was Lyndon Johnson from Texas."

Mike Monroney: "We were going into wartime price control legislation, and it was very important whether we had uncontrolled inflation during World War II or whether we would keep the dollar as stable as possible.

"The oil people of Texas and Oklahoma were violent at the fact that they would lose money at a dollar thirty a barrel. They got through the Senate a bill legislating a price increase of thirty-five cents a barrel for oil. It passed the Senate and came over to the House. I took the floor to point out that we would lose control of almost all prices—that there would be runaway inflation. If we legislated for oil we'd legislate for all other commodities. And here was Lyndon Johnson—and the state of Texas had even more oil than the state of Oklahoma—fighting side by side with me against the oil interests.

"Lyndon came from a sparsely settled part of west Texas, and after his oil vote he didn't enjoy too great a popularity among the oil barons of Dallas and Houston. He always said that I got him out on that limb, but he never regretted his vote."

Porter: "Johnson told me that he could not conscientiously support this increase while our boys were dying in foxholes. Such an increase—he had read our report carefully— would have pyramided the cost of fuel and its derivative products and would probably have added billions to the cost of World War II.

"I remember that many commentators said that here were Lyndon Johnson and Mike Monroney signing their political death warrants."

As the 1944 Texas primaries approached, it looked as if Lyndon might actually have done just that. Right-wing anti-Roosevelt Democrats mounted a campaign to steal control of the party in Texas. Roosevelt was being cagey about his own intentions, and there were conservative Democratic factions throughout the South who were opposed to a fourth term in general, Roosevelt and Wallace in particular.

At the Texas state convention in May, Lyndon was booed as Roosevelt's "pinup" boy. He was obviously not the most popular Texas congressman up for reelection in 1944.

Connally: "They ran a very mean campaign against Lyndon in 1944. I wasn't there; I was in the Pacific. But a man named Buck Taylor, who was a nobody, a ne'er-do-well, kind of a political hanger-on, ran against Lyndon with the support of a great many people. The only reason they ran him was to try to cut Lyndon up. They knew that he wouldn't win, but they wanted to try to destroy Lyndon."

The campaign, which was unusually dirty even for Texas, had, as Connally said, a predictable outcome. Lyndon carried nine of the ten counties in his district, winning easily in the primaries, which left him free to campaign along with the other Roosevelt stalwarts—Rayburn, Wright Patman, and Jimmy Allred—for the president's reelection to a fourth term. In November Roosevelt carried Texas by more than eight hundred thousand votes.

A major event in 1944, long-awaited and ardently desired, was the birth of the Johnsons' first child on March 19 in Washington. Lady Bird had suffered three miscarriages, and the doctor spoke pessimistically of her chances for more children, so Lyndon suggested they name the baby for them both, himself first, of course, and Bird rather than Claudia in order to keep the initials intact.

Willard Deason: "It was on a Sunday and I was out visiting with Lyndon and Lady Bird at their home on Thirtieth Place. Along about the middle of the afternoon Lady Bird said, 'Dear, I believe the time has arrived.' He said, 'You sure?' 'I think I'm sure.'

"So we took her to the hospital. Sat around in the waiting room and of course he was pacing around. The nurse in the waiting room said, 'It may be hours before that baby's born. Why don't you go home?' I think she wanted to get rid of us.

"So we took the hint and went on home and started playing dominoes. We always played dominoes on Sunday. After we played a game or two or three I could see his mind wasn't on the game.

"We got in the car and went back to the hospital. He asked the lady at the desk, 'What's the news on Mrs. Johnson?' She said, 'I think they took her up to the delivery room some time ago.' He said, 'Where's the delivery room?' She says, 'It's in the back end of the hospital, but . . .' He didn't wait for the rest of the 'but'—he took off for the back of the hospital. And as we were going down one of those long corridors, here came a nurse with a baby on her arm which was obviously just out of the delivery room and had not been cleaned up. Looked sort of like a piece of liver lying in the fold of the arm. LBJ straddled his legs out and planted himself right in front of that nurse, and said, 'Is that my baby?' She said, 'Hell, I don't know. It belongs to somebody.' And she just swept right on and kept going.

"It was one of the few times in my lifetime that I saw him nonplussed. He didn't know what to say next.

"They brought Lady Bird out directly and apparently she had had a lot of trouble, and we stayed and saw her and saw the baby through the window.

"I don't think he minded that it was a girl."

On February 1, 1945, as the war seemed to be winding down at last, the "Work or Fight" bill was at last passed by the House.

Two years before Lyndon had submitted an amendment to a House bill that would have required each navy yard or station to submit quarterly reports on absenteeism. The reports would cover all employees of navy contractors who were subject to the jurisdiction of the draft board. But H.R. 1876 died in the Rules Committee and never came up on the floor of the House.

A similar bill, however, H.R. 1752, sponsored by Andrew May of Kentucky and known as the "Work or Fight" bill, did come up before the House soon after Congress reconvened in 1945. It was bitterly opposed by both the AFL and the CIO because it permitted managers to fire war plant workers with high absentee records, making them, the young male ones anyway, subject to the draft. Lyndon, of course, was a strong supporter. When his old friend Jim Rowe, under the prodding of labor interests, wrote to him proposing that the bill be recommitted to committee because it might promote disunity and impede the war effort, Lyndon answered:

"Jim, there ain't any arguments against the government keeping a record on its employees when they are absent from their post and duty, and there ain't any wrong in that record being made available to any other government agency, particularly the agency that has the responsibility for saying where a man is needed most. If you can't take the pressure of a few autocratic, misguided, self-appointed . . . vultures who prey on the misfortunes of the working man, then pitch in your chips, pack up the wife and baby, and come on down to Texas where we believe in country and God and working man—and bosses and recommital afterward."

The bill passed the House on February 1, 1945, then went to the Senate where it passed in a different form, and it was mired in the conference committee when the war ended, making the point moot. But the labor leaders would not forget Lyndon's stand when he ran for the Senate three years later.

Then on April 12, 1945, less than a month before Germany surrendered to the Allies, President Franklin Roosevelt died in Warm Springs, Georgia.

William S. White, a young Washington correspondent to the *New York Times*, was told by his superior to get over to the Hill posthaste and interview a few of "Roosevelt's boys." White made a beeline for his friend and fellow Texan Lyndon Johnson, whom he described in the first paragraph of the article which appeared on page three of the *Times* next day as "a 36-year-old Representative from Texas and a typical Representative, too, of a hundred formerly obscure young men whose leap into national prominence had been immeasurably aided by President Roosevelt's paternal coaching."

He found Lyndon, White said, in "a gloomy Capitol corridor," standing with "tears in his eyes," a "shaking jaw," and "a white cigarette holder" in his hand. "There are plenty of us left here to try to block and run interference, as he had taught us," White reported Lyndon saying, "but the man who carried the ball is gone—gone."

White went on to describe Lyndon as a leading member of FDR's "Young Guard," which also included William O. Douglas, Tommy Corcoran, and Ben Cohen. Lyndon, apparently, had been with Mister Sam when the news came. "'I was in the Speaker's office. . . . The phone rang, and the Speaker answered. He didn't say anything at all that I could hear—just a kind of gulp. Then he hung up and looked at me. Finally, he said the president was dead.

"'I was just looking up at a cartoon on the wall—a cartoon showing the president with that cigarette holder and his jaw stuck out like it always was. He had his head cocked back, you know. And then I thought of all the little folks, and what they had lost.

"'He was just like a daddy to me always.'"

Lady Bird: "The day Roosevelt was buried the whole town was just immobile, frozen, stunned, almost disbelieving, almost angry that it could have happened to them. Lyndon actually went to bed, and I myself wanted to go down and stand on the street corner and watch the cortege pass by. I am still mad at myself because I didn't do it, but I was not a very adventurous person. I said, 'Let's go down,' and he turned to me almost with hostility and said something about how he just didn't see why, did I think it was a show, or something like that? Yes, it was a show. It was a magnificent show of great affection and devotion.

"I'm still sorry I didn't. So we just sat glued to the radio. It was virtually all we did."

Dorothy Nichols: "The day after President Roosevelt died, I said, 'He's gone; who do we have now?' And Johnson said, 'Honey, we've got Truman.' I don't remember what I said, but he said, 'There is going to be the damnedest scramble for power in this man's town in the next two weeks that anybody ever saw in their lives.'"

KTBC

During the depression years Lyndon's abundant energy had been largely occupied with his various jobs—first, running Dick Kleberg's office, then running the NYA in Texas, then running for Congress, finally being a congressman, some said the most active on the Hill, running all over Washington getting the many benefits of the New Deal offered his constituents. He wanted them all and got most of them. Running, running. No time to stop.

He was an ardent New Dealer, and he loved being the kind of can-do congressman that was less rare than it is in Washington today. Congressmen today have numerous assistants to do the running for them.

Lyndon and Bird didn't have much money in those days. No matter; they were both frugal people. Sam Houston Johnson once said, "They were always careful with money. I wouldn't say tight—careful. And Lyndon didn't have to wait to get to the White House to start turning off lights; he was always turning off lights. He'd get home late, and I'd be reading. He'd say, 'What are you trying to do, Sam Houston? Keep the electric company in business?' Then off with the light."

The Johnsons always rented their Washington apartment before going back to Texas for the summer, turning off the lights there, too. But in those days nobody had any money; everybody lived frugally.

The war had changed that. Suddenly there were lucrative defense contracts available, and Lyndon got more than what some considered his share for his constituents in the Tenth Congressional District and, since he was always planning to run for the Senate again, for his would-be constituents in other parts of the state. Suddenly there was money to be had if you produced something, almost anything would do, to help the war effort.

Thus people in Texas were getting rich, very rich indeed, people who only a year or two before lived the same way everyone did, frugally. Not only rich but getting richer, and they did not hesitate to display their opulence—mink coats, diamonds, huge ranches, Cadillacs. It was said that in Texas they did not ask what kind of car you were going to buy. They asked only, "What color?"

And Lyndon, when he came back from his Pacific tour and saw the feverish "me, too—I'm getting mine while the getting's good" atmosphere of the Texas home front, saw at once what that particular pie was all about, and, to be sure, he wanted a piece of it.

But being in politics made that more difficult. One's constituents were apt to look with disfavor upon their congressman benefiting materially from connections he had acquired from their votes freely offered, and they were also unlikely to condone his devoting time to furthering his own interests rather than theirs. The road to wealth for a heretofore poor politician was very rocky.

Lyndon consulted his old mentor Alvin Wirtz. What, he asked, did Wirtz think he might do to share in the new wealth of his constituents without offending them?

Communications, said Wirtz.

Actually, communications—*media* was a word not yet in wide usage—was a route Lyndon himself had considered; a number of his friends in Congress owned small newspapers or radio stations and reaped benefits usually far in excess of their congressional salaries. So when Lady Bird came into $21,000 cash from her inheritance, not an inconsiderable amount in those days, she and Lyndon looked first into the possible purchase of a small Texas newspaper, a venture that appealed to Bird with her journalism background. Lyndon, however, who always preferred the spoken word to the written, favored radio. An Austin station would obviously be the most practical choice, and there was one, floundering along, losing money annually, obviously in need of help if it were to survive at all. Station KTBC.

There are many versions of the sale of KTBC to Lady Bird Johnson in the winter of 1942–43. One frequently trotted forth—that Lyndon used Lady Bird as a cover for ownership of a potentially lucrative operation and pulled all kinds of strings to get government approval of same—ignores the facts that the funds involved were entirely Lady Bird's own; that she, five years married and still to her dismay childless, was looking for a business opportunity to employ her own considerable talents; and that the station itself had been in a state of flux and financial difficulty for all three years of its existence.

KTBC-Austin was started in 1939 as one of a half dozen Texas Broadcasting Company stations owned by a certain James G. Ulmer. Ulmer sold the station later that year to Robert A. Stuart, a state senator, A. W. Walker, a law professor at the University of Texas, and Robert B. Anderson, then a twenty-four-year-old state tax commissioner who would later, then many times a millionaire, serve in President Eisenhower's cabinet. It was not much of a station; its transmitting power was only 250 watts, and it had to share wavelengths with a very active Texas A and M campus station. Its new owners intended to lobby the Federal Communications Commission for a power increase, but they found themselves unable to give the necessary attention to the matter, and in turn sold it, or thought they sold it, to Texas multimillionaire Jim West.

West, however, could not get FCC approval to buy the station. He already owned the *Austin Tribune*, which made him subject to the charge of attempting to control the media in the Texas capital, and besides his right-wing politics were not at all pleasing to Roosevelt's New Deal appointees on the FCC. The matter went back and forth, and when West died in 1942, it was still not resolved.

Jim West's son, Wesley W. West, inherited the situation, and he passed on the purchase option to an Austin businessman's association of which a certain E.G. Kingsbery was a member. Kingsbery was about to submit an application requesting the FCC to allow the syndicate to purchase the station when Lyndon and Lady Bird entered the picture. Kingsbery was, of course, a constituent of Lyndon's and Lyndon had in fact only recently secured an appointment to Annapolis for Kingsbery's son, so perhaps, Lyndon reasoned, Kingsbery and friends could be persuaded to relinquish their option in Lyndon's, or rather Lady Bird's, direction.

They did allow themselves to be so persuaded. Then Lyndon had only to convince Wesley West to reassign the purchase option to Lady Bird and, when that was accomplished, to agree on a price with Stuart, Walker and Anderson who had begun to feel that they never would be rid of this particular white elephant. The station had loans from practically every bank in Austin, not to mention other debts about town, and was running at a considerable deficit. The figure $17,500 was eventually agreed upon, with Alvin Wirtz acting as counsel for the Johnsons.

Much has been made of the fact that Lady Bird's application to the FCC in January 1943 was approved within a month of its submission whereas Jim West's had had so much difficulty. But the difference obviously lay more with the FCC's reluctance to approve a right-wing newspaper owner than with any particular inclination toward the Johnsons. It is unlikely that Lyndon had to make *any* overt move to get FCC approval. The FCC chairman, James Fly of Dallas, was an energetic New Dealer, as was the majority of the commission, including Lyndon's old friend Clifford Durr. Their sympathies would naturally lie with an equally ardent New Dealer like Lyndon. Since the station was being purchased by Lady Bird, with what was clearly Lady Bird's money, and since she could show a personal balance sheet indicating a net worth of $64,332, it might indeed have been difficult for the FCC to find a reason *not* to approve the purchase. As to how it was accomplished so quickly, although one cannot entirely rule out a possible suggestion from the White House to hurry things along a little "for my old friend Lyndon," it might just as easily have been the simple predisposition of a band of New Dealers for one of their own.

Clifford Durr, who was a member of the FCC during the forties, said: "I don't remember Lyndon coming around the FCC. I never got any pressures at all from him.

"What I remember is this: Bird came to me and said there was a chance to buy this radio station in Austin, and as I recall, she said for about $22,000. She could raise that much money, and she wanted to know whether I thought it would be a wise investment. So I gave her some figures on the earnings of well-run stations at the time. They were making an awful lot of money.

"I heard generally around the FCC that this was a very poorly run station. I told her that it seemed to me if she could get that station on its feet and get it well managed, it ought to be a very good investment. That was my connection with it.

"Now there wasn't any skullduggery that I ever saw at the FCC. It was more or less the routine approval of the purchase of a station. Those had to be approved by the FCC, but nobody else was in the picture.

"About the time she bought that station, Bird virtually moved back to Austin. She would come to Washington on visits, but she devoted almost full time to getting that station on its feet."

Lady Bird: "We finally got the approval from the FCC in February of '43. The staff was infected with a sense of failure and uncertainty, and sloppiness had become a way of life in that little area, so we just gave it a good thorough cleaning up. I think it kind of improved everybody's spirits. It certainly did mine."

Bird did, as has often been written, literally clean up the station with a mop and pail. She was, of course, still in her twenties, the war was on, and help was scarce. Many of us cleaned our own offices—and barracks—in 1943.

Elizabeth Goldschmidt: "I remember her sitting there at their dining room table in Washington with all the books of the station laid out in front of her. She really worked very hard at running that station, and she was a very astute businesswoman."

Robert Kintner: "The business person of the family was Mrs. Johnson. I used to sit up with her, with a little pad you'd buy at the five-and-ten, trying to iron out the problems of the station.

"Mrs. Johnson used to come visit me when I was president of ABC about her station down in Austin. They were affiliated with CBS, but they were the only station in town. She was always interested in business. As to her business acumen, I was impressed."

Leonard Marks: "It was her station—don't let anybody tell you to the contrary. Over the years, as the station prospered, I would go up to visit them at their home on Thirtieth Place on a Sunday. She'd call and ask if I wouldn't mind coming by, and she would have the reports of the week's sales, the list of expenses, and we'd go over them. She could read a balance sheet the way a truck driver reads a road map."

Bird's assiduousness and industry was, however, only half the story. It might have been Bird's station, but it was also Lyndon's personal road to riches, and as such his attentions to it were second only to his obsession with his political career. It was he who, right after the FCC granted approval of the purchase, traveled to New York seeking network affiliation. David Halberstam in *The Powers That Be* describes how Lyndon went to see William Paley, and how Paley's secretary announced "that there was a very tall Texan waiting out there in a big hat and boots who said he was a congressman." Paley, says Halberstam, turned Lyndon over to a young staff member by the name of Frank Stanton who listened carefully to his request to become a CBS affiliate, consulted a map, and decided that neither their station in Dallas nor their one in San Antonio would be adversely affected by a third one smack in the middle, i.e., Austin, just as CBS would not be adversely affected by having congressional connections. No matter that at that moment the station operated on only 250 watts; it was clear to Stanton, and he no doubt made it clear to Paley, that any young Texan with as much brash ambition as this one would have that problem solved in no time.

With network affiliation taken care of, there still remained the matter of staff. The station had more or less to do the best it could until the war ended, but no sooner had his old friends started to return home than Lyndon started to recruit them.

Sherman Birdwell: "After the war we were all seeking work. I ran into Mr. Johnson on the street one day in Austin and he said, 'I need you over there at KTBC. We're going to really get cranked up, and I want you to go over there and go to work.' So I went as assistant office manager to Jesse Kellam and as special sales representative.

"KTBC began to pick up from the time Mr. Johnson took it over. He had great leadership ability and persuasive powers, and he would get the sales people all charged up. I think that his being congressman did help—the fact that he was well liked and that local businessmen knew that the Johnsons owned the station. But I don't think the success was due to any great extent to the fact that he was congressman. I think that was just helpful.

"He was always very interested in the station. He would go over the financial statements with me—what did this mean, and why were we spending this much for so-and-so?"

Others also came along—John Connally, Robert Phinney, Jake Pickle—KTBC became a place where just-mustered-out buddies of Lyndon Johnson worked a few months until they decided what they wanted to do next. In this sense, "next" for most of them became their own station, KVET, a potential rival, whose conception Lyndon attended, perhaps fathered, certainly midwifed into existence.

Jake Pickle: "I was one of the incorporators of KVET. John Connally was the main incorporator.[1] We made application for the station, put it together, and called it KVET—we were all veterans, ten of us. While the application was pending, a lot of people said, 'Well, you made application and you are Johnson people, and it will be no one but Johnson.' But that wasn't so. Mr. Johnson knew that from the growth of the city it would be inevitable that another station would come in because the size of the town demanded it. Mr. Johnson said he'd rather have friendly competitors than somebody trying to beat him in every way."

Robert Phinney: "Johnson advised us on our application to the FCC and helped us all the way through in spite of the fact that his wife Lady Bird's station was going to be our competitor."

Paul A. Porter: "After the 1944 election, I was appointed by Roosevelt as chairman of the FCC. Lady Bird was running those radio properties down there at the time, with Lyndon sort of hovering in the background. There was going to be another radio station dropped into Austin, and I will say in all the time that I was chairman of the FCC, my brief tenure there, Lyndon *never* approached me about any matter involving the Johnson family interests in this broadcast property except this one. He said, 'I know it is inevitable that a new station is coming into Austin. As a matter of inquiry, how many applicants do you have?' I said, 'I don't know, Lyndon, but I will check on it.' And he said, 'Well, if I am going to have competition down there, I want responsible, able competition.'"

By 1947, with KTBC flourishing in spite of its competition, Lady Bird, who had up to this point personally held the license to her station, decided to incorporate and applied to the FCC for permission to do so. When permission was granted she "sold" her personal ownership to the newly created Texas Broadcasting Corporation, allowing only two shares to go "outside," one each to two of her employees who shared managerial positions. Lyndon owned none of it outright, but was inextricably involved because of Texas community property law.

Then in 1948, with television just beginning to move west, the FCC began a study of which cities should be allocated TV channels, and how many. The study continued for four years, at the conclusion of which the FCC published its findings, complete with maps. How many stations a particular city was allowed depended on its population as of the 1950 census, and Austin, with only 132,459 inhabitants, was thereby limited to one.

As it happened, there was on file with the FCC only one application for a television station in Austin; the application was for channel 7. Coincidentally, 7 was the channel the FCC assigned to Austin. The applicant was Lady Bird Johnson.

Jack Valenti: "Mrs. Johnson applied for the station with the FCC. No one else in Austin applied. For four months it lay unattended by any other applicants. The FCC put out additional importunings and askings, and no one else applied. Now, with all the enemies Johnson had in Austin, somebody must have wanted the station, and if they wanted it, they could have applied for it. No one did."

David Susskind: "If the wife of a senator of the state has applied for the license and you would kind of like the license yourself, wouldn't it kind of look like a waste of your time to apply?" [2]

In 1964, Louis Kohlmeier, staff reporter for the *Wall Street Journal*, wrote a series of articles titled "The Johnson Wealth" in which he explored the rise of the Johnson fortune in general and the family radio and television empire in particular. The series extended over many months and eventually won a Pulitzer Prize for Kohlmeier. He specifically asked FCC personnel why no one else sought the choice standard television channel in Austin. Kohlmeier wrote:

"An FCC aide remarks it 'looks funny now,' but explains that 'apparently' they were not eager to do battle against the strong Johnson bid before a Federal agency when the UHF channels were available as an alternative and at a time when UHF's competitive disadvantages had not become apparent."

Kohlmeier also interviewed Tom Potter who built, he said, the first television station in Texas, and who applied for, and received, one of the two UHF channels in Austin. Potter said:

"Lyndon was in a favorable position to get that station even if somebody had contested it. Politics is politics."

While waiting for the FCC verdict, the Texas Broadcasting Corporation settled the matter of network affiliation. NBC was tied up in nearby San Antonio, but CBS eagerly accepted. After that the success of KTBC-TV was almost inevitable.

THE HOUSE ON DILLMAN STREET

One of the difficulties of postwar Washington was adjusting to Harry Truman; Lyndon had, after all, been in Washington before Franklin Roosevelt was first elected, and except for a few months at the end of Hoover's reign, had never served under another president. He strongly opposed Truman on the cold war, the Marshall Plan, and the Truman Doctrine; through the latter Harry thought to stave off Soviet aggression by military and economic assistance to Greece and Turkey. "The only thing a bully understands is force, and the only thing he fears is courage," Lyndon said in the debate that preceded passage. But Truman matched his foreign policy conservatism with a domestic liberalism that Lyndon, however he felt about it privately, knew he himself could not afford publicly.

Lyndon felt strongly the lack of a friend in the White House. No one called him the president's pinup boy any more, but no one considered him a person who had the president's ear either. Of course, Sam Rayburn was still there for support, and he helped Lyndon get on the Select House Committee on Postwar Military Policy and later on the Joint Atomic Energy Committee, from which vantage points Lyndon fought to keep defense plants from closing up and argued for an independent air force. But he was on his own as never before, and in postwar Texas the key to survival was conservatism.

Allan Shivers: "Johnson began to take that turn because he saw that shift in power from the Roosevelt era on to a more conservative approach to politics."

Elizabeth Rowe: "I was working for the International Labor Office on Jackson Place and the CIO was right down the street. Lyndon Johnson was running for reelection. He called me up one day, and he said, 'Elizabeth, do you know anybody well in the labor movement down the street?' I said, 'I know them pretty well.'

"He said, 'Well, do you suppose you could get them to come out against me?' I said, 'What do you mean?'

"He said, 'A little while ago I came home one night and I said to Bird, "I'm tired of voting the way I think I should vote to stay in the Congress and not voting the way I really feel when an issue comes up." She said, "Just vote the way your conscience tells you and forget about being pragmatic and surviving."' So he said, 'The next vote that came up was for the Dies committee.' You know the Dies committee—the Red-chasing committee. 'It was a vote for the appropriation. I voted against it,' he said, 'and do you know what's happening to me?' The *New Republic's* got out a special supplement supporting me in my district in Texas, and I need something to balance it out. Do you think your friends at the CIO would come out against me?'

"I talked to a few people. They didn't come out against him, but anyway he got elected."

In 1946 a recently discharged army colonel and district judge, Hardy Hollers, decided that a great many veterans of the Tenth District were dissatisfied with the way things had been handled while they were away and might, if given a choice, prefer to be represented by someone else in Congress, namely himself.

Hollers, said to be an able lawyer, and competent judge, campaigned on two issues only. One, that he was a veteran; two, that Lyndon was a crook. There was a great deal of talk about radio station KTBC, "allegedly owned by Mrs. Johnson,"[1] and a duplex Hollers often referred to as a "mansion" on Dillman Street in Austin, plus what he claimed was a sudden "acquisition of rental property in Austin" and "a mushrooming personal fortune."

Willard Deason: "The 1946 campaign was very bitter, not on Mr. Johnson's part, but on the part of his opponent. He accused Lyndon of everything under the sun, including his war record. He said he'd been in the army for four years, and Lyndon had been in the navy for just a few months. And that while he hadn't been making any money Lyndon had been getting rich, and he accused him of being too close to Roosevelt and then too close to Truman, and so on.

Jake Pickle: "All kinds of rumors were floating around town, that Lyndon owned *this* building and he owned *that* apartment house; and that he was the front man for several big investors and was growing rich in office. That was the theme used more than any other. No charges, just implied statements that he had feathered his nest and was getting rich.

"Mr. Johnson felt that it was a campaign by some of the major oil companies that didn't like some of his votes, and he in turn attacked the oil companies and campaigned against them far more than he campaigned against Colonel Hollers, who was an able attorney and well liked around town.

Walter Jenkins: "The house on Dillman Street was a big issue in 1946. It's a big house, but they never mentioned that there were three apartments and that the Johnsons occupied one while there were numerous other people in the other two.

"Hollers would say, 'I went out there to look at that mansion he's living in.'

"Well, at the time I was living in one apartment and John Connally had one. People would drive by and stare at the house, not knowing that. It's not all that much of a house anyway, and it's certainly far from a mansion."

Lyndon gave the major speech of his campaign in Austin on July 6 at Wooldridge Park. He spoke with the air of a man who has lately been much weighed down with the world's problems and is glad to be back among his dear friends with whom he can be himself.

"It is good to be home," he said, "to breathe Texas air again and be among Texas friends. All of you know me. Many of you know me personally. I have walked into your front room without knocking. We have sat together in your yards and watched the lawn sprinklers and talked."

The preliminaries of friendship out of the way, he talked on various themes, including the mud-slinging tactics of his opponent, and at one point reminded his constituents of the oil price increase he had voted against in 1943. "The petroleum boys said they were starving and they had to have the Disney bill to give them another thirty-five cents per barrel. Those ragged, barefoot boys from Houston flew their personal air planes to Washington to tell their tear-jerking story. They said, 'Vote against the Disney bill at your own risk.' I said, 'I'll take that risk.' I did take it. Their stake was one billion dollars. No wonder the order has come down from Wall Street—the order which reads, 'GET JOHNSON.'"

It was the last campaign, however, in which Lyndon would make reference to this vote against the oil issues. When he campaigned for the Senate two years later, he just hoped everyone had forgotten all about it.

Finally he appealed to their hearts. "There's an old popular song," he said, and his voice became somewhat hushed at this point, "which goes 'Did you ever see a dream walking? Well, I did.'

"You come home and see, in the eyes of folks you grew up with, their confidence and affection. Your old college president puts his arm around you and says he's proud of you. The kids who worked for you and never beefed about long hours or low pay go away to war and come back with their chests covered with medals, and they go to bat for you to defend your good name. A farm woman writes with a pencil on tablet paper to say, 'I have lights now.' You stand by the bedside of a dying father who opens his eyes long enough to see his son in uniform, flown in from the South Pacific at your request, and that father says, 'Thank God you got here, son.'

"Those are some of the dreams I have seen walking.

"I will appreciate it if those of you who believe in me will come forward, look me in the eye, shake my hand, and meet my mother and my wife."

Pickle: "One thing I remember he said: 'Now they don't challenge my record. They don't challenge my votes. They don't challenge my record for getting things done. They don't challenge my concern for people or my compassion.

"'All they want to make you believe is that I've got rich in this office. Now I think that ought to be a matter of record, and everybody ought to know what the facts are.' He said, 'Now I have here with me tonight sworn records on every business transaction that I have participated in in the last ten years. Here are the records for any and all to see, and I want anybody in this audience tonight or any time to come up here and look at these records. Come on.'

"He said, 'My opponent is bound to have *somebody* who wants to.'

"Well, nobody did. Nobody came up, and the Hollers balloon just went poof.

"He finished his speech by attacking the oil barons, and he attacked all the men in smoke-filled rooms making secret deals, and of course, people ate it up.

"Then he got down in front, took off his coat, and he shook hands with people as they went through the line that night.

"The campaign was all over at that point. It was just a question of how much he'd win by. And he did carry the district with 65 percent of the vote."

Margaret Mayer: "After the campaign Lyndon was feeling very good, very expansive, and he insisted I go to Dallas with them. I think it was John and Nellie Connally, the Jesse Kellams, Bird and I.

"We went to Nieman-Marcus, and Stanley Marcus had the clerk stay after the store closed because Lyndon wasn't through buying clothes for Bird. He was picking out clothes for her, and he insisted that Nellie and I also needed suits. He bought Bird a tremendous number of clothes. I remember a white leather coat that he bought for her. White leather was pretty fancy back in 1946."

Lyndon no doubt was pampering Lady Bird a little in those days. Lynda Bird was barely a toddler, and Lady Bird had overruled her doctor's suggestion that she have no more children and during 1946 underwent a tubular pregnancy which ended in another miscarriage and nearly cost her her life. By the end of 1946 she was pregnant again, and on July 2, 1947, Lucy Baines was born.

Otherwise, 1947 was not a banner year. Although he generally supported Truman on foreign policy, Lyndon opposed the president on so many domestic bills that at times one would hardly have thought they belonged to the same party. He voted for the Taft-Hartley Act, in opposition to both Truman and Sam Rayburn, and when Truman vetoed it, Lyndon voted with the majority to override the veto, an act that was to assume major significance the following year when he ran for the Senate.

Hank Brown: "I think that this vote on Taft-Hartley hurt him all through his lifetime. Ever since then, whenever people were evaluating him, as late as 1960 when he was vying for the presidency, the one thing that people would always use against him when they lacked anything else was that he was one of those that gutted us in 1947."

And as was to be expected, Lyndon opposed any and all of Truman's civil rights bills.

Congressman Johnson was ready, and eager, to move on. But another try for the Senate would require money, and where was it to come from when the oil barons in Texas were still suspicious of him? However, the aircraft industry was growing in Texas as almost nowhere else, and Lyndon, whose Naval Affairs Committee had, after 1946, become a part of the House Armed Services Committee, had always been convinced that air power was absolutely essential to the country's future security. Now he had a second reason to continue his support of a strong defense policy.

So, with the clout of ten years of defense preparedness behind him, Johnson came out against Truman's reluctance to spend money on more bombers right after the war. Truman wasn't sure how much the country needed them, and besides, they took away funds for which he had other plans. But Lyndon avidly supported the air force chief of staff, General Hoyt Vandenberg, and Secretary of the Air Force Stuart Symington when they asked Truman for bombers, and Symington, when he placed his orders with Texas plants, never hesitated to mention his, and their, indebtedness to their representative from the Tenth District who, by the way, might be thinking of running for the Senate before long.

As for the oil barons, while Lyndon's reputation with them in general was at a low point, he did have two friends there who stood him in good stead before, as he had them: a long-standing relationship and one likely to continue; though it was destined to cause some public controversy in later years.

George and Herman Brown of the Brown and Root Company were brothers who started a contracting firm in the twenties in partnership with Herman's brother-in-law Dan Root, who died not long after. At the beginning of the depression they fell upon bad times and lost all their equipment; to save them from bankruptcy Alvin Wirtz, their lawyer, obtained a lucrative contract for them in one part of Texas, quietly borrowed county equipment for them from another part of Texas, and as quietly returned it when the job was done. This certainly illegal but friendly act on Wirtz's part saved the brothers from financial ruin and, of course, put them in line for future expansion.

Lyndon met the Browns through Wirtz. It was Wirtz, not Lyndon, who saw that they got contracts with the Lower Colorado River Authority to build or enlarge certain dams, such as the Marshall Ford (Mansfield) Dam in 1937.

By the late thirties, Brown and Root was well on its feet and accumulating capital, so it was not surprising that when Wirtz looked about for money for his young friend Lyndon's campaign, he looked directly to the Brown brothers. And they were most cooperative. They agreed with Wirtz that Lyndon showed extraordinary political promise, and they were quite willing to do their part to see that he had a chance to fulfill that promise. They helped in 1937, and they helped again, even more substantially, during the 1941 Senate race. And Lyndon, of course, when the matter of a government contract for the construction of the naval air training base at Corpus Christi came up, was successful in swinging the contract their way.

D.B. Hardeman: "I never knew Herman Brown; I knew George Brown slightly. He was an elegant man. I think they were both really first-rate men. A lot of polish, a lot of brain power. Lyndon helped them and they helped him through the years. Then Herman died, and George Brown continued.

"I've always heard that Brown and Root were very competent contractors. They could really get it done. In these things somebody is going to get the contract, so you try to get it to your friends. A lot of the liberals looked on that as something evil and bad."

Terrell Maverick Webb: "The liberals didn't have any money; that's the trouble with liberals. They elect a man, and then many of them don't stay with him. Lyndon needed money and Herman Brown and George Brown and all these people were old, old friends. Margaret Brown, Herman's wife, told me, 'I remember when I wasn't rich.' Well, Lyndon had known them when they weren't rich, and when he wasn't rich either."

By the end of the war, however, there was no doubt but that Brown and Root of Houston was very, very rich. The naval base at Corpus Christi had mushroomed from modest beginnings to a $100 million project extending over three counties, and although Brown and Root received only a third of that contract, $33 million in the mid-forties was a considerable amount. The company went from that to similar cost-plus government projects, and then, as an offshoot, founded the Brown Shipbuilding Company and began production of destroyers and escorts. By 1945 hundreds of these had come out of their twenty-five-thousand-employee Houston shipyard. Immediately after the war the Browns with several associates founded the Texas Eastern Company on the strength of having bought from the U.S. government the Big and Little Inch pipelines and having converted the latter into a natural gas conduit to the East Coast.

One reason for Lyndon's tireless attention to Brown and Root was that he had inadvertently gotten them into considerable difficulties with the IRS and cost them rather a lot of money. During Lyndon's 1941 campaign for the Senate, Brown and Root had poured money into the race through various channels of questionable legality. Complaints from the opposition led to an investigation by the IRS as to why, for example, in 1941 Brown and Root should have awarded Christmas bonuses to its executives the previous spring, and how it was that the amounts awarded tallied almost exactly with the amounts those same executives contributed to Lyndon's campaign. The company, busy with its defense plants, put on an injured air and complained, in turn, that their concentration on the war effort was being seriously hampered by IRS persecution tactics. Eventually Wirtz, then in Washington as undersecretary of the interior, and Lyndon went in to see Roosevelt personally about the delicate problem of their patriotic constituents, and Roosevelt suggested to the IRS that it complete its investigation, file its report, and come to a settlement. The report, when filed, charged Brown and Root with a liability of more than a million dollars, accompanied by a penalty of half again that much for fraud. Somehow a settlement of $327,000 was arrived at, and promptly paid by the relieved defendants. But Lyndon, whose total assets at that time were considerably below that figure, must often have had that in mind when he picked up the phone to make a call on behalf of his benefactors.

THE GERIATRIC PROBLEMS OF 1948

Horace Busby: "In November 1947 Congress was nearing the end of the longest peacetime session in its history; it even went over into December of that year. Lyndon spent a good deal of time in Washington reflecting on his future, which he often did. After all, he was thirty-nine years old. He believed, and he believed it really quite sincerely for a number of years, that when a man reached forty, it was all over. And he was going to be forty in 1948.

"And there was no bill ever passed by Congress, that bore his name; he had done very little in his life. He thought he probably should get out of Congress and into some steady line of work. And he was kind of angry with some of his young friends, including Mr. Pickle and Mr. Connally, because they had gone off to the war and then didn't come back to his office. And he was up there alone.

"And he came back here and met with his inner circle, such as it was, and he told them that he had reached a decision. Early in the new year, early in 1948, he was going to announce his retirement from public life. Probably on January 1. He would manage the radio station or go back to teaching school or something like that.

"You have to understand that across a long span of Lyndon Johnson's career, one expected at least once a year to go through one of these sessions in which he was going to quit public life. The accepted way to handle this, if you were one of his friends or assistants, was always to say, 'Yes, sir, we think that's fine. That's right. Roosevelt's dead. You don't have any future. You couldn't get elected to anything in Texas.'"

W. Lee ("Pappy") O'Daniel, whose Senate term was due to expire the following year, had his problems. He was publicly ignored and privately ridiculed by his colleagues as well as by much of the rest of official Washington.

He was also in trouble back among his beloved rural Texans, an enormous number of whom by now either had or were about to move from the country to one city or another. But even among those tho stayed behind on the farm, Pappy's appeal had dwindled. The country folk were no longer so enchanted by talk about the golden rule, and Molly had, it was said, lost her looks. Pappy's audiences were smaller and, in numerous locations, urban and rural; rotten eggs and overripe tomatoes were thrown in his direction, sometimes reaching their mark. What's more, by June 1947, the Belden poll showed that former governor Coke Stevenson, who the year before had left the governor's mansion after five and a half popular years there, would have 55 percent of the vote should he decide to run for the Senate. But Coke always declared, "I'm just not fitted for the Washington picture."

Should Lyndon decide to run, and as yet he had no comment on the subject, he had a Belden rating of 24 percent; Pappy had only 21 percent.

On January 1, 1948, a day on which most Texans were concerned with hangovers and football, Coke Stevenson announced that he had changed his mind about the Senate. He was a candidate after all.

Stevenson was a slow-moving, slow-talking, deliberate man, never without a pipe in his mouth, and during the height of the campaign, Lyndon entertained the good folks of south Texas by borrowing a pipe from someone in the audience. He would stick it in his mouth and say, "With one eye on the labor bosses in Fort Worth and one on the millionaires in Houston, he sits and smokes." Then with his hands on his hips Lyndon would swing back and forth and murmur through the pipe stem, "I'm for states' rights; I'm for states' rights."

Stevenson, in announcing his candidacy, said he was also for "the complete destruction of the Communist movement in this country" and for a cut in federal spending. Oh, yes, and an *increase* in Social Security payments.

Stevenson was not quite sixty years old, but since Lyndon thought that at thirty-nine his problem was geriatrics, it is perhaps not surprising that in the heat of the campaign, he considered his principal opponent was too old to cope with the strains of the Senate job. Lyndon was not, he said, "going to sling mud in this campaign," although he did feel called upon to mention that, "One of my opponents is *sixty-one* [emphasis Lyndon's], and I am *not* for the fifteen-thousand-dollar pension you'd give him if you elected him." Fifteen thousand dollars a year was what senators were paid in those days.

T. Kellis Dibrell: "I don't know that I ever heard Coke raise his voice. His nickname was 'Calculating Coke,' because if you asked him a question, he'd light up his pipe, puff on it a few minutes, and then he would give you a very slow and deliberate answer."

In 1947, John Gunther, doing the research for *Inside U.S.A.*, asked Coke to recall his greatest decision. "Never had any," said Coke, puffing on his pipe.

By the June 2 deadline for filing, ten candidates had announced for the Senate race. Pappy O'Daniel was not among them, and it was generally agreed that "Calculating Coke" was the man to beat.

Jake Pickle: "Taking on Coke Stevenson was a very tricky thing to do. He was very popular in Texas. One of those strong silent cowboy types. A typical rancher, and while he was governor, there hadn't seemed to be many problems. There was great wartime prosperity, and he came out looking good without having done anything much. When he left the governor's office, he had made very few enemies, and he left the state with a surplus, having gone in with a deficit.

"Another thing that made the race risky was that Lyndon represented just one district; he wasn't widely known all over the state."

In February Stevenson had led over Johnson four to one; in March the lead was cut to three to one. Alvin Wirtz told Lyndon that was vastly encouraging; Lyndon was too depressed to agree. Wirtz said that even if he lost this time, the publicity gained by such a campaign would be invaluable for a campaign in 1954. "1954?" said Lyndon. "By 1954 I'll be fifty-five years old." He was often imprecise about precise things like mathematics.

John B. Connally: "Five or six of us met with him to discuss whether or not he should be a candidate. This was in May, May 10 or 11, 1948, and we met at the house on Dillman Street. And Lyndon kept raising all these objections about why he shouldn't run. I'm not sure he hadn't already made up his mind long before, but he wanted to be persuaded."

Busby: "He went through this session at length, and when he said he wasn't going to run, the crowd around him said, 'Congressman, that's really the right decision. We really think you ought to step aside and let us put forward a younger man that can carry on this great tradition. And he said, 'Who'd you have in mind?' They said, 'Well, we're going to run John Connally. And if you'll just step aside, we'll start running John.' He said, 'Well, just a minute. Let me think about this a little bit.'"

Lyndon announced his candidacy on the afternoon of May 12 in the penthouse of the Driskill Hotel in Austin. And on May 22 in Wooldridge Park in Austin, he made his first campaign speech. The crowd was small. In it was a young man who was to become attorney general in the Johnson cabinet.

Ramsey Clark: "There was a little cupola thing down there, like a small bandstand. He stood up in that. And what he did—it struck me even as a kid as being the corniest thing I'd ever seen—he took his hat off and said, 'I throw my hat in the ring.' Wow! he probably had a twenty-five-dollar Stetson on or something, and he sailed it out in the air."

Lyndon's campaign theme, he said that night, was peace, preparedness, and progress. He was against selfish labor, *and* he was against selfish capital. He was, to be sure, for leaving to the states those things "which are state functions, such as civil rights."

Lyndon said, "The civil rights program is a farce and a sham—an effort to set up a police state in the guise of liberty. I am opposed to that program. I have voted AGAINST the so-called poll tax repeal bill; the poll tax should be repealed by those states which enacted them. I have voted AGAINST the so-called antilynching bill; the state can, and DOES, enforce the law against murder. I have voted AGAINST the FEPC; if a man can tell you whom you must hire, he can tell you whom you can't hire."

Lyndon also said he was against socialized medicine, and he mentioned, with an air of pride and to the only cheers of the evening, that he had voted for and supported the Taft-Hartley Act. "With the utmost enthusiasm," he added.

Harry Truman, who had always called the Eightieth Congress a "do-nothing Congress," deplored the Taft-Hartley Act, saying that it was about all the Congress had accomplished—and that was negative. Sam Rayburn had called it "a punitive labor bill."

Truman and Rayburn aside, there was a good deal of antilabor feeling all over the country in 1948. Although almost all labor unions had agreed not to strike during the war, after hostilities ended there were a great many walkouts, affecting steel, coal, and the railroad industries, among others. The Taft-Hartley bill was basically a response to all that. Lyndon's support of the bill was always considered by many liberals and union members—not that they are necessarily the same—as a black mark against him.

In any event, Lyndon's campaign did not get off to what could be called an impressive start. There was very little notice in the press of the Wooldridge Park speech. What was there to notice?

Alvin Wirtz mentioned to John Connally that Lyndon was depressed; he was afraid that such depression might lead to an illness. It often had in the past. Connally said the idea was ridiculous. But on May 26, while campaigning in the Texas panhandle, Lyndon experienced "severe pain."

Connally: "Johnson got really ill in Dallas. We were all in Austin at the headquarters, and he didn't want anything said about it. He was ill, and he was going to the Mayo Clinic and Jacqueline Cochran, the famous aviator, was going to fly him there.

"I don't know how, but for some reason he thought he could keep the whole thing quiet. I thought it was a mistake. There was nothing wrong with his being ill; he had a kidney stone. So I told him we were going to release it. He said, 'If you do, I'll resign from the campaign, I'll withdraw.' And I said, 'Well, you're going to have to withdraw because we're going to release it.' And we did."

On his being admitted to the Mayo Clinic, Lyndon almost immediately became its star patient and leading pain in the ass. He stayed a week until his kidney stone was dissolved, but although a doctor there at the time said that a poll of the staff would undoubtedly have recorded that the period seemed more like a year. He demanded, and got, three telephones in his room; he had two radio sets, God alone knows how many nurses to shout at, and doctors who issued—it seemed on an hourly basis—statements saying that he was not about to die, that he was still in the campaign, and that his energy was undiminished. Statements nobody around at the time could deny. One nurse swore that he made sixty-four telephone calls in a twenty-four-hour period.

Walter Jenkins: "Of course, Mr. Johnson didn't start with the helicopter until he got back from Rochester. The first plane was a Sikorsky, which Mr. Johnson called the Johnson City Windmill. That's what he called the second plane, too, which was a Bell helicopter. The Sikorsky carried five men, as I recall, but the Bell was a small, three-man bubble-top helicopter."[1]

Thomas G. Corcoran: "There was Lyndon flying overhead in that goddamn machine saying, 'Come to whatever the county seat was and hear Lyndon Johnson.' And they'd come to hear him. Of course, mostly they came to see the helicopter. They'd never seen one before. Christ, it was brilliant as hell."

Joe Mashman: "In the early spring of 1948 the founder of our company, Larry Bell, called me into his office and said, 'Joe, I want you to take a helicopter down to Texas and fly this young congressman around who wants to become a senator.

"Mr. Johnson was considered a young, forward-thinking congressman. He was close to congressmen, senators, involved in the development of new materials. And, of course, our technological breakthroughs are usually initially funded and started because of military developments. But I am quite sure that Larry Bell didn't know him at all.

"We first went to Austin. Immediately upon arrival, KTBC, the Johnson station radio engineers, came out to the airport to install a loudspeaker system.

"That gave us a weight problem that affected the aircraft's performance, especially during the warm spring weather. I hadn't met the congressman up until then, and I was dismayed to find out how much he weighed, his size. Coupled with my size and weight—I was up at about 185—I knew that performance was going to be very marginal. But I still didn't know what sort of places we were going to be flying in and out of."

Pickle: "We spent more money on gas for that plane than you can imagine. Gasoline was the biggest problem. Being at the right place with the right amount of aviation gasoline in a community that had never seen a helicopter before—much less have gasoline for it—that became, shall we say, difficult.

"You had to travel ahead of it, and you had to be sure you had a place to land, because there were telephone wires everywhere. And when you'd go in and land in the heart of the city, we had to be sure the landing spot was cleared and roped off.

"It took quite a crew to get permission to land, get the gasoline there, bring it on, get the helicopter started, and then the advance crew would take off for the next town.

"Say it was Georgetown and the meeting was at the football field out there at the college. He'd circle the crowd, and then he'd speak over the big PA system. 'This is Lyndon Johnson, your next United States senator, and I'll land in just minute. I want to shake hands with all of you.'

"And then he'd come down; the helicopter would make one last swoop, and he'd open the door of the helicopter, wave his big cowboy hat at the crowd, and then throw his hat from the helicopter. And everybody whooped and hollered, but somebody in our crowd had to get the hat. You had to get the hat or there was hell to pay. I guess we had to retrieve it a hundred times or more."

Mashman: "We covered as many as thirty towns a day and some little towns we'd just fly over, because if we were going from one speaking town to another, we would pass a number of smaller towns on the way. In the list of activities for the day, we'd have perhaps the names of one or two of the individuals in the little town who at one time or other had written to the congressman. As we'd fly over the town we'd slow down and after a few weeks I'd just about memorized what he'd say, 'Hello, there, Mr. Jones. This is your friend, Lyndon Johnson. I'm sorry we can't land today, but I want you to know that I'm up here thinking of you and appreciate your kind letter and comments. I just want you to be sure and tell your friends to vote for me at election time.' And then we'd go on.

"It was all planned and programmed, but we did have unscheduled stops. Sometimes on the way if he'd see, say, a railroad repair crew working there on the railroad tracks— there was, you know, four or five men there—we'd stop and land there and talk to them, especially if it was an area close to the highway where the press was bound to be, keeping up with us. We'd land there so the press could get a story."

Dorothy Nichols: "It was hot, and they had to take the doors off the helicopter. I know the sand blew in, and you can imagine how dirty Johnson was when he came down for the noon rest stop. A lot of that time he didn't have any rest, but he always had a shower.

"Mostly what I remember about that campaign was that we had about three hours' sleep a night, every night. He'd get up at five in the morning to make radio broadcasts to the farmers, and he wouldn't get to bed until two or three, six or seven days a week. He never let up for a minute."

On June 22 at its annual convention in Fort Worth the conservative American Federation of Labor endorsed the conservative Coke Stevenson. True, Coke had consistently spoken against organized labor of any kind and voted against it, but he had not voted for Taft-Hartley. He had not been in a position to; that was a congressional matter.

Charles Boatner: "I was with Coke the day he got word that labor had endorsed him. We were preparing to leave. We went out and sat down in the car for ten minutes and didn't say a word. Then he said, turning to me, 'Well, I'm going to accept it. It will do me less harm to accept it than to fight it. Is that your opinion?' I said, 'That's your problem, I'm no politician.'"

In one speech Lyndon went on to accuse the leaders of the Texas American Federation of Labor of a "secret agreement with Coke that they couldn't get out of Lyndon Johnson and the other candidates." In another he said: "The workingmen of Texas know that I have been their friend. They have today annointed a candidate who was yesterday morning consorting with the big rich at the Houston Club."

Jenkins: "Lyndon was widely criticized for his vote on Taft-Hartley, particularly in 1960 at the Democratic convention. But I think it was that vote that won the election for him in 1948. A great many voters in Texas, except for that vote, were convinced that he was just too far to the left.

"And what helped Mr. Johnson was not only the way he voted, it was that he took a position and tried to get Stevenson to take one. That was practically the whole campaign. Stevenson was the great conservative, and you'd have thought he was for Taft-Hartley, and I'm sure he was. But he got the support of labor simply because they were unhappy with Mr. Johnson's position.

"In every speech Mr. Johnson would say, 'Do you want to vote for a man who won't tell you where he stands?' Stevenson still refused until finally, very near the end of the campaign, when he wrote to the editor of a little-known and little-read newspaper, saying that if he had been in the Senate at the time, he would have voted for Taft-Hartley. But by then it was too late; Lyndon had convinced most voters that Coke was a fence-straddler."

The primary was on July 24, and Coke Stevenson was ahead from the beginning. Eventually he had 477,077 votes, 40 percent of the total; Lyndon had 405,617, 34 percent; and a third candidate, George Peddy had 237,195, 20 percent.

Peddy withdrew the next day, and there were those who thought that Lyndon would and should do that, too. He did not. Instead he was forcing a runoff vote for the nomination. Whoever won would assuredly win the election, since no Republican could then hope to take such a race. Perhaps he thought that since he was going to be forty next month, after which he would have no future anyway, he might as well go for broke. Besides, while Lyndon was always indecisive about entering a race, once he was in there was never any question but that he would stay.

On July 25, the day after the primary, both Lyndon and Coke took off for Washington, Lyndon by plane to attend Harry Truman's "turnip day"[2] session of Congress and Coke by train to demonstrate that in a few days in Washington he could pick up all a senator needed to know about foreign affairs.

Soon after he arrived, Coke announced that he was not an isolationist. Then he had a talk with Senator Tom Connally of Texas, the foremost Democratic leader on foreign affairs; he also met with Robert Lovett, undersecretary of state, and he had brief chats with James Forrestal, secretary of defense, and Senator Arthur Vandenberg of Michigan, the Republican leader in foreign affairs.

Coke then said that having learned all he could about American foreign policy he was now able to deal with it competently. He also said, just as he had said before his trip to Washington, that such matters were totally nonpolitical. And he was delighted to find he was right.

Pickle: "It was a big mistake for Coke to go to Washington. He gave people the impression that he was sort of going to look over his office space in the Senate Office Building, and a lot of people thought he ought to wait until he was elected before doing that. People don't like to have their vote taken for granted."

Before he left Washington Coke made another mistake; he called two press conferences. Coke was used to the Texas press, by and large a down-home group. Hardly anyone there ever asked an embarrassing question. Lyndon mentioned to Drew Pearson that just in case the Washington press corps ran out of questions, they might inquire about Coke's views on Taft-Hartley, and Pearson passed on that suggestion to Jack Anderson, his assistant.

At the press conference on August 9 Anderson told Coke that a thorough search of Texas news files had revealed no commitment by Coke one way or the other on the Taft-Hartley Act. "A lot of Texans still say they don't know where you stand on the act, governor."

Coke: "I have already made a statement carried by the United Press."

Jack Anderson: "But why do you object to repeating your stand? Has it changed?"

Coke: "All my notes and papers are back in Texas. I am facing these questions without any material."

Anderson: "But all we ask is your position. It should be fairly simple to say whether you are for or against the Taft-Hartley Act."

Coke: "No, I want to repeat my statement word for word, and I might leave out some words."

Pearson's column later reported: "Ex-governor Coke Stevenson of Texas . . . on a recent trip to Washington evaded more issues and dodged more questions than any recent performer in a city noted for question dodging."

In Washington Lyndon was exuberant at Stevenson's gaffes, but after his return to Texas he was, as Walter Jenkins said, "As depressed as I have ever seen him, and Lyndon always ran scared during a campaign and was always depressed during a campaign. This was a special depth, though, and people who think he thought he had the election won or that he could finagle a victory are wrong. Lyndon thought there was no chance, and then, little by little, he began to regain some confidence, but never much."

Rhetoric did not notably improve during the runoff campaign. Stevenson said that in Congress Lyndon had three times voted against investigating communism, although he was vague about details. Naturally, Lyndon kept on mentioning Taft-Hartley. "My opponent has not yet made a public statement as to just where he stands on this measure that bans communistic control of unions."

Actually, Taft-Hartley had very little to do with communism, but such intricacies were ignored in the runoff.

In Washington the heads of the four railroad brotherhoods announced that they were endorsing Johnson in the runoff. Johnson greeted this news with caution. He said that he welcomed the support of all laboring men, both in and out of unions, and quickly added, "I do not seek the support of any labor bosses dictating to free men anywhere, any time."

August 11 was "Lyndon Johnson Day" in Johnson City. All the businesses closed their doors, and a sixty-eight-car caravan with two hundred persons drove from Austin to New Braunfels.

Pickle: "We organized a lot of automobile caravans during the runoff campaign. We'd go out with Lyndon Johnson signs on our cars and with a P.A. system that played band music on top. And we'd drive into a town and people would get out of the cars, say fifty to a hundred people in a town of two thousand or three thousand. That really made an impression.

"We'd shake hands and tell people why we were for Lyndon and hand out literature, and then after a while we'd get in our cars and drive away. It was really very effective."

Lyndon's opponent ran a very different brand of campaign. According to T. Kellis Dibrell, "Coke had an old Ford car, and he'd drive from city to city. There wasn't any advance scheduling; it was a very old-time campaign. He'd come to town, and we'd take him over to the courthouse, and he'd shake hands with all the public officials.

"I don't think Coke ever asked anybody to vote for him. He'd go in and they'd say, 'Well, governor, how do you feel about a certain issue?' And he'd answer it, and then he'd say, 'Well, have y'all had any rain?' and then they'd talk about cattle, or start reminiscing."

Allan Shivers: "Stevenson barely campaigned. As I remember, Booth Mooney was traveling with him, writing his speeches and driving the car and arranging the whole schedule and about the only campaign organization that Governor Stevenson had.

"Johnson always worked in his campaigns, and he did in that one. I remember on election day—most candidates in those days figured if you hadn't won the race by election day, you might as well forget it. But on election day in that particular race he left Austin early in the morning and went over to San Antonio and made the rounds of the boxes in south San Antonio—some of the very crucial boxes where he thought he could pick up a lot of votes and did. He just continued to work right on through the day."

THE DUKE OF DUVAL AND ALICE

Lady Bird: "That 1948 campaign was one that just didn't end. It just went on and on.

"Ordinarily, on the morning when the primary's over, you breathe a sigh of relief; you've won and the other race is just a formality. But this time there was the runoff and then one crisis after another right on up to the swearing in in January 1949."

John B. Connally: "I remember the day of the runoff vote very clearly. We, Johnson and I, had been in San Antonio campaigning, and he kept saying he was going to lose the big cities. I told him I thought the cities were destined to vote against him, but I thought the rural areas of Texas were going to support him. I said, 'Paradoxically, you carried the cities against O'Daniel in 1941 and lost the rural areas. This time it'll be the other way round.'

"I said, 'During the runoff campaign you made a great issue of Taft-Hartley and the labor issue, and that's where you're going to come across with the rural voters. Stevenson, being a conservative, expects to carry the rural vote, but I don't think he will. I think you will.'

"And, of course, that's exactly what happened."

Walter Jenkins: "I was back in Austin that evening, getting reports from all over the state. We had key men in each county who were calling in. We had much better information that the Texas Election Bureau."

George E. Reedy: "What you have to understand is that the Texas Election Bureau is not official at all. It's a newspaper organization. The figures put out by the bureau are merely figures gathered by newspapermen who have made various informal relationships with the candidates themselves. In fact, generally the candidates are putting out those figures themselves, and of course what they used to do, they'd hold back certain votes to see how many votes the other man had.

"In 1941 the Johnson forces had made the mistake of reporting the votes as fast as they got them, which gave Pappy O'Daniel and his forces a clue as to how many he had to steal, which they did."

Jenkins: "In 1948 we didn't urge anyone to get their votes in early because we knew the kind of shenanigans that might happen and did happen all the time, everywhere. One of the first indications was when we got a call from a woman in Eastland County who was a supporter of Mr. Johnson and a telephone operator there. She called and said, 'I shouldn't listen in on conversations, but I just heard two men talking and they're going to take two hundred votes away from you in Eastland County tonight in a revision of the votes.' I told Mr. Johnson, and he asked me to call our manager out there and tell him what we'd heard. I did, and he said, 'That's impossible. There's no way it could happen. I sat in on the count.'

"But some time during the night it did happen. We got a revised count from the Texas

Election Bureau. We called our manager back, and he said, 'Well, I was wrong. They made a mistake the first time and they convinced me that there is no theft involved. This vote is the correct one, two hundred more votes for Coke Stevenson than we found the first time.'

"We said, 'That's very odd. How do you know you're going to make a mistake of the exact number of votes ahead of time?' But that's the way it was. We never got those two hundred votes back."

Reedy: "You see, every time the Stevenson forces would come through with some votes, Connally would top it. And then came the count from Jim Wells County, and Coke couldn't top it. You can't really just make votes up. There has to be something written on a sheet of paper, even if it's the forged signature of a dead man."[1]

T. Kellis Dibrell: "On Saturday night we all went to sleep thinking Coke was the winner. Then Sunday night I received a call from Coke. He told me that they had checked with their campaign managers in the various counties and they had gotten their returns, the same as the Texas Election Bureau, and that we had won the election. But that an effort would be made at the time of canvassing the returns, which to my recollection would be the following Wednesday; that there would be some changes made, and that the changes would probably come somewhere in south Texas."

Much of south Texas—notably Duval and Jim Wells counties—was controlled by the Parr machine, which always before had backed Coke Stevenson; that is until Coke refused to appoint a particular man, blatantly inappropriate, as district attorney. The man had been recommended by George Parr.

Dibrell: "Before 1948 Coke had accepted the vote of south Texas when he ran for governor. If you look at those returns, Coke won by gigantic majorities. And in those days George Parr would endorse a man, and he would get a vote like 2,001 to zero for his opponent."

Reedy: "Now you must understand that the population of Parr's territory was largely Mexican, almost totally illiterate, and Parr would give the voters three names—two that were essential to him as boss and dictator, and another for somebody he wanted to do a favor, or perhaps the opponent of someone he wanted to get even with as in this case.

"Ideology had nothing whatever to do with it. Liberals, conservatives, George Parr didn't care. He just wanted to be left alone to run things the way he wanted to run them, and that's all he wanted."

Callan Graham: "The Parr machine, and all of those people in those machines, they never supported or opposed anybody on the basis of political philosophy or public issue. It was always, 'What's good for the machine?' Johnson didn't have to steal that election; it was stolen for him.

"Parr would have supported *whoever* was on the other side. The fact that it was Lyndon in 1948 was incidental.

"I know because I sat in on a conversation when Coke Stevenson solicited Parr's vote in that race. In 1947 when Coke and I drove through Laredo Coke said, 'I know it won't do any good, but I don't want people to say that I didn't solicit their support; so let's go to see George Parr and the others.'

"So we did. I've forgotten who all was in the room; but they were all very friendly.

They said, 'Coke, we've liked you, and we supported you in the past many times, but we cannot tolerate a governor failing to go along with our patronage appointments. We're going to have to be all out against you. We're not against you personally. This is just what we have to do.'

"We drove on to Corpus Christi, and Coke said, 'Well, that's just what I expected to hear, but at least they can't say I haven't asked.'

"Now you have to understand I was for Coke and against Lyndon Johnson. But I was never among those who said or inferred that Lyndon Johnson was personally culpable or stole that election. What happened was going to happen whoever the other candidate was. The Parr machine had to demonstrate that *nobody* could stand up against them."

By Sunday, September 5, eight days after the election, the election bureau was able to report that Johnson was ahead by 162 votes. Lyndon was said to have 494,158 votes, while Coke's total was said to be 493,996.

In Brown County there was a dispute between two county judges, each of whom accused the other of illegal "string pulling." Later a district judge threw out six ballot boxes because two election judges had refused to sign the returns. Their refusal meant a loss of 468 votes for Coke; yet he neither protested nor brought the matter to court. In Jack County the vote totals were switched in the official canvass, so that the vote reported was 894 for Stevenson, 879 for Johnson. Johnson didn't contest that one except in a radio broadcast. And one Lloyd Croslin said that the entire vote in Borden County should be thrown out because the ballot box had been left unsealed in a filling station all night election night. If the county had been thrown out, it would have meant a net gain of 17 votes for Johnson.

Reedy: "One thing that is just not understood about Texas primaries in those days. There was *no* requirement for counting the vote until the state Democratic convention met in the fall.

"The vote counts that you got right after the election were not official tabulations; there was nothing official until the state convention met. Those were the only *official* tabulations. Most people, even most Texans, tended to overlook that."

On Monday night, September 6, Lyndon, with Lady Bird sitting beside him, spoke to the people of Texas over the radio saying that he was the winner of the election runoff. He described how after election night, when the big-city vote had put his opponent ahead, the trend set in in his favor—except for substantial revisions and corrections in favor of his opponent. Such revisions, he said, took 400 votes away from him in a northeast county, 225 more in a west central county, and 213 more in two Gulf counties. The same thing happened in Dallas County, he said, to the amount of 2,000 votes.

Lyndon went on to charge that his opponents talked only of bloc votes in one county and were "strangely silent" about the bloc votes in their favor from the three big cities and other areas, including "the bloc vote in a box behind the gates of King Ranch where not one single vote went to me," and "the precinct along millionaires' row, the River Oaks box of Houston, where Stevenson got eight out of every ten votes." Even in his own Hill Country, he added, the vote was eight to one against him.

"Isn't it strange," he said, "that the greatest part of the venom has been vented against me because of one county where the population is largely Latin-American."

Of course the "bloc" vote that was causing Lyndon's enemies so much concern and making so many headlines, by that time all over the country, was the bloc of 200-odd votes that suddenly, and somewhat belatedly, had appeared in Jim Wells County in south Texas.

Coke decided to have some of his men look into the matter.

Dibrell: "Coke asked me then if we would go down to south Texas to try to find out if there were to be changes in the election returns—where they would occur and what could be done about it. Coke thought that if you had formerly been with the FBI [as Dibrell had been], you could work miracles, or you could reach into it and get information. Well, I had no badge or gun; I was just a young lawyer. It was an awful big assignment, and I didn't know where to start."

Dibrell started by going down to Laredo where his friend the chief of police told him Laredo would not be the spot. "If there are any changes," he said, "they'll be where George Parr is."

George Parr was in Duval and Jim Wells counties; bordering the two counties was a town called Alice.

On September 7, the day after Lyndon's radio speech, Dibrell and Graham[2] went down to Alice to investigate the electoral procedure of Precinct Thirteen.

Graham: "We zeroed in on Precinct Thirteen for one reason. The vote had see-sawed back and forth for a week, with Coke being ahead, and then Lyndon being in the lead. And then all of a sudden Lyndon was in the lead—it looked like to stay—for 202 votes. The last 'corrected' total added 200 votes to Lyndon and 1 to Coke. This certainly threw the election, or 'tilted' it, in Lyndon's direction.

"Dibrell and I talked all the way down in the car about what we were going to do. I remember before we left Austin people around headquarters told us not to wear a suit coat—of course it was summertime—because it might be dangerous. They said, 'Be sure there are no coats, so they can see you don't have a gun."

According to Graham's account, he and Dibrell managed to persuade the newly elected Democratic County Chairman, one Harry Lee Adams, to prevail upon the previous incumbent to unlock for all of five minutes the bank vault in which the voting list for Precinct Thirteen had been stored. Under instruction from Graham and Dibrell who were working under the asusmption that 202 names had been added to the poll list, Adams was to count each 202 names from the bottom, write down that name, and then go one above that—the name, they figured, of the last legitimate voter. Then he was to write down the last name on the list and as many in between as he had time for.

Adams had time to jot down some eleven names before the list was whisked away again. He also had time to verify that the last 202 names, unlike those before them, were all written in the same handwriting with the same color ink.

Graham: "Within a matter of minutes we hit the town and got the addresses of all those eleven people. They were all alive—there weren't any graveyard votes among them, but none of them had voted."

Dibrell: "One lady who would have been a legitimate voter testified that she went to the polls one minute before closing time, 6:59 P.M., and that when she was there no other voter was there, and that when she left there was no other voter coming. Her name appeared on the list, and there were 202 names afterwards. So we felt we had something.

"And then the first vote after that—his name was like Ancerra. And we interviewed him, and he said that he had not voted."

Graham: "Then we got the next one who was alleged to have voted on this list and talked to him. He had not voted. The total of eleven said, 'No.'

"So then we knew to our own satisfaction that the 202 votes had been added after the election."

Then late one night the two investigators received a phone call from the secretary to the county Democratic executive committee, Clarence Martens, who had unthinkingly signed a vote canvas certificate presented to him, and was now convinced that the document was false.

Graham and Dibrell managed to persuade Martens to come back to the hotel with them to type up a new certificate putting the returns back to where they had been before the 202 added votes.

Graham: "Before I could finish typing it, the door—I won't say it was broken in. I don't know whether it was locked or not. But it was jammed in, and some fellow came in and grabbed Martens by the scruff of the neck and marched him right out of there. I don't know who the man was that did it. But outside in the hall was Ed Lloyd, the lawyer for the Parr group there. I knew who he was; I had met him before. He was out in the hall when this guy came in and just literally lifted Martens out of the room.

"There wasn't anything to do. He was gone."

The next move, Coke's friends decided, was to suggest that he himself come to Alice and personally examine the poll list. Coke was, after all, the former governor; Tom Donald, the still incumbent county chairman, could hardly refuse. So Coke came, accompanied by Frank Hamer, who, in his heyday as a young Texas Ranger, had been responsible for the shoot-out deaths of Bonnie and Clyde.

Dibrell: "He appeared to be an extremely old man. He walked with us from the hotel room to the bank. He had tremendous confidence. Down there there were a lot of special deputies or otherwise, and everywhere you turned there were people with guns on. But when Frank Hamer walked down the street, those clusters of people parted."

Later this same walk was described in the book *"I'm Frank Hamer": The Life of a Texas Peace Officer*[3]:

> The bank was surrounded by armed men who refused to allow anyone to enter. Hamer and Governor Stevenson approached the bank on foot, and Hamer stepped up to the guards.
>
> "Git!" he told the first group, most of whom knew him and his reputation as a peace officer. They moved away.
>
> Hamer and the Governor then went up to the bank door, which was guarded by another group of armed men. "Fall back!" Hamer ordered. They did.
>
> The Governor and his party were allowed to enter the bank and to inspect the

ballots briefly. A political controversy of no small significance ranged for some time thereafter.

Between the primary—or, as was often the case, the primary runoff—and the general election in November, Texas procedure called for a meeting of the state Democratic convention to certify the nominees of the party to the Texas secretary of state, who would in turn put their names on the ballot for the election. Decidedly more important than the convention itself, however, was its executive committee. Made up of one man and one woman from each of the electoral districts, the state Democratic executive committee, met a day or two in advance of the convention itself; in this case on Monday, September 13, at the Blackstone Hotel in Fort Worth. It was their job to make recommendations to the convention as a whole.

Byron Skelton: "Stevenson announced that he was going to take a contest of the election to the state Democratic executive committee and ask them to recommend to the convention that he be certified as the nominee instead of Lyndon Johnson, alleging fraud and chicanery and illegal votes and all of that."

Jenkins: "Of course, all the top people on the committee were Stevenson people appointed by Stevenson and kept in office by Stevenson. We never thought it would be easy. We talked to as many of them as we could, presenting the facts to them. But since they were Stevenson people, *facts* lots of times didn't interest them very much."

Stuart Long: "One of the funniest things happened. It was really tragic, but the Austin member of the state Democratic executive committee was Jerome Sneed, a very prominent attorney and a Johnson supporter. It was a very hot, argumentative sort of a situation, and Mr. Sneed had a heart attack in the lobby of the hotel. There are those who swear this to be true—that another quick-thinking Johnson representative, Everett Looney, scrawled out a proxy on the back of an envelope and got Jerome Sneed to sign it before he called an ambulance for him.

"And as it turned out this was important, because in the state executive committee meeting the motion to substitute a report which would have recommended Stevenson instead of Johnson failed by one vote.

"The deciding vote was cast at the end of the roll call by Charlie Gibson from Amarillo, the committeeman from District Thirty-one, who had been down drinking a cup of coffee and came in just in time to cast the deciding vote."

There are those who insist that Gibson burst into the room shouting, "Let me in! I demand to be admitted—I am Charlie Gibson from Amarillo!" and that he had not been in the coffee shop, but in the Blackstone bar not too many steps, or lurches, away.

In any case, he shouted the crucial words, blurred somewhat, "I vote for Lyndon Johnson."

The vote was twenty–nine to twenty–eight in favor of Lyndon.

· The next day when the convention officially opened, two rival delegations showed up from Fort Worth, from Dallas, and from Houston. In each case, one of the delegations refused to swear that it would support the nominees of the Democratic National Convention, that is Harry Truman and Alben Barkley, in November; presumably it might also refuse to support the Democratic senatorial nominee. (This was the year Strom Thurmond and Fielding Wright marched out of the convention and formed the States' Rights party. Their supporters at the Fort Worth convention were numerous and noisy.)

Long: "The test vote in the state convention came on refusing to seat these delegations which had violated party law. The law said you couldn't participate in the Democratic convention unless you signed an agreement to support the nominees. And the roll call vote was to seat the three loyalist delegations from those three big counties instead of the 'Texas Regulars' (Coke Stevenson supporters). Of course, the loyalist delegations were Johnson delegations.

"So the regulars marched out and took the furniture with them. The Fort Worth Regulars, who had arranged for the convention, had borrowed furniture for the stage—adding machines, tables, chairs, desks, typwriters—and when they were evicted, they sent people in to pick the furniture up.

"I remember Sam Rayburn sitting there in front of a table, and they took the table away, and when he got up to protest, they carried his chair away.

"Finally, someone backstage found a barrel and brought it on stage. We put our typewriters and other paraphernalia on it. Someone started singing 'Roll Out the Barrel,' and that's what happened.

"Governor Allred announced that we were going to have to pay the rent for the hall, and he was going to pass the hat, which he did. As a matter of fact, they passed several hats, and we collected more than enough to pay the rent."

The convention, by a voice vote, agreed to accept the recommendation of the executive committee that Lyndon was, indeed, the winner of the primary runoff by eighty seven votes, and to certify him as the party nominee, to be placed on the ballot for election in November.

Lyndon himself showed up a little later and spoke of a hundred days of campaigning, one of the longest political campaigns in Texas history, he said, which was true. He added that he would "spend the next six years making Texas as good a United States senator as I possibly can."

Although he had just passed his fortieth birthday, he told a group of newspaper men that he felt twenty. "Except up here," he said, pointing to his forehead. "I've learned a little."

But at the time all this was happening in Fort Worth, other events pertinent to the situation were occurring in east Texas.

THE LAW IS THE LAW

Early on the morning of the opening of the Texas State Democratic Convention—between 3:00 and 4:00 A.M.—an old man vacationing at his sister's lakeside cottage in east Texas was awakened by Coke Stevenson's close associates T. Kellis Dibrell and Connie Renfrew. The old man had planned to do some fishing that day, but he was Federal District Court Judge Whitfield ("Tiddy Winks") Davidson of Dallas, and his friend Coke Stevenson needed him. While he sat over coffee on the porch, Davidson was handed a petition from Stevenson's lawyers asking for a temporary restraining order that would prohibit the secretary of state of Texas from placing Lyndon's name on the ballot in November.

Davidson signed the restraining order and set a hearing for September 21 in the federal court in Fort Worth.

George E. Reedy: "The significant thing about the 1948 runoff was that if Stevenson had really wanted an honest count of the ballots, he would have gone, as Texas law clearly provided, and made an immediate appeal to the Texas Supreme Court, and all the ballots would immediately have been impounded. Stevenson did not take that route. Instead he went to a close friend of his, a very old man and a very conservative man."

Walter Jenkins: "We thought it was rather peculiar that a fellow who talked so strongly about states' rights all during the campaign would try to go into federal court to present an election contest. I've never understood for sure why he did, because I think his attorneys might well have reached the conclusion that the courts would determine that it was a state matter and not a federal matter—which they finally did."

Alvin Wirtz: "Stevenson would not resort to the state courts because he knew that there all of the facts regarding illegal votes would be brought to light, and Johnson would win by at least two thousand instead of eighty seven. He knew that no state judge would issue an injunction to keep Johnson's name off the ticket until all illegal votes had been thrown out."

At Judge Davidson's hearing in Fort Worth on September 21 there was testimony from four of the eleven names uncovered by Callan Graham and his associates, all of whom swore that they had not voted in the runoff. And there were many affidavits from people saying they had stayed home that day.

Callan Graham: "One of the first times I ever remember seeing Lyndon was sitting in the courtroom in Fort Worth. His argument was that it was a party primary, not a general election, strictly a party affair, and the federal courts had no jurisdiction over it.

"They said, 'We can't validate or invalidate all the votes in Texas, and we can't act on the basis of one precinct where 200 votes were added and none other.'"

Lyndon's forces were not alone in that opinion. Price Daniel, attorney general for Texas at the time, agreed that no, one could not act only on one precinct, and yes, there was evidence of other, perhaps equally extensive, irregularities.

Jenkins: "Mr. Johnson kept inviting Stevenson to go into a statewide election contest under the jurisdiction of the state court—an invitation which he did not accept. It put us in a rather anomalous position. We were refusing to give information to the federal court, refusing to answer the charges. It made us look like we had something to hide. But the attorneys, particularly Abe Fortas, who was advising, strongly suggested that if we ever answered anything in the federal court, we were accepting the position that they had a right to be there."

After hearing the testimony, Davidson ruled on September 21 that the evidence made a "prima-facie showning of fraud." He granted an injunction and appointed two masters in chancery to go to Jim Wells County to look into things.

Graham: "So we went back to Alice. The master in chancery presided over another hearing.[1] Again we presented our evidence. All the lawyers were there. It was more lawyers, I believe, than had ever been in that little courtroom.

"Then we moved that we look in the Precinct Thirteen ballot box, and they brought the ballot box in. I knew what was in there. They brought it in, and it was locked. It had not been locked when we saw it a week or two before. But now it was securely locked, and nobody had a key. So the master in chancery ordered somebody to go get a locksmith and bring him up there to cut the lock off. They did—cut it open, opened the box, and it was absolutely empty. A very dramatic moment—we opened the ballot box and nothing was there!

"Almost at this moment we received a telegram, or rather the master in chancery did, to cease proceedings, that the federal courts had no jurisdiction. Justice Black of the United States Supreme Court was so holding."

Meanwhile, the Lyndon Johnson forces had not been idle.

Joseph L. Rauh, Jr.: "I got a call from Tommy Corcoran. He said, 'We've got to save Lyndon Johnson's seat.' So I went over—they had about ten or twelve of the best lawyers I ever saw. I figured, you know, what the hell am I doing here? What do they need another lawyer for? But that was Tommy's position. He believed in crowd scenes."

Luther E. Jones, Jr.: "Each of these lawyers was famous in his own right, and the reminiscing was just awful because it stopped the work.

"Mr. Johnson was getting impatient because they were not producing the pleading that was needed. Nobody could agree on how to do it. Judge Allred wrote one; Mr. Johnny Crooker wrote one; Mr. Cofer wrote one; Everett Looney wrote one. The day moved on and night came and they still had not agreed on the opposition paper."

Stanley Marcus: "Abe Fortas was visiting me, and I got a phone call, and Lyndon's voice said, 'Do you know where in hell I can put my hands on Abe Fortas?' And I said, 'He's right here.' Then Abe got on the phone and talked to Lyndon.

"Abe went to Fort Worth that night, and he was the first one who said they shouldn't be thinking about politics. They should be thinking about *law*. He said, 'What's the *law* on this?'"

Abe Fortas: "Judge Davidson had entered an injunction or restraining order to prevent Mr. Johnson's name from appearing on the ballot. Time was very short—just a few days—and the question was how a decision could be obtained from the appellate court soon enough to permit Mr. Johnson's name to appear on the ballot. It seemed to be agreed that unless his name could appear on the ballot at that time, that any subsequent relief would be of no help.

"The critical move was the decision to present this in a summary way to the court of appeals and then to go to the senior circuit court justice, who was Associate Justice Hugo Black.[2] I had had considerable experience with Supreme Court procedure, I felt very strongly that if we tried to go directly to the Supreme Court from the district court, we would be rebuffed, and that would mean the loss of some precious days. So we did it the other way, and it did prove to be the correct procedure."

Jones: "Abe was a brilliant lawyer, and this federal civil procedure was his specialty. It was a thing of beauty to watch the way he handled it. He listened to all of them for perhaps an hour, took all their work, got a secretary, and in ten minutes came back with a one-page opposition, or two pages—a very brief one. It was just exactly what was needed."

On September 24 Allred flew to New Orleans where the Fifth Circuit Court of Appeals was located and asked Judge J.C. Hutcheson to dismiss Davidson's restraining order. Hutcheson said that he could not do so until he sat with his two fellow circuit court judges on October 14. But that, Allred said, would be too late to meet the deadline for the printing of the absentee ballots.

Fortas: "The next step was Hugo Black, senior circuit justice. There was no alternative. If the circuit justice had been Mr. Justice Satan, you'd have had to go to him."

Paul A. Porter: "So we drafted an application to Justice Black. I remember after the pleadings were drafted I told Judge Arnold, 'Thurman, you and I had better go up and file this personally' and we did. We drove up to the Supreme Court. The Court was in recess, but Hugo Black, who was in charge of the Fifth Circuit, was in town.

"The next day we got a call from Justice Black's clerk that he would hear us the following day provided we notified the adverse parties that they, too, could appear. He wouldn't receive us *ex parte*. Well, of course we were delighted because at least we had gotten a justice to hear us. So we notified Dan Moody. Governor Moody came up on behalf of Coke Stevenson, and we all went over to the courthouse, and Abe Fortas presented the case.

"Well, Justice Black—I don't know whether he'd spent the night in the library or his clerk did, but he knew more of these reconstruction cases than any of us had had an opportunity to research. His questions were sharp and relevant, and after listening to the argument, he said, 'Well, gentlemen, I am disposed to grant the stay. Submit an order.'

We came back to our office—we already had an order drafted—and I recall that Wesley West had his airplane up here—the one oil friend probably that Johnson had in the state of Texas at that time. And we flew the order down, went before a good circuit judge in Austin, and got a mandatory order directing the secretary of state to certify Lyndon Baines Johnson's name as the Democratic nominee."[3]

Fortas: "With all respect to Coke Stevenson and his lawyers, there really was no question about the merits of the case. The injunction was improvidently entered; that is, the federal judge enjoining the state election under these circumstances was just plain wrong.

"It made no difference who Lyndon Johnson was. The law is the law."

But if that would seem to tie up the loose ends, nothing could be further from the truth. The various ramifications of the 1948 election would continue to plague Lyndon, in one form or another, through charges and countercharges, accusations and rebuttals, until his death and even after it. Because no one could prove anything.

In October 1948 two U.S. Senate investigators arrived in Texas. Fourteen subpoenas were issued to officers in Jim Hogg, Starr, Duval, Zapata, and Jim Wells counties for the preservation of ballots and records; only seven were actually served. All the ballots and records in Duval County had already been destroyed, and some were missing in other counties.

In the end there was no real investigation. Crucial persons were not to be found; necessary evidence had gone up in smoke. Literally. It was widely rumored that the ballots from box thirteen had been burned; certainly various persons from Alice and its environs took unexpected vacations in Mexico that fall.

Reedy: "Because Coke did not go to the state courts, Parr was able to burn the ballots. Nobody could stop him. If Coke had gone directly to the Texas Supreme Court, as the law provided, the ballots would have been impounded immediately and there could have been a recount. And there were an awful lot of very interesting counties over in east Texas where a recount might have produced all sorts of things."

On September 25, the day after Lyndon's case was argued before Judge Hutcheson of the U.S. Court of Appeals, and postponed, President Harry Truman's "whistle-stop" train arrived in El Paso from a quick trip through New Mexico. The president told the several thousand people at the station that the Republicans were on the run, and he said they were scared and he planned to keep them that way.

As the declared winner of the Democratic primary, Lyndon could, of course, campaign with Harry, even though at that time the Texas secretary of state was still enjoined from placing Lyndon's name on the ballot. Everybody knew the old man didn't have a chance though, and the prudent politician stayed as far away from the train and from him as possible. So what if he was president? He wouldn't be for long.

Creekmore Fath: "Lyndon got on in San Antonio. The train came in from the west to Uvalde and then we went to San Antonio and started up through Texas and got to Fort Worth where we got off the train and got into cars. I think President Truman was in the first car with Sam Rayburn, and I think Senator Tom Connally was in the second car.

"In any event, in the third car Lyndon was in the front seat with the driver so that he could sit and wave. And the caravan went all the way to Dallas, from Fort Worth to Dallas. There was a solid line of people, five or six deep, on both sides of the road all the way. Later it was estimated that half a million people were lined up there.

"We stopped at Garland, and Truman stood up and made his speech. Lyndon looked around and said, 'Just goes to show you the great respect people have for the presidency of the United States. Isn't it a shame they won't vote for Harry Truman!'"

Jonathan Daniels: "I think the most dramatic time I ever saw Lyndon Johnson was on that trip. As you remember, a lot of Democrats were holding off from Truman. Some of them didn't even want to get on his train. And we got down to Texas, and he came aboard, looking like the damnedest tramp I ever saw in my life. He couldn't have shaved in at least two days, and he looked sick as hell. At that moment I don't think he knew whether he was a pocketful of votes ahead or a pocketful of votes behind.

"If he lost at that point, he was pretty well licked for the rest of his life. He was going to be a great man or just another Texan, and at that point he didn't know and nobody else knew which it was going to be.

"But he had guts enough to come aboard the train. And the president had been in the same spot before that Lyndon was in; he'd been awful close in his reelection to the Senate. And I'm sure that the old man had a great deal of sympathy for Lyndon in his unshaven, worn-looking condition.

"I didn't know I was looking at a potential president. I didn't even know whether I was looking at a potential senator!"

While only a footnote in history, the 1948 Senate election has always been a subject of controversy among Lyndon Johnson watchers; nearly thirty years after the fact, certain events transpired to keep the controversy alive.

In April 1975 George B. Parr, facing a federal prison sentence of five years and fourteen thousand dollars in fines for perjury and income tax evasion, drove to his sister's ranch near Alice and put a bullet through his head. Two years later, on July 31, 1977, a reporter named James W. Mangan from the Dallas bureau of the Associated Press, released a story which made the front page of almost every newspaper in the country and which quoted one Luis Salas, then seventy-six, who had been associated with Parr since 1940.

Salas, who had been one of the election judges in Alice in 1948, told Mangan that he wanted to unburden himself before he died. He said that three days after the primary runoff, on Tuesday, September 7, Lyndon Johnson went down to Jim Wells County for a meeting with Parr, Parr's lawyer, Ed Lloyd, the Alice city commissioner, and himself. Salas said that Lyndon announced at the meeting that he needed 200 more votes to win, and that Parr then ordered him, Salas, to add the 200 votes.

Salas also told Mangan that most of the same Jim Wells County cast, plus Lyndon, boarded Harry Truman's campaign train in Corsicana, Texas, on the morning of September 29 and informed Harry that his friend Lyndon might be defeated in the court battle and thus lose the election. Mangan continued the story: "Black's telegram ordering a halt to the probe came the same day, in midafternoon."

Mangan said Salas had told him: "That was all it took to give the election to Johnson. A telephone call from Truman to Hugo Black. That's the way it works in party politics."[4]

Salas didn't say who told him about that telephone call, and Mangan apparently didn't ask. All the participants—Parr, Ed Lloyd, Lyndon Johnson, and Harry Truman—were dead as was Justice Black. Salas, for whatever reason, waited to tell his story until there was no one left who could refute it.

Not only that, but after the AP story was published, Mangan and Salas had a couple of New York agents submit it to various publishers, accompanied by a letter saying that the two were willing and able to turn the whole thing into a book. The book never materialized, but Salas did appear on several television programs where he repeated the story, with a few embellishments here and there.

However, the Truman train was not even in Texas on September 29; it was, by then, in the state of Oklahoma, a fact verified by the Truman Library and by the *New York Times* account of the whistle-stop campaign. Moreover, the Truman Library has a record, which it considers to be complete, of everyone who boarded that train in Texas and elsewhere; there is no mention of Parr, Lloyd and Co., Lyndon Johnson, yes— boarding the train at San Antonio, not Corsicana.

Ed Lloyd's brother and long-time law partner, Frank—who is, by the way, still very much alive and practicing law in Alice—said when interviewed:

"You can say for sure that Ed was never on that train. And you can say that Lyndon was never down here at the time that old man says he was. You couldn't have Lyndon come anywhere near this place without everybody knowing it.

"If Ed had been on that train with the president, don't you think he'd have mentioned it to *me*? We practiced law together from 1926 on until his death.

"That's a wholly made-up story by Luis Salas, and I don't know why he did it. But he's an old man, and I guess he wanted to make a little more glory out of his life than he'd had. And maybe make some money."

Graham: "I saw Salas on the TV, and I was shocked because I knew what he was saying wasn't true. My judgment was that he was an old man and that in his old age he wanted to have played a bigger part in things that he did play. He didn't need to do that. He didn't need to lie. He played the biggest part anyway. He's the guy that did the actual vote stealing. He knew that all the time. The 202 votes are in his handwriting; no question of that, never was."

Several books published recently have stated that John B. Connally went to Jim Wells County in Lyndon's behalf.

John B. Connally: "I did not. It's a complete falsehood. And I know Lyndon wasn't there the day that old man said he was. I was with him. He didn't go down there at all during that campaign. I know that."

Graham: "There was no reason in the world for anybody to go down there. What you've got to bear in mind about the Parr machine and all those machines—they never opposed anybody on the basis of political philosophy or public issues. It was always, what's good for this machine?"

The Salas story was also denied by Walter Meek, who was seventy-seven in 1977 and who had before his retirement been Duval County auditor for sixteen years. He said, "There's no question about the thing being rigged. But I really don't think Lyndon Johnson had a thing to do with it."

The story was also denied by Mary Rather and Walter Jenkins, both of whom were with Lyndon on the day he was supposed to have gone to San Diego.

And Bo Byers, head of the Austin bureau of the *Houston Chronicle* who as an Associated Press reporter—how small the world—covered Johnson's campaign; he also denied any possibility of Lyndon's having gone to Jim Wells County. He said he could not help but have known if that had happened. "I was at the door of his [Lyndon's] house from early each morning until late each night throughout that week."

As a result of the Salas story, the Lyndon Baines Johnson Library opened the entire files on the 1948 goings-on—eight huge boxes with five thousand documents. There was no evidence to confirm or, for that matter, deny the old man's account of what happened.

Perhaps the best comment on the Salas story came from Harry Middleton, director of the library: "I know Johnson didn't do what Salas said because that would have been *dumb.*"

Fath: "When I got to be friends with Tom Miller, who, as you know, was mayor of Austin, I said, 'Tom, who really won the 1948 election?' He said, 'Well, I'll tell you. We were picking up votes in east Texas. Only God knows who actually won the election, but I suspect that Coke was stealing as many votes as we were.'

"I've always accepted what Tom said, that both sides were stealing, and Lyndon won. And hell, he was, I suppose, a *somewhat* better senator than Coke would have been."

2

Mastering the Senate

TREADING LIGHTLY

Hubert H. Humphrey: "The class of 1948, so called, meaning those that were serving their first term in Congress, included besides Johnson and myself, Estes Kefauver of Tennessee, Paul Douglas of Illinois, Robert Kerr of Oklahoma, and Clinton Anderson of New Mexico, in the Senate; and I remember in the House Gene McCarthy, also of Minnesota, Gerald Ford of Michigan, Dick Bolling of Missouri, and Sid Yates of Illinois. A very interesting group of newcomers, but as always Lyndon stood out.

"I think Lyndon came to the Senate knowing what I had yet to learn, that the Eighty-first Congress was really very conservative. Truman had won a great and as you know surprising victory in 1948. When the class of 1948 was sworn in, there were eighteeen new senators, fourteen of them Democrats. But they were not necessarily Truman Democrats.

"Lyndon was well aware of that, and he was, I think, biding his time and building his contacts. Not breaking with the South but rather bending the southern attitude somewhat to his will, staying close enough to the southern leadership so that they trusted him and so that he could work with them."

Walter Jenkins: "Mr. Johnson took to the Senate as if he'd been born there. From the first day on it was obvious that it was *his* place—just the right size; he was at his best with small groups, and at that time he was one of only 96 senators, while in the House he had been one of 435, a group in which it was much more difficult to make his influence felt, to be effective. But with only 95 others—he *knew* he could manage that. And, of course, too, he knew practically all the other senators of importance; he had met many of them through Sam Rayburn. In those days almost all the important senators were southerners, the heads of almost all the important committees."

Michael Janeway: "Johnson came to the Senate in 1949 . . . treading lightly wherever he went. He was anxious to please Georgia's Senator Richard Russell, on whose Armed Services Committee he hoped to continue his preparedness work,[1] and one of his first actions was to line up with the southerners . . . against liberalizing the Senate filibuster rule."[2]

Bobby Baker: "Lyndon was always very smart at knowing where the seat of power was, and he recognized that at that time, in a predominately southern Senate, Dick Russell was *the* power, and he also recognized that Russell, who was no longer so young, was a bachelor and lonely, and he started his Senate career by cultivating him, no, *courting* him—courting is the word. To the Johnson girls it was always 'Uncle Dick.' Lyndon took the trouble at least to try to make him part of the Johnson family, and he flattered him outrageously.

"I first met Johnson in December of 1948. He had just been elected to the Senate, and I was twenty years old and had been in Washington as a Senate page boy since just after my fourteenth birthday. I had been given the title of chief telephone page, kind of an honorary title; before that I had been chief page.

"I remember when Johnson called me and said, 'I understand you know all the senators, their strengths and their weaknesses, and I'd appreciate it if you'd come by my office and talk to me.' It was a novel way of introducing himself."

Baker was the smallest and one of the youngest of the Senate pages and thus subject to many humiliations, and he hated the uniform, the knickers in particular. He disliked being called "boy" and being ordered to do something like bring "a bill stretcher" to a senator—a joke (there was no such thing as a "bill stretcher") that always brought down the house, the Senate anyway. Only Harry Truman called him "young man" and asked rather than ordered him to do whatever it was.

Baker: "Lyndon and I became very close very quickly because we both knew how to count, and he was very quick to learn all there was to know about each and every senator. I soon became known as 'Little Lyndon,' but that was after he became majority leader and really made use of me."

One can imagine Senator Russell's surprise when he first called together the southern caucus of the Eighty-first Congress to find two freshman senators from southern states noticeably absent; well, Estes Kefauver, notably unpredictable, yes, to be expected—but where was Lyndon?

Lyndon was somewhere else, anywhere else; he was, as noted, "treading lightly." He had established himself in the good graces of his southern colleagues and was determined to work hard on their committees. He had acquired a much sought-after place on the Tydings-Russell Armed Services Committee and another on Ed Johnson's Interstate and Foreign Commerce Committee. He was one of them, and if his ultimate goal had been no more than to rise in the southern-dominated Senate hierarchy, then Lyndon would no doubt have attended the caucus, too, right on time. But the clearest indicator that he was already, in January 1949 at age forty, thinking beyond that, was his absence. Because a southerner who was first, last, and always a southerner, or who was identified as such, could forget the national political scene right then.

Lyndon was, as always, keeping his options open.

Humphrey: "Our little group of twenty-five or so liberal senators were very suspicious of Johnson in those early years, very suspicious. I was maybe the one that looked on him with more friendship, more acceptance. I always felt that he was a lot more liberal than he ever acted. I felt that early."

Humphrey may have been right, but the dissenting views of the Paul Douglases of the Senate were understandable, especially considering that Lyndon's maiden speech in the Senate was a straight down-the-line anti-civil-rights diatribe that filled more than eight pages of the *Congressional Record* and placed him squarely in the middle of the southern bloc.

The civil rights issue came up at once because every new Senate session begins with the adoption of the rules, and a perennial issue was Rule 22 which allowed cloture—that is a vote to end debate—only by a two-thirds vote of the entire Senate membership. The liberals always hoped to relax that percentage to, say, three-fifths of the membership. The liberals always failed, but they never failed to try, and in 1949, encouraged by Truman's unexpected victory, and hoping against hope that that victory would make feasible new civil rights legislation, they made a more concerted effort than ever before.

The southerners answered the challenge with a filibuster, and when the South filibusters, all hands are needed and no southerner is excused. If Lyndon minded that his Senate debut was on so sectional and controversial an issue, it was not apparent from the ardor of his speech. He may, perhaps, have felt the need to mollify Russell after shunning his southern caucus. In any case, the speech he gave on March 9 could well have been delivered by Russell himself, or any of the southern diehards.

"We of the South," he said clearly, and went on at some length about the "right of free speech," meaning the option to filibuster. He attacked Truman's civil rights program unmercifully, repeating his long-stated opinion that it was the states' duty, rather than the federal government's, to outlaw the poll tax and enforce laws against lynchers.

Finally, Lyndon strongly denounced the FEPC (Fair Employment Practices Commission); that, too, he had done three years before in the House. There was, in fact, little if anything in the speech that he had not said or advocated before, and his detractors were wrong to call him inconsistent. What wounded many of his more liberal supporters was the promptness with which the new senator aired these views, less than two weeks after he took his oath.

Public response to the speech back home reminded Lyndon that now, however, as a senator for the whole state of Texas, he was responsible to a considerable number of black as well as white constituents.

Monroe Billington: "Although Johnson rationalized that he was not speaking against blacks, reaction from the minority race in Texas was immediate. The executive secretary of the Houston branch of the NAACP telegraphed: 'THE NEGROES WHO SENT YOU TO CONGRESS ARE ASHAMED TO KNOW THAT YOU HAVE STOOD ON THE FLOOR AGAINST THEM TODAY. DO NOT FORGET THAT YOU WENT TO WASHINGTON BY A SMALL MAJORITY VOTE AND THAT WAS BECAUSE OF THE NEGRO VOTE. THERE WILL BE ANOTHER ELECTION AND WE WILL BE REMEMBERING WHAT YOU HAD TO SAY TODAY.'

"Johnson's reply, which leaned heavily on the general principle of unlimited debate, was unacceptable, and a delegation of Houston blacks traveled to Washington to protest. The confrontation ended unsatisfactorily after heated words had been exchanged between the visitors and the new senator. Other NAACP chapters passed resolutions censoring Johnson for his remarks."[3]

The whole episode of Lyndon's first Senate speech—his willingness to accept what he saw as political necessity and his emotional response to the inevitable criticism from less pragmatic friends and supporters—set the pattern for what would recur again and again during the next twelve years. The young man who had thrown himself heart and soul behind his president, who had not wavered at the unpopularity of Roosevelt's Court-packing plan or his wartime wage and price guidelines, who had seen to it that black students were the equal recipients with white of NYA projects—that Lyndon was difficult to find in the man who stood on the floor of the Senate attacking Truman's civil rights program. And no one had a harder time facing that change than Lyndon himself.

Lyndon's problem was that he wanted his old friends, his liberal supporters, to accept his change of direction with like equanimity. When they did not, he felt betrayed. Unlike the Paul Douglases and, on the other side, the Richard Russells of the Senate, Lyndon could no longer trust his early instincts and survive, and that fact created in him an inner contradiction that was not to be resolved until he became president.

And yet there were still the isolated cases where the old Lyndon, the Lyndon who had bought baseballs and bats for the Mexican-American children and had spearheaded the Austin housing project, appeared.

D. B. Hardeman: "In January 1949, shortly after he became a senator, the funeral home of a Texas town called Three Rivers wouldn't allow the burial service for a Mexican-American soldier killed in the Philippines during World War II. The family was bringing his body back for reburial in his hometown, Three Rivers. When Johnson heard that he went off like a sky rocket."

Dr. Hector Garcia: "Mrs. Longoria, the soldier's widow, wanted him buried in Three Rivers, and she was trying to make the arrangements with the Rice Funeral Home there, but they refused the use of the chapel.

"We tried to convince everyone that it was wrong, but the funeral director wouldn't change. In desperation somebody said, 'Call Senator Johnson. He'll help you. He's a fair man, and he likes Mexican people.'

"I had never met Senator Johnson, but I put in a call to him in Washington. He said, 'Well, Dr. Garcia, let me assure you, you tell Mrs. Longoria I'll help.' He said, 'I promise you this. Try to talk to everyone and see if Felix can be buried in Three Rivers; if not, I promise you that we'll bury him with full military honors at the National Cemetery in Arlington.'

"We continued without success, and eventually the body was taken directly to Washington where with the help of Senator Johnson and President Truman, Felix Longoria was buried in Arlington with full military honors."

Lady Bird: "I remember that the day of the burial service was a cold, dreary day in Arlington. Lyndon said he wanted me to go. We both went. It was drizzling. President Truman sent his military aide, who in the course of his life came in for some unhappy publicity, but who was really a staunch Truman lover, General Vaughan.[4]

"I remember seeing him in a sort of trench coat standing there by the grave, very stiff and military, and how much Lyndon appreciated the president's sending him. I can remember Lyndon saying, 'Harry Vaughan stood in the icy sleet at attention with a red wreath he brought to place on the grave of the Mexican boy. He stood there for an hour because he wanted to do it, and I have never said anything against him—and I never will.'"

Hardeman: "At that time what he did could only hurt him politically in Texas. But what the people in Three Rivers did outraged him, and it was I think one of the things that led to the famous speech in his early presidency in which he talked about teaching little Mexican children, about prejudice and discrimination, saying, 'If ever I get the power, I said I'm going to do something about it, and now I've got the power, and I am going to do something.' Or words to that effect.

"I was on the floor of the House that night, and I think that was one of the great speeches of American history. I never heard him deliver a speech with more power than that. Of course, he felt deeply what he was saying. And the thing hit you like a double whammy.

"I think that was the real Lyndon Johnson."

But the same man capable of such concern and compassion, who stood in the cold and sleet by a Mexican-American grave, could with apparent unconcern and complete lack of compassion attack another man equally innocent, if perhaps less appealing, and one whose cause he himself always claimed, usually with justice, as his own. This man was Leland Olds; his cause was governmental regulation of public utilities.

Early in 1949 Harry Truman reappointed Leland Olds to the chairmanship of the Federal Power Commission. Senate confirmation of that appointment came under the jurisdiction of the Interstate and Foreign Commerce Committee; a subcommittee was appointed to conduct hearings, and Lyndon, who had from the beginning exhibited unusual capacity for hard work on his committees, was named subcommittee chairman, his first chairmanship as a senator.

Michael Gillette: "Leland Olds was not a Communist, nor had he ever been. Nonetheless, in the political climate of 1949, he was extremely vulnerable to anti-Communist attacks on the basis of his radical writings and associations with Communist-related institutions during the 1920s. The political atmosphere in October 1949 was one of suspicion against leftist government officials. The Hiss trial was in the headlines; two days after the Senate vote, eleven leaders of the American Communist party were convicted of conspiring to advocate the overthrow of the government. Only four months later, Senator Joseph McCarthy would address a Republican women's club in Wheeling, West Virginia.

"At that time most senators were far less interested in determining the accuracy of every accusation against Olds than they were in letting the public know and having the record show that they themselves did not vote for a man who was accused of being a Communist."[5]

With Lyndon, however, for whom the next election was a good five years away, other matters weighed equally in his decision to play the Grand Inquisitor. In light of his narrow election margin the year before, he was particularly anxious to solidify his position with the powerful Texas oil and gas interests, and they, of course, were adamantly opposed to a consumer-advocate like Olds. Mail from Texas was heavily anti-Olds, and Lyndon no doubt appreciated his good fortune at having so ideal an opportunity to prove himself so soon after his election.

So when he opened his subcommittee hearings shortly after the Labor Day recess, his own interrogation centered around Olds's record as a public utilities regulator and his, Lyndon's, disagreement with same. He made sure that Texas newspapers were barraged with press releases emphasizing the major role their new senator was playing in the opposition to this "prejudiced crusader," as he referred to him, who "has pursued a meandering but relentless course toward nationalization of the nation's fundamental power industries." He left the red-baiting to other subcommittee members, most particularly to the conservative Republican Homer Capehart of Indiana.

When in October the matter moved to the Senate floor, however, after a seven to nothing vote against Olds in the subcommittee, Lyndon took a new line. Public utilities regulation may be of prime interest to Texans, but to the country as a whole it was pretty boring, and he was aware that it was Capehart with his attacks who had been receiving national attention. The Texas press, too, could not very well be expected to repeat the same line endlessly. So to the great consternation of his old liberal buddies like Jim Rowe and Tommy Corcoran, Lyndon on the Senate floor joined the red-baiters.

Except for his desire to step into the limelight, there seems to be no other explanation for Lyndon's action. Olds had a few loyal supporters left but his confirmation was clearly doomed to defeat. Lyndon had successfully established his position in Texas to much applause from the nonliberals. But he wanted something more, some indefinable acceptance of himself as somehow special, a notch above the other freshman senators, someone to watch out for. In his Senate attack on Olds he broke his resolve to "tread lightly," and the consequences would plague him for many years.

Lyndon's final words on the Senate floor were, "I do not charge that Mr. Olds is a Communist, although I recognize the line that he followed, the phrases he used, the causes he espoused, resemble the party line today . . ."

The voice was Lyndon's; the rhetoric was to become Joe McCarthy's.

On October 12 the Senate voted fifty-three to fifteen against confirmation.[6] Joseph L. Rauh, Jr., years later said: "Lyndon Johnson almost alone was responsible for the defeat, the humiliation of Leland Olds. And he did that as a freshman senator. People kept telling me that he was a new kind of Texan, a liberal Texan, but I never saw any evidence of it, and to me the Olds case was a typical example.

"My conjecture is that Lyndon would still have been for public power, but the oil people also had interests in the federal power commission by this time. It must be that the oil companies came into this. The paradox—why does this pro-public-power guy jump on Olds. The only thing I can quickly think of is that the federal power commission regulated natural gas which is also owned by the oil people.

"I think the key is Abe Fortas. You have to know who Abe represented when he got Lyndon to fight Olds to really know the answer."

Janeway: "The Olds affair sets the stage for Johnson's behavior in the nineteen fifties. As his power grew in the Senate, he devised a way of balancing Washington positions with Texas positions, which was the other side of the coin from his effort to bring the liberal wing of the Senate Democratic caucus into productive communication with the conservative wing. . . .

"But it is inaccurate to say that Johnson was doing anything so palpable as 'delivering' for oil and gas interests in the Olds fight, or in his later efforts on behalf of eliminating federal regulation of natural gas producers, or in his votes to give the tidelands to the states, or in his defense of the oil producers' 27½ percent depletion allowance. These were examples of a man making clear to thousands of suspicious constituents his concern for the interests of a state which felt increasingly hostile to the directions of national policy on social and economic matters.

"To be 'for' the well-being and protection of Texas's richest industry, and its most important source of revenue, is not simply to be 'for' special privileges for selfish, reactionary oil producers, but to be 'for' the economic health of the state as well.

"For a Texas politician . . . to be 'against' the industry, pure and simple, would be as senseless as a West Virginia politician being against the mining of coal."[7]

Jenkins: "I think Mr. Johnson was *very* aware of the conservatism of his constituency; in my opinion it was his vote *for* the Taft-Hartley bill that elected him to the Senate. The so-called liberals were not a great power in Texas in those days."

Ralph Huitt: "As a Texan in Washington I used to be amused at the liberals who were always hostile toward Johnson because he supported the oil-depletion allowance. I'd say, 'Look, what would happen if one of your guys in Wisconsin voted against the dairy industry?' But those fellows never could equate oil and cows. They felt that cows were more wholesome than oil."

GETTING AHEAD

Paul H. Douglas: "Johnson was an intensely ambitious man, anxious to get power and hold on to it, a rather curious mixture of pragmatism and idealism. He had a progressive background, and I think this had entered into his spirit and was a fundamental feature of his character.

"But Texas after Roosevelt was a very different place than it had been. Gas and oil came to the fore. That gas was tapped instead of running wild, and there were still large native deposits of oil. The men who owned these resources were the economic barons of Texas, and they were supported by the cattle owners of the big ranches and the sugar planters of the more tropical sections of the state. They had become intensely anti-Roosevelt and antiprogressive, and yet they were the dominant characters in the state and in the Democratic party. These were interests which profited greatly from the activities of the federal government in taxation. They had put through, at an earlier period, the depletion allowance, which gave them relative immunity from taxation, even though their profits had been large. They were powerful and strong, and no one could rise in Texas politics, apparently, if they opposed them. Johnson, therefore, had this struggle within himself of his native tendencies, his Roosevelt idealism, faced with the hard facts of power politics and economic power. He wanted to get ahead, and he could not get ahead if he took an opposition point of view to the big gas-oil-cattle-sugar interests.

"So I, who believed in the more adequate system of taxation without any loopholes or truckholes, as I call them, who believed that special privilege in taxation should be eliminated, clashed with him."

Gerald Siegel: "I think of Johnson as a populist. Liberal labels, I think, early became anathema to him because they represented a very exclusive club to which he didn't belong; his credentials weren't in order. He got, understandably, damned mad at people who he felt were probably less liberal right in the gut than he, but who because they were fortunate enough to be born in a different part of the country, were widely accepted in the international liberal circles."

D.B. Hardeman: "In his early days in the Senate he was cut by the extreme conservatives on the one hand and the extreme liberals on the other. In fact, that was true from the day he came to the Senate until the end. It was tough to stay in the middle, a very difficult thing to manage, but he did. I don't know how.

"And you must remember, he never had any control of Texas the way Harry Byrd did of Virginia. With Lyndon it was always a tumultuous political career, always."

At the height of the cold war, which was already heated enough, largely by bellicose rhetoric and the enormous expenditure of defense funds, came Korea, the war nobody expected or wanted. Not only Texas but the whole of the country, already conservative, almost immediately took a frightening move toward the right. You could feel it in the air you breathed, in the jobs you lost because you had once back in the . . . Leland Olds had only been the beginning.

News of Korea came unexpectedly, like Pearl Harbor on a Sunday morning, and it was frightening. Harry Truman reminded everyone of what Hitler and Mussolini and the Japanese had done to the League of Nations, and he was determined, he said, that the Communists were not going to do the same to the U.N. So he immediately called up troops and instituted, almost single-handedly, a United Nations "police action" to "stop aggression and to prevent a big war."

Johnson agreed wholeheartedly. He not only agreed, he welcomed the opportunity the conflict offered to turn his attention back to his old specialty, defense preparedness, a subject considerably less controversial than oil and gas. Inwardly Lyndon was getting a little weary of being labeled a conservative, and in 1950 even the liberals, most of them anyway, were for being prepared.

Since this was a police action, Congress was never called upon to declare or not to declare war, but it swung into action in other respects. The Armed Services Committee of the Senate and its opposite number in the House were alarmed that only untried divisions of soldiers were immediately available. And so Truman sent down his Universal

Military Training Bill to the Senate, the merits of which were decidedly debatable. The country had never had a peacetime draft before; still, the country was not, as Truman kept reminding us, at war.

It was high time, Lyndon decided, for the Armed Services Committee to investigate the matter in depth, and after some maneuvering, he managed to convince Chairman Russell that a defense preparedness subcommittee might be set up to do just that—with Lyndon at its head, and all this within a month of Truman's commitment of American troops to Korea.

Most freshmen senators would have been content with that but Lyndon, still having in mind how much Truman's committee—the Committee to Investigate the National Defense Program—had done for the senator from Missouri politically, conceived the idea of recreating it in his own newly established subcommittee. There was just one possible problem: the Government Operations Committee and Joe McCarthy.

Horace Busby: "The investigatory function of government programs was supposed to fall to the Government Operations Committee. But Joe McCarthy was on Government Operations, and Johnson pointed out to Harry Truman that if Armed Services didn't do this—create this committee and pre-empt the investigatory role—it would fall to Government Operations and you'd have Joe McCarthy on it.

"So Truman agreed with Johnson that the defense preparedness subcommittee should be the reincarnation of the Truman committee. After that every time I was with Johnson and Truman, Johnson brought up the fact that he had chaired the second Truman committee."

But however much Lyndon was occupied with his subcommittee chairmanships, he kept up his "hobby" of accumulating vital information about the personalities and habits of his fellow senators. He had little use for any of that information as yet, but he hoarded it against the day, which he was sure would come, when he might need it.

Hubert H. Humphrey: "Early on in our Senate days, Lyndon started inviting me up to his office, and we'd talk. From the very beginning, it seemed to me, he understood the most intricate workings of the Senate. It seemed that he got there aware of the backgrounds of most of the members, and he took the trouble to find out about the ones he didn't know about. He was like a novelist, a psychiatrist. He didn't stop until he knew how to appeal to every single senator and how to win him over."

Warren Magnuson: "He just paid attention to every little thing. He was very accommodating to people. He put a lot of IOUs in the bank, and when he needed them for something he really wanted, he could pull them out." Lyndon was to pull some of the IOUs out very soon.

In the November elections of 1950 Lyndon observed with interest that the Senate majority leader, Scott Lucas, Democrat of Illinois, lost heavily to Republican Everett Dirksen. Francis Myers of Pennsylvania, Democratic whip, was also defeated. The routine duties of those posts made it difficult for the senators who held them to spend much time campaigning, and the result was often sadly predictable. The positions were not, therefore, much sought after, and, besides, they held no power. Richard Russell had the power.

It was not easy when the Democrats met in the late fall after the election to find anyone to replace Lucas. Conservative Ernest McFarland of Arizona—old easy-to-please Ernest—was finally persuaded, against the advice of all his friends, to take no part. Ernest was nice, but he was not overly bright.

The position of Democratic whip was less prone to disaster, and Robert Kerr, the rich, reactionary Democrat of Oklahoma, wanted Lyndon to consider it. Kerr, a man of intense vulgarity and greed, was anxious to have a contact in the Democratic hierarchy, and his Texas friend seemed to be the likeliest possibility.

True, being whip was not to have power, but it was a position that could be the next step to power, and Lyndon was never not aware of the next step. The next dozen steps.

Sam Shaffer: "At that time the assistant leadership was little more than an honorary degree. But to Lyndon it lifted him out of the rut of freshman senator, and he would sit in the leadership councils until the majority leader was out in the hustings campaigning, making a speech, and then he would be in charge of the fort. He would be noticed. Other senators would be aware of him."

So Kerr, not without some difficulty, persuaded Russell, and Mister Sam helped out by getting in touch with twelve Democratic senators who had been members of the House and urging them to back his Texas friend. And when on January 2, 1951, the Democrats caucused and formally voted Ernest McFarland their new majority leader, they simultaneously selected as majority whip Lyndon Johnson of Texas—by acclamation.

Meanwhile, as the police action in Korea continued, the generalship of Douglas MacArthur began to cause concern in the White House. Under orders from Washington to limit the war to Korea and under no circumstances to cross Soviet or Manchurian borders, MacArthur was simultaneously under pressure from Chiang Kai-shek and other nationalist Chinese to expand the war into mainland China at the first opportunity, a proposal he himself favored.

MacArthur's reluctance to confine the war as ordered led first to a disastrous military defeat when he allowed his forces to advance deep into North Korea where they were surrounded by Red Chinese troops pouring over the Yalu River from China, and second to a confrontation with his commander in chief when, after painstakingly winning back the territory he had lost by his military blunder, he announced that he himself would dictate terms for a peace treaty and would meet personally with the Red Chinese commander to arrange a settlement. The implication was that if his terms were not met, he would then expand the war.

It was at this point—April 1951—that Truman, with the unanimous agreement of his Joint Chiefs of Staff, fired him.

In spite of the public outcry against Truman's action, there is little doubt but that Lyndon agreed with him. He was present at the joint session of Congress when MacArthur, standing ramrod straight, delivered his "old soldiers never die" speech. And he could not help but rejoice when that same Congress, in response to its generally outraged electorate, designated the Senate Foreign Affairs and Armed Services committees to hold joint hearings on MacArthur's recall. True, it was the senior senator from Texas, Tom Connally, chairman of the Foreign Affairs Committee, who along with

Richard Russell, chairman of Armed Services, would formally conduct the hearings, but there would no doubt be a prominent spot for Lyndon just one seat down, assiduous in his preparation and prompt in his attendance, never far from the eye of the camera or the notepad of the nearest reporter.

Siegel: "In the investigation, the staff of the Senate preparedness investigating subcommittee did the night work of processing every bit of the day's transcript and putting back on the desk of Senator Russell in the morning, through Senator Johnson, questions for the next day's session.

"It went on for weeks, and it was an enormous task. We literally worked through the night. We'd go home, sleep in the daytime, and come back in the late afternoon and pick up the transcript and begin to process it.

"Then Senator Johnson and Don Cook would take the product of our night's work and brief Senator Russell in the early part of the morning before that day's hearings began."

George E. Reedy: "They set up a series of closed hearings at which we had the reporters who had security clearances from the Defense Department. As rapidly as the hearings were transcribed, a censor would delete the absolute security information that had come out, and the pages went to the press sometimes within a half hour after the actual testimony was given. A whole series of witnesses were heard exhaustively; great care was taken to see that all sides of the controversy had full opportunity to vent their attitudes. I think that paid off, because at the conclusion of the hearings, the tremendous wave of emotionalism that had swept the United States when MacArthur returned seemed to have subsided."

At the same time Lyndon was also actively continuing the hearings of his defense preparedness subcommittee, seemingly unmindful that it was a president of his own party at whom he almost daily leveled his guns and that he was thereby offering ammunition to the Republicans for an election now less than a year away. His committee became known in an approving press as the "watchdog committee" and Lyndon, according to *Newsweek* in December 1951 when he was on their cover, was "watchdog in chief."

He was, of course, no longer thought of as a freshman senator, and then suddenly even his position as junior senator from Texas seemed about to change. Senator Tom Connally, who had come to Congress before the Allies entered World War I, decided to give up his Senate seat, a decision that was not entirely his own idea.

The governor of Texas at that time was a conservative by the name of Allan Shivers, and his attorney general, equally conservative, was Price Daniel. Shivers and Daniel were unhappy, or so they said, that their senior senator had become so involved with Senate affairs, in particular with his role as chairman of the Foreign Relations Committee, that he had little time to devote to the particular concerns of his state. In actual fact Shivers's unhappiness had as much to do with his inability to exert any control over a senator so long independent and so deeply entrenched in national affairs as was Tom Connally.

Tom Connally: "When I came home to look into my prospects, friends told me that Price Daniel had got word from Shivers to run against me. Shivers had promised him the support of the state Democratic organization, and for insurance Daniel had gone ahead to organize his forty deputy attorneys around the state as his local campaign managers against me.

"I also found out that Lyndon Johnson had been over to talk with Shivers and promised to support Price Daniel."[1]

Price Daniel: "I do not believe that I talked it over with Senator Johnson. I knew where he would stand. He would have to support his colleague in the Senate. But the feeling throughout Texas was that Tom Connally was full-time chairman of the Senate Foreign Relations Committee and wasn't a senator from Texas at all."

In any case, Connally assessed his chances, concluded that they were slim, and announced his retirement. Daniel won the primary easily, assuring his eventual victory, and then went on to join Shivers in backing the Republican candidate for the presidency.

Daniel: "Senator Johnson had plenty of friends who supported Eisenhower in 1952. He was and is a great man to try to heal any breaches or misunderstandings and to forgive and meet anybody halfway or more than halfway. So he never chided me about it at all, about supporting Eisenhower.

"When I went to Washington, there was no office space left for me because one of the defeated senators who was having to move hadn't moved. So Senator Johnson gave me a desk in his office and the free run of his staff. The day that the Democratic caucus met, he asked me to go with him, and I entered the door with his arm around me."

Of course. The senior senator from Texas was delighted to introduce his new colleague around.

By the summer of 1952 it had been determined that Adlai Stevenson and Dwight Eisenhower would be opposing each other in November, but whom the Texas Democrats would back depended upon the candidates' positions on the controversial matter of the tidelands.

Two years before, on June 5, 1950, the U.S. Supreme Court had ruled that the submerged lands off the coasts of Texas and Louisiana, said to be rich in oil deposits, were owned not by Texas and Louisiana but by the federal government.

Twice since then, bills had come before Congress proposing to return the tidelands to their respective states. Both times Lyndon had, of course, supported the bills, along with a majority from both the Senate and the House—states' rights still prevailed in those days. Both times the bills had passed Congress only to be vetoed by President Truman. In 1952 there was new legislation pending. The question uppermost in the minds of most Texas Democrats in 1952, then, was what position would the new Democratic candidate for the presidency take? Would he, too, veto the tidelands bills?

Actually, that was only half of the question. Conservative Texans like Governor Shivers were not at all pleased with their party's nominee and were more than anxious for an excuse not to support him.

Reedy: "In 1952 Mr. Rayburn had extracted a promise from Governor Shivers that he would attend the national convention and support the national ticket.

"Then after the convention Shivers made a special trip to Springfield, Illinois, and it was quite clear to all of us that Shivers was going there for one reason and one reason only. And that was to provoke Adlai Stevenson into taking a stand on tidelands that would make it possible for Shivers to come out for Eisenhower.

"None of us were trying to talk Stevenson into taking a stand that was contrary to whatever principal position he had, but we did want him to phrase it in such a way that Shivers would not be able to come home and say, 'I just can't stand this; this man is taking away the sacred heritage of Texas, and I'm for Ike.'"

That, however, is precisely what happened. Shivers asked the Democratic candidate what he would do if a tidelands bill were passed again, and the Democratic candidate said he'd veto it.

Adrian Spears: "When Governor Shivers defected, he took most of the members of the state Democratic executive committee with him. Then Sam Rayburn and Lyndon Johnson and others got together and tried to put the Democratic party together again. It was a shambles. There was no organization, no leadership, except for what was provided at the last minute."

Reedy: "It put Johnson in an extremely difficult position. He was up for reelection in 1954. The emotion in Texas over the tidelands issue was incredible!

"The average Texan interpreted the northern position on tidelands as being one of taking money away from his schools, and the education of his children was at stake, and he reacted violently. Consequently, it took genuine courage of a very high order to support Stevenson that year."

Booth Mooney: "Johnson spoke . . . of people who would never forgive him for his support of Adlai Stevenson in 1952.

"'Amon Carter's one of them,' he said shrilly. 'The Fort Worth *Star-Telegram* was always for me till last year. Strongest paper in the state and my best supporter. But when I was committed to Rayburn to introduce Adlai Stevenson when he appeared in Texas, Amon Carter called me and asked me—no, he didn't; he *told* me—not to do it. I explained about my commitment and said I'd have to live up to it, and I did. Now Old Man Carter won't even accept my telephone calls. He even scratched me off his Christmas list."[2]

Hardeman: "Johnson was roundly criticized by a lot of the liberals because he didn't take a more aggressive part in supporting Stevenson, but I never did go for that.

"Johnson introduced him in Fort Worth and was on the platform with him in Dallas, and that wasn't easy. Except for one statewide official, everybody else endorsed Eisenhower or ran for cover. They went to the hospital or they went to the mountains of New Mexico. They scattered like quail."

On November 4, 1952, Adlai Stevenson was roundly defeated by Dwight Eisenhower. Texas did its part; Ike carried the state with 53 percent of the vote. There had not been a Republican in the White House for twenty years, and that change was profoundly to affect the career of the now senior senator from Texas.

MINORITY LEADER

The election of a Republican president for the first time in twenty-four years was not the only event of the 1952 election that would have a major effect on Congress in general and the newly senior senator from Texas in particular. There was also the matter of the defection from the Republican party, but not to the Democratic party, of Wayne Morse of Oregon, more's the pity, they said in the cloakroom, which pared the Republican majority down to one vote. And there was the defeat of Ernest McFarland in Arizona, which meant that for the third time in six years the Democrats were without a leader.[1]

It also meant that new candidates for the position had better review their options. Scott Lucas had assumed the leadership in '49 only to be defeated in the '50 election; McFarland had taken it on in '51 and been defeated in '52. Would it be wise for anyone to take it on in '53 who had to face reelection in '54, particularly if his position in his home state were as precarious as was Lyndon Johnson's in Texas?

Ralph Huitt: "I remember that when word came over the television and radio in 1952 that McFarland had lost in Arizona to Barry Goldwater, the liberals began musing on what they would do when they got back to Washington, whom they were going to support.

"Long before they ever got around to doing something, Johnson had the job nailed down. He and Russell were on the telephone all night long, and he had the job."

Bobby Baker: "The senators were all committed in a block to Russell, but once Russell didn't take it and indicated he would vote for Johnson, well, I started lining up the vote.
"Of course, Humphrey wanted it; he and Johnson came in at the same time, 1949, but Humphrey couldn't get the votes. Humphrey had made a big mistake when he first got to the Senate. He got up and said that Senator Harry Byrd [Democrat of Virginia] was a no-good sonofabitch, and they almost kicked him out of the Senate for that."

Sam Houston Johnson: "The minute the southerners heard that Humphrey wanted it and Russell didn't, they came flocking to Lyndon. They remembered that civil rights speech that Hubert had made at the 1948 Democratic convention and were not about to have him get into any position of leadership.

"I remember Kennedy, Jack Kennedy, that is—he'd just been elected in 1952—stopped by Lyndon's office to tell him he was going to vote for him. Lyndon said he looked like a nice kid and probably had some future in politics."

Hubert H. Humphrey: "Lyndon called me on the telephone at my home and said, 'How are you going to vote on the Democratic leader?' I said, 'I can't vote for you.' The tidelands fight had been on, and we'd had a couple of civil rights battles. And he said, 'Well, I'm sorry. You know, I'm going to win. You liberals haven't got even as many votes as you think you have. Some of the people that are telling you they're going to vote against me are going to vote for me.'

"Later on he said, 'Well, who are you going to run, you liberals?' I said, 'We're going to run Jim Murray. I know he's not going to get elected, but we thought we'd put up a good showing for Jim. He's an old-timer around here, and he symbolizes a lot of the spirit that we have amongst the liberals in Congress.'

"He said, 'Well, who do you think is going to vote for him?' I gave him the list that I had, and he went right down it and said, '*He* isn't going to vote for him, *he* isn't, and *he* isn't. These fellows are going to vote for me.' I said, 'I can't believe that. They've already told Paul Douglas or Estes Kefauver or somebody else that they're going to vote for Murray.' He said, 'Well, you'll find out.'

"I'll never forget it—when we had our caucus, he was just as right as day. They voted for Johnson. And I then moved to make the nomination unanimous, because I didn't want Jim Murray to be humiliated. When we got all through with that, Johnson said, 'Come down and see me. I want to talk to you.'

"I went down and he said, 'Now let me tell you something. You and I can get along fine. I know we don't agree on a number of things, but at least we can get along. You're an open-minded man. Some of those damn fools that you're with I don't want to have anything to do with. Now, who do you want on the policy committee?'

"I said, 'We ought to put Jim Murray on there.' He said, 'All right. It's a damned fool selection, but if you want to do it, go ahead.' I said, 'Why is it a damned fool selection?' He said, 'He's too old. He's going to go along with me on everything I want. You know that. You ought to pick somebody who, if you want to have somebody stand up and fight with the leader, will do it.'"

George E. Reedy: "The policy committee grew out of the LaFollette-Monroney Act of 1947, and no one quite knew what to do with it. It was the product of some academic political thinking concerned with establishing a leadership committee in the Senate that would state party positions for the Republicans and the Democrats. Well, that is simply an impossible thing. Under our political system you are never going to have clear-cut political positions that you can call Democratic or Republican in either the Senate or the House.

"But Senator Johnson was not the kind to take over a useless organization and just let it lie there. What he did with it was to use it as a nucleus for a staff that could be very helpful in shaping legislation so it could pass the Senate. He also used it as a gathering point for the leadership of the Senate to discuss legislation, to work out some of the necessary compromises.

"In the modern Congress, a senator does not have enough time to sit down and analyze arguments. In the policy committee we could go through the reports of the standing legislative committees with a fine-tooth comb. We'd be able to call individual senators who were objecting to something in a bill, and we'd explore their thinking and determine what would meet their objections. And we were able to come up with some positions that evoked a remarkable degree of unanimity which had been almost impossible in the past."

Huitt: "When Johnson assumed the leadership of the party it was broken all to pieces, and the business of putting it back together was the first job.

"There were forty-eight Republicans, forty-seven Democrats and one Wayne Morse. Morse was the Independent party of the United States of America, and he used to rise on Friday afternoon and talk for about three hours telling the people what the Independent party of the United States of America wanted to *do*.

"This minority was, I think, fortuitous for the leader because it meant that for two years he had precious time to pull his party back together without having to take initiatives. As a minority leader he could not be forced by some president to do something which was divisive to the party."

When he was vice-president, Johnson recalled his analysis of the situation at the time he became Democratic leader: "We are now in the minority. I have never agreed with the statement that it is 'the business of the opposition to oppose.' I do not believe that the American people have sent us here to obstruct.

"I believe we are here to fight for a positive program—a program geared *not* just to opposing the majority, but to serving America. I think that is the real desire of every Democrat—even though we may disagree as to methods."

One of Lyndon's methods with which the liberals in his party heartily disagreed was his application of a "unanimous consent rule" to the Democratic policy committee. Lyndon's opinion was that a minority party should not bring bills onto the Senate floor that it was not solidly behind—at least 90 percent of the members of the policy committee, and if possible 100 percent, should endorse the bill first.

Of course since the policy committee was basically southern and conservative, what that meant in practice was that a lot of bills initiated by liberals never made it onto the floor. Which would make senators like Herbert Lehman and Paul Douglas and Albert Gore furious; they knew many of their bills were popular with the folks back home, and they wanted those folks to hear about the bills, and they wanted to make political mileage out of forcing Republicans to go on record in opposition. But Lyndon, because there would be Democrats also forced into the same opposition, refused. He considered there was more mileage to be gained by a party that *appeared* unified, even when it most assuredly was not.

Douglass Cater: "During those Eisenhower years, I dare say that Congress would have been at a complete standstill if it hadn't been for Johnson. Seeking a consensus was not a negative act for him. It wasn't the lowest common denominator, or what just any old body would agree on. It was trying to find what was the maximum that you could get a majority to support."

Gerald Siegel: "Throughout that first year as minority leader, Johnson picked his positions carefully. He recognized that we had a very popular president at that time, Eisenhower, and that the worst thing that could happen for the Democrats was to get bloodied and lose a lot of skirmishes with him in the Senate. We were just beginning to see daylight out of Korea and getting that behind us, and I think he wanted to see some constructive, peaceful periods of cooperation.

"Senator Taft and Johnson worked very well. Knowland, who succeeded Taft,[2] was never a match for Johnson, intellectually or otherwise.

"Of course Johnson dominated this whole period from '53 to '60. His performance as Senate Democratic leader was really virtuoso. Even Dirksen, who was pretty slick, was not really a match for him. Knowland clearly wasn't."

From his very early days in the Senate Lyndon knew that one of the cardinal rules for getting ahead was to become an authority in one, or at most two, fields. His experience on the House Naval Affairs Committee had set the groundwork for his specialty in defense, so that when he came to the Senate he was anxious to continue that specialization by joining the Armed Services Committee. But the Armed Services Committee was one of the "desirable" committees; normally only senators with considerable seniority were members, and it was only by dint of his unusual persuasive powers that Lyndon had wangled himself a place on it.

Looking at the Senate objectively from his new position as Democratic leader, Lyndon could see all the drawbacks in such a system. Since many southern states had at that time only one viable party—Democratic—and seldom challenged an incumbent in Congress, the senators from those states were, to all intents and purposes, elected for life. That meant, of course, that the "desirable" committees were dominated by southerners, and that a new senator, from wherever, could expect to serve a long apprenticeship on such unimportant committees as the District of Columbia Committee before moving on to one where he could begin to build a reputation.

Such a system, Lyndon decided, was anachronistic, and now he was leader of his party and in a position to do something about it. He called a meeting of the Steering Committee of which, as leader, he was automatically chairman, and, by way of softening what would be an unpopular proposal, related a story he was to repeat many times in varying versions and under varying circumstances:

"When I was a boy in Texas, I was a good friend of the Crider boys, Ben and Otto. Now Ben was older, and he was kind of sturdy and outgoing and popular among the boys, and Otto, well he was more shy and retiring.

"So one day I was over there at the Crider house, and it was the weekend and no school the next day, and I asked Otto if he could come over to my house for a day or two. But Miz Crider, when we asked her, she said, 'No.' No reason, she just said, 'No.'

"And Otto, he began to protest, and he said, 'But, mama, why can't I go? Ben, he's already been twowheres, and I ain't never been nowheres!'"

And then, in case the analogy had escaped anyone, Johnson went on to correlate the less desirable committees with nowheres, and particularly this year when there was such a good crop of new Democratic senators—John Kennedy of Massachusetts and Stuart Symington of Missouri and Mike Mansfield of Montana, to name a few—wouldn't it be a good idea to revise—not scrap, mind you, just revise—the seniority system to provide that no Democratic senator could be on two good committees until all were on at least one good committee?

Michael Janeway: "It was a classic Rooseveltian compromise, right down to the more doctrinaire among the liberals looking back to it and deciding that they had been betrayed by a wolf in sheep's clothing. Because the southerner's domination of 'the Club,' that mysterious directorate of the Senate, was not destroyed. Like the capitalistic system in the 1930s, it was made more viable and more productive, for men like Richard L. Neuberger, Mike Mansfield, and Eugene McCarthy could now walk the bridge Johnson had built for them into 'the Club.'"[3]

Perhaps the most complex issue to face the Senate during Lyndon's minority leadership was the Bricker amendment. Senator John Bricker, Republican of Ohio, even more conservative than Taft, measured the dangers inherent in Yalta's and United Nations' human rights covenants and proposed a resolution calling for an amendment to the Constitution that would prevent such disasters in the future by curtailing the president's capacity to control foreign policy.

The resolution, conservative Republican in philosophy, was strongly opposed by Eisenhower, and although it appeared totally at odds with Roosevelt-Truman Democratic principles, was cosponsored by many Democrats and favored by others, including initially Lyndon Johnson. It was one of those issues that took on emotional ramifications in the populace at large far beyond any real effects it could possibly have had. In 1953, when Bricker first introduced it, and 1954, when the Senate Judiciary Committee reported it out favorably and it came before the Senate, the American people were particularly subject to emotionalism in matters dealing with foreign policy.

Reedy: "The Bricker amendment was probably the most divisive political proposal of the mid-fifties. Nobody was quite certain what it would do. The proponents were convinced that it would prevent American boys from having their hands chopped off in Saudi Arabia and being sentenced to five years solitary confinement in France, and the antagonists were absolutely convinced that if it were adopted, it would make a complete hash out of American foreign policy. And really, in all the years that I've been around the Congress, and that goes back to 1938, I don't know of any other single legislative issue that has aroused such intense emotion.

"It got to the Senate, and it became apparent from the start that it could not be defeated on a straight-out vote. No one could vote against the Bricker amendment with impunity, and very few could vote against it and survive at all—at least, so they thought."

Eisenhower objected to the resolution because of its encroachment on executive authority, and to one clause, known as the "which clause," in particular because it stipulated that Congress would have to pass special legislation in each case before a treaty could "become effective as internal law." Almost nobody seemed to know what that meant, but it was clearly antiexecutive. So the Republican leadership proposed an alternative to the "which clause" more acceptable to the president, and the Democratic leadership—Lyndon had obviously had second thoughts on the matter—counterproposed a substitute to the entire amendment, sponsored by Senator George.

Siegel: "I had prepared a research memo on the Bricker amendment for Senator Johnson. Then he called me into a meeting that was going on between himself, Bill White, and Walter George.

"I sat there and witnessed Johnson, with just a quick reading of the memo, talk to the substance of the issue and persuade Walter George that he should not lead a massive fight in favor of the Bricker amendment. It was a rapid-fire, almost uninterrupted monologue. It wasn't a give-and-take discussion. It was Johnson expressing just about every point of view that he thought would be effective. I'm sure he probably went back and talked about how Walter George's mother and father might feel.

"Finally, after long discussion, Senator George of Georgia, who was probably the most respected conservative member of the Senate, agreed to introduce a substitute for the Bricker amendment which stated simply that no treaty would be superior to the laws of the United States. Now this was a rather subtle distinction, but a number of legal experts looked at it and decided it was harmless.

"So Senator George introduced his amendment."

At this point the scenario became, if possible, even more complicated. Bricker altered his original amendment to a strengthened version of the George substitute which, opposed by the Republican leadership, was voted down on the Senate floor. Next the Senate approved the Republican-sponsored alternative to the "which clause," and finally came to the vote on the Democrat-sponsored substitute. The George amendment required two votes—a simple majority vote to substitute it for the Bricker amendment, and a two-thirds vote to adopt it. The substitution was made, but the George amendment itself failed by one vote.

There has always remained some question as to whether Lyndon Johnson meant for that to happen.

One reason Lyndon was having such early success in his role as minority leader was because he had extensively revised the job of Democratic whip and then had handpicked the man to fill it. Having held the position himself when it was little more than honorary, he understood how useless it had been and, more important, how useful it could become. With the right kind of whip, twice as much could be accomplished.

The right kind of whip would, of course, be junior to the leader, in Senate years if not in age, and yet would have served at least one term so that the workings of the Senate were not new to him. In Lyndon's case, therefore, the whip had to come from the class of 1950, and from that class there was one senator whose potential usefulness was immediately apparent. Earle Clements of Kentucky was one of a rare breed of southern liberal. As a southerner of good family he was accepted, even liked, by the Russells and the Georges, although his voting record was solidly liberal, and because his voting record was liberal he was also accepted, even liked, by the Lehmans and the Douglases.

Not only that, but Clements was also in the good graces of the national party structure because having been in ideological agreement with Adlai Stevenson he had enjoyed campaigning for him, and he had done so strenuously.

Earle Clements was, Lyndon decided, the perfect whip.

Kenneth Birkhead: "Clements had a great sensitivity to what Johnson was trying to do. When a particular action of some kind was coming up, Johnson would explain to Clements in three sentences what he wanted, and Clements would just get the full picture. It might take him an hour to give me my orders—I was leg man for the whip—but three sentences were enough from Johnson.

"My specific assignment was to be sure that we knew where all the Democrats were, and where they were going to be at the time a vote might come, and how to find them.

"I remember once on Republican amendments to the Taft-Hartley Act, there had been agreement as to a time certain for voting. The time came, and Mr. Johnson had every one of the Democratic members sitting in their seats—you know, just an unheard-of thing—not some in the chamber, some of them back in the cloakrooms or anything, but every one of them sitting in their seats when the vote started, including Harry Byrd of Virginia and some real mavericks in the party, ready to vote to hold back on these amendments."

The minority leader was, of course, keeping a weather eye on his own prospects for reelection in 1954. With the first Republican president in twenty years in the White House, along with a Republican majority in Congress, Lyndon, where others would have seen disaster, saw only opportunities. He immediately realized that the situation now offered him the possibility of becoming the most visible Democrat in the country. He would, he planned, deal with the new president, possibly the most idolized and beloved man in the country, by allying himself and his Democratic minority as firmly in the Eisenhower camp as possible. After all, Ike wasn't your usual run-of-the-mill regressive Republican. And he certainly had gotten those votes in Texas, hadn't he?

Within two months of the opening of Congress in 1953, Lyndon had his chance. Certain Republican members of Congress had waited eight years for their party to take control of Congress and "do something" about the Democrats' "sellout" to the Russians at Yalta and again at Potsdam in 1945. Ike, who had had some hand in these agreements in his role as Allied supreme commander, was naturally reluctant; he compensated by submitting to Congress a relatively harmless resolution that did little more than condemn Soviet "enslavement" of Eastern Europe. Senator Taft, although barely able to continue in his role as majority leader, was not about to give in that easily and insisted that the language be stiffened to indicate that the pacts entered into with the Russians under a Democratic administration, might actually be legally invalid.

Lyndon was quick to see the double advantage of pleasing his own liberal Senate Democrats, who naturally defended the Yalta and Potsdam agreements, and at the same time aligning the Democratic party with the popular president against the Taft conservatives, whom he denounced as attempting to "divide us in the face of the enemy." Eisenhower had, Lyndon said, issued "a clear call for America to speak with a united voice against the Soviet enslavement of free peoples." He himself intended to join with his president; he would not think of treating this as a partisan matter that might "jeopardize the president's prestige before the country and the world."

Stalin's death on March 5 interrupted the progress of this little drama, and then Taft's illness forced him to leave his post. When it was back to business as usual, the conservative Republicans had run out of steam. In the end no resolution of any kind was passed. But Lyndon had his new public role down pat—that of defender of the president against the majority of his own party.

But for all his newfound stature, Lyndon never forgot his constituents, the folks back home who had sent him to Washington and would, God willing, continue to do so. Every week he taped a radio broadcast which was carried over various Texas stations. In his July 6 talk he praised Ike, the "good soldier," whom he must safeguard by "an unusual form of bipartisanship . . . a combination between the president, some elements of his own party, and the Democrats against large groups of Republicans who tried to sabotage his program up and down the line."[1]

Lyndon had no intention of suffering the same fate as the two previous Senate Democratic leaders who had lost their bids for reelection.

SUMMER OF '54

George E. Reedy: "Actually Johnson won the 1954 election in 1953. There were many candidates who were reported to be ready to run against him, including at one time a rumor that Shivers might.

"There was quite a bit of thought that Johnson would be beat in '54, and what we did was arrange a whirlwind tour of Texas in 1953. He visited every major city. We estimated that he shook about 225,000 hands, made two or three speeches a day; he was hitting big towns, small towns, cities, villages, hamlets. He went through east Texas cafés drinking coffee with people. He hit Amarillo, Lufkin, Tyler; he hit just about everything you could think of."

Carroll Keach: "He came to Robstown and made a speech at the high school. Going up the steps, he turned around to Cliff Carter and he said, 'Cliff, I want to see every schoolchild in Robstown.'

"Cliff said, 'Senator, do you realize that we are on a very tight schedule and we've worked for months to get you a place to speak before the General Baptist Convention of Texas in Corpus Christi?'

"And he turned around to Cliff, and he said, 'Are we going to join the "Can't Do It Club" right here on the steps of the Robstown High School?'

"There was a young police officer standing there. Lyndon said, 'Son, go out there and get on that police radio and tell every school in Robstown, parochial and otherwise, that Lyndon Johnson is coming by and wants to greet the schoolchildren.' And he did.

"He started out at the Negro school. They had them lined up on the sidewalk, and he got out and made a little talk. He went by the two parochial schools. We visited every public school.

"He told them all to tell their mothers and daddies they saw a United States senator today and they wanted them to vote for Lyndon Johnson."

Reedy: "At the end of that tour, nobody wanted to run against him. Except for Dudley T. Dougherty. Which is the sort of thing you dream and pray will happen."

Dudley T. Dougherty was at the time thirty years old; he was a freshman in the state legislature, and although he had given Adlai Stevenson financial support in 1952, when he announced his candidacy for the U.S. Senate in the July 24 primary, he appeared to be far to the right of Pappy O'Daniel. He said that he was an isolationist, that the United States must immediately withdraw from the United Nations, that diplomatic relations with the Soviet Union must be severed at once, that Franklin Roosevelt, who was senile at the time, had sold out the United States at Yalta, that Harry Truman, who may also have been of unsound mind, had done the same thing at Potsdam. Besides, both Truman and Roosevelt were pro-Communist and possibly secret members of the Communist party. He said that except for himself, all other politicians in Texas were "afraid of sinister, hidden powers. Against me are the press, the vested interests, and all political machines."

Dougherty began his campaign with a telethon that lasted twenty-nine hours; it was to have been the first of three telethons. There never was another.

Creekmore Fath: "Maury Maverick[1] called me the next day, and said, 'Did you watch the telethon?' I said, 'No, Maury, I didn't because he didn't buy Lyndon's station. You couldn't see it here in Austin.'[2]

"Maury said, 'Lyndon Johnson's the luckiest sonofabitch in the world.' And I said, 'Why?' He said, 'You're going to have to vote for him.' And I said, 'Why?' He said, 'Last night in answer to a question Dudley Dougherty called Eleanor Roosevelt "an old witch." And that is only the beginning.' I said, 'You're not serious.' But sure enough he was, and so—this was Lyndon's genius in politics—I had to vote for the sonofabitch every time he was on the ballot because his opposition was always so goddamn much worse than Lyndon was.

"Dudley—well, he was rich; his daddy was a lawyer, and he handled a lot of the oil lease business in south Texas. So when his daddy died, Dudley's mother inherited something like eighty million, and Dudley was put on an allowance of something like eight hundred thousand dollars a year. In the 1954 campaign he ran around the state in a red fire truck and spoke from the back of it, with the bells clanging. His campaign slogan was 'Clean the Godless Communists Out of the State Department.'"

Reedy: "Johnson made only a single speech in Texas during that whole campaign. He never mentioned Dudley Dougherty's name, did not put out any campaign literature, and he only took out one ad—you always take out one ad in all of the weekly papers; that's expected of you."

Willie Day Taylor: "I ran an office in Austin for Lyndon in 1954. Lots of people called in about the campaign. One lady in particular, who had worked in his previous campaigns, called and wanted to work. And I said, 'I'm sorry; we have no campaign.' She said, 'Well, just send me some literature.' 'I'm sorry, we have no campaign literature.' She said, 'Well, just send me some cards, some pins, something I can pass out.' I said, 'I'm sorry, we don't have any cards, or pins, or anything.' She said, 'Well, where are Lyndon and Bird, or would you know?'"

Not only did Lyndon not campaign, but his office issued frequent statements saying that he was so concerned with the affairs of the nation and the world that it was simply impossible for him to leave Washington. Indeed, he voted by absentee ballot—to save time, his office said.

The primary on July 24 ended with 875,000 votes for Lyndon, 350,000 for Dougherty.

Gerald Siegel: "I remember the night that Johnson won the primary in '54. The first man to get up and congratulate him in the Senate was Goldwater."

The other event of major portent in the summer of '54 was the arrival on the Washington scene of Billy Don Moyers of Marshall, Texas, a sophomore journalism major from North Texas State College. Moyers wrote Johnson a two-page letter requesting a summer job in the senator's office, and offering as credentials three years of training as a reporter for the well-known east Texas newspaper publisher Millard Cope.

Bill Moyers: "How the letter got to Johnson, I don't know. Walter Jenkins probably pulled it out and said, 'Here's someone from Lady Bird's hometown.' Johnson called Millard Cope and asked him, 'What about this fellow who wrote me this letter? Is he all right?' Millard Cope said, 'Yes, he's all right.' So I got a call saying, 'Come on up.'

"I went to see Walter Jenkins in the old Senate Office Building. After we talked he said, 'Let's go meet Senator Johnson.' So we took the elevator down to the basement, and we took the train across, and just as we ended our little subway trip, LBJ came out of the elevator and walked toward us. Walter said, 'Mr. Johnson, I'd like you to meet Bill Moyers.' And Johnson stuck out his hand. And my first impression of Lyndon Johnson was that huge hand that just enveloped mine. He said, 'Millard Cope's friend.' I said, 'Yes, sir.' He said, 'Well, I hope you're not as conservative as Millard, but I hope you're as loyal.'

"I was sent downstairs to the basement to address 125,000 envelopes to his Texas constituents. But suddenly after two weeks they got an overload of mail, and someone asked me to answer some of it. So in addition to what I was doing during the day, I would stay at night drafting replies to mail. And there my experience in the newspaper helped, and in two or three weeks I wound up in P38, sitting at a desk just outside his office, answering mail.

"Late in the day I'd be the only one left in the office, and he'd call me in, and I'd sit there—I wouldn't breathe—I'd just sit there and listen."

But the summer of '54 was remarkable for other reasons besides the fact that Lyndon captured the Texas Democratic primary and added Billy D. Moyers to his intimate circle. On June 16 a phenomenon called the Army-McCarthy hearings drew to a close. And on August 3 a bipartisan committee of senators brought together by Lyndon was authorized to look into the affairs of the senator from Wisconsin, Joseph Raymond McCarthy.

JOSEPH RAYMOND McCARTHY

William S. White: "I never said to Johnson except on one occasion, 'I think you ought to do such and such.' This was in the time of Joseph McCarthy when I was very, very upset about McCarthy.

"I thought he was destroying civil liberties in this country. I went to Johnson and said, 'You really must do something about this damned fellow.'

"He said, 'Bill, that's a good point, but let me explain something to you. If I commit the Democratic party to the destruction of McCarthy'—what he meant was an attempt at something like censure, something of that sort—'first of all, in the present atmosphere of the Senate we will all lose and he will win. Then he'll be more powerful than ever. At this juncture I'm not about to commit the Democratic party to a high school debate on the subject "Resolved, that communism is good for the United States," with my party taking the affirmative.'

"Now, later on, Johnson did indeed go after him and he got him in the sense that he brought about the creation of the select committee that investigated McCarthy. But he waited until the atmosphere was right."

It was to be quite a while before the atmosphere was right. McCarthy seemed to be exactly what a large number of Americans wanted at the time. He was fighting communism, wasn't he? So what if his methods were sometimes a little rough? It took a brave man to ferret out the Commies and the sissies in the State Department who were selling this country down the river.

As the cold war grew colder and then heated up in Korea, the mood of the majority was bitter, and many people were frightened. What Winston Churchill called an iron curtain sliced Europe more or less in half, and when the Soviets detonated their own atomic bomb in 1949, the fright increased noticeably. It was generally agreed that agents in this country must have been passing the crucial diagrams and formulae out through an incredibly complicated spy network. The greatest danger to our security, most Americans felt, was not Soviet scientific expertise, but what was referred to as "the Communist conspiracy" in our very midst.

True, most nuclear scientists said that it was not necessary to steal anything; once it was known that such bombs were possible, scientists in any country would figure out how to build one. But then it was also said that most nuclear scientists were Communists themselves. Dr. J. Robert Oppenheimer, sometimes called "the father of the atom bomb," had once been intimately associated with members of the Communist party, and was, many thought, a party member and/or spy. And what about Alger Hiss, who most people thought had been an assistant secretary of state *at least*.[1]

Moreover, it was believed that a whole atomic bomb could easily be smuggled into the United States in a small briefcase, and once it was detonated, half, maybe three-quarters of the population would be wiped out. It is easy now to scoff at such ideas, but they were real enough at the time. The members of "the Communist conspiracy" had to be exposed and punished. The few that the FBI had succeeded in arresting were obviously only the tip of a gigantic iceberg. Those others, those clever people against whom the FBI could unearth no real evidence, those were the people so rightly subpoenaed to appear before our ever-watchful congressional committees—the House Un-American Activities Committee, for example, or the Senate Subcommittee on Internal Security, or the Senate Permanent Subcommittee on Investigations. Or sometimes all three. And it looked for a while as if the only man who knew how to deal with the menace of domestic Communism was Joseph Raymond McCarthy.

First elected to the Senate in 1946, on his second try, McCarthy seems to have been oblivious to the political potential of the domestic Communist issue until late in January 1950 when he had dinner with three acquaintances, one of whom was Dean Edmund A. Walsh of the Georgetown School of Foreign Service.

Joe confessed that he was worried; he would be up for reelection in 1952, and his Senate record so far was most undistinguished; there had been certain charges, true unproven, of illegal money coming to him, and he had introduced no legislation of importance. Then too, he felt he didn't have a single issue on which to campaign.

Dean Walsh, considered something of an expert in the fields of both domestic and foreign communism, asked why Joe didn't take on the issue of the subversion and danger of American Communists. Joe thought he would try it out on February 9 when he spoke to the Republican Women's Club in Wheeling, West Virginia.

Joe's speech in Wheeling was pieced together from a *Chicago Tribune* editorial, a recent address in the House by Congressman Richard M. Nixon, and a report written back in 1946 by James F. Byrnes, then secretary of state, on which departmental employees had or had not been discharged from the department as a result of proved or alleged disloyalty. Byrnes said that 79 out of some 3,000 department employees had been dismissed; 285 had been accused of something or other; of those, 204 were still working for the department. Later McCarthy said it was 205, sometimes 206. He did not take the trouble to find out what, if anything, had happened in the more than four years since; these employees, he told the Republican ladies, were still making State Department policy. No wonder, he said, we had lost China to the Reds!

The speech evoked a minimum of excitement across the United States, and even in Wheeling the local radio station got so little reaction on broadcasting the speech that the next day it followed its usual practice and "scrubbed" the tape. Thus nobody, including McCarthy himself, was ever sure of exactly what he had said.

Coincidentally, and of enormous help to the establishment of McCarthy's credibility, was the release only the day after the Wheeling speech of the testimony of one Klaus Fuchs, then residing in Waldsworth Prison, England, who confessed that he had indeed spied to obtain atomic secrets for the Soviet Union and that among those working with him had been David Greenglass, Harry Gold, Morton Sobel, and Julius and Ethel Rosenberg.

That same day McCarthy arrived in Denver and was surprised and delighted to see the number of reporters waiting to question him about those Communists still working in the State Department. Could he produce the list? McCarthy said that of course he could, but the plane for Salt Lake City, his next destination, was already boarding and he must hurry.

In Salt Lake City in a television interview, he said he had told the women in Wheeling that he had a list of seventy-six "card-carrying Communists still working for State."[2] When not long thereafter Lincoln White, who was press officer for the department, asked to see the list, McCarthy sent a telegram not to White but to President Truman telling the president that in case he didn't know, he himself could call Dean Acheson and get the list—"or a much longer list of those whom your loyalty board found as being disloyal and who are still working for the department." He also asked Truman to make available to Congress any information they might need to help in exposing Communists. And he added, "Failure on your part will label the Democratic party as being the bedfellow of international communism. Certainly this label is not deserved by hundreds of thousands of loyal Democrats throughout the nation and by the sizable number of able and loyal Democrats in both the Senate and the House."

After that whenever he appeared in public, whether on the Senate floor or not, Joe was never without a list in his hands, usually waving it in front of his audience, and his desk in the Senate was always piled high with "documents" that he said proved his charges.

Also after that until his downfall what he said was almost daily front-page news. In those innocent days almost nobody ever asked to see proof of his increasingly wild charges. And the power of the senator from Wisconsin continued to grow—not that he seemed eager to use it for much of anything except to make more and more accusations.

George E. Reedy: "There were some things about McCarthy Johnson couldn't understand. He recognized him as a menace, but I think he thought that McCarthy was just a northern version of a southern demagogue. Now with the southern demagogue, once he had established his position, you could make a deal with him. But you couldn't make a deal with McCarthy. Just to begin with, he didn't really have any set goals. He could always get plenty of money, from the rich and from the poor: from certain of the rich, including a good many rich Texans, he could get whatever he asked for, and from the poor, thousands of letters poured into his office every week, many of them containing a few dollars in cash or a small check.

"Joe did, I think, want power, but the kind of power he wanted was very vague. I don't think he ever thought far enough ahead to consider that he might be a man on a white horse riding into the White House.

"Some people criticized Johnson for not acting quickly enough. But most people don't understand the Senate. At that time there was a feeling that if the people of a state wanted to send a sonofabitch to the Senate, that was their business, and the Senate was very, very reluctant to attack a guy like McCarthy. Not through fear. I don't think many, if any, of those senators were afraid of McCarthy. McCarthy may have thought they were, but they weren't."

Hubert H. Humphrey: "Lyndon kept saying that we had to wait until McCarthy began attacking the more conservative, the respected, the senators of what you might call the old school.

"He'd say—I heard him say it about other things, too, it was one of his favorite expressions—he'd say, 'If you're going to kill a snake with a hoe, you have to get it with one blow at the head.' And he'd give a dramatic demonstration of what he meant with his hands, those hands that were just like a couple of great big shovels coming down."

Senator Carl Hayden of Arizona was a quiet man, a student of American history, and chairman of the Senate Rules Committee. As early as April 1952 he spoke against the junior senator from Wisconsin after McCarthy attacked the chief clerk of the Rules Committee, Darrell St. Claire, who had also once been a member of the State Department's loyalty board. McCarthy said that in the latter capacity St. Claire had voted to clear a man named Edward G. Postinak, an economist in the department, although McCarthy said St. Claire had seen "twelve separate FBI reports" opposing Postinak's clearance.

On the floor of the Senate, Hayden said, "The name of Darrell St. Claire has been dragged into this dispute without any basis of fact at all."

Hayden received a chorus of support from Senators Margaret Chase Smith, Mike Monroney, Hubert Humphrey and Herbert Lehman.

Publicly that day Lyndon said nothing at all, but that night he told friends in the press, "Joe has made a lifelong and powerful enemy in Carl Hayden, and Carl is not a man who forgets easily."

Still, he told colleagues, the time had not yet come to move against Joe.

Gerald Siegel: "He kept saying to those people who were impatient, 'Now just wait a minute. The time will come, and when we've got enough votes to be sure we'll win, we'll move.'"

Whatever the mood of the Senate, when November 1952 rolled around McCarthy had no difficulty being reelected; moreover, the overall Republican victory secured for

McCarthy the chairmanship of the Permanent Subcommittee on Investigations of the Senate Government Operations Committee, a position of dubious merit for which Joe, however, had long been hankering. Never mind that past activities of the subcommittee had generally revolved around such dry material as departmental bookkeeping. Joe had other plans for it. First he fired the subcommittee's chief counsel, then hired a dark-haired young man who had been known as a kind of prodigy—Roy Marcus Cohn, age twenty-six. Another contender for the spot had been young Bobby Kennedy, age twenty-seven, whose father had personally telephoned McCarthy to request the job for his son. It was not an unnatural request: the Kennedys had been entertaining Joe socially for some time, and one Irishman always deserves the support of another at campaign time, and afterward.

William O. Douglas: "Jack Kennedy would always dismiss McCarthy as, 'Well, he's an old friend. Known him for a long time.' And he treated him as a sort of screwball guy that needed some help.

"But there was some tie there. The Kennedys were financing McCarthy in some of his campaigns—how much, I don't know. I think Jack realized that the man was dealing in excesses and stepping over the bounds of propriety. But I think he was too close to McCarthy to make a really objective analysis of what was taking place."

Then, in November 1953, Roy Cohn's friend and coworker on the Subcommittee on Investigation, G. David Schine, was drafted into the army and sent to Fort Dix. Although the army had publicly promised to treat him like any other draftee, he nevertheless received a great many privileges. Still, Cohn was furious; he felt that Schine should be investigating communism at Fort Dix or elsewhere and should at the very least have the rank of lieutenant. Cohn made his feelings known to the army, but except for its tender treatment, Private Schine was left to laze around Fort Dix without even one stripe on his sleeve.

Into the midst of this from Cohn's point of view less than idyllic situation, came the case of one Major Irving Peress, a chubby, forty-year-old dentist hailing from that "bubbling, fomenting hot-bed of Communist conspiracy"—New York City. Peress, on his induction into the U.S. Army Dental Corps in late October 1952, had invoked the Fifth Amendment when filling out a loyalty form in which he was asked, as were all such inductees, whether he had ever been a Fascist, a Communist, or a member of any other group advocating the overthrow of the U.S. government. Approximately a year later Peress was promoted to major in accordance with a law that automatically provided for such promotion.

When the news of Peress's promotion and his perfidy in invoking the Fifth Amendment reached McCarthy and Cohn, Peress was asked to appear at the Federal Courthouse in Foley Square, New York City. That day—January 30, 1954—Peress refused to answer any questions about possible Communist affiliations not once but twenty-four times. When Peress served out his allotted time at Camp Kilmer, New Jersey, McCarthy and Cohn tried to prevent his honorable discharge. But by the time McCarthy's letter demanding that Peress be retained at Kilmer arrived, Citizen Peress was discharged and gone.

A few days later McCarthy summoned to a private hearing the commandant of Camp Kilmer, Brigadier General Ralph W. Zwicker, a veteran of D-Day on Normandy Beach, commander of the Second Infantry Division during the Battle of the Bulge, winner of the Legion of Merit with Oak Leaf Cluster and of the French Legion of Honor with the Croix de Guerre with Palm. McCarthy proceeded to scream and shout, rant and rave at Zwicker for not interfering either with Peress's promotion or his honorable discharge, declaring that the general was "not fit to wear the uniform."

A great many people were shocked by McCarthy's treatment of General Zwicker, people who had previously felt that while Joe's methods might at times be a little rough, they were perhaps not altogether inappropriate. After all, he had largely been dealing with unknown people with strange names or State Department officials who were and are thought to be both perverse and, isn't it almost the same thing, subversive. But a war hero, that was something else again. And although thousands of letters of support continued to reach McCarthy's office every week, a perceptible swell of anger and apprehension began to be apparent among many people who were by no means orthodox liberals.

The reaction in the country that Lyndon had predicted was slowly beginning to happen.

The further investigations into the Peress case and the army's alleged attempt to conceal espionage activities within its own ranks—popularly known as the Army-McCarthy hearings—were scheduled to begin on April 22.

In 1954, and for a long time thereafter, there were only two major networks and neither of them would consider the idea of broadcasting the entire proceedings. But what was known as the third network, the American Broadcasting Company, succumbed to the persuasions of Senator John McClellan, one of the three Democratic members of McCarthy's subcommittee, and Lyndon Johnson, who had first impressed McClellan with the importance of national exposure.

Sam Houston Johnson: "Lyndon didn't have any special fondness for the military, but he knew that what McCarthy was doing was a very dangerous thing for this country. And he knew that the newspapers alone and two minutes a night on television during the army hearings wasn't enough. McCarthy had to be seen day after day during the entire hearings on the army. He thought that would make people see what the bastard was up to, and it did."

As plans for the hearings by the subcommittee continued, its members, already sharply divided along party lines,[3] became positively polarized as to the nature and intent of the investigations. Not only would the committee look into charges against the army concerning the presence of Communists within its ranks and its alleged attitude of lenience toward same—McCarthy's issue, supported by the other Republicans on the committee—but it would also turn about and investigate the army's countercharge of "grave misconduct" against McCarthy himself and Chief Counsel Cohn for interference with the army in the matter of preferential treatment to Schine.

That the three sets of charges bore little relation to each other did not seem to be sufficient reason for not lumping them all together. It was untidy, to say the least.

The army's counsel for the hearings, who was serving without fee, was Joseph Hye Welch of the prestigious Boston firm of Hale and Dorr. Welch, a small man of most unmilitary bearing, spoke with what might be called a semi-Boston accent, and spoke it slowly, sometimes as if he were half asleep. There was, however, nothing either small or sleepy about his mind.

The hearings were held in the Senate caucus room. McCarthy was in rare form, interrupting repeatedly, exasperating his fellow senators, not to mention the army brass, and always playing to that invisible audience in all those living rooms across America.

At the end of the second week of hearings Lyndon's friend Bill White, then Senate correspondent for the *New York Times*, wrote that the hearings were a mess, and that none of the combatants remained unscathed. A great many senators—and from their mail it would appear a great many voters as well—were incensed that the hearings, held at the taxpayers' expense, appeared to be largely dealing with a private who made frequent trips to New York nightclubs with a brassiere model on his arm when other privates at Fort Dix were confined to the base.

By June, the confusion of issues in the Senate caucus room had reached such a point that the Republicans, at least, would have been glad to suspend the hearings indefinitely, but the army would not give ground, and the Democrats, led of course by Lyndon, backed them up, sure that if McCarthy kept on long enough he would bring about his own downfall.

That day came, as many who watched the hearings will remember, when McCarthy, incensed by Welch's success in confounding Cohn in the witness chair and making him look particularly foolish, counterattacked by suddenly introducing into the fray the name of a young man in Welch's firm who, McCarthy said, had dubious connections. Welch must be, McCarthy insinuated, a tool of the Communist conspiracy himself or he would not have attempted to force on the committee as counsel a certain Fred Fisher who had once been a member of a suspiciously leftist organization called the National Lawyer's Guild.

Senator Mundt, acting chairman, interrupted to say he had no recollection of Mr. Welch having recommended Mr. Fisher as counsel, but McCarthy, ignoring Mundt, instructed his aide to get the story of Fisher and his Communist-front organization out to the press at once.

Welch rose and, after a dramatic pause, defended young Fred Fisher, who had, Welch said dryly, removed himself from consideration as assistant counsel by openly volunteering his past association with the National Lawyer's Guild. "I said," Welch told the committee, "'Fred, I just don't think I'm going to ask you to work on this case. If I do, one of these days that will come out and go over national television and hurt you like the dickens.'"

With another pause for the irony of it all to settle in, Welch turned back to McCarthy.

"Little did I dream that you could be so reckless and so cruel," he said in a voice for the first time touched with emotion. "I like to think I'm a gentle man, but your forgiveness will have to come from someone other than me. . . . Have you no sense of decency, sir? At long last, have you left no sense of decency?"

There was, when he finished speaking, a long moment of silence, after which the entire room, with a few obvious exceptions, rose to prolonged applause. Chairman Mundt called for a five-minute recess.

That was, those who were there and many who watched agreed, the beginning of the end.

But yet another factor was to figure in McCarthy's downfall. Almost a year before the Army-McCarthy hearings finally concluded on June 16, a reporter from the *Washington Post* came across an article by one J.B. Matthews in the July 1953 issue of the *American Mercury* entitled "Reds in the Churches," in which Matthews said:

> The largest group supporting the Communist apparatus in the United States today is Protestant. Since the beginning of the first Cold War in April, 1948, the Communist Party of this country has placed more and more reliance on the ranks of the Communist clergy to provide the party's subversive apparatus with its agents, stooges, dupes, front men, and fellow travellers.

On July 4, a story about the article and about Matthews himself—a former Methodist minister who, it turned out, had been hired by the McCarthy subcommittee as a Communist expert—appeared on the front page of the *Washington Post*. More than a hundred names had been mentioned in the article, including the heads of almost every Protestant theological seminary in the country. There were also some who were unnamed but unmistakably indicated, among them Bishop G. Bromley Oxnam, Methodist bishop of Washington, D.C., who was identified only as a man who had helped the Communists by speaking out against "self-appointed vigilantes masquerading in patriotic robes."

Humphrey: "The story about Matthews was, of course, picked up by the wire services, and that morning when Johnson walked into the Senate cloak room, he went over to the ticker tapes where the AP and UPI dispatches that had been pulled off the machines were put.

"When I came in, he waved his arms at me and said, 'Come on over here.' And he showed me this story about Matthews. He said, 'I've told you, when you let one of these demagogues go long enough, he gets in trouble. This is the beginning of the end for Joe McCarthy. Now Bishop Oxnam is a friend of Harry Byrd's. In attacking Bishop Oxnam, McCarthy has struck at the heart of the Senate. Because Harry Byrd, who is a powerful man, is going to take this personally. And that is going to be a fatal blow.

"'They've all been saying I was never going to do anything about McCarthy, and I wasn't—not until the time came. Well, now it has.'

"I've never forgotten how he put it. He said, 'As long as McCarthy was eating up you ADA bomb throwers, as long as he was just on the generals and the State Department, that was raw meat for him. He was making all kinds of headway and you couldn't stop him. But with all these bishops, especially Bishop Oxnam, he picked the wrong guys.'"

Lyndon was right; Harry Byrd, the powerful Virginian who could and did treat the state as a duchy, did what he rarely found it necessary to do: he spoke on the floor of the Senate. Clearly angry, he demanded that Matthews "give names and facts to sustain his charges or stand convicted as a cheap demagogue, willing to blacken the character of his fellow Americans for his own notoriety and personal gain." All three Democratic members of the subcommittee attacked Matthews for what he had written. They were joined by Senator Charles E. Potter of Michigan, and Matthews was dismissed from McCarthy's subcommittee by a vote of four to three.

Humphrey: "Lyndon still took his time. As I say, he was attacked for it and abused for it, but he never ever jumped at a decision. He spent weeks and months on every political decision he made while he was in the 'Senate. He felt his way through. It was like walking through a mine field; he found out where every one was planted before he put down his foot to take the first step."

Even before the army hearings opened, Lyndon had started his study of Senate records on how those senators who appeared to have broken Senate rules had been dealt with in the past.

Humphrey: "I don't remember when he first mentioned appointing a select committee to deal with McCarthy, but it was soon after the Matthews incident, and he mentioned it to other senators, too, preparing them for what he had in mind."

On August 3, 1954, a bipartisan "select committee" was authorized by a vote of seventy-five to twelve. Eight senators did not vote; McCarthy voted present.

Humphrey: "Lyndon kept discussing who was going to be on 'that committee to go after McCarthy,' as he described it. Naturally, the traditional liberal response was to assume the membership would be and ought to be the people of ideological purity. But that was wrong, of course. That would be, as Lyndon said, just grist for McCarthy's mill.

"I was in his office one day when he said. 'I'm going to put John Stennis on the committee. He's a former judge, and he's fair. I'd trust him with my wife. He is basically a political conservative, but he's patriotic, and he understands the Senate.'

"Then he said he was going to put Ed Johnson of Colorado on the committee for the Democrats, and the new senator from North Carolina, who'd also been a judge, Sam Ervin, Jr.

"Senator Knowland, who was the majority leader then, chose his three members with a good deal of help and prodding from Johnson; Knowland was really against the whole thing, you know—afterwards he went back on them and voted against the censure.

"But the committee chairman was, I always thought, a very good choice—a Mormon, a conservative, a very reserved but also fair man—Arthur V. Watkins of Utah. Most respected. The other two Republicans, also conservative, also difficult if not impossible for McCarthy to attack, were Francis Case of South Dakota and Frank Carlson of Kansas.

"McCarthy couldn't say they were Communists, but he did end up by saying that Watkins was 'stupid' and that the committee had been the 'unwitting'—or 'unwilling,' I forget which—'handmaiden of the Communist party.' He said that the Senate debate on the committee report was a 'lynching bee.'

"Johnson had told me a long time before—told me point-blank—that the one thing that would trip McCarthy up was to violate the code of the Senate. He said, 'He can attack people all over this country, but when he picks on the conservatives and violates the rules of the Senate, he's through.'"

Chairman Arthur V. Watkins, the Utah Mormon, allowed no television or movie cameras in the caucus room when the hearings of the select committee began on August 31, 1954. Watkins, who was sixty-six, told newspapermen, "Let us get off the front pages and back among the obituaries. That would suit us fine."

Reedy: "The thing that interested me was an awareness of strength in men that I myself didn't know was there. I'd always liked Watkins, but I hadn't realized what a very shrewd man and what a very strong man he was. It would never have occurred to me, although it occurred to Johnson immediately, that Watkins was one of the ideal men to have on that McCarthy committee. And it had never occurred to me that anybody as gentle as John Stennis could actually get up in a cross-floor debate and not only hold his own but mop up the floor with an Irish brawler like Joe McCarthy, which Stennis did. I think Joe McCarthy was cleaning blood off himself for two weeks after he made the mistake of trying to tangle with Stennis."

There were nine days of hearings, from the last day of August until mid-September. Edward Bennett Williams, McCarthy's expensive attorney, was allowed to speak; the Senator was not.

After the 1954 November election a special session of the Senate convened to debate the recommendations of the select committee. In the end it was agreed McCarthy should not be "censured" but "condemned" for failing to appear before a committee that had been looking into his private financial matters and for his treatment of General Ralph W. Zwicker. During the Senate debate even these mild charges were softened, and about all Joe was really "condemned" and "censured" for was that he had said that Watkins was "stupid"; that the select committee hearings had been a "lynching bee;" and that its members were the "unwitting handmaidens," and "the attorneys in fact of the Communist party." And his wrist was ever so gently slapped for not having discussed his finances with the proper Senate committee.

Humphrey: "The resolution to condemn was mild, but at the time any resolution at all was a miracle."

Sixty-six Democrats voted for the condemnation (the only Democratic nonvote was that of Senator John F. Kennedy of Massachusetts, who was confined to the hospital after a back operation; of course he could have paired, but chose not to. Except in wartime such Democratic unity was unprecedented.

Paul H. Douglas: "Johnson was responsible for the Democratic vote. With the northerners it was easy; with the southerners, including the mossbacks, I just don't know. But I'll tell you this. He was magnificent in that fight. Simply magnificent."

Price Daniel: "Most of the letters I received from Texas were in favor of McCarthy, and especially after I voted to censure him, I received some from I'd say a half dozen old friends that just threw me overboard after I voted to censure McCarthy. You know McCarthy would never have been censured at all if he'd gotten up and apologized to the United States Senate. Barry Goldwater and I went to him and tried to get him to do that, and he just wouldn't do it."

In 1954, the year of the Senate vote, a *Fortune* magazine survey showed that McCarthy's popularity among Texas businessmen was higher than any place else in the United States—except Chicago. According to a Gallup poll, 36 percent of Americans still supported McCarthy after the vote, and more than a thousand of his supporters, including little old ladies in tennis shoes and mink coats, arrived in Washington with a petition bearing, it was said, a million names lauding the senator and his good works. These were, they said, the vanguard of "Ten Million Americans Mobilizing for Justice."

No matter. It was over.

Harry McPherson: "He never recovered. I'm not sure why. I would just see him lurch down the halls in the mornings, and he had a kind of bloated face with heavy jowls; he really looked terrible. And he would make those long, awful, incomprehensible speeches, seconded by other Republican drunks. He was clearly finished."

Elizabeth Rowe: "Lyndon used to say to me, 'You see, you always wanted me to hurry, to speed it up, but I kept telling you, you can't speed it up. You have got to know when the time has come for you to win.

"'Now I was right, wasn't I? We've done it. We've got him. He's finished.'"

MAJORITY LEADER

In the 1954 congressional elections, the forty-eight to forty-seven Republican majority in the Senate had exactly reversed itself to the Democrats, and at age forty-seven, Lyndon Johnson took his front row center aisle seat as the youngest majority leader in the history of the Senate.

True, Wayne Morse of Oregon, that indefatigable Independent, was once again in possession of the crucial vote. Without his vote on their side, the Democrats could not be sure of a majority. However, it is unlikely that Lyndon was ever more than moderately uneasy about that. Morse had, after all, been sitting on the Democratic side of the aisle for two years now, and he had almost registered as a Democrat that summer. Moreover, the Oregon Independent had, with his defection from the Republican party two years before, lost his influential committee assignments, a situation akin to banishment from the French court to the provinces in the seventeenth century, and the feeling definitely was that he would more than welcome a seat on the coveted Foreign Relations Committee, not to mention his old position on the Labor Committee, if the majority leader saw fit. And the majority leader would, of course, be happy to oblige—*if* the Independent party of one voted Democratic.

As majority leader, Lyndon again proceeded to demonstrate his genius for taking a position of small inherent power[1] and building from it his own position of enormous power. The title of majority leader itself, as evidenced by the men who had held it in the decade before Lyndon, meant virtually nothing. One would have to reach back all the way to Joe Robinson of Arkansas, majority leader from 1928 to 1937, who died in office the first year Lyndon was in Congress, to find a man who derived anything like the same kind of power from the job. Lyndon had observed Robinson while he, Lyndon, was in Washington as Kleberg's secretary; as a young congressman he had attended Robinson's funeral, listened to the eulogies, and rubbed shoulders with men of influence. The Senate of the mid-fifties was a far different place from that of the mid-thirties, and Lyndon Johnson as a person bore little resemblance to Joe Robinson, but with both the Senate *produced* as it had not before and has not since.

How Lyndon managed that came to be known as the "Johnson method" or "system," both of which incorporated the "Johnson network" and the "Johnson treatment." Through his method or system Lyndon controlled, for example, who was put on what committee and, sometimes more important, who was *not* put there. He also decided, once a bill was out of committee, when it should come to the floor and, once on the floor, when it should come up for the vote. He decided which of the president's bills the Democrats should back, and which not, and he decided when a bill was, and when it was not, worth risking defeat on.

The Johnson network consisted of those people Lyndon could, to varying degrees, depend upon for advice, help, and, whenever possible, actual votes. The network, although heavily Democratic, included a few Republicans—Styles Bridges, for example. It included conservative Democrats like Robert Kerr and liberals like Humphrey and Morse. It included men of influence like Richard Russell and men of almost none like Allen Frear of Delaware. Sam Rayburn, from his vantage point in the House, was part of the network. Bobby Baker was part of the network.

Then there was the Johnson treatment.

Benjamin C. Bradlee: "When Johnson wanted to persuade you of something, when you got the 'Johnson treatment,' you really felt as if a St. Bernard had licked your face for an hour, had pawed you all over.

"When he was in the Senate, especially as majority leader, it was like going to the zoo. He never just shook hands with you. One hand was shaking your hand; the other hand was always someplace else, exploring you, examining you.

"And of course he was a great actor, bar fucking none the greatest. He'd be feeling up Katharine Graham and bumping Meg Greensfield on the boobs. And at the same time he'd be trying to persuade you of something, sometimes something that he knew and I knew was not so, and there was just the trace of a little smile on his face. It was just a miraculous performance."

William Jorden: "His ability to knock heads together—to get two men who basically didn't share the same views, who just fundamentally disagreed with each other and perhaps didn't like each other personally—he could be standing there, kind of defiant, with two members of the Senate, just insisting that they come to some type of accommodation with each other. Not tomorrow, not next week, but right then, right there.

"When he talked to somebody, Johnson used to get right up close and poke him in the chest; at the same time he would drop his head and cock it to one side and really come in to talk to you with his head coming in under your face. And he would poke you in the chest with his finger and cock his head under and look up at you and talk, all at the same time."

Robert S. Allen: "Humphrey told me how Johnson gave him pep talks and Humphrey demonstrated saying, 'He'd grab me by the lapels and say, "Now, Hubert, I want you to do this and that and get going,"' and with that he would kick him in the shins hard. Then Humphrey added, 'Look,' and he pulled up his trouser leg and, sure enough, he had some scars there. He had a couple of scars on his shins where Lyndon had kicked him and said, 'Get going now.'"

But the Johnson treatment and the Johnson network involved considerably more than personal theatrics.

Sam Shaffer: "I've covered Congress for twenty-eight years, and Lyndon Johnson was the only man I would call a genius—an authentic legislative genius. In calling him a genius I mean he had an extraordinary extension of the political talents that we associate with competent politicians.

"In other words, Hubert Humphrey was a very able politician. Styles Bridges of New Hampshire was one of the ablest, good in getting legislation through, achieving compromises, and so forth. Everett Dirksen was even shrewder and slicker. But none of these men had that touch of genius."

J. William Fulbright: "When Lyndon was majority leader he was a master at managing the Senate and at reconciling people with diametrically opposed views. Nobody could match him. He knew every personal interest of every member of the Senate just like he knew the palm of his hand. He knew how to bring people together, because he could appeal to their different interests. If he asked Harry Byrd to do something, he always knew what it was that Harry wanted in return."

Hubert H. Humphrey: "He'd come on just like a tidal wave sweeping all over the place. He went through walls. He'd come through a door, and he'd take the whole room over. Just like that. Everything.

"He was not delicate. There was nothing delicate about him. He was not a ballet dancer. He was a downfield blocker and a running fullback *all the time*."

Although Lyndon's majority on the Senate floor was slim, it was enough if managed properly, and no one knew better than the senior senator from Texas how to do that. Besides, since Eisenhower was still at loggerheads with his own party while popular as ever with the country at large, there was political advantage to be gained from making it appear that Ike and the Democrats marched to the same drum, quite splendidly, while the Republicans were forever out of step.

Lyndon, after Eisenhower's State of the Union address on January 6, 1955, said, "The president correctly states a Democratic premise when he says that the general good should be our yardstick on every great issue of our time. We will consider his program in that spirit."

Not everything went swimmingly, however. On January 9, his whole being emanating peace and goodwill and the spirit of cooperation, Lyndon went blithely, if painfully, off to the Mayo Clinic for a kidney stone operation. In his absence, and much to his dismay, even horror, his old friend Sam Rayburn accepted the call of the Democratic National Committee chairman Paul Butler to an immediate showdown with Ike on a proposed tax cut. Eisenhower, mindful that the following year would bring presidential elections, produced his own tax reduction plans, but of course *that* one, Rayburn said, benefited corporations and rich people, not the rest of us. The Speaker offered his own bill, a twenty dollar across-the-board tax cut for every man, woman, and child in the land.

Lyndon's dilemma was acute. Eisenhower called the Rayburn plan "some kind of a height in fiscal irresponsibility," a sentiment with which Lyndon privately agreed, and with which he had little doubt about the concurrence of a majority of senators on both sides of the aisle. But the lines were drawn, and he had to support Rayburn. Moreover, the weeks he might have spent effecting one of his famous compromises were spent in shuttling back and forth to the Mayo Clinic and in convalescence. When he finally returned to the Senate on March 9, his back in a brace and his energies sapped, it was too late. The lame little compromise he managed—the same twenty-dollar tax cut for heads of households but only ten dollars for dependents and none at all for dependent spouses—was hardly the sort of thing to appeal to the five conservative Democrats, led by Harry Byrd and Walter George, who had committed themselves to Ike.

So with his first major bill as majority leader, Lyndon went down to defeat.

However, that incident was an exception in a generally unbroken series of successes. A major success was the minimum wage bill.

Humphrey: "In 1955 the issue came up in which the minimum wage was increased to a dollar from seventy-five cents. That was the time that Spessard Holland of Florida was the leader against it. It was late in the afternoon and I was there with Johnson on the floor, and I remember him looking around and saying to me, 'I think we'll pass that minimum wage bill now.' He had a little short quorum call. Zip, zip. He called it up, and it passed just like that—voice vote—zip. And boy, oh boy, Spessard Holland came charging out of the Senate dining room, and he wanted to know what had happened here. Oh, he was just jumping, screaming, hollering and pounding the desk. Johnson said, 'Well, Spessard, I had a little quorum call. If you fellows aren't on the job around here, I've got legislation to pass.' He just slipped it right on through there. Zip! Oh boy, they were furious with him."

Warren Magnuson: "Timing—he learned that from Roosevelt. If you haven't got the votes, what's the use of butting your head against a stone wall. The theory being that if you have a bill you want passed and you bring it up, you're going to be all righteous, 'I'm going to fight this until my doomsday. This is *right*,' and if you lose it, you are set way back. You'll never have a chance to do it again.

"If you haven't got the votes, wait a little while. Maybe you can pick them up."

The majority leader's influence extended into other areas as well, as was evidenced by a situation Aubrey Williams, Lyndon's old boss from the NYA, and their mutual friend Virginia Foster Durr found themselves in in 1955. Although by then McCarthy's own influence was almost nonexistent, McCarthy-like activities were far from over, and Williams and Durr were subpoenaed to appear in New Orleans before the Jenner committee, a subcommittee of the Senate Judiciary Committee on Internal Security, because of their connections with the Southern Conference for Human Welfare which had been organized by the Roosevelts in the forties.

Virginia Foster Durr: "The first person I called was Lyndon. I tried to get him all day long. 'The majority leader is in conference.' 'The majority leader is in Mr. Rayburn's office.' 'The majority leader is on the floor.'"

She finally reached him that night: "Bird woke Lyndon up and he got on the telephone. I said, 'What do you mean, letting this happen? You're the majority leader, and sending this Jim Eastland down to rake us over the coals this way?' He said, 'Well, honey, I don't know one thing in the world about it. What can I do?'

"I said, 'Well, Lyndon, in the first place, you can see that no Democrat comes with Jim Eastland. Let Jim Eastland come by himself.' The thing was, if a great big Senate committee came down, it would be real difficult not to be cited for contempt or get in real bad trouble, but I thought we might be able to handle Jim Eastland because he was so unpopular in the Senate as well.

"Well, Lyndon didn't say what he would do. He never made any declaration. 'Well, sweetie-pie, I love you; I'll do what I can.' But when Jim Eastland got to New Orleans, no Democrat was with him."

The most the Jenner committee could come up with were accusations consisting of epithets like "comrade" and "fellow traveler," for which there was, embarrassingly, no proof whatsoever.

John Kenneth Galbraith: "Several years later I went down to spend a weekend with the Johnsons at the Ranch. And we were reminiscing about the Durrs. Johnson told me with some pride, and I think more accuracy than some of the things you occasionally got from him, that he had intervened to make the Jenner committee lay off the Durrs. He said, 'That's one of the best things I've done in the Senate!' And he used the word *forced*— 'forced them to lay off the Durrs.' As majority leader he had enough leverage to do just that, and I'm sure he did do it."

Booth Mooney: "Johnson deplored Eastland's militant racism and laughed privately at his internal security subcommittee's obsession with the subversive threat to America posed by international communism. But he admired the political astuteness of the man from Mississippi and knew he could depend on him for support of legislation designed to benefit the rural areas of the nation.

"He sometimes entertained me and other staff members by telling us how he would expect Eastland to react to various situations. His Texas twang would disappear to be replaced by a heavy southern drawl.

"'Jim Eastland could be standing right in the middle of the worst Mississippi flood ever known,' he joked on one occasion, 'and he'd say the niggers caused it, helped out some by the Communists.'"[2]

If Lyndon had a guiding principle in the early majority leader years, it was flexibility. In the fifties the spectrum of political belief encompassed by the Democratic party was enormous. Lyndon had to deal with the Senator Eastlands of the party, and half an hour later he would be confronted by the liberals. He was anxious, this first year of his majority leadership, to please them, or at least appease them, and how better to do that than by guiding through the Senate some bill dear to their hearts for which they had given up hope?

He chose John Sparkman's public housing bill which proposed to construct a hundred and thirty-five thousand housing units a year. Homer Capehart, with Eisenhower's blessing, offered an amendment reducing the number to thirty-five thousand and the Republicans were confident that conservative southern Democrats would join them on this one. Minority leader William Knowland was complacent, Capehart positively cocky, and Lyndon feigned defeatism.

George E. Reedy: "Capehart thought that for once he had Lyndon Johnson beaten, so much so that shortly before the vote he actually walked over to him and said, 'Lyndon, this is one time I've really got you. I'm going to rub your nose in it!'

"He'd counted the votes, and he'd figured there were enough southern Democrats that would vote against public housing that, combined with the Republicans, he'd carry the day. He didn't know that we'd been up almost every night talking to southern Democrats. When he got to the roll call, the first southern Democratic vote was no against the Capehart amendment. I was sitting up in the gallery, and Capehart's chin almost bounced off the desk. He turned around, and sure enough they went down bing, bing, bing, bing, bing—every southern Democrat, even the most conservative. And Capehart was roundly defeated. The press gallery nearly collapsed out of sheer shock, because they'd all written stories that morning predicting that this would be a major defeat for Lyndon Johnson as Democratic leader.

"What we had done was quite simple. We'd explained to the southern Democrats that they might just as well vote against the Capehart amendment, because it was a public housing amendment, too. And the fact that it only called for thirty-five thousand was just the same thing as saying, 'Well, my daughter is only a little bit pregnant.' We persuaded them that the best tactic was to vote against the Capehart amendment for thirty-five thousand public housing units, and then vote against the whole bill. That would take care of their problems down home. We didn't mind their voting against the whole bill because we knew that after the amendment was out of the way the Republicans would have to turn around and vote for the whole bill.[3]

"And it worked exactly that way."

Humphrey: "When the vote came on the Capehart amendment, I was on my way back from Minnesota. The planes were stacked up over Washington. It was a tight vote, and Johnson stalled the debate in the Senate as long as he could, and in the meantime he was on the phone with the control tower out here at National Airport telling them to get that plane in here that had Humphrey on it. And he did get the plane in; there was a car waiting for me and it rushed me on into the Senate so I could cast my vote."

The Capehart amendment failed thirty-eight to forty-four, and the bill itself, which the liberals had virtually written off, passed by a comfortable sixty to twenty-five. Even Paul Douglas, the least compromising of all Senate liberals, joined the victory celebration, on the fringes anyway.

*   *   *

John Stennis: "From my experience with him, in all those ballots we had when I was on the same side with him or against him, he never did tell me anything false about the bill or what was in it. Or what he would or wouldn't do.

"He just didn't do it. And therefore he could always come back to you. And I think that was one of the mainstays of his influence.

"Another thing. He was very skillful in taking an issue and getting a group, like a conservative group, to have a prominent conclusion about certain phases of the bill, and then he could influence the liberals with some other parts of it or some other emphasis. In that way he could gradually narrow the gap as far as getting the vote. As long as you're honest about it—I think that was one of the great secrets of his success."

Gale McGee: "Lyndon Johnson knew how to count. He didn't care where you stood on a bill; he wanted to know that you were going to stand there so that he could count. And if it was a close type of thing and you were in a position where it would be embarrassing to you, many times he came to me and said, 'Now I need your vote on this, but don't you dare give me your vote because it would ruin you in Wyoming. I know Wyoming.'

"He was always very straightforward that way, and I appreciated that fact and was always cooperative where I could be.

"On the other hand, where it was a matter that could have no deep and abiding concern to Wyoming, he was most persuasive as he would tower over you and get his head down close to your nose and really work you over in terms of trying to get you to take a position that he favored."

With the Capehart amendment victory, Lyndon's status among his colleagues was at a high-water point. The conservatives approved his cooperative attitude with Ike, and the liberals were getting more than they had expected. Lyndon basked in the rare esteem and approval.

True, he was sometimes more tired these days than he had ever been, more than he really cared to admit to himself. But then he had been doing more than he had ever done. True also, Dr. Cain at the Mayo Clinic had warned him all the way back in March to slow down; well, he might do that when things slowed down a bit for him, though they never seemed to. And now that the warm months were upon them all, tempers began to be frayed, Lyndon's most of all. And the end of the session was still a long way off.

THE LONG SHADOWS

He was smoking at least three packs of cigarettes a day, sometimes more. He now never had lunch unless a legislative matter was being discussed. And Zephyr Wright remembers that he missed dinner more often than not, and when he did make it home, usually as late as ten or eleven, he was almost never alone, and he sometimes scarcely touched the meal. He was drinking more than usual, too, and despite his haphazard diet, he was putting on weight; he weighed 225 pounds.

He was also even more short-tempered and impatient than usual, "and that," said a former staff member, "was very short-tempered and impatient indeed. Usually he made up for his temper by later being extra attentive and loving, but he didn't seem to have time for that anymore."

On the night of July 1, 1955, after a particularly hectic day in the Senate, he had a late dinner with Sam Rayburn and Senator Stuart Symington. Rayburn, noting that Johnson's drinks were darker and larger and more numerous than usual and that the circles under his eyes were also unusually dark, told him, mildly, it was almost always mildly from Mister Sam, that he ought to take it easy. Lyndon said that he would, just as soon as the session ended. Sam Rayburn started to say that would perhaps not be soon enough, but he did not say it.

It was after midnight when Lyndon got home, but the next morning he was at his Senate office at a little after nine, somewhat later than usual, even on Saturday. He had two meetings with Senate staff members and then went to his tailor and was measured for two suits, one brown, one navy blue, both double-breasted. His suits were always double-breasted in those days and they always looked as if they had too much cloth in them. Later he was to wonder, often and audibly, why his clothes didn't look as trim as those of John F. Kennedy. They cost just as much, sometimes more. Why? He always felt not only that he was, as Dean Acheson put it, not a likeable man but one who was downright unattractive as well.

At noon Lyndon had lunch, the wrong lunch, two frankfurters on buns, beans, and half a cantaloupe. After lunch he held a brief, tumultuous press conference in which he had planned to describe the not unimpressive accomplishments of the Senate since he had become majority leader. During the press conference—he was never without a cigarette—he was especially irritated by a series of questions on the McCarran-Walter Act, which Senator Herbert Lehman, the esteemed New York Democrat, was proposing to repeal.[1] The Associated Press reporter was insistent. How, he wanted to know, could Lyndon, who like everyone else except Kefauver had voted for the bill when it was first passed, now be, as he claimed to be, or did he, for its repeal? "Could you explain that to us, sir? I should be very curious."

William Theis: "And that reporter, a quiet, soft-spoken man, who incidentally still covers the Senate, pressed Mr. Johnson curiously on why he wouldn't be more forthcoming on this one issue. Tremendously agitated, Johnson exploded—roaring resentment at the reporter's inquiry and his persistence.

"The outburst, so clearly out of character, concerned and shocked us all. He quickly broke off the session. He left almost immediately to go to the George Brown estate in nearby Virginia."

Lyndon had arranged to spend what was left of the July Fourth weekend at George Brown's in Middleburg, Virginia, a fancy community where fox hunting still abounds.

Lady Bird was to join him the next day; on Saturday Lucy (not yet Luci) was celebrating her eighth birthday.

Lyndon started for Middleburg around five.

Lyndon: "I was alone in the car with the driver, Norman Edwards. I remember it suddenly began to seem terribly close, and I told Norman to turn on the air conditioner. He said it was already on, and I said to turn it on full steam, and he said it was already on full steam and was getting very cold.

"I was an hour late, and I was trying to make it up, and there was this sense of pressure. My chest hurt, and I thought to myself, if only I hadn't eaten that cantaloupe at lunch. About twenty miles away from George Brown's place, my chest really began to hurt, as though there were two hundred pounds on it. Then I belched a little and felt better. But when we arrived I told Norman I didn't feel well and to stay around a bit because I might have to go back.

"Well, I had some baking soda—all along I thought I had indigestion—and I went to bed. But I got this feeling that I couldn't breathe."

Clinton P. Anderson: "When we came into the house, George Brown said, 'You better go in and see your buddy. He's not very well.' I didn't think he was serious about it, but Lyndon was stretched out. I asked him what his trouble was, and he said, 'Well, I ate some bad food.' They were giving him baking soda. Well, that's all right for heartburn, I guess. But by then I thought I saw the symptoms of heart trouble. I told him to go to a hospital and have a doctor examine him. And he was furious about that. He didn't want any doctor.

"I found out later that he knew there was a story coming out in the *Washington Post* about him as a possibility for the presidency. He didn't want to knock it in the head, kill it right at the beginning."

Lyndon: "Clint Anderson was there, too, and he said, 'Lyndon, I think you may be having a heart attack.' He'd had one himself. I said, 'Don't scare me, Clint,' but he was serious, and we sent for the doctor. The doctor thought I was having a heart attack, too. He said, 'You'll probably go into deep shock in about one and a half hours, which just gives us time to get you back into town.'

"On the road in, I still felt as though I had someone stepping on me, but I was able to talk all right. I got out a cigarette, I remember, and the doctor told me to put it away, but I said, 'Let me have just one more, and then I'll never have another.' So I had that cigarette, and it's the last I've ever had. [2]

Lyndon, accompanied by the doctor, went by ambulance to Bethesda Naval Hospital where he was whisked to the cardiac section on the seventeenth floor.

Lyndon: "When I got to the hospital, they were all there. I gave Bird my keys and the money out of my pocket. I had them call Earle Clements, who was the Democratic whip then, and to tell him to take over the leadership for the rest of the session. Then I began to go into shock. I felt sort of addled. I was conscious part of the time, or half conscious anyway."

As much as it sounds like something somebody (probably Lyndon) made up, Lady Bird remembers that he told her to go to the tailor at Connecticut and K.

"Tell him to go ahead with the blue suit," he said. "We can use that no matter what happens."

Lyndon went into shock at ten thirty that night. During the night he came close to dying, and the next day his chances of survival were considered no better than fifty-fifty.

Lady Bird moved into a room next to his and stayed the entire time he was in the hospital.

On the morning of July 5 Earle Clements, who interrupted his campaign for reelection to return to Washington, read a statement to the Senate dictated by Dr. James Cain, Lyndon's personal physician: "Senator Lyndon B. Johnson has had a myocardial infarction of a moderately severe character. He was quite critically ill immediately following the attack, but his recovery has been satisfactory. He should be able to return to the Senate in January."

Still, there were positive aspects. The executive, legislative, and judicial branches of the government vied in expressions of concern. Letters arrived from the president, the vice-president, every member of Eisenhower's cabinet, most of the ninety-five other senators and many of the congressmen, half the Supreme Court, Bernard Baruch, Walter Winchell. The floor of the Senate echoed with praise from such otherwise divergent quarters as Ellender of Louisiana, Morse of Oregon, and Margaret Chase Smith of Maine. Herbert Lehman of New York called for a standing prayer and said that Lyndon was beloved by his colleagues. The *New York Times* cited him for his "matchless tactical skill"; Humphrey called it "legislative genius." Dick Neuberger said: "He is as liberal as he *can* be."

Dr. Cain: "Lady Bird, after his heart attack, wanted to know if he should retire from the Senate. There was a great deal of talk and thought about this. The main thing she wanted to know was, 'Do you think that his staying in the Senate will shorten his life in any way?' We both recognized that he could not do it in moderation, and the question of whether or not he would continue as majority leader—we thought about this some. I remember telling her that I didn't think he should retire from politics, that I thought if he were sitting on the porch at the LBJ Ranch whittling toothpicks, he'd have to whittle more toothpicks than anybody else in the country. Politics had been his life. It was what he knew, what he liked; and I told her that we had no evidence that continuing on working with a *degree* of moderation would shorten his life a bit."

As before Lyndon was an impossible patient. As soon as he got out from under the oxygen tent he ordered a radio, and Dr. Willis Hurst, who was caring for him at Bethesda, agreed to let him have one on the condition that he not listen to any news, which might prove upsetting; Lyndon promised and, of course, listened only to news, switching from station to station. He had a habit of shouting back at newscasters when what they said did not please him, and his nurses reported that they almost immediately acquired larger vocabularies, though few of the words they learned were suitable for use in mixed company.

Lady Bird turned her room into an office. No matter. Within a week Lyndon demanded that key members of his staff, Walter Jenkins and George Reedy and occasionally others, be on constant call. His staff took over the office of the floor physician.

Lyndon decided one radio was not enough; he demanded and got a transistor with an earphone. He frequently had on both radios at the same time. He was visited for fifteen minutes by President Eisenhower, who was on his way to a summit conference at Geneva. Vice-President Nixon came; he stayed for an hour. Rebekah came, stayed for several days, and granted a series of interviews during which she told a number of stories, some of them true, about her illustrious son; many of them were cleaned-up versions of stories that Lyndon told about himself.

And Homer Thornberry, who had been a page in the state legislature when Lyndon visited his father there, and who succeeded Lyndon as congressman from the Tenth District, was a frequent visitor: "I played a whole lot of dominoes with him when he was recovering. We used to play every night, and he said I let him beat me. I'm not sure about that. He was a shrewd domino player and very tough to beat, very."

On August 7, to the relief of many of those of the staff at Bethesda, Lyndon was discharged. The report said that there had been "no complications" and that "he has made steady improvement."

Lyndon told reporters that the doctors expected him "to be as good as new in January" when Congress reconvened.

On August 27, his forty-seventh birthday, Lyndon, Lady Bird, Sam Houston, and Dr. Hurst flew to Fredericksburg for Lyndon's return to the Ranch.

Mary Rather: "I drove up to Fredericksburg at the time the plane was supposed to land, and they came off. He was the thinnest thing you have ever seen, and his clothes were just hanging on him. And of course Mrs. Johnson looked bad, too."

Lady Bird: "One of the first things we did, we put in a swimming pool. It was very clear that one might as well spend what one had and not wait for later, because there might not be any later. So we put in the swimming pool, and it was great exercise for Lyndon."

Willard Deason: "Up until that point he had always been very much in a hurry in everything that he did; he was always impatient to move on. I think during his recuperative period there was a change in his philosophy and his thinking. He became more deliberate, more thoughtful of people of lesser energy.

"During that period of recovery he played cards with his daughters—they were children at the time, and he had time to talk and visit with them where heretofore it had been, 'Daddy loves you, kiss me,' and run. He moved into a more nearly normal family relationship, had more time for his children; realized the value of having hours with them."

Rather: "He woke up at dawn. We had a milk cow up there, a Jersey that mooed right under the window nearly every morning until somebody came and milked it. I'd get up and go across the river to pick up the mail and the newspapers. Sometimes we would sit under the trees and eat breakfast.

"I remember those long shadows, and the skies kind of hazy sometimes like they are in the fall. It was way out in the country, and it was so quiet and still. The awareness of his heart attack made it such a long, sad time, four months, I guess it was—September, October, November, December. He didn't talk about it, not to me, but you knew that his mind was working and knew that his whole career was at stake, whether to return to

Washington, or whether to resign from Congress. Being the kind of man he was, he wouldn't have gone back and been a less active member.

"He didn't know how much his condition could stand. Although when he began to recuperate, began to get better and stronger, he got more cheerful."

George E. Reedy: "He made only two speeches that fall—one up at Dallas introducing Sam Rayburn, and then this big speech at Whitney. And that was an experience that I'll never forget; that's where he laid down a thirteen-point program for the Democratic party, which included a number of things—an extended Social Security bill, a tax revision benefiting low income groups, hospital and school construction programs, a public roads program and a farm program and a housing program. They were unhappy with it in the North because it advocated removing natural gas pipelines from federal price control. But he also had a number of things in it like the poll tax elimination, and it was really a very good national program."

Jake Pickle: "There was a gymnasium in Whitney, and it would hold more than five thousand people. I took a leave of absence from my job, and we went to all the communities around Whitney within, say a fifty- or seventy-five-mile radius. It became a matter of honor for everybody to do all he could to show we were glad Lyndon was back on the job. It would have been a success no matter what because that part of Texas is naturally a Democratic stronghold. But this was something special. There was a great crowd. There must have been at least seven thousand people there."[3]

Rather: "It was such a stimulating, exciting thing. He had been running hot and cold on his speech all November. He said, 'Nobody even knows where Whitney, Texas, is.' He kept working on his speech, though, and he even rewrote it as we drove from the Ranch to Whitney, and I had to type it again at the last minute. George Reedy had been staying up nights writing it. I don't know any speech that got rewritten so many times."

Reedy: "The response to that speech in Whitney was intense. The people that were there reacted—it was virtually a mass orgasm. People walked out of the armory with their eyes glazed as though they had just seen a vision of the Coming. This had given Johnson, I think, perhaps the strongest and most emotional popular following that he ever had in his whole career.

"I'm not trying to plug the speech, but it is a fact that it spread through the state, and it somehow crystallized the feelings that many Texans had, who had voted for Eisenhower but who had come to the conclusion that it was one thing to vote for Eisenhower, and it was another thing to convert the Democratic organization into a vehicle for the Republican campaign."

Pickle: "He gave them a good Democratic hand-clapping, hip-slapping speech that certainly demonstrated beyond doubt that he was back and ready to go. It was then that a lot of people started saying that Lyndon could go all the way."

A great many political figures visited the Ranch in the fall and early winter of 1955, among them Adlai Stevenson, who was consistently upstaged by Lyndon, Senator Hubert Humphrey, who was Lyndon's friend, some said captive, Estes Kefauver, who was given what was described as the "Z" treatment and Senator Robert Kerr of Oklahoma.

Then Lyndon got on the phone again, and magazine and newspaper correspondents began dropping by.

He was on hand for the reopening of Congress on January 3, but for a time, at least, he took the doctor's advice and went back to his job displaying as much moderation as was possible for him. He usually didn't get to his office until ten, and most afternoons he managed a two-hour nap, and wherever he went he had in his wallet an electrocardiogram, a habit that continued until the end of his life.

James H. Rowe, Jr.: "He came back to Washington after his heart attack at the beginning of 1956, and what he did is typical Johnson, vintage Johnson. He called me up and said he needed my help. He was just getting started and he desperately needed me. So I told him I'd give him a day a week. He said, 'No, that's not enough. I need you all the time.' I said that that was just impossible.

"The next thing that happened, Corcoran⁴ came in and he said, 'You can't do this to Lyndon. Don't you worry about the firm. We'll take care of that, but you've got to help out Lyndon.' I said, 'I don't want to work for Lyndon full time.'

"But after that everywhere I went and everyone I saw said, 'How can you let Lyndon down?' Or, 'Why are you doing this to Lyndon?' Everywhere, everybody. And, finally, would you believe it, one night my wife said, 'How can you do this to Lyndon?'

"But I still told him I couldn't do it. And then he put on his act. He started weeping, and he said, 'You know I am going to die, and nobody cares. You don't care. It's typically selfish. Nobody cares.'

"And so on. A sensational performance. Finally, I said, 'All right, goddamn it, I'll do it.'

"And within seconds the tears were gone. He straightened up in his chair, and he said, 'All right, but just remember I make the decisions, you don't.'"

THE SOUTHERN MANIFESTO

When Lyndon returned to the Senate in January of 1956, he was resigned to the prospect of operating the majority leadership by delegation, in part anyway. Besides the superbly competent and experienced Jim Rowe, he had lined up several other younger men, law school graduates, men of clear ability to serve as legal advisers to the policy committee or the conference committee or wherever he could ostensibly attach them. Usually, like Harry McPherson and James W. Wilson, they were transplanted Texans, although Gerald Siegel was from Iowa, almost as good, said Lyndon. George Reedy was still there, of course, and in the office that handled the problems of his Texas constituents, Walter Jenkins—good old dependable Walter.

James W. Wilson: "The Senate would go into session at noon. Senator Johnson would usually have a little press conference right ahead of time."

Harry McPherson: "Senators, especially those in the Establishment—the Club, as it's called in the Senate—have a great deal of respect for the leader. The maintenance of a strong leader is quite important to them. Bills that they personally oppose on policy grounds they frequently clear because they know that the leader has to take them up for one reason or another."

For example, the natural gas bill.

Of the thirteen points in 'his "Program with a Heart" speech in Whitney, Texas, passage of a natural gas bill to return to the oil and gas industry the right to set prices as high as it chose had been number seven, exactly in the middle, right where Johnson calculated it might be passed over by the country at large. There was no danger of Texans' not noticing it; in Whitney it had been applauded vociferously. But it was not a popular bill among many Democrats in Congress; it was too obviously one in which Texas's gain was everybody else's loss. Sam Rayburn had, however, through considerable personal effort, managed to squeak it through the House the previous summer;[1] Lyndon was determined to do the same in the Senate.

McPherson: "What Johnson was doing in the Natural Gas Act of 1956 was to do just enough to keep them off his back down in Texas, to keep a lot of oil money from going against him in the next election. He was never a friend of the oil and gas industry. He was never a believer in an ideological sense of the 27½ percent depletion allowance. He was not a disbeliever; it was just something that he resolved was a fact of life for any Texas senator."

Actually in January of 1956 prospects for the Harris-Fulbright Natural Gas Act were more favorable than ever before. Unlike his predecessor in the White House,[2] Eisenhower viewed the bill benignly, and a coalition of Republicans and southern Democrats assured passage. The liberals, however, would have their say, and proceeded to do so at great length.

True, Lyndon could have put pressure on his colleagues to limit the quantity of their opposition, but he was basking in the certainty of passage and was no doubt delighted to have an issue on which the liberals could vent their energies so early in the session. His sanguine attitude changed abruptly, however. On the afternoon of February 3, Francis Case, Republican of South Dakota, listed on Lyndon's tally in the yea column, rose on the Senate floor to announce that he could no longer support the bill. He had just been informed, said Case, that the Superior Oil Company had forwarded to him a "campaign contribution" of twenty-five hundred dollars—cash, needless to say—as a token of their approval of his stand, and in light of such blatant pressure on the part of the oil and gas lobby, he must in all conscience change his vote.

If Case hoped to lead a vanguard of similarly insulted knights in shining armor, he was disappointed, because no fellow senators came forth with a like experience, and as far as the world at large was concerned, Superior Oil's action was an isolated case and one no doubt frowned upon by Humble Oil, Kerr-McGee, Phillips Petroleum, and Brown and Root, among others. Lyndon stormed about, but Case, of course, was a member of the minority and relatively immune to Lyndon's attacks; anyway, there was little indication that Case's fussiness would persuade his fellow Republicans. When the vote came three days later, Lyndon's side carried the day by an easy fifty-three to thirty-eight.

But if Lyndon thought the Case episode closed and victory won at last, he was soon to find out he was mistaken. Eisenhower, although he reiterated his approval of the bill itself, announced that he would veto it because of lobbying practices clearly "in defiance of acceptable standards of propriety."

Lyndon: "When a gas and oil bill comes in here, everybody says it's crooked, for the same reason they think a girl on the street after midnight is probably up to something. But for me, I don't accuse a girl until I see her doing more than walking."

The trouble was, no one outside of Texas ever believed for a moment that Lyndon's girl was only walking.

In March of that year, an election year although not for Lyndon, the southerners struck back in their first united opposition to the Supreme Court decisions of 1954 and 1955, which declared unconstitutional racial segregation in the public schools and in publicly financed parks, playgrounds, and golf courses. The Southern Manifesto—the brainchild of Strom Thurmond of South Carolina, probably the Senate's most avid white supremacist—was composed and/or supported with varying degrees of enthusiasm by the more respected southern powers—John Stennis, Sam Ervin, Richard Russell, Harry Byrd, and Walter George. Formally titled Declaration of Constitutional Principles, it was a cleverly formulated document designed to couple "change" with "unconstitutionality" and "civil rights" with "subversion" in the public mind.

Albert Gore: "It was a dangerous, deceptive propaganda move which encouraged southerners to defy the government and to disobey its laws, particularly orders of the federal courts."[3]

Gore surprised many of his Tennessee constituents by his refusal to sign the document. They had expected such maverick behavior only from their senior senator, Estes Kefauver, and he did not disappoint them. The other southern senator who did not sign was Lyndon Johnson.

McPherson: "The Southern Manifesto was an expression of rage and resentment at the Brown decision. Johnson recognized its potential for tearing up his own party. At the same time he knew that the Republicans had a great opportunity. If Eisenhower wished to, he could capture the black vote in the United States for the first time since Al Smith. We think of the black vote as a Democratic vote, but if you recall throughout the nineteenth century it was a Republican vote; indeed, up to Al Smith and Roosevelt it was a Republican vote.

"There was a great deal of pressure for the Republicans to seize that opportunity. At the same time there was a deep personal and political tie between the conservative Republicans and the southerners. They didn't want to rock the boat."

When asked by the Texas press to comment on why he had not signed the Manifesto, Lyndon stressed that he was "not a civil rights advocate," but that his position as majority leader of all the Democrats did not allow him to be too closely identified with any one particular geographical division. He also talked a lot about the tradition of the law of the land.

Hubert H. Humphrey: "He told me once, 'I want you to notice who signed the Southern Manifesto and who didn't. Now all your bomb throwers over there think I am the worst thing that came down here. They're all cheering Bill Fulbright because they think he's got great connections overseas. He's a Rhodes scholar, and he's got the Fulbright Act,' and so on and so on. He said, 'But he signed the Southern Manifesto, didn't he? He signed that Southern Manifesto. I didn't.'"

John Stennis: "Just senator to senator, of course, we wanted him to sign it, but at the same time we recognized that he wasn't just a senator from Texas, he was a leader and had a different responsibility in that degree. It wasn't held against him, I'll put it that way, by the southerners, that he did not sign it."

On the other hand, few senators, from the South or elsewhere, agreed with Richard Neuberger that Lyndon's action or nonaction, was "one of the most courageous acts of political valor I have ever seen take place in my adult life." More seasoned colleagues, while not questioning Lyndon's courage in general, knew him to be more frequently moved by other considerations. Few would have disagreed with Stennis that "he was politically ambitious," just as few were surprised when, at the Democratic nominating convention five months later, three Southerners put their names forward for national office: Senators Gore, Kefauver, and Johnson.

But before the convention, there still loomed the considerable press of business before the Congress. Social Security, for one. Almost every election year one could count on a Social Security bill of one kind or another coming up in Congress, but in 1956 the bill included a very real departure from the whole existing Social Security program, and senators started lining up on one side or the other very early.

The controversial issue was the disability amendment which would allow disabled workers to retire with full Social Security benefits at age fifty instead of age sixty-five. The plight of the disabled laborer was not, of course, the real problem. The real issue was whether Social Security should be used for wider purposes than mere retirement benefits, for if it were once, for the disabled, then would it not be twice, for some other group, and three times, and you know where it would lead. Directly to a Social Security-financed national health program.

Or so said the AMA, meaning our very own family doctors. Eisenhower listened and agreed. Lyndon, however, was not feeling particularly sympathetic toward Ike's sentiments considering his recent veto of the natural gas bill. Extension of Social Security had been number one in Lyndon's "Program with a Heart," and although the disabled had not been the focus of his proposal, he could see it would do quite well as an opener.

The bill, including the disability amendment, had passed the House in 1955, but the Senate, generally more conservative, was another matter.

Elizabeth Goldschmidt: "Lyndon was very close to Senator Kerr who was very much influenced by the AMA in Oklahoma. The House had added disability insurance to the bill, but when it came out of the Senate Finance Committee, owing to the opposition of Senator Kerr, it had been dropped.

"I wrote a memorandum at that time to Johnson on the political implications of the disability amendment. Of course, I said that he would have to get Kerr's agreement, that Kerr was the person who had to be persuaded. Never heard another word, but when the bill came up on the floor, to everybody's astonishment, Senator Kerr led the fight on the floor to reinstate disability insurance."

George E. Reedy: "The bill provided for widows to receive pensions at age sixty-two; it provided a disability compensation at age fifty. It was the largest single revision that had been made in the Social Security Act since it was launched, and the administration really did put on the heat to defeat that bill. I can recall we'd wake up in the morning with about a ten-vote margin on some issue, and by two or three in the afternoon it would have dropped to about three, and then it would shrink to one."

But shaky though the prospects appeared, there was, Lyndon and Bobby Baker agreed, an outside chance for passage. The clue was to find a few wavering Republicans. The positions of most were already declared, but far to the conservative right were a few whose negative votes had been taken for granted. Such as, for example, George W. ("Molly") Malone; such as the drunk, the dying Joe McCarthy.

Malone cared almost nothing about any issues not related to mining, which meant about almost nothing at all, and he had no real interest in Social Security anyway. He did, however, have a tungsten subsidy bill coming up. Tungsten subsidy was hardly an issue dear to many Democrats, but on the special request of the majority leader, when the bill came to the floor such unlikely persons as Lehman of New York, Humphrey of Minnesota, and Kennedy of Massachusetts found their hearts committed to tungsten subsidy. And when Bobby Baker marked his tally on the disability amendment, he changed Malone to aye. He marked Joe McCarthy aye, too, but Knowland got wind of that one, and asked Joe who it was, Lyndon or himself, who had voted against his censure? And Joe, easily persuaded in those days, changed his vote back again.

Lyndon later reported to George Meany that he had spent "about twelve hours a day on the Senate floor for the last four or five days" during debate on the disability amendment. On July 17 it at last came up for a vote.

Wilbur J. Cohen: "As the vote occurred, the majority leader was there keeping a record, and he saw it get to forty to forty, and forty-one to forty-one, and forty-two to forty-two, and forty-three to forty-two, and forty-four to forty-three, back and forth, which took some time. He was holding Senator Earle Clements in the Democratic cloakroom. Senator Clements would have been opposed to the legislation, coming from the state of Kentucky where the tobacco and other interests were allied with the American Medical Association in opposition to the legislation. But he was whip, and he had told the leader that if he needed his vote, he would have it.[4]

"When the vote got to be about forty-six to forty-six, after a long interlude, various senators would get up to say, 'How am I recorded as voting?' which is a technique to stall for time. And that happened for quite a long time until Mr. Johnson could see that he needed one extra vote. And after about five minutes of this jockeying back and forth, he brought Earle Clements out from the cloakroom. He had voted nay but at Johnson's request he changed his vote to aye and the bill passed, forty-seven to forty-five."[5]

The Johnson system that saved the Social Security bill was repeated, less dramatically perhaps, again and again during that period.

Humphrey: "I recall that a number of measures had passed the House to limit the powers of the Court. This was after the Supreme Court decision on school desegregation—the Brown decision—and a number of other Court decisions relating to civil liberties, what we called the Warren Court decisions.

"Now the Committee on the Judiciary in the House had passed very restrictive legislation on the Court. Those bills had come over to the Senate, and John McClellan and Jim Eastland handled those bills, and Ev Dirksen. And about four or five bills had been reported out of committee and were put on the Senate calendar.

"Johnson said, 'What we need to do to defeat them is put them all in one package—an omnibus bill.'

"On this the liberals just said no. We had a meeting of about fifteen or sixteen liberal senators. Paul Douglas was there, Herbert Lehman, Estes Kefauver, Clint Anderson, Burdick, Johnny Carroll, Frank Church—a number of them. I went to them after Johnson had talked to me and said, 'Now, look, what the leader wants to do is put these four or five bills into one bill. In other words, he will take a bill, and each of the other bills will be an amendment to it, and put it all in one package. He thinks that way we've got a better chance of defeating it, because each bill, while it has friends, it also has enemies.'

"Well, our group were just beside themselves on that. They said, 'This will mean that Johnson will ram this whole thing through, Hubert. You're being taken. If you pile them all together, it's going to get so much momentum that we can't stop them.'

"So I reported this back to him. He said, 'Well, you guys go ahead and screw around now, and see what happens.'

"One night after that, we were in session, and he left. He had told me, 'You make damned sure that there are no votes tonight, because if you get votes tonight, you're going to get beat.'

"So help me, we had a late session. He was gone, and one of the Court bills came through, got the votes. Our people had disappeared, which was always a problem. And the opposition just wore us down, and by the time there were no speakers, nobody to do it, and they called the third reading of the bill, and bango, the bill was passed. But I was able to have a quorum called, and we finally got our people back, and we got Johnson back.

"I remember he was so mad, he said, 'Well, there you are, I told you what would happen. That bunch that you're associated with just won't take any orders; they will not march together; they will not listen to a program of action. They just want to go their own way. And now you see what happened.'

"So I went back to the group and told them that I'd had another meeting with Johnson, and I said, 'Now listen, we've got to follow his advice.' And they finally agreed. And so the bill was drawn up, all the diverse elements on one bill, and then Johnson took control of it. I'll never forget that, because this was a major civil liberties fight. And Johnson was able to defeat all those bills at one fell swoop—which was to me a masterful display of strategy."

By the summer of 1956 the Johnson-Eisenhower "spirit of cooperation" was decidedly on the wane. Eisenhower had vetoed Lyndon's natural gas bill, and Lyndon had confounded the president with the addition of the disability amendment to a Social Security bill that Ike could not afford to veto in an election year. Then in the final days before adjournment of Congress, Eisenhower's civil rights bill[6] passed the House in a somewhat transformed state and was sent to the Senate.

The situation was a touchy one. A civil rights bill, the first in decades, reaches the Senate at the end of a session when important bills long awaiting action are still pending and the opening of the nominating conventions looms in the foreground. Ordinarily under such circumstances a new bill would almost automatically have been deferred to the next session.

But the leading liberals, although they could not have hoped for passage, and although their motive in otherwise tying up the Senate seems unclear, were nevertheless unwilling to allow the bill simply to pass to committee. They were no doubt acting from experience. The committee concerned was Senator Eastland's Judiciary Committee, and they had seen many bills, their kind of bills, consigned to its depths never to emerge again. The first step was to prevent the bill from going to committee, and after that they would play it by ear.

So the liberals schemed, and on July 23, when Eisenhower's bill, considerably diluted, at last cleared the House, and by a large majority of 279 to 126, Senator Douglas set off on foot personally to accompany it from the House to the Senate floor. Senator Lehman, meanwhile, stood guard in the Senate to prevent anything untoward happening.

But Lyndon had gotten wind of their plan—some say Hubert told him—and as majority leader it was his concern to see that the last days of the session proceeded as planned and the necessary bills got passed. There were no doubt other ways to accomplish this, but Lyndon always preferred to beat a man at his own game. Almost before Rayburn's signature had dried, and a good quarter of an hour before Douglas reached the House, the bill had been spirited out a side door and was on its way at a fast trot to the Senate. Unsuspecting Senator Lehman, knowing his friend could not walk *that* fast, allowed himself to be briefly decoyed off the floor, and in that interim, with a sympathetic Lister Hill of Alabama presiding as planned, the bill was brought on the floor, read through twice without pause, and referred to committee.

Lyndon felt very good about the whole thing. The Johnson method had worked yet again, and the leader was sure that the eyes of the nation were on him, that his cleverness would be widely applauded. The facts were not quite like that. The eyes of the nation were anywhere but on a smart move by the Senate majority leader. Liberals saw the move as a delaying tactic to put off civil rights legislation yet again. And while Lyndon felt that he had emerged as a national figure, a potential Democratic presidential nominee even, clearer eyes saw that Lyndon was still hampered by his being a Texan, and that Adlai Stevenson, who had not had to have a civil rights record, would once more be the nominee. Adlai was also unhindered by a recent heart attack and a Texas accent.

ADLAI AGAIN

Of course, long before the congressional events of 1956 there was no question in the mind of almost any Republican about who their candidate would be—except, possibly, in the mind of Dwight David Eisenhower himself. At almost every press conference the general said, seemed to say anyway, that he was very likely not going to be a candidate, probably. And Adlai once more was being reluctant. He would or he wouldn't. It depended.

On the other hand, as early as September of 1955, Sam Rayburn wrote a friend, "It looks to me that Stevenson is way out in the lead for the Democratic nomination, and I believe he can defeat any man the Republicans can nominate, since it appears that Mr. Eisenhower will not make a second race."[1]

That same month Mister Sam wrote another friend, "I agree with you that if Lyndon Johnson were in good health he would make a splendid candidate in 1956. Whether or not he would want to take on that load at that time is another matter. He is young and would still be good for 1960 or 1964."[2]

One of Lyndon's visitors back at the Ranch in September 1955, when he was recovering from his heart attack, had been Adlai Stevenson, who was his usual urbane self, although Lyndon's enthusiasm for him was, again as usual, restrained. When, however, Adlai spoke at what was then the only University of Texas, in Austin, he received a standing ovation from the students and faculty and townspeople present.

The speech was without wit—Adlai had again been warned against that subversive tendency, especially in Texas—and what he said was filled with ponderous phrases calling for help for the farmer, embracing labor unions, collective bargaining, graduated income taxes, and mass purchasing, meaning more money for the poor to spend on this and that. There was not an idea that had not been part of Democratic dogma since the days of Franklin Roosevelt.

Sam Houston Johnson recalled that Lyndon said, "Pretty damn good speech. Now if all you had to do to run for and be president was talk, Adlai'd be best. But it ain't."

Only four days before Adlai's Austin speech, the chances of a Democratic victory in 1956 had improved greatly. President Eisenhower on one of his frequent golfing vacations had suffered a severe heart attack and was under an oxygen tent. That meant that Richard Nixon was the almost certain Republican nominee, and even in those relatively halcyon days, Nixon was a man for whom most Republicans, almost all Independents and Democrats, and even Dwight Eisenhower showed little enthusiasm.

Newton Minow: "After Governor Stevenson's speech, Stevenson, Mr. Rayburn, Grace Tully, and I drove to the Ranch in Johnson City. Grace Tully was, at the time, I think, one of LBJ's secretaries; she had, of course, been FDR's secretary. We drove through the night, and we expected that when we arrived, because it was quite late, the Johnsons would be asleep. But instead we found them all waiting for us out on the front porch there. I could see Mrs. Johnson was upset, very properly so, because her husband was still recuperating from his heart attack, and here he had stayed up to greet us."

Mary Rather: "It was a beautiful, beautiful night with a great big moon, a nice gentle little breeze, and we sat out in the yard until they arrived about 10:30 or 11:00 P.M., and talked for about an hour after they got there. It was kind of an unusual meeting, you know, to be out in the moonlight under the big oak trees and to have a man who had been a presidential candidate and might be again sitting in the front yard."

Minow: "Johnson said to Adlai, 'Now there are about fifteen reporters here who, because Ike is sick, have descended upon us and who think that you, Adlai, and you, Mister Sam, and I are here plotting about how to take over the government while Ike is dying. And we're not going to let them do that.

"'We'll have a very early breakfast tomorrow. We're not going to let them think we're sitting here plotting. We're going to take a tour of the Ranch and invite them to come along.' Which is exactly what we did. Governor Stevenson, Mister Sam, and Senator Johnson had a private visit for a while, and after lunch we left.

"Governor Stevenson and I went back to Chicago, and we were talking about it in the airplane. He said, 'Do you know what Lyndon and Sam told me?' I said, 'I'll bet they told you that if you are going to run for president, you're going to have to really run in the primaries and become an active candidate.' He said, 'That's right,' and he said, 'I'm not going to do it. If the party wants me, I'll run again, but I'm not going to run around like I did before to all those shopping centers like I'm running for sheriff. The hell with it.'

"I knew that he didn't really mean it, but that was the net advice that he got from them at that time, and of course, subsequently, he did have to go out and run in the primaries and everything else."

A few days later Estes Kefauver, another possible Democratic nominee in 1956, also visited the Ranch; one had, it was only polite, to pay one's official respects to the recovering Senate majority leader.

Apparently, Kefauver's visit did not go entirely unnoticed. Not long thereafter Lyndon received a phone call from Massachusetts.

Lyndon: "In the fall of '55, when I was at the Ranch, Joe Kennedy called me and he said that he had talked to Senator John Kennedy and they had concluded that they would like to support me for president in the '56 election, and they wanted the go-ahead to do so. And I told them that I had no ambition to be president, that I would not be a candidate for the presidency, that I thought it would be a mistake for me to be a candidate."

The two men hung up, Joe Kennedy no doubt conjecturing on just how categorical was that denial, and Lyndon possibly pondering exactly what had been Joe Kennedy's real motives for the call.

Meanwhile, Texas seemed doomed to repeat its 1952 internal problems, and Lyndon and Allan Shivers were by no means political colleagues.

James Nash: "I tried my damndest to get those two together. They just couldn't get along no way. In 1956 it was in all the papers that Lyndon wanted to lead the delegation to the Democratic convention *and* to be Texas's favorite son. Shivers was against that. He was perfectly willing for Lyndon to be the favorite son but not head of the delegation.

"Well, big-hearted old me, I thought I could get this straightened out. This was not long before the Texas convention. So I invited them both to breakfast, just the three of us at my house.

"But they did nothing but fight for three hours, from seven in the morning until just about ten. They started the argument the minute they bit into their grapefruit, and it never stopped."

Jerry Holleman: "In 1956 I was executive secretary of the AFL. We had been active in what was called the Democrats of Texas [DOT], which Mr. Rayburn set up to try to win back the party from Allan Shivers. Remember that in 1952 Allan Shivers had taken the Democratic party and endorsed Eisenhower for president, and Mr. Rayburn didn't intend for that to happen again.

"So we built a coalition. The Democrats of Texas was made up of all the liberal groups—the Negroes, the Latins, the independent liberals, the loyal Democrats. We put the whole thing together: we broke the state down into areas and raised the money and hired organizers to go out and get every county ready to win its county convention to come to the state convention. It was a tough fight, because Allan Shivers didn't give up easily.

"Then Sam Rayburn tossed Lyndon Johnson into the fray by designating him as the state's favorite son for president. I think that perhaps Lyndon was not thrilled with that in the beginning, but he could not very well turn Mr. Rayburn down. So he was flung into the fight."

Booth Mooney: "Johnson kept saying, 'Suppose I lose?' and Rayburn kept telling him he wouldn't; but that he had to take that chance, that the future of the party was at stake. Finally, Lyndon agreed.

"Connally agreed to help, though not with much enthusiasm. In fact, few of the Texas Democrats seemed to be very enthusiastic that year. The main enthusiasm was among the right-wing people. They said that Johnson was a captive of the NAACP, the ADA, the CIO, and the Communist party. Not that some of those people thought there was much difference between them."

Hank Brown: "I think Johnson was always a very pragmatic politician. I think he felt, like many of us in 1956, that Shivers's day was ebbing, that his power was diminishing and waning, and that there was a new power coming in Texas. And by that time the Democrats of Texas was a growing factor—the first real coalition of Negroes and Mexican-Americans and labor. Plus he was moving nationally and was becoming more nationally oriented. Shivers was moving further to the right all the time, and I think Johnson felt that he had to take him on and help break Shivers's power in order to maintain credentials with labor and the Mexican-American and the Negro."

Margaret Carter: "Johnson was fully aware that he would never be available for a national nomination unless he could take to a national convention a delegation which did the opposite of what the delegation Shivers had led there in 1952 had done. He had to reverse the image of Texas in the minds of the kinds of people who attend national conventions from other states."

Reversing the image of a state as large as Texas was, Lyndon knew, not an easy task. Not that Democrats from other parts of the country agreed on what that image was. There was a nouveau-riche conservatism in Texas that was different from the old-family conservatism of the South in general, and totally unlike the nouveau riche or any other kind of liberalism of the North. There was a wild-and-woolly, anything-you-can-get-away-with atmosphere to Texas politics that made the state appear, to the Democratic politicos in general, *unreliable*. It was that image that Lyndon, for all his outward protestations of disinterest in national nomination, knew he had to change. And he knew there was no time to lose.

Booth Mooney wrote Lyndon's speech on May 5 at the Dallas convention to choose the state delegates to the national convention; it began, "We should not come here in bitterness and anger." But no sooner had the senator uttered the words than a voice from somewhere shouted, "We *do*, though." Boos, catcalls, angry shouts, and unprintable epithets followed. Shivers's supporters were not pleased with Lyndon's ascendancy.

That night in a meeting with his floor managers for the Dallas convention Lyndon said that whether he was defeated or victorious was their responsibility. As Mooney remembered it, Johnson warned them: "Don't even leave the floor except to go to the bathroom—and don't go there very often.

"Don't stay up late and get drunk. Don't stay up at all; go to bed as soon as you leave here. Don't sleep late tomorrow. Get out to the convention hall early. Just remember, they'll screw us nine ways from Sunday if they see an opening."[3]

The floor managers, within the range of human capability, did much as Lyndon asked. And he was indeed—true, without much enthusiasm—chosen both as Texas's favorite son and as head of the delegation.

The Democratic National Convention would open Monday, August 13, in Chicago. Stevenson was, of course, expected to win, although it had not been entirely smooth sailing through the primaries.

On March 20 Adlai lost in Minnesota to Kefauver. True, many of the Kefauver votes had come from Republicans who had crossed over. But as Lyndon many times said, "It doesn't matter how hard you explain it or how well, defeat is not the same as victory—and don't let anybody tell you different."

The day after the Minnesota defeat Stevenson held a press conference saying that he wasn't "out of politics at all," that indeed he was very much still in it. Some of the people still around him said he was a "new" Adlai Stevenson. "When something like this happens," said Adlai, "I don't feel bitter or that an injustice has been done. I feel simply that I have failed to communicate, and that I must try harder."

He then decided that he must get into the fray of the primaries, distasteful as that was. He did in fact try for a "new look," and in Florida he actually mingled with the voters during the tour. After leaving one Florida hamlet Adlai asked Harry Ashmore, who had accompanied him, how he had done. Ashmore said it hadn't been too bad, but perhaps Adlai still had a lesson or two to learn.

Ashmore said, "When you are shaking hands in a supermarket and a little girl in a starched dress steps out of the crowd and hands you a stuffed alligator, what you say is, 'Thanks very much. I've always wanted one of these for the mantelpiece at Libertyville.' What you don't say is what you did say, 'For Christ's sake, what's this?'" Ashmore added that Stevenson was so pleased with the lesson that he repeated it to his audience in the next town thus, no doubt, losing another hundred or so votes.[4]

Adlai did, however, win in Florida, and in the District of Columbia, Alaska, New

Jersey, and Oregon primaries. In California he won over Kefauver by almost two to one, and after nursing his wounds for a time, much to the relief of almost all his Senate colleagues, Kefauver finally withdrew.

Estes was not popular with other senators. He was better liked among party members in the House and in governors' mansions across the country because he was always ready to appear on a platform somewhere in support of a fellow Democrat, and his appearance never failed to draw attention. In the Senate some northerners suspected his acclaimed devotion to civil rights; his southern colleagues despised him for it, sincere or not. Many were jealous of the attention he had received when hearings of his Senate Special Committee to Investigate Organized Crime were nationally televised before an estimated twenty-million potential voters. He was a boozer, a womanizer, and an eager accepter of bribes from almost any source, pursuits not unknown in Senate circles, but he was also a loner, decidedly not a member of the Club.

In addition Estes often failed to remember the details of legislation on which he was to vote. On those rare occasions when he did vote, he would usually turn to whoever was standing nearby, often a Senate page boy, and ask, "What's my position on this one?" In the Senate he was called "The Hand" because it was always out to grasp that of a potential voter.

Sam Shaffer: "Johnson didn't like Kefauver, which is why when there was an opening on the Senate Foreign Relations Committee he gave it to Jack Kennedy. They both had presidential ambitions, and Johnson knew it, and Kefauver had seniority, but Johnson didn't like Kefauver because he was a very independent-minded person, and in the Senate he did not carry his share of the legislation."

James H. Rowe, Jr.: "One of Johnson's best stories had to do with a campaign trip Kefauver took in 1956 through parts of Texas. He said Kefauver almost always kept every audience waiting an hour or more, and in every town he made some fool mistake. Like he said, 'The greatest senator we ever had from Texas is Sam Rayburn.' Or he would say, 'Lyndon Johnson is a great Speaker.' And he would say, 'Wixahoochie' instead of 'Waxahachie,' and so forth.

"And Johnson said, 'He went through every town insulting my people, and still they looked at him with admiration, and at first I couldn't figure it out. But I remember we went to bed in Waco, and in the middle of the night I woke up Bird, and I said, "Bird, I finally figured out what it is that he's got." I told her that everybody looked at him and listened to him and said, "He is running for vice-president, and by God if he can be Vice President, I can." And that's the answer.'"

When Lyndon got back to Washington after his mitigated triumph at the Dallas convention, he was treated by his Senate colleagues as a conquering hero. Perhaps despite his unpredictable health, despite his declaration of disinterest, he would be the Democratic presidential nominee. After all, Ike, in spite of his illness and his original hope of serving only one term, had given way to his party's need for a November victory. And despite the general feeling of Ike's invulnerability, for the time Lyndon seemed to go along with the idea. Or was he only kidding? For instance, he said to Senator Walter

George of Georgia, who was tired, sick, and aging, "Walter, I guess you'll have to be my secretary of state."

Walter Jenkins: "I don't think he ever thought he was going to be either the vice-presidential or the presidential nominee in 1956. All he thought, as nearly as I could see, was that he and Mr. Rayburn might exert some influence on what happened at the convention."

The convention opened on Monday, August 13, and very few delegates thought that there was more than one candidate for the presidential nomination, although Averell Harriman continued to act like a candidate with Harry Truman's support.

Hale Boggs: "Lyndon continued to act like a candidate too; he certainly wanted to be more than a favorite son, although I do believe he thought Adlai would be nominated."

Shaffer: "On the first day of the convention in the basement of the Conrad Hilton Hotel, Johnson called a press conference and announced that he was a candidate for president of the United States. We were all flabbergasted. This Texan, this southerner. Outside of the Senate, who was he? True, he dominated the Senate almost entirely, but that was of importance only to other senators. His manager for that almost stillborn effort was John Connally, but I don't think either of them saw more than a deadlock, with Johnson possibly emerging as the dark horse."

John B. Connally: "I guess all of us hoped that he might get one nomination or the other, but I don't think any of us were kidding ourselves about the odds. Still, you never know what's going to happen at a convention. So we certainly wanted to advance his name in nomination, hoping, clearly vainly, that something would happen."

Arthur Krock: "I think Lyndon came to the convention to discover whether, as some people told him, the party was so reluctant to nominate Stevenson. Truman was trying to prevent this, as you know, and Lyndon thought that there might be a chance for him.

"He came to discover otherwise. It didn't take him more than a couple of hours to find out. So it was then, feeling as he did that Stevenson's campaigning was on the wrong basis entirely and that he needed help, it was then that he sent word over that he and Rayburn were available for the vice-presidential nomination in case Stevenson thought that he might find them necessary. And Stevenson indicated, 'Thank you very much,' but he didn't have that in mind."

The master of the 1956 national convention was James Aloysius Finnegan, of Philadelphia. He ran Stevenson's draft movement in 1952, and those who knew him agree with Jim Rowe that he was the master politician of his day.

Rowe: "Finnegan kept talking to me and to Lyndon, head of the Texas delegation's seventy-six votes, the favorite son, and all. Finnegan would say, 'I have been telling the Michigan people—Walter Reuther and "Soapy" Williams [then governor of Michigan], "Well, if you want to lose to Lyndon Johnson and all those Texans, then they'll have all the say for Stevenson.'

"And then Finnegan would say the same thing to us: 'Well, if you want all those Michigan people to make the first break over to Stevenson and get all the power. . . .'

"And that's what happened; Johnson and the Texas delegation did lose the balance of power to Michigan. But first I remember a significant, very significant moment— Finnegan and Adlai came to see Johnson. I was with him; just four of us were in the room. Stevenson and Finnegan asked for support. Johnson said, 'I have got to have something on civil rights that will not hurt my people too much.' Adlai said, 'Well, I would like to think about that.'

"Finnegan just said, 'No.' Johnson said, 'What did you say?' And Finnegan repeated, 'I said no. We are not going to give you anything.' Johnson said, 'Why not?' Finnegan said, 'Look, all we're asking for is a shotgun. If we don't give the crowd in the North that, they are going to use machine guns. The answer is no.'

"Johnson said, 'All right,' and they left.

"I later heard Johnson tell Dick Russell, who had not been in the room, 'Well, you know, I was really making some real progress with Adlai. I took my knife and held it right against him, and all of a sudden I felt some steel in my ribs, and I looked around and Finnegan had a knife in my ribs.' He laughed, and Russell said, 'Finnegan is a pro,' and that was it.

"But as I say Johnson didn't move toward Stevenson, and, again, I suppose it was because the Texas delegation knew that Adlai was going to be against gas and oil again."

In any case, on Wednesday morning at two thirty Governor Soapy Williams, himself a favorite son, turned over most of Michigan's forty-four delegates to Stevenson, and a little later Robert Meyner of New Jersey, also a favorite son, pledged that state's thirty-six votes to Adlai.

By that time a first-ballot nomination was a certainty.

The third day of the convention was nominating day. The roll call of the states was at the halfway point when the junior senator from Massachusetts stood up to nominate Adlai Stevenson. Kennedy's speech—he had rejected the draft prepared by the Stevenson staff and had, with Ted Sorensen's aid, written his own—was graceful, urbane, witty, appropriate to its subject, and was wildly cheered. Averell Harriman's nomination was seconded by old Harry—the first ex-president to accommodate a friend so—and that speech, too, or anyway the speaker, was loudly applauded.

Booth Mooney: "On nominating day Connally gave a riproaring, southern-politician– type speech (which he had rehearsed over and over in my and Reedy's room the night before) placing Johnson's name before the convention.[5] An extended and wildly enthusiastic demonstration by delegates followed. Television commentators noted with some surprise—*had they missed something?*—that participants were by no means confined to the whooping Texans and their southern neighbors. It appeared that almost every state's banner was paraded around the hall. All such demonstrations are basically sham and this one was perhaps more so than most. The show for LBJ had been organized by several Texas congressmen who went around to their House colleagues in other delegations to remind them that Sam Rayburn would keep right on being Speaker. No doubt he would be watching with interest, and would remember, which states helped to add to the fervor of the convention demonstration for his friend."[6]

Jerry Holleman: "We marched around the convention hall at least three times, wearing our 'Love That Lyndon' buttons and banners, and so forth. But it became obvious before the first roll call was over that Adlai Stevenson was going to be the nominee. The Texas delegation wanted to switch over from Lyndon and change its vote, cast its final vote for Stevenson and be on the bandwagon. Sure, they loved Lyndon Johnson, but they weren't serious in believing that he could win the nomination.

"They were after John Connally, and John was on the phone talking to Lyndon, desperately trying to get Lyndon's permission to let them ask for the floor to switch their vote over to Adlai Stevenson. Remember, Mr. Rayburn was the chairman of the convention; he was the man with the gavel. He wanted Texas to switch its vote, and he waited and he waited and he waited for Texas to change its vote before he finally dropped that gavel, and Texas wouldn't change its vote because it couldn't get a release from Lyndon. It was committed until he released it.

"So Texas never did cast its vote for Adlai Stevenson."

Very early on the morning after the nomination Adlai took a group of friends including Lyndon, Mister Sam, Governor Ribicoff of Connecticut, and Jim Finnegan to the Stockyard Inn for some food and drink; he told them that he had decided that for the first time in history he was going to throw the vice-presidential nomination open to the delegates. To a man his listeners objected. Johnson and Mr. Sam were particularly vehement, certain that since Kefauver had the best and tightest organization, that meant turning the nomination over to him. Nevertheless, Adlai was adamant.

Besides the ubiquitous Kefauver, the leading vice-presidential candidates were Kennedy, Humphrey, and Gore. Kennedy and Kefauver had plenty of money to spend and had sent large staffs to Chicago. Hubert, as always, had a small, incompetent staff and almost no money.

Senator Gore didn't have much money either, but he was acceptable to most northern liberals and had a reasonably liberal voting record, somewhat more cohesive than that of Estes.

Hubert H. Humphrey: "Not too long after his defeat in Minnesota in March, Stevenson, Max Kampelman, Jim Finnegan, and I met. Stevenson talked about the vice-presidential nomination and indicated—no said, very bluntly, too—that he did not want Kefauver. He mentioned several other people he did like. Gore, also a senator from Tennessee, was one and there were others. Then he said, 'And how about you, Hubert?' I said that, of course, I was interested but that there would be considerable southern opposition. He said that Jim Finnegan would take care of that with some southern leaders. I considered that a commitment; and by the time of the Chicago convention was working on an acceptance speech and making plans for a campaign.

"Then we heard that Stevenson had thrown the nomination open to the delegates."

George E. Reedy: "I was in the Texas caucus, so I remember very well. The feeling was definitely anti-Kefauver. Southerners didn't like Kefauver; they thought he was a traitor to the region.

"Johnson quite early decided he would push the delegation to Humphrey. And he and

Humphrey talked. I was there in the corridor somewhere and he said, 'If I can get this delegation for you I'm going to get it.'

"Johnson was trying to maneuver to Humphrey, but it was clear that Humphrey just didn't get going. So the choice was between Kennedy and Kefauver, and Johnson said, 'I think we've just got to go with Kennedy.' And he got Rayburn to make a speech about 'all these fine young men,' but it was clear, at least you got the impression, that the old man was putting the hand on Kennedy.

"And then Johnson, who arranged this God knows how, had a Mexican-American get up and say, 'I must speak for John Kennedy,' and so forth. And finally you could see it would be Kennedy, though nobody was very optimistic."

Jack Bell: "This was really a wild night. Kefauver and Kennedy were dashing about in the hotel corridors and in the basement and everywhere else, going from one caucus to another, each making his pitch. At one point, I was going down one corridor, and Kennedy came barging around a corner. Kefauver was standing with a bunch of cables around him giving a two-minute thing on TV taping. Kennedy almost collided with him as he came around the corner. They solemnly shook hands and wished each other good luck, and Kennedy went on the lope over to another caucus.

"All of this, of course, as far as Kennedy was concerned, was spearheaded by Lyndon Johnson, who at that point decided he would be a king-maker. He liked this young fellow, Kennedy, and Lyndon thought he could use him in the future, politically.

"The governor of Oklahoma, Raymond Gary, had the key votes. If the Kennedy team could have gotten Oklahoma, they might possibly have gotten the nomination for Kennedy. I happened to be there when the governor told Johnson's emissary, 'No, we won't vote for Kennedy.' His reason was that Kennedy had voted against the farm bill.

"That was the political burial of Estes, who became a defeated vice-presidential candidate. Kennedy once told me, 'My God, I didn't know how lucky I was not to win that because I would have been buried with Stevenson and the ticket, and they probably would never have heard of me again.'"[7]

A FIRST STEP

The 1956 election had a variety of interesting repercussions for Johnson, not the least of which was that it almost cost him his job—if not as leader, at least as leader of the majority. Whether or not the Democrats could retain numerical superiority in the Senate was in the fall of 1956 a very questionable matter.

For all his insistence that the Texas Democrats unite behind the party candidate, Lyndon did little to help Adlai's cause in Texas when, in a turnabout of his Dallas stand in May, he supported the conservatives against the liberals at the Fort Worth governor's convention in September to the extent that liberals who had been legitimately nominated to the next state Democratic executive committee were ousted in favor of conservative candidates. As a result, Adlai decided against campaigning in Texas at all, considering it a lost cause, an opinion few would have disagreed with; indeed Eisenhower won Texas for the second time and by an even greater majority.

But the Eisenhower victory left the Democrats with the same narrow Senate margin—forty-nine to forty-seven—that they had held in the Eighty-fourth Congress. And there were two threats to that margin.

The first came from Texas itself. The junior senator, Price Daniel, had run for the governorship, which Allan Shivers was vacating and, with Lyndon's help, he had won. Since Daniel's term in the Senate still had two years to go, a special election would have to be called to replace him, but that was not scheduled until the following year, and in the meantime it was up to the governor—still, in the fall of 1956, Allan Shivers—to appoint a successor. This was a matter of no small concern to Lyndon, because on the party membership of that successor hung the balance of power in the Senate. And Shivers had strongly supported the Republican presidential nominee.

Single-handedly, Shivers could reduce Johnson to minority leader. That thought also occurred to Eisenhower. According to Shivers, Ike came down to Texas after the election and asked Shivers what he was going to do.

Allan Shivers: "Eisenhower said, 'Well, I'm sure you're going to get a lot of pressure to appoint a Republican with the situation in Washington like it is.'

"I said, 'Well, I don't think I can do that.'"

Shivers added that he really never seriously considered appointing a Republican, and that he called Lyndon and told him so.[1]

The second threat occurred after Congress convened. Conservative Ohio had elected a Democratic senator, not so surprising considering that it was ex-governor Frank Lausche, a man almost more Republican than most Republicans. There was, in fact, talk that Lausche might actually move to that side of the aisle. Such rumors were fed by his unexplained and, in Lyndon's view, highly injudicious absence at the first Democratic caucus. When the Senate convened, the issue was apparently still in doubt, and both Republicans and Democrats put forward their spokesmen—William Knowland and Lyndon respectively—as candidates for majority leader. The motion on Knowland came first. If Lausche should vote with the Republicans, the Democrats would go down to minority status. Lausche, savoring the suspense, made no answer when his name first was read in the roll call vote; on the second call he said in a loud voice, "NO." Lyndon to his relief was still majority leader.

Yet another repercussion of the 1956 election was the formation, against the strong opposition of Lyndon and Mister Sam, of the Democratic Advisory Council.

John Kenneth Galbraith: "The DAC, as it was called, was set up as a place where the then very substantial number of Democrats who weren't in office could express themselves, these being Stevenson, Harriman, Finletter, Acheson, Herbert Lehman [who had retired from the Senate], etc., with the further idea that such a conclave would take, as it was then said, some of the Texas image off the party—inasmuch as Lyndon Johnson was majority leader and Sam Rayburn was Speaker. I was co-chairman of the DAC—to be specific, Acheson was chairman for foreign policy and I was chairman for domestic policy."

Kenneth Birkhead: "Basically it was Paul Butler's idea. He and a lot of leaders of the party felt terribly frustrated. They felt the Democratic National Committee ought to be more than just a caretaker, fund-raising operation. Many of them felt that the position taken by the leadership on the Hill, particularly Mr. Johnson and Mr. Rayburn, was too friendly to the Eisenhower administration, too conservative on some issues."

Newton Minow: "Johnson and Rayburn thought that the place for the Democratic party to set policy was in the Congress, and that the best politics was to go along with Eisenhower whenever possible and fight with him only when they thought it was very, very important. Stevenson, on the other hand, felt that the party could be rebuilt only by taking a very vigorous stand and going after the issues."

To do him credit, Paul Butler never intended that the DAC should be a body separate from the congressional Democrats. One of the first things he did was to send invitations to join to twenty top Democrats, Lyndon and Mister Sam heading the list.

As majority leader, Lyndon foresaw the difficulties of getting Republican support for legislation put forward not by fellow congressmen but by "a committee whose sole objective is to sponsor a Democratic program that will elect a Democratic Congress in 1958 and a Democratic president in 1960." He saw his role as the Great Compromiser threatened. He also foresaw, and no doubt correctly, that the committee's public statements would emphasize ideological divisions within the party, leaving an impression of disunity. And with a two-vote Senate margin, an impression of disunity could hardly be desirable.

Only two of the twenty congressional invitees—Humphrey and Kefauver—accepted, but Butler decided to push ahead anyway. The Speaker and majority leader had tacitly agreed to hear out the DAC's recommendations, perhaps occasionally even to consider them. It was difficult to do less when outside members included Adlai Stevenson, Harry Truman, and Mrs. Eleanor Roosevelt, and besides, the recommendations those three alone could agree upon would obviously be few in number.

In any case a lot of prestigious names were involved, and Lyndon considered it quite possible that he might want to draw upon them for other matters. It would be just as well if they all remained on friendly terms. And they had managed to raise an impressive three hundred thousand dollars, with more coming in, and such talents were not to be sneezed at.

Galbraith: "Johnson took steps to cultivate us to some degree. He would have various people, myself included, down to the Ranch. It's a wonderful place to go, I may say.

"In the case of Arthur Schlesinger, he got Arthur down to his office—spent a whole morning with him—from half-past nine in the morning till half-past one. Johnson went over every member of the Senate—his drinking habits, his sex habits, his intellectual capacity, reliability, how you manage him. Arthur said, 'Most informative morning I ever spent. Never got a word in edgewise.'

"Not very long afterwards, Johnson and I spent a weekend together down at the Ranch. Johnson said, 'I've been meeting with your friend, Arthur Schlesinger. Really had a very good meeting. We had a long talk. He's a right smart fellow. But, damn fellow talks too much.'"

"I was never so pleased with anything in my life as coming back to tell Arthur that."

✻   ✻   ✻

Of course the DAC was perfectly right that Lyndon, and Mister Sam, were "friendly to the Eisenhower administration." Just how friendly was "too friendly" depended on who was doing the measuring. But in the fall of 1956 two events had occurred—the overthrow of the Hungarian uprising by the Soviet regime and the controversy over the Suez Canal—that caused Americans in general to unite behind their president, and Lyndon saw no reason to run counter to this tide. As a result of the Suez upheaval, the president formulated his Eisenhower Doctrine, by which he proposed to send military and economic aid to any Middle Eastern country that requested it in order to fortify the area against Communist aggression. Lyndon was for that, too, with a few reservations.[2]

The following year the president saw the first test of his Middle East resolution when rioting broke out in Tripoli and Beirut in Lebanon—ironically the only Arab nation to have accepted the Eisenhower Doctrine—against President Chamoun and his pro-West policies. Chamoun asked Eisenhower to send American troops, and the president decided to comply.

James Hagerty: "Eisenhower had a joint congressional leaders meeting and told them that we had received a request from the president of Lebanon—Chamoun—that he was going to honor. I remember Mr. Rayburn said, 'Mr. President, so that's your decision. Fine. Thank you for telling us about it, but it's your decision.' And he left it that way."

Everett Dirksen: "Of course, Sam Rayburn stood up for what the president was doing, and so did Lyndon Johnson."

Erv S. Duggan: "Johnson would say, 'Don't you believe all this foolishness you hear about Eisenhower being stupid. I dealt with him, Mr. Rayburn and I, when we were the congressional leadership, and we felt that he always knew what he was doing.'

"And he said that Eisenhower understood the Constitution and that before he sent troops to Lebanon he got congressional approval. And he said that was the reason he was so careful to get a piece of paper in his pocket on the Tonkin Gulf; he was following Eisenhower's example."

Hagerty: "There was a very warm and close feeling between the Democratic leaders of the Congress and President Eisenhower. Both the Speaker and the senator were perfectly candid and frank with Mr. Eisenhower. If he was going to get votes that he needed for legislation, they would tell him. If he was not going to get the votes, they also would tell him. There was no double-talk.

"I think Mr. Eisenhower was quite proud of his Texas ancestry. They used to kid each other quite a little—'us three Texans got to stand together.'"

Harry McPherson: "Senator Johnson and Speaker Rayburn gave the country the feeling that they wanted to *help* Eisenhower do things. Johnson thought the presidency of the United States was the one great office of the system. He thought that to attack the president inevitably was to attack the presidency. And so he said that he was not going to pull Eisenhower down in order to make issue with him and make him look bad and to try to win in 1960. He said, 'We tell old Ike what to do, and if he does it we give him a twenty-one-gun salute.'"

D. B. Hardeman: "If you say, and many people did and do, that Lyndon Johnson was the most powerful man in the United States for a time, even more powerful at times it seemed than President Eisenhower, then you must also say that Sam Rayburn was the second most powerful.

"That decade, 1951 to 1961, was the peak of Texas influence in Washington. Rayburn and LBJ led the Congress as it will probably never be led by two men from the same state again. They were quite different in many respects. Rayburn was sixty-nine, Johnson forty-three as the decade began. Rayburn was five feet six, but he growled to an audience one night, 'Napoleon was just five feet four!' Johnson was a large man. Both were tireless workers, totally immersed in their calling. Rayburn was quiet, terse, carefully disciplined, stingy of time. Johnson had a large measure of theatricality. The Speaker said he once told him, 'Lyndon, I don't run around and wave my arms half as much as you do, but I think I get just as much done.'

Richard Bolling: "I didn't have much consciousness of Johnson till I got close enough to Rayburn to trot along behind him when we'd go to the Senate and Johnson would come over and kiss him on top of his bald head and sit down and have a drink with him, when he was majority leader."

Hardeman: "Rayburn was simple and down-to-earth, and Johnson loved the modern and the grandiose. When dial telephones were installed, Rayburn made them leave the old-fashioned phone on his desk so the operator could get the number for him. Johnson had an elaborate console of buttons to push.

"Johnson used to say of Rayburn, 'He operates his office out of his back-ass pocket. He doesn't know how to use a staff, and in this modern world you have to operate through a staff. And he doesn't anticipate crises and try to head them off. He waits for them to arrive, and then he deals with them.'

"Then he laughed out loud and recalled a conversation with Rayburn in the 'board of education' room. 'Mr. Speaker,' I said, 'this is a bad crisis. This is a real one. You've got to do something.' Rayburn jiggled the ice in his glass and said, 'Well, I've seen damn few of them in forty years that I couldn't sit out.'"

Robert Waldron: "To come to Washington and have your state men running the nation was incredible to a Texan. I came for one year on my way to New York; it lasted ten. I could not have come at a more exciting moment in history, when Mr. Johnson ran the Senate, Rayburn ran the House, and with the cooperation of the Texas delegation they ran the nation."

More than his part in the McCarthy censure, more than any other action prior to Vietnam, it was Lyndon's role in the passage of the 1957 civil rights bill that sharply divided his supporters from his detractors, those who thought he had worked a miracle from those who thought he had gutted what might have been a miracle.

In 1956 the Eisenhower administration in the person of Herbert Brownell, Ike's attorney general, drafted a civil rights bill which, as we have seen, passed the House with virtually no changes but arrived in the Senate too late to be properly considered. Then in the national election that took place, a significant number of Negroes, traditionally Democratic, voted Republican for the first time since Reconstruction days. The message to the Republicans was clear: build up party strength by appealing to the minorities. The message to the Democrats was equally clear: if we, the majority party, do not pass a civil rights bill in Congress, we will answer for it in the next election.

So when the administration bill was submitted to the new Congress, it again sailed through the House with no substantive changes. It was reported out of committee on April 1, was sent to the House floor by the Rules Committee on May 21, where it passed by more than two to one on June 18.

The Senate, however, was a different matter. There the Senate Judiciary Constitutional Rights Subcommittee held hearings now and then, mostly then, through February and March, after which the bill went to the full Judiciary Committee. In June, when the House bill reached the Senate and no bill had yet been reported out by the Judiciary Committee, Minority Leader William Knowland and Senator Paul Douglas, in an almost unprecedented alliance, decided to try to bypass the Judiciary Committee by placing the House bill on the Senate calendar at once where it could be called up for debate by majority vote at any time.

The motion to bypass the Judiciary Committee was successful, forty-five to thirty-nine, although Lyndon voted against it. Knowland then moved that the Senate "proceed to the consideration of H.R. 6127." Eight days of debate followed, during which southern senators voiced almost solid opposition to the bill. On July 16 came the vote on whether to take the bill off the Senate calendar and bring it up for debate; that, too, passed. This time Lyndon was one of the seventy-one senators to vote aye.

The story behind Lyndon's conflicting votes and the crowded events of the week of July 8–16 started before the opening of the Eighty-fifth Congress.

Gerald Siegel: "Near the time Congress was going back into session, Lyndon and I were discussing the civil rights issue. I remember saying that the time had come when the Senate had to act on civil rights and that it couldn't act without his taking the leadership. I said that I recognized his problem, the problem with his conservative Texas constituency, but I still thought he should be the one to make the motion to take up that bill.

"He looked at me in the way that he had when he was annoyed, and he said, 'Why, Gerry, you couldn't run for dog-catcher of Blanco County with the political judgment you've got.'"

Nevertheless, only a week or two after that conversation, rumors began to circulate that Lyndon had warned the southerners that a civil rights bill would go through this session, absolutely no doubt about it, and they had better address themselves not to whether or not they wanted a bill, but to what kind of bill they would settle for.

Clearly the old coalition between Republican conservative and southern Democrat was not going to work this year, not on civil rights anyway. And if the Democratic moderates in the Senate—men like Clinton Anderson of New Mexico and Mike Mansfield of Montana and Joseph O'Mahoney of Wyoming—did not have some leadership offered them, they would be forced to look for it to the more extreme liberals like Paul Douglas and Jacob Javits, resulting either in a bill somewhat punitive to the South, which would split the party, or in months of discord and at the end of it no bill at all.

So when the initial vote came on the motion to refer the bill back to the Judiciary Committee, Lyndon, well aware that the vote would fail, and anxious to keep open his avenues of communication to the southerners and not to show his hand too early, voted aye. He had, however, already spent much of the winter and spring planning the stages toward the successful passage of a bill that everybody—well, all the Democrats anyway—could live with.

George E. Reedy: "I convinced Johnson that it would be possible to pass a civil rights bill if you limited it to voting rights. Because I had a sense that the southerners felt guilty about depriving the Negroes of voting. They didn't feel at all guilty about depriving them of jobs, they didn't feel sensitive about housing, but they were defensive about the vote thing. That they couldn't justify.

"One of the characteristics of southerners is they really do believe in the Constitution as written. And when they have to take some stand that is clearly unconstitutional, it worries them. Well, it was clearly unconstitutional to deprive these blacks of their votes. And the southerners knew that."

But Reedy had not only to convince Lyndon that the South would capitulate; he had also to convince him that he, Lyndon, was the person to make that happen. "The Senate Democratic leader is the only bridge between the South and the moderate elements of the North," Reedy reminded him in a lengthy memorandum. It was up to him, Lyndon Johnson, to hold the northern extremists in check. Furthermore, only if he voted for the motion to take up the bill would his arguments for moderation be accepted by the North, which then, and only then, would understand the political risk he was personally willing to take.

Lyndon agreed. He also knew, a matter which Reedy did not go into but which was never far from Lyndon's mind, that if he was to broaden his own political appeal beyond the South, if he was ever to enter the mainstream of American politics, he must be irretrievably connected with a successful civil rights measure. No matter that the next election was almost four years away—the time to begin was now.

So on July 8 when the first stage of the Senate debate opened—the week-long debate preceding the vote on whether to bring the bill onto the floor for debate—Lyndon kept a low profile although his presence was unmistakable. On the eleventh he surfaced to warn the press against speculating about a compromise to avoid a filibuster—above all he did not want the bill to appear to have been *arranged*. At the same time he complimented the Senate on its statesmanlike behavior. He inserted an article by Walter Lippman into the *Congressional Record* which recommended a voting rights bill only. He also hinted to Jacob Javits, who had only that winter assumed Herbert Lehman's New York Senate seat and might not yet understand such matters, that the passage of the civil rights bill might not be totally unconnected with the passage of his Niagara bill.

On the twelfth Lyndon read into the *Record* a newspaper editorial favoring a voting rights bill. He also proposed that the Senate limit itself to three more days of debate before voting on the motion; the Senate agreed.

On the thirteenth, a Saturday, several more southern senators voiced their opposition. Karl Mundt of South Dakota then suggested several moderating amendments on which, he hinted, the majority leader had already been consulted and was in agreement. Sunday the Senate did not meet. On Monday, Lyndon praised the Senate further for its statesmanlike approach. He inserted into the *Record* an article by Roscoe Drummond commending the southerners for not resorting to filibuster; he also inserted similar articles by Arthur Krock and James Reston.

On the sixteenth, the day set for the vote, Paul Douglas read into the *Record* editorials opposing compromise on the bill. Lyndon was quoted in favor of compromise in the *Philadelphia Enquirer*. Harry Byrd of Virginia denounced the whole business. Several other southern senators who had not yet voiced their opposition did so. Finally Lyndon rose to announce—should anyone still be in doubt, and with Lyndon's penchant for surprise perhaps a few still did doubt—that he would vote *for* the motion to bring the civil rights bill to the floor for debate. Then at 4:00 P.M. he suggested the absence of a quorum; bells were rung, and eighty-nine senators answered the quorum call. The vote was called for and the motion passed, seventy-one to eighteen.

The first phase of the battle—which had started out as Eisenhower's and was rapidly becoming Lyndon's—was over.

Meanwhile a certain amount of confusion understandably existed in Texas as to just where the senior senator stood on this damnable civil rights bill. Telegrams such as the one Lyndon received from the Texas Citizens Council in Houston were frequent: "WE ARE TOLD YOU ARE READY TO SELL OUT THE SOUTH STOP IS THIS TRUE?"

Lyndon responded to all such enquiries with a carefully worded form letter:

> I do not know where you could have gotten the idea that I am supporting the "so-called bill for civil rights legislation now before Congress." Certainly I have made no statement to that effect nor have I intimated to anyone that I plan such support.
>
> The bill that has been introduced is one to which I am very much opposed, as I do not believe it would advance any legitimate cause.

Technically, the letter was quite accurate. The bill that stood before the Senate did not have his support, for the certain reason, among others, that he knew it could not pass. H.R. 6127 would, he was convinced, have to be amended, at which point it would become a different bill, no longer the one "that has been introduced . . . to which I am very much opposed."

There were four sections of H.R. 6127, called, interchangeably, titles or parts. Parts I and II created a bipartisan commission empowered to investigate civil rights violations and proposed a special civil rights division in the Department of Justice under the charge of a specially appointed assistant attorney general. Crucial to Part I was the section empowering the attorney general to seek a court injunction against anyone obstructing or depriving anyone else of his right to vote. That right had, of course, been guaranteed by the Fifteenth Amendment since 1870, a fact that had always been widely ignored.

The enforcement of voting rights, as George Reedy had predicted, caused little problem with the southerners; in some measure that was because they found parts III and IV so much more objectionable.

Part III of H.R. 6127 provided even broader powers for the attorney general. Under its provisions he could file civil suits for injunctions against anyone who deprived anyone else of any civil right. Inherent in this, and of utmost concern to southerners, was the school desegregation issue.

In a speech on the floor of the Senate, Richard Russell brought all his ammunition to bear against part III. It would, he said, allow the attorney general to employ "the whole might of the federal government, including the armed forces if necessary, to force a comingling of white and Negro children in the state-supported schools of the South."

In the course of their many private consultations that spring, Russell had advised Lyndon that the South would not under any circumstances accept part III; they would filibuster first, he personally would lead the filibuster, and not only would Lyndon find it very difficult to pass a bill, he would find himself in an extremely ticklish position as regards Texas. On the other hand, should part III be deleted . . .

Reedy: "I'm quite convinced in my own mind that the Eisenhower administration was not aware of just what they were proposing with title III.

"The bill could not be passed with title III in it. The southern senators would have stood up and fought, and you would have had to kill all of them to get the bill through with title III. It evoked all the old spectors of Reconstruction."

Although H.R. 6127 was a bill Eisenhower had submitted to Congress for two years in a row, there did seem to be considerable question as to whether he had ever given it more than a passing glance. In domestic matters he was conservative, a great believer in moving slowly. He was not at all in accordance with the Supreme Court on the Brown decision—"with all deliberate speed," whatever that meant, was too fast for him, and he said so. But he had allowed Attorney General Brownell, a true civil rightist, by Republican standards anyway, to draft a bill that he knew to be politically expedient in 1956. He had watched approvingly as that bill passed the House twice, but it was not until the Senate debate that he woke up to what its provisions might actually *mean*.

Then, without informing the Republican leader of his possible change of heart, the president suggested at a press conference that he perhaps was not so committed to part III as he had imagined himself to be.

Ike apparently continued to ruminate over the pros and cons because on the day of the Senate vote, July 24, he informed Knowland that he did not, after all, want part III eliminated. He was not exactly 100 percent for it, but he certainly was not quite opposed to it.

But if that was supposed to be a rallying cry—not much of one at best—to his fellow Republicans, it was too late. An amendment had been offered by Clinton Anderson and cosponsored, at Lyndon's suggestion, by George Aiken—a "good" Republican—to eliminate part III from the bill. Lyndon cashed in a lot of IOUs that day, and the vote on the amendment was fifty-two to thirty-eight. The southerners were, of course, highly pleased; the liberals were outraged.

Joseph L. Rauh, Jr.: "When Johnson took part III out of the House bill, he set back integration in the South for seven years. Part III passed in '64—the part III that was taken out in 1957 in essence became a title of the '64 law. But for seven years there was no federal power to bring injunction suits to integrate schools."

Siegel: "Senator Johnson tried to keep the lines of communication open between himself and the southern group, the rump group of southern senators who were standing fast, and the liberal senators, who were determined to try to pass as strong a civil rights bill as they could.

"Well, the fact is that he didn't close the lines in either direction. The liberals, unfortunately, closed the line between them and Senator Johnson. I suspect we possibly could have gotten a somewhat stronger bill had that not occurred, but they made it necessary for Senator Johnson to put together, in order to pass anything, a coalition of the more conservative members rather than the moderates and the liberals. And he simply had to include, in many instances, the southern senators.

"Now, you know, he clearly used a lot of strong-arm tactics of persuasion. His approach to the southern senators was, 'Well, if you don't allow progress on this issue, you're going to lose everything. There's going to be cloture; and your opportunity to delay or to slow down and to bring some kind of order or change will be gone.'

"They recognized this was a possibility, and it had an effect. The problem, I think, with dealing with the liberals was that they weren't scared of anything. They didn't have anything to lose, in a sense. They'd never passed a civil rights bill. There'd never been any progress, really, made except in the Court. So what could he tell them they might lose, except any bill at all? That's the only argument he could make: 'Look, if you press too hard, if you insist on perfection, you'll get it, but the bill won't be passed.'"

Roy Wilkins: "The NAACP disagreed with Mr. Johnson on leaving part III out of the bill. There was considerable debate on that. There was a split between the then senators from Massachusetts—Senator John F. Kennedy, a Democrat, and Senator Leverett Saltonstall, a Republican; Kennedy voted against deleting part III. There was heated debate and sharp difference of opinion. Mr. Johnson with his well-known predilection for consensus and for the 'possibility of what you could get through' felt that part III was a stumbling block on which the whole bill would founder. We differed with him, and we went our separate ways. He won; we didn't."

There remained the matter of part IV, which involved the old American right of trial by jury.

Hubert H. Humphrey: "Title IV as proposed by the Eisenhower administration provided for trials by federal judges in cases involving civil rights contempt charges; Johnson was positive that such a provision would never be accepted by the South. So he got Joe O'Mahoney of Wyoming, Estes Kefauver of Tennessee, and Frank Church of Idaho to sponsor a substitute amendment[3] allowing jury trials in all criminal contempt but not civil contempt cases.

Frank Church: "When I first came to the Senate in 1957, I had no sooner taken the oath and stepped down and started to walk up the central aisle to my seat in the rear of the chamber when I encountered this long arm of Lyndon Johnson reaching out and grabbing me as I passed and pulling me in to his desk there, front and center, and saying to me, 'Now, Frank, you are the youngest member of this Senate, and you have a great future. There's lots going for you. But the first thing you ought to learn is that in Congress you get along by going along.'

"The old Rayburn axiom. He said, 'Now, we've got a motion here that Clinton Anderson offered and it relates to a matter that is not important to your state. People of your state don't care how you vote on this, one way or the other, but the leadership cares. It means a lot to me. So I just point this up to you. Your first vote is coming up, and I hope you'll keep it in mind, because I like you, and I see big things in your future, and I want for you to get off on the right foot in the Senate.'

"I simply said that I would study it further and try to make up my own mind.

"But apparently I left Senator Johnson with the impression that I would vote with him, and he never came back to me for a second time before the vote. I remember he was taking down the vote on a little pad. When he got to my name and I didn't vote with him, he threw his pen down on his desk, and I didn't see him pick it up again. I knew then that I was in deep trouble with the majority leader.

"For the next six months he never spoke to me. He said nothing to me that was insulting, he just simply ignored me. When I was present with other senators, he talked to the other senators. It was clear to me that I was *persona non grata* with Lyndon Johnson.

"Then came the Civil Rights Act of 1957, and the key to the passage of that act was the jury trial amendment which was proposed by Senator O'Mahoney. The ardent civil rights spokesmen were contemptuous of the amendment, contending that it would gut the bill, that in any effort to enforce the bill through criminal proceedings and to punish those who violated the provisions of the act, their acquittal was assured by all-white, nonsympathetic juries.

"On the other hand, the argument for the amendment was equally strong, since this was not a matter of civil action where an injunction could require compliance with the law and where a willingness to comply would result in automatic release from penalty, but rather a criminal action that had to do with punishment of a past act which could not be undone. And here the tradition of allowing men so accused to be judged by their peers was a very strong one. As I studied it, it occurred to me that perhaps the addendum that was needed to the amendment was one that would put an end to the practice of all-white juries which had developed in the federal procedure. So I suggested that the federal code be amended in such a way as to guarantee that in the selection of a jury, it would not be possible to secure an all-white jury. And this addendum became the key to the passage of the act.

"After my role in the passage of that civil rights legislation, Lyndon Johnson was warmly and massively grateful, so much so that I was almost stifled in his embrace. He would pick you up and just squeezee all the air out. All at once I was in the Garden of Eden, and Lyndon Johnson could not be lavish enough."

During the debate on the amendment Eisenhower suggested he might openly fight against it, but Knowland was afraid that moderate northern Democrats would then feel compelled to vote for it. So Ike contented himself with sending Nixon out to contact each Republican who had voted to eliminate part III and tell them to stand firm on part IV.

The final vote on the jury trial amendment came just after midnight on August 2. It passed on a fifty-one to forty-two roll call vote. Nixon's legwork had apparently had some effect, because six of the eighteen Republicans who had voted against part III returned to the administration fold on part IV. But it was not enough. Lyndon's tenacity and patient courting had whittled away at Knowland's original majority until it no longer existed as such. Then when his head count showed he would carry the day, Lyndon called for the question and won with votes to spare.

Eisenhower commented that the jury trial amendment made the bill "largely ineffective." He had not decided, he said, whether he would veto the bill if the House accepted the Senate version.

The House did, with some minor improvements, and the bill returned to the Senate, where it passed again. Then it was sent to the White House.

Bolling: "My impression always was that Bill Rogers, the deputy attorney general, and Nixon were working to kill the bill. The counter to that was to get to Eisenhower and convince him that what we had to do was have a compromise, to get Bill Knowland convinced that that's what we should do and then send him in the back door to see the president in the White House.

"So what happened? Johnson just talked to Knowland himself. I wasn't there for the conversation, but I have a memory that he talked to him early in the morning from his limousine—he loved that telephone in the limousine. I think he talked to Bill Knowland very early and got Knowland to go see the president and convince him."

President Eisenhower signed the bill into law on September 2.

William S. White: "It was actually the most skillful single legislative job of leadership I ever saw, because Johnson of course had to deal with his southern friends who had up to that point formed the basis really of his constituency in the Senate. And yet he left them on this in their view.

"He managed to get this thing through with a bipartisan effort, and it's not now recognized how enormously hard that was. That was, after all, with all its shortcomings, the first genuine civil rights measure since Reconstruction."

Bayard Rustin: "I felt that the 1957 civil rights bill was a weak, but a very important bill. And while we had considerable questions about it, we all supported it on the basis that this would establish a very important precedent."

Roger Wilkins: "In 1957 I was a case worker in Cleveland, Ohio, and if you're trying to get your news of what happens in the House and Senate from the Cleveland, Ohio, newspapers, you don't get very much. But I had the feeling that in order to get the bill, he pulled teeth out."

Richard H. Rovere: "The astonishing thing is that the bill passed with only a small part of its original substance gone, and the lesson that must evidently be drawn from this is that in law, as in real estate, it is a good idea to begin negotiations with a stiff asking price."[4]

Lyndon was not satisfied with the bill, but it was a start, and as he so often said, sometimes crediting the unknown Chinese philosopher who first said it, more often not, "The longest journey begins with one step."

Lyndon: "Maybe I voted wrong on some civil rights bills in the past, but I'm learning all the time. I got all I could on civil rights in 1957. Next year I'll get a little more, and the year after that I'll get a little more. The difference between me and some of my northern friends is that I believe you can't force these things on the South overnight. You advance a little and consolidate; then you advance again. I think in the long run my way may prove to be faster than theirs."

ONE BIG HAPPY FAMILY

Willie Day Taylor: "I remember on one occasion—I don't know what it was about—he had said something very harsh to me that I thought was unjust and I didn't say anything, but tears came in my eyes. And he looked around at me in complete astonishment, and tears came to his eyes. And he said, 'But goddamnit, honey, I told you I love you.' And so when he loves you, you're part of the family. When he yells he's not yelling at you, he's yelling at events over which he has no control. He does prefer that you act with semi-intelligence; he greatly dislikes stupidity and sloppy work, but as Gene Williams once described it, 'Mr. Johnson's not hard to work for; Mr. Johnson just wants things done right.'"

One of the reasons for Lyndon's success as majority leader was that he was able to delegate authority to a staff that was exceptionally well trained and, generally speaking, content. A few, notably Walter Jenkins, had been with him since House days, others he inherited from former Texas senators. Often they came in pairs. At one time or another during the Senate period Lyndon's staff included Glynn and Mildred Stegall, John and Ann Leonard, Jack and Nell Hight, Dick and Jo Stansberry, Glen and Marie Wilson, and Bill and Nadine Brammer.

Glen Wilson: "Congressional staffs work long hours. We're never certain exactly what time a workday will end. The men work every day but Sunday, and the women get Saturdays off only twice a month. It's easy to see that a staff member has less friction at home if the wife or husband keeps the same hours and isn't waiting impatiently at home."[1]

Mary Margaret Wylie Valenti: "We had to work on Saturdays. I remember one Saturday night leaving about seven o'clock; I had a date. Apparently he didn't like it, and the word got back to me that he didn't like it. I learned that when you worked for him, you worked for *him*. You didn't just check out at seven o'clock on a Saturday night. You left when he said, 'O.K., be on your way.' I remember one night at nine o'clock he buzzed me, said, 'O.K., honey, now go on and have your date.' But by nine o'clock my date was burned up."

Most of Lyndon's staff he recruited—from Texas, of course. Lyndon also inherited staff occasionally, the most notable example being Grace Tully, who for many years had worked for Franklin Roosevelt but had fallen on hard times.

John Skuce: "Grace Tully owes her life to Lyndon Johnson. He picked her up and gave her the best appointment she ever had, congressional and executive. He made very sure that Grace Tully, never as long as she lived, had to be concerned about employment.

"You know, the humanity of Johnson, the things he did, these gestures—I think of them as being enormously southern. I don't know of anybody who has a greater expression of all the finest southern qualities than Lyndon Johnson."

Ashton Gonella: "When you worked for him, you were treated as practically a member of his family, and he treats you that way. He was as interested in what I was doing, what I did on weekends, what the children were doing, how they were doing in school, when they had the mumps, the measles, the chicken pox, as if they had been his own.

"Working for Senator Johnson was full of surprises. Every day was different. It usually started around nine thirty and, as I say, would always go until seven thirty or eight and sometimes much later, depending on the Senate business. As the sessions would get into the year, the actual day's work was longer. Then, on the weekends, I think one of the happiest things was that every Sunday a lot of the staff members would go out to the Johnson house and we'd sit and talk. They used to call it the 'Johnson togetherness' because we just seemed to be a little clan all of our own."

When Lyndon was majority leader his office sometimes received as many as six hundred letters a day and if, say, forty-five went unanswered, he would say, "There's forty-five people who didn't get the service they deserved today."

Booth Mooney: "Some days Johnson would sit down at the end of the day and read all the letters that were going out. Most often Walter Jenkins read them. Walter was really the indispensable man for Johnson.

"But personal letters, like eating a leisurely meal, Johnson never found the time for. Somebody had to, though, and somebody did, some members of the staff; after all, writing letters was part of what they were paid for, wasn't it?"

One recent biographer spent a great deal of time psychoanalyzing those letters and concluded that Lyndon had more of a mother-fixation than was healthy.

Walter Jenkins: "I got a great kick out of reading that because almost all of those letters were written by other people. For years every Monday morning Gene Latimer had to write to Lyndon's mother. L.E. Jones had to write his mother. A lot of people had to write his mother. So I guess this would show that all of us who wrote those letters had a mother-fixation on Lyndon's mother."

Skuce: "Johnson as senator could be quite cruel at times. After a morning telephone call from Johnson at home, if it seemed it was going to be a bad day, Carmen Johnson, his sister-in-law, who was the office manager, would bustle up from around her desk and say, 'All right, has everybody got the work they need for today?'; which was like waving a red flag, and instant spastic tension occurred. Harry McPherson would get up and go to the bathroom. That was the first thing that happened. Reedy would pop out of his door and say, 'Carmen, what did you say?' Then, the door would blow open and Johnson— Jesus God, he filled up the whole room the minute he came in, and if he was really in a bad mood, he would be so excruciatingly rude I would gasp."

Richard Bolling: "He burned his staff up a lot of times. I've seen him practically whip members of his staff. I mean, almost literally if he'd had a whip in his hand I'm sure he'd have given them a couple of lashes with it."

Mooney: "I never had what I would consider any difficulty working for Johnson. I think maybe it was because I took a somewhat impervious attitude. For example, I went home every evening at six. And he complained about that, but not to me.

"However, I've seen him bawl out Reedy, and Stegall, and even Walter at times. He could be surprisingly and deeply considerate of people and, also, just give them hell. For example, he was fully capable of saying, as he did about Bobby Baker on the floor, that 'He's my right-hand man, the last man I see at night, the first man I see in the morning,' and so on. Then saying to somebody else in a private conversation, 'Sometimes I think Bobby's just a cheap conversationalist.'"

Bobby Baker, of course, was never actually an employee of Lyndon's; his title, from 1955 on anyway, was secretary for the majority, and technically speaking he was hired and salaried by the Democratic caucus. He was not part of the "family," various of whom strongly disliked him, but he was necessary to the system as Lyndon saw it. He saw Lyndon daily when he was in Washington and when the Johnsons were in Texas he was in regular contact.

To say that Bobby Baker was indispensable to Lyndon was simply to say that he filled a crucial role in the Senate structure as it existed under Lyndon Johnson and probably filled it better than just about anyone else could have. He helped Lyndon keep track of where this senator was, when, and for how long, and he was available to pass on bits of information like "April 21, 1956, Senator Eastland personally requests you not to consider S. 2875 No. 1813, a bill to revise the Civil Service Retirement Act. He is very anxious to vote for this bill and due to the cat fishing season it will be impossible for him to be here Thursday and Friday of next week."[2]

Ralph Huitt: "I think that Bobby Baker was a great tool in a fine hand. Bobby Baker did not get into trouble while he worked for Lyndon Johnson. Never had time to. My God, when would he have done it—after midnight? Two o'clock in the morning?"

Virginia Foster Durr: "I think that Lyndon was taken in by people like Bobby Baker. Of course, if you want my honest opinion, I think he was also taken in by John Connally. John was so servile to him with his 'Yes, senator,' and 'No, senator.' He was a man who was always on the make, always buttering up people he thought could help him. I never did like him. I thought him a cold-blooded opportunist. But I think Lyndon liked him. I think Lyndon loved him. I think he thought John—and Bobby Baker, too—had the same relationship to him that he had had to Sam Rayburn."

Elizabeth Rowe: "I always thought Bobby Baker was terrible. I couldn't stand him. Harry McPherson called him a Snopes, and that's the best description I can think of him. Now I know Johnson relied on him because he was very bright, active, and a good head counter in the Senate, and that sort of thing. But to me he was just poison.

"He arrogated to himself that he was Johnson's right hand, and he would 'straighten Johnson out' on anything."

James W. Wilson: "Senator Johnson would have what he called staff conferences every morning—or a couple of mornings a week, maybe. He would get Walter Jenkins and George Reedy and me—sometimes Horace Busby—ostensibly to get advice and suggestions, but they were nothing but occasions for him to let off steam. He would just talk for maybe a couple of hours. Much of them were kind of mass chewing-outs—because we weren't inventive enough, ingenious enough, and weren't coming up with new ideas and programs and so forth. But on the whole they were good-humored, and this is when I saw him most kind of being himself.

"Very frankly, after about the first six months, I just didn't enjoy being around Senator Johnson as much as others did. He'd just talk and talk and talk, and you'd hear the same stories over and over and over, and the 'retinue,' so to speak, they thought there was nothing greater than to sit in a circle around him and hear him expound for hours and hours.

"The loyalty of the people around Lyndon Johnson seemed to me really an odd kind of loyalty, more like the lover relationship. They would just take the worst sort of abuse from him and just come back for more. This was something I had never encountered before in my life, and I didn't like it.

"People who worked for Johnson who were other than just secretaries and mail people—people who were in a staff position of any significance—it seemed to me that everybody was in sort of concentric circles, and you were constantly maneuvering to try to get into the next closer circle. Then something would happen, and you would go to the next circle out, and your competitor would come in, and there was just, well, what you read about palace intrigue. And very frankly, this more than anything was the reason I left."

Valenti: "As demanding and difficult as he could be, there were rewards. He would ask me to do things that he wasn't feeling quite up to. He would ask my judgment, my opinion on issues, and I was flattered that he asked. He didn't mean to be patronizing; it was that he sincerely felt I might be capable of giving him a judgment that might be worthwhile.

"He did this with a good many people on the staff. He had that way of drawing out people. But it also made all of us grow, trying to follow someone who thinks you have potential."

Robert Waldron: "I think we felt under the influence of this one human being. When you were in his presence, and worked for him, you felt there was something going on—with a future to it. And you might have threatened to quit, but you felt, well, I'll be the loser."

SPUTNIK AND OTHER MATTERS

On October 4, 1957, with the Congress adjourned and most senators, certainly Lyndon, relaxing in their home states after their marathon civil rights summer, the Soviet Union broke into the general calm by launching *Sputnik I.*

D.B. Hardeman: "Psychologically the greatest shock I felt during the fifties was the success of the Russian *Sputniks*, while our own fell into the sea. Historian Tom Bailey called it a psychological Pearl Harbor. Speaker Rayburn was deeply grieved. 'They tell us we have the greatest engineers in the world, and we send tons of money to the Pentagon, but something is badly wrong.'"

George E. Reedy: "I wrote Johnson, who was in Texas, a rather strong memo, saying that he had the natural vehicle to get into the space issue, which was the Senate Preparedness Subcommittee, which had been relatively inactive in recent months. He got in touch with Dick Russell, and Russell thought it over and was rather favorably inclined toward the idea. So Johnson just stepped into it and it followed from there.

"The Eisenhower administration was very sour on it. Eisenhower purportedly made some remark about 'Lyndon Johnson can have his head in the clouds. I'm going to keep my feet on the ground.' Sherman Adams made some nasty crack about playing outer-space basketball. In '57 it was quite an issue, and Eisenhower was sort of ignoring it."

Then on November 2 the Soviet Union sent *Sputnik II* into orbit. *Sputnik II* was ten times heavier than *Sputnik I*, and it carried a dog inside.

The Preparedness Subcommittee hearings, the first major hearings of the committee since Korea, opened on Wednesday, November 25. They would continue for two months, and in that time more than two hundred scientists, the country's best, and government officials would testify to the whys and wherefores of the country's deficiencies in the space field.

The hearings were barely into their second week when, on December 6, the United States launched its own satellite, *Vanguard I*, apparently premature; the object, considerably smaller even than *Sputnik I*, exploded almost at once and fell back to earth. "How long, how long, O God," said Lyndon publicly, "how long will it take us to catch up with the Russians?"

Besides hearing witnesses, the subcommittee was also examining the question of whether the space program, when there was one worth considering, should be under military or civilian control. Eisenhower was reviewing the same options, but Lyndon was not about to wait around for that decision, any more than he had waited for the president's State of the Union message. On January 7, 1958, the day before the president addressed Congress, Lyndon delivered his own state of the union speech before the Democratic caucus. Space, and the ultimate control of it, was, not surprisingly, the focus. Then, on January 23 Lyndon outlined before the Senate six conclusions that the subcommittees had derived from the testimony it had heard, and seventeen recommendations on which the committee was in agreement that decisive action should be taken; these ranged from an acceleration program in missile development to reorganization of the Defense Department.

Finally, on January 31 the United States launched *Explorer I*, successfully. The country at large, led by its president, relaxed just a little.

Having done all he could, for the time being, about the future of space, Lyndon continued to preoccupy himself with the more immediate, and earthbound, future of the country. The congressional elections of 1958, however, even more lopsided than had been predicted, brought about some major changes in his power and influence. When Congress convened in January of 1959, there were nearly twice as many Democrats as Republicans in the House, and in the Senate the majority increased from two to thirty. Lyndon's problem was no longer having enough votes. Now the problem was to keep those votes in line.

Perhaps partly to make his position of power a little more apparent to the new arrivals, Lyndon moved out of his old, smallish, relatively simple majority leader's office into a new one, actually a suite of rooms, directly off the Senate floor, which he had decorated by a New York concern in green and gold.

Sam Shaffer: "It was a magnificent affair; we newsmen used to call it the Taj Mahal. As soon as you entered the door, you saw over the fireplace a life-size photograph of Lyndon, standing up, leaning against a case of law books. Huge and impressive. Overwhelming, you might say.

"And this is where Lyndon would see a new senator to find out how he stood on various issues."

The first issue to come up in a new Congress, always, was the rules issue, specifically Rule 22, which allowed cloture only by a two-thirds vote of the entire Senate. The liberals lived in perpetual hope of relaxing that rule, and at the beginning of the Eighty-sixth Congress, there was new hope that this time they might succeed. Paul Douglas noted that there were fifteen newcomers to whom to appeal, and appeal he no doubt did, but Lyndon, in the southern camp since the beginning on any rule that protected the filibuster, held a lot more trump cards, not the least of which was the promise of desirable committee assignments. What had Douglas to offer, after all, beyond a pat on the back?

However, Lyndon, the Great Conciliator, was anxious to start out the new session on a note of unity if possible. The southerners, in the face of such enlarged opposition, were more ready to consider a slight relaxing of the cloture rule—never to a mere majority, heaven forbid, but to, say, two-thirds of *those present and voting*. One by one Lyndon called the newly elected senators into the Taj Mahal for a friendly chat—we must unite against the Republicans, he told them; divisiveness is what they're hoping for. Now here, right off, was a compromise, a new senator's first opportunity to help his party, and all on a mere procedural matter, no trouble back home with that sort of thing. And while the senator was here, had he noted down somewhere, anywhere, his committee preferences?

Shaffer: "Ed Muskie came in 1959, and he was a bright new face on the horizon and had a lot of promise. Johnson called him up to the Taj Mahal and said, 'Well, Ed, there are a lot of issues where you have to know how you will vote before the roll is called. And there are some issues that are very difficult.' And so on. Then Johnson said, 'By the way, how do you stand on Rule 22?'

"Muskie said, 'I think I'll wait on that one until the roll call gets to the M's.' Well, Johnson was furious. He saw to it that Muskie didn't get a decent committee assignment during his entire first term in the Senate."[1]

Muskie, of course, voted with six freshman senators who defied Lyndon, joined the liberal die-hards, and went down to defeat. Lyndon's compromise passed seventy-two to twenty-two.

Besides his new majority, there were two other major changes in the "system" as it affected Lyndon at the beginning of the Eighty-sixth Congress. One was the departure from the Senate of William Knowland to run, unsuccessfully, for governor of California, and his replacement as minority leader by Everett Dirksen of Illinois.

Hubert H. Humphrey: "Johnson knew Dirksen was a good speaker; Dirksen was smart, he was agile, he was Machiavellian, and he was always willing to make a deal. Johnson liked that, and even as president Johnson worked closely with Dirksen.

"Johnson knew how to woo people. He was a born political lover. Many people looked upon him as a heavy-handed man. That was not really true. He was sort of like a cowboy making love."

The other major change in the political scene was a hardening of the opposition, led by Eisenhower himself, suddenly no longer the indecisive figure of the previous six years. Faced with a majority of Democrats hungry for issues to use in the 1960 election against the Republicans, Eisenhower, once again the general, summoned his forces, laid the strategy for the defense of his most beloved issue—a balanced budget—and prepared for the siege.

The guns started at once. For the second year in a row, Lyndon delivered his own state of the union address before the Democratic caucus the day before Eisenhower addressed Congress. He let it be known that a balanced budget was no concern of his, nor should it be of the Democratic party; what mattered was that Democratic-sponsored bills, a number of which he named, most of which involved considerable amounts of money, be passed, the sooner the better, preferably by Easter. But such was not to be the case.

Every offensive he launched was met with an impenetrable defense called the veto, and the two-thirds necessary to override a veto was not so simple a thing. While the Republican army was solid, his own was far from it. His forces were splintered into conservatives, moderates, liberals, and ultraliberals, not to mention a few mavericks like Wayne Morse and William Proxmire who did not conveniently fit anywhere and could hardly be trusted to march at all. Poor Lyndon. He was a great general, but then Robert E. Lee had also been a great general.

James W. Wilson: "In '57 and '58 he had just unbelievable success as the leader. And in '59 he was expecting even greater things, but Eisenhower had learned the formula, so to speak, and started this budget-busting thing. Everything that the Democrats would propose, well, the Republicans would not oppose them on the merits; they would simply oppose them on the proposition that they were exceeding the budget, and this was inflationary, and so forth."

Eisenhower's very concentration on economy became a problem. If the word *Republican* became synonymous with *thrift* in the public mind, then the word *Democrat* would almost automatically be associated with such unhappy terms as *wasteful*, *profligate*, and *extravagant*. Such appellations were a matter of concern to Democratic senators, many of whom had a sneaking suspicion that in this one matter a high proportion of their constituents agreed with the president.

So Lyndon was forced early into a tactical retreat.

Fortunately for his morale, not all the bills that came before the Senate dealt with funds; there was an occasional bill on which he and Eisenhower actually agreed, and on rare occasions one in which he and the Democratic liberals and the president all agreed, and then Lyndon could perform his accustomed wizardry with some prospect of success. Such were the statehood bills for Hawaii and Alaska, which had recurred with some frequency through the fifties, and in 1958 had come up again.

Susan Bartlett: "When my husband, Bob, decided to run for delegate to Congress from Alaska back in 1945, he said he would run on two planks: first, statehood for Alaska, which was practically unheard of at that time, and second a tuberculosis sanatorium for Alaskans, primarily Alaskan natives, because tuberculosis was decimating the Eskimo population. Within four years he had a hospital in Seward, Alaska. It took longer to get statehood.

"When Lyndon Johnson came to the Senate in 1948, Bob felt that there wasn't very much hope in having any support from him because it was an absolute fact that the South was against statehood for Alaska and statehood for Hawaii. Statehood for Hawaii on account of the mixed population, and therefore statehood for Alaska because if they let Alaska in, they would have to let Hawaii in.

"But by 1958 we had the votes for Alaska statehood, and the opposing faction decided to do the thing again that had been successful before: tack the Hawaii statehood bill onto the Alaska statehood bill. This then would defeat it because the South was against it. But the delegate from Hawaii, Mr. John Burns, refused to allow Hawaii statehood to be tacked to Alaska statehood because he knew that this would defeat the bill. He took this chance of ruining his political career—a great act of political bravery.

"With Alaska it was like a snowball rolling; it was coming fast. Pressures were coming in from all over the country.

"Sometime in February of 1958 Bob went to see Lyndon Johnson to talk to him about it. Johnson said he had always voted against Alaska statehood. He went on to say that he didn't know what he was going to do. He might even find it necessary to vote against the bill, but later he added that maybe what he wanted to do was to act as a midwife in getting the bill to the floor—just a midwife, he said, *not* a doctor. He was willing finally to do that, Johnson said, to take the bill to the floor.

"Anyway, Johnson saw to it that the bill was brought to the floor. The vote was taken, and Johnson was absent. He was in Texas. But he was recorded in favor of the bill. He didn't need to do that. He could have just been recorded absent, but he recorded himself in favor, which Bob had sincerely hoped for but hardly believed would come to pass. It was a sentimental thing with him; it meant a lot to him that Lyndon would do this.

"The day that the bill passed was a beautiful, sunny, hot day. There must have been a hundred Alaskans about, maybe more. The galleries were jammed. There was a real tense atmosphere. I think everybody thought 'This is it.' There were several tries at votes during the day and many quorum calls and each one would raise the pitch of excitement. Not only in the galleries—you felt it on the floor, too. The men that would occupy the chair would gavel the noise down time and time again, but with very little success. As the day wore on and the time allotment grew shorter and shorter, the excitement grew more and more. Finally the vote was taken, as I recall, about six o'clock. As the last vote was tallied, the people in the gallery just rose as one person."

On March 11, 1959, the Hawaii bill reached the Senate floor.

Bill Davidson: "For several days before the vote, Johnson conferred with members of his brain trust, who briefed him on all the possible objections to the bill. Then, methodically, he began to work on the senators who might be against it—using the horse trade, the face-to-face talk, and all his other stratagems. To the Republicans he said, 'The administration is in favor of this bill. Let's give the nation a show of real unity.' To the Democrats, 'The Republican governor of Hawaii is flying in to Washington at 8:00 P.M. on Wednesday. You wouldn't want *him* to take credit for getting this little old bill passed, would you? So let's put it through before he gets here.'

"At 3:34 P.M. on March 11, the day Governor William E. Quinn of Hawaii was due to arrive, Johnson brought the bill up on the floor of the Senate, and the speechmaking began. For the first three hours of the debate, Johnson wasn't even on the floor, having turned over the majority leader's duties temporarily to thirty-five-year-old Senator Frank Church of Idaho, one of his favorites.

"At 6:58 P.M. Johnson returned. He was impeccably dressed in an expensive gray suit, white shirt and conservative gray tie. He wore horn-rimmed glasses, as he always does except when being photographed.

"I was seated in the gallery with one of Johnson's assistants, who explained his every move. The assistant said, 'He's talking to Willis Robertson of Virginia and now to Olin Johnston of South Carolina and now to Harry Byrd of Virginia, all opponents of the bill. He's keeping them soothed down. Now he's talking to Wayne Morse of Oregon. Lyndon wants him to limit his speech to a few minutes. Morse nodded, so I guess he'll keep it short.'

"In the next ten minutes, Johnson crisscrossed the Senate floor six times, talking to various senators. Senator Morse and Senator Robertson made very short speeches. While they spoke, Johnson wandered from desk to desk, talking to about a dozen senators, both Democrats and Republicans, concentrating on the southerners.

"At 7:09 P.M., Johnson got involved in an animated discussion with Senator Johnston. A Senate employee later told me that the majority leader wanted Johnston to limit his speech to two minutes. Johnston wailed, 'But, Lyndon, Strom Thurmond spoke for twenty minutes. I went down there to Hawaii with the committee, and I saw all them Communists and now if Strom spoke for twenty minutes and I only speak for two minutes, what are the folks back home in South Carolina going to say? They're going to say that them Hawaiians came up to old Olin with their *leis* and they put them around his neck and they took old Olin in. That's what they're going to say.'

"The majority leader replied, 'Now, Olin, you don't want that Republican governor of Hawaii to come into Washington at eight o'clock and take all the credit for statehood. Why don't you speak for two minutes and tomorrow you can put your whole speech in the *Congressional Record*, and you can mail it to all the folks in South Carolina, and they won't know the difference.'

"'Why, I guess that's all right, Lyndon,' Johnston said, and the crisis was averted. He read his speech so quickly that he scarcely could be understood.

"At 7:19 P.M., the speeches were still going on, but little attention was being paid to them. Johnson was moving all over the floor. Suddenly, he stopped and twirled his fingers. His assistant said, 'That means he wants a fast roll call. All the pages are out rounding up the senators for a vote.' Senators began to pour through all the doors of the chamber, and in a matter of seconds, the room was filled for the first time since the debate began.

"At 7:36 P.M., Johnson himself got up to make the closing remarks. He said simply, 'This is an important thing for the people of Hawaii and the United States, and I request a vote.' The roll call began, and by 7:52 it was all over. Hawaii statehood had won by a vote of seventy-six to fifteen. In just over four hours Johnson had accomplished what no one had been able to do in forty years."[2]

But the honeymoon with Eisenhower over the Hawaii statehood bill was brief. Hardly a week passed before hearings began in the Senate Commerce Committee on the confirmation of Admiral Lewis Strauss (pronounced "straws') as secretary of commerce, and although, as Eisenhower said, "It should not have taken the Senate more than three minutes to confirm his appointment, the hearings dragged on for more than two months. Strauss had crowned a distinguished career with long service on the Atomic Energy Commission, to which he was appointed by Truman and reappointed by Eisenhower. There was no scandal connected with him, no suggestion of corruption, and few, Lyndon included, disagreed with a president's prerogative to choose his own cabinet; still it was clear from the start that Admiral Strauss was a special case.

To begin with, one reason Eisenhower was appointing him to his cabinet was that he did not dare attempt to reappoint him to the AEC. The AEC worked in close conjunction with the Joint Committee on Atomic Energy, whose chairman was Senator Clinton Anderson of New Mexico. To say that Strauss and Anderson did not get along would be a gross understatement. Anderson said that Strauss was "untrustworthy," that he "conveniently omitted mention" of pertinent facts not once but several times in testimony before the congressional committee—all true, but the major cause for disaffection was the clash of their personalities. When Eisenhower called Anderson personally to feel him out on the possibility of reappointing Strauss, Anderson let him know that the going would be very rough.

Instead Eisenhower appointed John McCone to the AEC, but in the fall of 1958 when the position of secretary of commerce became vacant, Eisenhower turned once again to Strauss. He foresaw no real difficulty, and in the fall of 1958 there probably would have been none. But by the spring of 1959 Eisenhower and the Senate Democrats, the liberals in particular and Lyndon especially, were in a constant collision.

Warren Magnuson: "I handled the Strauss nomination in my committee. Strauss was a very arrogant fellow. He's the only guy I know that could strut sitting down. We let Clint Anderson come into the committee and ask questions and Strauss was very arrogant in front of the Commerce Committee. We didn't think that he had the temperament to be a secretary of commerce. That's why he got defeated."

Lyndon did not take part in the hearings, but he was curious about what effect they were having, so he sent Bobby Baker out to take a head count. Bobby was to be sure to emphasize that the majority leader himself had not made up his mind. It appeared, at that point, that Strauss would make it, but only just, and that prediction was confirmed when on May 19 the committee voted nine to eight to recommend confirmation.

The debate then moved to the Senate floor where it became even more bitter. Those on the anti-Strauss side were labeled either Communists (some had supported Robert Oppenheimer against Strauss when Oppenheimer had come out against developing the hydrogen bomb and Strauss *for* developing it) or anti-Semites at the very least. Most people took neither allegation very seriously, but the latter gave pause to both Lyndon and John Kennedy, who had to consider how it might affect the Jewish vote in 1960. Kennedy's decision was further complicated by the fact that Admiral Strauss was yet another in a whole string of notables who had once been a close friend of his father's.

As the final vote approached, Lyndon, heretofore silent, took a greater part in the proceedings. He had Bobby Baker make another head count, this time strongly indicating to any still wavering colleagues, and to some Democrats who had already declared an affirmative vote, that their leader had decided that he would, after much soul-searching, be forced to vote no. Pro-Strauss senators suddenly found themselves scheduled to speak at off moments when the Senate chamber would be considerably less than full. Lyndon made no attempt to force the vote along party lines; the issue was too sensitive, and besides there were a few Republican votes he was after.

By the time the roll call vote at last began, at 12:35 A.M. on the morning of June 19, Lyndon was able to inform Anderson that his forces would win, that Strauss would not be confirmed. When his own name was called, he voted no, as was expected. John Kennedy, to hell with dad, also voted no. The final tally was forty-nine to forty-six against.

While Lyndon was undoubtedly the major power in the Senate, he didn't always get what he wanted.

Jerry Holleman: "As majority leader, Johnson developed the reputation of being able to play the Senate of the United States just like a concert organist would play the console of an organ. People said he was pulling the strings, he was pushing the buttons, and the Senate performed as he played it.

"Of course, nothing could be further from the truth. In 1959 when the Landrum-Griffin Act was up, I was there trying to prevent its passage. We sat in his office, and he pulled out a roll call sheet, a narrow long sheet of paper with the name of every senator on it and a yea or a nay and a blank spot for absent or not voting. He sat there and marked everyone of them, every senator, as to how he would vote on Landrum-Griffin, and he didn't miss one single one. He called every shot exactly as it would happen.

"Most people, seeing him do this, began to presume that he was causing that to happen. People began to believe that he wasn't just counting them, he was casting them, controlling how the senators were going to vote. But this was not true. The man did not have that power."

As early as 1957 Congress had begun an investigation into labor practices, most notably through the Select Committee on Improper Activities in the Labor and Management Fields—popularly known as the Senate Rackets Committee—under the chairmanship of Senator John L. McClellan of Arkansas. Witnesses before the Rackets Committee, or as it was sometimes known, the McClellan committee, described practices so corrupt, occasionally sadistic, certainly illegal, that the general public, who watched the hearings on nationwide television, was outraged. The unions, it appeared, were not always the benevolent protectors they were supposed to be; they were never promanagement, but they were sometimes not proworker either, often just prounion. So when John Kennedy, who was chairman of the Senate Labor and Public Welfare Subcommittee, sponsored a bill in 1958 designed merely to safeguard employee pension and welfare funds, there were shouts of "grossly inadequate" and "a surrender to the unions."

The Republicans—still in 1958 a sizable minority—supported by many southern Democrats, attempted to amend the Kennedy bill with tough anticorruption and collective bargaining provisions, but with Lyndon's help and the promise of a general labor anticorruption bill still to come that year, Kennedy was able to defeat the amendments. Kennedy's second bill passed in the Senate eighty-eight to one, but it failed in the House, defeated by a combination of conservatives who thought it too weak and liberals who considered it too strong.

But after the 1958 elections and the change to a heavily Democratic Congress, Kennedy, supported by Lyndon, resubmitted virtually the same bill to the Senate, assuming that this time it would make it through both houses. Instead it encountered obstacles everywhere. In the Senate McClellan, partly from conviction and partly from a wish to capitalize politically on his newfound expertise in labor affairs, introduced an amendment which he labeled a bill of rights for union members. Under its provisions unions would be considerably democratized; workers would be entitled *by federal law*, to the rights of union membership, voting, and free speech. Labor leaders, predicting chaos in union discipline, were violently opposed. Never mind, they were privately assured, the bill of rights amendment would never pass.

Only it did, not once, but twice. It passed first by a one-vote margin, forty-seven to forty-six, and on being put up for reconsideration, it passed again on a tie vote with Vice-President Nixon breaking the tie to vote in its favor. Kennedy, who had been assured by Bobby Baker that the votes were there to defeat it, was understandably upset. Lyndon, although he had voted with Kennedy, and although he was technically as responsible for the defeat as anyone, seemed strangely unperturbed. Labor, he knew, would ascribe its passage to Kennedy, and not soon forget it; neither would the country at large forget that Nixon had voted for the amendment. Nineteen sixty loomed ahead.

Whether Lyndon's action was one of commission or merely omission, the deed was done, and almost as an afterthought he decided perhaps he better be able to explain his vote—which was contrary to the vote of almost all the other southern conservatives—to his constituents back home. Well, that was what he had hired good young legal minds like James Wilson for. Only he did not at all expect what he got.

James Wilson: "Senator Johnson wanted me to come up with something that he could say to his Texas constituents. So I went back, and suddenly something dawned on me. McClellan had literally taken the bill of rights and converted it to a labor context. It had due process and equal protection and all this.

"So I wrote Johnson a one-page memorandum in which I said that the Senate the night before had just passed the strongest civil rights bill that anybody'd ever suggested. There were just all these *allusions* of integrating, on the basis of equal protection, integrating labor unions and forcing sort of a FEPC. And I'm convinced to this day, even though I was very much tongue-in-cheek, that it would have been used as such.

"I took it to him on the Senate floor. He was sitting in his seat—the debate was just going around—and he read it. And as he read it, he smiled. He turned around and looked, and the first person he took it to was Talmadge of Georgia.

"And this is significant, because Talmadge is probably the best lawyer among the southerners. He showed it to him, and Talmadge read it and turned white, didn't say a damned thing. Then Johnson started showing it around. I remember it really caused consternation among the southerners. Thurmond just went into a rage. I remember he was talking to Stennis, and he had some crazy objection, and Senator Stennis said, 'Oh, Strom, we'll never get away with that.'

"They really were in a position where, not realizing it, they had voted for a civil rights bill.

"Well, anyhow, Senator Clark of Pennsylvania and Humphrey and one of the southerners sat down the next day and rewrote it. And the portion of the labor law now which is comparable, which secures the rights of union members against the union, is the language which came out of this memorandum."

The Kennedy bill, thus amended, once again passed with only Goldwater dissenting, then moved to the House. But the mood of the House, despite its influx of Democrats was, if anything, more antilabor than before. Two congresssmen, Phillip Landrum, Democrat of Georgia, and Robert Griffin, Republican of Michigan, had already devised a much stronger bill, incorporating all the Taft-Hartley labor reform amendments that conservatives had been pressing for for years. They took the relatively mild Kennedy bill and more or less tucked it into theirs for good measure. Eisenhower was delighted with the House bill, so much so that he defended it on nationwide television, although he got parts of it confused with other parts so that the country's conception of just what it would do, when he finished, was not quite clear. But in any case most Americans were still enough incensed by their exposure to organized labor via the televised Senate rackets committee hearings that they were strongly for the bill, and let their congressmen know it.

The Landrum-Griffin bill—Kennedy would not put his name on it—passed the House in August by 229 to 201. Almost all the 153 Republicans in the House voted for it. Southern conservatives voted for it. Various other congressmen examined their mail and voted for it. Although Sam Rayburn urged its defeat and voted accordingly, and Lyndon had Walter Jenkins on the phone advising Texas congressmen to vote against it, 16 of the other 19 Texas members voted for Landrum-Griffin. Not long afterward the bill, with very slight modifications, passed the Senate, too.

George Meany: "We wound up, of course, with the Landrum-Griffin Act despite the fact that we had very strong support from the majority leader against it. If we had not had his support, the bill would have been even more drastically against labor."

Hank Brown: "National AFL leadership felt that Johnson did considerable foot dragging as far as labor was concerned—he and Mr. Rayburn both on the Landrum-Griffin laws. They felt that Rayburn and Johnson were saying the right things, but they just weren't pressing. This showed up, in my opinion, in 1960 as to why Johnson got very little help out of labor in his bid for the presidency."

Holleman: "Labor was vigorously opposed to it, but Johnson did not sympathize very much with us. He had counted the votes. 'You haven't got them.' He said, 'You get the votes and you'll have your way, but you get the votes. I'm not getting them for you, and you haven't got them.'

"It came through to me pretty clearly that both he and Mr. Rayburn felt that in order for the Democrats to win the presidential nomination in 1960, they needed to give labor a slap on the wrist, politically speaking. He never did say it just like that, but I've put all of the things he did say together. And we spent hours and hours and hours down in the 'board' room sipping his bourbon together."

IN THOSE DAYS AT LEAST YOU *KNEW*

Nineteen-sixty was going to be a difficult year for anybody in national politics. The man who as president had been compared to Queen Victoria, a reigning monarch but not too reigning, could not run again because his own party had made a third term impossible, though there were those in both parties who thought that, heart attacks and all, Ike still could have been reelected. There was little enthusiasm anywhere for Richard M. Nixon, the vice-president.

It did not look like a Republican year; it looked as if, if the Democrats could put up an *acceptable* candidate, he would be a shoo-in, because, then as now, more people were Democrats.

And there appeared to be numerous Democrats who wouldn't mind having the job, among them, it sometimes seemed, almost every Democratic member of the Senate—except, of course, those from the South. But there was Stuart Symington who, being from Missouri, wouldn't be considered a southerner. Another possible candidate was Pat Brown, the governor of California, and there was, of course, Hubert Humphrey, who had by now at least softened and largely silenced the southern outrage at his foolishness at the 1948 Democratic convention.

There was also young Jack Kennedy, but few, with the possible exception of the Kennedys and people who understood presidential nominations and how they were obtained, took Jack seriously. Most people, although aware that Jack was making speeches all over the place and not ignorant of the fact that his younger brother Bobby, the ruthless one, was said to be *trying* to line up state delegations, paid little attention. Jack was surely not a candidate for '60; '64 perhaps, '68 or '72. He was too *young*; he was forty-three.

Lyndon told everybody who would listen and some who were even a little impatient that, although Jack had said that he, Lyndon, was the most qualified candidate, his background—what most people assumed was his background, southern—made his candidacy impossible, although really he was a westerner and, besides, he wasn't interested. Who would want to be president when he could be the leader? There was in all of this, of course, a familiar litany of self-pity.

Meanwhile, he had the best job in the world, and he would continue to do it better than anyone else had ever done it. And, just to begin, this year, the year of the election, there had to be another civil rights bill. The Negro votes that had so long been dependably Democratic no longer were, as had been proved in 1956.

And civil rights was the leader's department, not to mention a thousand other issues that he and only he could handle quite so well.

But the word *compromise* acquired new depth of meaning for Lyndon when the second session of the Eighty-sixth Congress convened on January 6, 1960. Eisenhower was still adamant about his budget, still veto-happy when expenditures were concerned; now, in fact, even more so, with a national election looming and a philosophy of fiscal responsibility to leave as the hallmark of his party. With the certainty of vetoes on his right, Lyndon still had on his left his large contingent of liberal Democrats bearing bills labeled "medical care for the aged," "federal aid to education," "housing" (yes, again), and "increase in the minimum wage." He was sympathetic—more than sympathetic; they were his bills, too—but what could he do?

The only major issue to come before the Senate not requiring federal funding was another civil rights bill, one designed to correct many of the inadequacies of the 1957 bill, particularly with regard to voting rights. But here again Lyndon saw himself stymied—this time, of course, by southern Democrats. He already knew that the "deal," as his enemies called it, the "compromise," as his friends saw it, that he had worked out in 1957 to keep the southerners from filibustering would not be possible again. The average voter back home, it turned out, was not interested in the argument that a little something would keep a bigger something from happening. The way the average voter saw it, nothing need happen at all. All his senator had to do was talk—just keep on talking, for as long as was necessary to win.

As usual, Lyndon had his strategy, but few of his strategies worked with the Eighty-sixth Congress. After the 1958 election had brought in its large Democratic majorities, Lyndon, knowing that another civil rights bill was inevitable, thought to pass a mild one as quickly as possible before senator and voter alike were mesmerized by the imminence of another election. But the bill he devised and presented on January 20, 1959—a bill he saw as a workable compromise[1]—pleased no one; the liberals thought it unworthy and the southerners unnecessary. Lyndon was disappointed; the mere fact of offering the bill would, he knew, lose him many votes in the South, and he had hoped to gain correspondingly in the North. Eisenhower sent over his own bill, but the whole matter was, as usual, still bottled up in the Judiciary Committee when Congress adjourned in September. The best Lyndon could do was to join Minority Leader Dirksen in announcing that civil rights legislation would come up on the Senate floor for debate by February 15 of the following year.

Lyndon: "I remember I told—I believe it was Senator Javits of New York—that I would bring up a civil rights bill on a certain day and he could take my word for it. That was the end of one session, and I told him I'd bring it up in the next session at a certain time. As the day approached, I told Senator Russell that this was going to be the twelfth of the month or whatever the day was, and he was rather cool, aloof, and said, 'Yes, I understand that you let them jockey you into that position. I understand.' And a little later I reminded him again, and he said, 'Yes, I know that. Go ahead, do whatever your judgment tells you. That's your business, your responsibility. I'm not the leader.'

"So at the appointed day and the appointed hour, I got up and made a motion that we proceed to consideration of the civil rights bill. And as soon as I sat down, Senator Russell addressed the chair and got recognition and said, 'You have just heard a motion that I thought would never be made in this Senate by the leader of my party.' He said, 'This motion, if adopted, will result in legislative lynching.' He just took off there; he rose as he went along; he spoke for an hour or so. Every headline in America that afternoon—'Russell Charges Johnson with Legislative Lynching.' And lynching was a very ugly, nasty word, particularly in certain parts of the country.

"Well, we fought for weeks and weeks and weeks and finally passed the 1960 civil rights bill, but not with Senator Russell's vote and not with his support, and not without both of us feeling it."

Meanwhile, events in the country at large were not about to wait on the measured pace of legislative action.

On February 1, black students from North Carolina Agricultural and Technical College entered a Woolworth variety store in Greensboro and sat down at the lunch counter. Before that time Negroes could order food only while standing. The students were asked to leave; they refused and were arrested. Other students did the same at the local Kress store. Later that week the incidents were repeated at department and drugstore lunch counters in Charlotte, Durham, and Winston-Salem. By the middle of the month the sit-ins had spread to fifteen cities in five states. They were, at the beginning, nonviolent, but by the latter part of the month a major brawl had occurred in Portsmouth, Virginia, and riots had broken out in Chattanooga and Nashville, Tennessee. By the twenty-fifth of the month the sit-ins had reached the Deep South, and Governor John Patterson of Alabama warned against inevitable riots if Negroes "continue to provoke whites."

Back in the Senate, on February 8, Everett Dirksen presented the administration's civil rights bill. It authorized (1) the appointment of federal voting referees, (2) criminal penalties against those using force to obstruct federal court orders to desegregate schools, (3) aid to communities in their school integration programs, and (4) federal officers to aid in apprehending suspects in bombing cases. The bill was referred to the Senate Rules and Administration Committee, which had assumed investigation into civil rights issues after the southern-dominated Judiciary Committee had failed to act at all the previous year.

A week later Lyndon, determined to keep his promise to Javits and other liberals, in spite of the fact that the administration bill had not been, and did not seem about to be, reported out of the Senate Rules Committee, reverted to an alternate tactic. He obtained unanimous consent to bring to the Senate floor H.R. 8315, a bill passed by the House that, as it happened, allowed the Stella, Missouri, public school system free use of local army barracks until their burned-down school could be rebuilt. Then he invited his fellow senators to introduce civil rights amendments to H.R. 8315. "The Senate," Lyndon said, "[is] going to do what is right . . . even though we do not satisfy the extremists on either side."

It was then that Lyndon's old friend and mentor, Richard Russell, attacked him for what he called the "lynching of orderly procedure in the Senate." Russell's motion that debate be delayed for a week was defeated. "Feeling against the South has gotten to be almost a national disease," he said, and charged that northern senators "expect one standard from us, whereas those who harass the South can bring in amendments as they will."

Dirksen, as might be expected, offered the entire administration bill as an amendment to H.R. 8315.

On February 23 Lyndon announced that beginning February 29—1960 was a leap year—he would initiate round-the-clock sessions until the Senate could vote on the rights bill. On that same day the southerners began a filibuster.

Lyndon immediately determined to take all this lying down. In preparation for the filibuster, he had forty cots moved into Senate offices, committee rooms, wherever space was available, since fifty-one senators must always be available to answer a quorum call or the southern forces could adjourn the Senate. He was convinced that only by keeping the Senate in continuous session would the southern opposition be worn down. Ironically, the filibuster proved considerably harder on Lyndon's side. Russell had carefully divided his forces into teams of three that spelled each other with clocklike regularity; they, of course, didn't care whether the quorum was met or not, so after their eight hours in attendance, they went home for sixteen hours of rest and refreshment. It was Lyndon's team, the bedraggled, bleary-eyed majority, who had to be in constant readiness.

Lyndon: "We spent thirty-seven days and nights here. We had to get quorums at one o'clock in the morning, three o'clock in the morning. But we were determined to pass the bill, and we did pass it."

Harry McPherson: "During the 1960 civil rights debate, he tried to break it by letting it run for day after day, night after night. He described one night when he just had a feeling that Senator Russell might try to start something, and he had somebody on watch, but he wasn't sure the fellow he had watching would be quick enough or wouldn't be dozing off himself. So he dressed, put on his shoes and went out and pushed open one of the swinging doors at one end of the Senate. He looked around the chambers and heard the southerner speaking and saw his watchman sitting there, his head nodding.

"And at that very moment at the other end of the chamber he saw the door push open about two inches, and there was Dick Russell looking out, waiting for Johnson to pull a trick, cut this guy off, and pass the bill."

On March 2 the Senate was "dismissed" for fifteen minutes to allow for a hurried cleanup of the Senate chamber; continuous sessions were then resumed until 5:31 P.M., March 5. The filibuster had, at that point, continued for a record 125 hours, 31 minutes. Lyndon then recessed the Senate until noon March 7, and the round-the-clock sessions were called off entirely the next day when a coalition of twenty-three Democrats and eight Republicans moved to impose cloture. The motion was, Lyndon said, and Dirksen agreed, "premature," and on March 10 it was defeated fifty-three to forty-two.

Debate on the bill was not resumed, however, because another scheme had emerged as a better possibility for passage. On the same day debate began in the House on an omnibus civil rights bill, and word had it that since the House was likely to pass its bill and then send it to the Senate, the Senate might advisedly wait for that to happen. The House bill was known to be weaker than the Senate bill and would therefore be more palatable to the southern contingent. In the meantime, and just in case plans went awry, Lyndon and Attorney General William Rogers worked on watering down the administration bill, purging those sections concerning the desegregation of schools and jobs.

On March 24 the House-passed bill reached the Senate, and two weeks later, after various amendments, it was passed by the Senate seventy-one to eighteen. The eighteen were all southern Democrats.

The bill, which was decidedly weaker than the original administration bill, provided for minor penalties for infringement of various federal statutes. Its only real addition to the civil rights cause was to authorize federal courts to appoint "voting referees" to enroll Negroes in parts of the country where racial discrimination against voters was known to occur.[2]

The southerners, although they voted against it, were not entirely displeased. Noting that the "odious and obnoxious" original proposals had been eliminated, John McClellan of Arkansas said, "We have repelled . . . vicious assaults on the rights and liberties of our people." The liberals had, once again, suffered defeat. The bill was, said Senator Joseph Clark of Pennsylvania, "only a pale ghost of our hopes."

On April 21 the amended bill was approved by the House, and on May 6, when Eisenhower signed it, the Civil Rights Act of 1960 became law.[3]

Lyndon: "I know the liberals felt that I made too many compromises. I felt I got the best bill I could with the votes I had, and if they could have gotten a better bill, we would have gotten it. But I know there was a lot of feeling among the liberals that they ought to have the whole loaf. And a lot of us would like to have a whole loaf, but you don't always get what you want."

There were times, as the 1960 session went along, when Lyndon doubted his own ability as legislator. From the passage of the civil rights bill until July 3, when Congress adjourned for the national conventions, absolutely no significant legislation was passed. Having already announced that, unlike other presidential hopefuls, Kennedy and Symington in particular, *he* must stay and keep the Senate going, he of course had to do just that, but he might as well have been off in the hustings for all he was accomplishing.

Then the thought occurred to him that if the Senate reconvened after the conventions, everything might be different. It particularly occurred to him that if he were the Democratic candidate, things might be especially different, but even were he not, he might, with a newly spelled out Democratic party platform behind him, have more leverage. He hoped at least for more unity within his own party. He apparently forgot that he must expect the same from the other party.

Lyndon had another motive, less unselfish than the wish to pass needed legislation. He was aware that his own potential candidacy for the presidency—still unannounced—needed a power base behind it that he lacked. Still under the misapprehension that senators had a large influence with their state delegations, he saw himself gaining influence over delegate votes from the veiled threat of how he would manage a postconvention Senate. Why he thought senators would be overly concerned with his control of a postconvention session considering his record with the Eighty-sixth Congress up to that point . . . well, perhaps it was just a last-ditch, long-shot effort.

In any case, Lyndon decided not to adjourn the Senate, but only to recess it, on July 3, somewhat earlier than was absolutely necessary, under the conditions of its reconvening in August to wrap up unfinished business.

Probably the less said about that August "rump session," as the senators called it—Lyndon's last days in the Senate—the better. There were many items of unfinished business; some, such as the farm bill and additional defense appropriations, were scuttled from the start. The Senate should, Lyndon decided, concentrate on the four most important bills: federal aid to education, a raise in the minimum wage, medical aid to the aged, and housing. If he could pass these, he thought, his record for the session, a matter extremely important to him, would hold up.

But for once Lyndon had misjudged the Senate entirely. One-third of his colleagues, including many from his own party, were running for reelection, and were more than a little annoyed at having to be there in Washington, never pleasant in August, at all. Also, Lyndon now faced not just an omnipresent Eisenhower but an actually present Nixon, presiding over the Senate while he led the Republican opposition. The Republicans were not interested in supporting bills that had become part of the Democratic platform. And without virtually any Republican concessions toward compromise, and still the necessity of a two-thirds majority to override a veto, Lyndon was, if anything, in a worse position than he had been in that spring. One by one, though with varying approaches and degrees of anguish, the bills were defeated. And to top if off, Minority Leader Dirksen succeeded in further embarrassing the Democrats by moving that the Senate reconsider the two strong civil rights measures—faster desegregation of schools and jobs—which the Democrats had with such enormous effort managed to delete from the civil rights bill in the spring, a move which triggered an immediate filibuster from the southerners and could only be resolved by the Democrats' tabling the motion and facing the loss of Negro votes as a result.

About the only thing that was gained from the rump session was that Lyndon and Jack Kennedy got a little practice in working together, and although the turnabout in their relationship was not always easy for Lyndon to swallow, he apparently played his role well.

Peter Lisagor: "During the special session I watched to see how Johnson and Kennedy behaved together, with Johnson still the majority leader. I thought Johnson was very circumspect. He'd go back and chat with Kennedy, who sat in the back of the Senate floor. I thought Kennedy sort of played it cool, as he always did, and was sort of low-keyed about it all. It was just a kind of a tableau, a bit of ballet on the Senate floor."

Adrian Spears: "Later there was a good bit of talk about what bitter enemies Johnson and Kennedy were and how they didn't get along. But in 1956, when Stevenson was running for the second time, Johnson and Kennedy were at a motel on the edge of San Antonio. Kennedy was the main speaker at our rally there.

"I had the best suite in the motel set aside for Kennedy and Johnson. LBJ and Lady

Bird were there in one wing of the suite and John Kennedy was in the other wing. I was in there talking to them, and the picture that stands out in my mind is John Kennedy sitting in a bathtub filled with hot water to ease the pain in his back, and LBJ sitting on the side of the tub pouring water on his back. I never thought at that time that this would make such an impression on me, but it did, especially when people attempted to say that they did not get along."

With the end of the rump session, Lyndon's Senate years were over—though he wasn't quite sure of that yet. He had served twenty-four years in Congress—twelve in the Senate and twelve in the House. The nature of his personality and the at times roughshod method of his leadership had earned him enemies, but most of his colleagues were friendly, at the least, and quite a few were actually friends.

McPherson: "His closest friends in the Senate were Magnuson, whom he had known for years—a hard worker and very effective, a czar in his committee and a playboy on the side—Kerr, Russell, to some extent Lister Hill. He was close to Pastore and was increasingly close to Humphrey. Mike Monroney to some degree.

"Johnson's relations with Kerr were fascinating. Kerr had a razor-sharp mind and a razor-sharp tongue. He was the most devastating debater I think I have ever seen. He was frightening on the floor, and he had full command of political invective.

"Johnson was close to and arm's length with Kerr at the same time. They shared an awful lot of interests. Johnson, Kerr, Clinton Anderson, and Wayne Morse would sit over in the corner of the Senate during a debate and in the most querulous terms and also with enormous humor and invective would trade horses or cows. They sold each other animals all the time, I mean literally—the animals on their farms. Each of them had animals from the other's ranch or farm. To hear them tell it, they were always spavined or diseased, brought half of what they'd paid for them, and so on. Very rough country talk."

In the end, however, it was not a friend but one of Lyndon's bitterest opponents who, with remarkable objectivity, best summed up Lyndon's Senate years.

Barry Goldwater: "I'll say this about him. He was a very good majority leader. He worked the Senate. If he had a job to do, we didn't go home at five or six o'clock. We went home when we got the job done, and it might be two or three days later, having been there all night, several nights.

"Personally, I liked working that way. In those days at least you *knew*. When Lyndon Johnson said, 'This is going to be legislation,' you knew you weren't going to leave until it *was* legislation, until it was finished.

"These days you never know what is going to happen. It's nine fifteen and I don't know what we're going to be doing at twelve thirty. I much preferred it in every way with Lyndon Johnson."

3

The Vice-President

ARTHUR AND MODRED

Katharine Graham: "About 1958 Philip and I were having dinner at Joe Alsop's with Senator Kennedy, whom we did not know intimately at the time, in fact ever, although we got to know him much better later. After most of the people went home, several of us sat down, including, I believe, Mrs. Longworth and the Kennedys and ourselves and Joe. And my husband said to Senator Kennedy, 'Jack, you're awfully good. I'm sure you will be president someday, but I think you are too young to run and I hope you don't.'

"Kennedy said, 'Well, Phil, I'm sorry, but I'm running, and this is why. There are three reasons.' One was that if he didn't run now, somebody else would run and be in for eight years and probably dictate his successor. The second reason was that if he stayed eight years in the Senate intending to run, he'd end up being a lousy senator and a lousy candidate. And the third, he said, 'I think I'm better than any other of the possible candidates except Lyndon Johnson."

Hugh Sidey: "Kennedy was the only one that really wanted it above and beyond everything else, who was really organized and dedicated to the job of getting it, who kind of had the fire about him that it takes, and the know-how.

"Lyndon was very erratic—as he always was. He'd say, 'That Kennedy's really going. Look at the polls.' And of course never quite admitting that he, Lyndon, was interested in it."

Carroll Kilpatrick: "I was covering Nixon some in the late fifties. I had traveled out west with him, and late one night at the Denver airport there weren't but four or five reporters with him and he invited us into one of the airport rooms while we waited for the plane to be refueled. We sat there for an hour or so and we talked about Johnson, and I remember this very clearly, he said, 'He is the ablest one,' and I think he said, 'He would be a successful President.' 'But,' Nixon added, 'If he had only one strike against him, he might make it, but I don't think he can with two.'"

"At that point, I accepted that comment of Nixon's at face value. Then later a group of us had dinner in the National Press Club with John Kennedy—I would say it was the fall of 1959, because he told us quite frankly, 'I'm going to announce, I think, in January.'

We talked about all the candidates, Symington, Johnson, and so on, and he said, 'Lyndon would make the ablest president of any of us running, but he can't be elected.'"

James Hagerty: "Many times towards the end of the second term, Eisenhower would talk about who the candidates might be, and he always gave Mr. Johnson very high marks. We all felt that Stevenson was going to be renominated, and we didn't think it was much of a contest. But if Eisenhower had had his druthers, he told me this—he thought Lyndon Johnson would be the strongest man that the Democratic party could put up."

James H. Rowe, Jr.: "I remember in '58 I once said, 'Look, if you're going to run, you'd better get moving.' And he said that the country would look at the great, strong leader in the Senate working away while Kennedy and Humphrey were running around the country making noises.

"Well, the country didn't look at him at all. In my opinion, he didn't understand national politics. He wanted one thing. I think he wanted it so much his tongue was hanging out; then this other part of him said, 'This is impossible, and why get my hopes up? I'm not going to try. If I don't try, I won't fail.'"

And there were other considerations, too. Bobby Baker describes how they sat in the Senate chamber, just the two of them, one night after adjournment discussing the matter, and just as the lights, timed to go off thirty minutes after the session ended, went out, Lyndon said, "Bobby, you never had a heart attack. Every night I go to bed, and I never know if I'm going to wake up alive the next morning. I'm just not physically capable of running for the presidency."

Joseph L. Rauh, Jr.: "In January of '59 the Humphrey campaign started. He declared in January of '60, but we started back in '59 and set up our organization and went to work.

"There were two Humphrey camps rolled into one. One Humphrey camp was for Johnson and was 'Stop Kennedy,' and the other Humphrey camp was for Humphrey and against Johnson. We who were all for Humphrey a hundred percent—I guess we were more idealistic than practical. It was unlikely that Humphrey would get it, but we thought he *could* get it, and it was fun to try and do.

"The others were really for Johnson with Humphrey taking the vice-presidency or whatever crumbs he could get. So the Humphrey camp was not one camp but two, and quite bitter and unpleasant. It wasn't a very happy time."

The two candidates, Kennedy and Humphrey, did not actually confront each other until the Wisconsin primary on April 5.

Rauh: "We'd been campaigning out there, in Wisconsin and we thought things looked fairly good. It went badly. The *Catholic Worker* forgot about Humphrey's labor record and went for Kennedy and we got badly beaten. In the meeting in Humphrey's suite that night there was a question of whether to go on. We didn't have much money and so forth. But I guess everybody in the end was for going on figuring we'd recoup in West Virginia.[1]

"We did win in the District of Columbia. It gave Humphrey a terrific boost. But West Virginia was just a disaster, Kennedy got all the votes. That night the real fight between the 'Stop Kennedy' boys and the Humphrey boys occurred, in Hubert's bedroom.

"The 'Stop Kennedy' boys wanted to go on. They had to have a candidate until Johnson was ready, and Johnson wasn't ready yet. He tried to hold off right through the congressional session. The Humphrey people wanted Humphrey to get out and be generous. I had a perfectly simple theory—that Hubert could never be president of the United States through the primary route. He should be generous here to Kennedy, and he should be Kennedy's vice-presidential candidate.

"The theory on the other side was that Hubert still had some strength to stop Kennedy, and that should be done, and Johnson might someday get it.

"We won. Hubert issued our statement. It was very generous to Kennedy. I read it to Bobby Kennedy at the other hotel on the telephone, and he thanked us. About five minutes later downstairs the clerk tells the people in our suite that Mr. Kennedy's on his way up. Everybody thought it was going to be Jack, except Jack was on television claiming victory.

"I knew what was going to happen. I knew it was going to be Bobby, and I knew it was going to be terrible because the Humphrey crowd hated him. So when Bobby walked in that room, I thought I was going to die. Hubert and Muriel were at the other end of the room, and it was like the movie on the *Ten Commandments* when the Red Sea opens. A sea of people opened so Bobby could walk through. He walks over to Hubert and he leans down and kisses Muriel on the cheek. I thought she was going to hit him. She hated him. It's one of the reasons Hubert wasn't president after John Kennedy died, because the family hated the Kennedys so they tried to persuade Hubert not to run for vice-president with Jack Kennedy.

"At any rate, Hubert was out of the race, and it was May tenth."

The West Virginia primary had provided considerable reason for Muriel Humphrey's antagonism toward the Kennedys. There had been no lack of opportunity to spend money there, and the Kennedy forces had done just that, a move disastrous to his more impoverished opponent. It was well known that any West Virginia county sheriff, who always had a great deal to do with its voting pattern, was for sale for five hundred dollars or less. Franklin Roosevelt, Jr., with no objection from the Kennedy camp, openly branded Humphrey a "draft dodger" when in fact he had been refused a naval commission repeatedly because of color blindness, had flunked the physical for an enlisted man for the same reason, and had failed to be inducted into the army twice for a variety of physical reasons. Humphrey had hoped that his own role as "poor boy candidate" would appeal to the average Appalachian voter, but in fact the average Appalachian voter was fascinated by the wealth and glamour of the Kennedy image, as who was not? In the end the Catholic candidate won by 60 percent of a state that was 95 percent dyed-in-the-wool Protestant.

Back in October of 1959, Sam Rayburn had scheduled a press conference in Dallas in which he announced that the Johnson for President Committee would open in Austin under the auspices of Governor Daniel and himself. Publicly, anyway, Lyndon ignored this move.

James H. Rowe, Jr.: "I don't think there's any question that Rayburn was very anxious for Lyndon to run. He did not think any Roman Catholic could win the election."

Another person who in the fall of 1959 apparently had a few doubts on the same score was Joe Kennedy. Thomas G. Corcoran, in a letter to Lyndon dated October 9, 1965, referred back to a meeting he had—or as he put it, "a meeting I was summoned to in New York with Joe Kennedy and Bobby and Jim Landis"—in the fall of 1959.

Corcoran continued. "I bore you Joe's proffer to announce and work for you as the Kennedy candidate for *president* if you would tell him you would take Jack as *yours* for *vice*-president."

A startling suggestion considering that Jack was to announce a few months later. Perhaps Joe was just covering his bases.

On a Sunday morning in February 1960, Earle Clements, who had sacrificed his Senate career to provide the vote Lyndon needed for the passage of the Social Security amendment in 1956, called together a select group of Lyndon Johnson supporters— Senators Clinton Anderson of New Mexico and Robert Kerr of Oklahoma, Bill Brawley, a Senate staff employee from South Carolina, and John B. Connally—at the Sheraton-Carlton to discuss, over breakfast, how their friend Lyndon Johnson could achieve the Democratic presidential nomination.

Clements was convinced that Lyndon's position as majority leader had acquired for him immense influence with his fellow senators and congressmen which would inevitably, if properly directed, translate into votes at the convention in July. The other candidates, Clements argued, would battle it out in the primaries with John Kennedy emerging a scarred favorite, but his Catholicism would keep him from being chosen at Los Angeles where the delegates, exhausted after many ballots, would turn to Lyndon. Kerr and Anderson were unconvinced; they felt it was important to start "sewing up" some delegates. But that would require some kind of positive announcement from Lyndon, and Lyndon, supported by John Connally, was very much opposed to anything so public.

James Blundell: "In 1960, the early part of the year, Johnson said that Mr. Rayburn and a lot of his very strong friends were really pushing him to get into the presidential primary campaign. He said, 'I don't want to do it because I've got to run the Senate.' Then he made this statement: 'If Jack'—meaning John Kennedy—'wins West Virginia, the show's over anyway. Then it's not going to make any difference. If he wins West Virginia, he'll take the convention and the nomination.'

"I probably wasn't as realistic as Senator Johnson, because I got imbued in the campaign and we really talked ourselves into thinking we had a chance. But we were up against some real pros in a well-organized, well-financed, well-publicized operation."

Lloyd Hand: "There was an effort to secure New York's support for Johnson. I met with him and Carmine deSapio, Pendergast, Rayburn, and, if I'm not mistaken, the mayor of New York, who at that time was Bob Wagner. It was a very interesting meeting. And the net of it was, they really liked him. They thought he was a can-do man, a man of accomplishment. But they couldn't sell him. De Sapio and Pendergast told him that.

"Cliff Carter was working very hard along with a lot of other people in the delegate search. We had a lot of 'maybes' but I think we were selling our own soap to ourselves. The Kennedys just got out first, and they had more muscle; they had more money, and they were more sophisticated. Most of the people in the Johnson organization hadn't been involved in national delegate hunts before. Good men, able men—I loved them dearly, but getting a fellow from south Texas to go into Manhattan to talk to delegates . . . you know. A lot of people . . . they just hear some South in your mouth, and they automatically think that you're dumb. They think if you talk funny, you are funny."

Mary Lasker: "He came to New York in January or February in 1960, and he told me he wanted to run for president. He said to me, 'Now you know Mrs. Roosevelt and you know Dorothy Schiff. I want you to tell them I'm for civil rights. You know I'm for civil rights, and I want them to know it.' I did know it, and I went to Mrs. Roosevelt and said, 'You know Lyndon Johnson wants to run for president, and he's a very able man.' She said, 'What about civil rights?' I said, 'He's for civil rights.' She said, 'He's from the South, and it's impossible.'[2]

"The same thing happened when I went to see Mrs. Schiff, then publisher of the *New York Post*, and James Wechsler, who was then editor. It was very hard to convince people that he was a genuine liberal, as I was sure he was. Perhaps if he had come up here and spent time with people, he could have convinced them, but he was too busy as majority leader, and the convincing couldn't be done secondhand."

Charles Diggs: "Prior to the national convention, he sent some people up to Detroit to try to stimulate some interests in his behalf, but they weren't too successful. There was just a normal prejudice against southerners in that regard which has existed in this country ever since, I guess, the Civil War. Really about the only black friend he had was Hobart Taylor, who at that time was assistant prosecutor of Wayne County in charge of the Civil Division—who is a Texan, and a very prominent Texan."

Hobart Taylor, Jr.: "In 1960 when I looked over the thing, I concluded that I was going to be for Johnson which was, as one sage Texas newspaperman said, like being a Puritan in Babylon. There weren't many people in Michigan that were for Johnson, and I knew the realities of the situation, and I didn't war against them.

"I helped Johnson get some delegates. I think we could have done more if Senator Johnson had not taken the position that he shouldn't campaign openly and make promises because he was leader of the Senate and it would be divisive if he did so.

"But still, you know, you have to stand for something sometimes, and I stood for him."

India Edwards: "Oscar Chapman and I were supposed to round up citizen support for LBJ, but it was not easy to find men and women who knew Johnson outside the District of Columbia and Texas. . . . When I was trying to speak about LBJ's voting record in Minnesota there was so much laughter that one man got to his feet and said that they knew me well enough to know I would not support a man who was not liberal and they owed me the courtesy of at least listening to me. I doubt that LBJ or Sam Rayburn ever realized what an impossibility it was to expect LBJ to win the nomination in Los Angeles."[3]

Robert Nathan: "The Americans for Democratic Action was seriously concerned that Kennedy and Humphrey might come to a stalemate and Johnson would be nominated. ADA, without question, was very strongly against Lyndon Johnson for the presidency, although most of them just didn't believe it could happen.

"ADA had always been in quite serious conflict with the Senate majority leader because they felt that Lyndon Johnson was not 'all out,' that he was attempting to compromise and take what he could get, so to speak. They were worried about Kennedy's scope of experience and his youth, but it was nothing like the anti-Johnson position."

Jack Bell: "The Kennedys recognized that the way you become a presidential nominee is to get the votes of the state delegations. And Lyndon made a terrific mistake in this respect. He took the word of senators and House members. 'Don't worry about our state. We'll do it for you. We'll get you that convention vote.'

"Lyndon was raking Kennedy every day about missing Senate votes. Here he was— Lyndon, the great tower of strength of the Democratic party; he was there on the job passing legislation and casting votes. He forced roll call votes of all kinds, even on quorum calls. He'd have a dozen quorum calls in order to demonstrate that Kennedy was not around, and then he'd point out these absences. Of course, he didn't realize that nobody outside of the Senate knew what the hell a quorum call was, and whether Kennedy was there or wasn't there didn't make much difference to anybody. [4]

"Johnson fooled with it back and forth. He never got organized. He had a bunch of, to be perfectly blunt, incompetent Texans who were fouling things up around the country and never helping him any."

One Texan who had begun to figure in the events of 1960, was the ultraconservative oil billionaire, H.L. Hunt. Hunt had been anti-Lyndon ever since the war when Lyndon and Wright Patman were the only two Texas congressmen to vote against the Disney bill that would have raised the ceiling price of oil. In 1948 Hunt had contributed heavily to Coke Stevenson's campaign against Lyndon, as had other Houston oil barons.

But by 1960 Hunt's feelings about Lyndon had softened. First of all Lyndon had never again voted "wrong" on oil. Second, Lyndon had proved himself a strong figure in Congress, able to "lead those Democratic and Republican senators around as though they had rings in their noses,"[5] Hunt told Booth Mooney, who left the Johnson staff to join Hunt's in 1958. Hunt was sure Lyndon would be able to control what he viewed as the ever present threat of Communist subversion in the government. And finally, the man who had emerged as Lyndon's major opponent for the nomination was a Catholic, and Catholicism was an anathema to Hunt.

So by the time Lyndon's candidacy for the nomination was in as full swing as it was ever to be, Walter Jenkins was accepting, and putting to use, money from the Texas oil interests. Booth Mooney relates that on two occasions he personally carried packets of 100 hundred-dollar bills.[6] Well, *somebody* had to counteract the Kennedy millions, and probably Hunt was no less savory, only more famous, than many of the Kennedy supporters.

Arthur Krock: "From the moment he almost made the vice-presidential nomination in 1956, Jack Kennedy began to run for president. And in his way, looking around, there was Lyndon Johnson, a very formidable figure in the path, and that started, of course, a rivalry. Well, that brought it into existence.

"I first discovered it by Kennedy occasionally saying to me, 'Why do you give all that space to Lyndon Johnson's achievements? Why don't you think of some of us younger men?' It was always on a kidding basis.

"Johnson would complain about Kennedy and Kennedy's people and how he had given Kennedy the best committee assignments and helped him along, and then Kennedy's people were saying critical things about him, Johnson; how he had summoned Kennedy on a couple of occasions to tell him if his people went on with that, Johnson would take some steps to counteract. So this grew and grew.

"It reminds me of the lines from *Idylls of the King* called 'Arthur and Modred.' One day, as Tennyson relates it, Arthur and Modred were playing in the sand, and Modred built a sand castle, and Arthur kicked it away, and Tennyson says, 'But ever after, the small violence done/Rankled in him and ruffled all his heart/As the sharp wind that ruffles all day long/A little bitter pool about a stone/On the bare coast.'[7] It was sort of like that. Their relations were bound to be those of competitors."

Peter Lisagor: "I was on the *Face the Nation* program with Johnson in Oklahoma City before the convention. When we finished, Johnson invited us to ride back with him in his plane. During the long night of some five hours Johnson was up front talking about how many delegates he thought he would have at the convention. Finally he came back and I began to question him about the Kennedys, and all of the enmity and hostility that he felt for the Kennedys came out.

Sidey: "In the course of doing both Humphrey and Symington, I heard small cracks about Kennedy, but they were never bitter. They knew the game, and the closest they'd get to being bitter was that he was a rich, spoiled kid who had never had to make it. In all honesty, the most vicious evaluation of Senator Kennedy was from Johnson, and that got quite violent at times."

Lisagor: "Kennedy went to see Stevenson at Libertyville before the Democratic convention. Later Stevenson told me that Kennedy described Johnson to him at that meeting at Libertyville, and Kennedy, he said, used some pretty stiff language about Johnson and what would happen if he became the candidate and got elected. I had heard Johnson dwell on Kennedy before the convention, and I knew what Johnson told Stevenson. Stevenson never told me what Kennedy had said. He just said, 'The language was equally sulfurous.'"

For a long time, and indeed even into the convention itself, the specter of Stevenson as candidate loomed in all the contenders' minds.

John Sharon: "Lyndon Johnson had made a commitment to Stevenson. I was not in the room when it was made, but I was right outside the door. Johnson had told him that it was either going to be Johnson at the convention or it was going to be Stevenson. Kennedy couldn't make it; he, Johnson, had well over four hundred votes and probably close to five hundred, and that if he didn't have enough to crest over the top, why he was going to throw his support to Stevenson because he was the only man qualified in the international area to lead the country.

"Stevenson said he repeated to Johnson what his own views were—that he wasn't going to be a candidate,[8] he was going to stay neutral. That was all that Lyndon Johnson wanted to hear."

Newton Minow: "Stevenson didn't particularly like Kennedy, and he did have a couple of meetings with LBJ during this period. LBJ kept saying, 'Now, listen, Adlai, you just hang loose here. Don't make any commitments. You may still get it. Don't help that kid Kennedy. You just stay neutral.' And I believe that Governor Stevenson, at some point, made a commitment that he would do so.

"I think LBJ was using Governor Stevenson. I think he was attempting to keep the situation fluid in the hope that he, LBJ, might get nominated. Although in fairness I would say that I think he would have preferred Stevenson to Kennedy."

"But Governor Stevenson and I had a specific argument about whether or not he was being used by Johnson, and he did not think so. He thought Johnson was playing it straight."

In fact, Adlai Stevenson presented a double problem for the other presidential aspirants. Besides the possibility of his own last-minute candidacy, a draft perhaps, assuming there is such a thing in a presidential convention, there was the problem of his possible designation as secretary of state by whoever should happen to procure the nomination. It was clear that the pro-Stevenson faction would settle for nothing less, and they did not want to wait until after November for assurances.

Roger Kent: "In San Francisco in early June I attended a press conference where some newspaper guy asked Kennedy, 'Now if you are elected president, would you appoint Stevenson secretary of state?' And he said, 'I think any Democratic president would.'

Bill Moyers: "Johnson thought up until late in the preconvention era that Kennedy wouldn't get it—that the religious issue would focus against him and the press would turn on him. He thought Kennedy would have the momentum, but then he would stall short, and there would be a free-for-all in that Symington and Humphrey and other liberals would have knocked each other off and there would be the place for the Great Compromiser. That's how he saw himself.

"But I think by three or four weeks before the convention this perception had melted away, and he really saw that he was unlikely to take it. I think that happened with the Arizona convention when the delegates were chosen. Because he felt that old Senate hands like Carl Hayden and Ernest McFarland and others could get him the majority of the delegates. He didn't go out; he used the standard Washington 'tending the shop' approach. But the Kennedy people came in and took delegates away, western delegates, there in his own backyard. Johnson said, 'There I was, looking for the burglar coming in the front door, and little did I know that the fox was coming through the fence in back. When I woke up, the chickens were gone.'"

The Democratic convention was scheduled to open July 11 in Los Angeles. On July 5, in what surely must have been the anticlimax of the year, Lyndon formally and lugubriously announced his candidacy for the Democratic nomination for president from the theater of the newly completed Senate Office Building.

He spoke of the responsibility weighing heavily on the 6,000 delegates acting for the 179,000,000 Americans at the two national conventions about to take place. "But," he said, "after July the bandwagons will be silent; the dark horses will be out to pasture; and we will stand face to face with whatever destiny this century holds for us."

Lyndon emphasized that he had known intimately all the presidents since FDR in 1937—there had been three—and he went on to make "some observations of the presidency," many of them, one could say, transparently suggesting that the senator from Massachusetts was clearly unsuitable. "If he himself [a president] is narrowly partisan, if he himself is a divisive influence, if he himself is not seasoned and is inexperienced in making government work, he becomes a weak link in the whole chain of the free world," Lyndon said. "The next president is not going to be a talking president or a traveling president. He is going to be and should be a working president."

Walter Jenkins: "I thought that if Kennedy didn't get it on the first ballot, it would have been sort of open. Kennedy had to get it on the first ballot or not at all. Maryland, for instance, was going to vote for him on the first ballot and wasn't really for him. They were going to switch just as soon as the first ballot was over. So were a lot of other states; many of them, including Maryland, would have gone to Johnson.

Jim Rowe: "Johnson and I had dinner the night Frank Church delivered the keynote speech. And while Church was speaking, Johnson said to me, 'There's no way we can stop this fellow, is there?' Said it just as quietly as that. I don't think he had any illusions at all.

"Some of his people did, and he kept fighting, you know. He went through the motions of going down and having a debate with Kennedy and all, but I think he had no illusions."

"THE WORD IN LOS ANGELES IS . . ."

Lyndon and Lady Bird arrived in Los Angeles on Friday, July 8. John Kennedy did not arrive until Saturday, but in no other way could he be said to have been behind Lyndon. There were still some uncommitted delegates, the populous state of Pennsylvania comprising the largest plum still unplucked, and caucuses to attend, bosses to consult, people to persuade. But there was no real indication that the direction of the tide or the wind or the prairie fire, or whatever it was, would change.

Lyndon moved into a suite on the seventh floor of the Biltmore; Kennedy, when he arrived, acquired the same suite two floors above, but then that was only one of several domiciles he occupied during the next week. Stu Symington, who also arrived on Saturday, occupied yet another Biltmore suite in the same corner. Adlai Stevenson, disdaining to be in the thick of the fray, moved into the luxurious Beverly Hills, forty minutes away. He later exchanged that location for the Sheraton-West. Hubert Humphrey, he was at the Statler Hilton. Pleasant accommodations, but not where the action was.

One group with whom Lyndon was particularly anxious to meet, considering that they composed an almost solid front against him, was labor.

Albert Zack: "I flew out with George Meany to Los Angeles. It was quite a planeload of people. The Speaker of the House was on it. Everybody was going from Washington to Los Angeles. Mrs. Meany was also along, and as the plane landed and we were about to get off, Mrs. Meany took out of a bag a John F. Kennedy hat and put it on. Meany said to us, 'There goes my neutrality.'"

Hank Brown: "Very frankly, while I said, 'If Johnson gets the nomination, I'll be for him,' I was not going to help him get the nomination because I was still mad as a wet hen about Landrum-Griffin. It seems like the two times in his life that he really came to bat he had offended labor just before or during the period of engagement before the marriage. In 1948 he had offended us very deeply with his overriding the presidential veto on Taft-Hartley. Then in 1959 most of us believed that he had been foot-dragging on the Landrum-Griffin matter or that we could have substituted for it a bill that would have been better for the working people and for the labor unions of this country."

Zack: "George Meany took Andy Biemiller and me with him to see each of the three candidates. We saw Senator Symington first, and then Jack Kennedy, and then finally Lyndon Johnson. Mr. Meany wanted to explain what it was that labor was seeking, and why.

"Senator Symington was absolutely alone in his suite with the exception of a single secretary. He knew by that time that he was gone; he knew that he didn't have a chance, that the two chief candidates were going to be Johnson and Kennedy.

"Senator Kennedy's office was much different. It was very busy. We went into the parlor, which was almost stripped bare. The key thing was the telephone on the coffee table—one with a lot of buttons and a lot of lines, and it rang quite often. And Kennedy was talking, as we said afterwards, not like a candidate for the nomination, not even like a candidate for president, but like a man who knew he was in, and 'What will we do starting January to achieve these kind of goals?'

"We went from there to Mr. Johnson's suite. It was vastly different. There were a great many flowers. Mrs. Johnson was an advocate, even then, of beautifying what were pretty sterile hotel suites. Mr. Rayburn came over, and we had a long conversation about whether or not the trade unions should support Lyndon Johnson as a candidate for the nomination.

"Kennedy's suite was all business. Symington's suite all gloom. And Johnson's suite—Mrs. Johnson was there; they wanted to give us a drink, give us something to eat—'Have some fruit'—you know, a social event type of thing."

John Kenneth Galbraith: "I was of the old Stevenson group, but I had announced my support of Kennedy two years before. I went out to the convention not as a delegate but as the cochairman of the Democratic Advisory Council. Then the Kennedys discovered that they had nobody on the immediate Kennedy staff—Ted Sorensen apart—who wasn't either Irish Catholic or Jewish. They had no representative of the WASP minority. So I was whisked from the airport to the Kennedy headquarters, decked out with credentials, made into an instant political boss, and given charge of the delegations west of the Mississippi. Along with Jesse Unruh—Jesse had California.

"I was staying at a small hotel across from the Biltmore, and fairly early on in the convention I was coming out from a meeting in the Kennedy headquarters late one night, and there was a big crowd assembled at each side of the sidewalk, watching the notables coming in and out, including Kennedy, who a little earlier had come in from meetings. And as I came out, Johnson was coming in, and he was bowing to the crowd, and nobody recognized him. Kennedy's face and Stevenson's face and Hubert Humphrey's face were known to everybody, but Symington and Johnson were not.

"So we met halfway across this wide sidewalk. Lyndon stopped and pumped my hand and literally embraced me. There was never any doubt but that he was shocked at this lack of recognition. Obviously, in Washington or Texas everybody knew him. And you know, in the enlarged affability of politics, particularly where somebody on the other side is concerned, I stopped and said, 'Senator, great to see you!' He put his arm twice around me, as only Johnson could, and this caused a little reaction from the crowd and some clapping which pleased him very much."

Lyndon had not been in Los Angeles long before he recognized the primary political reality of the 1960 convention—stop Kennedy *first*, and *second* decide what the next step should be.

James H. Rowe, Jr.: "I set up the meeting with Johnson and Stevenson, the breakfast meeting. It was a secret meeting.

"But Rayburn talked Johnson out of keeping it, so we canceled it. Rayburn said that it wasn't wise—or maybe Johnson had second thoughts and said that Rayburn told him to cancel it."

Galbraith: "I was not aware of any liaison between the Stevenson supporters and the Johnson supporters, but I suppose there was such communication—it would be natural. Because, you know, Johnson could count, so could Stevenson. They had been in the same game by then for eight years."[1]

Rowe: "Johnson and I went over to see Humphrey to see if Humphrey could deliver some votes. Humphrey opened the door and Pat O'Connor[2] was there; I can't remember who else. And we were just talking back and forth. 'Hubert, what can you do for me?' Hubert was sort of indicating that maybe he could and maybe he couldn't, at which point there was a big banging on the door and this voice said, 'HUBERT!'

"It was Joe Rauh—we finally recognized the voice. And he said, 'HUBERT! I KNOW YOU'RE IN THERE!' So finally Pat O'Connor went to the door. Joe could see us, and then Joe said he wanted to get in, and O'Connor said, 'You can't come in!' And Rauh started in and poof! Pat hit him[3] and closed the door. That's all. That was the end of the discussion and Johnson and I left."

Joseph L. Rauh, Jr.: "I was by that time committed to Kennedy, but I also was committed to making Hubert the vice-president of the United States. I went back and forth between the Kennedy group and the Humphrey group. I really thought that they made an offer to Humphrey at one stage in June, and I really thought Humphrey had accepted it. Offers and acceptances are a little loose in politics, and Jack Kennedy subsequently said he'd never made an offer to Humphrey and Humphrey subsequently said he never accepted any offer. So I guess it never really took place.

"At any rate, on June 9 there was a fund raising for George McGovern for the Senate, and Jack Kennedy came as one of the speakers. I was helping. As Kennedy went out, he motioned to me to come with him. He was then the leading candidate for president. We got in a taxi. He said, 'There's something I want to talk to you about.'

"He said, 'Your friends on the *New York Post* are going to print a story tomorrow that I have an incurable disease. This will hurt me badly in the campaign. I think you ought to tell them that it isn't fair and that I am not using any suppressant drugs, and that I really am wholly healthy and able to take this job.'

"So I said I would relay the message. Then I said, 'I'd like to ask you a question. What is it going to be on the vice-presidency, because this means a great deal to me.' He said, 'It will be Hubert Humphrey or another midwestern liberal.' And then I simply said, 'Well, I guess that relieves my fears about Johnson.' And he said, 'There's no need for fears.'"

Sam Shaffer: "Before Johnson announced his candidacy John Connally and India Edwards came out to Los Angeles and held a press conference in which they said that John Kennedy suffered from a fatal disease—Addison's disease.[4] They held that press conference on the 4th of July. On the fifth Bob Kennedy held a press conference, denied it, had doctors' certificates. Said his brother suffered from an adrenaline insufficiency which is adequately handled by medication."[5]

Myer Feldman: "Rumors were circulated during the campaign prior to the India Edwards statement. She made the statement because she didn't think the rumors were getting enough attention or having enough effect, so she said it publicly. But we traced the rumors back to the Johnson camp, although we didn't trace them to Lyndon Johnson."

India Edwards: "If they had not held a press conference to deny what I said, the revelation would have caused only a mild ripple and not stirred up the storm it did. Many doctors and laymen have written about JFK's health problem, and all have agreed that he had Addison's disease."[6]

Clark Clifford: "Ambassador Kennedy, Senator Kennedy's father, was outraged by the charge. The entire family—Senator Kennedy, Bobby Kennedy, all the sisters, and all the rest of them—was embittered as far as Senator Johnson was concerned. They felt that it was grossly unfair."[7]

Of course, "grossly unfair" is what one candidate, or his supporters, always says about another candidate who has some advantage he has not exactly earned in the political hustings. Lyndon had enjoyed five years of good health since his heart attack and could not himself reasonably be labeled ill, meaning that the Kennedy forces could not answer in kind, although Bobby had done his best to play up Lyndon's heart condition. Harry Truman thought it "grossly unfair" that the Kennedys should be so rich, or rather that they should have so much money to use for political purposes, that old Joe should be able to, as he put it, buy the nomination for his son.

And quite a number of people thought it "grossly unfair" that Adlai Stevenson should not have another chance, that he should have twice been the victim to Eisenhower's popularity and never reaped his reward.

Elinor Green: "We had had a secret operation for Stevenson in New York State for about eight months and had raised about three hundred thousand dollars. We had about six thousand volunteers from all over the country come to Los Angeles. Paul Butler, the chairman for the Democratic National Committee, had given Stevenson a tiny office under the stairs in the Biltmore; it was dubbed Butler's pantry. He said Stevenson was not a candidate; so this was good enough.

"On one day thousands of people ringed the coliseum and marched round and round for Stevenson, about eight or ten deep, through which the delegates had to go to get in to the coliseum."

Mike Monroney: "I was terribly anxious to have Hubert Humphrey make the nominating speech for Stevenson because he was well known and he would have penetrated a lot of the liberal vote that was going for Kennedy because they felt Johnson was too conservative.

"Humphrey said he'd give anything in the world if he could do it. 'But if I do it,' he said, 'the Minnesota vote, which is tied up for me by the primary, would be automatically withdrawn.' That vote would then be cast by Orville Freeman for Senator Kennedy.

"I said, 'Good Lord, I need you badly. Who can we get?'

"He said, 'Why don't you try Gene McCarthy?' So this was the genesis of that great speech McCarthy wrote sitting on a folding chair in Leroy Collins's office with a pad of paper on his knee. It was one of the great speeches of our time."

On Monday, July 11, the convention officially opened. Paul Butler was much in evidence, as was LeRoy Collins, the affable governor of Florida, who was, as planned in advance by the outgoing chairman, Sam Rayburn, elected chairman of the convention.

Philip Graham, publisher of the *Washington Post*, had brought to Los Angeles not only his wife, Katherine, but an army of *Post* reporters, editors, and photographers. He was a close friend of both the leading contenders, but he had little doubt as to which would come out on top. On that Monday Graham and his friend Joe Alsop requested, and received, five minutes with Jack Kennedy, alone.

Philip Graham: "At Joe's request, I did the greatest portion of our talking and urged Kennedy to offer the vice-presidency to Johnson. He immediately agreed, so immediately as to leave me doubting the easy triumph, and I therefore restated the matter, urging him not to count on Johnson's turning it down but to offer the V-Pship so persuasively as to win Johnson over. Kennedy was decisive in saying that was his intention, pointing out that Johnson would help the ticket not only in the South but in important segments of the party all over the country.

"Joe and I were a bit shaken by his positiveness; his brother Bobby had told me earlier that Johnson would not be considered. We were more startled by his aplomb when he began asking about the party Joe was giving that night at Perino's, saying it was the one event of the convention his wife would really miss.

"On the basis of this I agreed with Al Friendly and Chal Roberts that the *Post* could write for Tuesday that 'the word in Los Angeles is that Kennedy will offer the V-Pship to Lyndon Johnson' but forbade them writing more strongly in order not to embarrass the Kennedy confidence."[8]

Rowe: "Phil Graham said to me, 'You know, Jack is talking about Lyndon as vice-president.' And I said, 'Oh, horseshit, Phil. He's offered that goddamned thing to at least thirty people out here. Don't bother with that nonsense. Tell Kennedy he can play those games with somebody else.' I did mention the conversation with Graham to Johnson, and I remember his reaction. He said, 'Oh, bullshit!'

"Then Graham had a lunch date with Johnson, really to press this vice-presidential thing, but Johnson was very bad-tempered about something that day, mad at Kennedy for something, and Graham didn't dare bring it up.

"But Graham was pushing it. Graham was telling Kennedy, 'The fellow you need is Johnson.' He was telling Johnson, 'By God, you ought to be vice-president. You don't want to be a southern senator all your life. This is your opportunity.' He was a very skillful fellow. Every time he went into a room he'd walk around, look at the phone numbers, and copy them. So at the end the fellow that could communicate with anyone was Phil Graham."

Meanwhile, entirely unknown to Graham, Alsop, and the inner coterie of the *Washington Post*, other forces were at work at the convention on a parallel path and toward the same goal.

Robert Notti: "The early part of June 1960 I went to work as a personal aide to Texas oil billionaire H.L. Hunt and he immediately assigned me to the Johnson-for-president staff. I went to Los Angeles on July 4 and promptly reported to the Citizens for Johnson headquarters in the Biltmore Hotel.

"Several days prior to the opening of the convention I advised Mr. Hunt that in my opinion Lyndon Johnson would not have the slightest chance to get the nomination. Mr. Hunt agreed with me. I then suggested that he should devote his efforts toward getting Johnson the nomination for vice-president.

"Early Tuesday morning, July 12, Mr. Hunt and Booth Mooney began to prepare a rough draft of a memorandum to Lyndon Johnson, to be signed by Booth Mooney, stating why Hunt believed Johnson should consider accepting second place on the ticket if he did not get the top spot. The memorandum also noted that 'The Kennedy people have been very active in seeking an audience with Mr. Hunt. He has not seen them as yet and has no plans to do so unless you ask him to, but he is in a position to get word to them about anything you have in mind.'

"While this draft was still in the typewriter—about 9:00 A.M.—Sargent Shriver, accompanied by Chicago oil man Robert W. O'Meara, an old friend of Hunt's and a friend and neighbor of Shriver's, came to Hunt's suite. Shriver and Hunt met privately, and after Shriver left, the following postscript was put on Mooney's memorandum to Lyndon B. Johnson: 'Since writing the above Mr. Sargent Shriver arrived at Mr. Hunt's room unannounced, and in the course of their conversation wondered if there was any possibility that you would accept the vice-presidential nomination in case Senator Kennedy is nominated for president. Mr. Hunt told him he had no idea but suggested that lines of communication be kept open.' The memorandum was retyped and promptly taken to Lyndon Johnson's suite by Booth Mooney."

The reason Lyndon was angry with Jack that day—Tuesday, July 12—was because the latter seemed about to back out of a commitment he had never actually meant to make, but which the Johnson forces had seized upon with delight. The Kennedy staff had, apparently by error, included the Texas delegation in a form telegram they had sent out to all delegations requesting an opportunity for their candidate to appear and meet the delegates. The Johnson staff had cleverly conceived the idea of the Texas and Massachusetts delegations coming together in a "joint caucus" to hear their respective candidates "debate the issues," whatever the "issues" by that time were. The whole thing could be televised, and how could anyone best the star debater of Southwest Texas State Teachers College anyway? Besides, the confrontation itself suggested that the two candidates were on equal terms in the race.

Graham: "The possibility of 'debate' had given Johnson a tremendous exhilaration. Once again he was a candidate for the presidency with a chance, even an unlikely one. But he was also bone tired from the long Senate session, from the days in Los Angeles, and especially from a grueling morning during which he had spoken before three or four delegations.

"I listened to his ideas about the forthcoming debate, which seemed a bit harsh and personal, and I finally persuaded him at 1:50 (after receiving several pleading notes from his staff) to take a nap until 2:20. A Negro couple from the Ranch were in the room throughout our lunch, and the three of us converged upon him, disrobed him, pajamaed him and got him to bed. As I was tucking him in he began talking in *ad hominem* terms about Kennedy, whereupon I told him 'No, we're not going to say that sort of thing. We're going to talk about the world. Walter Lippmann came out for Kennedy this morning, saying you were an ignoramus about the world, and we're going to show him he's wrong.' He was wonderfully surprised that 'his friend' Lippmann would say that— really unbelieving. Then I assured him I'd jot down some thoughts for him and have him awakened at 2:20. He went off to sleep with a quickness I shall always envy.

"At 2:50 I found Johnson still in pajamas and still sleepy in his bathroom, handed him the typed sheets, said I was still not sure Kennedy could appear, but suggested he scan the sheets in case the 'debate' occurred.

"At three o'clock in the Biltmore, Johnson appeared as though he had had a quiet morning in preparation for this occasion only. And soon after Kennedy appeared and made a fine speech. Johnson then rose and used my 'high road' for his opening, continuing on ad lib for some thrusts at Kennedy which he kept within the bounds of propriety."[9]

Hugh Sidey: "Senator Kennedy did not plan to go down, and then Lyndon went on TV, you know, on the challenge. As the crowd gathered, Fritz Hollings called up Senator Kennedy and said, 'You know, you'd better get down there. If you don't, Johnson's really going to give it to you.' This was just a few minutes before the time was due; Kennedy was about five minutes late, as I recall. He and Bob sat on the stage together, and I remember seeing Kennedy's trousers shake. I guess his leg just shook when he had nervous energy there."

Jake Jacobsen: "Kennedy did a tremendous job. He made a talk that was really very persuasive and nice and complimented Johnson. Just did a hell of a job and got Johnson to where, when he got up, there wasn't much to say. You couldn't argue with a man who was treating you so good, and really it didn't come off as we had expected it to.

"We had it televised. We figured if it went well, enough delegates would be watching it maybe to be persuaded, but the comparison between them was not as great as I'd hoped it would be. I would say that that was about our last gasp."

That was Tuesday. That night the delegates convened in the Los Angeles Sports Arena and approved a platform that included the toughest civil rights pledges in the history of the Democratic party. Southern members of the platform committee sent in a minority report repudiating the platform and attesting to "a calculated effort" by radicals to "drive the South from the Democratic party."

Meanwhile, thousands of people continued to ring the Sports arena carrying placards reading Stick with Stevenson, Adlai Is a Moral Man, etc., and chanting. Inside the arena the object of their enthusiasm—not a candidate, he still insisted, but still a bona fide delegate from the state of Illinois—took his seat on the floor and kindled an outburst of emotion in the galleries that portended what was to come the following night. Those who had infiltrated the floor boosted Adlai onto their shoulders.

The Kennedy staff was not worried. They were reasonably confident, with the confidence born of being clearly the largest and best-trained and most single-minded staff there.

James Symington: "I could see the Kennedy techniques of communication with their little radio beepers. They were in touch with every delegation. They knew much more, I think, about each delegate and what his spots were and his hopes and aspirations than any of the other people. The Kennedys really made a study of it in a very professional fashion.

"Whereas we were just sort of the good guys of America. We had, I think, one delegation the night before the roll call—what the devil was it? Kansas, I think. We had it by one vote and went to bed on it and woke up and that one vote had changed. I went and asked the guy, and he burst into tears right on the floor there, saying, 'Don't ask me; I can't tell you.' So we realized that we were really outclassed as far as professional performance is concerned."

David Lilienthal: "I particularly saw Robert Kennedy on the floor. He didn't make a very favorable impression on me. The word was spread—you know how the emotional temperature is at a convention—that Robert Kennedy was bearing down on people, meaning something a little more than just persuasion."

But business was conducted not only on the convention floor. Hotels, restaurants, and private homes from Beverly Hills to Malibu were the scenes of gala parties that went on well into the wee small hours and almost overlapped with the equally gala breakfasts of the following day. At one such breakfast at the Huntington-Sheraton in Pasadena the Pennsylvania delegation—eighty-one votes—listened to the avowals of Senators Symington, Johnson and Kennedy, after which three-quarters of them followed Governor David Lawrence in endorsing Kennedy. At a less crucial but somewhat larger affair, Perle Mesta invited seven thousand people—all the delegates plus those of her friends who were in town—to meet Senator and Mrs. Johnson over orange juice, coffee, or whatever liquid refreshment they preferred.

At approximately 3:00 P.M. Pacific Daylight Time—5:00 P.M. in Johnson City, Texas, and 6:00 P.M. in Hyannis Port, Massachusetts—thousands of people began to file into the Sports Arena, among them 1,520 delegates who that night would nominate the Democratic candidate for president of the United States.

WEDNESDAY NIGHT

There was ample room on the floor of the Los Angeles Sports Arena to seat the delegates, alternates, and other persons of prominence, altogether numbering in the neighborhood of two thousand. Another 15,600 could be seated in the balconies. The press, of course, had a large section of the floor to itself, and if in the crowd you couldn't see what was happening, you had only to look up at the giant TV screen to see the speaker, enlarged ten times.

Directly opposite the rostrum where LeRoy Collins presided, from where Frank Church had delivered the keynote speech on Monday night and Adlai Stevenson had acknowledged the applause on Tuesday, was the VIP box, occupied that night by Eleanor Roosevelt and Herbert Lehman, and with a place where Harry Truman would have sat had he attended the convention.[1] In the exact center of the floor, halfway between the rostrum and the VIP box, a platform supported the large TV cameras on their swivel bases. Everything was laid out according to plan, but with several thousand people milling around, banners, flags, and balloons everywhere, and the incessant noise, it hardly appeared so.

Outside the arena were grassy areas and the inevitable palm tree, one. A home show had taken place at the arena just before the convention, and builders had constructed two rather ample "cottages" just to the left of the rear entrance. The Kennedy forces had requisitioned one for their headquarters and the Johnson forces the other. Opposite them were two trailers from which the smaller Stevenson and Symington staffs operated.

The nominations began about four o'clock. John Kennedy was nominated by Orville Freeman. Sam Rayburn, to be sure, nominated Lyndon. Rayburn was not quite the robust figure that had chaired past conventions. The House had recessed only ten days before, and he was still tired, but he spoke with the old fervor of "these times of terrible trial, of grave risk . . . somber, sobering hours in which we gather here to select the man who must lead the forces of freedom."

The thrust of his speech was the same as Lyndon's announcing his candidacy the week before: "This is no time to experiment. We must offer a man who has demonstrated that he can lead. He must not be just a man who wants to lead; he must be a man who has proved that he knows how to lead." Emphasis on *demonstrated, proved,* and *knows how;* the words *lead, leader,* and *leadership* recurred thirty-eight times during the speech.

Rayburn spoke of Lyndon as "a poor boy who dreamed great dreams," emphasis on *poor.* He described him as a man who "has demonstrated a priceless capacity for getting people to work together," who "lives by Isaiah's advice—'Come, let us reason together.'" With the hint of a quaver in his voice, Rayburn said, "I have been a member of the Congress of the United States for nearly half a century. I have worked beside more than three thousand members of Congress from every nook and cranny of America. Every giant of the past half century in this country I have known personally. I think I know a great leader when I see him. . . .

"This is a man for all Americans," Rayburn concluded, "a leader matured by long experience, a soldier seasoned in many battles, a tall, sun-crowned man who stands ready now to lead America. . . . With great confidence in your judgment, I give you the name of the proven leader which these anxious times demand—

"Your friend, and my friend, LYNDON B. JOHNSON OF TEXAS."

Stuart Symington was also nominated that day, and various of the favorite sons, including Hubert Humphrey, whose Minnesota delegation was still pledged to him in spite of the fact that its governor, Orville Freeman, nominated Kennedy, and its other senator, Eugene McCarthy, nominated Adlai Stevenson.

Although he never did announce as a candidate and could not be a favorite son because almost the entire Illinois delegation, under his old friend Mayor Daley, was pledged to Kennedy, Stevenson had decided to allow his name to be placed in nomination *just in case*; there was always the possibility that a compromise candidate might be needed after all. And this was, of course, the real reason—not previous commitments of neutrality at all—that he had declined to nominate Kennedy.

The high point of the nominations was Eugene McCarthy's ringing plea for Stevenson's nomination. "Do not reject this man who has made us all proud to be Democrats. Do not leave this prophet without honor in his own party." The appeal continued, McCarthy's resonant voice and sense of timing holding his audience as no convention speech had done for many years.

Mike Monroney: "Dore Schary was in charge of the Stevenson demonstration. Somehow when word got out that Stevenson was going to come in, the galleries started filling up with Stevenson people. I've always had the feeling—I couldn't prove it—that Dore Schary, who had been a great movie producer, had counterfeited the Pinkerton uniforms and put them on his own men and removed the guards from the door by order so that these Stevenson people were allowed to come in."

Robert Fratkin: "We held a thirty-minute demonstration. LeRoy Collins kept turning the lights out and turning the lights on. We didn't stop until Mike Monroney, the senator from Oklahoma, said, 'We're not gaining ground; we're losing ground.' And Bobby Kennedy kept saying, 'It doesn't matter how many people demonstrate or how much noise they make. The votes are down there'—pointing to the floor where the delegates were—'and all this hasn't changed one single vote.'"

The delegates, who were in a hurry for the end of tedious nominations and the beginning of their own act in the play, were obviously restless, a fact lost upon the demonstrators but not on the more politically canny like McCarthy and Eleanor Roosevelt, both of whom joined Collins in trying to stop the goings-on.

When at last it was over, the balloting began. Up until Illinois Lyndon kept even pace with Kennedy, but the optimism of the Johnson camp, expressed in loud cheers each time a new bloc of votes was acquired, faded with the second half of the alphabet, and any hope that a second ballot might be in the offing was soon ended.

Mike Manatos: "Senator O'Mahoney, because of his health, was unable to go to the convention, and he asked the Wyoming Democratic convention whether I could be designated delegate in his place. He had only one instruction: he wanted me to vote for Lyndon Johnson on the first ballot; if it went to the second ballot, it was up to me.

"As the roll call of the states approached Wyoming, New Jersey, which had originally passed,[2] came over and asked if we could defer to them when it came Wyoming's time to cast its vote. We were just a little too alert to the possibilities we had to do that.

"Tracy McCraken, who was then chairman of the convention delegation, and Joe Hickey, governor of Wyoming, who were sitting in front on me, turned around and asked, 'Well, what are you going to do?'—knowing full well that I was a Johnson delegate.

"I recall that my contribution to the hasty conference on the floor was that we would be absolutely foolish to pass up this opportunity to nominate the next president. It was obvious it was going to be John F. Kennedy. Right behind us was the District of Columbia delegation, and if we didn't nominate Kennedy, they sure were going to."

The candidates, the major ones anyway, were watching the proceedings on television. Lyndon, with Lady Bird, Lynda, and Luci, were settled in cushioned comfort in their suite at the Biltmore. In the living room a large group of reporters, photographers, and TV personnel gathered; Lyndon joked with them, offered them drinks, ordered sandwiches sent up, then retired to the bedroom to watch the balloting.

Stevenson and Symington were also in seclusion with members of their families. Kennedy had watched the nominations with his parents in the luxurious Beverly Hills villa they had leased from Marion Davies for the week, but before the balloting began he returned with Dave Powers, an old friend, to his hideaway apartment on North Rossmore Boulevard. On the other side of the country, overlooking another ocean, Jackie, her mother and stepfather, with Caroline asleep in the next room, also watched. When the vote reached Wyoming, the television camera zoomed in on a widely grinning Teddy in the center of the Wyoming delegation. Mike Manatos's hasty conference had been successful, and Tracy McCraken, unable to disguise the jubilation in her voice, reported into the microphone that Wyoming cast "all fifteen votes for the next president of the United States."

After that it was bedlam.[3]

Booth Mooney: "After Kennedy was nominated, Johnson snapped off the television and said, 'Well, that's that. Tomorrow we can do something we really want to do—go to Disneyland, maybe.'"

Rayburn's tall, sun-crowned candidate lounged in pajamas, received close friends, sipped Scotch and water, chatted amiably and appeared to regret nothing.

Rayburn himself, exhausted from the tension of the evening, anxious to retire for the night, still had one thing on his mind. He put in a call to Lyndon. He had a premonition, he told his friend, that John Kennedy would offer Lyndon the vice-presidential nomination in the morning. He must not take it, Rayburn said. Lyndon told him to rest easy, that he didn't think Kennedy was going to do anything of the sort, but if Kennedy did, he would give no answer before consulting Mister Sam.

One more thing Lyndon did that night. He sent a telegram of congratulations to John Kennedy.

Bill Moyers: "He knew that no matter what was going to happen at the convention, the glory days of the majority leadership, in which he reveled, were over. That is, if a Democrat got the nomination and won the election, then that Democrat was going to be Mr. Democrat in the nation. Not Lyndon Johnson.

"Second, if Nixon got the nomination for the Republican party and was elected, Nixon was not going to be Eisenhower. Eisenhower was benevolent, passive, cooperative, collaborative, as much a Democrat as a Republican. And the vacuum was there for Johnson to do what he had done as majority leader. On the other hand, if Nixon were president—partisan, narrow, an in-fighter, a vehement man, not given to collaboration, a loner, not trusting of the legislative process—Johnson knew that his relationship with the White House was over. And given his own feeling about the uncertainty of things, better to be ready to take advantage of a new situation than to hope to hold on to the old. Johnson was never one to believe that a train ran down the same track twice. If you wanted to get to where you were going, you didn't take the same train two days in a row. 'Keep moving,' he said. 'Keep moving, boy, if you're going somewhere—keep moving. Keep looking. Keep waiting. You miss one train—another will come by.'

"That was why he didn't have the sense of a tragic figure on the night of the nomination, nor was he exceedingly disillusioned. Disappointed and exhausted, yes, but he didn't feel it was the end of the world. Boats leave tomorrow. Trains run all the time. No, the moment that that roll call was finished, I think he began to say, 'What do I do now?'"

AND THURSDAY MORNING

Theodore C. Sorensen: "I had great respect for Johnson. I think he was an unusual person. Had great heart, great energy, wanted to do great things. I think he was an asset to the Kennedy ticket in 1960.

"The selection of a vice-president is not the writing on the clean slate that one thinks it is. After a while, you get down to the choice of who is going to hurt you the least. So the list narrows down by itself rather quickly. In the 1960 case it was particularly important that the vice-presidential candidate be a Protestant and not be from the Northeast. Of those ending up on my list as viable possibilities, I ranked Johnson at the top.

"I do not want to exaggerate the importance of my list in Kennedy's selection. I'm sure he got many lists and in the end made up his own mind.[1]

"I think it is true to say that Kennedy did not expect Johnson to say yes, and it would be inaccurate to say that he was hoping Johnson would say no. Johnson was the logical person to ask. He was the runner-up at the convention. He was the leader of that segment of the party where Kennedy had very little strength—the South, and to some extent the West. He was the leader of the party in the Senate. He was a man with whom Kennedy had worked and knew he could work. Compatible. And he was a man whom Kennedy admired. Had the greatness, the stature.

"So for all those reasons, it was logical to go first to Lyndon Johnson and ask him if he would be vice-president."

Clark Clifford: "Shortly after Senator Kennedy was nominated, I got a message to meet with him in a private room he had, at which time he told me that he'd discussed the matter in considerable detail with his advisers and had decided to ask Senator Symington to be his running mate, and that I was to convey that to Senator Symington and tell him he was the choice. And he was to consider it and give his answer as promptly as possible to Senator Kennedy.[2]

"I met that night with Senator Symington and his wife and his sons and their wives, and the matter was discussed at great length, and Senator Symington finally made the decision that he would accept the offer, and I then conveyed that word to Senator Kennedy.

James Symington: "We went to bed in a troubled state of mind, fully expecting to wake up and find ourselves Little Goody Shoes in the trail of the Kennedy crowd, number two, and all being patted on the head. Well, the first headline that I saw was 'Symington the Choice.' That was the Los Angeles paper—one of them. And then the thing began to take a little longer. We weren't so sure. And then we finally saw Kennedy on television.

"It looked as if he'd really been through a night, and apparently he had, and at that time he announced that Lyndon Johnson was his choice."

Richard Scammon: "One must never forget that Jack Kennedy was essentially a very smart politician. Because of the tragedy of his death, many people ascribed to Kennedy a whole framework of attitudes and patterns of behaviour which simply weren't there. Kennedy was really not the great emotionalist that some people think he was. He was a pretty hardheaded guy. He was also political right down to his fingertips. I think he recognized that in a tight fight, as a Roman Catholic, he needed all the help he could get, and that Johnson in a sense epitomized the viewpoint of a group in the Democratic party and in the country at large.

"There are a hundred stories about who talked to whom on what telephone at what hour of what night. You know, you can almost pick your choice there. With his death, we'll never know what went through his mind."

Lady Bird: "I remember we went to sleep that night after Kennedy had won the nomination, and we were relaxed and ready to sleep around the clock. *That* was over with.

"Then my recollection is that I was awakened the next morning by the telephone, and it was Senator Kennedy himself, to talk to Lyndon."

Bill Moyers: "I remember very distinctly on the morning after the nomination the phone ringing. I was up, and I walked into their bedroom to get them up. As I walked into the darkened bedroom, Mrs. Johnson answered it. She said, 'Just a minute,' and she shook Mr. Johnson awake and said, 'Lyndon, it's Senator Kennedy, and he wants to talk to you.' And Johnson sat up in bed, said, 'Yes, yes, yes, yes sure, come down about ten thirty.' And he handed the phone back to Lady Bird and she put it back in the cradle.

"Lady Bird said, 'I wonder what he wants.'"

Homer Thornberry: "The next morning after Kennedy was nominated I called Lyndon and said that I wanted him to know that while I was sorry, maybe the situation would work out best for him, and to know that I was still his friend and still had confidence in him—something along those lines. He thanked me and he said, 'Kennedy's coming to see me in a little while. He may be wanting to talk to me about the vice-presidency. What do you think?'

"I said, 'Oh, you can't do that. It's just not something that you'd want to do. And you'll upset so many people back home; I just don't believe you should do that.'

"He said, 'Well, here's my problem. If I refuse it and go back as majority leader and Kennedy chooses somebody else, and he loses, they'll blame me for it, and then my position as majority leader might be in jeopardy. If he wins, they'll say, "He won without your help," and then I'll have some problems. Finally, I may owe a responsibility to try to carry this country for the Democratic party.'

"I said, 'Well, I just don't know. My advice to you is not to do it. I just don't believe I'd do it.' He said, 'You think about it.' Something like that.

"I went back. I was shaving. I got to thinking about it, and I went back to the phone, and I got his suite, and I told whoever answered, I said, 'Will you deliver a message to Senator Johnson? Just say to him that I believe I was mistaken and I've changed my mind.'

"In a minute he came on the phone, and I repeated what I'd just said. And he said, 'Well, what do we do about Mr. Rayburn?' I said, 'That's not your job. That's up to Kennedy. If he asks you to do it and you accept, then it's up to Kennedy to talk to Mr. Rayburn.'"

Hale Boggs: "The morning after the night Kennedy was nominated I got a telephone call from Tommy Corcoran asking me if I could get down to the Biltmore right quick. I did, and I woke up D.B. Hardeman, who was then associated with Mr. Rayburn, and we went down to Mr. Rayburn's room. Mr. Rayburn was there with only John Holton, his administrative assistant. Mr. Rayburn said, 'What do you think about this?' I said, 'Well, do you want Nixon to be president of the United States?' I knew that this was one thing that he didn't want to happen. That's a gross understatement. And he said, 'You know I don't.'

"'Well,' I said, 'unless you approve of Lyndon taking the nomination, that's what's going to happen.' 'Well,' he said, 'that's right. He's got to do it.' That's about how much discussion there was.

"And in his political mind, and he had a remarkable mind, he immediately started realizing the handicaps and he knew that already the opposition had set in. And he said, 'Get Senator Kennedy down here so we can decide *immediately*.' So I wound my way upstairs to Kennedy's suite.

"He was mobbed by people, and I just kind of eased on in, you know, and finally got next to him, and said, 'Look, you better go down there and talk to the Speaker right now.' He said, 'Yes. Where is he?' I told him where, and I said, 'You better come *now*— not a half an hour from now.' I said, 'Come *on*.'

"So I went on back, the old man was getting a little impatient. About that time Kennedy walked in with Kenny O'Donnell. Kennedy said to Mr. Rayburn something which implied, 'Would you like to have Hale here while I talk with you?' And I said, 'Why, senator, you and the Speaker talk. Kenny O'Donnell and I will talk.' I scarcely knew Kenny O'Donnell.

"Senator Kennedy walked out of the room positively exuberant. And from that point on, Mr. Rayburn was a hundred percent for the Kennedy-Johnson ticket."

Hugh Sidey: "Sam Rayburn went in there and said, 'You better take it. Kennedy wants you; he needs you; you better take it.' Johnson said, 'Mr. Rayburn, last night you told me not to take it.' And Rayburn said, 'I'm a wiser man this morning.'"

Buford Ellington: "Senator Johnson called me that morning: 'Come over here real quick.' "I got over there then in just a very few minutes. The halls were jammed, but the police got me down there. In a few minutes Bob Kerr got there, and John Stennis from Mississippi was brought in. A lot of boys like John Connally and Bobby Baker and Earle Clements were there.

"I remember very well Bob Kerr. When he walked in the door, Bob said, 'I know what's up, and I'll go get my long rifle. It ain't going to happen!'"

Oren Harris: "Senator Kerr said, 'Lyndon, they tell me that Jack Kennedy wants you to be his running mate. If you accept, I'll shoot you right between the eyes.'

"Sam Rayburn got to him immediately without any chance of further conversation, took him into the bathroom and closed the door.

"After some period of time, Bob Kerr came walking out of the bathroom, Sam Rayburn beside him. He said only one thing; he said, 'Lyndon, if Jack Kennedy asked you to be his running mate, and if you don't take it, I'll shoot you right between the eyes.'"

James H. Rowe, Jr.: "I remember one stage—Phil Graham and I in sort of a big living room, and Kerr yelling at Lyndon. I can't remember if Rayburn was in the room. There were two or three of what I would call powerful southern senators. They were just giving Lyndon hell. Price Daniel—I remember him talking—'Kennedy's just a boy, Lyndon. Don't pay any attention.' Pretty tough talk, to such an extent that Phil said to me, 'We're not southerners, Rowe; we better get the hell out of here.'

"And as I later learned, the same thing was going on in Kennedy's suite upstairs. Goldberg and all that crowd, yelling."

Walter Jenkins: "Kennedy came down, and he and Johnson went into another room and talked privately. And then he left, and Mr. Johnson came out and said that Kennedy had asked him to be vice-president. He said he had declined, but Kennedy had insisted. He said that then he told Kennedy that the vice-presidential candidate had to be the unanimous choice of the convention, and he could never be that. Kennedy said that he had already checked with David Lawrence, then governor of Pennsylvania, and with Carmine de Sapio, a political leader in New York City, and that they had approved of Johnson.

"Johnson said he then told Kennedy that he had better talk to people like Walter Reuther, head of the UAW, and Soapy Williams, governor of Michigan, because he knew they wouldn't approve of him. He told us that Kennedy had said he would do that, and that is the way it was left. After that we didn't hear anything for a long time, and we thought it was all over."

Albert Zack: "Early in the morning of that day Walter Reuther, Arthur Goldberg, [then counsel for the United Steel Workers], and Alex Rose [head of the hatters union and the New York Liberal party] went over to see Kennedy and to talk to him about vice-presidential candidates. Our choices would have been any one of a number of people. Symington would have been perfectly acceptable. A number of our people were for Scoop Jackson. Many were for Hubert Humphrey. It was a pretty wide choice. None of them would have said Lyndon Johnson.

"Before they left the room, as I understand it, Jack Kennedy took Arthur Goldberg into the men's room and told him that it was Johnson. He was the only one that knew anything about it, that Kennedy had even made the decision.

"Later, Bobby Kennedy went over to the Statler and told them that it was definite that the candidate had decided on Johnson. Either Rose or Reuther, I don't remember, said, 'Well, let's talk about it.' And Bobby said, 'There's nothing to talk about; the candidate has made up his mind,' and left."

Michael DiSalle: "The morning following the nomination Kennedy asked a group of people that supported him what they thought about Lyndon Johnson for the vice-presidency.

"There were two groups. Abe Ribicoff [governor of Connecticut], and I sat through both meetings. The first meeting was held with northern leaders, and in that group were Soapy Williams, Carmine de Sapio, Dick Daley, Pat Brown [governor of California], possibly Mike Pendergast from New York, John Bailey [Democratic National Chairman-elect], myself, and Ribicoff. Of that group the only person who spoke out in opposition to Johnson was Williams because of his strong labor organizations in Detroit and the fact that Johnson had opposed civil rights and liberal legislation generally—at least that's what they thought.

"Right after this meeting broke up came the southern leaders like Terry Sanford [soon-to-be-elected governor of North Carolina], Luther Hodges [then governor of North Carolina], Senator Ed Brown of South Carolina, Buford Ellington [governor of Tennessee], and of course they were unanimous in support of Johnson.

"As I was leaving the Biltmore, I ran into Art Goldberg and Walter Reuther. Both of them were furious. They had heard what was in the wind. They felt it would destroy the ticket, that labor would back away. They talked about a fight on the floor to keep the convention from accepting Johnson."

Leonard Woodcock: "We had a meeting of our Michigan delegation the morning following the presidential ballot. Governor Williams was our chairman, and he reported that he was just going to a discussion about the vice-presidential nominee, but it was quite certain that it would be Symington. So we broke up; I went down to have lunch at the Biltmore, came strolling back, to the Statler, and the first person I run into is Joe Rauh, who had tears literally rolling down his cheeks. Have I heard the news? I couldn't possibly imagine what was causing such consternation. It seemed the news was that Lyndon Johnson was Jack Kennedy's pick, and that Kennedy had betrayed us all. Well,

I, very frankly, was shocked, because our whole theme had been to unite behind Kennedy to stop Johnson.

"I went upstairs to Walter Reuther's suite, and quite a few of our people from around the country were sitting around with their chins hanging on their chests. Alex Rose was there, too, of the Liberal party and the hatters' union in New York. We were all sitting around as though it were a wake, and at this point one of the girls stuck her head in and said, 'Mr. David Dubinsky is calling from New York for Mr. Rose.' I remember Walter saying, 'Well, Alex, you're going to get your head taken off. As a matter of fact, just open the window—you'll be able to hear him.'"

David Dubinsky: "I was at my summer home in Hampton Bays on Long Island, when suddenly, on the day after Kennedy won the nomination, I got a call from Goldberg.

"Naturally, the first thing I asked him was, 'What's doing?' He said, 'Kennedy wants to nominate Johnson as vice-president.' I jumped. 'It's terrific,' I said, 'it's a winning ticket.' That was my instant reaction. 'Yes, but your friends don't think so,' said Goldberg. I asked, 'Who are my friends?' He replied, 'George Meany, Walter Reuther, Alex Rose.'

"'What,' I said. 'Alex too? I think he's crazy.' Goldberg answered, 'I think so too, but still and all that's the situation here. They want Hubert Humphrey or Stuart Symington, not Johnson.' So I said, 'I'm going to talk to them.'"[3]

Woodcock: "So Rose goes out to take the phone call, and at that point I said, 'Well, I was a delegate in '52, and I voted for John Sparkman for vice-president. Lyndon Johnson isn't a John Sparkman, and Texas isn't Alabama. And I'm not so sure that this is all that bad.' Walter picked it up, and some of our number sort of rallied around.

"We were just about to break up when Alex Rose came back in. He'd obviously had a lengthy conversation. And he said, 'Dave Dubinsky thinks that this is the smartest thing that could ever have happened. It's wonderful! It's great!'"

John Kenneth Galbraith: "The night Kennedy was nominated was the last time in my life I think I never went to bed at all. I got back to the hotel about 10:00 A.M., and as I started to get into bed the telephone rang and it was Bobby saying, 'Get back out to the convention hall—it's going to be Lyndon Johnson.' I said, 'What do you mean?' He said, 'Well, Jack's decided and you've got a revolt on your hands. You'd better go out there and see what you can do.'

"So I lay down on the bed for a few minutes, then struggled out, went over to the Biltmore, and rode out to the convention with Eunice and Pat and Sarge. And all of them very, very quiet. We never talked all the way out. I was figuring out what I was going to do.

"So I put in a solid couple of hours with all of the delegations where I thought I had some influence. The argument I was using was, 'Look, nobody objected when FDR made a deal that took along John Nance Garner, and here's JFK taking along a man a hundred years in advance of Garner. It's not the man we chose for president, but it's not Garner, so for God's sake give Kennedy the same right that you would have automatically given FDR!' You see, it was only fifteen years after FDR. And that argument—so far as any argument is ever useful—worked. And I went from one delegation to the next with that short argument. And you could see the temperature go down. People were looking, really, for an excuse to go along and not have the fight."

Philip Graham: "On Thursday, about 1:45 P.M., I went to Johnson's suite in the Biltmore. The Los Angeles papers and the press corps in general were prophesying Symington. On entering Johnson's suite, he at once seized my arm and took me into his bedroom, alone with Lady Bird. He said that Bobby Kennedy was with Sam Rayburn in another part of the suite. . . .

"We sat on a bed, the three of us, about as composed as three Mexican jumping beans. Lady Bird tried to leave. Johnson and I lunged after her, saying she was needed on this one. I tried to duck LBJ's inquiry, but finally said I felt he had to take it. Lady Bird was somewhere between negative and neutral. At that point Sam Rayburn entered and said Bobby wanted to talk directly to LBJ. Lady Bird intervened, apologizing by saying she had never yet argued with Mister Sam, but saying she now felt LBJ should not see Bobby.

"LBJ asked my advice—the while all of us were pacing around the bedroom, in and out of the bathroom, etc., 'No,' I said, 'you shouldn't see him,' and then repeating LBJ's expression on the bed previously, 'You don't want it, you won't negotiate for it, you'll only take it if Jack drafts you, and you won't discuss it with anyone else.'"[4]

Jenkins: "Mr. Johnson didn't talk to Bobby. When he came and announced that he wanted to see Mr. Johnson, Mrs. Johnson was very wise and said Mr. Johnson shouldn't see him. She said, 'If Jack wants to talk with you, that's one thing, but I don't think you should see anybody else. Send him to Mr. Rayburn or John or somebody.' So Bobby saw Mr. Rayburn.[5]

"Now exactly what was said I don't know, but I believe it was that there was too much opposition against Mr. Johnson. I know whatever was said by Bobby made Mr. Rayburn even more convinced that Johnson should take it."[6]

Graham: "Finally it was decided. Mr. Sam was to tell Bobby LBJ's position and why he wouldn't see Bobby. I was to go phone Jack LBJ's position. I dragged Jim Rowe along as witness and we went out through thirty or so press people in the hall, down into a vacant bedroom."

Rowe: "I was in the room when he called. He said to Kennedy, 'Johnson hasn't heard from you.' Kennedy said to Graham, 'Well, I'm under terrific pressure against Johnson here.' And Graham—he could be very tough—said, 'Do you want to be another Adlai Stevenson? Are you going to go back and forth?' In effect, are you a man or a mouse? That's the way Graham talked. He said, 'You call Johnson.' And Kennedy said that he would."

Rowe reports only one telephone conversation between Phil Graham and Kennedy that afternoon; Graham in his memorandum says he made three. In the first call Kennedy mentioned "a general mess because some liberals were against LBJ," and asked Graham to call back "in three minutes." Graham says he stretched the three minutes to ten and called back, at which time Kennedy said, according to Graham, "It's all set. Tell Lyndon I want him and will have Lawrence nominate him." He also asked Graham to call Adlai Stevenson and inform him of his decision, which Graham did.

Then, Graham says, Lyndon sent for him to say that still no call had come from Kennedy. Graham took down the number of Lyndon's bedroom phone and said he'd call

Jack again, which he did. Kennedy, when reached, said he'd call at once, but then again mentioned the opposition to Lyndon and asked for Graham's judgment. "I said something to the effect that the southern gains would more than offset liberal losses, and added that anyway it was too late to be mind-changing and that he should remember 'You ain't no Adlai.' He agreed about the finality of things."

Still the call from Kennedy did not come.

Rowe: "I went down to make sure Johnson didn't wander off—to make sure he was at the phone. A few minutes later Kennedy called. Bird was in the room, and Johnson took the call sitting on one bed; I was on the other. Kennedy said—I could hear him, 'This is the statement I'm going to issue,' and he read it.

"Johnson's only comment was, as I remember it, 'Do you really want me?' And Kennedy said, 'Yes, I do.' Johnson said, 'Well, if you really want me, I'll do it.' And everybody sort of relaxed, thought it was all settled.

"About ten minutes later Graham and I were back in the room down the hall talking to Adlai—he was being difficult in his usual way—when Bill Moyers came up yelling, 'Graham, my God, Bobby is in the room!'"

Sorensen: "Bobby's position, as expressed to me later, was that he was primarily a messenger boy.

"First, he was a messenger boy to go clear the Johnson appointment with all the various powers to be. Second, a messenger boy that came back to Kennedy and told about a lot of trouble from the AFL-CIO, Soapy Williams, the Liberal party, Joe Rauh, and so on. And third, a messenger boy when Kennedy said, 'Well, go tell Johnson that. Maybe he doesn't want to have a fight either. Maybe he'd rather be chairman of the Democratic National Committee.'

"Bobby merely felt that he was carrying those messages. Johnson felt that it was Bobby creating those messages, creating the opposition. Bobby hadn't created the opposition; he was merely repeating it. He brought the bad news and he was nearly beheaded for it—just like in the old days."

Rowe: "My own theory is that Bobby had left Jack Kennedy's suite to tell Johnson that there was a hell of a lot of pressure against him. While he was gone, Graham called Jack and then Jack called Lyndon. But Bobby didn't know that Jack had just called and made the final commitment. It was just a matter of bad timing, but Johnson thought that Bobby was out to get him, to do him in.

"Johnson came in to where I was and said, 'Bobby's in the other room, and he says Kennedy doesn't want me. It will break up the party and so forth. What am I going to do?' I'd never seen him in such a state of—not panic—confusion."

Graham: "LBJ seemed about to jump out of his skin. He shouted at me that Bobby Kennedy had just come in and told Rayburn and him that there was such opposition and that Lyndon should withdraw for the sake of the party.

"There was considerable milling about and hubbub, and finally Mr. Rayburn said, 'Phil, call Jack.'"

Rowe: "Phil stepped over to the phone, looked in his little notebook, found the number, and finally got through to Kennedy and said, 'Bobby's down here saying such-and-such.' And Kennedy said, 'Well, Bobby's not up-to-date.'

"There were about five or six of us in the room. Kennedy just said, 'Bobby's not up-to-date.' He said to Graham, 'I've already announced that Johnson is the candidate.' Then Jack said, 'Put Lyndon on the phone.' So Lyndon picked up the phone. I really don't know what Kennedy said then, but Johnson sort of grunted and said, 'All right. Let me go outside and accept.'

"Bobby had come in, and I think Jack said to Lyndon, 'Put Bobby on the phone.' Bobby got on the phone and said, 'Well, all right.' And hung up. Everybody left except Bobby and me. And Bobby sort of looked at me, and said, 'Jim, I guess we were all too tired.' And then he said, 'Don't you think Symington or Jackson would be better?'"

There is, at this point, yet one more final difference of opinion concerning the star actors of this drama. Kennedy, according to Walter Jenkins, made yet another trip down two flights at the Biltmore to speak to Lyndon; Lyndon, according to Evans and Novak, made his first trip upstairs to confirm the agreement with a handshake; neither, according to Phil Graham and Jim Rowe, did anything of the sort. Thursday was apparently just one of those bewitched days when completely contradictory events occurred at exactly the same moment in time in the most unlikely places. Some days are like that.

Graham: "In the entrance hall of the suite LBJ and Lady Bird were standing, looking as though they had just survived an airplane crash, with Lyndon holding a typed statement accepting the V-Pship. 'I was just going to read this on TV when Bobby came in, and now I don't know what I ought to do.'

"With more ham than I ever suspected myself of, I suddenly blurted: 'Of course you know what you're going to do. Throw your shoulders back and your chin out and go out and make that announcement. And then go and win. Everything's wonderful.'"

Luther Holcomb: "I remember Senator Johnson stepping out into the corridor of the hotel right by his door and standing on a chair. And of course the press were on their tiptoes, trying to get pictures. That was when he said, 'If my country thinks I can serve better as a private, I want to serve. If they want me to serve as a general . . . whatever my country wants.'

"Then he said, 'Jack Kennedy has asked me to serve. I accept.'"

FROM BOSTON TO AUSTIN

> And then that little ole Massachusetts boy took his little ole torpedo boat and rammed into the side of a Japanese cruiser, and there wasn't nobody around askin' what religion he was. And when he was savin' those American boys that was in his crew, they didn't ask what church he belonged to.
>
> Basic Lyndon Johnson campaign speech in 1960.

There was, after Los Angeles, a week or two for both candidates to pause and reflect, regroup their support, and reestablish, momentarily, family ties before the return to the capital for the August rump session that Lyndon had, it now appeared, so unwisely scheduled. Kennedy returned to Hyannis Port, and Lyndon, after a few days' vacation in Acapulco, to the Ranch. The staff of the former still muttered protest at their running mate, and the Texas buddies of the latter were even more voluble in their disappointment and frustration. Meanwhile, in Chicago, to no one's surprise, Richard Nixon was named Republican nominee, and also to no one's surprise, although for this there was some desultory competition, the vice-presidential nomination was offered to, and accepted by, Henry Cabot Lodge. Which put Massachusetts, if only briefly, in the undecided column right along with California and Texas.

For Kennedy the two months between Labor Day, September 5 that year, and election day, November 8, were largely a stepped-up version of what he had already been doing since January. The game was the same, only now the team was enlarged, and as a lot of people kept pointing out, it was "a whole different ball park." Nothing was "sewed up" anymore; nothing could be counted upon absolutely; instead of 561 delegates, there was a whole country to persuade.

For Lyndon the roughly two months of the campaign would be quite new. He had never even been in half those states that he must now convince to want him as their vice-president. His religion, not something he was accustomed to giving much thought to, was suddenly of particular value, and the geographical accident of his birth, only a few weeks before his greatest drawback, had become his prime asset. A less welcome reversal was the change in status between himself and the junior senator from Massachusetts, but the pact that he made with the nominee that fateful Thursday morning dictated, by necessity, a new relationship in that regard, and to the best of my knowledge no one ever again reported that Lyndon Johnson spoke ill of John Kennedy.

Lyndon also understood that his whole political future, whether or not he and Kennedy won in November, depended upon his ability to deliver the South to the Democrats. So his first move as nominee was to call a "unity meeting" of all southern governors in Nashville. His good friend Buford Ellington opened up the governor's mansion of Tennessee for the occasion, and although several governors were conspicuous by their absence, Lyndon did not allow that fact to detract from his enthusiasm. They must all work together, he told them; it was "all the way with JFK" now; past prejudices were just that, *past*. As Governor LeRoy Collins of Florida said, "There wasn't anything said there that couldn't have been printed on the front page of a newspaper."

But all that sweetness and light faded—diminished anyway—rather quickly once the realities of campaigning became clearer.

James H. Rowe, Jr.: "Right after the convention I went up to Hyannis Port and helped make the first schedule. I'm an old scheduler. Logistic problems of how you get a candidate around are very difficult, because where you put your candidate depends upon where the electoral votes are and whether you think you can do well or not. Everybody wants the campaign in October and nobody wants it in September.

"I met with Jack, Bobby, Kenny O'Donnell, and Dick McGuire, who was Kennedy's scheduler. We made out his schedule for the whole two months. Bobby then asked, 'How much time can you give us during the campaign?' I said, 'I can't very well give you any, because I have to do it for Lyndon.'

"I came into Hyannis Port about three weeks later with Lyndon to coordinate their campaigns.¹ I did the schedule for Lyndon for his first week in New England where he made his first Boston-Austin speech—'And you Irishmen helped us Texans win World War II, and now we're going to help you elect the president.'

"Kennedy wanted to start in Hawaii, then go to Alaska and then come into Detroit. The only commitment he had made to get the nomination was that if Alaska voted for him, he'd begin his campaign there. So we had to scratch Hawaii. Some way or other, he got Johnson in line to go to Hawaii.

"So I had Johnson on the way to Hawaii—you have to do these things pretty fast. The next day I went in to finish up the schedule. I began, 'After Hawaii , , ,' 'Who said I was going to Hawaii?' 'Well, senator, you said yesterday you were going to Hawaii.' Walter Jenkins, my old friend, was sitting there. Johnson said, 'Walter, did you hear me say I was going to Hawaii?' 'No, I didn't.' So I got a little upset about it. I said, 'My God, you've given Kennedy a commitment.' He said, 'I'm not so sure about that.'

"This was after he was back in his Senate office. Johnson said, 'Let's go talk to Kennedy about it.' So in we went, O'Donnell and Lyndon and I all sat down. Johnson said, 'I've been talking to the Hawaiian senators. They don't think it's advisable for me to go to Hawaii.' He gave some reason. Then he said, 'Well, maybe I'll go out in late October.' Kennedy looked at him in absolute amazement, and said, 'Lyndon, Hawaii? Three votes? In October?' Johnson didn't go at all."

"I was so exhausted after one week of scheduling Johnson that I quit. 'Get somebody else. I've scheduled Adlai, Kefauver, and Kennedy, but all three of them gave me less trouble in the whole business than you've given me in one week,' I said. I called him a Mongol emperor. He didn't like that a damn bit."

James Blundell: "I got to discussing the schedule with him. I said, 'The main thing we want to do is coordinate your schedule with Kennedy's. We don't want you both on the East Coast at the same time. From the standpoint of press coverage, when he's in the East, we want you in the West.'

"He said, 'Now, Jimmy, there's three places I will not go.' I said, 'Really, where's that?' He said, 'I will not go to Chicago, California, and New York City.' I said, 'Well, you just mentioned the three largest voting centers in the country.'

"He said, 'Well, I'm not going to let the liberals cut me up and embarrass Jack Kennedy. And they will, just because I'm a Texan and a southerner.'

"I said, 'You're the boss. We'll do the best we can.' Of course, he went to all three places and was very successful."

Elizabeth Rowe: "He started his campaigning in Boston. Lined up at the Boston airport were a dozen and more little dumpy women, all with great big cowboy hats on. They were all Italian, all good Democrats, and all absolutely overpowered by these great big hats. He came down, twice the size of any of them.

"Then we got in a series of limousines to drive through downtown Boston at lunch hour. We got over to the Copley Plaza and there was a policeman directing traffic on a horse. Johnson just said to the policeman, 'If you will get off that horse, I'll get on.' So he got on the horse and pranced around in the square a little while. That was the starting of 'from Boston to Austin.'"

Jim Rowe: "Walter Jenkins came back with Johnson from the campaign from New England down, Connecticut and finally—New York, Washington, ending up at Johnson's house. Walter, Lady Bird, and I were there. Johnson sent Walter upstairs to get something, and Lady Bird said, 'Walter is so exhausted. It will kill him unless you tell him to take time off.'

"Johnson got up and talked a little more. Walter took it down in shorthand. Everything Johnson wanted to tell someone, Walter took down.

"Finally we started to bed and Johnson said, 'Now, Walter, you're working too hard, and I've told you eighteen hundred times—I want you to get the hell out of here for two or three days.' We got halfway up the stairs, and he turned around and said, 'Walt, by the way,' and then he dictated halfway up the steps for forty-five minutes to Walter, with Walter writing it all down."

On September 9, 150 Protestant clergymen congregated in Washington under the divine leadership of the Reverend Dr. Norman Vincent Peale and issued a statement warning of the pernicious influence of the Vatican foreign policy on a Catholic president. He would, the clergyman said, be "under extreme pressure by the hierarchy of his church" and "duty bound to admit to its direction." The religious issue, the statement concluded, was the most important of the campaign.

Norman Vincent was not, it should be noted, joined in this endeavor by Billy Graham, who back in early August had written to Lyndon assuring him that, contrary to rumor, he had no intention of raising the religious issue publicly. Graham had always been, and always intended to be, a friend to presidents, and it was not at all clear who the next president would be.

When on September 12 Kennedy and Johnson were greeted at the Alamo by pickets carrying signs that read We want the Bible and the Constitution and We Don't Want the Kremlin or the Vatican, Lyndon countered by introducing Kennedy with his "little ole war hero" speech. Kennedy's speech, appropriate for the Alamo, said, among other things, that "side by side with Bowie and Crockett died McCafferty and Bailey and Corey, but no one knows whether they were Catholics or not. For there was no religious test at the Alamo."

The applause was thunderous; many, though not all, of the pickets put down their signs.

That evening Kennedy was scheduled to meet the religious issue head on in Houston; he had accepted an invitation from the Greater Houston Ministerial Association to discuss the relevancy of his religion to the presidency. The confrontation was planned for eight thirty on the neutral ground of the Rice Hotel.

Luther Holcomb: "There was a strong anti-Catholic feeling in Texas. One of the leading businessmen in Dallas throughout that campaign bought radio time—he himself would come on the air I think every morning at six thirty and make a speech. And every kind of pamphlet—the state was literally flooded with wild speculation. All the old stories of maybe there being a pope moving into the White House. All the prejudices of 1928 were brought up to date."

Myer Feldman: "Ted Sorensen and I talked for a long time about whether or not

Kennedy should accept the invitation. Johnson was all for it, but he said that it was like going through mine fields. He told Jack to watch his step."

Theodore C. Sorensen: "Writing the speech for those ministers wasn't easy. It went through many drafts. But when the time came, he delivered it, and it was his best speech during the campaign. It made a great impression. It was telecast not only in Texas but all over the country."

The speech *was* impressive; it still is. "I believe in an America where the separation of Church and State is absolute—where no Catholic prelate would tell the president, should he be a Catholic, how to act, and no Protestant minister would tell his parishioners for whom to vote. . . .

"I believe in an America that is officially neither Catholic, Protestant nor Jewish . . . foɪ while this year it may be a Catholic against whom the finger of suspicion is pointed, in other years it has been, and may someday be again, a Jew—or a Quaker—or a Unitarian—or a Baptist."

Approximately three hundred ministers and an equal number of others listened. The atmosphere, noticeably tense when he began, relaxed and warmed as Kennedy spoke the clear, reasoned prose, and the applause was, if not unanimously enthusiastic, certainly respectful.

In October Lyndon conducted a whistle-stop tour of the South.

Lindy Boggs: "Although I don't think there were advance teams in 1948, Lyndon decided that in 1960 advance teams were necessary, and he decided that in the South in a year when there were civil rights difficulties the only way he could send a team out and be sure it was met with politeness was if he had women on it."

"So six of us went. We wore these costumes that we thought were a little silly—blue blazers, navy blue and white pleated skirts, white blouses, and red hats. We took along Kennedy-Johnson buttons to explain why we were wearing these silly outfits.

"We flew in advance of the train—the LBJ Special it was called. And everything worked out beautifully. What southern gentleman is not going to receive southern ladies when they are coming to his state and his city?"

Virginia Foster Durr: "We got word that the LBJ Special was coming through Montgomery, Alabama, and I went down to see the train come in and try to wave to Bird and let her know that I was with her. It was a very dark and extremely cold and miserable day and the group at the station was very small, and many of them were Republicans with signs derogatory to the president saying, The *Yellow* Rose of Texas, etc. There was a very bad, small and dreadful little high school band that was all out of tune and the whole atmosphere was one of just real tension and no enthusiasm and no warmth and no kind feeling at all.

"So when the train pulled in there was only a very small scattering of applause. Mrs. Hale Boggs had come up ahead of time trying to organize reception committees and passing out the hats and streamers, but it was a very cold reception and a very cold day. All the politicians that came out, like the mayor and the governor and the senators and the congressmen, you could see they were scared to death because they thought Alabama was probably going Republican and by being publicly on record for Kennedy-Johnson they might be cutting their own political throats, so their speeches were not very enthusiastic either.

"Then Lyndon came out. By that time he was a pretty tired man, and I'm sure he did the best he could, but he didn't draw out the crowd. So then he introduced Lady Bird, and she came out in a very bright red suit and she began to speak in that very soft, you know, southern Alabama accent about how she came up every summer to Alabama, came up from Texas, and how she loved Alabama, how she loved to go in the creek and eat blackberries and watermelon and go to the barbecues. And then all of a sudden she looked into the crowd, and she saw an old woman, and she called, 'Oh, Cousin Elaine.' And the woman came up, and she said, 'Come up here.' Then she hugged and kissed her and stood her by her. Then she looked over and saw another cousin and called, 'Cousin Effie and Cousin Carolyn! Come here.' Finally, I think she had six or eight on the platform with her, and it got to be a regular family reunion.

"Well, all this stirred the crowd into the first enthusiasm they had because, you see, this was being true to our own kin, being true to your family, being true to your state. The crowd really went wild with enthusiasm and Bird saved the day."

Blundell: "Senator Johnson said he only wanted to make three speeches a day, and that was my biggest problem, because any time you got six people together, that man was going to make a speech.

"If the Kiwanis Club had a meeting that day, well, the local people are going to insist that Senator Johnson appear at that luncheon club. And maybe there were two or three meetings; they wanted him at all of them.

"And he objected and objected, but he always did it. The primary thing was not selling himself but selling Jack Kennedy. His entire theme all through the South was that you don't make an issue of a man's religion. And he would always tell the story of Jack Kennedy's brother, Joe Junior, going down in that airplane with a copilot from New Braunfels, Texas, and he said, 'I'm sure that they didn't ask each other what church they went to. They both died for their country.' He made a lot of points with that story."

It was in the 1960 campaign that it first became obvious how different the Kennedy style was from the Johnson. To begin with, Kennedy, having trusted his staff to bring about his initial victory in Los Angeles, trusted them again to bring about eventual victory at the polls. Lyndon was always ready to seize upon some minor mishap to explain why things had not gone quite so well somewhere as he would have wished them to. Kennedy always delivered the speech he was handed for a particular occasion. Lyndon generally had two or more people independently writing a speech for a single occasion so he would have a choice; then he made his own changes to the preferred one, and occasionally at the last minute scrapped it entirely.

Campaign funds was another area in which their differences of approach were particularly apparent.

Jim Rowe: "After Kennedy and Johnson had been nominated, a lot of people would come in with cash or checks. One day some fellow came into the Senate cloakroom and said to Kennedy, 'I want to give you this, senator.' Johnson said, 'Not here! Let's get out of this building.'[2] Kennedy looked at him, grabbed the money, and put it in his pocket.

"Kennedy was not so finicky; he would take money anyplace. I don't mean personally. Steve Smith, who was his treasurer in 1960, said that once a week he left his office, went out to Kennedy's house, and went through every suit, just collecting money. He collected cash, checks, etc., in all of Kennedy's suits, all contributions, and took them back and used them. He used to collect thousands of dollars."

Robert Waldron: "Lyndon was always saying to us, 'Now don't let me speak more than fifteen minutes.' One time—as I recall we were in Indiana—we went to this rally, and he said, 'Now don't let me speak but fifteen minutes. I'm only going to speak fifteen minutes.'

"Mrs. Johnson let him have an extra five minutes; then she sent him a note, 'Dear— You've gone overtime; you've been talking twenty minutes.' But he kept right on, and Mary Margaret Wylie sent him a note saying, 'You've been on thirty minutes.' But he still didn't stop. It was just one of those speeches where he was reminiscing and telling stories, and finally he'd been on forty minutes, and Mrs. Johnson wrote him another note and then started tugging on his coat, and he said, 'Now I want to keep on talking to you good people, but my wife and staff tell me I've talked too long.' The crowd shouted, 'No, no, no!' But he stopped, blaming it on us. Said he had been just delighted to talk to these good country people, but *we* wouldn't let him go on. Made us look like absolute beasts for shutting him off."

Blundell: "During the campaign, Johnson kept saying to me, 'Nixon and Lodge are always making joint appearances. When am I going to appear with Jack?' I could tell he was very sensitive about it.

"I don't think Jack ever said this or felt it, but some members of the Kennedy staff felt that Johnson wasn't as *refined* as Kennedy and maybe they shouldn't appear together. I'm not going to get into any personal things, but there was some of that feeling."

Leonard Marks: "The press began writing stories about the middle of October that LBJ and Jack Kennedy were not getting along and that they hadn't talked. Well, in order to put that rumor to rest we agreed that we'd have them meet in New York. Kennedy was coming down from Connecticut, and LBJ was on the West Coast. So I got him to agree to come to New York for that evening. There would be a parade down Broadway, and we would wind up at Columbus Circle for a nationwide TV program at which they would both appear. We were to rendezvous at six o'clock at the Biltmore Hotel.

"They first wanted to give LBJ two minutes on the telecast. I said, 'He's the majority leader; he's the vice-presidential candidate, and you don't give him just two minutes, not to come across the country for that. Kennedy will have twenty minutes. He ought to have at least ten.' Well, finally, we compromised on five, and I had to break the news to him. And he said, 'But I've got an eight-minute speech.'

"I said, 'Look, they may think you're going to talk for five minutes, but I'm going to have the cue cards for you, and I'm going to miss three minutes.' Which is what happened. He made an eight-minute speech.

"But that was only the beginning. The Kennedy caravan was running two hours late, and then we got a report that they were lost."

Blundell: "I said, 'What do you mean lost? Out of communication? How can they be lost? He's got the police commissioner with him; he *can't* be lost.' I was told nevertheless that they were."

Marks: "We were all supposed to meet at the Biltmore and I had rooms reserved for both parties and our party was already there. Then I got word—not only were they lost and it was getting later and raining harder than ever; I got word that they were going to the Carlyle and not the Biltmore. So I got in a cab and rushed up to the Carlyle. Dave Powers was there and he had ordered Kennedy's dinner and had his clothes laid out.

"So I hurried around and ordered rooms at the Carlyle for our party. No sooner had I done that than I got word that the Kennedy party was not coming to the Carlyle after all. They were going to the Biltmore, as originally planned.

"It was all like a Marx brothers movie. It is hard to believe. We got cabs; we vacated the rooms at the Carlyle and went back to the Biltmore, and LBJ and I went to the rooms Kennedy was occupying. He had just got out of the shower and was toweling himself dry when the waitress came in with his second dinner.

"The waitress took one look at him, stark naked, and knowing who he was and all, this poor gal sort of screams and drops his whole dinner on the floor.

"Kennedy says, 'Christ, after all this I won't even get anything to eat!'"

Blundell: "Lyndon went in and talked to him and stayed about fifteen minutes. He came out shaking his head. He said, 'That's the maddest man I've seen in my life, and I don't blame him. They got lost, and he said he had to stop the car himself at a filling station. He said, 'I had to tell them, stop this damn car.' And they stopped and he went into a filling station himself to find out where the hell they were. The Democratic candidate for president of the United States. And then they brought his clothes to the wrong damn hotel."

Marks: "He bawled out the advance man, calling him everything he could think of. They always talk about Johnson's temper and the way he treated his staff. I never heard anything like that in my life.

"And he said to Lyndon, 'Thank God you've got intelligent people working for you.' Lyndon said, 'Yeah, yeah.' I don't think he was too displeased."

Blundell: "There were twenty-five thousand people waiting at Columbus Circle,[3] and they'd been waiting for hours, I don't know how long. But there wasn't anybody to introduce Lyndon; that had been overlooked, so I told Bill Moyers, I said, 'Bill, get up there and introduce him.

"Here's this boy from Marshall, Texas, going up on the platform cold, without any warning, before twenty-five thousand people of New York City. And he made the best damned introduction I ever heard—of Johnson, Mrs. Johnson, and the girls. They came up on the stage, and Johnson made his speech. He told the story about Joe Junior, and the boy from Texas being shot down and the part about nobody asking what their religion was. I could see that Kennedy, who was waiting to go on, was very moved."

As the end of the campaign neared the Kennedy forces felt increasingly justified in their choice of Johnson as a running mate. He may have been difficult, very often impossible, to work with, but he was incredibly hardworking and he was a crowd pleaser, no mistaking that. The LBJ Special had been a marked success. Lyndon had reversed the opinion of many eastern liberals about him, and in several areas, noticeably southern California, he had done much better than JFK himself.

The only place his promise seemed less than what it should be was his own Texas. Texas had not come round; Texas might go one way, might go another, no one knew.

So for the last week of the campaign Lyndon returned to Texas. After all, the South in general, Texas in particular, was what it had all been about that Thursday morning in Los Angeles.

D.B. Hardeman: "Of course you never know what wins or loses a campaign. But I think what happened at the Adolphus Hotel in Dallas had a lot to do with the Kennedy-Johnson victory, slim as it was.

"Bruce Alger, the only Republican congressman from Texas, took credit, if credit is the word, for the whole thing. It was on November 4.

"Alger was carrying a big sign that said LBJ Sold Out to Yankee Socialists. And I'm told somebody else had a sign that said Beat Judas.

"A lot of those involved in what happened were Junior Leaguers, and they were wearing the Nixon uniform, straw hats, and red-white-and-blue dresses. They had just been at a Nixon rally at the Baker Hotel across the street. And Alger was very proud of having all those Junior Leaguers with their campaign buttons."

Carl L. Phinney: "We had arranged a speaking engagement for Senator Johnson at the Adolphus Hotel.

"I met him in Fort Worth and brought him back. As we were coming into the city limits of Dallas, one of the policemen rode up by the side of me and said, 'General Phinney, they're having a little disturbance at the Baker Hotel and we want to take you around and put you on the Akard Street entrance instead of the Commerce Street entrance.'

"I said, 'Well, I don't like to vary this schedule, and I know Senator Johnson wouldn't want it done.' And he said, 'I think it's best.' I said, 'Well, go ahead.'

"So we drove up on the Akard Street entrance of the hotel, and I didn't realize the extent of the hatred that had been built up until one of the women grabbed Mrs. Johnson's gloves out of her hands and threw them in the gutter. Then there was Alger, Congressman Alger, with this ugly sign about Senator Johnson. We got into the Baker Hotel lobby, and they had an elevator waiting to take us up to the suite where he and Mrs. Johnson could freshen up before we took them over to the luncheon at the Adolphus. They were jeering him and booing him.

"It was preorganized. Alger had put all those signs in the Baker Hotel the night before. I had a lot of trouble with Senator Johnson; he wanted to go out and make them a speech. I finally got him in the elevator with Mrs. Johnson and we took him on up. While I was there I got a call that they thought I ought to surreptitiously take him out through the automobile entrance and get him in a car and take him around and secretly put him into the Adolphus Hotel.

"I said, 'Well, I'm not even going to suggest that because I know the senator well enough to know that he's not afraid of anything, and we'll come down and walk just like we planned to.'

"Of course, a tremendous crowd had gathered on Commerce Street between the two hotels. We really didn't encounter too much trouble until we got into the lobby of the Adolphus, and I was trying to get them moving through this crowd as much as I could. Senator Johnson asked me not to push him. He said, in fact, 'I want you to get away from me.' He also asked the police to leave. He said, 'If the time has come when I can't walk through the lobby of a hotel in Dallas with my lady without a police escort, I want to know it.'"

Charles Boatner: "All of them were anti-Johnson people. They were muttering, and audibly saying things, and it was one of the few times, the only time publicly, that I ever saw Mrs. Johnson lose her temper. She started to answer one woman—one girl rather; most of them were young, Junior League types—and Mr. Johnson kind of put his hand over her mouth and stopped that and brought her right on along. Of course he looked like I.B. Hale packing Davy O'Brien,[4] he's so big. He had her gathered that close."

Lady Bird: "It was just about as bad an hour in politics that I can ever remember. It's had worse successors, but that was *my* worst.

"It was a complete, overwhelming surprise. If a whole bunch of Martians had suddenly dropped down out of the sky, I would not have been more surprised, because these were the people that we had been working for for twelve years in the Senate."

Bill Moyers: "Mrs. Johnson was frightened. You see, he could see over the crowd; she could only see up."

Hardeman: "LBJ and Lady Bird could have gone through that lobby and got on that elevator in five minutes, but LBJ took thirty minutes to go through that crowd, and it was all being recorded and photographed for television and radio and the newspapers, and he knew it and played it for all it was worth. They say he never learned how to use the media effectively, but that day he did."

Moyers: "He knew it got votes for him. He could never have calculated that scene or fixed that situation or arranged for it. He didn't know how he was going to carry Texas, and he greatly feared losing Texas because he thought it would discredit him totally in the nation and with Kennedy. If he could have thought this up, he would have thought it up. Tried to invent it. But the moment it happened, he knew."

Phinney: "That night before they went on to Houston one of the senators from Kentucky called Johnson while we were eating dinner. He was a Republican,[5] and he apologized that a Republican member of the House would stoop to such things as Alger had done."

Ashton Gonella: "Texas had not really been that much for Kennedy-Johnson. They're sort of a conservative state and a lot of people felt that Mr. Johnson had deserted them by going on the ticket. But for some reason, after Dallas the people felt, 'This is disgraceful. They've done something to our people.' We were told ahead of time that Houston was really going to be ugly to us because they were very conservative and were at that time anti-Kennedy-Johnson. We got to Houston. It couldn't have been more overwhelming. Everybody had signs: We Apologize; We Love You."

Boatner: "Senator Johnson had asked Senator Russell to join him the last week or ten days of the campaign—and this had rocked along more or less forgotten. But when the

Adolphus story got out, immediately this wire came from Russell that he was going to join us the last two days of the campaign. And he was in Houston the next morning when we arrived."

There is seldom any one thing that can be pinpointed as *the* reason that a campaign is won or lost; most people, remembering back now, would say "the Kennedy-Nixon debates, of course" and look puzzled at mention of "the Adolphus Hotel incident." But its effect was enormous, not just in Texas, not just in the South where thousands of voters switched loyalties when they saw their sacred concepts of courtesy and hospitality so violated. But in the North, too, previously unconvinced liberals watched the man they had castigated for his conservatism being attacked physically, in his own backyard, for his *liberalism*.

By the time the campaign ended, Lyndon's absorption into the political scene, always greater than almost anyone else's, was total, absolute. Nothing else intruded very far into his consciousness, as those who encountered him at the time well remember.

Monk Willis: "In 1960, just before the election, Lady Bird's father, T. J. Taylor, died. I live in a little town called Longview, just a few miles from Lady Bird's hometown, Karnack, and of course I went to the funeral because I cared greatly about Lyndon and Lady Bird.

"The burial was over in the cemetery in Marshall, a few miles away. We went over to the cemetery. There wasn't any order—you know how you walk up to a grave. I happened to stand right next to Lyndon during the commital service. I've forgotten the prayers—very simple, 'earth to earth, ashes to ashes, dust to dust,' and all that. And then the grace of our Lord, the benediction. The minister said, 'Amen.'

"Johnson looked up and said to me, 'Monk, how's that damn county of yours doing?'"

A JOYLESS VICTORY

Photographs on the front pages of almost every newspaper in the country on November 9 showed John F. Kennedy and Lyndon each displaying a full set of teeth in what were described as victory smiles. They had bested—triumphed seems hardly the word— Richard M. Nixon and Henry Cabot Lodge by the narrowest of margins, 112,881 votes, 112,881 votes out of 66,832,818 cast, a fact that was to haunt Kennedy throughout his brief administration.

But even that meager lead was viewed skeptically by a great many. Out of four million votes cast, the president- and vice-president-elect carried Illinois by fewer than 9,000 votes, many of them coming from the outer reaches of Richard Daley's Chicago precincts, and they were slow, very slow in coming in. And some said that there was—as when was there not?—evidence of fraud in the Texas returns. Nevertheless, Texas was officially in the Democratic column once again, by 46,233 votes out of more than two million cast. Lyndon, who also ran for reelection to the Senate, won that race with 1,210,386 votes, not so remarkable when you consider that John Tower, an obscure conservative Republican, got 41 percent of the total. The next year Tower was elected to what had been Lyndon's seat, the first Republican senator from Texas since Reconstruction.

Lyndon's good fortune in being able to run for two offices at the same time in 1960 was made possible when the amiable state legislature passed a law allowing him to do so; it was widely known as Lyndon's law. When it was challenged in a Texas court, the equally amiable court upheld it. No matter what happened in the election, Lyndon, who had won the Democratic primary in May, would not have been unemployed in November.

Lyndon's presence on the national Democratic ticket undoubtedly contributed largely to its carrying most (not Mississippi) of the Deep South. Governor LeRoy Collins, however, was unable to persuade the majority of Florida voters to support the candidates chosen at the Los Angeles convention, which he had chaired, and Governor Almond of Virginia failed to bring enough Virginians along; the majority followed old Harry Byrd, who voted Republican. The border states split, and what was the result of a clearly anti-Catholic bias carried Kentucky, Tennessee, and Oklahoma for Nixon.

Lyndon's part in the tenuous victory warmed, although in most cases only temporarily, the hearts of even the most vocal of his detractors in the Kennedy inner circle. Clinton Anderson said outright that without Lyndon, New Mexico would have gone Republican, and nobody anywhere said that he was responsible for the *loss* of a state.

Lady Bird was happy; she was going to enjoy being Second Lady, she thought, and she did. Besides, she was *always* glad when a campaign was over, victorious or not. Lyndon? Did he hoot and holler? Did he even smile except for the photographers? He did not. He was demonstrably morose.

Margaret Mayer: "The night he was elected vice-president—very late, when it was quite apparent that he and Kennedy had been elected—I don't think I ever saw a more unhappy man. He had been at the Driskill Hotel with the Homer Thornberrys, the Connallys, Jesse Kellam, and sometime after midnight, maybe one in the morning, they all came downstairs and went across the street to an all-night café on Seventh Street.

"There was no jubilation. Lyndon looked as if he'd lost his last friend on earth, and later he was rude to me, very rude, and I tried to remind myself that he was unhappy, but he did the same thing the next day in the TV station. He was rude to just about everybody. Now I've known Lyndon a great many years, and I've never known him to act like that.

"It was clear to me and a lot of other people that even then he didn't want to be vice-president."

Eight days after the election Kennedy visited the Ranch, accompanied by a planeload of reporters and some staff members. Lyndon's dark mood of election night had passed, and he was smiling and genuinely pleased to see Jack; he was also, as almost always, graciously hospitable. He climbed in his favorite Lincoln convertible, top down, put Kennedy on his right with Lady Bird in the middle and a few Secret Service men in back and gave his guest a brief after-dark tour of his domain. He drove somewhat slower than usual but only somewhat. The next day's talks were sandwiched between what seemed to be an extraordinary number of hearty Texas meals, and there was a more extensive tour that included a visit to Cousin Oriole who had a small house on the Ranch, and a deer hunt during which, Lyndon said, his boss had felled a deer from a distance of four hundred yards, which veteran deer hunters doubted, and some cynics were willing to bet that, as had often happened before, Johnson shot at the same deer at the same time as his guest.[1]

Lyndon and Lady Bird also flew, by invitation, to Massachusetts.

Jacqueline Kennedy Onassis: "They came to stay with us in Hyannis. It's a rather small house we have there, and we wanted them to be comfortable; so we gave them our bedroom. But we didn't want them to know it was our bedroom, because we thought they might feel they were putting us to trouble. There was a lot of moving things out of closets so there'd be no trace of anybody's toothbrush anywhere.

"I remember that evening how impressed I was with Mrs. Johnson. She and my sister and I were sitting in one part of the room, and Jack and Vice-President-elect Johnson and some men were in the other part of the room. Mrs. Johnson had a little spiral pad and when she'd hear a name mentioned, she'd jot it down. Sometimes if Mr. Johnson wanted her, he'd say, 'Bird, do you know so-and-so's number?' And she'd always have it down. Yet she would sit talking with us, looking so calm. I was very impressed by that."

Essentially both calls were courtesy calls, a certain cementing of relations between the First and Second families. Lyndon was not really a part of the launching of the New Frontier; although, accompanied by Mister Sam, he went down to Palm Beach, he was not present at any of the crucial meetings of the Kennedy circle there, or at the house in Georgetown or the penthouse of the Carlyle Hotel in New York.

Even when his old friend John B. Connally was placed in nomination as secretary of the navy it was not at Lyndon's instigation. Kennedy had at first wanted to appoint Franklin Roosevelt, Jr., to the position. Robert McNamara, already nominated as secretary of defense, did not want Roosevelt.[2] He called Kennedy in Palm Beach, suggested Connally, and the president-elect said that clearing the appointment with the vice-president was no problem since Lyndon was sitting right there. Lyndon, of course, did not disagree, and it was done. Big John was in except for some sharp questioning by that eternal gadfly, Senator William Proxmire, who wanted to and did ask Connally a few pointed questions. For instance, should a man like Connally, so closely related to oil men and himself an oil man and unregistered lobbyist for oil interests, be given a position closely related to oil?

When asked whether he could serve without a conflict of interest, Connally, who after all had played in *Liliom* at the University of Texas with Eli Wallach in the starring role, kept a perfectly straight face as he said, "Without any question of a doubt."

And the majority of the Senate agreed.

Lyndon did, however, make his feelings known about several appointments, most especially his preference for J. William Fulbright for secretary of state. Two years before he had persuaded the aging Senator Green to retire as chairman of the Foreign Relations Committee so that Fulbright could inherit that post. Although his feelings would change drastically, Lyndon at this time was a Fulbright fan. But here as elsewhere he was informed of decisions rather than consulted, and often neither. It became increasingly clear that wherever on the East Coast Kennedy happened to be, it was very far from the Texas Ranch.

Robert F. Kennedy: "It finally came down in the last three or four days to Fulbright and Rusk. The president was quite taken with having Fulbright, and I really stopped Fulbright because of his coming from Arkansas. With so many problems with newly developed nations—so many problems on racial difficulties—I thought you could never get over the fact that you had selected a senator from Arkansas to be secretary of state who had signed the manifesto and who had been tied up on all segregation votes."

William Lawrence: "The president did tell me that Fulbright was pushed very, very hard by Johnson, among others, for the post of secretary of state, and that when he decided on Dean Rusk, as a matter of courtesy he had Rusk telephone Johnson in Texas. He said that Johnson was so mad that it wasn't Fulbright that he barely was polite with Rusk on the telephone. Rusk offered to come out to Texas and talk to him about the whole range of foreign problems, but Johnson said no, not to bother, he'd probably see him in Washington sometime—or words to that effect."

Eleanor Roosevelt was also very much upset by Kennedy's choice of Rusk—as were all of Adlai Stevenson's loyal supporters, as was Adlai himself. But then Adlai had lost his chance for that prestigious position in Los Angeles with his meander, however half-hearted, toward the presidential nomination. Neither Jack nor Bobby were forgivers.

Lyndon spent the greater part of December relaxing at the Ranch, his mind actively searching for an answer to the question that now most plagued him—how to circumvent the traditional powerlessness of the vice-presidency. Unsure of his executive role as yet, he determined to try to hold on to a certain amount of the legislative privilege to which he was so accustomed.

The inauguration was on January 20, but the Senate, as always, convened right after the new year. Lyndon was sworn in for his third term as senator, and he, of course, resigned—but not until after the meeting of the Democratic caucus. It met on January 5, 1961, and Lyndon, whose ambition must be considered to have overtaken his good sense and certain knowledge, brought upon himself his first humiliation as vice-president.

John Kennedy recognized that Mike Mansfield of Montana was not an assertive man—pipe smokers often are not—but was nevertheless greatly respected by his colleagues and had not made enemies among the southerners. Kennedy persuaded him, not easily, to accept the majority leadership. The caucus raised no objection, but then Mansfield suggested that the vice-president, who not coincidentally was seated beside him, be invited to attend and preside over future caucus meetings. Mansfield had not discussed the matter with anybody but Lyndon, but he later said he thought the job would be purely "honorary." Who could object to that?

A great many senators did, strenuously. First of all, in seventeen days Lyndon would be vice-president, a member of the executive, not the legislative, branch of the U.S. government. It seemed like freshman civics, high school freshman civics; yet neither Lyndon, that greatest of legislative maneuverers, nor Mansfield seemed to have grasped it. Among those who immediately opposed Mansfield's suggestion was Senator Joe Clark of Pennsylvania, a longtime antagonist of Lyndon's. Another was Albert Gore. "We might as well ask Jack Kennedy to come back to the Senate and take his turn at presiding," said Gore. Even Clinton Anderson of New Mexico, also a liberal and always considered a friend of Lyndon's, announced his opposition. As did Johnson's old ally, Mike Monroney.

The first vote was taken on whether or not to postpone a decision. Postponement was defeated, forty-five to eighteen. The second vote was on the Mansfield resolution itself, forty-six aye votes and seventeen nays, which, although not an outright defeat, was nevertheless a humiliation to the former majority leader, who wanted and expected unanimity from his former colleagues. Besides, it was obvious that many Democratic senators who voted for the resolution did so reluctantly.

Lyndon did not speak again during the meeting. On leaving the caucus that day, he was widely reported to have remarked, "I now know the difference between a caucus and a cactus. In a cactus all the pricks are on the outside." He did appear at the caucus's next session but turned the gavel back to Mansfield, and never returned thereafter.

On January 20, a brisk day in the district, Lyndon joined John Kennedy, Chief Justice Earl Warren, Harry Truman, outgoing President Eisenhower, Jackie, Lady Bird, and, among others, Marian Anderson and Robert Frost, for the inauguration. At 12:40 P.M., using a Bible given him by Rebekah, Lyndon was sworn in as the thirty-seventh vice-president of the United States by Mister Sam. It was the first time a Speaker of the House had ever sworn in a vice-president, but it was generally agreed that it was appropriate. Sam Rayburn, feeling the chill acutely, said that he would not have been anywhere else that day. If there was bitterness in him because he had not in his long career been sworn into executive office, he never expressed it. But then he was not a man who allowed himself such emotions.

Lyndon later watched the inaugural parade, and that night he and Bird attended several of the inaugural balls. Lyndon danced with numerous ladies, though far fewer than the new president.

Mrs. Hugh Auchincloss, Jackie's mother, with whom he danced, said that she thought Lyndon was very courtly and gallant.

Then, on January 21, Lyndon took up the gavel of presiding officer of the Senate, which he had so often said he would not take up. He had never wanted the vice-presidency; he did not now, and there is no evidence that in his few years in that position he changed his mind. He was not, however, going to be another John Nance Garner; he was not going to be disloyal to his president, and there is no evidence that he ever was, publicly or privately. Disgruntled, yes; disgusted, very often, but for a man who usually wore all his feelings in public, who was often described as one great big open bleeding wound, he was remarkably successful in concealing his emotions. Loyalty. It was a sacred word; he expected it from his subordinates, and he knew that Jack expected it of him—and he gave it.

KEEPING LYNDON HAPPY

Hubert H. Humphrey: "There is the old story about the mother who had two sons. One went to sea, and the other became vice-president, and neither was ever heard of again."

Lyndon: "The first thing when a man is elected vice-president, you media fellows start talking about, 'Well, what's happened to Lyndon, the vice-president? Where is Lyndon Johnson?' And the press plays it up, and it's cruel and inhuman, I think.

"So the vice-president can't be as effective as he should because of all these doubts. President Kennedy was very good to me and tried his best to elevate the office in any way he could."

And Kennedy did try. He promptly named Lyndon chairman of his Presidential Committee on Equal Opportunity, in which position the vice-president had considerable opportunity to pursue his concerns for civil rights. And although he did not feel justified in turning NASA over to Lyndon, which Lyndon had audaciously requested, he was pleased to deliver up the chairmanship of the Space Council—the perfect spot, he thought, for his vice-president, whom he was anxious to keep busy and, if possible, happy.

The National Aeronautics and Space Council had been created in 1958 with the enactment by Congress, under Lyndon's direction, of the Space Act. It was designed to be the executive finger in the space pie, which also accommodated the aforementioned Senate Committee on Space, the Department of Defense, the Federal Communications Commission, and NASA. The Space Act had avoided possible conflict by designating the president as chairman of the Space Council, but Eisenhower had expressed little interest in the council and none at all in leading it. Kennedy was interested, but Lyndon—well, Lyndon had to do *something*.

The function of the council, said its new chairman, was "to advise the president, upon his request, of what this nation's space policy should be," and Lyndon wasted no time presenting his first bit of advice. His Senate committee had strongly advocated improving the country's propulsion capability with what was called the big booster. Eisenhower had vetoed that project, but Kennedy was prevailed upon to give the big booster a try.

That accomplished, the council began, at a slightly more leisurely pace—that is, within a week or two—to hold hearings and review the space program as a whole. The hysteria of *Sputnik* had worn off, but the country had yet to produce anything comparably dramatic. Such an event was, Kennedy felt, overdue, and surely it should occur sometime within his projected eight years in office. So on the twentieth of April he wrote Lyndon a letter in which he asked him, among other things, what project could the United States probably beat the Russians at?

Lyndon's answer came on May 5, a few days before he took off for the Far East, when he carried into the Oval Office a manila envelope containing the first major report of the National Aeronautics and Space Council. The best possibility for the United States, the report advised, was the lunar project. The Russians had, it was true, already achieved a rocket capability for putting a multimanned laboratory into space and had crash-landed a rocket on the moon, but the experts nevertheless predicted that they were probably not much closer to actually landing a man on the moon and bringing him back than was the United States. If the point was to win, and to win within the foreseeable future, then the lunar project was probably the likeliest prospect.

Kennedy was pleased with the report and approved it. He had been less pleased a few weeks before when Lyndon had requested permission to accompany astronaut John Glenn on his tickertape parade down Broadway in New York, but Lyndon had managed to convince him that it would be entirely appropriate for the new chairman of the Space Council to do just that. Lyndon was clearly still testing his ropes and Kennedy was still wary, but the rapport between them had not diminished. Kennedy liked to tell the story of how he and Lyndon had watched Glenn's takeoff together from his office, and how, when the countdown began and they were both watching very tensely, Lyndon suddenly turned to him and said, "If John Glenn were only a Negro!"

The Space Council chairmanship was, however, only briefly satisfying for Lyndon. Once the present program had been evaluated, new directives issued and the revised program set into motion, there was little for him to do. There was not even any way he could make it move faster.

Angier Biddle Duke: "The president brought me into his office and said, 'I want you to take care of the vice-president and Mrs. Johnson. I want you to watch over them and see that they're not ignored, not only when you see them but at all other occasions.' I said, 'What do you mean?' He said, 'Because I'm going to forget. My staff is going to forget. We're all going to forget. We've got too much to do around here. We move so fast from one thing to another that I'm going to forget, and I want you to remember.'"

Jacqueline Kennedy Onassis: "Jack thought it would be a very frustrating job, and I think he tried to do everything to make Vice-President Johnson feel as comfortable in it as possible. One thing Prime Minister Macmillan of England had said to Jack about President Eisenhower and Vice-President Nixon—that Eisenhower never let Nixon on the place—impressed Jack a lot. Every time there was a state dinner, he wanted Vice-President and Mrs. Johnson to come, too. They would always come upstairs. We would then walk down with the color guard so that we would receive the state guests as a foursome.

"Every time we had a private party, which was about five times I think in the time we were there, we'd always ask the Johnsons to be with us and our friends who weren't political friends."

Duke: "The real problems were when the president would have some of the 'in-group' parties for Arthur Schlesinger, Mac Bundy, Kenneth Galbraith, and his friends that would come down from New York. I would get the list pretty late and see that the vice-president wasn't on it, and call the White House—it was often in the afternoon of the day of the party—and remind—usually it was Kenny O'Donnell, that the president himself would have to invite the Johnsons.

"He would and they would come. I say this in all respectfulness, not about Lyndon

Johnson, but about the post of vice-president. Nobody was terribly interested in him."

Elizabeth Gatov: "There were a lot of small parties, informal kinds, dinners that were given by Kennedy people for other Kennedy people. You know, just twelve people in for dinner, all part of the administration, in some way or another. No press, no long white gloves, and just talking. Really, it was brutal, the stories that they were passing, and the jokes, and the inside nasty stuff about Lyndon. I didn't protest—I don't want to pretend that I did—but it seemed unnecessary to me at the time. It was a pretty heady period and they were young people mostly, and they were going to run the country for the next decade."

Dean Rusk: "I had long been used to the favorite indoor sport around Washington—making fun of vice-presidents. But I never saw the slightest trace of that in John F. Kennedy. He always spoke of Lyndon Johnson with understanding and respect, although some of his staff people used to throw barbs at the vice-president.

"Johnson showed great self-discipline and strength. I think it was a major effort of self-control to fit into that role—with all that volcanic force that was part of his very being."

Charles Bartlett: "There was never any word that ever drifted back to Jack Kennedy of any criticism from Lyndon Johnson. I don't think Kennedy knew how tough certain members of his staff were being on the Vice President, but there certainly was not one word—and I'm very sure of this—of disloyalty that the vice-president ever uttered."

Arthur Krock: "As far as Kennedy himself was concerned, he was not a hater. He was a historian, too, and I don't think he quite accepted the ogre picture of Johnson that seemed to appeal to many of those around him."

That Lyndon, who always wanted *everybody* to like him, suffered under the barely concealed scorn of certain of the president's staff cannot be questioned, but he would not have minded that, perhaps hardly have noticed it, had he held any actual power over events and had any real outlet for his reined-in energy. But he did not; even at meetings of the cabinet or the National Security Council he was unsure whether Kennedy's requests for his opinion, among the others', were real or merely perfunctory. And on top of that he had the bad luck to be out of the country and not even available to *give* an opinion when the first major crisis of the Kennedy administration—the Bay of Pigs fiasco—occurred.

Exactly how much Lyndon knew beforehand about the abortive invasion of Cuba is unclear; Kennedy once said, "Lyndon's been in on every major decision except, that is, for the Bay of Pigs."[1] Lyndon, on the other hand, held a long conversation with Carroll Kilpatrick of the *Washington Post* on the subject. In this account, which Kilpatrick reported to Phil Graham in a letter, Lyndon was an important, almost pivotal figure in the decision.

What is certain, however, is that Lyndon was in Africa during the crucial week before the actual invasion and on his return flew almost immediately to the Ranch where he was host to Chancellor Konrad Adenauer of Germany. Lyndon liked Adenauer, but all the while that he was listening to German hymns sung in German, of course, at the little Fredericksburg church, and entertaining fourth- and fifth-generation German-speaking

Hill Country Texans at a barbecue, he was chafing that, as seemed always to be the case now, the action was one place and he was another.

Lady Bird: "When he became vice-president, I had a ball. I loved it. I had a great time once I was in it. We bought a beautiful home.[2] We took a sizable share of entertaining the visitors; we did a lot of traveling—all things I enjoy and had done very little of before. But I would not say Lyndon shared my feeling. It was a life that was not nearly as pleasant for him as it was for me."

Duke: "Let's say there was going to be a meeting of the National Security Council and that afterwards everybody went down to the Rose Garden to have a few photographs. There was no problem at times like that, because the vice-president was a member of the National Security Council and would naturally be in the photographs.

"The vice-president would always hang in the back as if he felt he was unwanted.

"Whenever I was around, I would say in a loud voice, 'Mr. Vice-President, Mr. Vice-President,' and then the president would look around and say, 'Where's Lyndon? Where's Lyndon?' Johnson liked that, and he'd come up front."

Krock: "Kennedy often said, 'I don't know what to do with Lyndon. I've got to keep him happy somehow. My big job is to keep Lyndon happy.'"

THE MAN WITH NO SHIRT

Lyndon's career as vice-president was by no means confined to Washington. While a vice-president of the United States may lack power, he never lacks status; his rank is similar to that of a crown prince, though his succession is considerably less certain.

Lyndon was, of course, accustomed to status in Washington, but he had never had occasion to try it out on an international level before, and his feelings on the subject were mixed. Except for a NATO conference the previous fall, he had hardly been out of the country, barring Mexico, since his brief European trip in 1945. He spoke no foreign language, although he had retained a vague familiarity with Mexican Spanish and Hill Country German. His understanding of the culture of almost any country outside his own was sketchy at best.

There were, on the other hand, various points in his favor. If he had little knowledge, he also had few, if any, prejudices. He had a natural sympathy with people; to him, the workingman, particularly the ordinary farmer, was just a variation of the Texas farmer he had always known and identified with and tried to help. Any drawbacks his Texas accent might have at the Court of St. James' or along the eastern seaboard of his own country were minimal among people who did not understand English in any form, and he emanated a kind of expansive *caring* that was heightened by the fact that he was about twice the size of the Asians, Africans, Indians, etc., he moved among.

During the thirty-five months he was vice-president, Lyndon embarked on a new "tour" on an average of every three months, visited dozens of foreign countries, conferred with the leaders of each, shook God alone knows how many hundreds of thousands, maybe millions of hands of varied colors, hooted and hollered, even in the Taj Mahal, spoke of the poverty of his youth, especially to the dispossessed, which was almost everybody, got out of official cars and walked among and shook the hands of the multitudes, and acted for all the world as if he were running for reelection to the Senate in Texas. When he was in India, John Kenneth Galbraith, then ambassador there, had to find him a translator. "I told him, 'If Lyndon forgets and asks for votes, leave that out.'"

Robert Waldron: "In his campaigns he was always handing out cards admitting people to the Senate gallery and telling them to be sure and come visit him in Washington. It was the same in the 1960 campaign. He said to people, 'Now you-all come to see us in Washington when we get to be vice-president.'

"And it was pretty much the same when he was vice-president and traveling all over the world. He'd tell everyone he met, practically everyone he shook hands with, 'Now you-all come to see me in Washington.'

"We used to joke about it, about what would happen if all the people he'd invited showed up, what would he do?"

With the possible exception of his trip to Pakistan in 1962, Lyndon as traveling ambassador was most effective during the first year of his vice-presidency. There were several reasons for this. In the first year he tried harder, was fresher, less travel-weary, more *interested*. He was not yet aware of the highly negative views that many career officers in the State Department came in time to have, with some justification, of his travel style. But even more, as Lyndon in Washington became increasingly constrained and frustrated and subdued in his vice-presidential role, Lyndon out of Washington, and particularly out of the country, reacted with a characteristic lack of restraint that left his hosts, although frequently charmed, at the same time bewildered and often dismayed.

But that was later. In April 1961, when he left for Senegal, he was in his best form, a little apprehensive perhaps, but *expectant*.

The Senegalese were celebrating their independence as a new African country, and Lyndon was to represent the United States at the ceremonies in Dakar.

William Crockett: "The ambassador and his wife briefed Mr. Johnson and our people on behavior, and one of the things they said was 'Don't get out among these people because they're dirty; they have disease and among everything else, don't shake hands with them unless you wear gloves.' Well, you know, telling Lyndon Johnson this was like waving a red flag at a bull. It was hot, it was dirty, and it was dusty, but he went among the people."

On the second day of their stay, while the ambassador and his wife were still asleep, Lyndon and Lady Bird were up at four thirty in the morning and visited a fishing village called Kayar where the annual per capita income was one hundred dollars.

Lyndon told the villagers that when he was a boy the annual income in rural Texas was $180. "Now," he said, "it is $1,800."

Naturally, he shook many hands, without wearing gloves. He tasted the raw fish; he kissed many babies, and Lady Bird, seeing the great baskets of peanuts said, "Why, it's just like Texas."

Lyndon told the village chief, "I came to Kayar because I was a farm boy, too, in Texas. It's a long way from Texas to Kayar, but we both produce peanuts and both want the same thing: a higher standard of living for the people!"

The Johnsons were not soon forgotten in Kayar.

Roy Wilkins: "I remember remarking to Mr. Johnson on the photographs of his trip to Senegal, and he said something that I haven't yet been able to forget. It seemed to me to attach to the man himself and not to the administration. He said, 'You know, in Senegal, when I looked in the eyes of the mothers there they had the same look as the mothers in Texas. All mothers want the best for their children. And the mothers in Senegal were no different from the mothers in Texas.'"

Lyndon returned from Senegal via Geneva where the nuclear test ban talks were in progress, Spain where he unwittingly caused much consternation when the Spanish government deduced that the American military base he visited must be one rumored to be closing, and Paris where he spoke at the tenth-anniversary celebration of SHAPE. It was a very full week, and John Kennedy was apparently pleased by the results because the vice-president was hardly back before Kennedy wanted to send him off again, this time on a considerably more important mission—a fact-finding and morale-boosting trip to Southeast Asia.

Lyndon, however, was reluctant. Kennedy would press it and Lyndon would balk, he would say things like how embarrassing it would be for the president if the vice-president got his head blown off in Saigon. Since there was little likelihood of that occurring in the spring of 1961 and since it was very unlike Lyndon to express fears for his own safety to the ex-captain of PT boat 109, it is probable that Lyndon was not looking forward to defending the administration in the wake of the Bay of Pigs fiasco as well as reacting to rumored mumblings from the State Department about his general "conduct" on trips abroad. In such matters Lyndon's opinions and those of State Department career officers were diametrically opposed.

Crockett: "When we were going to the Far East, some State Department guy talked about the Asians being small people, and Johnson, I remember said, 'These State Department people think I'm going to go out there, and pat a little guy on the head and say, "Little man, do this." They don't give me any credit for having any sense about how to treat people.' But this was always a fear—that he would go out and say something, or do something, or commit to something—of the foreign service people. But I would like to make the point it was not the fear of Dean Rusk. Dean Rusk liked Johnson, trusted Johnson, appreciated Johnson.

"Rusk called me in one time and said, 'Now, you're going on this trip, and I want you to make sure that one thing happens. I want you to make sure that he sees the heads of state personally and alone. There is no person in America that can equal Johnson in knee-to-knee conversation with another man.' He said, 'I want you to make sure that he gets some personal, alone time with each of these people.'"

Whatever Lyndon's fears actually were about the Far East trip, they were apparently allayed by Kennedy's suggestion that he send his sister Jean and her husband, Stephen Smith, along with the party. Lyndon liked Jack's sisters, and besides, the presence of the Smiths might relieve him of some of the disagreeable attention to protocol.

The tour, which was to last two weeks in all, began on May 5 and included stopovers in Honolulu, Wake Island, and Guam on the way to the primary destination, Saigon. Lyndon met with chief of state Ngo Dinh Diem on May 12. General Diem was pleased when Lyndon told him that President Kennedy planned to increase U.S. aid to his country by about $40 million, but when Lyndon went on to some possible uses of that $40 million—water and electrification in the country villages, for example—Diem seemed not to hear.

George E. Reedy: "The basic purpose of the trip was to convince Diem that he simply had to institute some social and fiscal reforms if he were to survive. Diem was an absolute autocrat, and he'd been holed up in his palace for so many years that he'd gotten quite far from the people. I don't believe he himself realized how shaky his position was."

Later Lyndon was reported to have had a strong admiration for Diem, publicly comparing him to Winston Churchill, and he was, it is true, opposed to the coup that overthrew Diem. But his evaluation of Diem in his subsequent report criticized him for being "remote from the people" and described his advisers as "persons less admirable and capable than he."

Carroll Kilpatrick: "One day outside Saigon Johnson walked off the road into a hut where people were living in almost unimaginable circumstances. As we were going back to the cars he walked up from behind, put his arms around my shoulders and said: 'You don't have to worry about your children living like that. We're going to see to it that yours and a lot of others never will.'

"People who think Johnson is not a sentimentalist or is not genuinely moved by human suffering are fools. . . . You have to have guns to keep off the marauders but as Johnson said time and again, you have to give these people bread and medicine and education or you are certain to lose."[1]

The next major stop of the trip was Bangkok, but Lyndon and his party spent a night each in Manila, Taipei, and Hong Kong en route. In Manila he reassured President Carlos Garcia that of course the United States understood that the safety of the Philippines depended upon a no-retreat policy in Southeast Asia. Then, much to the dismay of the U.S. ambassador there, he toured Manila Lyndon-style.

Dr. James Cain, his personal physician who accompanied the vice-president on most of his trips, described the scene: "As we came to a crowd Lyndon told the driver to stop the car so he could get out to shake hands with the people. The ambassador sat there just frigid, almost frightened to death and said, 'You can't do that; you just don't *do* that in this country.' So I got out of my own car and went up there where Lyndon was. The ambassador sat right there in the car, afraid to get out.

"Then we drove on about half a mile, and the vice-president did it again, and this time this State Department fellow did look out the window to see what was going on.

"The third time we stopped, he was out as quick as the vice-president and shaking hands with all the population."

Kilpatrick: "That trip went like so many Johnson trips. It was hectic and frenzied. He wouldn't keep to his schedule; and wouldn't tell us his schedule in advance.

"I remember that we had all gotten to Bangkok and we had all gotten to bed late, late at night, and I don't know, two o'clock in the morning we got telephone calls that Johnson was having a press conference. He was in a hotel in one end of the city and we were in the other. So they rallied us all out of bed, and we found cabs and got across to his hotel room, and there he was in his pajamas. He was very annoyed by something so he was having a press conference and was making a statement to clarify it.

"The next night I know they told us to be 'at the such and such dock at seven o'clock in the morning because he's going on the tour of the Klongs, the water market.' I remember getting awakened in the middle of the night and told, 'The trip has been canceled; he is not going.' Then later at six or six thirty or so, being awakened again and saying, 'You missed the trip because you didn't get there in time. He's already gone!'"

The next stop on the itinerary, and second in importance only to Saigon, was India where John Kenneth Galbraith had recently assumed duties as ambassador. Galbraith and Lyndon knew and liked each other. They were the same age, and both had had childhoods in which luxury was not abundant. Both had also gone to colleges that were, shall we say, without much éclat.

John Kenneth Galbraith: "I used to tell LBJ that whatever doubts he had about that college in San Marcos, I could double and redouble as regards Ontario Agricultural College."[2]

Galbraith and his wife, Catherine, went to Bangkok to accompany the vice-president's party to New Delhi.

Galbraith: "I was a little apprehensive about the whole thing; there were to be two planeloads of them, about fifty people. Also, they were our first guests since I had become ambassador.

"And then we talked with the State Department people who were with the vice-president. Everybody appeared to be angry with everybody else, Johnson people with the State Department people, and vice versa.

"We got back to New Delhi late, two hours late at least, but Nehru was at the airport to meet Johnson. There was an honor guard of Sikhs, and then we all rode into town. We had dinner with the prime minister, and later he and LBJ talked for a long time, until about one in the morning.

"That first meeting between Johnson and Nehru—well, the heads of state always meet under conditions of very great difficulty, because if they seem to agree on anything, that becomes a commitment. So they are likely to become extraordinarily cautious and sometimes find it difficult to have anything to talk about.

"Now this was particularly true in the case of Nehru because he was a man who was given to long silences. If you had to ask Nehru for something he didn't want to give you, he would just remain silent. You would ask him again and he would remain silent. By the time you asked him a third time, you would be yearning for him to say no, to bring the torture to an end. And in his first meeting with Johnson there were long silences on Nehru's part.

"This was coupled with the fact that there wasn't really any appreciable business to transact. But finally after fifteen minutes they hit upon a subject that they could discuss fervently, aggressively, and on which they could reach a full conclusion. And that was the matter of rural electrification—which they were both in favor of.

"The evening ended about one in the morning, I'd guess, and they agreed to issue a joint communiqué of no startling importance."

The trip to India also had its lighter side. The Galbraiths escorted the Johnsons to the Taj Mahal, and many in the State Department were duly upset, although not surprised they said, when Lyndon not only kissed Lady Bird—kissing at the Taj is strictly forbidden—but also gave his Texas yell inside to test the echo. Galbraith was not upset. The yell was said to be sacrilegious, Galbraith said, although it is not at all unusual. Tourist guides do it every hour on the hour. The Taj Mahal is a monument, not a mosque.[3]

But the vice-president, the State Department pointed out, is not a tourist guide.

At the Taj Lyndon was also reported to have said to Jean Smith, "Jean, I hope you will build something like this for Stephen one day."

The final stop of the tour was Pakistan. One could not, after all, go to India and not go to Pakistan, even if only for twenty-four hours.

Reedy: "He was touring Karachi and the crowds were really tremendous that day— much different from how they had been in India. The Indians, the Hindus, are a very quiet, almost docile people and it somewhat breaks your heart. But Pakistanis are Mohammedans, and they're much more emotional and much more likely to turn out and shout and yell and scream."

Walter Jenkins: "In that motorcade from the airport into town, there were literally thousands and thousands of people lining the streets to the point that we had to stop and let them open the way. And he got out and shook hands. Standing on one side was a camel driver, sort of alone with his camel. And something prompted Mr. Johnson to leave this big crowd and go over to shake hands with this fellow. Mr. Johnson, with his normal ebullience, said, 'Why don't you come over to the United States?' and the photographers had a field day."

Reedy: "This man did have an unusual face, a very fine face, a sort of Santa Claus face that looked like a tremendous amount of humanity. The vice-president had a little conversation with him through an interpreter. And in the course of the conversation he said, 'I've enjoyed so much visiting your country and meeting your people; and I hope someday that you will have the opportunity to visit our country and meet our people.' Then he went about his business.

"Well, the next day the newspaper *Dawn* came out with a huge article lauding the vice-president to the skies. The article said, 'He reaches out to the man with no shirt on his back.' And in one of the paragraphs it said, 'And all the bazaars are talking about his invitation to Bashir, the camel driver, to come to the United States and stay in the Waldorf-Astoria in New York City.' How the Waldorf got into it I don't know.

"He didn't think too much of it at the time, but later on after we returned to the United States we got an almost panicky cablegram from the American embassy in Pakistan, saying that this matter of Bashir Ahmad the camel driver had become a major *cause celèbre* in the country; and if, by God, Bashir the camel driver wasn't brought to the United States and put up in the Waldorf, the vice-president was going to look like the biggest fourflusher in history. So he kind of groaned and said, 'Okay, bring him on.'

"And the embassy went out to Bashir's home—he lived in a little mud hut in the center of Karachi under really horrible conditions—to find him and he was gone, with no explanation—just that the police had come and taken him away. And the only thing we could guess was that the Pakistani authorities had decided they didn't want their country to be disgraced by having this illiterate camel driver, who couldn't even sign his own name, receiving so much prominent attention in the United States as a representative of Pakistan.

"Well, a few months later, Ayub Khan came to the United States with his daughter, and on the trip visited the Ranch. While he was at the Ranch, the vice-president had a little talk with him and said, 'We'd better get Bashir the camel driver over here,' and explained to Ayub that he would not disgrace the Pakistani, that he'd probably be very warmly received. And so it was arranged. And Bashir turned out to be—from a public relations standpoint—a marvelous find, one of those things that you walk into every once in a while without realizing the gods have been good to you because Bashir was a very appealing man. He was extraordinarily gentle; he had this marvelous face. And he was a very devout Mohammedan and didn't drink. He was past the age where he would chase women, if he ever had chased women. He really loved small children, and they responded to him. He handled himself with considerable dignity. And then we had this marvelous interpreter who was very quick, and, as I said, rendered into highly literate English whatever Bashir was saying."

Waldron: "Still we thought it was just as well that of all those thousands of people, maybe tens of thousands that Mr. Johnson invited to Washington, only one ever showed up."

AMERICANS IN BERLIN

Lyndon's most dramatic trip as vice-president was during the Berlin crisis that burst upon the Kennedy administration that first summer. On the evening of August 16, 1961, Kennedy phoned Lyndon at Sam Rayburn's Washington apartment where Lyndon was visiting his old friend, who was obviously very ill, although Lyndon did not openly dispute the Speaker when he said he was suffering from nothing more than a bad case of "lumbago," and refused to be examined by doctors.

"Lyndon," asked Kennedy, "are you available to go to Berlin?" He wanted, he said, for his vice-president to go to assure the Berliners, in fact the world, that Berlin was not about to be abandoned to the Communists.

A few days after Kennedy's inauguration, the Soviet Union had released two U.S. Air Force officers shot down in July 1960 over Russia, and subsequently imprisoned on charges associated with the U-2 crisis. Premier Khrushchev announced that in return for their release he expected American concessions, in particular action on the unending Soviet demands concerning West Berlin and the humiliating hundred-mile Helmstedt corridor through the Russian zone leading to it. Khrushchev also indicated that he would sign a separate peace treaty with East Germany before the year was out—one that would do away with Western autonomy in West Berlin.

When Kennedy met with the Soviet leader in Vienna that June, Khrushchev again mentioned the separate peace treaty he intended to sign, he said, regardless of whether the United States would go to war on the issue.

Kennedy's reply was, "It's going to be a very cold winter."

Lyndon, who had advised against the "Vienna summit," felt vindicated by the clearly negative results of the meeting. The Russian leader had treated Kennedy with a combination of contempt, bravado, and condescension, and the president returned to Washington in a state of shock and gloom.

Kennedy's immediate official response was to ask Congress for more of everything in West Germany—more troops and more weapons. The Western powers, he said, must take a "firm stand" in Berlin; he asked for an immediate addition of $3.25 billion to U.S. defense funds and called up the reserves.[1]

In reply, Khrushchev mentioned that the Soviets had a 100-megaton nuclear warhead, as yet untested, and said that it would be easy indeed for him to order the mobilization of all Russian troops.

Then, beginning on August 13, and for the next four days, the Russians proceeded to erect a wall inside the entire length of the twenty-five-mile border between West and East Berlin. The reason eluded many outsiders. Was it a threat to the Western powers, in particular, of course, the United States? Most observers agreed that the wall was probably built to inhibit the exodus of East Berliners into West Berlin.

Nobody knew for sure—except maybe the West Berlin officials, who weren't discussing it—how many East Berliners had already crossed from East to West Berlin, though it was rumored that during the first ten days in August alone nearly seventeen thousand had crossed the border.

By the time the Western powers got around to making a formal protest about the wall it was virtually complete.

On August 17 Lyndon met with the president and General Lucius D. Clay in an upstairs study of the White House. General Clay had directed the Berlin airlift in 1948 and '49 and was a great hero to the West Berliners. Also present were Charles E. Bohlen, known to his friends as "Chip," past ambassador to the Soviet Union and an expert on its politics, Secretary of State Rusk, McGeorge Bundy, Ted Sorensen, and press secretary Pierre Salinger. They reviewed the strategy of the trip and the drafts of the speeches that Lyndon was to deliver.

Also under discussion that day was the matter of sending additional combat troops into Berlin through the West Berlin corridor, not so much because anyone thought they might be needed—no one, for example, was proposing to attempt to tear down the Wall—but just to reestablish the right-of-access of the Western powers and their determination to protect and defend the city.

On the other hand there was the question of whether such action might be interpreted as aggressive and provoke retaliatory action on the part of the Soviets. Clay later discussed Kennedy's dilemma with Lyndon. "I'm impressed all over again with the awful loneliness of the president," Clay said. "You noticed in that meeting President Kennedy was twisting a paper in his hands, and then after a while he asked to see me alone. And we went into the next room, and he said, 'General, I've heard all the advice pro and con. What do you think I should do?' I said, 'I think you should let the tanks roll.' He smoothed out the paper, and it was the order for the tanks to roll, and Kennedy had already signed it."[2]

The "tanks" in question were not the World War II variety, but actual armored trucks that would convey fifteen hundred additional American troops down the Autobahn through the Helmstedt corridor into West Berlin. Then for added dramatic impact, it was suggested that the timing should be such that the troops would arrive in Berlin while the vice-president was there to greet them personally, and the pros and cons of that plan, too, were discussed.

Jack Bell: "Lyndon loved it. This was the first real thing that Kennedy had given him, really the first big show. Kennedy thought of going to Berlin himself, but he realized something might happen to him, or could, easily, and they couldn't protect him too well. So he called on Lyndon."

Walter Jenkins: "I think Mr. Johnson realized the seriousness of the Berlin crisis from the beginning and that the trip to Berlin was not like the others he had taken for President Kennedy, and that if anything went wrong, it might lead to a third world war. He was very conscious of that."

To complicate the matter still further, West Germany was at that time in the throes of a political campaign. Konrad Adenauer was a candidate for reelection as chancellor, and Willy Brandt, mayor of West Berlin, was opposing him.

Lucius D. Clay: "It was decided that Vice-President Johnson would stop and call on the chancellor, but that we would have to very politely let the chancellor know that this was an American visit and that he would not be asked to go along. It wasn't in any way intended to slight the chancellor, but it was felt that this was the only way in which this trip could be made without it being interpreted as possibly being an invasion into the political campaign."

The flight to Germany left at eight o'clock on the next evening, August 18. The passengers in the 707 included the vice-president, General Clay, Ambassador Bohlen, several other advisers, and numerous reporters. When they arrived in Bonn the following morning, Chancellor Adenauer was, to be sure, among those waiting to meet the vice-president, politely offering to accompany Lyndon to Berlin. Just as politely the vice-president turned down the chancellor's offer. Nonetheless, when the plane flew on to Tempelhof Airport in Berlin, Lyndon had to contend with the complaints of Mayor Willy Brandt who pointed out to the vice-president that Adenauer was capitalizing on his visit to the Johnson Ranch earlier that year. Lyndon then did lose his temper; this hardly seemed the time or the place to involve the vice-president of the United States in a German election, he said. Besides, Brandt himself had visited the Ranch in 1954, and so on.[3]

Bell: "When we left Tempelhof there started the goddamndest seven miles of motoring that I've ever seen in this world. We were riding in one of these Volkswagen buses immediately behind Lyndon's car. He stopped the car to get out and kiss babies and shake hands—everything just like he was campaigning in Texas. But it got a tremendous response. It was terrific. I estimated about a million people were out in Berlin. He drove up to the Wall. He didn't get too close, but we all walked up and took a look at the Wall."

Then they continued on to the *Ratskeller* (city hall). Lyndon went in and made a speech to the Parliament, which was gathered inside, and then he went outside and made another:

> I have come to Berlin by direction of President Kennedy. . . . To the survival and to the creative future of this city we Americans have pledged, in effect, what our ancestors pledged in forming the United States: "our lives, our fortunes, and our sacred honor." This island does not stand alone.

Although the speech made no new commitments it was exactly what the people of West Berlin needed to hear.

Bell: "I estimated there were seventy-five thousand people in that square.[4] God, they gave it back to him! I mean every time he'd say it in English—most of those people understood English—wham! the applause would come back to him. And then they'd translate it into German for the 25 percent who didn't know English. Then they'd yell. Everybody else would yell again. It was terrific. West Berlin's spirit was revived, and this was what Kennedy wanted to do—give them something to hang on to. Khrushchev was threatening to sign a treaty with East Germany, and the East Germans might march over.

"Actually, Kennedy told somebody at one point, 'This is touch and go. We may lose the whole thing.'"

While Lyndon spoke, the fifteen hundred additional American troops were on their way to Berlin: the "tanks" would soon roll through the Helmstedt corridor, a 104-mile stretch of Autobahn. There were a dozen places where that token force could have been stopped—a force that could have stood up against the Russians for "let's say an hour at most," an American colonel was quoted as saying.

The West Berliners began arriving at the Helmstedt entrance to Berlin early on Sunday morning, August 20. In Washington Jack Kennedy had postponed leaving for his usual summer weekend at Hyannis Port until he heard. Lyndon and General Clay arrived around nine o'clock, and at ten they proudly greeted the first American soldiers.

Glover S. Johns, Jr., commander of the troop, was pelted with flowers as he jumped out of his jeep to shake hands with the vice-president and with General Clay. Johns said that the demonstration that followed was "the most exciting and impressive thing I've ever seen in my life, with the possible exception of the liberation of Paris."

Clay: "Meeting the combat team added a very dramatic moment to the vice-president's visit, because he was actually there, took the watch as the combat team came into the city. It did a great deal to restore morale.

"Subsequent to that I set up a series of convoys so that there was almost constant military movement on the highways between Germany and Berlin."

As dramatic and exhilarating as the Berlin mission was for him, Lyndon nonetheless returned to sadness, to an event which, however expected, affected him as deeply as the loss of a parent.

Lady Bird: "When I went out to the airport to meet him, I found Speaker Rayburn there. I hadn't seen the Speaker in several weeks and my heart was in my throat at the way he looked. He looked *sick*. But he wanted to pay that deference to his friend and leader, to welcome him back. It must have been a considerable effort for him to come. He left within a few days, never to return."

Hale Boggs: "The last year that Mr. Rayburn was here, none of us realized how sick he was. Oftentimes when you are very close to a person, you just don't see it; it's insidious, and he would complain about things—he nearly always talked about a pain in his back, talking about having lumbago, which was an expression I hadn't heard in years, kind of a country disease. I realized how very ill he was in July of that year when I went down to Tennessee with him to the county in which he was born where they named a bridge for him. He loved to fish; we went fishing in one of the Tennessee Valley lakes, and he was just miserable all the time. I knew that he was very sick."

Charles Boatner: "When Mr. Rayburn was so ill with cancer back in Texas, Mr. Johnson would say, 'Now, I'm not going to Texas this weekend. I'm just not going.' I would say, 'Yes, sir' and I would make plans with my wife for the weekend. Then on about Thursday afternoon: 'I don't know whether I shouldn't go down there next weekend.' Well, I just put a big X on the side of wishful thinking. He was going to go down there every weekend.

"And after Rayburn's death it was hard for him to go back. Every death was hard on him. You could see it in him for two or three days. He was more somber. Deaths hurt him, and especially those who were people close to him. At times like that he'd tell that story about his father wanting to go back to the Pedernales where people thought about you when you were sick and cared when you died."

D.B. Hardeman: "Mister Sam used to say he came 'within a gnat's ear of being a tenant farmer.' He'd say, thinking about his career, 'It's a fur piece from Flag Springs.'"

Lady Bird: "He had a keen feeling about how close he was to having lived a life that was flat and unproductive, just sitting there in Flag Springs for fifty years. I think he marveled all the time at how far he'd gone. I remember coming home—Lyndon and I and the Speaker—from down in Virginia on a Sunday drive, and getting to sort of a rise in the land, and looking down on the Potomac and the dome of the Capitol. It was a quiet, contemplative moment, and then he looked around at us, and he said, 'How do you like my Capitol?' What he meant was every American's Capitol, and his very especially."

AUGUST IN ANKARA

Several events occurred in 1962 that were viewed with some concern by the rest of the world. In March the United States announced that it would not commit itself to any agreement that prohibited stationing nuclear weapons on the territory of its allies. A little later Secretary of Defense Robert McNamara admitted that there had been "occasions" when U.S. "training personnel" had "returned the fire" of Communist guerrilla forces in South Vietnam. And shortly thereafter the Defense Department announced that the federal government planned to construct a number of fallout shelters across the country, just in case.

None of this information endeared us to non-Americans. No wonder Kennedy decided that a goodwill trip was necessary to that always troubled spot—the Middle East. The president was too busy to go himself, but there was Lyndon. What could Lyndon have to do in Washington, in *August?*

Robert Komer: "They called in LBJ and they said, 'We want you to go on this trip to the Middle East.' 'Representing me,' said Jack Kennedy. Lyndon said, 'I'm not going on another trip. When I went on this Far East trip the State Department guys wouldn't let me say anything, and when I *did* say something they hated me,' etc., etc.

"But Kennedy and Bundy persisted, and finally Johnson's compromise was, 'I will only go if you will let Mac Bundy go with me. I want one of your people at my elbow. Under those circumstances and no other way. I'm *not* going to be at the mercy of the State Department.'

"At which point Mac Bundy and Jack Kennedy apparently both said the same thing. It's wonderful how the protective instinct works. Kennedy said, 'You don't want Bundy. Bundy doesn't know anything about the Middle East—there's a guy named Komer who works for Bundy.' LBJ said, 'Who?'

"So Kennedy and Bundy sold LBJ on the idea that *the* White House Middle East guy was some bird named Bob Komer.[1]

"The first time I knew what was going on was when I was called up to Mac Bundy, who said, 'You are going to the Middle East in forty-eight hours. And you are going over to see the vice-president this afternoon at five o'clock.'

"I spent the next seven hours of that day trying to find out about Lyndon Johnson. To me he was a name in the newspapers, and I had read all those fearsome stories about his behavior.

"But at five o'clock I presented myself at the Capitol and after a number of false starts was ushered into a room that was I think the largest office I ever saw outside of the movies. I remember a huge crystal chandelier, and in this room was a table that seemed to be forty feet long. There were lots of chairs but only two people. At the far end was

Lyndon; and sitting at the other end was my old friend Phil Talbot, assistant secretary of state for Near Eastern and South Asia affairs, appointed by Kennedy. Talbot was a particular specialist on India and Pakistan.

"Johnson pulled out a chair and said, 'You sit down up here,' meaning near him. It wasn't an invitation; it was an order.

"Then Johnson said, 'I'm having an argument with the representative of the State Department here. He's trying to tell me about Pakistan and about the Pakistanis needing even treatment with the Indians.'

"Well, that was an issue on which Talbot and I disagreed. Phil Talbot always believed in being much more even-handed in the matter of foreign aid than I did—fifty-fifty, or even sixty-forty, which would have satisfied the Paks. I thought it should be more like seventy-thirty, with the seventy for the Indians. I didn't know from the vice-president's question that he was on the side of the Pakistanis. I told him that I was on the side of the Indians, and he didn't like that. But he liked it that I was willing to argue with the State Department; that I was my own man.

"And at that point he turned and shouted down to Talbot: 'SEE? I TOLD YOU SO. EVEN THE HIGH-RANKING KENNEDY MEN DON'T AGREE WITH THE STATE DEPART-MENT ON THIS PAKISTAN-INDIA BUSINESS.'

"And that was my start with Lyndon Johnson.

"We hit it off from the beginning. Of course, when a president sends a vice-president off on a trip that the vice-president doesn't want to go on, he does it with style. At least Kennedy did it with style. There we were at the helicopter on the White House grounds—this was on August 22—the departure ceremony from the Rose Garden. And this was the first time my wife and kids had ever seen a president and a vice-president, much less met them. Then Kennedy put his arm around me as we walked out there and said, 'Well, now, Bob . . .' They knew they were sending me to my death! I was the sacrificial lamb. And I will say this about Kennedy and Bundy—they were very nice to me as I went off to the slaughter in the helicopter. It was great. My family watched me lift off from the ground—they thought I was an important fellow.

"And we flew in Air Force One. Not Air Force Two or Three but Air Force One. When you're sending the vice-president of the United States off on a fool's errand, you send him on Air Force One."

Lyndon, Lady Bird, Komer, and party arrived in Beirut the next morning, August 23 at eleven thirty, and, of course, there were huge crowds everywhere. Lyndon got out of the car several times, as always, to press the flesh. From Beirut they flew to Teheran, and from there to Ankara.

Komer: "They said in Iran that if he had wanted to run for shah, he could have been elected—of course, that looked like a desirable job at the time. Johnson shook about thirty thousand hands; somebody said he shook three hundred in five minutes. The shah really got them out.

"Now Ankara was the third stop, and the State Department man from Washington, Ben Barnes, had been sent from Teheran by the Ambassador with one mission only, to deliver a message to the vice-president which was first, that everybody leaves Ankara in

August because it's a ghastly place, and second, the Turks are a stolid and undemonstrative people.

"Well, Barnes, after Beirut and Teheran, was afraid to tell the vice-president that he was not going to be mobbed. I said, 'That's what I'm for on this trip. I'll tell him.'

"So I went in to see him, and I said, 'Mr. Vice-President, you know, I'm a Turkish expert; I studied the only course in Ottoman history in the United States before World War II, and I want to tell you about the Turks. They are not going to give you a big show like in Beirut and Teheran. And the airport is eighteen miles from Ankara; nobody ever comes to it. It is a mess. And anyway, everybody leaves Ankara in August who can run or crawl because it's so damned hot.

"'It is just sad in August.'

"Anyway, we arrive, and there is Turkish protocol, of course; the president of Turkey is out there and a few other high officials, and we get in this long line of decrepit limousines to go into town. And nobody's there except the inevitable gendarmes standing on hilltops about every two hundred yards.

"We are riding along, and I am thinking, 'Thank God I told the vice-president that there will be no more demonstrations.' Then we run into a little group of people with little flags—women with baggy pants and so on. By the time we get about ten miles out of town there's sort of a thin line on both sides. Then we get about eight miles out of town—I haven't seen that many people in quite a while. We get about six miles—haven't even gotten to the city limits yet—and, my God, the place is absolutely mobbed.

"I was traveling in the second or third car, and at that point, Lyndon Johnson gets out and starts to press the flesh. And the security people came up and said, 'It is wall-to-wall people from here'—for the last six miles into the hotel.

"So I turn around and go a back way to the hotel. I check in, all alone. Freedom Square in front is just wall-to-wall people. I go up and have a shower. I order a double and then I walk out on the balcony just in time to see Lyndon Johnson. And he's walking. And, Christ, there's just billions of people, and he's loving it, just loving it. So I thought, 'Jesus Christ, those bastards at the State Department—they screwed me again.'"

Raymond Hare, American ambassador to Turkey: "The Turks were sort of surprised, this technique of talking to people and being in contact with people. I remember the last night we were in Istanbul, we went to see the vice-president and his wife and had dinner with them. They were in sports clothes. And the vice-president pulled up his trousers and showed us, I think it was his right thigh, and it was just burned from friction, from the crowds. And if he hadn't been a big man, he couldn't have done what he did. He'd stand, bracing himself, and put one leg out in front. That leg that stood out in front was actually burned from friction of people pressing against him."

On August 29, Lyndon departed for Nicosia, Cyprus, where he was showered with flowers on his arrival. The road was paved with laurel branches, an old Cypriot custom, and the crowds were huge. He was stopped five times along the way into town. The next day he addressed Parliament, after which he shook every member's hand. Outside there were more crowds.

On August 31 he arrived in Athens. There again were more crowds. Huge crowds.

Lyndon was in his favorite element, and it was all his aides could do to get him to rest sometimes.

William Crockett: "I always thought of his health as being a little precarious after his heart attack, and it always frightened me how hard he worked. He did rest occasionally, but he never stinted on what he had to do. As for food, he was a good sport. He generally ate before they went somewhere, so that he really wasn't hungry and could play with the food.

"I was interested in the contrast of his never having lost the need to save money, yet seemingly not worrying about how much money was spent. For example, we might have taken a whole floor or a whole hotel, and he didn't complain about that, and it may have cost us an awful lot of money on the changes we made in the plumbing or in air conditioning. But, you know, he was capable of going around and saying, 'Now, Bill, I told you to put everybody two to a room. I don't expect the taxpayer to pay for single rooms and all these guys living in style over here at the taxpayers' expense.'

"On our trip to the Middle East, he briefed all of us that went with him, and he said, 'Now, I don't expect this to be a big buying spree. I don't want any of you to come home with a bunch of rugs over one arm and a bunch of camel saddles over the other when we get off this airplane.'"

On September 4 the Johnsons flew to Rome, back to a world of technical competence and sophisticated people, and not entirely happily.

George E. Reedy: "He was always at his best with very poor people, people who were really at the end of their rope, who were deprived, and with whom he could establish a channel of communication.

"I saw this happen in Vietnam. I saw it happen in Thailand, in Turkey, and in Iran. I saw it happen in Greece. He always got much greater response from the poor—in Naples, for instance. In Rome the crowds were very, very small, and they paid very little attention to him. But Naples turned out a tumultuous welcome—a delightful combination of garlic and grease and sweating, screaming, yelling, smiling, happy people. And I think this may reveal something about him—he did have this capacity to reach out to poor people, did not do so well in a somewhat more technical or sophisticated or highly commercialized milieu. He did not do as well in the Scandinavian countries as he did in the Middle East or in Southeast Asia.

"He would do very well with government officials—not quite so well with diplomats. You know, the diplomat lives in a rather straitjacketed world in which life must proceed according to the exigencies of protocol, in which every action must be preplanned, preplotted, and predetermined."

In Rome the vice-president had discussions with the Italian prime minister and the chiefs of cabinet and visited Pope John XXIII. Then at 3:00 P.M. on September 7 Air Force One left for Washington, arriving at eleven that night. Everybody agreed, including Kennedy, that the trip had been a resounding success—well no, not everybody. Most of the foreign service people didn't; Bobby didn't; members of the Irish Mafia didn't. McGeorge Bundy did.

Komer: "Bundy was effusive in his praise—mostly, I imagine, because my presence had spared him the trip.

"And, of course, my Ankara *faux pas* made me a lifelong friend of LBJ.[2] If it had been the other way around and I had said there would be huge crowds and there weren't—I don't even like to think."

THE 101st SENATOR

For a while, quite a long while, it looked as if Bobby Baker was invincible. And if Lyndon had stayed on in the Senate, he might have been; Bobby says in his autobiography[1] that he spent many a sleepless night wondering if his trouble would have happened if Lyndon had not, on the advice of Bobby, among others, accepted the vice-presidential nomination. In the first place, in the view of many, Baker probably wouldn't have had time to get into trouble, and in the second, Lyndon, who, unhappily, never helped Bobby become rich, was succeeded by Senator Mike Mansfield as majority leader, and Mansfield, more often than not, was off in a hideaway smoking his pipe and reading a book.

Bobby could understand and deal with senators who were hard drinkers, who were, to use a euphemism of the time, skirt chasers, who were anxious for bribes, begged for them even, accepted them almost without exception. But a *book reader!* Who could deal with a man like that?

So Bobby took up with Senator Robert Kerr of Oklahoma, also a member of Lyndon's class of 1948, in Paul Douglas' words, "the uncrowned king of the Senate." Kerr not only gave Bobby advice on the proper stocks to invest in; if Bobby was without visible cash, he lent him money from one of his several Oklahoma banks.

Everything went beautifully—depending, of course, on one's definition of beauty—until October 1963. Bobby was a part owner of twenty-two corporations, motels, vending machine companies, housing developments, insurance, whatever was profitable. He could arrange an abortion for a senator's girl friend. He could also provide a girl for the night, the week, or even ten minutes, though he claims to have done the latter infrequently and with pangs of Baptist guilt. It was difficult to find anybody in the Senate of the United States who would speak ill of Bobby, publicly anyway. For one thing, he had the goods on most of them, and no senator doubted in the least that Bobby would use what he knew if he were pressed.

People said he was the 101st senator and that, though he had never run for public office, he had more power than any of the others, maybe more than all the others.

But in October 1963, it all began unraveling.

The first hint that Bobby was not invincible came when a certain Ralph Hill, owner of the Capitol Vending Company, brought a civil law suit against him, alleging Bobby to be in violation of a contract with him by virtue of canceling, or threatening to cancel— these matters are never clear—a vending machine contract. Hill, a thin, nervous man, alleged that Bobby was also heavily involved in, perhaps owned outright, a California vending machine operation called Serve-U and used his political influence to place them in defense plants across the country.

When Bobby told Mike Mansfield about the impending suit, Mansfield put down his book and pipe, though only momentarily, and said that he had complete faith in the secretary of the majority. He said almost the same thing to the *New York Times* the next day.

But a soft-spoken senator from Delaware, "Whispering John" Williams—who had uncovered the deep freezes that embarrassed Harry Truman and felled General Harry Vaughan, as well as the misdeeds of Eisenhower's Sherman Adams with his vicuna coats and vacations paid for by Bernard Goldfine—decided to look into the Bobby matter and asked that those who knew anything about Bobby's misdeeds to come forward and tell all they knew.

On October 7, 1963, Bobby, after a four-martini lunch, resigned his Senate position, thinking, he says in his book, that the matter would end there. It did not.

George E. Reedy: "Bobby Baker had the biggest ears for such a small man of anybody that ever lived. He was constantly listening, constantly snooping. And he did know the workings of the Senate.

"All the senators liked Bobby because he was useful. Very useful. He'd trade information back and forth. You know, Bobby had a quick pair of feet and a boundless supply of energy. And he was constantly running around, talking to people, exchanging gossip, getting things for them—got himself in position where he could deliver money to them during political campaigns. They all liked him. But that was all he knew, the workings of the Senate. To him the Senate was a mechanism that cranked out good things for Bobby Baker if he played it right."

Harry McPherson: "His great flaw was his ambition. He wanted desperately to improve his financial situation, and he did. He would sometimes come running in and ask if we could take up a certain bill. And I would say we took it up two hours ago and passed it. He would look shocked and run outside, get on the phone, and call someone and tell them, 'I just got your bill through.'

"Johnson, even though he embraced him, was also aware that Bobby was running on thin ice. He had heard too much—rumors about his serving many clients—and he told him to quit and go out into private practice. But Mansfield said, 'I'll quit as leader if you quit as secretary of the majority. I can't run the Senate without you.'

"But it always struck me as very ironic, unfair even, that Johnson got nailed as the guy to whom Bobby was the greatest close crony and that Mansfield escaped any criticism at all. Frankly I don't think either one of them deserved criticism, because Bobby was not doing the things that he was later charged with doing under their scrutiny at all. They knew nothing about it. Johnson literally did not know a damned thing about the operations that Bobby got himself tied up in, and I know that to be the case.

"The Senate is both close and permissive. And also willingly obtuse about such things. I mean if you hear that X is doing something that somebody rumors is not absolutely straight and skinny, but X comes to you and says, 'Going to have a party for you. We're going to charge a hundred dollars a plate; going to get you reelected,' and you say, 'Hot damn!' Then it all just sort of gets lost. You know, the rumors get put on the side, and he's a good fellow and he's helping you out and you're a good liberal and you want to get reelected. The friends of Bobby Baker were not just Mike Mansfield, Lyndon Johnson, and Bob Kerr—those of the Establishment. They included virtually every liberal in the place."

On November 22, the day of the Kennedy assassination, Don B. Reynolds, head of Don Reynolds Associates in Silver Spring, Maryland, testified before two investigators of the Senate Rules Committee, to which the Bobby Baker case had been referred, that Baker was an honorary vice-president of his firm and had received a part commission for procuring, among other life insurance policies, two $100,000 policies on the life of Lyndon Johnson; understandably, more orthodox insurance companies were not anxious to take such a risk on the life of a man who had only a few years before suffered a nearly fatal heart attack.

As a result of the sale, for which his honorary vice-president was solely responsible, Reynolds gave Bobby a part of the commission and said he accepted the advice of Walter Jenkins to do some $1,200 worth of advertising on Lyndon's—sorry, Bird's—television station.

The Senate investigators that day agreed that since Reynolds' testimony was so fascinating, they would not adjourn for lunch, and thus they did not learn until late afternoon that Jack Kennedy had been assassinated and Lyndon Johnson had become president, which changed things considerably. It is, or was then, one thing to look into the affairs of a vice-president, and quite another to examine those of a president, particularly when he had become president under such adverse circumstances.

Before they learned they had a new president, however, the investigators were told by Reynolds that he had sent the Johnson family a $585 Magnavox stereo set chosen, he said, by Mrs. Johnson. And he had a copy of a receipt—he kept a copy of everything, as men of his kind often do—which showed that the set had in fact been charged to him and had been shipped in a government car to 4921 Thirtieth Place, where the Johnsons had lived.

Naturally, all of Reynolds' testimony was leaked to the press, but it might have made larger headlines had Lyndon Johnson still been a largely powerless vice-president. Now most newspapers were inclined to play down the stories.

Most of the new president's advisers told him to ignore Reynolds, but Abe Fortas counseled him to tell his story to the public. So Johnson called a press conference in which he said that the Baker family had given the Johnson family the stereo. He said the families frequently exchanged gifts; he said further that he and Lady Bird had used the stereo for a period. What happened after that was rather vague; apparently the set had been given to some other friendly family. Who, why, and whether or not the Baker family often sent such expensive gifts to the Johnson family would forever remain a mystery.[2]

Fortunately, Senator Kerr had died on January 1 of that year and thus was spared the personal embarrassment of the committee's investigation of his affairs.

Lyndon was also busy denying that he had ever had much if indeed anything to do with Baker, whose name he sometimes could scarcely remember—Bakerly, Bakey, Beggerly. Something like that.

Reedy: "Johnson adopted this line that he hardly knew Bobby Baker, and I think he tried to convince himself that the line was true. You know, one of the things about Lyndon Johnson that you always have to be careful about—whatever Johnson tells you at any given moment he thinks is the truth. The first victim of the Johnson whopper is always Lyndon Baines Johnson. In his own mind I don't think the man ever told a whopper in his whole life. And once he came out with that line that he hardly knew Bobby Baker, I think he decided in his own mind that he didn't.

"Abe Fortas gave Johnson very poor advice when he told him to say he hardly knew Bobby Baker. But Johnson really panicked. I think if he'd just accepted the thing calmly and revealed the facts as they came out, I don't believe he could have been touched.

"Of course there was no question that Johnson felt they, Bobby Kennedy in particular, used Bobby Baker to get at him, and there's no question in my mind that Lyndon Johnson was innocent as the driven snow where Bobby Baker was concerned. I don't believe that he ever got into one crooked deal with Bobby, and I don't think he was aware of Bobby's crooked deals. And for that matter I don't think Bobby did very many crooked things when he was working for Johnson.

"All the other things—all the stuff about the wild women and what have you—all that came after Johnson gave up the leadership and Bobby was under the somewhat more relaxed regime of Mike Mansfield.

"I never knew, and I don't to this day, the extent to which Bobby was guilty of the things with which he was charged, and the extent to which a lot of it was merely Bobby talking big, and Bobby always talked big. He never wanted to talk in terms of less than $100,000. And I know of my knowledge frequently that $100,000 wasn't there, wasn't anywhere near the place."

Robert F. Kennedy: "I hadn't gotten really involved in the Bobby Baker case [in the capacity of Attorney General] until after a good number of newspaper stories had appeared about it and there really wasn't any choice but to look into some of the allegations, which were violations of the law. Some weeks after that I called him, I suppose sometime in November, and said that I just wanted to assure him that he'd get a fair shake, that he could send his lawyers to the Department of Justice and he'd be fairly treated. There were a lot of stories then, after November 22, that the Bobby Baker case was really stimulated by me and that this was part of my plan to get something on Johnson. That wasn't correct."

Charles Bartlett: "I didn't have the sense that Bobby Kennedy was trying to use the Baker thing as a sword to destroy Johnson. In a conversation maybe a week or two before the assassination, I asked Bobby how the investigation was going. He had a lot of stuff about what Baker had done, investments he'd made, loans, etc., but he said he didn't think it really tied in to Johnson at all. He said that very flatly."

The whole Bobby Baker affair was no problem during the 1964 presidential campaign; indeed, in April 1964 a Lou Harris poll reported that 73 percent of the American people were indifferent to the Baker case, even though Barry Goldwater said the whole thing led straight to the White House. And for reasons that I prefer not to explore 3 percent of the populace said that the whole investigation of Baker had increased their high regard for Lyndon.

Bobby's troubles were, however, by no means over even after Lyndon's triumph in 1964. On January 5, 1966, he was indicted by a federal grand jury on nine counts—including income tax evasion, conspiracy to defraud the federal government, theft, and misappropriating $100,000 in campaign funds. In January 1967, a U.S. District Court convicted him of most of those charges, and Bobby went off to Lewisburg Federal Prison on January 12, 1971; he was sentenced to three years and served half that time.

Before his death, Lyndon had one final conversation with Bobby at the Ranch, highly romanticized in the Baker autobiography, all very forgiving on Lyndon's part.

Bobby Baker: "He understood the presidency, and I understood the presidency, and had he tried to do anything, the press would literally have run him out of this town. There were a few minor scandals, but nothing that ever involved him. He was impeccably honest as far as I was concerned."

"MILDRED WICKS HAS CANCELED"

Besides the Bobby Baker case, another matter that continued to plague Lyndon, both before and during the presidency, was the question of how much his position in the federal government positively affected the fortunes of station KTBC, Lady Bird's station in Austin.

Exactly how large a part in the affairs of the station Lyndon played is open to conjecture. It was quite likely sporadic, but almost certainly it was more than he was willing to admit. Lady Bird's attention was continuous, whether she was in Austin or Washington. The station was managed by Jesse Kellam and Oscar Bobbitt, Lyndon's brother-in-law. The stock was held almost entirely by Lady Bird, Lynda and Luci, and Walter Jenkins, a surrogate family member if ever there was one, served as corporate treasurer (although he was also on the public payroll as Lyndon's administrative assistant) until the presidency.

So Lyndon could hardly have escaped involvement even if he had wanted to, which he really did not, although he always pretended to. He saw to it that the corporate name was changed to the LBJ Company in 1956 (it returned to the Texas Broadcasting Corporation after he became president). He kept close tabs on the sponsors, and he was always on the lookout for fresh talent, particularly Texas talent.

John Henry Faulk: "One time in February 1955, Walter Jenkins came to see me. He came to take care of some business, and we had lunch together. He said, 'The senator is very interested, Johnny, in having a conversation down in Washington.' That was on a Friday. On Saturday night I told a friend, Palmer Webber, about it.

"Palmer said, 'Well, here's the score. Lyndon has looked after everything very well.

Lyndon goes around with a basket under the trees, and he never shakes them; he just lets the fruit fall. Lyndon never shakes a tree.'

"He said, 'Lyndon's great failing is that he is not only suspicious, but he is also very nervous around the eastern Establishment. And he is enchanted with the fact that you have as close friends Ed Murrow and Walter Cronkite and the boys at the *New York Times* and the *New York Herald Tribune.* Oh, you've done well. And what Lyndon is doing, he's fixing to run in 1956, he and Averell Harriman, the only two men that've got enough money, on the Democratic ticket. They're going to get beat anyhow. But what Lyndon wants to do is to get you lined up. He's interested in your contacts and the fact that you've made it up here on the eastern seaboard.'

"He said, 'What you do is, you call Jenkins, tell him that you will get off one Sunday and come talk with the senator, and that you respect him highly. But for Lyndon, remember this one thing—Lyndon will always do right if it doesn't cost him anything. He is a genuine man, but he is also an opportunist and a man of expediency. And that's the reason the left wing scares him so. He's always scared to death; they're not for sale. They'll go with him when he's right, but they won't go with him when he's wrong. They won't go down to the spring to get water when it ain't time to get water.'

"He said, 'Yes, you get off one Sunday and go down. And I'll tell you exactly what's going to happen. Senator Johnson's going to court you. You haven't been courted like Senator Johnson's going to court you. He's going to have you just by yourself; nobody else is going to be with you. And I want you to say one thing; I want you to say, "Senator Johnson, I just turned twenty-one when Roosevelt became president, so I was not able to participate in that great and historic event. But I've supported and voted for you since '38, and if I thought there was a chance that you would ever run for president, I would be willing to give up a great deal in my own personal life to support you, sir." And then Lyndon will run his legs out in front of him and look you in the face and say, "I seek no other office than that to serve the people of Texas, Johnny. I appreciate your point of view." But you will know by that time that you have got the hook in his jaws. He will recognize you as a very smart and perceptive man. And you can then discuss what you want from Lyndon. But don't discuss it till you say that.'

"And it was the damndest thing. I flew down there, one o'clock one Sunday afternoon. And I could tell that the senator couldn't wait to have our conversation.

"So then the senator and I sat down and he poured me a drink and ran his legs out in front of him just like Palmer said. And I said, 'Senator Johnson, the reason I'm down here . . .' and then word for word, like Palmer told me, 'I'm not interested in radio and television in Texas, but if I thought there were an opportunity you could be persuaded to run for the presidency, the slightest opportunity of that, then the prestige and joy of signing autographs in New York would mean nothing to me.'

"And then Lyndon, as though Palmer Webber were standing over his shoulder, said, 'Johnny, I seek no other office than to serve the people of Texas who have placed their trust in me, and they mean to see me senator of Texas. But I deeply appreciate . . . Johnny, you come from the same kind of people I come from. We're born up the creek from each other. Johnson City is just forty miles from where your own place is.'

"Then he launched into what Bird was acquiring, how they were building a radio-television empire. And he said, 'What do you want, Johnny?' And I said, 'Well, senator, I'm very happy where I am. You see, Texas radio and television can't pay what New York does.' Palmer had said that to feel him out about taking a salary and also taking an interest. So I said, 'If I should make this move that you're suggesting, I would want to have some stock.'

"He said, 'Johnny, let me tell you about Texas Broadcasting Corporation. I don't own a penny of the stock. After Bird and I got married, she had the good fortune to have ten thousand dollars and KTBC was up for sale. Well, we gambled. We bought it.'

"Then Lyndon goes on to tell me about how nobody but Bird has any stock in it. But, 'We want to talk about this, Johnny; we want to see you. And if it works out, you can be assured that you'll be taken care of.'

"Now understand, up to this time I have never discussed with Bird Johnson one damn thing about radio and television. Only with Senator Johnson, who 'had no interest whatever in television.' Quote, unquote. So I said, 'I'll think about it,' and flew back, all expenses paid.

"Then one Thursday Walter Jenkins called me, very excited, and said, 'Johnny, the senator apologized for calling so late, but could you possibly come down tomorrow night because Saturday is Sam Rayburn Day in Washington. Great big birthday party for the Speaker.'

"So I went down and Walter met me and took me out to the senator's house. 'Now, Johnny, you go to bed early because we've got a very, very important day tomorrow.' Lyndon was to be the host at a breakfast in the Senate dining room for the Democratic National Committee at seven o'clock, and then at nine o'clock we were to go to a breakfast for Mister Sam given by the Texas Club. And then after this we were to rest, and then at six o'clock that night we were to go to a reception at the armory with former president Truman and his wife, Dean Acheson, Mrs. Roosevelt, and then a big dinner for Sam Rayburn after the reception at which Lyndon and Harry Truman were to speak.

"Well, we went to both breakfasts, and we had a big time. Lyndon was courting me, and he introduced me to everyone. By noon we'd gone back to his office and I said I was going on back out to the house and get some sleep. I was tired as hell. So I took a nap, and at six o'clock I'm dressed in my tuxedo. He's dressed in his tuxedo. We go out to this damn reception, and here is Dean Acheson, Mrs. Roosevelt, the whole Democratic party. And we have a wonderful reception. Go to the dinner, and it's a wonderful dinner.

"About one o'clock we went home. My tailgate was really dragging, and I could scarcely get out of that car, I was so tired. Although I'd had a nap in the middle of the day. The senator had had nothing. He said, 'Bird, you go on up to bed. John and I want to talk a minute.' Which was desolating news because I didn't want to talk. He said, 'I got something here I want to show you, Johnny.' He had this thick air-mail special delivery, from KTBC—their last two weeks' receipts.

"Now this is the majority leader of the United States Senate, whose principal interest in life was running that damn Senate, who 'had no interest whatever in radio and television,' quote, unquote, and he gave a dissection of the commercial status of KTBC that I do not think another American radio and television station owner could have done. And there was a woman, an evangelist, named Mildred Wicks who laid the hands on and cured people, and she bought commercial time on KTBC at night, after eleven o'clock, for fifty cents a minute—that was what radio time cost then in Austin, Texas, on a local station. Well, she had canceled her Wednesday and Thursday night commercials, and he picked up on this from the whole two-week section. 'Well, I'll be damned. Mildred Wicks has canceled.' This represented one dollar in the company account.

"That scared the hell out of me. It really got me wide awake all of a sudden. I realized I was sitting in the presence of an utterly unbelievable man. That he could pick this up at the end of a fifteen-hour day when he'd been meeting with Dean Acheson and Harry Truman and all of the Democrats and had made a speech at the dinner . . . absolutely unbelievable."

Throughout the fifties and well into the sixties the Johnson radio-television enterprise continued to grow. In 1955, after a complicated series of behind-the-scenes moves, it succeeded in acquiring a controlling interest in KWTX Broadcasting Company in Waco, Texas, north of Austin. Due south on the Mexican border in a town called Weslaco, the floundering station of KRGV-TV was scooped up by the LBJ Company, set upon its feet, and then sold at a handsome profit. Although the details of these two ventures are too complicated to be of interest here, they involved various rulings by the FCC, which were always prompt and always favorable.

Louis Kohlmeier, in his 1964 Pulitzer Prize-winning series for the *Wall Street Journal* titled "The Johnson Wealth," wrote on March 23:

> Unlike most businesses, a broadcasting enterprise can exist and expand only with government approval. From the very beginning and repeatedly thereafter, the fate of the Johnson family fortune has inevitably hung not only upon business acumen but also upon favorable rulings by the Federal Communications Commission. Yet FCC public records show not a single intervention by Representative, Senator, Vice-President, or President Johnson in quest of a favor for his wife's company.
>
> Quite apparently, there was no need for it. Mrs. Johnson was able to present the FCC with a record of solid business success, whenever that was relevant to government decisions. When it was not relevant, she was—as one official of the agency remarks—consistently "lucky." The practical effect—disregarding intent—of a long series of FCC rulings has been to create the Johnson local TV broadcasting monopoly, expand its sphere, and defend it against incursion.

Barry Goldwater, however, was more skeptical:

"There could be a beautiful story written about the members of the Commerce Committee, especially those attached to the subcommittee having jurisdiction over the FAA and FCC and FDC, of what they've come out of those things with. Members have gotten licenses; members own portions of stations.

"How could a man, almost penniless, come to Washington and die a man worth over $20 million? I can't understand how a man can become a multimillionaire."

The question of why, as the years went on, Austin should continue to have only one standard television station was one that persisted right up until the station was finally sold in 1972. Although Austin is not far from San Antonio, which has three, there are other cities equally close to larger cities which have two or three. On the other hand Austin is not entirely unique; there are also other cities of comparable size—Topeka, Kansas, for example—close to larger cities, that still have only one.

Lyndon was always sensitive to charges of a "TV monopoly." In 1964 a Goldwater supporter—ironically the man for whom almost a quarter century before Lyndon had obtained a commission to Annapolis, the same man whose father had turned over his option on KTBC to Lyndon, John Russell Kingsbery—began construction on a second large television tower for a rival TV station. True, the intruder was not a standard VHF station, but a UHF station, by then economically feasible, which took over one of the UHF channels originally assigned to Austin and therefore not requiring any further FCC ruling.

But then, as Kohlmeier reported, "A serious search of FCC public files discloses no instance in which either Mr. Johnson or his wife's company demanded that Austin be denied a second TV station. And the agency never expressed any desire to maintain the local Johnson TV broadcasting monopoly."

Kohlmeier continued:

> While Mr. Johnson happily displayed his friendships with network officials, he constantly avoided any appearance of espousing network causes—or the cause of the Johnson Company—when broadcasting matters were before Congress. The official index to records of Congressional debate back to 1950 discloses not a single instance of the Senator taking the floor to comment on broadcasting affairs. Men who served with him on the Senate Commerce Committee say Mr. Johnson carefully refrained from using his influence to push or oppose broadcasting legislation.

Leonard Marks, who served as legal counsel for the Johnson radio and TV interests for thirty years, said:

"I decided almost from the beginning that Lyndon Johnson was going to be president and that I must never do anything as a lawyer, ask for any favors, that could in any way raise questions politically. Only once did we ask for any special consideration, and that one time we were turned down. One time involved moving a tower from point A to point B. And we asked that it be expedited because the lease was running out on point A. We asked the FCC, and they turned us down.

"In his campaign for the Senate, and when he ran for president, his opponents went through the FCC record with a vacuum cleaner and a fine-tooth comb. They questioned everybody on the staff and they questioned commissioners, former and present, and they couldn't find one single thing, for the simple reason that we never did anything. And all this business that Goldwater raised in the '64 campaign—that he must have used his influence as a senator to get his permit—is absolute nonsense. It's been investigated so much that it's pretty well established that everything that was done was done on the merits. And LBJ wanted it that way."

When Lyndon, as Marks had predicted, acceded to the presidency, the LBJ Company and all its holdings were put into trust. Lady Bird resigned as chairman and the name reverted back to the Texas Broadcasting Corporation. Revenues involved could no longer be used by the Johnson family, but of course they did not disappear—they simply sat there accumulating until the presidency should be over and the old life resume its course.

During his presidency Lyndon courted the media, increased his intimacy with network presidents Frank Stanton of CBS and Robert Kintner of NBC.

During the 1964 campaign, in response to repeated questions on the extent of his fortune, Lyndon had the national accounting firm of Haskins and Sells of New York prepare a financial statement. The nine-page document, although greatly detailed, merely spawned more questions. By figuring net worth on the basis of original cost rather than current market value, the firm came up with the almost ridiculously low figure of $3,484,098 for the Johnson family "capital." Everyone in Texas, anyway, knew that the television holdings alone were worth approximately twice that amount. The $3 million figure was "legally acceptable," but of course no legal matter was involved. What was involved was a presidential incumbent trying to convince the American people that he was as honest, if not as middle-income, as the rest of them, and the American people quite rightly remained unconvinced.

Hugh Sidey: "*Life* sent a team of reporters down, and they had come up with the fact that Johnson was worth $14 million. Johnson was just horrified. He tried to persuade them, and then he tried to intimidate them not to run it, to change it. He was apparently very uptight about it, and very concerned."

In some ways this denial of wealth in the last decade of his life was typical of the later Lyndon, torn by his dual desire to be a Texas big shot, to sit among the kings, and his feeling of identity with the struggling poor of America. He did not really want to lose his association with that latter group, at least theoretically he did not. Perhaps he thought they would disclaim him if his true wealth were known. Perhaps they would not believe him when he talked about all the things he wanted to do for them.

For the sake of his image in their eyes, he wanted to keep his humble beginnings, to play down his good fortune in which they had not shared.

DUMPING LYNDON

By the time Lyndon was into the third year of his vice-presidency, certain patterns had been established. He presided, with some regularity, over the Senate; he delivered prepared speeches around the country on appropriate occasions; he traveled extensively, not only on major trips, but briefer ones such as to Dag Hammarskjöld's funeral in Stockholm, to an Independence Day fete in Jamaica, and to the Dominican Republic for the inauguration of the new president, Juan Bosch. He tried to represent his country and his president well. And in his free hours, of which he had more than he had ever had before, he asked himself whether he could endure six more years of semiretirement.

Harry McPherson: "It was a time of deprivation. He grew very fat and drank a lot. He took up golf some, I recall, but not with enthusiasm.

"But he was very scrupulous in his relations with President Kennedy, a scrupulousness which I think has not been generally recognized. He did not talk with anybody who might have published any of his negative thoughts about Kennedy. He would tell *me* how Jack Kennedy and Bobby had failed to do whatever it was to meet congressional problems. And how the stories about the midnight parties at Bobby's swimming pool were doing the administration harm, which I think was probably true."

Outwardly he and the president were still friends, but anti-Lyndon sentiment was rife among the inner Kennedy circle, and Lyndon no doubt felt that Kennedy could have controlled his troops better if he'd tried. Kennedy, on the other hand, disappointed with congressional inaction on his legislative program, was no doubt convinced that Lyndon could have helped him out there if he had tried.

Whether or not Lyndon did try, and just how much, depended considerably on the point from which one was observing.

Elizabeth Goldschmidt: "Many people thought that he would become a great aide to the president in getting his legislation through the Congress. But in actual fact, Lyndon didn't touch it. He had to sit there, to the extent that he did, and observe controversies and frustrations which for years he had managed and be totally passive."

McPherson: "I remember one day I was coming off the Senate floor, and I passed him coming out of an elevator wearing a hat. That was a very unusual thing. He looked distinguished in a hat, should have worn one more frequently.

"He had a briefcase and looked very businesslike. And I asked him where he had been. He said he had been in a meeting of the Smithsonian Board of Regents talking about the zoo. I thought, 'My God, I don't believe it. Lyndon Johnson and the zoo.'"

Wilbur Mills: "Kennedy made a very grievous and serious mistake in not utilizing the vice-president. I had the feeling that the president had more or less shelved the vice-president, or, as we say in Texas and Arkansas, 'turned him out to pasture.'"

Jack Bell: "When Kennedy wanted something, Johnson did what he could for Kennedy in trying to get it, but he had none of the old power left. He couldn't punish anybody really; he couldn't promise anybody anything. A man in that position can't do too much in politics. While Johnson could tell Kennedy, 'Okay, this guy's against you; this guy is for you, and this guy's going to do that,' he couldn't produce because he had no power."

The truth was that after the lesson of the Democratic caucus of January 1961, Lyndon had virtually given up any thought of trying to reexercise power. He had long reconciled himself to the fact that the only power that counted in the executive was in the Oval Office and in the few men who had freest access there—of which he was never one.

Bell: "As he told me one day, 'Every time they have a conference, don't kid anybody about who is the top adviser. It isn't McNamara, the chiefs of staff, or anybody else like that. Bobby is first in, last out. And Bobby is the boy he listens to.'"

It was Bobby's opinion that Lyndon was no help at all. But often Lyndon was glad to help, if asked. He was seldom asked; or if he was, it was usually after the initial mistakes had been made and there was no undoing them.

For example, on June 3, 1963, after Kennedy's civil rights bill had been sitting in committee and getting nowhere, Ted Sorensen finally made a call to Lyndon, whose experience with getting civil rights bills through Congress was hardly unknown. Lyndon's advice on the subject, when transcribed (the call was taped) ran to twenty-seven pages. Although, as Lyndon pointed out, he had not been asked to sit in on any of the conferences with senators on the bill—"I'd just as soon be included out on all these things," he said defensively—he would, since asked at last, tell Sorensen just what he thought Kennedy should do, which was to go personally to the South and lay it on the line.

"I wouldn't have him go down there and meet Wallace and get in a tussle with him," Lyndon told Sorensen. "I'd pick my own time and my own place. The hell with confronting those people. But I think he ought to talk frankly and freely, rather understandingly and maybe fatherly. He should stick to the moral issue and he should do it without equivocation.

"I know these risks are great and it might cost us the South," Lyndon went on, "but those sorts of states may be lost anyway. The difference is: if your president just enforces court decrees, the South will feel it's yielded to force. But if he goes down there and looks them in the eyes and states the moral issue and the Christian issue, and he does it face to face, these southerners at least respect his courage. They feel that they're on the losing side of an issue of conscience."

There was a lot more of it, more about how *after* he had gone to the South, the president should then tackle the Congress, and this was how he should do *that*, and so on. Obviously Lyndon was so pleased finally to have been consulted that he could not restrain himself. And the advice, as Sorensen noted, wasn't half bad, might have worked. (It worked fine, as we shall see, for Lyndon a year later.)

But advice wasn't Bobby's idea of help at all. And Lyndon knew that Bobby was saying, and saying openly, that Jack had wanted Lyndon to be vice-president not because he had wanted him to be vice-president, but because he had *not* wanted him to be majority leader during his presidency.

Foreign affairs, however, was another matter. Whatever Lyndon's ambivalence about helping the president with his domestic problems, he really wanted to do his part in the international arena, and to do it properly. He was well aware of his own inadequacies in diplomatic circles, of his limited background in, and grasp of, foreign affairs, and whatever deficiencies he had not already suspected, the State Department did not hesitate to make known to him, often directly. On the other hand he considered the State Department the source of many of his problems.

Angier Biddle Duke: "He came up to New York to speak at a UN dinner for Adlai Stevenson. It was a hard-line speech, and the Iron Curtain country ambassadors—first the Czech, and then the Pole—all started to get up and go. He looked bewildered, but he kept on. He finished the darn speech, and he sent a note down the table to me saying, 'Come to my room after.'

"And he got hold of Adlai Stevenson and said, 'What was wrong? What happened? Gee whiz, why didn't you guys tell me? I cleared this with the State Department.' Adlai said, 'Don't you worry about it. It'll be okay,' and sort of eased him into the car.

"We went back to my room, and he threw all his attention on me. He said, 'I want you to get Dean Rusk on the phone, and I want to know why when I get clearance from the State Department, why can't I trust it? Do I have to rewrite speeches myself? I mean, what's State Department clearance mean anyway?' We got Dean Rusk, and then he said, 'Get the president on the phone.' I got Ted Clifton, the military aide, at the White House, and we got the president up at some god-awful hour. He was not very happy about it.

"I don't know why the eastern Europeans, who must have heard lots of those speeches, were offended. I think it was the occasion rather than the substance of the speech. It was a UN dinner for Adlai at some hotel in New York, and all of them were there. Some of them were on the dais. The Soviet ambassador was on the dais. He got up and walked out.

"Now that hurt Lyndon Johnson. He wanted to play on the president's team. He wanted to be a help to him. He said, 'I don't want to have any blurring of the image of the United States in its foreign policy.' He thought I was very close to the president, and he said, 'I want you to get that point over to him that I'm not playing any games here. I'm sincere. I would like to be part of his team and to play on the team. If he thinks I'm out playing for myself, carving out areas of foreign policy, it's not so. How can I get that through to him?

"'After all, I'm sent out to speak all over the country, and then when I do, I get myself knocked on the head as I did tonight, and it's just not fair.'

"He was like a dog worrying at a bone."

Lyndon's reticence in National Security Council meetings was another effort on his part to be "part of the team." He never spoke unless his opinion was directly asked for, and then he was careful, at least while the meeting was in progress, not to differ too sharply with what he understood to be the administration viewpoint. Occasionally, if he felt strongly on a particular matter, he would stay afterwards to argue it in private with the president.

Charles Bartlett: "One of the weaknesses of the Kennedy White House staff was that individuals became rather arrogant. This was certainly not true of Jack Kennedy, who kept a very humble sense of his own role all the way through. But I do remember one instance when Johnson was going off on that last trip as vice-president to Scandinavia. The vice-president indicated to Kenneth O'Donnell that he'd like to see the president before he went and have a little bit of a send-off from the president to boost his own role.

"O'Donnell said it was impossible. Ted Clifton heard about it and felt this was not the way that John Kennedy would really want it, so he made the arrangements for Lyndon Johnson to visit the president just before he departed.

"They met in Hyannis Port. Apparently it was a very touching visit. Johnson came, and Kennedy said, 'What are you going to say over there?' Johnson had George Reedy produce the speeches that had been drafted for the trip, and they read through some of them, and Kennedy made a few suggestions. Johnson was very formal and sat on the edge of his chair. Red Fay was there; he said that Johnson was playing the vice-president with the president in a very formal way, an almost deferential way, and was very grateful for the conversation."

In spite of repeated denials by the president, there was, by the time of the midterm congressional elections in 1962, talk, discussion, hints, what-have-you, that Lyndon would be dumped from the reelection ticket in 1964.

Burke Marshall: "The only thing I can remember about the question of whether Lyndon would be on the ticket in 1964—I was sort of an ambassador for a while with Evelyn Lincoln. Mrs. Lincoln wrote a book[1] in which she claimed that President Kennedy came in to her and said something like, 'We're going to dump Lyndon Johnson and nominate Terry Sanford in 1964.' I remember Bobby commented on that to me—'that was a silly, absurd story,' I think he said. 'Of course we had no intention of doing that.' And in addition, he said, 'Can you just imagine that president coming in and telling Mrs. Lincoln something like that?'"

Max Frankel: "I have never encountered anything that corroborates that story. My own guess is that it would have depended on Kennedy's sense of his political standing and whether he really needed the South still. I would guess that John Kennedy never forgot he would not have been elected if not for Lyndon Johnson. Whether he would have, therefore, been capable of the ultimate, really, destruction of Lyndon Johnson—I would doubt it.

"Lyndon Johnson always made a point of saying how much more cordial his relations were with John. I think he had a fundamental respect for John Kennedy that he could never get for Robert."

Arthur Krock: "The thought of Johnson as president—I don't think Kennedy *ever* would have groomed Johnson as his successor had he been allowed to have two terms. Certainly he would have built up somebody else for the leader to succeed him. But I don't think he intended to dump Johnson in '64."

Bartlett: "In the swimming pool, and I can't remember at what point in 1963 this was, but it wasn't too long before the assassination, I said to Kennedy, 'Why don't you get another vice-president in 1964?' Kennedy turned on me in the pool, and he was furious and said, 'Why would I do a thing like that? That would be absolutely crazy. It would tear up the relationship and hurt me in Texas. That would be the most foolish thing I could do."

Hubert H. Humphrey: "Of course there were a few hotheads around; there are in any administration. There were those who just didn't like him at all, and a group of them met. I got a full report on the meeting, and they were going to dump Johnson. I know Arthur Schlesinger was one of them. They had the meeting out in Georgetown. And there was another meeting shortly after Kennedy was assassinated; this time they didn't want Johnson nominated in 1964.

"I know Schlesinger was at one if not both meetings. I don't know if Bobby was there or not, but I'm sure he wouldn't have gone along with them while his brother was still alive. It would not have been intelligent to dump Johnson as vice-president."

Robert F. Kennedy: "There were a lot of stories that my brother and I were interested in dumping Lyndon Johnson and that I'd started the Bobby Baker case in order to give us a handle. Well, there was no plan to dump Lyndon Johnson."

Arthur Schlesinger, Jr.: "There was, so far as I know, no discussion before Dallas of dumping LBJ in 1964. This idea is total fantasy."

The other question, of course, although it was seldom discussed and hardly ever written about, was whether Lyndon wanted to remain on the ticket in 1964. The Kennedy people, having long since decided that he was a man mad for power, insatiable in his political ambitions, dismissed the idea that "Uncle Corn Pone" would leave a soft spot one heartbeat away from . . . would even consider stepping aside and down.

But he did consider it.

Orville Freeman: "He hinted on a number of occasions that he was thinking seriously of doing something else. He had apparently some offers from colleges that he was interested in, that were asking him if he might be a president."

Horace Busby: "In Brussels on November 8, 1963, he was talking about Kennedy and about his own future. And the latter seemed very bleak to him—another four years as vice-president. That was not a happy prospect for him. And he said what he thought he wanted to do was to become a publisher, the publisher of a progressive, a forward-looking Texas daily. He said he'd be the publisher and I'd be the editor. He got very excited about the whole thing; he was going to reform the state.

"I saw him again on Sunday night, after we got back to the United States. As I was leaving, he said, 'I'm going to look into that newspaper business.'

"And in the middle of the next week I found out that he had approached Harry Provence, editor of the *Tribune-Herald* in Waco, Texas."

Ed Clark: "I discussed the newspaper business with Lyndon many times, including when he was vice-president. He seemed quite knowledgeable on the subject, and I advised him as to what papers might be on the market or coming on the market. But I don't think his interest in publishing a newspaper came just when he was vice-president. I think he'd have bought a paper any time from 1937 on if the price was right and its future seemed lucrative enough to him. He also would have bought, under the same criteria, ranches, banks, cattle."

Lyndon, in any case, never became a publisher. And even if there had been the slightest hope in the minds of members of the Irish Mafia that he would be dropped as the vice-presidential nominee, events, as they were forever saying in eighteenth- and nineteenth-century English novels, intervened.

NOVEMBER 22, 1963

Bill Moyers: "In October of '63, when I was deputy director of the Peace Corps, Kenneth O'Donnell called and said, 'We're going to Texas. There's a fight between the Yarborough[1] forces, the Connally forces, and the Johnson forces. We need a faith-healer. We hear the Connally people accept you, the Yarborough people like you, and you are part of the Johnson people. Would you go down and coordinate this trip for us?'"

George E. Reedy: "The conservative forces in Texas were definitely on the rise, and all the indications were that the administration was heading into real trouble in that state. It was strongly felt by the Kennedy people that he had to make an appearance in the state in order to recapture lost ground.

"I don't know what Johnson could have done to smooth the split in Texas, because this was not an organizational question at all. It was a question of popular feeling. John Connally had no control over the type of people who made up the John Birch Society, and the right-wing sentiment in Texas was growing rapidly."

Henry Gonzalez: "The main purpose for that trip was to lay pledges for money on the coming campaign. They weren't looking for votes in Dallas, they were looking for money, and Dallas had the money."

Stanley Marcus: "The day before the trip, when they were due to come to Dallas, I called Johnson and said, 'I've got the money, Mr. Vice-President, but I sure wish to hell you'd persuade Kennedy not to come. It is a grave mistake to come to Dallas.' There was a very hostile atmosphere, and I was afraid he would be embarrassed. Johnson said, 'Look, it doesn't make a damn bit of difference what you think or I think, the president is coming to Dallas. So get the money to whoever needs it.' Purely for local entertainment—garlands and flags and so forth. 'Put on a big show.'"

Gene Worley: "I called a good friend of mine the day before Kennedy and Johnson went to Texas; he was in the life insurance business in Dallas. I said, 'Incidentally, what are you-all going to do when they get to Dallas, shoot them?' 'Aw, no, Gene,' he said, 'we're going to roll out the red carpet for them.' I said, 'Are you serious?' And he said, 'I sure am. This is a fine day. Great thing for Dallas. Heal all those wounds and everything else.'

"Preston Smith was in his office at the time—that was when Preston was lieutenant governor—and I said, 'What about those nitwits and beatniks?' And he said, 'Aw, we've got them tied down.' I said, 'You mean the right-wingers and the left-wingers, too?' He said, 'Oh, yeah, there'll be no trouble.'"

Hale Boggs: "What I said to President Kennedy was that politics in Texas are so disturbed—at that time they were really in a terrible factional fight—that it looked to me as if he was apt to get into trouble. I didn't mean that somebody was going to try to shoot him. I meant politically. And I remember he sort of laughed about that and said, 'Well, that makes it more interesting.'"

Jacqueline Kennedy Onassis: "I know he was warned before not to go by Senator Fulbright, by Adlai Stevenson, by Bobby, to whom they—Texas politicians, I think—had given messages."

Lyndon: "Mrs. Kennedy had never been to Texas before. She was interested in Texas. I think that she was anxious to do what she could to show confidence and help the president with his political problems. He told me with great pride that she had agreed to come and he was so pleased that she was coming. And she was coming to spend a night here at the Ranch and to ride the next day. We had planned to have some friends in for lunch, and to have a little western show for her. They were going to enjoy the relaxation and the countryside.

"And she was so glad that she came. That was one of the things she said—after the tragedy—if something like this had to happen, she was so glad she was here. Right by his side to the last."

Air Force One arrived in San Antonio, the first leg of the trip, the afternoon of November 21. President and Mrs. Kennedy were given a very warm reception. There were large crowds lining the streets from the airport to Brooks Aerospace Medical Center where Kennedy was to speak. From there they went on to Houston.

Charles Roberts: "One of the things that sticks out in my memory is the fact that this was the first political trip Jackie had made with him since the primaries of '60 and the fact that she was getting such an acclaim everywhere. People were asking 'Where's Jackie?' and there were as many yells for Jackie as there were for Jack."

Jacqueline Kennedy Onassis: "Vice-President Johnson came to our hotel room in Houston the night before we went to Fort Worth. There was all of this about people not wanting to ride in the car with him. I forget if John Connally wouldn't ride in the car or Senator Yarborough wouldn't.

"I remember asking Jack that night in Houston what the trouble was. He said that John Connally wanted to show that he was independent and could run on his own and was making friends with a lot of . . . I think he might have said 'Republican fat cats,' and he wanted to show that he didn't need Lyndon Johnson, or something. And that part of the trouble of the trip was him trying to show that he had his own constituency.'"

From Houston the president and First Lady flew to Fort Worth where they landed shortly after midnight. Again there were large crowds at the airport. In Fort Worth, Senator Yarborough agreed to do what he had refused to do in San Antonio and again in Houston—ride in the same car with the vice-president. Yarborough's change of heart may have had something to do with what a Texas congressman overheard Kennedy say to Yarborough: "If you don't ride with Johnson—you'll walk."

The activities of November 22 began early and in a drizzling rain. Lady Bird accompanied Lyndon to a prebreakfast reception at the Hotel Texas at 8:20 A.M., during the course of which the president, vice-president, Senator Yarborough, and Governor Connally absented themselves briefly to greet the crowd that had gathered in the parking lot across the street. Lyndon introduced Kennedy, but the people, many of whom had been standing for more than an hour in the rain, were disappointed at not seeing the First Lady with him. They started shouting, "Where's Jackie?" To which he replied, "Mrs. Kennedy is organizing herself. It takes longer, but of course she looks better than we do when she does it."

After breakfast Lyndon asked Kennedy if he might bring his youngest sister, Lucia, to meet him, and the president suggested they come up to his suite where he wanted to change his shirt before getting on the plane. He was pleased by the whole trip so far. He told Lyndon, "You can be sure of one thing—we're going to carry two states next year: Massachusetts and Texas." And Lyndon said, "We're going to carry a lot more than those two!"

After which, as Lyndon said later, "He told my sister good-bye, glad he met her, and we went down to our plane, and he went to his."

Lyndon: "We left Fort Worth ahead of Air Force One. We landed in Dallas around eleven thirty. Mrs. Johnson and I got off the plane and shook hands with the group that was there to receive the president, and we moved back with the dignitaries and welcomed the president and Mrs. Kennedy as they came off the plane. He was happy, smiling, and I think stimulated by the Fort Worth experience that morning. And Mrs. Kennedy was radiant and looked charming and beautiful in her pink hat and pink suit."

Kenneth O'Donnell: "We landed in Dallas with everybody on the plane in love with each other. When we were riding through Dallas on our way from the airport to the Trade Mart luncheon I said to Dave Powers, 'There's certainly nothing wrong with this crowd.'"

That morning, however, the *Dallas Morning News* had carried a full-page ad, bordered in black, accusing the president of being pro-Communist. The ad had been placed by Bernard Weissman, chairman of something called the American Fact Finding Committee.

Liz Carpenter: "Dallas had been, I think, in the minds of everyone, a questionable spot. If we made a good show there, it really meant that all of the Goldwater talk was nothing, because it was the most anti-Johnson, the most anti-Democratic, and the most anti-everything city in Texas.

"Everyone was delighted there was such a large turnout at the airport. There were a few ugly signs again. However, the fabulous thing about the Dallas reception was that it was not at all as we had envisioned—just thousands of people. They outdid San Antonio and outdid Houston and outdid Fort Worth."

Moyers: "I wanted approval from the Secret Service and the people running the campaign in Dallas to publish the route of the motorcade. The Secret Service didn't want to, and the politicians of course wanted to. They wanted a crowd. It was a very easy decision to make—yes, publish the motorcade. I had made the decision the night before in Dallas. So that morning the *Dallas News* carried the map of the motorcade."

Lyndon: "They got in a big Lincoln with Governor Connally. The president rides with the first man of the state when the first man of the nation comes to visit. They drove away, and Mrs. Johnson and Senator Yarborough and I got in the car that was driven by a patrolman, and Rufus Youngblood was our Secret Service escort."

Roberts: "I remember on the press bus there was a Dallas reporter, and when the question of security came up, he said there wouldn't be any security problem because of what had happened to Adlai Stevenson there just about two weeks before when he got spat on and hit over the head with a placard. He said, 'The cops won't let them get near him today because of the Stevenson incident.'

"I remember looking up at the sign on this building as we came to a park and sort of turned to the right to go down this incline under the triple underpass. I saw the words 'Texas Schoolbook Depository' and thought it was a weird name for a building."

Jack Bell: "It was a wonderful day, beautiful weather. He came down Dallas's Main Street in a motorcade. Kennedy had overruled the Secret Service, which wanted to take him directly from the airport to the Trade Mart where he was supposed to make a speech. Johnson had not wanted that. He wanted Kennedy to go through Dallas and demonstrate to these people—and to the world—that Dallas loved Kennedy. The people did. Out on the streets they gave him a terrific hand. Jackie was beautiful, and the people were rushing out to lay a hand at least on the car if they couldn't get to the president. We turned a corner, and there was the Texas Schoolbook Depository."

Rufus Youngblood: "Suddenly there was an explosive noise—distinct, sharp, resounding. Nothing that could be mistaken for the incessant popping and backfiring of the motorcycles, but in the instant I heard it I could not be certain if it had been a firecracker, bullet, bomb, or some other explosive. I looked around quickly and saw nothing to indicate its source.

"But the movements in the president's car were not normal. Kennedy seemed to be falling to his left, and there was sudden movement among the agents in the car directly ahead of us. I turned instinctively in my seat and with my left hand I grasped Lyndon Johnson's right shoulder and with all the leverage I could exert from a sitting position I forced him downward.

"*'Get down!'* I shouted. *'Get down!'*

"The vice-president reacted immediately. Still not seeing the source of the explosion, I swung across the back seat and sat on top of him. There were two more explosions in rapid succession, only seconds after the first. . . . People along the sides of the street were scattering in panic. . . .

[Over the radio] "*'Halfback* [code name for the presidential follow-up car] . . . *Halfback* to Lawson! The President's been hit! Get us to a hospital, fast but safe.'"[2]

Lyndon: "He got on top of me and he put his body between me and the crowd. He had his knees in my back and his elbows in my back and a good two hundred pounds all over me. And the car was speeded up. He had a microphone from the front seat that he'd pulled over with him, a two-way radio and there was a lot of traffic on the radio and you could hear them talking back and forth, and one of them said: 'Let's get out of here quick.'

"The next thing we were on the way to the hospital."

Bell: "I thought somebody had set off a cherry bomb. I thought to myself, 'My God, those Texans don't ever know when to quit. They've given the man everything they could. Here they are shooting off firecrackers and cherry bombs.' About three seconds later there was another report, and then there was a third one. By that time, everybody thought this was a rifle shooting. So we started to jump out of the car. We didn't know what was happening because Kennedy's car was four cars ahead and we couldn't see it clearly.

"Then the motorcade began to move, so we all jumped back in the car. It moved very fast. We went tearing up a freeway. All we could see was the president's car about a hundred yards ahead of us and the 'Queen Mary,' the Secret Service car, with an agent sitting in the back with a machine gun and looking around in the sky."

Roberts: "Bob Pierpoint, who was sitting next to me, said, 'That sounded like gunfire.' And as he said it, I looked off to my left and saw a man sprawl over what I think was his daughter. Our bus came to a halt. Everybody started screaming different advice to the bus driver: 'Open the door.' 'No, close the door.' 'Let's go.' 'Stop the bus.' 'Let us out.' What he did do was open the door for a few minutes and a few of us jumped out. I jumped back aboard and we were held up then by the police for I guess about five minutes.

"There's no precedent. When somebody shoots at the president, there simply is no precedent for what you do with the press. But within a few minutes they released the press bus and we went on to the hall where the president was to speak—the Dallas Trade Mart.

"We lumbered up to the back of the Trade Mart, burst into this hall, literally pushed those double doors open and swarmed into the place. And this was kind of an other-worldly scene. They were sitting there with no knowledge of what had happened, and the water fountains playing softly. I think there was music piped into the place. And here were perhaps a thousand lunch guests sitting there waiting for the president, and they looked up at us like we were men from Mars or nuts of some kind. And we couldn't get out of them what had happened, of course, because they knew even less than we did."

Judge Sarah Hughes: "I was seated downstairs next to Jan Sanders, Mrs. Barefoot Sanders, and we were waiting. The press came in, and we kept on waiting, and Jan began to get worried. She said, 'Something has happened.' I said, 'Oh, no—no, it can't be.' And she actually began to cry even before we knew.

"Then Eric Johnson, who was chairman of the luncheon, got up and said, 'We've had news of an accident, and the president and Governor Connally have been taken to Parkland. We'll give you information as soon as we have it.'

"Of course we all waited, and in about ten minutes he said, 'It has been a serious accident. We don't know how serious, but it is serious and we will adjourn.' Then he called on Luther Holcomb for a blessing and we all left."

Luther Holcomb: "To be sure, I had prepared an invocation, but if I ever offered a prayer that came from my heart I did it on that day."

Lyndon: "They just almost shoved us into the hospital, into the first room that they'd come to down the corridor. They pulled all the shades in the room, closed the door, and we sat there and endured the agony and waited for reports that came in from time to time."

Bell: "We pulled into the ambulance entrance and we all boiled out of the car to see what had happened. Governor Connally was helped out of the car. His shirt was red in front with blood. Johnson was getting out of his car. I ran up to the White House limousine. There the president was lying on his face in the back seat, and there were pools of blood—an inch of blood maybe—over the floor of the car. There were some twisted roses lying in it. I turned to the Secret Service man who was standing as a sort of sentinel there, and I said, 'That is the president, isn't it?' He said, 'Yes.' I said, 'Is he dead?' He said, 'I don't think so, but I don't know.'"

Roberts: "At 12:57 P.M. a Roman Catholic priest, later identified as the Reverend Oscar Huber, was whisked through the guarded doors into the emergency room, where, we were now informed, the mortally wounded president was still lying on a portable bed. 'That means the last rites,' a cop said."

Cliff Carter: "At 1:10 P.M. Agent Emory Roberts of presidential detail entered the room where Vice President and Mrs. Johnson were waiting and told the vice-president that he thought plans should be made to get back to Washington immediately. The VP replied that he thought those wishes ought to come from both Ken O'Donnell and the Secret Service.

"At 1:20 P.M. Agent Emory Roberts came into the room again and notified the vice-president that the president was dead. In the room were Congressman Thornberry, Rufus Youngblood, Lem Johns, Jerry Kivett, and myself.

"At 1:22 Ken O'Donnell came in. Ken said, 'He's gone.'"[3]

Lyndon: "The greatest shock that I can recall was one of the men saying, 'He's gone.'

"I asked that the announcement be made after we had left the room and were in an unmarked car en route to the presidential plane, so that if it were an international conspiracy and they were out to destroy our form of government and the leaders in that government, that we would minimize the opportunity for doing so.

"I think the first thought I had was that this is a terrifying thing that may have international consequences, that this might be an international conspiracy of some kind. And I knew, of course, that I was on my own and that it was my responsibility and it was a thing that had to be dealt with very quickly and as calmly as could be. And I tried to think it out, recognize the problems that faced me and the necessity of giving the nation and the world confidence as soon as I could."

Lady Bird: "It was Lyndon who spoke of it first, although I knew I would not leave without doing it. He said, 'You had better try to see Jackie and Nellie.' We didn't know what had happened to John.

"I asked the Secret Service if I could be taken to them. They began to lead me up one corridor and down another. Suddenly I found myself face to face with Jackie in a small hallway. I believe it was right outside the operating room. You always think of someone like her as being insulated, protected. She was quite alone. I don't think I ever saw anyone so much alone in my life. I went up to her, put my arms around her, and said something to her. I'm sure it was something like 'God, help us all,' because my feelings for her were too tumultuous to put into words."[4]

Roberts: "At the door of the hospital was a hearse from this O'Neal undertaking parlor—funeral home. O'Neal was sitting in the front seat of this hearse, and he said, 'They expect me to take this body out to the airport and put it aboard a plane, and I can't take the body out to the airport because I don't have a certificate or a permit.'

"They brought the president's body out in the bronze casket that O'Neal had brought in that hearse.

"Mrs. Kennedy was walking on the right side of it. She was walking with her left hand on the casket and was really in a state of what I would call medical shock, with an almost glazed look on her face. She seemed almost unaware of what was happening and, curiously, had a kind of a little frozen smile on her face. I had the feeling that if somebody had literally fired a pistol in front of her face that she would just have blinked. It seemed that she was absolutely out of this world."

Lyndon: "When I got to the plane I called the president's brother, the attorney general, Bobby Kennedy, and asked his advice and judgment on where the oath should be taken, under the circumstances, and who should administer it. He gave me his immediate reaction, that the oath should be taken in Dallas at once. I said, 'Well, I don't have the oath.' He said, 'I'll have it given to you right away.' And very businesslike, although I guess he must have been suffering more than almost anyone except Mrs. Kennedy."

Walter Jenkins: "I began to get calls from President Johnson, who was on the plane which was sitting on the ground in Dallas.

"The first question was whether he should be sworn in right away. He asked me to get a hold of Bobby Kennedy and ask him, which I did. He was for the swearing in. He said that there is no question but that he is president, but we don't know but that this is an international conspiracy and maybe there are others that are going to be attacked, and that he should be sworn in as quickly as possible. And then he talked to Mr. Johnson and reiterated what he had said to me.

"Then there was a question of the oath. Johnson wanted me to find Sarah Hughes, which I did. I knew her closest friend was Irving Goldberg, so I called him, and he was able to locate her and get her to the plane. He said, 'She may not know the oath for the president of the United States.' So we had to get a copy and read it to them. Somebody dug it out from the White House archives and it was given over the phone to Jack Valenti, who wrote it down on an invoice and gave it to Judge Hughes."

While these events were taking place aboard Air Force One in Dallas, half the Kennedy cabinet was on jet aircraft 86972 en route between Honolulu and Tokyo where they were to attend the Japan Economic Conference. Secretary of State Rusk was about to prepare an agenda for talks with the Japanese prime minister when the news from Dallas reached him. The plane turned back immediately, planning to refuel in Honolulu and continue to Dallas, but after it was learned all the principals in Dallas were returning to Washington, 86972 also headed for the capital.

Stewart Udall: "I was on that plane going to Japan. The word came in over the teletype that the president had been shot. You had the feeling on the plane, because all the Kennedy people were there and a lot of his cabinet, that the roof had just fallen in—you know, that something had ended, like a crushing weight falling on you.

"After we had turned around and were coming back, somebody said, 'I wonder what kind of a president Johnson will make?'"

At the same time at the LBJ Ranch preparations were in full swing for the presidential visit that evening.

Cactus Pryor: "We were down at the Ranch, getting ready for President Kennedy, and Dale Malechek drove up in his pickup and said, 'Mr. Kennedy's been shot! Mr. Kennedy's been shot!' Then Mary Davis, who was the cook at the Ranch, came running out the front door yelling that the president had been shot. So we all rushed into the kitchen of the ranch house and watched Walter Cronkite report the news on the set in the kitchen, Secret Service men included. Some of them were back at the communications trailer behind the Ranch; they would bring in reports that hadn't yet been received on national television.

"Immediately they placed the Ranch on what they call a 'presidential alert,' because Johnson then, they assumed, was president. They sealed off the Ranch just like that. Cousin Oriole came down and they weren't going to let her in, even though she's the cousin of the president. She took great issue with this and she said, 'No young fellow is going to keep *me* out of this house.'

"But the reality of the situation didn't really strike us until Mary Davis took some pecan pies out of the stove and she said, 'Well, these pies were for President Kennedy. What do I do with them now?'"

Lynda: "I was in my sophomore year at the university in Austin. I had come home to eat lunch in the college dorm. As soon as I got there my former roommate, Warrie Lynn Smith, called and said, 'Stay right where you are, I am coming right over.' I'm not sure if she was the one who gave me the word or we turned on the radio together. I just remember how horrifying it was. I remember getting down on the floor in front of the radio and praying. This was while we thought he was still alive.

"That night we were going to have this big dinner there in Austin. The president was coming. I had my ticket, and everybody was excited. I had gotten a friend a ticket. I wanted everything to go well in Texas. Of course, my parents had had that bad situation before, at the Adolphus. So we were all kind of on pins and needles.

"Then, of course, this was a dormitory for girls and those were the days when men could not come in the dorms—upstairs, no men—except, I guess, if there was a broken pipe. But one of the house mothers brought this man up to my room. She asked everybody to leave the room, and there was a Secret Service man with her, and he said, 'I am going to be with you for a little while.'

"I also made the decision then to leave the dorm and go to the governor's mansion. I called down there and asked how the Connally children were because I was very close to the family and John Connally had been shot and was in dreadful condition. Mrs. Connally was with him, of course. Young John was a teenager, so it wasn't that they needed a baby-sitter; it was just that we all wanted to be together and offer each other some sort of comfort. So I went there—also, I guess, for protection. We didn't know what the situation was, and there were state police outside the mansion."

Luci: "At school a girl came in and said, 'I just heard on the radio President Kennedy's been shot.' She was the sort of girl who was a little flippant, and a good friend of mine turned around and said, 'Oh, my gosh, don't say something like that; look who's in the room!'—looking at me, and recognizing that President Kennedy was my friend and my father was the vice-president and that would be a dreadful thing to say. I said, 'What did you hear?' And she said, 'Well, I've just heard he's been shot.'

"This of course started a great deal of buzzing and conversation among the sixteen-year-old students, and then all of a sudden, bells started to ring, the bells of the National Cathedral. They rang and rang, and four hundred girls got up without a word and walked out single file from their classrooms downstairs to the gymnasium, which we used as a chapel as well, without any conversation.

"My closest friend from the eighth grade was in another class down the hall. I remember looking over my shoulder, and she was trying to wind her way down to me. She came over and she put her arms around me and said, 'Oh, Luci!' And that's all she said. Then another friend came and put her arm around my waist. We walked down to the gymnasium and the four hundred girls came in and knelt, and the announcement was made that the president had indeed been shot. We did not know whether he was still alive or not, but it did appear grave, and we were asked immediately for our prayers. And of course, my first reaction was, my gosh, this man is a friend of mine, somebody I know! It wasn't really until I walked out of the gymnasium to go back to class that I realized my father was there, too, and nobody had said anything about him, and was he all right? There were shots—Governor Connally had been hurt—but I didn't know anything about my father.

"Then as I walked over to talk to the principal, here was a man walking up, and he was a Secret Service agent. I knew him; they tried to send someone I would know and not be afraid of or uneasy about.

"He and the principal took me into one of the counselor's rooms, and it was at that point they told me that my father was fine and my mother was fine but that President Kennedy was dead. I kept saying, 'No, it can't be; it can't be.' Then they told me to get in the car, and I could take a couple of friends to The Elms with me."

Helene Lindow Gordon: "Luci asked if I could be allowed to come with her, and Kitty McGee, who was a friend of hers from Texas. I remember going through the gates of The Elms, and people standing outside the gates. The gates were closed for the first time that we'd ever seen them."

Lyndon, meanwhile, waiting on Air Force One for Judge Sarah Hughes to arrive, had swallowed a bowl of vegetable soup with crackers, dictated some notes to Marie Fehmer, and acknowledged the arrival of Bill Moyers, who, on hearing the news in Austin, had chartered a plane and flown immediately to Dallas. Moyers, who found himself suddenly blocked at the midsection of the plane by security, sent Lyndon a note saying, "I'm here if there's anything I can do." Lyndon replied, "There will be. Just hang around."

Lyndon later wrote that the most unbearable moment of that day was when Jackie Kennedy arrived at the plane with the president's body. He had not seen her since they had left Love Field by motorcade that morning—hardly more than two hours before.

Lyndon: "It was a tragic thing to observe Mrs. Kennedy. Here was this delicate, beautiful lady, always elegant, always fastidious, always the fashion plate. And I remember her getting off the plane in Dallas a few hours before and contrasting that with how she looked when she got back on the plane after that trip through the streets of Dallas. What that morning was a beautiful, unsoiled, nicely pressed pink garment that was the last word in fashion and style was now streaked and caked and soiled throughout with her husband's blood. Mrs. Johnson asked her if she wouldn't come in and let her help change her clothes and she said no."

Sid Davis: "Sarah Hughes of Dallas was there with an oath and said we ought to proceed. Johnson said, 'No, let's see if Mrs. Kennedy can stand this.' And so they went back, and she said she'd like to come out and she did."

Judge Hughes: "When Mrs. Kennedy came into the compartment, Vice-President Johnson told her to stand on his left and Mrs. Johnson on his right. And I leaned over to Mrs. Kennedy and said, 'I loved your husband very much.'

"Mr. Johnson turned to her and told her who I was, that I was a district judge who had been appointed by her husband. Then I read the oath of office, which somebody had handed to me, and the vice-president repeated it after me.

"Now the oath of office is in the Constitution, but it does not contain the words, 'So help me God.' Every oath I had ever given ended up with 'So help me God,' so it was automatic, and I said, 'So help me God.' He immediately leaned over and kissed his wife and Mrs. Kennedy. He turned around and said to the pilot, 'Let's be airborne.'"

Davis: "And they revved up the engines. And it was starting to get cold in Dallas."

THE FLIGHT BACK

Merriam Smith, in a UPI dispatch the next day: "Colonel James Swindal, pilot of the plane, a big gleaming silver and blue fan-jet, cut on the starboard engines immediately. At 3:47 P.M. EST,[1] the wheels of Air Force One cleared the runway. Swindal roared the big ship up to an unusually high cruising altitude of 41,000 feet where at 625 miles an hour, ground speed, the jet hurtled toward Andrews Air Force Base.

"When the president's plane reached operating altitude, Mrs. Kennedy left her bedchamber and walked to the rear compartment of the plane. This was the so-called family living room, a private area where she and the Kennedy family and friends had spent many happy airborne hours chatting and dining together.

"Kennedy's casket had been placed in this compartment, carried aboard by a group of Secret Service agents.

"Mrs. Kennedy went into the rear lounge and took a chair beside the coffin. There she remained throughout the flight."

Charles Roberts: "The ride was like going back in a tunnel. All of the shades were drawn when we got aboard, I suppose for security reasons. Someone must have figured, 'Well, if there's a gunman up in the terminal, he's not going to be able to see through those windows and pick out another target.' And for some reason those curtains stayed down all the way back.

"There was not the tension, the crackling white hot tension aboard this plane between a Kennedy faction and a Johnson faction that appears in Bill Manchester's version[2] of the thing. Bill talked to a lot of people much later who must have misled him with statements like, 'Not a member of Kennedy's staff would even watch the swearing-in.' They were either blinded by grief or sorrow or their prejudice against Johnson into saying that Johnson's takeover was rough and crude and that he appropriated the plane and that there was a great tension aboard the plane. It simply didn't exist.

"Kenny O'Donnell and Godfrey McHugh had been obsessed with the idea of getting the plane off the ground, because the county medical examiner had told them that the body couldn't be flown out without an autopsy, and they were determined to get that plane in the air. There's no question about that. McHugh, who was a brigadier general in the air force and Kennedy's air force aide, went flitting up and down the aisle trying to get the pilot to get the plane off the ground, because his president was aboard and he didn't care whether the new president got sworn in or not.

"But it was not like two armed camps aboard, waging a feud over who was going to be aboard the plane and when it was going to take off. That just didn't happen."

Charles Bartlett: "I personally think that the bitterness that developed from the whole airplane ride was largely due to the real shock of the Kennedy staff who had seen their president destroyed. And they had a hard time adjusting to it. But in all the piecing together I could do, I couldn't really find any real ugliness or insensitivity on Johnson's part."

Roberts: "To me, Johnson's conduct in that period—I think we took two hours and twelve minutes—was perhaps his finest hour. He couldn't have been more considerate, not only of Jackie but of all the Kennedy people. He was thoughtful. He was thinking ahead. There was nothing unseemly at all about his takeover. It was not a grasping for power. It would have been of course utterly absurd for him to fly all the way back to Washington without taking the oath, for the country for two hours and twelve minutes not to have a constitutionally sworn president. It would have been absurd for him not to take Air Force One, because it had better communications equipment, decoding, coding, and so forth. He was the president. He should have flown on the plane with the best equipment. Furthermore, if he had left Jackie behind to fly back on either plane with just a corporal's guard of mourners and get off alone with the casket—if he hadn't stayed by the widow and paid Kennedy the honor of accompanying the body back—he would have been criticized forever after. So all of those things that he did were right, and yet the people who never did like the man and never will found some way to criticize him for all of the right things that he did, all of the compassionate things."

Communications between Air Force One and Washington increased as the plane neared the capital. There were, as might be expected, decisions to be made. Would the body go to Bethesda Naval Medical Center or Walter Reed for the postmortem? Would it travel by helicopter or ambulance? Would Mrs. Kennedy accompany the body or return to the White House? Would the casket be removed from the plane by forklift or carried down the ramp? Where would the press be situated?

These were decisions made by the Kennedy party, but there were directives from Lyndon, too. General Clifton, military aide to the president, informed Bundy that the new president would meet with those few members of the cabinet not on the plane to Japan on arrival, and with the congressional leadership of both parties at seven thirty.

Clifton also informed Bundy that either the Cabinet Room or the Fish Room would be satisfactory to meet in, but that the new president did not want to go into the mansion or the Oval Office.

Before the plane landed, Lyndon asked to speak with Mrs. Rose Kennedy. "We're grieving with you," he told her. "Thank you very much," said Kennedy's mother. "Thank you . . . Mr. President."

Liz Carpenter: "The Johnsons spent some time with Mrs. Kennedy and then came back to the state room where the phone calls were going on. Mrs. Johnson sent for me and she said to me with a little notebook in her hand, 'Liz, I have tried to start making some notes on the events as they have happened.' The notes were mostly about Mrs.

Kennedy, who, she said, looked like a 'heap of helpless pink.' And putting out her arms to her—then going on upstairs in the hospital to spend some time with Mrs. Connally.

"I said to Mrs. Johnson, 'As soon as we land in Washington the press is going to be all over the place and you will be asked to say something and perhaps you'd better think of something to say.'

"And she said, 'I just feel like it's all been a dreadful nightmare but somehow we've got to find the strength to go on.'

"I said, 'Nothing could be better than that,' and I wrote it down on a piece of paper and in a few moments she showed it to Mr. Johnson and he approved it."

Walter Jenkins: "I was making decisions about who would go out to meet him, what they'd drive in, whether they'd use helicopters—things that the Kennedy staff had been used to doing. I was ill-prepared to do it, because I didn't know anything about how you accomplished those things. But I did go out on the helicopter and rode back with him. There was quite a large crowd out there. If there was tight security, they made a lot of exceptions because there were hundreds of people."

Carpenter: "The plane landed, and as we stood there flattened against the walls of the plane, I suddenly was aware that pushing through us was Bobby Kennedy. He didn't look to the left or the right and his face looked streaked with tears and absolutely stricken. He said, 'Where's Jackie? I want to be with Jackie.' And he pushed through and we got him to her.

"There was quite a delay at the door of the plane in getting a lift up that could take the casket of the dead president down. Mr. Johnson said, 'Some of you men here help them.' And so Sergeant Glynn and some of the others went to the back to help them lift the casket.

"The lights of the television cameras at the field were on the door and we waited while the casket and the different members of the Kennedy staff got off.

"The steps for the plane were pushed up and we walked down them—the new president, Lady Bird, myself, Marie Fehmer, Jack Valenti, and then the Texas congressmen, as he had suggested. At the foot of the plane there was a very disorganized group of people waiting—congressmen, just looking expressionless, members of the cabinet, all of the members of diplomatic corps."

Roberts: "We stood by while the president's casket was removed by that lift truck. They backed it up to the rear door, and I can remember how astonished I was, having come down the front ramp, to see Bobby Kennedy appear in that rear door.

"Somehow he had bounded aboard that plane, probably by the rear door, just as we taxied up. And as soon as I got down on the ground and looked up to the rear door, there was Bobby with Larry O'Brien, Kenny O'Donnell, and Dave Powers, and the other Kennedy people who had spent, by the way, the whole trip in that rear compartment. I think that Larry O'Brien was the only one of the holdover staff members who conferred on any substantive matters with the new president on the way back."

Roberts: "President Johnson, after this gray navy ambulance had taken the casket, walked over to a battery of TV cameras and lights—by then it was dark, and things were a little eerie in that light—and read the statement he had prepared on the plane. I remember I was looking at Mac Bundy because I was wondering if he had any word of what had happened in the world while we were in transit, whether this assassination was part of a plot. And he told me later that what he reported to the president during that flight back was that the whole world was stunned, but there was no evidence of a conspiracy at all."

Hale Boggs: "Of course, the whole evening was a tragic one—watching the plane land at Andrews, seeing that beautiful girl, the blood-spattered dress, a moonlit night, and the battered ambulance from Bethesda Naval Hospital. There was a man I'd seen two days before, vibrant and full of life. He always gave you the impression of being totally alive, and then to see a casket moved out and the look of utter disbelief on people's faces. I think I was the first one really to greet President and Mrs. Johnson. And I watched Jackie open the door to that ambulance. She opened it herself. The casket went in there. I remember every bit of it so vividly."

Jenkins: "Mr. Johnson waited until they had actually left. Then he came down and went down the line shaking hands with the dignitaries that were there, then went over to the microphone and made a very short statement."

What the new president said, standing under the floodlights, trying to make his voice heard over the roar of the engines, was the following:

> This is a sad time for all people. We have suffered a loss that cannot be weighed. For me it is a deep personal tragedy. I know that the world shares the sorrow that Mrs. Kennedy and her family bear. I will do my best. That is all I can do. I ask for your help—and God's.

Then, almost abruptly, he walked over to the first helicopter and got in. He was followed by Mrs. Johnson, McGeorge Bundy, Robert McNamara, George Ball, Walter Jenkins, Liz Carpenter, and Bill Moyers. The ride back, according to Walter Jenkins, was very quiet.

George W. Ball: "At that moment there were only about three of us in Washington who had any stature in the key departments. That is, Bob McNamara, Mac Bundy, and myself, because the cabinet, all of those who had particularly dealt with foreign affairs, were on their way to Japan. And so Mac and Bob and I got to Andrews Air Force Base when the vice-president newly become president arrived.

"And we greeted him and got in the helicopter with him and Lady Bird, and we talked on the way in. He said that it was absolutely essential that we stay with him and give him moral support and that we were going to be effective, and so on.

"When we got to the Cabinet Room through outside doors, we sat and talked for a few minutes at the cabinet table, and then some of the congressional leaders came, and we all had a lot of work to be done. But beginning that night he was in charge.

"What had happened had obviously been an enormous experience, like a load of hay had fallen on him, as in the case of Harry Truman. He was certainly aware that something enormous had happened, and he was genuinely very moved.

"But, above all, he was in charge."

Carpenter: "We landed on the White House lawn and got out of the helicopter. Again there was a battery of newspaper people. The Secret Service man motioned to Mrs.

Johnson's car in front of the White House—and the president said to me, 'Stay with Lady Bird and help her all you can.'

"I got into the car and we started driving through the night to The Elms—rolling up the window so we could talk.

"Both of us were well aware of the difficult days ahead—made even more difficult because this had occurred in the home state of the vice-president.

"And I said to her, 'It's a terrible thing to say but the salvation of Texas is that the governor was hit.'

"And she said, 'Don't think I haven't thought of that. I only wish it could have been me.'"

Bill Moyers: "When we got to the south grounds of the White House, we walked in the dark across the grounds just below the Rose Garden, toward the Oval Office. We got to the porch outside the Executive Office Building. I was walking immediately behind Mr. Johnson, and he didn't stop. He just veered to the right and hit my shoulder with his right shoulder. I remember two or three people saying, 'Don't you want to go in?' The doors were open, and you could see the president's desk.

"He said, 'I'll use my office in the EOB.'"

Boggs: "When the joint leadership of Congress meeting was called that night, there was some confusion as to where to go—whether to the Cabinet Room, where we usually met, or whether we would go to the office of the vice-president in the Executive Office Building.

"I looked into the Cabinet Room, and there wasn't anybody there, so I walked into the president's office, but the place was completely empty. And I looked about and I knew that it would be difficult from then on, that somebody else would be there. I looked at all the mementos of the man, and then I went into the Fish Room and there, by himself, was Ted Sorensen. Not another person around. And he was watching the playback on television of the Fort Worth speech that morning, the breakfast group. It was a marvelous speech. And he greeted me and said, 'They wouldn't even let him have three years.' That's all."

According to the daily log, the meeting with congressional leaders, scheduled for seven thirty, actually began ten minutes later. Before the meeting Lyndon took out two sheets of White House stationery and wrote out, in longhand, a brief message to each of the Kennedy children:

> November 22, 1963
> 7:20 Friday Night
>
> Dear John—
>   It will be many years before you understand fully what a great man your father was. His loss is a deep personal tragedy for all of us, but I wanted you particularly to know that I share your grief—
>   You can always be proud of him.
>
> Affectionately,
> Lyndon B. Johnson

Friday Night 7:30
November 22, 1963

Dearest Caroline—
Your father's death has been a great tragedy for the nation, as well as for you,
and I wanted you to know how much my thoughts are with you at this time.
He was a wise and devoted man. You can always be proud of what he did for
his country—

Affectionately
Lyndon B. Johnson

Except for his meeting with the congressional leaders, Lyndon, typically, spent most of the rest of the evening on the phone. He tried to get Herbert Hoover at the Waldorf Towers, but Hoover had already gone to bed and they wouldn't wake him. He did talk to Eisenhower and Truman, asking them for their help and advice. Both men announced their intention of coming to Washington the next day to offer their services. Lyndon also called J. Edgar Hoover, and Ted Kennedy, and Sarge Shriver, who was then director of the Peace Corps. And Bill Fulbright and Averell Harriman came by that evening to see him.

Around eight he called Keith Funston, president of the New York Stock Exchange, to thank him for closing the exchange after the assassination. Funston, in the first and last humor of the day, said, "Thanks, Mr. President. Nobody has complimented the stock exchange for anything in a long while."

The next day when he did reach Mr. Herbert Hoover, the eldest of the living presidents told him, "I'll take any assignment you give me, from office boy on up."

Lyndon: "They promised their help, to do anything they could. The thing that concerned me and those around me very much was trying to give the world a picture of stability and confidence worthy of their recognition and their support.

"The press was following all of this very carefully, and of course that went out to the country."

Luci: "It was very late when he got back. He looked like he'd been run over by a truck. And yet very strong. Like a paradox—he looked like part of him had been gutted and another part of him was just as strong and sturdy as an Olympic champion. My mother was very, very pale and in control."

Horace Busby: "When the president finally returned home, he was met in the foyer by Mrs. Johnson. They spoke with each other briefly; she returned to her bedroom upstairs, and he came into the sitting room. At one point he asked that the television be turned on. We flicked through the channels and came to a retrospective on Kennedy. He watched it for a few minutes, and then he said, 'I guess I know less than anybody about what's happening in the United States.' After looking for a while, he kind of put his hands over his eyes and said, 'Turn it off. It's all too fresh. I can't watch it.'"

Moyers: "Above the television set was a painting of Sam Rayburn. And Johnson was drinking a glass of carbonated orange soda. He raised his glass and said, as if there was nobody else around, 'Oh, Mister Sam, I wish you were here now. How I need you.'"

Busby: "Eventually the president went upstairs to his bedroom, accompanied by Dr. Hurst. I remember Dr. Hurst speaking to him about possibly taking mild sedation so that he could sleep. The president was emphatic in rejecting this advice, being still quite concerned about whether there might still be more trauma to unfold in conjunction with the day's events.

"I was considering leaving when one of the servants came down from the bedroom and said that Mr. Johnson wanted to see me. I had a long episode with him in the bedroom during which he was resting, but each time I tried to leave he called me back. I finally departed. I was the first to leave. Bill Moyers, Clifton Carter, and Jack Valenti, all of whom had come in with the president, were scattered around at various places in the house talking on the telephones."

Jack Valenti: "At some time during the evening, I remember the president saying to me, 'Get hold of your wife and get some clothes sent up here. You can stay here. You can stay in the guest bedroom down the hall. I want you to work on my staff.'

"We stayed with him until about three in the morning, at which time we let him go to sleep, and I went to the guest bedroom. Bill Moyers and Cliff Carter went up on the third floor to sleep."

Moyers: "That whole night he seemed to have several chambers of his mind operating simultaneously. It was formidable, very formidable.

"About three I went to the upstairs bedroom, and I looked down and could see shadowy figures moving through the grounds. The Secret Service had on a heavy guard."

4

"Not a Fluke of History, but a President"

THE LONG WEEKEND

Four hours after he went to bed Lyndon was having breakfast with Lady Bird. It was Saturday, November 23, his first full day as president, and it would be a long one. By 8:40 Lyndon, Moyers, Carter, Valenti, with Homer Thornberry, who had come over that morning, left The Elms for the EOB. On the way Lyndon stopped by the White House and the Oval Office where he encountered Bobby Kennedy and Evelyn Lincoln, President Kennedy's private secretary. The meeting was, not surprisingly, tense.[1]

From there Lyndon went directly to the Situation Room in the White House basement, where he met with McGeorge Bundy and John McCone, director of the CIA, and was briefed on the current state of the world.

Actually, except for a little activity, whatever one wanted to call it, in Southeast Asia, the world seemed to be relatively quiet.

Back in his office in the EOB across from the White House on West Executive Avenue, Lyndon spent most of the next hour on the phone.

At about eleven he and Lady Bird went across to the East Room of the White House, where the body of President Kennedy lay in state.

Lady Bird: "Lyndon walked slowly past the President's body in the East Room. The catafalque was in the center and on it the casket, draped with the American flag. At each corner there was a large candle and a very rigid military man, representing each of the services. . . .

"After we left the White House we went to a brief service at St. John's Episcopal Church, right across from Lafayette Square, a very 'high church'—a stern, rigid church—but most fitting for the day."[2]

True to his promise of the evening before, President Eisenhower drove down from his farm at Gettysburg to Washington that morning. Lyndon spent almost an hour with the former president, whose eight years as a Republican in the White House had coincided with his own eight years as Democratic leader on the Hill, whose policies he had alternately supported and combatted, but who now was ready, eager in fact, to put aside any partisan feelings to be of service to a man whose unexpected responsibilities he well understood. After their talk, Eisenhower jotted down on a yellow tablet notes on what he, Ike, would do if he were in Lyndon's place, including calling a joint session of Congress, and thoughts on what he might say to them.

Ike also suggested that Lyndon confer with Robert B. Anderson on fiscal matters. Anderson, a Texan of great wealth and extreme conservatism, had frequently been a lobbyist before Congress representing Texas oil. He had served Eisenhower as secretary of the navy and later of the treasury. Johnson did consult with him; indeed the next day they had a four-hour conference that was not listed in the official White House log, nor were other visits later.

Anderson advised the new president to abandon Kennedy's proposed tax cut of $11 billion and slash the budget drastically. Johnson refused on the former but went along on the latter. It was probably at this time that he began to think of the economies in government that he was to become increasingly preoccupied with in the months to come.

Meanwhile, Lyndon had called a cabinet meeting for 2:30.

Lyndon: "The men at the top had sat with Kennedy in dozens, I guess hundreds, of meetings. Men like Secretary Rusk, Secretary McNamara, McGeorge Bundy, George Ball—all those men had worked very closely with the President on a variety of problems. I was present at the Security Council meetings, so I knew each of the men and I respected them. In the top echelon I had no desire to replace any of them. I wanted all of them to stay.

"Frankly, if I'd been picking a cabinet, fresh from an election myself, I don't think I would have done that. And, in retrospect, I don't think I would do it again."

George E. Reedy: "I got a call from the president that said, 'George, you and Bill Moyers come on over.' So the two of us walked across the street to the cabinet session.[3] I can recall the cabinet session opening with a minute of silent prayer. Then Adlai Stevenson, describing himself as the senior member, which I guess in a way he was, made a statement telling the president of the absolute loyalty of the cabinet and their realization of the tremendous problems before the country. The president made a very brief speech, to the effect that he needed their help and wanted them all to stay on. I'm under the impression that Bobby Kennedy came in a bit late."[4]

Clark Clifford: "When you come in as president under those circumstances, so suddenly and so quickly, you want to keep the team together. You can't organize a team in a matter of days or weeks or even months.

"Also, it was very clear that after the assassination, President Kennedy's popularity grew all the time; he was revered in a manner after his death that perhaps didn't exist before his death. He had become a martyr president, and I think President Johnson felt that it was advisable to keep that team.

"As time went on, it was very obvious that some of them weren't ever going to be digested into the new administration. They couldn't get over it. Kenneth O'Donnell,

Ted Sorensen, Arthur Schlesinger, those fellows were very close to President Kennedy and could not make the adjustment. On the other hand there were some, like McGeorge Bundy and Larry O'Brien, who made the adjustment very well."

Of course the person who found it most difficult to make the adjustment was the attorney general. No other president in the history of the country inherited his predecessor's brother in a cabinet post, and few brothers were so fanatically devoted as was Robert Kennedy. Lyndon included Bobby in his blanket request to the Kennedy cabinet to remain at their posts; he could hardly have done otherwise. Bobby, on the other hand, could have resigned, pleading grief and, perhaps, an inability to transfer loyalties, which everyone would have understood and which would have saved both himself and the president many hours of later turmoil. But Bobby saw that as deserting his post; he felt himself essential to the continuation of his brother's ideals and goals, both practically and symbolically.

So Bobby gritted his teeth and stayed on, determined to carry the banner into the fray, and certain there were snipers and booby traps on every side. Most overt actions are subject to a variety of interpretations. From the moment Air Force One landed in Washington, and progressively in the days and weeks that followed, Bobby was ready to see slights to his brother, his brother's widow, or himself in whatever Lyndon did or didn't do. His own feeling was that if Kennedy people stayed on into the Johnson administration, it should be not so much to serve the new president and the country, as to carry on the image of the dead president.

At this time, however, Lyndon was assured that his great plea for continuity had been honored; the entire cabinet[5] had agreed to stay on, at least for the foreseeable future, and he could move ahead as events carried him. He had still that day to meet with President Truman, who had flown in from Kansas City; Harry's offers of aid had perhaps more psychological than practical value, but they were nonetheless welcome.

One of the new president's visitors during his first full day in office was Ambassador Lodge, who had returned from Saigon before the assassination.

William H. Lawrence: "As I waited on West Executive Avenue with a live television camera, I saw Henry Cabot Lodge . . . coming out of the EOB. . . . Lodge had been called back from Saigon for consultations by President Kennedy, he said, but his appointment now had been with the new president. The president had authorized him to say he had reached his first decision of substance—that American aid to the Saigon regime would continue at present levels.

"Lodge went on to observe that this demonstrated the continuity of American foreign policy even as Johnson's other moves already had proved domestic continuity. It was obvious to me that LBJ had hoped for just such an opportunity—a live television interview with Lodge as he left the new president's office so the ambassador could tell about the first foreign policy decision of the new administration."[6]

All together that first day Lyndon made thirty-two telephone calls and, in addition to Lodge, was visited by eleven persons; he called in some, McGeorge Bundy, for instance, three or four times. And no doubt for the first time in history an incumbent president found the renowned White House telephone service unsatisfactory; it had, he said, taken him ten minutes to get Dean Rusk at one time, and Rusk was right there in town; the service had to be speeded up. But then, what didn't?

Dinner that night was at ten. About eleven Lyndon retired upstairs for a massage and to discuss privately with Horace Busby the events of the day, in particular the cabinet meeting. Horace was an astute observer, and at the same time a comforting presence.

On Sunday after an early-morning consultation at The Elms with Mac Bundy and John McCone, Lyndon and Lady Bird, accompanied by Luci and Homer Thornberry, went—as did many in America that Sunday—to church.

Harry McPherson: "I had just flown back from Tokyo, and Sunday morning I went to church, St. Mark's Episcopal, up on Capitol Hill. And lo and behold, the new president and his family came in. The place was swarming with Secret Service agents—God, there must have been twenty in the church, and there were cops on the top of the Library of Congress annex with rifles, and a massive crowd outdoors.

"The service was very simple and very powerful. I remember the sermon hymn was 'America,' and I remember Lyndon Johnson got his handkerchief out and held it over his face and was rubbing at his face. It was so overwhelming. And Bill Baxter, with a very steady voice, preached a hell of a sermon about how we were held together in this moment and that it would pass quickly, but it was vital that we understand the dimensions of our being held, of our unity, understand what it meant to be 'one people.'

"When it was over, the Johnsons decided to go back into the parish hall where everyone went after church to have coffee. And they stood around shaking hands. The Secret Service was going crazy. But it was very comforting to him, quite obviously, to shake hands. Very plain people, old women and kids and everybody just going up and taking his hand. And a lot of people crying and holding his arm. It was immensely strengthening, this crowd of just ordinary people, and he drank about three cups of coffee, just inhaling them.

"Then he and I stood toe to toe for a long time, and we just talked very quietly about what he was doing. He said, 'Come on, walk me out to the car.' The family had already gone. So we walked back through the church, a completely dark, empty church, and you could see every five feet a Secret Service man standing.

"We got to the door of the church, and just as we did, I felt a heel go right down on my foot and an elbow come into my gut, and it just paralyzed me. It was a Secret Service man, and what he was going to do was get Lyndon Johnson out that door and into that car without getting shot. There were about a thousand people in the street, and Rufus Youngblood or Clint Hill or one of them just took him by the elbow and with great strength moved him right down those stairs and into the car.

"I then went back into the church, and it seemed not five minutes before somebody came up and said, 'Jesus Christ, they've shot Oswald.'"

Early that afternoon, the new president and Mrs. Johnson rode with Jacqueline Kennedy, the attorney general, Caroline, and John John from the White House to the Hill.

Lady Bird: "As soon as we emerged from the gates of the White House, I became aware of that sea of faces stretching away on every side—silent, watching faces. I wanted to cry for them and with them, but it was impossible to permit the catharsis of tears. I don't know quite why, except that perhaps continuity of strength demands restraint. . . .

"After that interminable drive we reached the Capitol and entered the Rotunda. In the center, directly underneath the dome, stood the flag-draped coffin with the honor guard around it. There were eulogies by Chief Justice Earl Warren, by Speaker John McCormack, and by Senator Mansfield. . . .

"Lyndon went forward and laid a wreath at the foot of the casket. Then Mrs. Kennedy went over and knelt. I remember how carefully she knelt and kissed the casket, and Caroline by her side simply put her little hand on the flag—sort of underneath the flag. John John had disappeared. And then we left in separate cars."[7]

Lyndon went directly to the EOB where he met with Rusk, McNamara, and George Ball to discuss Southeast Asia. Then after his lengthy consultation with Robert B. Anderson, he began to see some of the people who were assembling in Washington from all over the world to represent their countries at the funeral the next day.

On Monday, the national day of mourning, the casket was brought from the Rotunda down the steep steps of the Capitol by the honor guard and loaded onto the caisson. The navy band once again played "Hail to the Chief" and the navy hymn, "Oh hear us when we cry to Thee, for those in peril on the sea." By that time more than a quarter of a million people had walked past the flag-draped casket and tens of millions more had looked at it on television, watched the procession from the Hill to St. Matthew's Cathedral, listened to the solemn service conducted by Richard Cardinal Cushing, an old Kennedy family friend from Boston, and followed it then to the burial in Arlington.

Marya Mannes: "I followed the caisson every step it went down the broad avenues from home to Hill, from Hill to home and from home to earth. The simplicity of that box with the flag on it, the great loneliness of the executive in death as in life, were made just bearable by the sturdy gray horses, nuzzling and jerking against their traces, by the beautifully ridden lead horse with his high head and rhythmic gait, by the fretting and rearing riderless black horse behind, by the single sailor with the president's flag. I was grateful every inch of the way for these traditions, for the awful solemnity of the muffled drums; I was proud of the silence they beat in and the grief they echoed."[8]

Members of the Kennedy family, including the widow, walked behind the casket. President and Mrs. Johnson, Lynda, and Luci were just behind, followed by the largest assembly of foreign dignitaries gathered, it was said, since the funeral of Edward VII in 1910—among many others, Charles de Gaulle, Anastas Mikoyan, deputy premier of the Soviet Union, Sir Alex Douglas-Home, prime minister of England, and Prince Philip, Ludwig Erhard, chancellor of West Germany, Haile Selassie of Ethiopia. They in turn were followed by members of the Supreme Court, the cabinet, Congress, and the state governors.

Lyndon: "Walking in the procession was one of the more difficult decisions I made. The FBI people and in particular the Secret Service felt that in the atmosphere at that time that it would be injudicious and unwise for the American president to expose himself by walking along the avenue with all the buildings on each side, until we collected ourselves and knew a little bit about what was happening. Under no circumstances should the American president take that risk. I finally concluded, though, that it was something I wanted to do, should do, and would do; and did so."

John Kenneth Galbraith: "Then there was the problem that developed with all the foreign ministers, looking after them *after* they came in, meeting them. You couldn't have an assistant secretary of state go out and meet de Gaulle, who would regard an assistant secretary of state as a clerk. Perhaps rightly so in some cases."

Angier Biddle Duke: "I handled the foreign guests for the funeral and handled the reception that the new president gave the heads of state and chiefs of government.

"The reception was at the State Department. It was the day of the funeral, Monday, November 25, and it was at five o'clock in the afternoon, and after we came from Arlington. There were eleven chiefs of state and other royalty and ministers from seventy countries, and the order of rank was alphabetical, by country, in the English language, and that put the king of Belgium in the first place. We went to the White House first. We lined them up in two rooms, the chiefs of state in one room, then the chiefs of government, prime ministers, and then the heads of delegations.

"Then we brought them in. The thing went pretty well."

Benjamin Read: "It was an incredible throng of foreign leaders. The president had had a terribly busy day, doing the thousand-and-one things that he needed to do in those desperate early days.[9] And the briefing time was just nonexistent.

"We were able to put on little five-by-eight cards the essence of what we thought would be useful for him to say to U Thant, to de Gaulle, to Mikoyan. And when he was receiving upstairs this incredible panoply of leaders, we would put these little cards into his hands just moments before he would be greeting these people. And he handled it just extraordinarily skillfully; grasping the essence of it, he would work into the conversation the points we had suggested.

"And then after the reception, as it was concluding, he retired down to the seventh-floor office of Secretary Rusk and met five or six of the real heavyweights in private sessions there. We had really quite a sight. I remember de Gaulle in one anteroom and Haile Selassie in another. And they were just practically falling all over each other. The president had his private time with them in the secretary's room, and we'd have to interrupt and say, 'De Gaulle is ready,' and he'd say good-bye to the king of Belgium or whoever it might have been. It was quite a show."

Duke: "I know that they were taking the measure of the man at the time. He was really listening and talking and awfully good at it. I've seen him impatient with foreign affairs and somewhat bored, but I think he understood what was going on and how he was being measured by them and he was marvelous. It gave him a sense of confidence, a sort of security, and he came away with a good strong, firm hand on the presidency and with a good deal of respect."

That evening at eight thirty the new president, not yet at the end of what must have seemed an interminable day, spoke in his office at the EOB to those governors who had come to Washington to attend the funeral. Then, more than a dozen other telephone calls later, he got back to The Elms and went to sleep, shortly afterwards, at 1:00 A.M. When he returned to his office the next morning, there was a long handwritten note delivered by messenger from Mrs. Jacqueline Kennedy:

Dear Mr. President:

Thank you for walking yesterday—behind Jack. You did not have to do that—I am sure many people forbid you to take such a risk—but you did it anyway.

Thank you for your letters to my children. What those letters will mean to them later—you can imagine. The touching thing is, they have always loved you so much, they were most moved to have a letter from you now.

And most of all, Mr. President, thank you for the way you have always treated me—the way you and Lady Bird have always been to me—before, when Jack was alive, and now as President.

I think the relationship of the Presidential and Vice Presidential families could be a rather strained one. From the history I have been reading ever since I came to the White House, I gather it often was in the past.

But you were Jack's right arm—and I always thought the greatest act of a gentleman that I had seen on this earth—was how you—the Majority Leader when he came to the Senate as just another little freshman who looked up to you and took orders from you, could then serve as Vice President to a man who had served under you and had been taught by you.

But more than that we were friends, all four of us. All you did for me as a friend and the happy times we had. I always thought way before the nomination that Lady Bird should be First Lady—but I don't need to tell you here what I think of her qualities—her extraordinary grace of character—her willingness to assume every burden—She assumed so many for me and I love her very much—and I love your two daughters—Lynda Bird most because I know her best—and we first met when neither of us could get a seat to hear President Eisenhower's State of the Union message and someone found us a place on one of the steps on the aisle where we sat together. If we had known then what our relationship would be now.

It was so strange—last night I was wandering through this house—

There in the Treaty Room is your chandelier, and I had had it framed—the paper we all signed—you—Senator Dirksen and Mike Mansfield—underneath I had written "The day the Vice President brought the East Room chandelier back from the Capitol."

Then in the library I showed Bobby the Lincoln Record Book you gave—

You see all you gave—and now you are called upon to give so much more.

Your office—you are the first President to sit in it as it looks today. Jack always wanted a re-doing and I had curtains designed for it that I thought were as dignified as they should be for a President's office—

Late last night a moving man asked me if I wanted Jack's ship pictures left on the wall for you (they were cleaning the office to make room for you)—I said no because I remembered all the fun Jack had those first few days hanging pictures of things he liked, setting out his collection of whale's teeth, etc.

But of course, they are there only waiting for you to ask for them if the walls look too bare. I thought you would want to put things from Texas on it—I pictured some gleaming long horns—I hope you put them somewhere—

It mustn't be very much help to you your first day in office—to hear children on the lawn at recess. It is just one more example of your kindness that you let them stay—I promise they will soon be gone.[10]

Thank you, Mr. President
Respectfully,
Jackie

BUILDING BRIDGES

Of course after he had made his brief statement at Andrews the night of the assassination, everybody in the world who had access to a television set knew what he looked and sounded like: a huge Texan with preposterous ears and a Texas twang. But beyond that most people knew very little about him, and many of those who did, or thought they did, didn't care much for what they knew. True, he may have been a master legislator, a giant among senators, and a Democratic majority leader of skill and power, but the legislative process is widely misunderstood in the United States and has never been popular. Most people—conservatives, liberals, reactionaries, radicals—maybe everybody, wants *all* of what he or she wants, *immediately*, and a legislative maneuverer, a wheeler-dealer, if you will, has to say, "But getting it all is impossible because other people, who are also allowed to vote, have other quite different things in mind. At best, you can have *some* of what you want, and you'll have to wait a time to get even that because I have to persuade those who hate your guts and your ideas to give in just a little, and you in turn will have to . . ."

That was the impression almost everybody had of the new president.

Bill Moyers: "He knew that he was not a legitimate president. Constitutionally, he was president, because this is the way the Constitution chose successors. Politically, he had not been asked into that office by the people. This made him uncomfortable.

"He also knew many of the people who had been for Kennedy considered him an intruder. On one of the rides in from The Elms, one morning before Kennedy had yet been buried, he said, 'I always felt sorry for Harry Truman and the way he got the presidency, but at least his man wasn't murdered.'"

The people had to get to know him as *president*, and everybody around him agreed that Lyndon would have to make an appearance, some kind of speech during which hundreds of millions of people could see him, hear him at some length, and judge him.

Some of his advisers thought that the speech ought to be from the White House with

Lyndon alone at his desk in the solemn and symbolic Oval Office; others, Lyndon included, felt that he ought to speak before a live audience. And what could be better than Eisenhower's suggestion—an address to the assembled members of both houses of Congress?

The latter prevailed, but then there was the question of what the new president would say. It would, everybody knew, be the most important speech of his career. If it failed, all the doubts, oh, more than doubts, all the suspicion of him would only be fortified, and nothing he said in the future would ever erase that original mistake.

God and perhaps Lyndon knew how many people worked on that address—anyone within shouting, telephoning, cajoling, persuading, listening distance certainly.

John Kenneth Galbraith: "The day after the assassination I met LBJ between the West Wing of the White House and the Executive Office Building. He grabbed me by the arm, and we went over to his office. He wanted to talk a little bit about the issues he faced, but mostly he wanted to talk about his speech to the Congress.

"I remember first he said, 'Look, Ken, put your mind on it. What do you think I have to worry about the most?'

"And I said, 'Well, I think there are two things, one domestic, one foreign. Domestically, the whole liberal community is going to be watching you like a hawk on civil rights. Put your mind at rest on that. There's no problem there.'

"As for the foreign problem, I said that he had to worry about the military and about Indochina. Having been in India I was much more exposed than people in Washington to the kind of trouble most of the so-called strategic minds could get you into. But on that second observation I got no response at all from Johnson. His response to the first was very immediate and warm, but on the second, nothing."

Abe Fortas: "A great issue was whether he would recommend congressional action in respect to civil rights—the voting rights act. And if so, whether he should put that as a number one item.

"At one point there were a lot of us sitting around at the table at The Elms discussing that with him for hours. And the incident that I remember, which renewed my pride in him, was this. One of the wise, fine, practical people around the table said, 'Mr. President, you ought not to urge Congress to pass this. You oughtn't to make this one of the imperatives of your program because the presidency has only a certain amount of coinage to expend, and you oughtn't to expend it on this. It will never get through.'

"There was a moment of silence as I recall, and Johnson looked at this fellow—'Well, what the hell's the presidency for?'"

On Tuesday evening Hubert Humphrey and Abe Fortas were invited to the Elms. During dinner Lyndon produced several drafts of the speech he was to deliver the next afternoon; there had, he said, been others, but these, which included something of Adlai Stevenson, a good deal of Ted Sorensen, some Horace Busby, a little Valenti, and more than a little John Kenneth Galbraith, were his favorites. They had, he said, to be melded, and he wanted Hubert and Abe to do it.

Hubert H. Humphrey: "He insisted that we produce something that he could deliver the next day before Congress. Others worked on it, but Abe and I prevailed until the end, which was at least two thirty in the morning. I wrote the line 'Let us continue,' which later became famous, being a familiar reference to Kennedy's inaugural speech in which he said, 'Let us begin.'"

Robert Waldron: "When the final, supposedly the final, draft was finished the president read it. Then he handed the speech to Lynda, then a sophomore at the University of Texas, and she read the speech and pointed out a word that she considered too restricted to Texas and to the South. She said, 'Father, tomorrow you're going to be speaking to the world. I think we should change this word.' I forget what it was, but he did change it. Then he said, 'Well, I think the speech is done, and if you gentlemen agree, that's it.' And he got up and went to bed.

"I drove the final draft[1] down to the White House and handed it in at the gate so that it could be reproduced for the press."

On the way to the Capitol at noon Johnson, who was accompanied by Larry O'Brien, Pierre Salinger and Ted Sorensen, gave credit for the speech to Sorensen, handing him a copy of the final draft. Sorensen said that on the contrary, only about 50 percent of what remained was his.

"But that's the best 50 percent," said Lyndon.

He began speaking so quietly that those in the back rows had to strain to hear him.

All I have I would have given gladly not to be standing here today.

The greatest leader of our time has been struck down by the foulest deed of our time. Today John Fitzgerald Kennedy lives on in the immortal words and works that he left behind. He lives on in the hearts of his countrymen.

No words are sad enough to express our sense of loss. No words are strong enough to express our determination to continue the forward thrust of America that he began.

Reassured by the first round of applause, Lyndon continued.

The dream of conquering the vastness of space . . . the dream of partnership across the Atlantic, and across the Pacific as well—the dream of a Peace Corps in less developed nations . . . of education for all of our children . . . of jobs . . . of care for our elderly . . . of equal rights for all Americans, whatever their race or color—these and other American dreams have been vitalized by his drive and by his dedication. . . .

On the twentieth day of January, in 1961, John F. Kennedy told his countrymen that our national work would not be finished "in the first thousand days, nor in the lifetime of this administration, nor even perhaps in our lifetime on this planet." But, he said, "let us begin."

Today, in this moment of new resolve, I would say to my fellow Americans, let us continue.

The southerners sat forward in their seats when he began the next part:

No memorial oration or eulogy could more eloquently honor President Kennedy's memory than the earliest possible passage of the civil rights bill for which he fought so long. We have talked long enough in this country about equal rights. We have talked for one hundred years or more. It is time now to write the next chapter—and to write it in the books of law.

I urge you again, as I did in 1957 and again in 1960, to enact a civil rights law so that we can move forward to eliminate from this nation every trace of discrimination and oppression that is based upon race or color. There could be no greater source of strength to this nation both at home and abroad.

There was enthusiastic applause after that, although the southerners, including Lyndon's old friend Dick Russell, sat silent.

But the president pleaded against division:

We will serve all of the Nation, not one section or one sector, or one group, but all Americans. These are the United States—a united people with a united purpose. Our American unity does not depend upon unanimity. We have differences; but now, as in the past, we can derive from these differences strength, not weakness, wisdom, not despair. Both as a people and as a Government, we can unite upon a program, a program which is wise, just, enlightened, and constructive.

There was more, including a plea for the passage of Kennedy's tax bill, and there were many interruptions for applause while the television cameras focused on one after another of the members of Congress on the floor of the chamber or the foreign dignitaries and members of the diplomatic corps in the balcony. Lady Bird, Lynda, and Luci received their share of attention, but almost equally proud, if less observed, were the members of Lyndon's staff, many of whom, headed by Walter Jenkins, had been with him since he was a member of that same House at whose podium he now stood.

Finally Lyndon concluded:

I profoundly hope that the tragedy and the torment of these terrible days will bind us together in new fellowship, making us one people in our hour of sorrow. So let us here highly resolve that John Fitzgerald Kennedy did not live—or die— in vain. And on this Thanksgiving Eve, as we gather to ask the Lord's blessing, and give him our thanks, let us unite in those familiar and cherished words:

America, America,
God shed his grace on thee,
And crown thy good
With brotherhood
From sea to shining sea.

The standing ovation at the end was thunderous; now even the southerners joined in. Jack Kennedy would never have used those concluding words, but Ted Sorensen had thought that they were appropriate for the occasion, and they were. And if most members of Congress felt there was some doubt that their new president could accomplish all he had asked of them, they did not say so then.

Even the *New York Herald Tribune*, which rarely had a good word for any Democrat, particularly a Democratic president—hadn't Jack Kennedy himself, in a moment of fury, canceled the White House subscription?—said of the address, "Fine words, fitting words, at times inspiring words. As he stood before Congress and the nation not a fluke of history but a president."

And Dick Gregory said, "As soon as Lyndon Johnson finished his speech before Congress, twenty million of us unpacked."

Would there ever again be so triumphant an hour? No, there would not. All new presidents have a honeymoon with Congress and with the public; Lyndon's was perhaps the shortest in our history.

Charles Roberts: "During the month of mourning for Kennedy, I think one of the wisest things he did—without violating good taste or anything else—he used that period of mourning to call in people and to build bridges to the business community that Kennedy had destroyed, in the steel industry for instance, by calling them sonsofbitches. Johnson called in businessmen, he called in labor people, he called in church people, and he called in ethnic groups. He had literally hundreds of organizations representing millions of people in the White House during that month and told them, 'I need you. I need your help more than Jack Kennedy did, and I'm the only president you've got.' He enlisted their sympathy, understanding, made them feel that they had a friend in the White House, and he built a fantastic base that way.

"The meetings were all off the record. But in retrospect I know that it made him a lot of friends. It made a lot of organizations and whole communities friendly to him—people that didn't understand him. I don't think he had a great rapport with the Negro community—they were suspicious of him because he was a Democrat. Liberals were suspicious of him because he was a Texan. And, as I say, labor was suspicious of him. And he, I think, allayed a lot of those fears and really convinced them, 'I need your help.' And it wasn't just a show.

"Of course, this guy was on the phone more than any president in history. He made the phone an instrument of national policy."

George Meany: "He contacted me at home one morning after the assassination, somewhere between eight and nine o'clock on Saturday morning, and told me that he had this heavy responsibility and that we had to keep moving forward even though we were all certainly grief-stricken and so on. Of course he was very anxious to have the full cooperation of the AFL-CIO, and I would say that he got their cooperation."

Horace Busby: "In addition to talking to labor leaders, he talked to a group of businessmen; there must have been eighty, ninety, maybe a hundred businessmen there.[2] This was to him some kind of mountain he had to climb up. He had to get them in his stable. He needed their support while he accomplished this revolution that they didn't normally want to accomplish. And he just kind of went over the mountains by himself, and it dazzled them. Sidney Weinberg, one of the most important Wall Street brokers, said that he had never heard any president be more impressive with businessmen, and he said he'd been listening to them for thirty years or so."

But perhaps Lyndon's most extended talks were with civil rights leaders.

Roy Wilkins: "After the assassination, a member of his staff called and said Mr. Johnson would like to hold a series of conferences on the civil rights situation beginning Friday morning, four days after the funeral."

A. Philip Randolph: "He called up all the civil rights leaders and asked them to come to the White House and talk with him.

"We went. He told us about his plans and so forth and said that he was committed to principles of civil rights. And I told those civil rights leaders then, 'We must help the president, cooperate with him to our fullest.'"

Whitney Young, Jr.: "The press got to me immediately after the assassination, and I remember my first comment when asked how did I feel about Lyndon Johnson as president. I said I had always felt that if ever I turned on the radio and heard the president of the United States speaking with a deep southern accent that I would panic. But I did not feel that way at all. I felt by that time that Lyndon Johnson would do exactly what he did."

James Farmer: "I saw him then in the White House on December 6, for an hour and a half or two hours I guess, and we discussed many things, including the civil rights bill, and he made countless phone calls and received countless phone calls from the Hill in the course of our conversation pertaining to the bill. He said he was running into great difficulty, but he's got to get that bill through, he's got to get it through; it is of vital importance and some of the southerners tell him that they'll buy the bill if he will take out the public accommodations section. But he can't do that, because that's the heart of the bill as far as he is concerned."

Then, too, in the first days and weeks of the presidency Lyndon consulted frequently with old friends.

Elizabeth Goldschmidt: "As soon as he became president, he was very eager to reactivate all his old connections. I think it's typical of presidents—they suddenly are subject to such overwhelming pressures of people with an ax to grind of one sort or another that they instinctively turn to their old friends.

"Abe Fortas did every kind of task for Johnson. He was constantly on the phone with Johnson—as soon as Johnson acceded to the presidency, he called upon Abe immediately."

But even among old friends, life was never again the same.

Walter Jenkins: "As soon as Mr. Johnson became president, I think that even people who had been with him a long time felt a little bit of restraint. I never called him by his first name, but I never did call him Mr. President either. Most of us who had been with him a long time had always called him Mr. Johnson, even in the days when he was senator. I continued to call him Mr. Johnson."

Peter Lisagor: "You know, it's an interesting thing about presidents. Even though

Lyndon Johnson had been in this town twenty to thirty years before he became president, the presidency is new to everybody that goes into it. They have to find out about it. There's no on-the-job training for a president."

Hugh Sidey: "Johnson in my judgment was probably the only man in the United States who could have handled that transition. He'd been in Washington since 1937. As an administrative aide, House representative, senator, vice-president, he'd lived through virtually every crisis in politics this country had had. He knew instinctively what to do."

STYLE AND SUBSTANCE

James H. Rowe, Jr.: "The one thing I used to say when Kennedy died and Johnson came into office—I used to say my boss Roosevelt had both style and substance. And Kennedy had style. And this fellow Johnson has substance. I still think this is true. Kennedy looked fine, made nice speeches, but he didn't get much done.

"They tell the story, the difference between Kennedy as president and Johnson as president. A senator would come to Kennedy and say, 'I'd love to go along with you, Mr. President, but it would give me serious trouble back home.' Kennedy would always say, 'I understand.'

"Now Johnson knew damn well the senator was going to tell him that, and he never let the senator get to the point of his troubles back home. He would tell him about the flag, and by God, the story of the country, and he'd get them by the lapels and they were out the door. That's why he got so much done so fast.

"Roosevelt would do that, too. He would do it, let's say, with more charm than Johnson, but they'd get the same results. They'd get what they wanted."

John Kenneth Galbraith: "There should be no doubt about it—Johnson was very much more a part of the liberal instinct of the times than John F. Kennedy was. Also, in comparison with John Kennedy he had a greater sense of what he could get away with and what he could do on the Hill. Johnson used his leverage with Congress to the hilt and more. Kennedy's tendency, particularly during the last two years he lived, was to underestimate his strength."

Myer Feldman: "I'm a little prejudiced in Kennedy's favor. I don't think Kennedy had vices. I think he only had virtues. I think Lyndon Johnson had great virtues and great vices, depending upon whether that particular day he was emphasizing the vices or the virtues, you liked or disliked him. You couldn't say that you liked Lyndon Johnson all the time. It was equally impossible to say that you disliked Lyndon Johnson all the time—but he was a very strong personality, and he had big swings.

"Almost everybody I know feels that way and if they are honest will say the same thing. I have talked with Walter Jenkins, Jack Valenti, and Bill Moyers about whether they liked Johnson, and they all reacted the same way. They did not, could not like him all the time."

Robert Kintner: "Johnson always lived in the shadow of Kennedy, a suave, very popular, able speaker, well dressed, a class boy with his Boston-Irish accent. That contrast had a terrible effect on Johnson, in one respect, that he tried to emulate Jack, and he wasn't like Jack at all.

"Even Jack's war record bothered him—a record that now turns out to be partly fictional. But Johnson always had the feeling that Jack was doing these incredibly brave things on that wonderful torpedo boat, medals all over, while all he [Johnson] did was sit in Melbourne, Australia."

Lloyd Cutler: "I think the comparisons relate primarily to the different ways in which the two of them were brought up. Lyndon Johnson was a man who had to fight for everything he got. He had very little either formal training or other schooling in how to behave and what were regarded as admirable qualities of restraint and self-deprecation and moderation. In the part of the world where he lived and grew up those were not great qualities. Canniness, craftiness, exuberance were regarded as great qualities where he lived, and he showed that through his life. He lived by his standards."

Benjamin C. Bradlee: "I tell you what the things I've read about him don't have is— and it haunted him all his life—was that Kennedy had more style. If you read the dictionary about style the fact is that Johnson had more style than Kennedy. If style is individuality—that individuality by which one distinguishes a person—he was just a goddamn bank vault of style."

Max Frankel: "In my experience the Kennedys played rougher. They had many more favorites in the press corps in Washington. They had a much more rigorous sorting out of who was their friend and who was not. Lyndon Johnson made those calculations, but he never quite strained your independence and loyalty the way Kennedy did around the White House. There were fellows around the Johnson White House, Jim Dealin and others, who had written just fierce stuff about the president. I don't think they came to the Ranch, and I don't think he had much respect for them or liking for them, but day in and day out they were able to do their jobs at the White House without undue pressure.

"The Kennedys were much more abrupt about this, and they tried to sort out who was with them and then bestow favors and access and private interviews and so on. Life is not fair and covering a president is not fair. But, all in all, I don't think anybody would ever suggest that Lyndon Johnson was unfair in his dealings with the press, although he certainly tried to influence the product to the best of his ability, as does every president."

Harrison Salisbury: "There is an illusion that Jack Kennedy liked the press while Johnson was hostile. The truth is that Truman and Roosevelt and Kennedy were every bit as hostile to the press as Johnson.

"The greatest con game in the world was done by Kennedy so that many people thought that he just loved the press. I knew Jack Kennedy very well, and I know he hated the press. It's very normal for a president to have that attitude. I don't think there is any other way for a president to be, but I often smile—a sweet sad smile—when I listen to some of my colleagues who regarded themselves close to Jack."

Galbraith: "Johnson was the master of the political show, political panache of every kind. Which, coming out of Harvard, I rejoiced at and loved. Kennedy saw it as another version of larger-than-life style of the last hurrah, by which he was revolted, from which he was separating himself. He was not as amused, and he would not be as amused by Johnson's vulgar language, which Johnson would use in my presence because he knew I liked it. He would never use it in Kennedy's presence or Jackie's presence.

"In private Kennedy often uttered four-letter words, which was considered part of his charm; when Johnson used the same words he was described as vulgar."

Erv S. Duggan: "De Gaulle once said that Kennedy was a mask on the face of America while Lyndon Johnson *was* America, and I think that's true. And it goes back in a sense to liberalism in this country. Johnson used to say, and he said it again and again, I think he originally got it from Carl Hayden, who once told him, 'Son, there are two kinds of horses; there are show horses, and there are work horses, and you've got to decide in the United States Senate whether you want to be a show horse or a work horse.'

"And I think in liberalism there is the liberalism of style—the liberalism of substance. Both in the Senate and in the White House Johnson was always the latter and Kennedy was always the former. Roosevelt had both, but I don't think there's been a president since who has.

"Liberals, in general, I think, are inclined to favor style over substance. Compare the way the Kennedys and the Johnsons ran the White House. Under Kennedy and his wife it was a salon and the style was European/British, and interestingly enough that is the style that appealed to liberals—the elegance of it all.

"Under the Johnsons the White House was like a mom and pop store, and there is probably no more American institution than the mom and pop store, whether it's the Jewish couple in New York or the couple in Alabama running a rural store—mom at the cash register, pop in the meat market, and they were America."

John P. Roche: "They were very different men.

"Kennedy was incapable of any kind of intimacy. That's why the stories about all the women, those casual things that went on, are no surprise. They were all old news in Massachusetts anyway.

"But the one thing Jack Kennedy didn't want was an intimate relationship. Except maybe with Bobby. Maybe. But Ted Sorensen points out in his book that he himself was never invited over to the mansion for dinner.

"Now Johnson was completely open in the sense that he would call you up and say, 'What are you doing? Come on over.' You'd say you were working, and he'd say, 'You're not working. All you're doing is sitting there playing with some lousy speech your liberal friends want me to give.' Anybody to the left of Barry Goldwater was *your liberal friend*.

"And so you'd end up sitting over in the mansion having coffee, having one of those— what I call therapy sessions in which he talked about everything."

Elspeth Rostow: "When Kennedy was with daytime people he was busy, on the job, charming, funny, but after hours he saw different people and lived differently.

"With Johnson it was a continuous web. Everybody was part of the act. He'd bring secretaries to supper; there was no upstairs, downstairs.

"This doesn't mean that one was right and the other was wrong. They simply had different styles."

Andrew Young: "Dr. King used to say that when you'd go to talk with President

Kennedy he made you do all the talking. But when you talked to President Johnson, he did all the talking. Of course, Dr. King was a talker himself, so that no personal relationship ever developed, as I think it did with President Kennedy, in that there was a give-and-take kind of relationship."

Norman Cousins: "Kennedy was a great listener. As he listened his eyes got larger, and he looked at you, and you knew you'd been looked at and listened to.

"Johnson sometimes squinted, and you couldn't be quite sure if he was looking at you or staring off into space. But you always knew he was listening, because what he said later indicated he had heard and understood every word. He would be sitting with his hand against his cheek, very thoughtfully."

Robert Hardesty: "Kennedy started things, an awful lot, good things, too, but he could never get the bills passed. There are those who say he would have done it if he'd had more time, but I don't think so. I don't think he knew how or ever cared very passionately. Johnson did."

Robert C. Weaver: "I think Kennedy had an intellectual commitment for civil rights and a broad view of social legislation. Johnson had a gut commitment for changing the entire social fabric of this country, and after the 1964 election he had a large majority and was an adroit strategist.

"I don't think we would ever have got the civil rights legislation we did without Johnson. I don't think Kennedy could have done it. He would have gone for it, but he was a lot more cautious than Johnson. And his caution may be an element of his having had such a small margin in 1960."

Eugene V. Rostow: "Dean Rusk, who is very, very careful and very correct, once remarked that you could never get President Kennedy to think beyond what he had to do at nine o'clock tomorrow morning, whereas with Johnson it was always, 'Well, where are we going to be ten years from now? And if we move in this direction, would this foreclose my successor from any options?' "

Leon H. Keyserling: "To be sure, Kennedy had less than three years, but the history of every great president is that he has struck in his first year. Jefferson and Jackson and the others, too.

"Kennedy was virtually at a stalemate before his assassination; he couldn't get any of his programs through. There's no use speculating what would have happened if he had lived.

"Then Johnson came along. In my view, he was much more activist, aggressive, and managerially competent than Kennedy, and he got through a very broad and creative domestic legislative program.

"The truth of the matter is that every good president in American history has pushed beyond the bounds of what is politically possible."

Liz Carpenter: "I have really always thought that you could describe presidents in almost a word. Kennedy inspired, which Johnson was not capable of doing, and Johnson delivered."

Hubert H. Humphrey: "Kennedy became much more of a hero as he became much more of a martyr. The fact is that his weakness and flaws were quickly forgotten, particularly by the Democrats. Johnson was constantly compared to Kennedy, and that was like comparing a heavyweight boxer to a ballet dancer.

"Of course, every presidency has its own personality. Kennedy's had great grace and charm and class. Johnson's presidency was more like a developer moving into an area that needs rehabilitation, renovation, rebuilding. It isn't very pretty at times. There's a lot of debris laying around, but all at once you see new structures coming up, and it may not be all quite finished, but the structures are there.

"He was a builder, above all. He was a muscular, glandular, political man. Not an intellectual, but bright. Not a talker, a doer. Kennedy was more a talker.

"But I think when you look back, you will see that with Johnson—he didn't get all the little paintings on the wall, and he didn't get the gold plate on the dome and didn't shine up the doorknobs, but he got the foundations in, got the sidewalks up, got the beams put across. The structure was there."

THE WARREN COMMISSION

During that first month, few matters of the slightest national relevance or concern escaped Lyndon's attention. Two matters that he had referred to in his speech before the joint session—the civil rights bill and the tax cut—he had his staff working away on, but he knew that their resolution would have to wait until the next session of Congress. There were, however, several concerns that required immediate executive action—an address before the UN General Assembly, the foreign aid appropriations bill, the Medal of Freedom awards, and, looming largest and most pressing to the new president from Texas, the investigation of the assassination itself.

John Tower: "I think that was the grimmest experience I've ever had in my life, the aftermath of the assassination. A lot of people blamed the city of Dallas for it. Of course, Dallas was not responsible, but there was a hate campaign against Dallas which I think weighed heavily on all of us from Texas."

Something had to be done quickly; it was clear that the Texas authorities, even though the state attorney general had proposed an investigation, would not do; neither would the Texas Rangers, and certainly not the Dallas police force. Nobody from Texas could be considered, since many people thought that Lyndon himself had planned the whole thing; indeed, sometime later a young playwright rewrote *Macbeth*, not very well, accusing Lady Bird, too, of complicity.

It was almost equally apparent that the FBI, particularly its director, was in many circles far too suspect of totalitarian tendencies to be trusted with what might be a totalitarian plot; besides, Hoover hated Bobby Kennedy, the victim's brother, and was hated back.

The idea of a national commission, unconnected with Congress, the executive, or the judiciary, apparently occurred to various people independently. Lyndon said the idea was first mentioned to him on Sunday, after Oswald was shot, by Eugene Debs Rostow of the Yale Law School, and not long afterwards by Dean Rusk and Joseph Alsop. Abe Fortas later said that it was his idea, as did Hale Boggs, the House Democratic whip.

So the Special Commission to Investigate the Assassination of President Kennedy was established, and the president chose all of its members—save the chairman—very quickly. He asked Hale Boggs to serve, and Hale agreed; so did the Republican from Michigan who came to the House the year Lyndon arrived in the Senate, Gerald Ford. One Republican, one Democrat, both from the House. Lyndon's old friend Dick Russell said that he was too sick, too old, and too tired to accept the appointment. Lyndon said he was sorry to hear it, but he needed him and he had already released the news to the press, which was not quite true. Lyndon also persuaded John Sherman Cooper, a highly regarded Republican senator from Kentucky, to serve. Again, this time from the Senate, one Republican, one (albeit ailing) Democrat.

Allen Dulles, who was for so long head of the CIA, was asked and agreed. So did John Jay McCloy, a man considered at the very center of the American Establishment.[1]

But the chairman? He had to be a man of world renown and worldwide respect. There were not too many such around; but Abe Fortas, the always present Abe, says he came up with that name, too—the man Abe was for one hopeful moment named to succeed, Earl Warren, chief justice of the United States.

True, Chief Justice Warren had enemies. There were zealots all over the country who felt that because of Warren's rulings, particularly in the Brown case, he should be impeached and indeed Birchites and Minutemen and their ilk erected billboards all over the country saying simply, Impeach Warren!

Most reasonable people, however, had the greatest respect for his achievements not only as chief justice but as attorney general and governor of California.

Lyndon agreed at once that Earl Warren was the man for the job.

Earl Warren: "The solicitor general and the deputy attorney general [Archibald Cox and Nicholas deB. Katzenbach, respectively] told me that the president was contemplating setting up a commission to investigate the assassination of President Kennedy, and they asked me if I would be chairman of it. I told them that I thought I should not do that; that we had discussed many times in the Court that it was not wise for members to accept positions on presidential commissions. I had personally expressed that view and I still think that as a general thing it's a sound rule. Because in the first place, we have enough work to do here; and in the second place, it does get you over into another department of government which is supposed to be separate.

"So I told them that, and thought that was the end of it. Then in about an hour I got a phone call from the White House and was asked if I could come up and see the president. So I went up there. And the president told me that he was greatly disturbed by the rumors that were going around the world about a conspiracy and so forth, and he thought because it involved both Khrushchev and Castro, that it might even catapult us into a nuclear war if it got a head start.

"He said that he had just been talking to McNamara, and to the leaders of both parties of Congress. And he said, 'I think this thing is of such great importance that the world is entitled to have it presided over by the highest judicial officer of the United States.'

"And I said, 'Well, Mr. President, I've told you what my views are but,' I said, 'things can get to a place where your own personal views shouldn't count. And if you think it is this important that I should do it, why, I'll do it.'

"I got them to rent the building right across the street here from the Court and I would come for every session of the Court, then run over there and work until maybe midnight. It lasted for ten months.

"The White House never gave us any instruction—never even looked at our work until I took it to the president. The president never once in any way, shape or form, made any suggestions; no limitations of any kind were put on us.

"So far as getting evidence is concerned, we had no problems at all. Even Jack Ruby— I went down and took Jack Ruby's testimony myself—he wouldn't talk to anybody but me. And he wanted the FBI to give him a lie detector test, and I think the FBI did, and he cleared it all right. I was satisfied myself that he didn't know Oswald, never had heard of him. But the fellow was clearly delusional when I talked to him. He took me aside and he said, 'Hear those voices, hear those voices?' He thought they were Jewish children and Jewish women who were being put to death in the building there."

So the Special Commission to Investigate the Assassination of President Kennedy, always known, despite its namesake's original misgivings, as "the Warren Commission," concluded that Lee Harvey Oswald, "without advice or assistance," killed John F. Kennedy, that Jack Ruby acted likewise when he killed Oswald, and that there was no conspiracy involved in the actions of either man.

The commission also concluded that Oswald might have been crazy, was probably a Marxist, was certainly possessed of "profound alienation from the world in which he lived," and had a "strong concern for his place in history." He had not, the commission decided, cared much for his environment, wherever it was, and had talked about that dislike "with an apparent disregard for possible consequences." All of which contributed to "the character of a man capable of assassinating President Kennedy."

Warren: "The conspiracy theory of assassination—it's historical, particularly with Europeans. Most of their assassinations grew out of palace guard defections and things of that kind. It's the same in South America. Here on the contrary practically all of our assassins have just been demented people."

Henry Brandon: "It was absolutely fantastic the impact that this assassination had made in the Soviet Union. The first Russian virtually I talked to asked me, 'Do you think Johnson organized the assassination?' Now with their conspiratorial mind and their history this is not an unusual question to ask."

Warren: "When the report was finished, we just walked in there and I handed it to the president. I gave him just the report, not the evidence. The evidence is twenty-six volumes, but the report is a single volume. I just handed it to him and asked to be discharged, and he made a few gracious remarks, and we went out."

The report was delivered to the White House on September 28, 1964, and it served its purpose, which was to convince most people that Lee Harvey Oswald, alone and unaided, slightly crazed, had assassinated Jack Kennedy. There were others who doubted that the report told the full story, and a great many still do. Among the doubters was the man who had created the Warren Commission.

A few days after the assassination Hubert Humphrey said that Lyndon, while passing a portrait of Ngo Dinh Diem in a hallway at The Elms, said, "We had a hand in killing him. Now it's happening here."

On his trip to Vietnam in 1961 Lyndon had not thought that Diem was perfect, far from it, but, he had said and thought that Diem was our best hope in South Vietnam, which later proved to have been a good observation.

Kennedy, on the other hand, allowed State Department officials to persuade him otherwise and, according to Thomas Powers in his biography of Richard Helms, *The Man Who Kept the Secrets*, "Kennedy bore a heavy moral responsibility for Diem's death, since the generals' coup which deposed him probably never would have occurred without American encouragement and assurances."[2]

Powers also reported that "not long after Johnson became president, Richard Helms was one of a small group that heard him claim that Kennedy's murder was an act of retribution . . . by unnamed persons seeking vengeance for the murder on November 1, 1963, of the president of South Vietnam, Ngo Dinh Diem."[3]

How long Lyndon held this view is not known. By spring of 1967 the CIA-Mafia involvement plots to kill Fidel Castro had emerged, and Drew Pearson had publicly stated that "President Johnson is sitting on a political H-bomb—an unconfirmed report that Senator Robert Kennedy may have approved an assassination plot which then possibly backfired against his late brother."[4]

By that time Lyndon knew that the Kennedys, both Jack and Bobby, had been heavily involved in a number of schemes to "eliminate" Castro. Lyndon, who according to Powers wanted no part of such schemes, was by then converted to the idea that it had been Castro, rather than Diem forces, behind Jack Kennedy's death. In any case, it seems unlikely that Lyndon himself ever believed the conclusions of the Warren Commission.

But all of that would come later. For the moment, Lyndon's primary concern was legislation, what he could pry out of a recalcitrant Congress, and his first confrontation with that body came almost immediately. The foreign aid appropriations bill was currently before the Congress; at issue was the administration's plan to sell surplus wheat to the Soviet bloc countries, and to allow them to buy it on credit, if necessary. In the Senate a prohibitive amendment concerning loan guarantees was introduced by cold warrior Karl Mundt of South Dakota, and was to come up for a vote the day after Kennedy's funeral.

Fully occupied with diplomatic duties himself, Lyndon sent Larry O'Brien over to the Senate to count heads and persuade. It was, Lyndon said, far too important a vote to leave to chance. Larry's efforts paid off in the Senate, but then three weeks later the House passed its bill with the same credit restrictions.

When the bill went to a Senate-House conference, Lyndon exerted enough pressure to keep the Mundt amendment from the bill, and a compromise was reached. The full

House, however, was not so easily tamed and refused to accept the compromise.

With Christmas only five days away, many proadministration congressmen had already left Washington. Never mind, said Lyndon, and called them back for another vote, waving his presidential stick in one hand and his carrot, in the form of a White House Christmas reception, in the other.

Thus it was that on the evening of December 23, in a White House newly relieved of the black mourning crepe that had swathed the chandeliers and hung over the doorways, Lyndon and Lady Bird entertained. And at 7:00 A.M. on the twenty-fourth, Christmas Eve, the House met to vote on a second conference report from which the Mundt amendment credit restrictions were still missing. Needless to say, no administration supporters overslept that morning, and the foreign aid bill passed.

Lyndon, Lady Bird, and a planeload of Texas congressmen left Washington almost immediately. In Austin the Johnsons stopped by the governor's mansion to check up on the progress of John Connally, his arm still in a sling, but mending.

The appearance of the Ranch when they at last arrived came as something of a shock. Two large radar screens scanned the sky near the little landing strip, and at night the house was ringed with searchlights. Guard house cubicles, chalk-white in the winter sun, were settled at every entrance to the Ranch and occupied by vigilant guardsmen. Secret Service people seemed to be everywhere. At first glance the Ranch appeared to be fortified against imminent attack.

Otherwise, Christmas came and went much as in previous years. Lady Bird delivered poinsettias about the neighborhood, as was her custom, although this time the station wagon was driven by a Secret Service man. The new president's kinfolks had been asked for Christmas dinner, and all three of Lyndon's sisters—Rebekah, Josefa, and Lucia— were there with their families, as was Cousin Oriole. The press was omnipresent, eager to record how the new First Family spent the day, and the dinner got cold while Lyndon gave them a tour of the ranch house and passed out ashtrays as Christmas presents.

It was, as Lady Bird said later, "the busiest Christmas day that I can remember."

Lyndon, during the week that followed, was full of stories of the wonders and woes of the presidency. He put on his Stetson and his cowboy boots and entertained old friends, and they found him little changed by the exalted office he held. He still drove the Lincoln Continental at the same break-neck speed whenever possible, meaning whenever Bird wasn't watching; he still ate forbidden foods when Bird was out of sight, and he still had really close friends bring him boxes of pralines, which he hid in various places, and which Bird more often than not found and caused to disappear.

And he was still the great raconteur. Some of his imitations of members of Kennedy's cabinet, which was now his, were hilarious. His friends at the Ranch could not vouch for their accuracy, but they recognized the old Lyndon flair.

Benno Eckert: "There's one thing I have to tell you that's always tickled me—this was right after Lyndon became president. A lady stopped at our garage for gasoline. Our oldest boy was waiting on her, and I was inside the shop, and she was raving how she wished she could shake hands with Lyndon Johnson. Sam, my son, told her, 'Well, if you meet him anywheres, he'll be glad to shake hands with you. He wouldn't mind!'

About that time Johnson drove up in that old '34 Ford without a top on, sloppy, Stetson hat on, and he got out and came in the garage. He wanted to talk to me about something—I don't remember what it was. Well, James didn't say anything to the lady, and after Johnson got through, he got back in the car and left. And she was still raving on about wanting to shake hands. And James said, 'Well, why didn't you?' And she said, 'Why, what do you mean?' James said, 'Well, he was here just a minute ago, and you had all the chance in the world to shake his hand if you'd wanted to.' She said, 'That wasn't him, was it?' She expected him to come up there in a full dress suit, you know."

Stella Glidden: "Here in Johnson City, even after he was president, we still called him Lyndon.

"I wrote him one time that I thought when a man loved his fellow man like he did, he had nothing to worry about, and his answer to me was, 'Oh, Miss Stella, everybody does the same.'

"But everybody doesn't, of course."

FIRST LADY

Just as there is no way to train for the presidency, so there is no way to train for becoming the president's wife either. You get there, and then you start coping, and some do it better than others. Or as Lady Bird told Nellie Connally the first week, "I feel like I am suddenly on stage for a part I never rehearsed."

Bird admired Eleanor Roosevelt more than any other First Lady of this country, and while she played a different role in relation to Lyndon from Eleanor's to Franklin, she had a great influence on what he thought and did. Like Eleanor, she had come a long way from the diffidence and withdrawnness of adolescence. Only being from Texas, Lady Bird had had a longer way to come.

Russell Morton Brown: "Lyndon and Lady Bird came up to Washington, and I mean this without deprecating them any, but they grew up in *Texas*. I mean, there was no theater. There were no symphonies. No opera. All that was a totally strange world to them, but Lady Bird had had good schooling and a good education and had an intellectual bent of her own.

"I remember one time she was talking about some of the symphonies she had read about, and composers. She had read about them, but she had never heard them actually spoken of, never heard their names pronounced. She said, 'I particularly want to hear some of the work of Beeth-oven.' That's the way she pronounced it—'Be-e-e-th-th-th-oven.' I mean no one in Texas had ever *said* it to her."

But it came naturally to Bird to pick up that extra bit of culture that had never come her way back in Texas. She surmounted Texas, she had no desire to put it behind her. She *loved* Texas, preferred it to Washington, felt, she once told me, "utterly secure and happy about being from Texas and, if anything, sorry for people who weren't."

Either place, though, her life was never easy. It took discipline, which everyone agrees she had well beyond the usual, and a willingness to let Lyndon's life be hers—to have, in fact, very little of her own. Even motherhood became somewhat of a luxury; there were periods when she had to choose between staying with the children or being with Lyndon, and Lyndon usually won.

Lady Bird: "One of the things about the White House is that you know from the moment you walk in there that this has a time limitation. You don't know exactly what it is; it may be the four years you were elected for, or death, but you know it's got a time limitation. And that's one reason why you do as much as you can do, because you know that this will never happen again, and you can drum up the energy from somewhere within you to go more, do more, learn more, for this limited time."

One reason Lady Bird was able to "go more, do more," was because she was so organized. And she never let the unexpected faze her.

Ashton Gonella: "She was not a complaining type female. If he came in at three o'clock and said, 'We're going to Texas at four,' she didn't say, 'Oh, I haven't had my hair done,' or 'Oh, I've got this to do or that to do,' or 'I haven't packed.' She just got up and did it. And was on the plane at four."

Sometimes, of course, Lyndon couldn't plan ahead, but much of the time he just didn't want to. From the earliest days of their marriage Lady Bird never knew when he might come home for dinner, or how many he might bring with him when he did. She learned very early to plan expandable dinners. "He would say, 'I'm not coming home,'" McGeorge Bundy said of the presidential years. "Then he'd call, 'I'll be home for a hamburger at seven, dear.' At nine he'd arrive with twelve speech writers for dinner."

As First Lady, Bird came into her own as never before. At first there were just small trips—to Appalachia, for instance, to dedicate a school. But after she got her "beautification program" going, there were trips all over the country in that regard, and speeches.

Gonella: "I would watch her when she had a speech to make. She would do her homework. She would sit down and read all about wherever she was going. Then she would tell Liz Carpenter, who did most of her speeches, what she wanted to say. Liz would put it down, then bring it back to her, and she would change it. Then she would get a speech teacher to come, and she would actually rehearse it for two or three hours until she had it down to perfection. She put this much work into every speech that she did, whether it be five or thirty minutes. She wanted everything absolutely perfect."

Lady Bird's beautification program was her contribution to the country as First Lady; it caused, at the time, not a few snickers, but she stuck to it. She was sure that in the end people would be glad for it. It was a double program, locally involving improvements in the District itself, and nationally concerned with highway beautification.

Katharine Graham: "The District beautification program I worried about at first, because Washington has so many real problems that I felt we didn't really need bushes. I felt that people would even resent it and not give money to it, because when we were all being asked for money for ghetto problems, educational problems, school problems, health problems, you just felt embarrassed going to people and saying, 'Will you give a garden?'

"But fundamentally I think it did something very real for the city, and it brought in an awful lot of outside money and outside resources that the city would not have had.

"One day my mother wanted to see one of the playgrounds, and I drove her down there. We were just looking at it when Lady Bird drove up, and she said that she often just rode around looking at things that she was doing and enjoying them. I think her heart got terribly involved in this program, both here and in the country."

John L. Sweeney: "On the highway beautification program, we were really caught between this remarkably tenacious distaff side of the White House and an absolutely adamant Congress. I have never had a rougher time in all the time I have ever spent dealing with clearance from senators than on that beautification program.

"The big objection was that the little business men of the country were going to be done in by the restrictions on billboard advertising. Those little associations of motel owners, tavern keepers, roadside standers, and resort operators—you know, the backbone of the middle class of a lot of rural counties and rural congressional districts in this country—did us in. If they would just have written letters, that would have been great. But they came up here in droves.

"A congressman would get back to his district, and he would be surrounded by these people saying, 'Don't you let them pass the bill that says I've got to take my signs down. How am I going to live? How are people going to know where I am?'

"But Lady Bird and Lyndon Baines wanted them signs down. And by God, they were going to come down!

"We stuck it out, and it went through by the skinniest of skinny votes. We won it by one vote in the last go-round. One single vote, and it was done by the most incredible of sources—Mendel Rivers, who went out and switched four votes on the floor, got four of his southern buddies to swing off no and onto yes. It was just unbelievable.

"It had gotten to the stage where it became a matter of personal honor to the president. There were times, I know, when she was willing to draw back from some parts of the bill, and I know damn well he was saying, 'No we are going to stick with this. Ain't nobody going to be able to write a headline saying that Congress administers defeat to Lady Bird!'"

Virginia Foster Durr: "Everybody knew how Lyndon adored Bird, that Lyndon was wild about Bird and depended on her for everything. But you never heard Lyndon say it.

"Of course, he worked her to death! A lot of her women friends used to get mad at him because he would bring shoals of people home at a minute's notice. Her cousins in Alabama would say, 'We're just crazy about Bird, but that Lyndon! We think the way he works Bird is just terrible.'

"And he did, you know. He took her completely for granted, and he expected her to devote every waking hour to him, which she did. I don't know how she lived through it."

Bess Abell: "I look at Mrs. Johnson and I think that she is perhaps the only woman who ever lived who could have been married to him for that many years and remained a person.

"She had a way of—I don't know maybe one of the ways she survived it, she had this great ability to be able to compartmentalize her life. We'd be working on something—maybe a trip, maybe a guest list, maybe a batch of mail—and one of the girls would come in from school, and she would shift gears and suddenly all of her attention was devoted to that child—that particular child, that problem, or the thing that was going to happen."

Wilbur J. Cohen: "Mrs. Johnson, I think, was the most valuable asset he had. She was the one person that could talk to him and he would listen, knowing that she had no ulterior purpose. He always looked at anything that anybody else said to him with this criteria—what is the self-interest, unspoken assumption on which that person is operating?

"One day the president bawled holy hell out of me. I was trying to appoint a man to a position in HEW, and he said to me, 'Mrs. Johnson and Mrs. Lasker and Mrs. Mahoney have come to talk to me about it. You put Mrs. Johnson up to it.'

"I said, 'Mr. President, I did not do that.' He said, 'You know you did. Don't tell me you didn't. You put her up to talking to me.' I said, 'No, I didn't. I didn't have to. She felt that way anyway.'"

William S. White: "Mrs. Johnson was extremely skillful at handling him, particularly when he was upset or angry or tired or depressed. She never frontally challenged him on anything, but she often had her way by a very soft manner of getting around him.

"He was a very old-fashioned type. He was very much pater familias in that house, both to his daughters and to his wife. It was not a Chinese household, but very much of a traditional 'Papa knows best' attitude. Mrs. Johnson, as I said, always managed— whatever way she got, she managed it by indirection. I don't think I ever heard her directly repudiate him in anything or directly dispute him.

"What she would do, for example, when he was angry and out of sorts, if he'd had a bad day as president, and had problems on the Hill and what not, and somebody had done him in, or so he thought—he'd say very harsh things about him, that person, and she'd say, 'Now, Lyndon, don't you think . . . don't you really believe . . .' and so on. And finally he would smile and sort of withdraw it.

"Mrs. Johnson had the gentleness that he lacked and was very often the agent for bringing him back together with people with whom he'd broken. She once said to me, 'I will not take on Lyndon's animosities or quarrels because I don't want him to lose any friends.' And whenever he seemed about to lose a friend, a genuine friend, she would invariably come into the picture in some way and bring him back together with that friend."

McGeorge Bundy: "Mrs. Johnson was very, very sensitive. John Connally and Johnson didn't see the world the same way. They would get mad at each other. Mrs. Johnson always could tell when these things were going on, and you can be certain during this period when he wasn't speaking to John, she was on the phone regularly with Mrs. Connally.

"That happened to us later. There was a time or two when he was annoyed with me, and we could tell when that had been perceived elsewhere by the sudden increase in invitations from Mrs. Johnson."

Harry McPherson: "There are not a great number of happy marriages among people where the husband is trying to be president or trying to be one of the great world leaders.

"But the Johnsons had a relationship that was really everything that one would hope to have in a marriage. He trusted her advice and judgment. But more than that, we'd be in a meeting—it might include the chairman of the Joint Chiefs and the secretary of state and a couple of staff people from the White House—and in the midst of a very intense conversation on issues, interrupted by phone calls and all that, she'd walk through. And he'd suddenly stop and say, 'Come here.' He'd look at her dress and say, 'I don't like the yoke on the neck of that dress. You were wearing a pink dress last Saturday that had the right kind of yoke for your neck and shoulders. Turn around. Let me see the back.'

"It was very unfeigned, unforced. He really related to her, and that's rare in my experience among public men. He loved her very much. Needed her. Depended on her."

Frank Church: "I always had the feeling that when she was exasperated enough, she would be able to stand up to him. I'm certain that her sense of control and patience was greater than most people's, but at the same time I think it was probably a mark of their marriage that if she really wanted to lay it down, she could and there wouldn't be any problem. I just always had the feeling that they had a very good marriage."

Hubert H. Humphrey: "She sublimated herself to Lyndon's needs, his passions, his hopes, his dreams, and his drives. But she was a marvelous wife for him. She understood him. And let me tell you, she had an affect on him, too. In her quiet way she made him come to heel. Lyndon Johnson would be bluffing and snorting around, and Lady Bird in her own nice quiet way would get that big old moose under control. I watched that many times.

"And when he was in the Presidency, she cut out her own swath, and she did the things that *she* wanted to do—that made *her* comfortable."

And she did, too. In *A White House Diary*, which she recorded evenings after very busy days, usually on the chintz-covered couch in the little upstairs sitting room she loved, she describes at length the things she did, and they are essentially comfortable kinds of things. She also describes a number of things she did because they were required of her, that she could not really have *wanted* to do, but in her words they became acts of grace if not of delight.

In his memoirs Richard Nixon describes how he encountered the president unexpectedly one day, and how Johnson asked him to come have coffee with him the following morning. When he arrived at the White House, properly attired we may be sure, he was shown up to the bedroom where Lyndon, still in his pajamas, had coffee served and conducted the conversation from his bed. In the middle of an exchange on Vietnam, in walked Lady Bird in her dressing gown; she welcomed him warmly, Nixon says, then climbed into bed beside her husband and joined in the remainder of the conversation. Nixon does not indicate his own reaction to the experience.

Erv S. Duggan said that the presidency under the Johnsons was like a ma and pa store. Which is another way of saying that Lady Bird, like Lyndon, was a pro. She was not only careful to know all she could about everyone invited to the White House, to meet them promptly and entertain them charmingly, but she knew the ins and outs of all the legislation Lyndon sent up to the Hill and could discuss it intelligently. And if her views were mostly carbon copies of his own, well, loyalty was a big thing to them both. They carried it east from Texas with them, and thirty-odd years later they carried it back intact.

During the postpresidency period the Johnsons were vacationing in Acapulco with Robert and Mary Hardesty, and Mary later described how among Lyndon's reminiscences was the story of how he had persuaded Bird to marry him after so brief a courtship. "He said there was no time to buy a ring. He sent his best man, a longtime friend, to Sears to pick out several rings so that Mrs. Johnson could use whichever fit.

"At this point he turned to Mrs. Johnson, seated on his right, and said, 'Why did you wait so long—a year or two you waited—to replace that ring? I kept telling you to go buy another one, a better one.'

"Mrs. Johnson blinked at him with loving affection, smiled, and replied in her soft, cultivated Texas voice, 'Why, darlin', I wanted to be sure the marriage was going to last.' Then she walked over to where he sat and kissed him.

"This was thirty-six years after they were married."[1]

Also during the postpresidency John Dodds went down to the Ranch to help Lady Bird edit her diary. She was, he said, as active as ever, happier than ever, back in her beloved Texas. "After she'd been working on the diary for four or five hours, she'd say, 'Let's all take a little walk,' and with that she'd jump up and throw on one of those crazy hats that are hanging there, and go tripping out of the room. And one morning when I'm sure that they had slept together—there was with both that kind of comfort and relaxation—she came down to breakfast in some kind of staggering housecoat, which was probably the gift of some potentate, or certainly Near Eastern somebody or other, swimming in perfume, sort of glistening and singing, and helping put the breakfast together."

Well, that was Lady Bird.

END OF THE FIRST HUNDRED DAYS

On New Year's Day, 1964, Lyndon sent greetings to Soviet Premier Nikita Khrushchev and President Leonid I. Brezhnev of the Soviet Union; it was the last time such a message would be directed toward Khrushchev, but Lyndon had no inkling of that. "In our hands have been placed the fortunes of peace and the hope of millions," he said. "It is my fervent hope that we are good stewards of that trust."

He also sent a message to the new government of South Vietnam in which he assured them of continued support against the Viet Cong.

He was rested from a week at the Ranch, even though the last couple of days had included intensive discussions with Chancellor Ludwig Erhard on U.S.-German relations. In their concluding communiqué the two leaders paid lip service to the ultimate goal of a reunified Germany and agreed, in the meantime, to the continuance of American combat forces in the West. With the passage of the foreign aid bill and the Soviet credit amendment, the new administration's foreign policy was definitely on its way. Even the polls were in agreement: A solid majority of the American people approved of the way their new president was conducting the affairs of the nation. And after three years of virtual powerlessness, it was a heady experience to be in charge again.

Barely seven weeks after he had stood before a joint session of Congress asking their help to continue, Lyndon appeared before them again, on January 8, to deliver the annual State of the Union message. He had in those seven weeks spent a good deal of time holed up with Ted Sorensen discussing what should go into the message, and where, and how. He kept a current copy—it went through many revisions—on his bedside table in case a thought should come to him before going to sleep or, perhaps, in a dream. The speech was finally cleared by no less than 123 people. Even so, Sorensen apparently felt very paternalistic about it.

Jack Valenti: "Sorensen was very upset about anybody tinkering or even looking over his prose on the State of the Union message. He was very zealously guarding his copy of the document. When we drove down to the Capitol for the delivery—Sorensen, Larry O'Brien, myself, and the president—Sorensen was clutching the only copy of the document in the car. And when I asked if I could see it, he said no; he was afraid that if I did I'd be changing some of the words at the last minute.

"Later on we became amused at that, but at that time he meant it. He wanted to be the chief architect of the presidential prose, as he had been under Kennedy."[1]

The explicit goals of the new president, enumerated in the message, were lofty. "Let this session of Congress be known as the session which did more for civil rights than the last hundred sessions combined," the president said. He also wanted, he said, "the most far-reaching war on human poverty and unemployment." *And* a major health program, *and* a reform of transportation policies, *and* the most effective, efficient foreign aid program ever, *and* the construction of more homes, schools, libraries, and hospitals "than any single session of Congress in the history of our Republic."

All this, Lyndon said, could be accomplished by summer, *this* summer, and without any increase in spending, and he pledged that toward that end his administration would be "efficient and honest and frugal."

A long discussion followed of just how he meant to go about eradicating poverty and unemployment, which concluded: "Above all, we must release $11 billion of tax reduction into the private spending stream to create new jobs and new markets in every area of this land."

There was much applause—particularly, of course, from Democrats, who were a decided majority, and many hands extended toward him as he walked back up the aisle.

Concerning that $11 billion tax reduction a budget of $102.2 billion had been drawn up and sent to Kennedy shortly before his death. But the estimated revenue for the same period was only $93.1 billion, showing a $9 billion deficit. The problem was to get the Senate even to look at a tax reduction bill in the face of a $9 billion deficit.

On the night of Kennedy's funeral after the State Department reception and his long talk with the governors, Lyndon had sat down to discuss the economy with his troika of economic advisers—Douglas Dillon, secretary of the treasury; Kermit Gordon, budget director; and Walter Heller, chairman of the President's Council of Economic Advisers. Also present were Gardner Ackley, a member of the same council; Henry Fowler, undersecretary of the treasury; Elmer Staats, deputy budget director; and, intermittently, Bill Moyers.

Gardner Ackley: "The president asked Dillon, 'What about your tax bill?' Almost immediately he answered his own question by saying that we wouldn't have the votes to get it to the Senate floor unless the budget was about $100 billion. The president indicated pretty clear knowledge of every vote. It was as simple as that—if you wanted to get an $11 billion tax cut, you were going to have to give up $1.5 billion of expenditures."

Obviously no one in the room that evening wanted to believe Lyndon was right and that they would have to trade a budget cut for a tax cut. Heller kept arguing that they needed the support of the liberals, which would be forfeited if too many of their programs were cut. Gordon kept reminding them that he had already cut back considerably in areas such as irrigation, reclamation, and REA. Dillon kept assessing how close they might inch toward $100 billion—say $100.6 or $100.7—and still pass. Finally, Heller advocated that the president stick with the $101.5 figure and stake his prestige on it.

Ackley: "The president retorted, '*I* can defend $101.5—*you* take on Senator Byrd.' He had talked with Ike, with Bob Anderson, with Congress. 'Unless you get that budget down around $100 billion, you won't pee one drop.'"

All right, Dillon agreed, if the price of an $11 billion tax reduction bill was subtracting $1.5 billion from the budget, then that's what they would do. Besides, once you had your budget, you could use it as you chose. Like Ike did, Lyndon said—talk economy and then spend away.

C. Douglas Dillon: "The problem was that Senator Byrd was holding out for some sort of gesture of saving money. He indicated that he wouldn't let the bill get out of his Finance Committee unless the budget for the coming year was under $100 billion. So President Johnson went to work, and he sent the budgets back to every department and said that they should review them and reduce them."

At the same time, Lyndon launched his own personal economy drive. He ordered all government departments to cut down on expenditures, in particular waste of materials and overstaffing of offices. On January 20 Lyndon paid a visit to the Budget Bureau and told them that since he had been in the White House, he had discovered all kinds of ways of saving money, including cutting down on the light bill. This prompted the heads of the other departments and agencies to issue their own directives against leaving lights burning, particularly in windows that faced the White House.

The next day Lyndon sent his economic message to Capitol Hill; $100 billion had been pared to a triumphant $97.9 billion.

After that the tax reduction bill seemed to have no problems moving out of Harry Byrd's Finance Committee and onto the Senate floor where it was debated and passed on February 7, seventy-seven to twenty-one. On February 26, after a House-Senate conference, the final $11.5 billion tax cut passed the Senate again. Later that day, amid no little fanfare, Lyndon signed it into law. A great many pens were handed out that day.

Shortly after Lyndon became president, Bird remarked to a friend, "I do hope there aren't too many problems in foreign affairs matters during Lyndon's administration." And, although he never said so, that was his hope as well. Why couldn't those foreigners leave him alone to build his domestic paradise?

It soon became apparent that they would not, and, since they all spoke odd languages, he could not, in most cases, pick up a phone and persuade them of his wisdom as he could, say, George Meany or Mike Mansfield. That was where his "strong right arms"—Bundy, Rusk, and a dozen other experts—came in. Bundy said that Lyndon referred to so many people as his "strong right arm" that it made him think of "one of those Hindu gods with all those arms—in this case, all right arms."

In January 1964, after he'd just got settled in the Oval Office, there was trouble in, of all places, Panama.

Panama, as a republic, had been tossed together in 1903 by that old empire builder, Theodore Roosevelt, who had used U.S. troops to support the area's revolt against Colombia. He wisely wanted authority over the canal link between the Atlantic and Pacific, and a treaty was signed granting the United States exclusive control over the Canal Zone in perpetuity. The ten-mile Canal Zone became American turf. It was Our Canal.

In addition to the soldiers stationed in the zone—it was for the most part far from hazardous duty—there were a large number of government employees, clerks, certified public accountants, engineers, persons adept at opening and closing the locks on canals. The American Legion and the Veterans of Foreign Wars had large memberships there, and everybody seemed to be aggressively patriotic. American flags were profusely displayed as was also, very often, contempt for the dark-skinned natives whose standard of living was always considerably beneath that of the patriots. Various American presidents had over the years doled out small and generally meaningless concessions to the natives; for example, in January 1963 President Kennedy and Panamanian president Roberto Chiari, a man mild of manner, had agreed that the Panamanians could have their very own postage stamp. They had also agreed that the Panamanian flag and the American flag would in the future be displayed side by side at all locations where the American flag was normally flown by civilian authorities. There were fifty such sites, eighteen of them at American schools.

Subsequently, it was wisely decided by American civilian authorities that rather than having two flag poles or two flags on one pole, they would gradually eliminate the sites where any flag would be flown. That was the situation when Lyndon came into the White House. On January 2, 1964, it was decreed that no American flag would be displayed at the Balboa High School. On January 7 the pupils of Balboa, who were not especially noted for their eagerness to study, for once got to school early and ran a good-sized American flag up the pole. Looking out of a window of his office the U.S. governor saw the flag and immediately ordered it removed.

Later the teenaged patriots of Balboa High ran up another, somewhat smaller flag; for some reason it was allowed to fly for the rest of that day. The theory apparently being that the Panamanians wouldn't mind a *small* flag. If so, the theory was wrong.

On January 9 some young Panamanians came into the Zone, marched to the Balboa High School, and raised their flag. The Americans routed the Panamanians, tore down their intolerable flag, and committed various indecencies with it and on it. Not surprisingly the violence was taken up by older Panamanians, and Molotov cocktails and guns appeared seemingly from nowhere. Snipers appeared on rooftops and wounded four Americans. At which point American soldiers started shooting back.

The riots lasted three days, and when they ended on January 12 twenty people, including three American soldiers, were dead. Hundreds had been injured, and property damage all over Panama, including the Zone, was considerable.

On Monday, January 13, the Organization of American States set up a military cooperation committee on which Panama and the United States would both be represented. The committee's purpose was to prevent the recurrence of violence. In the meantime the two sides lined up, most uncooperatively, for battle. The White House issued a statement, the intent of which was not entirely clear, saying that the United States would continue operating the canal and was not about to risk its security, and Panama issued a counterstatement that it intended to sever diplomatic relations with the United States, and would President Johnson please withdraw U.S. diplomats at once?

Lyndon, of course, then phoned Chiari, who spoke excellent English, and the two presidents agreed to go along with the suggestion of the OAS that the United States send a team to Panama to try to clear up the difficulties. But, Lyndon added, *nothing* could be done until law and order was restored in Panama. He seemed not to understand then or later that it was in Chiari's best interest to restore law and order, but that insofar as his own small constituency was concerned, Chiari could not take—*appear* to be taking— orders from that colossus to the north.

A delegation was sent down, but it immediately ran into trouble over whether the two countries should *discuss* or *negotiate*. In the English version of a proposed agreement between the United States and Panama the United States agreed to "discuss" a revision of the treaty and in the Spanish version the word was "*negociar.*" A great deal of time was wasted over that. Lyndon refused to "negotiate." Chiari declined to "discuss."

Finally, after a good many exchanges, most of them acrimonious on the part of both presidents, Lyndon arrived unannounced at a routine press briefing in George Reedy's office. The United States was, its president said, willing to "review" all problems and all difficulties.

God alone knows what Noah Webster would have made of the language. What most observers at the time and since made out of it was that the United States and its president had given—a little.

Lyndon did not, however, emerge from the fracas unscathed. For that matter neither did the United States. Latin American suspicions of the neighbor to the north increased noticeably.

Not a good beginning in the foreign area, and in addition to Panama, which may seem in retrospect to have been a petty squabble, there was another problem overseas, itself petty to many at the time, about which Lyndon and his "strong right arms" were becoming increasingly uncommunicative.

Domestically, however, there was no doubt but that things were moving along rapidly. On January 15 the White House sent to Capitol Hill a request for a $5.3 billion space budget for the coming year. On January 27 Lyndon delivered a request for a housing program. He asked specifically for legislation to deal with housing for minorities, low-income families, and the elderly, and he recommended an additional two-year $1.4

billion appropriation for urban renewal. On February 5 he sent yet another special message to Congress asking for a campaign to protect the consumer, and he suggested that Esther Peterson, appointed assistant secretary of labor on January 2, lead that campaign. And on February 10 he sent up a health message which, among other things, strongly recommended hospital insurance for the aged based upon social security payments.

Then, on Saturday, February 29, Lyndon held his first live televised news conference marking the completion of his first hundred days as president. He announced several appointments, among them that of William P. Bundy as assistant secretary of state for Far Eastern affairs, and Mrs. Frankie Muse Freeman as a new member of the Civil Rights Commission; Mrs. Freeman, a lawyer, Lyndon noted proudly, was both a woman and black. He discussed a new A-II experimental jet aircraft and the supersonic transport. After that, however, his willingness to communicate decreased sharply.

"Mr. President, sir, could you bring us up to date on the conflict in South Vietnam and North Vietnam, and whether or not you think that this conflict will be expanded? And, sir, are we losing there?"

Lyndon: "We have asked Secretary McNamara, who has made periodic visits to Saigon, to go to Vietnam in the next few days. He will go there and have his conferences and will bring back very valuable information.

"We think that Mr. McNamara will correctly appraise the situation on this trip and make such recommendations as he deems appropriate. I do not think that the speculation . . . that we are losing the fight in that area, or that things have gone to pot there, are at all justified. . . .

"Ambassador Lodge is in constant communication with us. He makes recommendations from time to time. We act promptly on those recommendations. We feel that we are following the proper course and that our national interests are being fully protected.

"Next question."

THE WAR ON POVERTY

John Gardner: "I see a society learning new ways as a baby learns to walk. He stands up, falls, stands again, falls and bumps his nose, cries, and tries again—and eventually walks. Some of the critics now sounding off about the Great Society would stop the baby after his first fall and say, 'That'll teach you. Stick to crawling.'"[1]

On the evening of November 23, the end of Lyndon's busy first day as president, Walter Heller, articulate and urbane economist from the University of Michigan, and head of the Council of Economic Advisers, had told the new president that Kennedy had asked him to help work out a detailed program on how his administration could deal with poverty. While he had been "very enthusiastic," said Heller, and wanted to introduce antipoverty legislation in 1964, Kennedy had not planned to push for its passage until after the election. Too controversial, and anyway, if he managed to get a civil rights bill and a tax bill through Congress before he took to the road to campaign, he would have accomplished a lot. That would leave poverty a subject to talk about during the campaign, vaguely. Not too much detail about how much it would cost or just how it would work. Poverty was something everybody was against, but in a prosperous America, who was poor?

Heller was delighted to find that Lyndon, from that first night, was as enthusiastic as Kennedy. Nothing had been done for the dispossessed since Franklin Roosevelt's time. Lyndon would be the president who eliminated poverty. What Heller seemed to be proposing was in the grand tradition of the NYA, the CCC, the WPA.

Hubert H. Humphrey: "Heller thought that poverty was not only wrong, it was something we could not afford. His argument was that poverty should be eliminated so that the poor could stand on their own and become contributing citizens.

"Johnson agreed with that. Investing in the poor to lift them up, to make them independent, was economically feasible. Eventually, as Heller said, it would reduce the costs of unemployment and welfare and help the economy."

Lyndon told Heller he would introduce antipoverty legislation shortly after his State of the Union message, mentioning it there, of course, and then he would push ahead and get it passed during that session of Congress. He said, "Give it the highest priority."

The discussion had continued at the Ranch over the Christmas holidays. Not only was Heller a guest; so was Kermit Gordon, director of the budget. A group of Texas cattlemen were also at the Ranch, there to teach these effete easterners the relationship between beef prices and imports. When the cattlemen heard what these economist fellows were talking about, they had not hesitated to express their collective and unanimous opinion—negative. They had repeated what they no doubt believed, that in this great country of ours there was no reason at all for anybody to be poor; jobs were abundantly available for all those who wanted them. Besides, weren't most of these so-called poor people . . . well, to put it politely, "colored"? Heller somewhat diffidently said that many were white as well.

How much was this program, this *handout*, going to cost? Well, said Heller, it just might—and this is only the roughest estimate, it could be a good deal less—it might cost, well, a billion dollars the first year.

The cattlemen looked at him with dismay and distrust. Heller was not a reassuring sight. He was wearing very elegant slacks, what Texans call "city-bought trousers," and a too large khaki shirt the president had lent him.

After the cattlemen left, Heller, Gordon, Bill Moyers, Jack Valenti, and Lyndon continued to talk about the poor. Lyndon, as always at this stage of the discussion of a new idea, raised the objections he was sure Congress would raise. Like, how extensive a program did the chief executive have in mind anyway? Answer: if the program was big enough, it would not merely benefit the poor in a material way, it would also strengthen the moral fiber of the whole country. "One thing, I did know," Lyndon told Douglass Cater later. "When I got through, no one in this country would be able to ignore the poverty in our midst."[2]

Lyndon: "I realized that a program as massive as the one we were contemplating might shake up many existing institutions, but I decided that some shaking up might be needed to get a bold new program moving. I thought that local governments had to be challenged to be awakened. The concept of community action became the first building block in our program to attack poverty."[3]

Elizabeth Goldschmidt: "The whole idea of declaring a big war on poverty and ending it for all time, all the rhetoric of it appealed to him very much. In fact, I think he built the rhetoric far beyond that which had been planned by his advisers."

Joseph A. Califano: "He thought of the War on Poverty as an extension of the New Deal as helping people get in positions where they could be on their own and where they could pull off their own share of the economic pie. That was the reason for all the vocational education, health, but especially the manpower training. It was a 'hand up' rather than a 'handout.'"

In his State of the Union message on January 8, 1964, Lyndon said:

> This administration today, here and now, declares unconditional war on poverty in America. I urge this Congress and all Americans to join with me in that effort.
>
> It will not be a short or easy struggle—no single weapon or strategy will suffice—but we shall not rest until that war is won.
>
> One thousand dollars invested in salvaging an unemployable youth can return forty thousand dollars or more in his lifetime.

As the massive program was being drafted, the big question was how it was to be administered. Willard Wirtz, secretary of labor, and Anthony Celebreze, secretary of HEW, and Orville Freeman, secretary of agriculture, thought that it should be handled by already existing departments, meaning their own. Lyndon, Heller, and Gordon did not agree; they thought that the war should be conducted by an independent, newly created agency, and on February 1 Lyndon announced that he had appointed Sargent Shriver, already director of the Peace Corps, to head that agency: the Office of Economic Opportunity.

In his March 16 message to Congress the president said that the OEO would "direct and coordinate youth programs, community action programs, antipoverty programs in rural areas, small business incentive loans, and work experience programs, in an effort to alleviate poverty." And more, aid to children in need, aid to migratory workers, and job training for about four hundred thousand disadvantaged young men. And more. And more.

The whole thing would only cost $970 million—about 1 percent of our national budget. "Not only that—every dollar I am proposing for this program is already included in the budget I sent to Congress in January."

In the Senate, after a great many telephone calls and some intensive lobbying by Larry O'Brien and Mike Mansfield, the bill passed by a vote of sixty-one to thirty-four. It passed despite a passionate speech by Barry Goldwater calling the whole thing "a Madison Avenue stunt."

In the House the fight was more difficult, although the program, after some presidential persuasion, was introduced and fought for by Philip Landrum, a conservative Georgian. Landrum had, of course, cosponsored the 1959 Landrum-Griffin Act, which won him no friends in the AFL-CIO, particularly George Meany. Meany was at first incredulous at Lyndon's choice of sponsors, but Lyndon reassured him. "After all, it's the result we're after." Certainly the labor leader would put his country above his personal prejudices, Lyndon said, wouldn't he? He would and did.

The bill was held up in the House Rules Committee for six weeks by Chairman Howard Smith of Virginia, who was then eighty-one. Would the Job Corps, which was similar to the Civilian Conservation Corps in Franklin Roosevelt's time, *force* white boys and *Negras* to be in the same camp? The boys in his state, he said, and in Landrum's, "have a very deep feeling about living with *Negras.*"

Nobody would be forcing anybody to do anything in the Job Corps, Phil Landrum replied; enrollment was strictly voluntary. Nevertheless, Smith did not allow the bill to be voted out until July. It was passed by the House on August 7, 226 votes for, 185 against.

After that, the real problems began to emerge.

The Volunteers in Service to America (VISTA) was designed to appeal, and did, to the same kind of people who volunteered for the Peace Corps, mostly the young, college graduates, idealistic, anxious to serve, anxious to change society, the kind of young who in 1968 were to be "Clean for Gene." And they caused a lot of trouble that at times seemed to threaten the entire program.

Califano: "If you send a group of college students or recent college graduates into a situation like that in the VISTA program, you can send them in to teach and to show people how to keep budgets and how to keep house and how to be sanitary and how to have hygienic conditions and so forth. But inevitably the VISTA people are going to see that in order to do something people are going to have to vote and they've got to get control of the city council or the sheriff's office or get on the local board of education or what have you.

"Johnson fully knew that. In my judgment that is what he wanted to happen. I think that part of the whole poverty program as he perceived it was getting people into the voting process. Just as it was basic to his thinking and what he did about civil rights. Vote, vote, vote; that was the key to progress.

"He got a lot of complaints from the Hill about the VISTA kids, that they were organizing political actions against incumbent mayors, incumbent school board members. We put out, I don't know how many directives to Shriver to stop that. We stopped them from doing that, the kids, but as I say, in my own judgment, he knew it was going to happen, and he wanted it to happen."

Kenneth Clark: "The conflict between the newly stimulated, indigenous poor and the entrenched political power brokers and controllers of political systems in local communities soon emerged as a major problem which had not been adequately anticipated or prepared for. The untrained poor sought to assert their power and found that, in fact, they really did not have the controlling power which the community-action programs . . . promised them. Antipoverty programs became political pork-barrel-type programs and were taken over by sophisticated middle-class bureaucrats. In some cases, upwardly mobile working-class individuals became either the products of or the puppets of the more sophisticated middle-class political controllers of these programs. Sometimes the upwardly mobile indigenous became sophisticated antipoverty hustlers."[4]

Wilbur J. Cohen: "It got out of hand. For instance, the community-action program. We extended community action in the poverty program from just about I think a hundred communities to eleven hundred. And that was just too many; that just could not be done.

"We had to do it to get congressional votes for the program itself, but it was a mistake. We tried to do too much in too many places in too short a time."

People say that Lyndon fought two wars, one in Vietnam, the other the War on Poverty; some people say that he lost both of them. But perhaps not entirely. Millions of preschool children from low- and middle-income families, both urban and rural, have taken and are still taking part in the Head Start program, which was part of the poverty war, the one part not killed by Nixon. Children, from the age of three until they enter kindergarten, get nutritious breakfasts and lunches, as well as acquiring rudimentary learning tools from block play, number games, etc. Many of them come from homes in which there are no toys, no paper, and, to be sure, no soap.

Hubert H. Humphrey: "There is a kind of easy assumption by some affluent Americans that people can find work if they wish. It is not just that simple or easy. On one visit to Chicago, in a job-training center, I saw surprising things. Young adults were being trained in personal grooming, how to use a public washroom neatly, how to punch a time clock. One might ask: How could they *not* know these things? There are people in America who do not have money for food, much less soap. Routine cleanliness is almost irrelevant in lives in which hot water for a bath is unavailable.

"It was a shock to visit a Job Corps camp and see adults who had been through some years of our public education system stare at a blackboard where a teacher was writing CAT or helping them write their own names. In another room, men were learning to tell time. What are you to make of the strange apparatus of a time clock if you can't tell time?"[5]

Califano: "In 1963 when John Kennedy died, the federal government was training seventy-five thousand people in manpower training programs. In January of 1969, when Lyndon Johnson left the White House, one and a half million people were being trained in federal training programs. A dramatic change in the government's role in that area."[6]

Robert C. Weaver: "Beginning with President Johnson's declaration of a war on poverty, magazines, newspapers, and television made common knowledge what urban professionals had known for some time. Our cities were filled with poorly housed, badly educated, underemployed, desperate, unhappy Americans—many of them black."

THE COURTSHIP OF EV DIRKSEN

It seems unlikely that Lyndon was much impressed with symbolism; yet the new president began the year 1964, the year of the historic civil rights bill, with a gesture that can only be considered symbolic.

The Forty Acres Club, the faculty club for the University of Texas in Austin, was segregated, and many of its members had resigned in protest. On that New Year's Eve, however, a party was given to honor Lyndon's longtime associate and friend, Horace Busby. Among those who attended, though with great reluctance, was E. Ernest Goldstein, then a professor of law at the university and a longtime Johnson observer and associate.

Ernest Goldstein: "I said, 'I feel very strongly about this segregation at the club. I'll come, but only because of Horace Busby.'

"So we got there. All of a sudden the Secret Service appeared. And in walked the president of the United States along with a very handsome black woman named Miss Gerri Whittington, then one of his secretaries. The sight of Miss Whittington was one to gladden my Yankee heart. And I went up to Bill Moyers and I said, 'Does the president know what he's doing?' He looked at me with a great twinkle—I should never have asked it in that stupid fashion—and he said, 'He always knows what he's doing!'

"And so after that magnificent evening, on the morning of January 2, I called the club and said we were having a meeting in the University Methodist Church, and I would like to reinstate my membership and bring in some of my Negro guests from the meeting next door. 'Oh,' they said, 'no problem at all.' And I said, 'Are we really integrated?' And he said, 'Yes, sir. The president of the United States integrated us on New Year's Eve.'"

Miss Whittington, when asked later about the incident, said that she had been not a little nervous and had asked, "Mr. President, do you know what you're doing?" To which Lyndon had replied, "I sure do. Half of them are going to think you're my wife, and that's just fine with me."

From the beginning of 1963 the Kennedy administration had been increasingly criticized by civil rights leaders for inaction. The Democratic platform of 1960 had promised much more than the 1960 Civil Rights Act had given, and in their campaigns both Kennedy and Lyndon had promised more, too.

Harry McPherson: "The first time I ever had a real sense of Johnson's commitment in civil rights—one that didn't have anything to do with the prestige or the political gain of getting a bill through—occurred one day in maybe the spring of 1963. Kennedy sent down the omnibus civil rights bill which became the Civil Rights Act of 1964. It had in it a title that prohibits discrimination in places of public accommodation. This was just as obnoxious as hell to the southerners. This was going against private property and it was telling people whom they had to associate with in cafés and restaurants and so on. It was a very, very hard subject and didn't seem to have any chance at all of passage.

"I was sitting up with Johnson at the chair of the vice-presidency in the Senate shortly after the bill had been sent down, and we were speculating about it. Senator Stennis walked by on his way out. Johnson asked him to come up to the chair, and Stennis did. Johnson said, 'How do you like that Title II of the civil rights bill, John?'

"Stennis said, 'Oh, Lyndon, well, you know, our people just can't take that kind of thing. It's just impossible. I mean, I believe that a man ought to have the right to—if he owns a store or owns a café—he ought to have the right to serve whom he wants to serve. Our people just never will take it.'

"Lyndon said, 'Then you don't think you'll support it.'

"'Oh, no, Lyndon, I don't think I'll support it at all.'

"Johnson said, 'Well you know, John, the other day a sad thing happened. Helen Williams and her husband, Gene, who have been working for me for many years, drove my official car from Washington down to Texas, the Cadillac limousine of the vice-president of the United States. They drove through your state, and when they got hungry, they stopped at grocery stores on the edge of town in colored areas and bought Vienna sausage and beans and ate them with a plastic spoon. And when they had to go to the bathroom, they would stop, pull off on a side road, and Helen Williams, an employee of the vice-president of the United States, would squat in the road to pee. And you know, John, that's just bad. That's wrong. And there ought to be something to change that. And it seems to me that if people in Mississippi don't change it voluntarily, that it's just going to be necessary to change it by law.'

"'Well, Lyndon, I'm sure that there are nice places where . . .'

"Then the vice-president just said, 'Uh-huh, uh-huh,' and sort of looked away vacantly and said, 'Well, thank you, John.' And Stennis left. Johnson turned around to me and winked. It represented, as I say, the first time I had ever really had the feeling that the comprehension of the simple indignity of discrimination was deep in Johnson."

The Kennedy bill had not made much progress in Congress. Jack Kennedy's inclination had been, in that area as in so many others, to put civil rights on a back burner until after the 1964 election. But Lyndon had given fair warning when he spoke before the joint session after the assassination. As far as legislative priority in 1964 was concerned, a comprehensive civil rights bill, all-inclusive, uncompromising, and uncompromised, must be passed without delay by both houses of Congress.

The House received the new Johnson-backed 1964 civil rights bill on January 31. The public accommodations section that the Kennedy bill had concentrated upon was there intact and expanded. Two new sections, or "titles," had been added with Lyndon's strong approval. The House Judiciary Committee had inserted into the bill that same part III, empowering the federal government to intervene in cases where a person's civil rights are threatened, that Lyndon as majority leader had with so much effort deleted from the 1957 bill. And on the House floor a section providing for a Fair Employment Practices Commission (FEPC) had been added—in spite of the opinion of the Kennedy staff the year before that that would be "politically impossible."

But the greatest difference between the 1964 civil rights bill as it would probably have been passed in that year under Kennedy, had he lived, and the one that actually passed under Lyndon was that Lyndon made sure he got everything he asked for. Kennedy, faced with inevitable Senate opposition, would almost surely have compromised somewhere, traded the deletion of one section, say, for the passage of the rest. Lyndon refused to delete, refused to compromise, anywhere.

The bill passed the House 290 to 130 on February 10.

Clarence Mitchell: "To show you how closely he was following this situation, when we got the bill through the House, Joe Rauh and I were in a footrace over to the Senate to start work there. The phone rang in one of those pay phone booths over in the House wing, and to our amazement it was the president calling—I don't know how he ever managed to get us on that phone, but he was calling to say, 'All right, you fellows, get on over there to the Senate because we've got it through the House, and now we've got the big job of getting it through the Senate!'"

Everybody, *everybody*, said that for the Senate Lyndon would have to take out the section on federal intervention in civil rights cases or the one on fair employment, maybe both; otherwise, the bill would be filibustered to death. Then, said Lyndon, the Senate must vote cloture on the bill, limiting the debate to, say, one hour per senator.

Cloture? The Senate had never voted cloture on a civil rights bill. It never would. Cloture was the one subject on which liberals and conservatives, northerners and southerners, were all agreed; it was sacred to the Senate, including some of the president's best friends and strongest supporters, like Carl Hayden of Arizona. Hayden, the grand old man who had been born in 1877 and was thirty-five years older than the state he represented, had many times said, publicly and privately, that he would never vote for cloture.

If it is necessary, said the new president, the Senate will vote cloture. Then he said, "Get me Hubert."

Hubert H. Humphrey: "He called me up on the telephone, and he said, 'You have this great opportunity now, Hubert, but you liberals will never deliver. You don't know the rules of the Senate, and your liberal friends will be off making speeches when they ought to be present. You've got a great opportunity here, but I'm afraid it's going to fall between the boards.'

"He said, 'No, your bomb-throwing friends will be out making speeches to the already converted—for a fee. And, Hubert, I'm not sure that you yourself . . .'

"He had sized me up. He knew very well that I would say, 'Damn you, I'll show you.' One thing about Johnson was that even when he conned me I knew what was happening to me. It was kind of enjoyable. I mean I knew what was going on, and he knew I knew.

"Then he said, 'Now you know that this bill can't pass unless you get Ev Dirksen.' And he said, 'You and I are going to get him. You make up your mind now that you've got to spend time with Ev Dirksen. You've got to let him have a piece of the action. He's got to look good all the time.'

"We really worked with Dirksen. I remember I was on *Meet the Press* in March when the civil rights bill had come on down. Dirksen had come out against what I believe was title II, which had to do with public accommodations, and title VII, the fair employment part of the bill.

"The problem was as difficult as it was clear; how do you get the support of Ev Dirksen for cloture without watering down titles II and VII.

"On *Meet the Press* I was asked the question, how did I think that Dirksen would vote for the bill when he had said that he was against those two sections?

"And I said, 'Well, I think Senator Dirksen is a reasonable man. Those are his current opinions and they are strongly held, but I think that as the debate goes on he'll see that there is reason for what we're trying to do.' And I said, 'Not only that, Senator Dirksen is not only a great senator, he is a great American, and he is going to see the necessity of this legislation. I predict that before this bill is through Senator Dirksen will be its champion.'

"Johnson called me after that and said, 'Boy, that was right. You're doing just right now. You just keep at that. Don't you let those bomb throwers, now, talk you out of seeing Dirksen. You get in there to see Dirksen! You drink with Dirksen! You talk to Dirksen! You listen to Dirksen!'"

Mitchell: "A southern senator, whose name I might just as well not mention, told me that the president had put so much pressure on everybody that there wasn't any doubt that the bill was going through. At the time he told me, he seemed almost to be feeling the pain of the pressure. We were riding together on a subway car from the Senate wing of the Capitol to the Senate Office Building. I'll never forget the expression on his face as he recalled what kind of pressures were being exerted."

Bayard Rustin: "He urged us to keep up the pressure on Congress, and said that he would do his part of the job if we did ours. Pressure on congressmen, pressure on the labor movement to put more people in, pressure on the churches for money for more lobbyists."

Joseph L. Rauh, Jr.: "Often you can honestly and truly and sincerely believe in something which is to your political best interest. Johnson really believed in this bill, and it's just impossible to say whether he believed in it solely because of politics or whether he believed in it for the country. I want to give him the benefit there, that he believed in it for both reasons.

"He made it clear to everybody that he wanted it, wanted it more than anything else, and that he wouldn't substitute anything for it; that if they filibustered, they could filibuster, but he didn't want *any other* bill."

Lyndon: "I made my position unmistakably clear: We are not prepared to compromise in any way. 'So far as this administration is concerned,' I told a press conference, 'its position is firm.' I wanted absolutely no room for bargaining. . . . I knew that the slightest wavering on my part would give hope to the opposition's strategy of amending the bill to death."[1]

On January 24, even before the bill reached the Senate, Dick Russell drew the battle line:

"I have no doubt that the president intends to throw the full weight of his powerful office and the full force of his personality—both of which are considerable—to secure passage of this program. . . .

"Although I differ, and differ vigorously, with President Johnson on this so-called civil rights question . . . I expect to support the president just as strongly when I think he is right as I intend to oppose him when I think he is wrong."

Bill Moyers: "Dick Russell would say to me, 'Now you tell Lyndon [publicly he said "Mr. President," but privately, "Lyndon"], You tell Lyndon that I've been expecting the rod for a long time, and I'm sorry that it's from his hand the rod must be wielded, but I'd rather it be his hand than anybody else's I know. Tell him to cry a little when he uses it.'"

On March 30 the Senate began to debate the bill, southern senators having already delayed for more than a month by various parliamentary tactics. Humphrey initiated the debate with a four-hour speech, saying in part—"Until racial justice and freedom is a reality in this land, our union will remain profoundly imperfect. . . . That is why the bill must become law. . . . The Negro is going to get justice or this society will be ripped apart."

Humphrey: "I knew from the beginning that I was in the fight of my life, and I knew I couldn't lose and didn't think I would lose, but I knew it would take all of my skills and all of my energy. I decided from the beginning that until the bill was passed I would devote all my time to it, and I did."

Mitchell: "I don't believe I ever thought we were going to lose. I'm sure I always felt that we had to fight to win.

"Of course, we all knew he had to have the support of Senator Dirksen. Other senators he had to get were from the old guard of the Republican party, like Senator Carl Curtis of Nebraska and Frank Carlson of Kansas and a few others like that. I think also Alan Bible of Nevada and Howard Cannon of Utah, because although both were Democrats, both came from states where they would have had all kinds of reasons for not voting for cloture; senators from states with small populations like that feel the need for the right to filibuster to keep them from being dominated and overwhelmed by the big states.

"Now we didn't try to get the real hundred-percent-opposition southerners, but we did discuss with the president the importance of trying to soften the quality of the debate and the kind of opposition they'd give. And he worked on them.

"Of course, another thing in our favor was the growing political strength of Negroes."

Humphrey: "We were well organized, very well organized. We issued a daily newsletter, I think for the first time in history, that reported what had happened the day before and gave our supporters answers to the arguments of the opposition. But the main thing was that we had complete liaison at all times with the White House, with the president himself, and he answered every question and so far as I can remember did everything we asked—and usually a lot more, too.

"We had a list of which senators were to be on duty at what times, so that we would never be without a quorum, and from March until the bill passed we never were except, I think, once. The lack of a quorum that day turned out not to be disastrous, but the next day we published in our newsletter the names of those senators who should have been there and weren't. Believe me, we never again lacked a quorum.

"In the meantime I never failed to stroke Ev Dirksen's ego; I don't know whether he realized what I was doing or not, but he liked it.

"I don't think a day went by when I didn't say, 'Everett, we can't pass this bill without you. We need your leadership in this fight, Everett.' And I'd say, 'With you in the lead, Everett, this bill will pass, and we will get cloture.' And I'd say, 'This will go down in history, Everett,' and that meant, of course, that *he* would go down in history, which interested him a great deal.

"Oh, I was shameless. But as I say he liked hearing it all, and I didn't mind saying it.

"The debate lasted seventy-five days, and on June 10 we had the crucial vote—on cloture. We had to have sixty-seven votes; I thought we had them, with two to spare. I passed a note to Phil Hart before the voting began saying that I thought we had sixty-nine, two more than we needed. But of course you never can be absolutely sure, not even if you were the kind of legislative genius Lyndon was.

"Anyway, it was a great moment, and when the voting was over, we had seventy-one votes, four more than were necessary, and Carl Hayden, for one, was waiting in the cloak room to vote with us, to vote for cloture if necessary.

"Of course *every* senator was there, including Clare Engle of California, who was dying of a brain tumor and could not speak. But he was wheeled onto the floor in a wheelchair and recorded his aye vote by pointing to his eyes."

After cloture was voted, no fewer than 115 amendments were presented and defeated, and there were still 106 roll call votes. But in the end the courtship of Ev Dirksen paid off—he presented a "revised" bill which was virtually the same as the first bill introduced in the House in January. It was passed on July 2, 73 to 27.

Since the bill was almost the same as the one passed by the House in February, there was no need for a conference, and on that same night Lyndon signed it into law and went on television to tell everyone about the new law and to remind them, as he often had before and often would again, that we are a law-abiding people: "This is why the civil rights act relies first on voluntary compliance, then on the efforts of local communities and states to secure the rights of citizens. It provides for the national authority to step in only when others cannot or will not do the job. So tonight I urge every public official, every religious leader, every business and professional man, every housewife—I urge every American to join in this effort to bring justice and hope to all our people, and bring peace to our land."

While it may seem little more than basic common sense now, the bill reached further than any civil rights bill in the country's history. The act outlawed "unequal application procedures"—meaning, essentially, that Negroes could not be asked what whites were not when they came in to register. The act prohibited discrimination in restaurants, motels, hotels, and places of amusement, although what was known as "Mrs. Murphy's clause" did not prevent discrimination in rooming houses with no more than five rooms to rent. Municipally or state-owned libraries, parks, playgrounds, and swimming pools were to be desegregated or sued. Schools were to be desegregated, which of course was no more than the Supreme Court had said ten years before. But in 1964 it was a *law*, not a decision.

A giant step forward, but not gigantic enough for Lyndon. Within days he was telling Nick Katzenbach about the bill he had in mind for passage in 1965; after, of course, he was reelected. "I want you to write me the goddamndest, toughest voting rights act that you can devise."[2]

Humphrey: "He used to tell me, 'Yes, yes, Hubert, I want all those other things—buses, restaurants, all of that—but the right to vote with no ifs, ands, or buts, that's the key. When the Negroes get that, they'll have every politician, north and south, east and west, kissing their ass, begging for their support.'"

Reactions of southern statesmen and politicians were varied. Dick Russell told his fellow Georgians that they must obey the law "as long as it is there," the implication being that he and other southern stalwarts would as soon as possible rush back to

Washington to get the damned thing repealed. Senator Allen J. Ellender told his Louisiana constituents that he had, as he had been careful to make sure they already knew, opposed the bill—if not quite to the death, nearly so—and had, of course, voted against it, but that resistance to the bill become law "must be within the framework of the orderly policies established by law. Any other course is foolhardy and indefensible."

Governor George Wallace of Alabama, already beginning to emerge as a national political figure and a powerful one, had told newspapermen a few weeks before the bill was passed, "It is not my responsibility to enforce the civil rights bill. My attitude will be to leave it alone. It will take a police state to enforce it."

But except for the deep South, the response to the Civil Rights Act of 1964 was positive, the mood of the country as a whole optimistic.

Ramsey Clark: "There was a glorious feeling about it, there really was. It just seemed like there was immense generosity in the American people, and goodwill, and they were going to do something about this great wrong."

UNVEILING THE GREAT SOCIETY

In case anyone was uncertain whether the Lyndon Baines Johnson imprimatur was yet engraved on the White House, after the railroad strike negotiations of April 1964, all doubts were erased from the mind. No other president would have, maybe even could have, behaved as he did. And it worked. In those days things did work for him. People listened and applauded, and there were ovations everywhere.

For more than four years railroad management had been pressing for revised contracts with labor that would alter what the railroads considered outmoded work rules. They wanted to end what they called "featherbedding"—the system which required, in their opinion, unnecessary firemen on diesel locomotives and an inordinate number of trainmen. Recommendations had been made by presidential commissions under both the Eisenhower and Kennedy administrations, but although accepted by management, they had always been refused by the brotherhoods. Finally the industry simply changed the work rules itself, an action which, when tested, the Supreme Court said it had a right to do.

On April 8 a strike call went out against Illinois Central, and when management announced retaliatory measures, the unions responded with the threat of a nationwide strike. Lyndon was horrified. A nationwide strike would add half a million workers to the unemployment rolls and adversely affect the program that was formulating in his mind, one that would, if he had his way, change the whole of American society, uplift it, improve it, edify it, and, to be sure, beautify it.

He called Willard Wirtz, secretary of labor, and told him that nothing, absolutely nothing, must stand in the way of a quick settlement.

Wirtz called an emergency meeting with management and labor to no effect. The strike deadline was midnight, April 9, and the strike would surely happen if the president did not personally intervene. Perhaps, said Wirtz, it would be better if the president did *not* intervene, but let matters settle themselves. There were times when a brief strike actually contributed beneficially toward a settlement. True, said Lyndon, but how could one be sure of a *brief* strike? What if it turned out to be a prolonged affair and the very food supply of a city like New York were affected—as predicted by the chairman of his Council of Economic Advisers, Walter Heller, for example.

The president had also to weigh the possibility of the unions rejecting his request for an extension, a contingency humiliating to contemplate. But against that possibility was the alternative one of emerging as the hero of the negotiating table, as Kennedy had in the steel dispute, and that image was too tantalizing to reject. So a mere six hours before the deadline Lyndon summoned to the Cabinet Room—the most awesome of the White House meeting rooms—the labor and management negotiators of the railroad industry.

And he laid it on. There is no other way to put it. All his Senate tactics stood him in good stead now, all the toe-to-toe, the finger-wagging, the arm draped across the shoulder. He pleaded. He cajoled. He persuaded. He spoke at length of the probable economic impact of the strike; he referred frequently to one's duties as a patriotic American. And interspersed among his dire predictions and admonitions were his pleas. "Have you lost faith in me?" No, of course they hadn't. "I am your president! Give me a chance!"

Any senator could have told the negotiators their options were over once they entered that room, and indeed they were. At 11:05 P.M. Lyndon went on nationwide television with the president of the Illinois Central and the grand chief engineer of the Locomotive Engineers Brotherhood jubilantly to inform the country that the strike had been postponed for fifteen[1] days to allow for renewed negotiations.

That was Thursday. The negotiators, tired from that day's efforts, assumed the talks would resume on Monday, but Lyndon would not hear of it. They must start the next day, Friday, and he would let them have a lovely and comfortable room in the EOB so they could have immediate access to him whenever they desired.

So the talks resumed on Friday, April 10, and needless to say Lyndon did not wait to be consulted. First he called everybody together in the Rose Garden bright and early to deliver a few encouraging remarks and to introduce White House appointed mediators George Taylor and Theodore Kheel whom he had, the night before, drafted into the fray. During the next two weeks he clucked about the group like a mother hen anxious about the progress of her unhatched eggs. He kept the public informed of the progress— he would not admit to the lack of it—in several news conferences, and he brushed off one reporter's suggestion that the "considerable weight of the presidency" was being used "against the public interest in the freedom to bargain." What was the presidency *for* anyway?

Then, as the talks appeared to stall, Lyndon, just as he used to do in the Senate, looked about for some seemingly minor point which, if settled to the satisfaction of the parties concerned, might result in concessions on major points. It was suggested to him that the railroad industry wanted more leeway in setting rates, but the bill to that effect was stalled in the House Rules Committee. It was also mentioned that the industry was anxious for more favorable consideration by the IRS in the matter of depreciation for bridge and tunnel construction. Lyndon lost no time assuring railroad management that yes, the bill surely could be pried loose from the House Rules Committee, and yes, it would certainly behoove the IRS to review their position. After which management again returned to the conference table.

On April 22, the fourteenth day of negotiations, Lyndon went to New York to speak at the opening of the New York World's Fair. When he returned that afternoon he went immediately into conference with the rail bosses who, despite the aforementioned promises from Lyndon, were balking. They were holding out for longer runs for train crews, a measure the brotherhoods refused to concede. Lyndon reminded them, somewhat loftily, that there was but one day left, and that he their president surely did want a settlement, he surely did. Those longer runs—well, they could be worked on and included in the next contract, could they not? Well, *couldn't* they?

Half an hour later the negotiator for management informed Lyndon that the industry had agreed to the compromise.

This time the television cameras were not prepared and waiting—the networks apparently had expected the talks to go right down to the wire the next day—and Lyndon, unwilling to wait the extra hour that it would have taken to set them up, ordered the White House limousine to take him, accompanied by the head negotiators for union and management, across town to station WTOP.

He marched in, beaming, made directly for the microphones and cameras where the newscasters were waiting to give the seven o'clock report. Flanked by his negotiators, he announced the settlement, piling praise on the brotherhoods (to his left) and on management (to his right), both of whom had, he said, "operated in full freedom of spirit" and had thereby proved, he said, "that free enterprise, free collective bargaining, really works in this country." Then, still beaming, he turned and marched out.

In the end neither the House Rules Committee nor the IRS followed Lyndon's suggestions, but by then the new contracts were signed, and everyone, train crewmen and presidents alike, was glad to have that dispute settled for a time.

When Lyndon went back to Texas for Easter that year, a goodly part of the press, of course, followed. He put them up at the Driskill in Austin, then owned by his friend George Brown, and transported them by bus to the Ranch by day.

Lyndon was in high spirits, and the weather was good, and one day he packed as many reporters as he could fit into his Lincoln Continental, the rest following in similar conveyances, and toured the Ranch and its environs at an exuberant ninety miles an hour. He had a paper cup of beer on the dashboard which he sipped at intervals, and when a woman reporter commented from the back seat on the possibly excessive speed, he placed his Stetson over the speedometer. The incident was much reported by those same press, with suitable concern expressed for the president's safety and remarks about how little actually did stand between the presidency and Speaker of the House John McCormack. The whole event would probably have received less play had it not been at such variance with the sober, ever reliable captain-at-the-helm image that Lyndon had been projecting since November.

Johnson was furious. Those reporters had been his *guests*, he insisted, and how could they have accepted his hospitality and then turned against him? It seemed not to occur to him that they had jobs to do and were not exactly in Texas by choice.

J. Russell Wiggins: "I've always thought that the president made a mistake in his opening days by trying to deal with the reporters as friends and colleagues. He thought that they could be his collaborators, not in a narrow selfish way, but for the good of the country, if he took them into his confidence and told them everything they asked him.

"Eisenhower had held the press at arm's length. He never went below his dignity. He had a sense of mystique, a reserve. Now the other technique which Johnson undertook to copy was Roosevelt's—the incredible technique of being open and communicative. Roosevelt had a certain razzle-dazzle with the press and got away with it. But Johnson arrived on the scene when the press was infinitely more sophisticated, cynical, and suspicious than it was in Roosevelt's day."

Marianne Means: "Johnson had his first press conference, and it was the usual nervous kind of a hullabaloo. By his second press conference he was really a very changed man. You could tell the difference between his first press conference with the nervous laughter and the jokes written out in advance and the second when he did pretty well.

"So I wrote a comparison between the first and the second press conference saying how much better he was. He was in command; you know, he seemed more like a president. So the next time I see him, what does he say? 'You didn't like my first press conference? What was wrong with it?'"

George E. Reedy: "The first six months he was in the White House he had the press eating out of his hand. But he kicked that away himself. He'd get mad at them for some reason, and they couldn't understand it.

"Everything was overdeveloped in Johnson. He simply could not understand why it was he could buy a reporter a drink and take him out to the Ranch, show him a good time, and that reporter would write a story he didn't like. Again, I think that's because Johnson had so little respect for the integrity of words. I think he thought words were just something you used as weapons.

"He himself really didn't know what a good story was. He thought a good story was something that began, 'Lyndon Baines Johnson is a calm, collected statesman who is the finest representative of the American dream.'"

As Lyndon's interim presidency neared its halfway mark and the elections loomed ahead, he became progressively concerned with finding his own hallmark, some phrase that would encompass his aims the way Roosevelt's New Deal, Truman's Fair Deal, and Kennedy's New Frontier had encompassed theirs. Some phrase that would catch on with the press, with the people, with the historians.

One afternoon in March he invited Bill Moyers and Dick Goodwin, among others, to join him in the White House swimming pool, and in the course of the general conversation—there was always more talking than swimming—he told his companions that now that the Kennedy legacy was safely disposed of, the tax bill and the civil rights bill, he was anxious to let the people know where he, Lyndon, intended to go from here. So would they please think about how and when and where he might best do that.

Moyers suggested that Goodwin might try to formulate just such a speech as the president was looking for, possibly to be used at the first presentation of the Eleanor Roosevelt Memorial Award, which Lyndon was to make on March 4 to Anna M. Kross, a New York judge.

It is generally agreed that the term Great Society as a Johnson label was conceived that night when Goodwin sat down at his typewriter to hammer out the memorial speech. Although that speech was discarded for a more female-oriented one, Lyndon remembered what he had read, and he suggested finding another occasion on the calendar for its use.

The event selected was the commencement address at the University of Michigan scheduled for May 22 at Ann Arbor.

Jack Valenti: "Goodwin redrafted the Eleanor Roosevelt speech, a jewel of a speech.[2] The president was pleased with it; he felt that it told in clear and sometimes ringing tones what he felt was the direction he wanted to take this country."

The university said afterward that the May 22, 1964, commencement was the world's largest. At least eighty thousand people were there; the black-robed faculty and administration on the special platform from which the president spoke, the new graduates—4,943 of them alone—on rows of chairs set up in the middle of the field, the fond parents, etc., filling the stadium seats. The day was sunny and hot.

Lyndon spoke for only twenty minutes, although even that was twice as long as had been originally suggested. There were few platitudes. He spoke of the "challenge of the next half century," and looking directly toward the new graduates, he said:

"Your imagination, your initiative, and your indignation will determine whether we build a society where progress is the servant of our needs, or a society where old values and new visions are buried under unbridled growth. For in your time we have the opportunity to move not only toward the rich society and the powerful society, but upward to the Great Society."

He went on to describe the goals of the Great Society. He promised "to assemble the best thought and the broadest knowledge from all over the world to find those answers for America." And he challenged the new graduates to "join in the battle to build the Great Society.

"There are," he warned, "those timid souls who say this battle cannot be won, that we are condemned to a soulless wealth." But he refused to concede that. And he closed, "So let us from this moment begin our work so that in the future men will look back and say: It was then, after a long and weary way, that man turned the exploits of his genius to the full enrichment of his life."

Charles Roberts: "The day I rode back from Ann Arbor to Washington in his plane— that was what I would call the president in his manic phase. I don't use that term critically. I just mean he was absolutely euphoric.

"He was popular then. Dick Goodwin had written him a hell of a speech, and he delivered it well. The crowd seemed to get the idea that he was laying out a new program, that this was the new Johnson program now coming on.

"When we got back on the plane, he was sweating and exuberant. He violated his old rule and had himself a drink, a Scotch highball, and came back to our press pool. Merriam Smith of UPI and Frank Cormier of the AP were the other poolers.

"Johnson asked, 'Well, what did you think of it?' I said, 'Well, you got a hell of a reception. There were twenty-seven interruptions for applause.' He said, 'No, no, there were twenty-nine.' I said, 'Well, I counted twenty-seven, Mr. President, but . . .' He said, 'Now wait a minute, there were twenty-nine. Jack . . .' And he called Valenti, and Valenti came up and he had a script just as reporters do on a speech like that. It turned out that Jack had marked the applause when he was introduced and the applause when he finished, which gave the difference.

"Then he took the script from Jack Valenti and read, with emphasis, portions of the speech to us. He wanted to make sure we got the story. He'd say, 'Now did you get this?' and 'Back here I said this and that.'

"That was the unveiling of the Great Society, his own program, the program he was going to run on the next fall.

"He was a compulsive talker mostly when he was in this buoyant, euphoric mood after giving a speech or when things were going right for him. And of course during all that great first year that he was so euphoric, the Vietnam thing was still just a cloud no bigger than a man's hand."

THE INHERITANCE

In the beginning and, indeed, for a long time thereafter, everybody except for a few long-haired malcontents supported our involvement in Vietnam. It was said that Franklin Roosevelt, had he lived, would not have, and it is true that Roosevelt was against colonialism—rhetorically, at least. It is also true that he had several times argued with Churchill about colonialism. Its time, he said, was over. The colonies should voluntarily be freed; otherwise they would fight for their freedom, and they would win.

At Yalta when he met separately with Stalin, Roosevelt told him that he was in favor of a UN trusteeship over both Korea and Indochina—which, if it had happened, might have prevented two disastrous wars. Might have, assuming that Roosevelt did not change his mind; he often changed his mind, and before his death was already speaking of his suspicions of the Communists and of Stalin in particular.

In any case, the French who had occupied Indochina from 1880 until the Japanese took over during World War II had other ideas. In 1945 they returned to Southeast Asia and so, although it was not widely noted at the time, did a slight, bearded Communist leader named Ho Chi Minh.

That year Ho wrote a declaration of independence for his country which said, among other things, "All men are created equal. They are endowed by their creator with certain inalienable rights, among them life, liberty, and the pursuit of happiness." In Vietnamese, of course. With the big war over, Ho even hoped that the United States would help him in a small war to oust the French.

Instead, American aid went to the French, almost half a billion dollars a year. That number increased greatly when Eisenhower became president and John Foster Dulles secretary of state. Despite considerable diplomatic camouflage, Dulles' subsequent invention, the Southeast Asia Treaty Organization (SEATO), was intended to aid economically and militarily the new state of South Vietnam, which had its headquarters in Saigon and was presided over by Ngo Dinh Diem.

After the fifty-six-day battle of Dienbienphu, which they lost, the French withdrew; the war had become as unpopular in France as it was later to become in the United States. But in the beginning our military and economic aid to Diem was widely applauded by every red-blooded American and by most northeastern elitist blue bloods as well. The only criticism came from those who felt that not enough was being done.

The day before his inauguration John F. Kennedy sat in the Cabinet Room with retiring President Eisenhower and Eisenhower's chief advisers.

Lyndon: "The last thing President Eisenhower told President Kennedy before he went out of office was this: 'During all of this election period our problems have accumulated in Laos and Southeast Asia. You are going to have to move with men there. I would have already moved with men except for the fact I don't want to bind you.'

"He also said, 'If Vietnam should become Communist, the free world would have lost some twelve million souls, and then the spread of communism throughout that part of the world would be almost inevitable.'"[1]

In other words, to use the jargon of the day: "the domino theory."

In a television interview with David Brinkley and Chet Huntley on September 9, 1963, President Kennedy was asked whether he had any reason to doubt the "domino theory."

John F. Kennedy: "No, I believe it. I believe it. I think that the struggle is close enough. China is so large, looms so high just beyond the frontiers, that if South Vietnam went, it would not only give them an improved geographic position for a guerrilla assault on Malaya but would also give the impression that the wave of the future in Southeast Asia was China and the Communists. So, I believe it."

Robert F. Kennedy: "The president [Kennedy] felt that the strong, overwhelming reason for being in Vietnam was that we should win the war in Vietnam or face the loss of all of Southeast Asia. It was quite clear that the rest of Southeast Asia would fall. Also, it would affect what happened in India, of course, which in turn has an effect on the Middle East.

"Everybody, including General MacArthur, felt that land conflicts between our troops, white troops, and Asians, would only lead to—would end in disaster. So we went in as advisers and tried to get the Vietnamese to fight themselves.

"The president was convinced that we had to stay in there and couldn't lose it. We were winning in 1962 and 1963—up until May or so of 1963. The situation was getting progressively better and then we had all the problems with the Buddhists, and Diem wouldn't make even the slightest concessions.[2] So the situation began to deteriorate in the spring of 1963.

". . . What was of great concern to all of us during this period of time—nobody liked

Diem particularly, but how to get rid of him and not split the country in two and therefore lose not only the war but the country. That was the great problem."[3]

Roger Hilsman: "I went out to Vietnam and, after having talked with R.K. Thompson,[4] came back convinced that it could be won but not by conventional military means. It had to be done by adopting the tactics of the guerrilla, by arming the villagers, by the strategic hamlet-type program.

"I talked to President Kennedy at great length about this. Kennedy said, 'I want you to go around and see Bobby and several other people and give them this briefing.' And he named the vice-president. So I set up an appointment to give him a full briefing on this whole new concept.

"I arrived at his office, and there was a political crisis going on in Texas. He was all tensed up; the telephone would ring every two minutes; he'd jump up and call a secretary. It was just a total flop. I think right there if it had worked out so that I could have had an hour with him he would have understood better the nature of the problem when he did become president."

Michael Forrestal: "Between May and the middle of July [1963], a series of things had begun happening in South Vietnam which caused a number of the so-called experts to get extremely worried about the capability—or the survivability—of President Diem.

"It was at that time that Johnson began to get nervous. He wanted to know, first of all, why the press was behaving in such a nonsensical way. He wanted to know why some civilians, both in the State Department and in the AID agency were beginning to look as though they were no longer supporting our policy in Vietnam, and what was their problem. He was anxious to know whether we had thought through what was going to happen if Diem did collapse. One of the statements he made in a larger meeting—it was very rare for him to say anything—he sort of wondered out loud: 'Shouldn't one be more frightened of the devil one doesn't know than the devil one does know?'

"In May just before the Buddhist problems in Hué, we were at what everybody thought was the high point, the high-water mark, of our success in Vietnam. All the statistics looked good, we were supposed to control more of the countryside, and so forth. When the Diem business started the worst that we contemplated happening was that there would be a terrible vacuum, a political vacuum. We thought, well, maybe he'll just abdicate and go away, and somebody else is going to have to be discovered to take over. It was obviously going to have to be a general, because they were the only ones that have the power over there. And the nervousness was that running that government by a committee of generals looked poor from a political point of view."

Roger Hilsman: "In the struggle over the whole Buddhist crisis with the military and the National Security Council—everybody was split. The CIA split down the middle, and the military wanted to go on with Diem. Vice-President Johnson had met Diem and liked him. I knew Diem and liked him, too. But being, by this time, assistant secretary and being very intimately concerned with the political side of the question, I went along with Averell Harriman and Dean Rusk and others in the State Department who became increasingly convinced that we couldn't sit still. We had to say something—had to do something."

*　　*　　*

Robert F. Kennedy: "Lyndon Johnson was against—strongly against—the coup. And so he was bitter about it.

"President Kennedy—he'd like to have gotten rid of Diem if he could get rid of him and get somebody proper to replace him. And he was against getting rid of him until you knew what was going to come along and whether the government that was going to replace it had any stability and, in fact, would be a successful coup. But he didn't know—I mean, other than the fact that there were rumors about coups all the time, he had no idea that this particular coup was going to take place."

On November 1, 1963, Diem and his unpopular brother, Nhu, were assassinated, ostensibly by officers, possibly some enlisted men of the South Vietnamese Army. Madame Nhu was spared, and she naturally and, as was not often the case with her, accurately said, "No one can seriously believe in the disclaimer that the Americans had nothing to do with the present situation in Vietnam." It was her belief her husband and brother-in-law were treacherously killed with either the official or unofficial blessing of the American government.

But even without Diem and Nhu, things didn't seem to get much better. By the fall of 1963 the United States was spending $3 billion a year—about $1.5 million a day—to support whatever government there would be in South Vietnam. On October 2 President Kennedy told the press that he and the National Security Council agreed that "the United States military task in Vietnam can be completed by the end of 1965."

It has now become part of the myth of Camelot that John F. Kennedy intended to withdraw from Vietnam after he had won the 1964 election. That myth was launched in an article in *Life* magazine by the president's longtime friend and White House associate Kenneth O'Donnell, who claimed that Kennedy had definitely told him so, and Senator Mike Mansfield had a similar recollection, dating from a conversation with the president early in 1963.

Dean Rusk: "Kennedy never said anything like that to me, and we discussed Vietnam—oh, I'd say hundreds of times. He never said it, never suggested it, never hinted at it, and I simply do not believe it."

In an interview with Michael Charlton, Rusk elaborated further:

If he had decided in 1962 or 1963 that he would take the troops out after the election of 1964 sometime during 1965, then that would have been a suggestion that he would leave Americans in uniform in a combat situation for domestic political purposes, and no president can do that. Now, President Kennedy was a man who liked to chew the fat and gossip with people and explore ideas; and I am not suggesting at all that Senator Mansfield was untruthful. But I am just saying that the president of the United States, in my judgment, did not reach any such conclusion, in 1962 or 1963.[5]

In the same Huntley–Brinkley television interview, Kennedy said: "What I am concerned about is that Americans will get impatient and say, because they don't like events in Southeast Asia or they don't like the government in Saigon, that we should withdraw. That only makes it easy for the Communists. I think we should stay."

George W. Ball: "By the time Kennedy was killed we had 16,500 men in Vietnam and there were two or three thousand more prepared to move. I think you can safely say that escalation was proceeding fairly rapidly before Johnson took office."

Erv S. Duggan: "Vietnam was very much Kennedy's war. The internal logic of Vietnam had already been set in motion. The momentum was already going before Kennedy was killed and liberals didn't really hold that against him."

Lyndon: "When I took over I believed that the president's policy was clear—namely, that we had a great interest in that area of the world; that we had soberly concluded that although it involved a great chance, we should inform any would-be aggressors that if, in the face of common danger, when parties to the Southeast Asia Treaty asked for help, when they found themselves confronted with invasion or aggression or threats to their security, that we would come to their assistance. I think President Kennedy felt very strongly that we should not permit Southeast Asia to fall into the hands of the Communists."

Max Frankel: "Johnson was very conscious of carrying on and continuity, especially before his own election. But even after that, there's a theory that much of his unconscious calculation about Vietnam had to do with the fact that 'This is something that Kennedy started.' And it was somehow incumbent on him not to let go.

"He was trying to live up to something. The fact that Kennedy had set a certain course and made certain commitments and, more important, that the Kennedy men around, whom he respected, would give him this kind of advice made it much harder for Johnson to disregard than otherwise."

Clark Clifford: "He inherited his senior advisers from President Kennedy. He had Secretary of State Rusk, and he had Secretary of Defense McNamara; he had General Maxwell Taylor, who was a separate consultant and adviser; he had the Joint Chiefs of Staff, who remained substantially the same.

"When President Johnson inherited them, these senior advisers to President Kennedy all felt that we were headed correctly in Vietnam."

TONKIN

August 2, 1964, was a sunny, relaxing Sunday in most parts of the country, relaxing until early afternoon, at least, when it was announced that an American destroyer in "international waters" almost nobody had ever heard of, the Tonkin Gulf or Bay, had been fired on by three torpedo boats. The destroyer, the U.S.S. *Maddox*, had been on a "routine patrol"; the attack was totally "unprovoked."

At first the identity of the attackers was said to be unknown. What was known, it was said, was that two of the torpedo boats, while damaged, had managed to escape. A third was said to be lying inert in "international waters," although its personnel appeared to be unharmed. Oddly enough, no prisoners had been taken to be questioned about this mysterious attack.

The enemy, whoever he was, was said to have fired several missiles at the *Maddox*, any one of which could, on contact, have sunk the destroyer. The enemy had also fired 37-mm shells, but apparently none struck the lucky ship, which went jauntily on its way in what was said to be a "southerly direction," though later there was doubt about that as well. Finally it was revealed that the attack had been twenty miles from North Vietnam and, sure enough, the attackers were North Vietnamese, representing what was surely one of the smallest navies in the world, attacking what was undeniably the largest. There were several theories as to the reasons behind such derring-do; but sheer insanity seemed to be the only sensible explanation.

The "Tonkin incident," as it was soon to be called, nevertheless raised some problems for the president, who was about to run as the "peace candidate," and who was already under attack by many Republicans, including Barry Goldwater, as being "soft on Vietnam." Goldwater almost immediately issued a press release saying, "We cannot allow the American flag to be shot at anywhere on earth if we are to retain our respect and prestige." Could any American disagree with that?

Lyndon the next morning chewed out his admirals. He is reported by ear witnesses to have shouted, "The whole goddamn navy is out there, all those ships and planes, and you can't even sink three little PT boats."

Well, of course not the whole navy, not even a sizable part of it, was in the Tonkin Gulf at the time, but it did turn out that the aircraft carrier *Ticonderoga*, which by good fortune was not far off, was able to dispatch four jet planes which fired on the torpedo boats with rocket missiles and cannon fire. That was when the two allegedly crippled PT boats escaped.

Why the hell were they not pursued? Lyndon wanted to know. The admirals explained to the president that under naval peacetime rules naval forces could shoot back if attacked but could not pursue the attackers.[1]

Okay. A little later that morning Lyndon issued a statement:

I have instructed the navy

(1) to continue the patrols in the Gulf of Tonkin off the coast of North Vietnam;

(2) to double the force by adding an additional destroyer to the one already on patrol;

(3) to provide a combat air patrol over the destroyers; and

(4) to issue orders to the commanders of the combat aircraft and the two destroyers (a) to attack any force which attacks them in international waters, and (b) to attack with the objective not only of driving off the force but of destroying it.

Quite a strong statement for a "peace" candidate for the presidency, but the nation was behind him, including most of its press.

*   *   *

What had happened on Sunday, though, was only the beginning. As more official releases revealed, there was considerable confusion about the time the attack had taken place. Then it appeared that shortly after the attack, the *Maddox* had met another destroyer, the *C. Turner Joy*, and the two of them had begun patrolling together.

On August 4, Tuesday, it was reported in the morning newspapers that the carrier *Constellation* had very suddenly left Hong Kong, so suddenly that many members of its crew had to be summarily plucked from various bars and, regrettably, houses of ill-repute. The *Constellation*, a so-called supercarrier, was already on its way to Tonkin. Nevertheless, that very day the North Vietnamese attacked the two destroyers *and* the *Ticonderoga*, with not only gunfire but torpedoes as well.

So the official releases revealed.

At lunch that day, Tuesday—it was the first of the Tuesday lunches[2]—McNamara, Rusk, and McGeorge Bundy, White House assistant for national security affairs, discussed the affair with Lyndon. Later, other experts joined in the deliberations, and it was decided that North Vietnamese naval bases would be attacked from the air—bombed, that is, the first bombing of the still non-war.

The National Security Council concurred, and when Lyndon called in sixteen congressional leaders from both parties, they did, too. There was, indeed, little to discuss. The president reminded the lawmakers that there would have to be something written down, a resolution of some sort passed by both houses of Congress to back up their commander in chief. He was assured that such a resolution would have no problems in Congress, none at all.

J. William Fulbright: "We had one meeting with Lyndon as I recall, before the resolution arrived at the Senate. McNamara and Rusk were there, and I think Wheeler came, too. I do not think they were very candid, not only about what just had or had not happened, but about what was on their minds for the future.

"I agreed to lead the debate—fight is hardly the word—for the resolution in the Senate. Not being a professional psychiatrist, all I can say is that I was deceived. The greatest mistake I made in my life was to accept Lyndon's account of what happened and those of his men."

Robert Hardesty: "We were talking once about the Gulf of Tonkin resolution and Johnson said, 'Fulbright said later that he didn't know what he was voting on.' And Johnson said, 'To think that a Rhodes scholar couldn't understand what was in that resolution is more than this hillbilly can understand.'"

On the night of August 4, at 11:36 P.M., Lyndon went on television to tell the people what was said to be going on.

"Repeated acts of violence against the armed forces of the United States must be met not only with alert defense, but with positive reply," he said. "That action is now in execution against gunboats and certain supporting facilities in North Vietnam which have been used in these hostile operations. . . .

"The determination of all to carry out our full commitment to the people and to the government of South Vietnam will be redoubled by this outrage. Yet our response, for the present, will be limited and fitting."

The president added that the congressmen he had met with agreed that it was necessary to have a resolution "making it clear that our government is united in its determination to take all necessary measures in support of freedom and in defense of peace in Southeast Asia.

"I have been given encouraging assurance by the leaders of both parties that such a resolution will be promptly introduced, freely and expeditiously debated, and passed with overwhelming support. And just a few minutes ago I was able to reach Senator Goldwater, and I am glad to say that he has expressed his support of the statement."

For once both the potential "peace candidate" and the senator who was called "the Air Force candidate" were agreed. Seldom had the nation been so united.

To be sure, a few foreign newspapers, including the Manchester *Guardian*, found it a kind of miracle that reaction had been so swift. The *Guardian* said, "Many people—not only Communists—will be tempted to suspect that the U.S. air attacks, and the great movement now proceeding of military power in Southeast Asia, had long been planned and required only a suitable occasion—easily manufactured—to set them off."

The next morning, Wednesday, in some American papers, if you could find it, was a statement from Hanoi saying that on the previous sunny Sunday, there was no mention of just when, North Vietnamese patrol craft "took action" and chased the *Maddox* out of its territorial waters. But as for the Tuesday battle, Hanoi said, that was "sheer fabrication" on the part of the Americans. No such battle had taken place. But few paid much attention to that disavowal—"nonsense," everyone, even the Russians, said. The Chinese supported Hanoi. Naturally.

The very next morning, Thursday, August 6, the intricate resolution was ready. It said, among other things, "The United States is . . . prepared, as the president determines, to take all necessary steps, including the use of armed force, to assist any member or protocol state of the Southeast Asia Collective Defense Treaty requesting assistance in defense of its freedom."

It also said, ". . . The Congress approves and supports the determination of the president, as commander in chief, to take all necessary measures to repel any armed attack against the forces of the United States and to prevent further aggression."

Senator Wayne Morse of Oregon, a former dean of the law school at the University of Oregon, pointed out that the resolution granted the power to declare war to the president, while the Constitution clearly granted that power to Congress, but nobody, including most newspapers, paid much attention to Morse, a well-known sorehead and malcontent, a Republican turned Democrat. He was joined in his protest by the first U.S. senator elected from Alaska, Ernest Gruening. But Gruening was old and, some now said, senile.

Happily, sounder minds in the Senate prevailed, and the bill that Lyndon was later to describe as being "like grandma's nightgown; it covered everything," passed the Senate with a minimum of discussion. Debate seems hardly the word, two votes against, an overwhelming ninety-eight in favor.

The House took forty minutes to decide 416 to 0 that the resolution was in the best interests of the nation and the commander in chief. Lyndon was a very secure president that night.

Erv S. Duggan: "Johnson said that the reason he got the Gulf of Tonkin Resolution was that he remembered how passionate Eisenhower was about not making a move without the full cooperation of the Congress, not doing anything that he could get in trouble with Congress about. And Johnson thought that was extremely shrewd of Eisenhower politically. And the reason he was so careful to get a piece of paper in his pocket on the Tonkin Gulf was that he was following Eisenhower's example."

Hubert H. Humphrey: "Some senators said later that they had been taken in, didn't understand. I asked at the time whether the resolution meant that we could end up with American men on the field of battle, whether it committed us to American armed intervention. Senator Fulbright, who handled the resolution on the floor, said, 'Yes.' There was no ambiguity, no question about what we were voting on."[3]

General Earle G. Wheeler:[4] "As far as I was concerned, there was no doubt as to what the commitment was, what we should do on the military side to carry out what seemed to be an authorization. It was probably constitutionally unnecessary, but what was actually passed by the Congress put the executive branch and the congressional branch in the same bed. As I say, there was no confusion in my mind. There seemed to be a confusion in a lot of other people's minds but not mine. Maybe I'm too simple.

"We had a couple of destroyers that were in international waters. They had been doing this for some time, going up the coast of North Vietnam but out in the waters. In fact, we even avoided going in closer than about thirteen miles. They claimed twelve miles as their territorial waters.

"Now I'm not trying to mislead you. These ships were equipped with electronic equipment so that we could keep an eye on the air order of battle and so on in North Vietnam, and also to pick up other interesting tidbits of information. I don't regard this as a provocation, unless you want to take it as a provocation that a Soviet intelligence collector sits right off the port of Charleston all the time. They have another that sits right off the runway in Guam, I've seen it myself. Now, is that a provocation, or isn't it?

"The president was understandably upset and I think angry that our vessel had been attacked on the high seas. This was by international law an act of war, and he wanted us to examine very carefully what our response should be. We agreed that we should undertake a retaliatory action, which we did."

Ernest Gruening: "The Tonkin Gulf Resolution was a deliberate fraud, as you know. None of us knew it at the time. Johnson had in his possession early in the afternoon of August 4 the telegram from Captain Herrick of the *Maddox*, which said in effect, 'Hold it—the earlier reports may be due to freak weather conditions and overeager sonar men. No visual sightings by the *Maddox*.' In other words, 'We've seen no torpedoes; we've seen no PT boats; suggest complete evaluation before action.'

"Johnson could have said to himself, 'Well, now, wait a minute. I've got to show this to the senators.' But he suppressed it. He was determined to find a pretext to go in. If that telegram hadn't been suppressed the Congress would never have voted the Tonkin Gulf Resolution."

Robert McNamara: "Well, obviously, we were concerned, and we immediately began to examine it [the telegram], and I have here a whole series of steps we took at that point as to what was done. I personally called Admiral Sharp and brought this to his attention, and said we obviously do not want to carry out retaliatory action unless we are 'damned sure what happened.' . . .⁵

"We discussed it and he [Admiral Sharp] stated that he was fully assured that the attack took place. I stated that I was then convinced it had, and I released the executive order on the strike."⁶

Later it was revealed that William P. Bundy, assistant secretary of state for Far Eastern Affairs, was in the process of writing a similar resolution before the incidents in the Tonkin Gulf had actually occurred. In his testimony before the Foreign Relations Committee in September of 1966, he explained this procedure was quite normal . . . simply a contingency plan just in case things took a turn for the worse.

McGeorge Bundy: "Johnson was worried about the unknown. He knew how many unknowns there were; he knew how complicated and uncertain life was. He knew that the way to avoid failure was to put yourself on guard against it, and he was, in that sense, the wariest man about whom to trust that I have ever encountered.

"On the other hand, he lived in a terribly short time frame; he lived in the belief that the legislative process was *the* decision. It may be a terrible exaggeration to say this, but when he got the Gulf of Tonkin Resolution, he thought he'd won the war. Because the world of real decision was the world of Congress and Congress was with him 514 to 2."

It was now Lyndon's war, all the way.

TO RUN OR NOT TO RUN

Before the events of Tonkin Gulf, in fact way back in the spring, Lyndon had started planning the 1964 Democratic campaign. Of course there was little doubt then as to the identity of the presidential candidate. That, astonishingly enough, was to come later. But the subject of Lyndon's running mate caused no end of debate, much of it stirred by Lyndon himself.

James H. Rowe, Jr.: "I sat in on a meeting of politicians months before the '64 convention. He went around the room and all of us were Catholics except Bill Moyers. Johnson said, 'Who should it be, Humphrey or McCarthy?' I said, 'Mr. President, you don't have to ask me. You know where I stand. So go ahead.' He went around the room and everybody voted for Senator Humphrey except for Walter Jenkins, who voted for McCarthy. John Connally, who wasn't in the room, was for McCarthy, too.

"They had two theories. One, since Jack Kennedy is gone, he probably ought to have a Catholic. Then the Kennedy people couldn't talk. The other thing, they were worried about Hubert and his big red flag of civil rights. McCarthy had all the virtues of Hubert and none of the handicaps."

Eugene McCarthy, the senator from Minnesota who was not Hubert Humphrey, was an acerbic man, an occasional poet, who had a roguish sense of humor and a negligible record as a senator.

Bill Moyers: "I thought maybe Shriver had a chance, and I talked to Lyndon Johnson about it. He weighed Shriver very carefully. He was of the Kennedys, but he was not a Kennedy. He was a Catholic and a northeasterner from a blue-blooded Maryland family, who had lived in Chicago. He was a businessman with business contacts. There were many things about him that Lyndon Johnson thought were politically valuable.

"But in another way Shriver was not acceptable, and that was *because* he was a member of the family. The message that filtered through from the family was that if you are going to take a Kennedy, it's got to be a *real* Kennedy, which Shriver isn't."

Marianne Means: "I don't think Gene McCarthy was ever under serious consideration as the vice-presidential nominee. I think Johnson may have got carried away in a conversation with McCarthy, and it may have pleased him to snow a man like McCarthy who's always snowing everybody else. But I think Johnson *always* knew the vice-presidential candidate would be the other senator from Minnesota."

Hubert H. Humphrey: "I had the feeling most of that summer that I would most likely make it. But I also knew that Johnson was a very pragmatic man and that if it looked to him like I couldn't be of any help to him or might be a hindrance to him or a load to carry, I don't think he'd have hesitated a minute to have said, 'Good-bye, Hubert.' Not that he wouldn't have liked me and so on—just as he liked Gene McCarthy.

"I remember one time a story was in the *Washington Post*, something to the effect that Mike Mansfield was being considered.

"And when I came over to the White House to one of those breakfasts we used to have when I was majority whip, I said, 'How about this Mike Mansfield talk?' And he said, 'Oh, hell, Hubert, you know you've got to keep up interest. I just like to throw a few pieces out there to the press and let them think about it a little bit.' But he said, 'Mike wouldn't even take it. I don't think he'd take it if you offered it to him.'"

And then there was Bobby.

Clark Clifford: "We were alone in the President's office and it was, I think, the first time he and I discussed how he would face up to the recurring suggestion that Bobby Kennedy should be in the second place on the ticket. I might say that I thought the suggestion had no merit at all. I thought that if by any chance it were to result in that, it would be a complete shambles.

"They were very unlike. I doubt that under the best of circumstances they could ever have developed much of a friendship. But also Bobby Kennedy seemed at the beginning very much to resent President Johnson. It was a curious attitude, completely illogical, wholly emotional. It seemed to irritate Bobby Kennedy when he saw President Johnson as president.

"My own private opinion is that the Kennedy family considered President Johnson an interloper. President John F. Kennedy had been elected to the spot; they saw themselves in a position they liked a great deal for a full eight years, by which time some other member of the family would be ready to receive the mantle as it was passed on, so they just had stars in their eyes about the future and they loved the light and all that went with it. And suddenly their hopes were all dashed and they looked upon President Johnson as a usurper of the job that really belonged to them."

Charles Bartlett: "Lyndon Johnson was convinced that there was a great conspiracy to try to steal the government back for the Kennedys. And on the other hand, I think that Bobby was absolutely convinced that Lyndon Johnson was out to destroy him in public life. So once you had these two convictions, there was really no way to bridge it.

"I had a feeling that J. Edgar Hoover played a large role. J. Edgar, who hated Bobby, was doing what he could to be sure that the president was convinced that there was a Kennedy conspiracy."

George E. Reedy: "Robert Kennedy was very strongly imbued with this concept of the family; he really regarded the family in the old Irish clan sense. 'The family' had captured the White House. And there was only one other man on the American scene that really represented in his mind any possibility, let alone threat, of taking this control away from the family. I believe that he definitely regarded Lyndon Johnson as a threat to the Kennedy dynasty or clan or whatever you want to call it."

Bobby meanwhile had been giving the vice-presidency a good deal of thought.

Charles Spalding: "The vice-presidency was one of the things that General Mac-Arthur, among other people, told him he must do. MacArthur was cheered by the notion that Mr. Johnson wasn't particularly well and said, 'Go and do it.' He thought that Mr. Johnson wasn't going to be able to serve out his term. I think probably what desisted Bobby really was that the considerations were so macabre. I mean to sit and figure out whether Johnson was going to live or not—on top of everything else, that was just too morbid.

"As opposed to that thought, I don't think that Bobby was so perfect that he didn't enjoy nettling Johnson a bit. The idea of Johnson and Bobby on the same ticket, in those sick days, was almost too much—you couldn't help but consider that with a certain amount of relish, I'm sure, if you were Bobby. It gave him a chance to turn the clock the other way.

"So I suppose he gave it a lot of consideration back and forth: first on a practical basis, and then, second, on as I say a somewhat ironical basis."

Lawrence F. O'Brien: "It was late July; I forget the exact date,[1] but Bob came to my office in the White House before he went to see the president. We had a pretty good idea of what was going to happen. He wanted the vice-presidential nomination, but we both realized there wasn't much chance that he'd get Johnson's support. Johnson didn't need him, and he didn't want him.

"So it was very simple. Bob saw the president, and Johnson told him that he was not going to pick anybody in his cabinet as the vice-presidential nominee."[2]

Lyndon's account of the meeting with Bobby was told many times to many people, with increasing detail and, unfortunately, decreasing discretion.

Edward T. Folliard: "I had lunch at the White House a few days after Bobby was dropped, on July 31. Jack Valenti was there; George Reedy was there. Doug Kiker, who was then with the *New York Herald Tribune*, was there, and Tom Wicker of the *Times*.

"Johnson said, 'When I got him in the Oval Office and told him it would be "inadvisable" for him to be on the ticket as the vice-presidential nominee, his face changed, and he started to swallow. He looked sick. His adam's apple bounded up and down like a yo-yo.'

"Johnson went on to say that Adlai Stevenson was the most qualified to be vice-president but that Stevenson would be seventy-two after Johnson had served another eight years. Later, of course, he claimed he'd *never* planned to serve two terms, but that certainly wasn't the case that day. He was in it for two full terms.

"He mentioned Humphrey and McCarthy and Mike Mansfield as possible vice-presidential candidates but said that Mansfield didn't want it.

"After running through a long list of names, LBJ told us that the polls and reports indicated that everyone he had mentioned would hurt him in some way. In other words, he would do better in the November election if he had no running mate. This left Wicker, Kiker, and me baffled—and that is just what the man evidently wanted us to be."

O'Brien: "It was quite a game while it lasted, and Johnson played it for all it was worth. Everybody thought the nominee was going to be Humphrey, but Johnson kept pretending he hadn't made up his mind. Humphrey kept coming to me to ask if I'd heard anything. He was very nervous. He kept wanting to know if he was still in it."

Walter Jenkins: "Of course, he was playing games with the vice-presidential nomination. I think he felt very strongly that we didn't have the greatest suspense for the TV audience that a convention ever had. He knew you had to have some suspense."

The 1964 Republican convention at the Cow Palace in San Francisco did not add luster to the party or to the Republic. The well-dressed delegates stamped their feet, hissed, booed, and spit when Nelson Rockefeller tried to speak to them. Then on the first ballot they nominated the man who was sure to lose, Senator Barry Goldwater, the silver-haired senator from Arizona.

Goldwater, who had already hired three Arizona friends with little political experience to manage his campaign, refused to consult either Eisenhower or Nixon about his vice-presidential nominee. To balance his ticket geographically he chose an almost unknown congressman from upstate New York, one William E. Miller.

Barry's campaign slogan was "In your heart, you know he's right," but almost immediately some subversive made up a substitute slogan that swept the country, "In your guts you know he's nuts." While most people wouldn't go *quite* that far, even before the campaign began it was clear that voters didn't think the senator was a conservative at all; they thought he was some kind of radical—of the right.

Strangely, so strangely it is hard to conceive, Lyndon had started fretting even before Goldwater's nomination. Should he run or shouldn't he run? He couldn't make up his mind, so he told almost everyone within hearing distance, although it was clear that there was almost no way of his not winning the nomination, possibly by acclamation, and of winning the election by a great sweep. Clear too that a president who was already campaigning and who concerned himself and everybody around him with the troubling question of his running mate ought certainly have made up his mind as to his own candidacy.

Nevertheless (said Lyndon) he was a man of limited education, an accidental president, a man ridiculed not only by the Georgetown "jelly beans" but by intellectuals and self-styled intellectuals on every campus in the country and by some who simply lived near campuses or read publications like the *New Republic*. Liberals—in other words, "red hots"—"to them my name is shit and always has been and always will be. I got their goddamn legislation passed for them, but they gave me no credit."

How, he would ask, could a man with such handicaps *unite* the country?

Reedy: "The night before the convention he walked around with me on the White House grounds saying he was going to announce his withdrawal the next day."

Zephyr Wright: "I didn't think Mr. Johnson was going to run. When we first moved into the White House, he said, 'We're going to be here for the rest of this term and then we're coming out.' And he kept saying that even after they started this convention in Atlantic City. He was supposed to go to Atlantic City, and I saw all these people coming into the White House, and I saw Mr. Humphrey, and I thought, 'Oh, my Lord, he's getting ready to tell them he's not going to run.' That was just what came to my mind.

"The next thing I knew he was on his way to Atlantic City. See, with him you never could tell."

Abe Fortas: "He wasn't just playing games with his intimates. He was playing games with himself, too. That is to say he was constantly rearguing the question with himself, constantly saying to himself, 'This is not the right thing to do. Maybe I won't do it after all. Maybe something will happen; the convention won't really want me, and even if they do want me, I shouldn't have it, shouldn't do it.'"

Later Lyndon described his misgivings at length, how he'd kept his options open to the end, had not made any final decisions until the day after the convention opened when, still in Washington, he wrote out a statement on a yellow pad from his desk in the Oval Office. The statement began with a sentimental observation or two about leaving the majority leadership to help unify the country and about doing his best since the "fateful day" he had accepted the responsibilities of the presidency. The times, however, he wrote, required a man who could lead *everybody*, and he was not such a man, so he would only serve until the election and then "go back home as I've wanted to since the day I took this job." A few teary smudges on the yellow pad.

Then he picked up the phone and read the statement to George Reedy, who was properly horrified and told him he would be just handing the country to Goldwater, and did he really think that *Goldwater* was a man who could lead everybody? Walter Jenkins was also consulted. You're too late, Walter told him, needlessly, one would have thought. Three or four months ago, maybe. But the convention, Mr. Johnson, opened *yesterday*.

Lady Bird, who understood that he needed reassurance more than reasoning, sent him a wifely note praising his strength and patience, for which, she said, the country, or most of it, honored him. Yes, he was burdened, but presidents always have been, and she knew he was "as brave as any of the thirty-five."

> *Beloved—*
> You are as brave a man as Harry Truman—or FDR—or Lincoln. You can go on to find some peace, some achievement amidst all the pain. You have been strong, patient, determined beyond any words of mine to express. I honor you for it. So does most of the country.
> To step out now would be *wrong* for your country, and I can see nothing but a lonely wasteland for your future. Your friends would be frozen in embarrassed silence and your enemies jeering.
> I am not afraid of *Time*³ or lies or losing money or defeat.
> In the final analysis I can't carry any of the burdens you talked of—so I know it's only *your* choice. But I know you are as brave as any of the thirty-five.⁴
> I love you always.
>
> *Bird*

Lady Bird: "The reason I wrote a letter instead of telling him was I wanted to think it through myself, and I wanted to get it down in black and white. I thought if I started talking to him, he would probably interrupt me and outtalk me whatever way he wanted to. I just wanted to put it in front of him, sort of inescapable.

"I did have reason to think he didn't want to run previous to 1964. He was wrestling with that demon very hard. I think he always would have, in the end, gone along with the machine which was already rolling. He would turn away from it, I think, simply because he knew how hard it was going to be and that it was going to get worse.

"I can't describe his feelings or why, except I think he had an extraordinary feeling of reverence for the job of president and a good conception of just how hard it would be and how some of those lowering clouds that were on the horizon might rise up to storm proportions."

A LOVELY CAMPAIGN

On Wednesday night, August 26, Lyndon, who had just been nominated by John Connally, Governor Pat Brown of California, and numerous others, arrived in time to listen to the hysterical approval of the delegates and the galleries. He let the cheering go on for what some considered an unseemly time, then entered in triumph and made his way through the applauding, cheering thousands to the rostrum where he took the gavel from Speaker John McCormack, who was presiding, and silenced the multitudes before letting them in on the not particularly well kept secret that Hubert Humphrey was his choice for vice-president and would, he hoped, be the choice of the convention.

If you select him, you can proudly say to the American people, "This is not a sectional choice. This is not just merely the way to balance the ticket. This is simply the best man in America for this job."

After which the cheering, stamping, and applause began again; glory be, it looked as if the convention might follow the wishes of its leader, and Lyndon handed the gavel back to McCormack, returned to the floor and once again made his way through the tumultuous delegates, stopping to press considerable flesh, and then got on a plane and returned to Washington.

The Mississippi Freedom Democratic party consisted of sixty-eight delegates and alternates, including four white civil rights workers. They demanded to be seated as full delegates with all the rights thereof although they had no legal status; the compromise finally reached was, it was said, on a "moral" basis.

There was, of course, the regular Mississippi delegation, pure white with a single exception and chosen by a political machine headed by the governor of Mississippi. As a gubernatorial candidate, Paul B. Johnson, Jr. had made speeches saying that the NAACP stood for "niggers, alligators, apes, coons, and possums."

As Joseph L. Rauh, Jr., the lawyer who represented the Freedom party asked, "Are we going to seat a delegation sent by a man like that?"

Rauh: "When Johnson found out that I was representing the MFDP, he used every pressure he could think of on me. He used Walter Reuther, who was my client, and Hubert Humphrey, who was my friend and political hero. He wanted to get me away from what looked like trouble for him and for the convention. So first he'd have Hubert call me, trying to get me out, and then Walter would call. This was before the convention, and it got to be a joke around my office. The girls would answer the phone and say to me, 'It's the other one calling.'

"Hubert would say, 'Joe, the president is very concerned about this. I've got to tell him something.' And I'd say, 'Well, Hubert, why don't you tell him I'm just a sonofabitch that you can't handle.' And he'd say, 'I don't think that would go down very well.'

"Now Walter was the other. That was the muscle. But I think really the most hysterical of all of the phone calls was the day Walter said, 'I've been talking to the president and we have agreed that if you go through with this—with trying to seat these people—we're going to lose the election.' I said, 'Are you serious? I mean, Goldwater has been nominated. How can you lose it?' He said, 'We both think the backlash is so tremendous that we're going to lose the election if you go through with this. You can't possibly win, but if you should win, the pictures of all the black delegates going in to replace the white is going to add to the backlash, and we are convinced Goldwater will be president.'

"I said, 'If I thought Goldwater could be elected I don't know what I'd do, but that just isn't possible. So I don't have to answer that question. He hasn't got a chance, and you two ought to know it.'

"At the beginning the credentials committee offered us absolutely nothing—tickets for the Freedom Democrats to get into the convention, nothing else.

"The real compromise offer came on Tuesday when the credentials committee offered to unseat the white delegates from Mississippi who wouldn't take the loyalty oath; two of the Freedom delegates would be seated, with one full vote each; the other sixty-six would be invited to sit on the floor as 'honored guests,' and the convention would resolve that any state party that discriminated against blacks would be refused a seat at future conventions.

"It wasn't a bad offer. Eventually, we accepted it, largely because of the promise that it would never happen again. A promise that, by the way, was carried out in Chicago in 1968 when the full inheritors of the Mississippi Freedom party were seated and the others were ousted. So we got in '68 what we should have got in '64, but we got it. That was the important thing."

On August 27 Lyndon flew back to Atlantic City to accept the nomination; it was his fifty-sixth birthday, and the speech was one of the worst he ever made, which meant it was very bad indeed.

He dwelled largely on domestic matters, though without too many specifics. There was not a word anywhere about Vietnam, although the nominee said, "I report tonight as president of the United States and as commander in chief of the armed forces on the strength of your country and tell you it is greater than any adversary. I assure you that it is greater than the combined might of all the nations, in all the wars, in all the history of this planet. And I report our superiority is growing."

That paragraph brought down the house; that was the stuff you fed the troops as well as the civilians in those days, liberals, conservatives, everybody.

Also on the twenty-seventh, before the huge birthday party, tickets to which cost $1,000, Robert Kennedy received an ovation that lasted twenty-two minutes. Bobby introduced the film about his brother that brought tears to almost everyone's eyes. He ended with the quotation from *Romeo and Juliet* which, said Bobby, Jacqueline had given him:

> When he shall die
> Take him and cut him out in little stars
> And he will make the face of heav'n so fine
> That all the world will be in love with Night
> And pay no worship to the garish Sun.

That day, too, Hubert gave his acceptance speech, which most people liked better than Lyndon's:

> Most Democrats and many Republicans in the United States Senate . . . are for the nuclear test ban treaty—
> but not Senator Goldwater.
> Most Democrats and most Republicans in the United States Senate voted for an $11.5 billion tax cut for the American people—
> but not Senator Goldwater.

Most Democrats and most Republicans in the United States Senate, in fact over four-fifths of the members of his own party, voted for the Civil Rights Act of 1964—

but not Senator Goldwater.

During the last half of his speech five thousand voices chanted "but not Senator Goldwater" along with the vice-presidential nominee.

After that the president cut into his mammoth birthday cake and ate a huge slice in front of Lady Bird, the television cameras and the world, after which three tons of fireworks were launched. And Carol Channing sang "Hello, Lyndon"—for perhaps the hundredth time.

Hubert H. Humphrey: "After it was over, a lot of people suggested that no campaign was necessary, that Lyndon and I could go home and sit on our front porches until after the election, but neither of us was in any way equipped to do that."

Katharine Graham: "I spent the weekend after the convention at the Ranch by a wild series of accidents. The convention had been hot and humid, and all I had was a suitcase full of dirty clothes.

"We had a company plane, and we were loading it. I was trying to get back down to my farm for the weekend, and I had some house guests. Then, just as we got the plane loaded, the helicopters landed with the president and the vice-presidential nominee. So, of course, I knew the field was locked up and we couldn't do anything about it. My daughter, who was then about eighteen, said, 'Ma, we can't leave, so let's go over and watch them.' Mrs. Drew Pearson, Luvie Pearson, also was with me. So we went over into this crowd of people watching them get out of the helicopter and into Air Force One. We were just standing there with the gaping sightseers, and my hair was so filthy and kinky from the humidity that I had a bandanna wrapped around it and no stockings on.

"He came shaking hands down the fence, which he used to do all the time. When he got to me, he looked at me and said, 'Hello, Kay, what are you doing here?'

"I said, 'Waiting for you to take off.'

"He said, 'Do you want a ride?'

"I didn't quite know what he meant. I had read he was going to Texas, but I got absentminded and thought, 'Oh well, he's going back to Washington.' So I said, 'Sure. Lally and Luvie are with me. Can they come, too?'

"He looked slightly surprised and said, 'Yes, but you know we are going to Texas?'

"I said, 'Texas. I can't go to Texas.'

"Luvie Pearson, being more present-minded than I was, gave me a large kick in the shins and said, 'Go!'

"So I immediately said, 'Of course, I'd love to go to Texas, Mr. President.'

"He grabbed me by the elbow and I went up the stairs, having no idea what I was doing, or where I was going, or what he wanted.

"That night Lady Bird reminded him that they had to go to something in Stonewall the next night. He chewed her out and said he had just gotten over a convention and that her press secretary had gotten him into this thing. Why did she do these things? He really was awful. The next morning, he was driving and the Humphreys were in the back seat. I was in the front seat with him. Somehow Lady Bird wasn't there. And he started in again about how Lady Bird had gotten him into this evening and how he didn't want to do it. And I said, rather bluntly, 'Yes, she did get you into this thing tonight, but she also got you where you are today.' He then started lighting into me, and I said, 'Oh, shut up!' I was horrified when I heard the words fall out of my mouth, and I thought, 'I wonder if I should add, "Mr. President."'

"The Humphreys, I must say, were delighted."

Humphrey: "He was very 'high' that weekend; I think that convention, which he'd managed every minute of, every movement, every motion, every gesture, everything; that was the greatest time of his presidency and I think of his life.

"He got me into a cowboy outfit at the Ranch which was much too large for me, and made me feel ridiculous, and I knew I looked ridiculous, and he made me get on a horse and go riding with him . . . it was his ranch, after all, and, vice-presidential nominee or not, you were going to do what he said.

"Then, of course, we had a staff meeting about the campaign."

The campaign got under way in earnest on the morning of September 28, in the alien land that he had avoided and feared before, New England. The first stop was at Brown University where Lyndon was received with great enthusiasm by the students, one of whom was Roland L. Guyotte: "He arrived an hour late and spoke to a great crowd of students, the Providence elite, and dignitaries robed in colorful academic drag—all in celebration of Brown's bicentennial that year.

"The president slowly drawled the speech, looking to the left, looking to the right, looking to the center—just like a speech teacher. At the close he stared into the television cameras and sonorously intoned his appreciation for the people of Rhode Island and how he would remember them when he returned to his 'lonely desk in the White House.'

"The students, the academics, and the elite all ate it up."

Later it was estimated that more than the population of Providence turned out to greet him in the streets, and as was to happen often that day, they shouted, applauded, cheered, screamed and tried to touch him. His campaigning style was not much different from the one he had always used in Texas, maybe a little more sophisticated but not much more. "I want to ask you just one question: Are you going to vote Democratic in November?"

A great shout of agreement.

Then Lyndon would cup his hand to his ear and say, "I didn't hear you. Did you say yes?"

This time the response was deafening—to every ear save Lyndon's; for him it was never loud enough. He made thirteen stops in Providence.

It was the same wherever he went that day—Hartford, at the airport in Burlington, Vermont, Portland, Maine, and Manchester, New Hampshire, where the conservative members of the Weekly Newspaper Editors Association gave him a standing ovation after he said, "I want to ask you in advance to give me your hand and your help, and give me your counsel, and give me your heart, and give me your prayers. . . ."

In Manchester on that hectic day Lyndon also made the remark that was to haunt him and many millions of others during the next few years. He said:

> I have not thought we were ready for American boys to do the fighting for Asian boys. What I have been trying to do, with the situation that I found, was to get the boys in Vietnam to do their own fighting with our advice and our equipment.

In Akron, Ohio, on October 21, he said:

> We are not about to send American boys away from home to do what Asian boys ought to be doing for themselves.

But that day in New England, the home of the "jelly beans," of the "Harvards," of the snot noses and the smart asses, the territory of the Kennedys—that was the day to warm a Texas heart.

Jack Valenti: "These were not crowds that could be manufactured by an advance man. You cannot generate hundreds of thousands of friendly people, thronging every street and every byway the president went down, and in the squares where he spoke. This was the first time we realized that we had a landslide in the making."

On the morning of October 6 at the railroad station in Alexandria, Virginia, Lyndon said, "Alexandria has been chosen as the first stop for one of the greatest campaigners in America, and I am very proud to announce that I am her husband."

Liz Carpenter: "The whistle-stop thing, both in 1960 and in 1964, was Harry Truman's idea. He told Lyndon there were still a lot of people in this country who didn't know where the airport was, but they did know where the depot was. And he said if we went there to these depots and let them know when we were coming, they'd come down to listen. And he was right. Mrs. Johnson made forty-seven stops in eight states."

Lady Bird: "I made a great many little speeches standing on the end of the platform at the depot of a lot of southern states, starting in Alexandria, Virginia, going down through North Carolina, South Carolina, Florida, Georgia, Mississippi, Alabama, and Louisiana."[1]

Scooter Miller: "The hostesses on the train wore uniforms, and our job was always to make a picture in front of Mrs. Johnson. We passed out the balloons and the Lady Bird whistles. Since this was a whistle-stop, we passed out whistles and candy kisses, banners, engineer hats.

"We didn't go into any of the easy towns. We went into the toughest, like Savannah. We went through the northern part of Florida; we went where the real 'against' people were.

"There were some ugly incidents, but, well, you know, chivalry is not dead in the

South. And I believe the reaction came. The constant thing we wanted Mrs. Johnson to remember was never to let anything ruffle her. And she didn't."

Lady Bird: "In Alabama I always saw relatives. The newspaper people got to asking, 'Is this a one-cousin town or a two-cousin town?' Sort of joking, you know. They were very loyal and dear about showing up everywhere that they possibly could.

"I think they could recognize me as one of them. I could certainly recognize them as mine. I had a very close affection for the whole South, and Alabama especially, and also a sort of anger that a lot of the nation just wanted to read them out of the whole American picture.

"I also felt intensely the hostility which certainly did exist, particularly in South Carolina—more in South Carolina than anywhere else by a long shot.

"There would be banners with unpleasant things like, Go Home, or Fly Home, Lady Bird, something like that. And then if you got up and started to make a speech, some people would begin to make so much noise that you couldn't be heard. It was not frightening. It was not bad, really, but it was enough hostility so that you could feel it, palpably, in the air.

"Interestingly enough, the silent town was one of the loveliest towns I know— Charleston, South Carolina. The train stopped for several hours there. Part of the day was planned as a sort of sight-seeing trip through the Battery area—lovely old houses along the waterfront where there were magnificent live oaks and stately white houses. As I went down the street in this open carriage with a liveried black driver, I kept noticing that all the houses were shuttered. All the shutters were closed tight. It looked like everybody had left town.

"Then I began to see signs in windows that said, This House Sold on Goldwater. Very occasionally I would see a face peering out from behind the curtains, but the only people I saw were a few small children in the yards accompanied by their black nurses.

"That's all I saw in that hour or two in that lovely area."

William S. White: "The president was both very pleased with her success and, I thought, in a slight way somewhat jealous of it. I think he didn't particularly like it when people suggested that she'd made a major contribution to the campaign."

Bill Brammer: "The highlight of the 1964 campaign, a highlight any way you look at it, was the speech in New Orleans, what people call the 'nigra, nigra, nigra' speech. It galvanized me. I was ready to go out and kill. That's how great he was."

Carpenter: "The president joined us for our last stop, in New Orleans, and he first met us at the station where there were thousands, tens of thousands of people, thousands of blacks alone, and they were all chanting, 'We want Lyndon.' 'We want Lyndon!' It was a very dramatic moment. Blacks and whites all mixed together."

At the station Lyndon said:

I am going to repeat here in Louisiana what I have said in every state that I have appeared in, and what I said the night that I walked to the White House to take over the awesome responsibilities that were mine: As long as I am your president, I am going to be president of all the people.

The blacks continued chanting, shouting, applauding, stamping their feet, and so did most of the whites. Later that night at a fund-raising dinner Lyndon said:

> Whatever your views are, we have a Constitution, and we have a Bill of Rights, and we have the law of the land,[2] and two-thirds of the Democrats in the Senate voted for it and three-fourths of the Republicans. I signed it, and I am going to enforce it . . . and I think that any man that is worthy of the high office of president is going to do the same. . . .
>
> I remember Sam Rayburn telling me about a certain southern senator[3] who came to him . . . and talked about how the South had always been at the mercy of outside economic interests. They exploited us. They had worked our women for five cents an hour, they had worked our men for a dollar a day, they had exploited our soil, they had taken everything out of the ground they could, and they have shipped it to other sections.
>
> The senator said, "What a great future the South could have if we could just meet our economic problems, if we could just take a look at the resources of the South and develop them."
>
> Wistfully, the old senator told Rayburn, "Sammy, I just wish I felt a little better. I would like to go back to ole ————," and I won't call the name of the state; it wasn't Louisiana, and it wasn't Texas—"I would like to go back down there and make them one more Democratic speech. The poor old state, they haven't heard a Democratic speech in thirty years. All they ever hear at election time is 'nigra, nigra, nigra.'"[4]

The ovation, when it came, lasted a full five minutes, but in November Lyndon lost Louisiana.

The two candidates were far apart on many issues, but the one that most clearly separated them was civil rights. Goldwater never apologized for voting against the Civil Rights Act of 1964.

Andrew Young: "We campaigned very heavily not only for President Johnson but against Goldwater. I've always thought that the anti-Goldwater tide was something that Dr. King helped to create, because we went around to every city mobilizing the black community against Goldwaterism. We really weren't looking too hard at President Johnson. We were just scared to death of Goldwater."

Predictions or no predictions, polls or no polls, Lyndon never stopped.

Bill Moyers: "You really can't understand that campaign if you haven't watched Johnson rise out of the back seat of a car at dusk on a wide boulevard in Phoenix and bring the whole caravan to a screeching halt. How he took a bullhorn and verbally caressed six spectators on a street corner until he had them in the palm of his hand.

"Once in Denver, he spoke for fifteen minutes to a small group of people who were standing on a street corner. They didn't know he was president of the United States, and they couldn't understand him because they were Chicanos who couldn't understand English. When we got back to the hotel Lady Bird admonished him, because she felt he was diminishing himself physically. He made me go get the Gideon Bible out of the hotel drawer and turn to that passage in the New Testament where it talks about: there may be ninety and nine all safely protected for the night, but the Lord worries about the one. He said, with that familiar twinkle in his eye, 'Now, Bird, if God worries about the one, you don't expect the president of the United States to forget him, do you?'"

Lyndon: "Lynda and Luci both went all over the nation alone, just a Secret Service agent most of the time, speaking to crowds of three to four thousand who paid fifteen to twenty dollars to come and hear them make campaign speeches. One night I woke up at three o'clock. I said, 'Who is that at the door?' And she said, 'Daddy, it's Luci.' I said, 'Come on in here. What are you doing coming in at three o'clock in the morning?' And she said, 'Well, I left here Friday.' This was Monday morning about three o'clock; she was just getting back in time for school. And she said, 'I've been in North Dakota, South Dakota, and Nebraska.' I said, 'How many speeches did you make?' She said, 'I made eleven speeches.' I said, 'What did you tell them?' And she told me what all she told them, and how she took questions and answers from them, all of them, and she said she believed she was going to carry all three states. And I thought, 'Oh, the optimism of youth.'

"But we really did carry all three states."

The one, however temporary, threat to the success of the campaign occurred in mid-October.

James H. Rowe, Jr.: "After the event it is, of course, very easy to see what was important and what was not, but at the time, in the heat of a campaign, people are inclined to panic over anything. The Jenkins affair turned out not to be important; indeed, I believe it resulted in a certain sympathy for the president, but that was not clear at the time."

Jenkins, who was the president's most trusted adviser and in many ways the most important, on October 7 attended a cocktail party in the newly opened Washington offices of *Newsweek*. Shortly after he left he was arrested in the men's room of the Washington YMCA, not far from the White House, along with another man; the charge was disorderly conduct.

On October 14 the assistant managing editor of the *Washington Star* called Liz Carpenter and told her that a *Star* reporter had uncovered the police record of the arrest. Mrs. Carpenter said that the story was ridiculous; she called the editor back a few minutes later to say that Jenkins himself would call the *Star* to issue a denial.

Instead, Jenkins went to see Abe Fortas.

Clark Clifford: "Abe and I decided it would be a good idea to go to the editor of the *Evening Star*, the paper that had the story.⁵ So we spent time with the *Star*; we then went to the *News*, and then to the *Post*. Our position was that the printing of a story without knowing the facts could destroy this man and his family; that he had been a loyal worker for twenty-five years, and we couldn't believe it was true. Sometime during the day we went back to Abe's house where Walter was, and we both talked with him.

"He was terribly agitated, terribly. We decided what he needed was a doctor more than anything, so during the course of the day we got a doctor for him, and the doctor, seeing the condition he was in, put him in the hospital.

"It was maybe later that day, toward dark I think, that somebody in making a further search of the records came across a previous instance of a very similar nature in which I think he'd posted bond and then forfeited the bond.

"Well, that changed the whole complexion. Then the papers were full of it. That evening we both got on the phone and talked with the president, and I believe I never talked to the president again about it. It was just as though the book was closed on it."

Valenti: "That evening Johnson was scheduled to address the Al Smith dinner in the Waldorf. He was staying on the thirty-fifth floor; I was with him at the Waldorf.

"He got a call telling him of Walter's arrest. He was very calm and I did not see him betray any noticeable emotion.

"Then he placed several other phone calls. I know one was to Abe Fortas, and then he talked to Mrs. Johnson. Then at some point after a series of phone calls the decision was made that it was best for all concerned if Walter were to resign immediately. I know the president was in a difficult situation because obviously this was going to be *the* big news story.

"Later on that evening he went down to the podium at the Waldorf and delivered a fine speech, engaging in conversation with people at the head table, and I daresay that there was no suspicion on their part that anything was wrong."

J. Russell Wiggins: "The only instance I know of where Lady Bird reacted independently was during the Walter Jenkins episode. All other times she would have followed Lyndon to the guillotine if it were necessary.

"At the time I was on the board of regents at George Washington, and so was Katharine Graham. We were attending a meeting and got a call from Mrs. Johnson's secretary. Would we come over to the White House when we left George Washington and meet her in the family sitting room? It was that little blue room way up on the top floor, and we were ushered in, and in came Lady Bird.

"My God, she was like a vessel under full sail. She came into that room, and she issued a statement declaring full loyalty to Walter Jenkins. She read it, and she said she wondered if we would print it.

"It was a great statement, and we did print it, of course. But I am practically certain that it was her own statement and that she issued it without talking to Lyndon. The only time."[6]

Elizabeth Goldschmidt: "When the Walter Jenkins thing happened, that was a terrible tragedy for Johnson—just a terrible tragedy in all respects. Walter was so indispensable to him."

The Jenkins story as it happened did not remain in the headlines for long. Within a few days after what had happened became public, the Chinese exploded their first nuclear bomb; the Tory government in England, which had been in power for thirteen years, was voted out of office, and Nikita Khrushchev was deposed.

Moyers: "I was responsible for the advertising campaign. After the Republican convention was over, Barry Goldwater was making a rush for respectability. He was trying to put behind him all the reckless statements of his past and make people think that now that he was the nominee of the Republican party he was a statesman.

"I remember calling in Lloyd Wright, who was at the Democratic National

Committee, and the people in the agency and saying to them, 'I want to remind folks of what Goldwater was saying *before* he got to be so respectable.' They developed a brilliant series of ads, Goldwater saying the eastern seaboard ought to be chopped off and floated out to sea, Goldwater cutting down or eliminating Social Security, that little girl picking petals off the daisy. That ad did not mention Goldwater. It didn't even quote his reckless statement on the nuclear bomb, saying we ought to lob one into the Kremlin.

"I think it ran on television on a Monday night at nine o'clock.[7] Millions of people saw it and the response was immediate. So immediate that I knew it had been a success.

"Johnson called me not too long after and said he'd been swamped with calls. Some of his own friends had gotten through to him, and there were some people having dinner with him. I could tell the moment he answered the phone that he was having a wonderful time putting on an act. He said, 'What in the hell do you mean putting on that ad that just ran? I've been swamped with calls, and the Goldwater people are calling it a low blow,' and on and on and on—typical, wonderful, Lyndon Johnson fashion. His voice was chuckling all the time. He said, 'You'd better come over here and tell me what you're going to do about this.'

"So I went over at ten o'clock, and he said, 'Don't you think that was pretty tough?' I said, 'Mr. President, we were just reminding people that at this time it might be a good idea to have an experienced hand on the button.' I said I had only ordered that it be run once. There were eight or nine people in the room.

"I turned and went back to the elevator, which is in a little alcove on the second floor, and I heard, 'Bill, Bill! Just a minute!' He got up out of his chair and came down to the alcove with his back to the group. He said, 'You sure we ought to run it just once?' I said, 'Yes, Mr. President.'"

Goldwater ended his campaign in Fredonia, Arizona, on the Utah border, where he made his last speeches in his two successful campaigns for the Senate.

He was never better. He said, "I think from time to time about Pipe Springs down the road here a piece. I think of the courage of those people who came here not knowing that the federal government could help them, but doing it on their own, standing off all kinds of abusive action, standing off the weather, but finally triumphing in raising cattle where cattle probably shouldn't have been raised, and living their lives as they felt God wanted them to. These are the things, the simple things that I have talked about and will continue to talk about as long as I live regardless of what God has in mind for me to do."

After, as usual, some internal debate—Washington or Austin—Lyndon, not surprisingly, decided on the latter for his final speech. And on election eve he spoke from the steps of the state capitol. It was agreed that this speech, largely Lyndon, was the best of his campaign:

> It was here as a barefoot boy[8] around my father's desk in that great hall of the House of Representatives where he served for six terms and where my grandfather served ahead of him that I first learned that government is not an enemy of the people. It is the people.
> The only attacks that I have resented in this campaign are the charges which

are based on the idea that the presidency is something apart from the people, opposed to them, against them.

I learned here when I was the NYA administrator that poverty and ignorance are the only basic weaknesses of a free society, and that both of them are only bad habits and can be stopped.

Those two speeches, Barry's and Lyndon's, really summed up what the campaign had been about. It was the people who settled in Pipe Springs "doing it on their own" against those people who believed that to preserve a free society there were things that the federal government, and only the federal government, could do, and that it should. As Harry Truman once said, "It took them a long time to discover that part in the Constitution where it talks about 'the general welfare of the people' being the responsibility of the government."

The next day the people decided overwhelmingly in favor of the government, big government if you will. Lyndon carried forty-four states and the District of Columbia; Goldwater won in six. Goldwater received 27,174,898 votes, and Lyndon 43,126,218 votes, 61 percent of the total. Goldwater won Alabama, Georgia, Louisiana, Mississippi, South Carolina, and his own Arizona. Lyndon carried Illinois by more than a million, Michigan, Ohio, and California by almost a million each, and New York by more than two million. The Republicans lost more than five hundred seats in state legislatures, thirty-seven in the House and two in the Senate.

At 1:40 A.M. Lyndon thanked the people for the mandate they had given him, and after a few remarks from Bird, Lynda, and Luci, he announced that Hubert and his charming wife, Muriel, were arriving the next day at noon. They were to be the guests of honor at—yes, a barbecue "out on the banks of the Pedernales."

A GOOD PLACE TO WALK

As always it was pleasant, necessary even, to spend time at the Ranch after a long campaign, even one that ended in triumph. The Johnsons stayed at the Ranch from November 5 to 15, returned to Washington for four days, went back to the Ranch until the twenty-ninth, once again shuttled to Washington, and finally back to the Ranch for Christmas.

Lady Bird: "This ranch is our heart's home. We began the purchase in the fall, and I think we signed the papers before Christmas, in '51. We moved in in '52. My recollection is we paid $12,000 for all the renovations that we did and thought that was a lot.

"The house[1] sits in the little valley of the Pedernales—the land sloping down gently to the river which is normally a very placid stream, and it rises slightly to the north through patches of alfalfa and sudan grass from which the view is beautiful."

Lyndon: "This is very beautiful country. A friend of ours who is a geologist says that this is old, old land that has been worn down by centuries of erosion. There have been no upheavals within the last good many thousands of years.

"Here the sun seems to be a little brighter and the climate a little warmer, the air a little fresher and the people a little kinder and more understanding. It's a dry country, but there's always a breeze blowing and there is always sun here. We don't have dreariness. We don't have those dull gray skies when you look up. Here you have birds singing, flowers growing, girls smiling. And I guess it's a good deal in what you're accustomed to, and I still like to eat the food my mother cooked when I was a little boy, the types of food she cooked, and I still like to visit the scenes of my childhood."

Lady Bird: "You just live with the seasons out here. You always remember when it's a full moon. Possibly, if I failed to look forward to the coming of spring and to look forward to the bright blue and gold days of October, then I'd know I was getting old. But it's a very full life."

Ephraim Evron: "On my first visit to the Ranch the country reminded me very much of some parts of lower Galilee. The low hills and the trees. There was a tree which looked very much like an olive tree. I remarked about it to the president later, and said that I felt a little at home at least by the scenery, that it reminded me of Israel.

"When Prime Minister Eshkol and his party and Dean Rusk came to the Ranch, the president immediately took the prime minister in his car to show him around the ranch; and the ambassador and I joined them. And since Mr. Eshkol was also a farmer—he was one of the early settlers of Israel and he was a member of one of the kibbutzim near Lake Tiberius—he felt very much at home. The president began telling him about his cattle and what he was growing there and we saw, as if it was prearranged, one of the cows just giving birth to a calf. Just as the car stopped there. The timing was perfect. And the president began telling us what kind of cow it was, what the calf would look like, and all the time he was patting the cow, rubbing its back, talking to it, trying to help it give birth."

Jack Valenti: "He used to say, 'I'm going to show you the greatest thing you ever saw, the greatest treasure that no money in the world can buy—sunset on the Pedernales.' And he really meant it. He was big on sunsets and sunrises and trees and grass and flowers and shrubs."

Elizabeth Rowe: "I went down to the ranch early in December of '66. The president rode us all over, and we investigated the state of the fences, took a look at everything.

"He had had one of those two-way radios in the station wagon he was driving, and if he found that a fence was in need of repair, he would report in that this fence needs a little attention. He explained all the different times and ways of feeding the wildlife, especially the deer which were all over the place. There were complicated pulley arrangements on some of the trees to let down at a certain time grain for deer to have that would supplement their regular diet. He was expansive and just loved it down there, just loved every foot of that Texas countryside."

Elspeth Rostow: "I don't think Washington was quite as comfortable a place for him ever, as Texas. The phrase that both he and Mrs. Johnson used to use was they were coming back to recharge their batteries. It was an accurate description."

Cactus Pryor: "Mostly at his parties the president liked a western atmosphere. Round tables with checkered tablecloths and coal oil lanterns. All of his help dressed in western attire. He had big old iron washpots full of melted butter in which you would dip your corn on the cob. It had all the look and feel of the 'chuck wagon' dinner. And we would depict in pageant form the settling of Texas, and of course, we were settled at first by the Spaniards. We actually had the early Spaniards in costume coming down the Pedernales River and the friars and the Indians meeting them. Then we had the settlers coming, and they came roaring down on horseback, shouting, the stagecoach coming full speed, the buckboards; and the settlers in their old costumes sang songs of windmills and cattle drives.

"There was one time in which I watched the president with apprehension during the first three numbers; he had been very worried about this entertainment because they were amateurs. During the first couple of numbers he was just casing the crowd with his political eye, and then as he saw the audience enjoying it, he began to enjoy it, and by the end of the performance he was laughing and clapping the loudest."

Jesse Kellam: "A few years after acquiring the Ranch, Lyndon decided to take up deer hunting. Bird was so delighted that her hardworking husband was at last showing an interest in a hobby that she, too, learned to shoot a rifle, with which she usually bags her quota each fall.

"Lyndon's idea of a hunting trip, however, was a mechanized safari in a fleet of air-conditioned cars equipped with intercommunications systems. He drove his cars as if they were cow ponies, and once, as Bird was following with guests at the wheel of the second car, trying to match his ninety-mile-an-hour pace, he suddenly zoomed up a forty-five degree embankment. As he did so, he bellowed gleefully into the intercom: 'Bird, you don't have to come up here if you're too scared to try.'

"With her usual serenity she replied: 'Of course, I'm coming, darlin'.' Her companions gritted their teeth while her car shot smoothly up the earth dam that was barely wide enough for the wheelbase."

Jake Pickle: "So many times when I came up there, it was associated with traveling over the Ranch to see the deer. Or if it was deer season, then we all had to go hunting. And if anybody was visiting, particularly if you were from the north or the east, you had to go get a deer. That was the test. And if you were able to get a deer, you had to be an excellent shot, because he'd trash you every way in the world. You'd be getting a fair shot, and he'd holler in your ear, or accelerate the car, or he'd scream and you'd look silly—well, he took great pleasure in that."

Lloyd Hand: "I look back on those days—the evenings—and it was just wonderful, warm, and with good food. After dinner we'd all walk down to Cousin Oriole's. Her house was about two hundred yards away. You walked down the path toward the graveyard—the house isn't there anymore—but it was just before you got to the cemetery. Cousin Oriole was well read, literate, a little zany lady, and he loved her, but he poked fun at her. He'd just knock on her door—ten thirty, eleven at night and shout, 'Cousin Oriole, got some friends I want you to meet—come on out—no, no, you come on out here in your nightgown.'

"And she'd put her robe on, come out, and humor him, and always good-naturedly.

But it was a ritual after dinner to walk down there. 'Let's go see Cousin Oriole,' he'd say. And everybody would walk along in the moonlight."

Stewart Alsop: "Visiting the LBJ Ranch, this reporter was reminded of another visit— to Chartwell, Sir Winston Churchill's country place—which may partly explain Johnson's quality of nonordinariness. Mr. Churchill was marvelously and unashamedly proud of everything about Chartwell, especially his own gadgets and contraptions. . . . But he was proudest of all of his goldfish pond. While a Scotland Yard man fed grubs to the monstrously fat goldfish, Churchill pointed to each fish in turn, named the price he had paid for it and estimated its current worth. 'See that one there,' he would say, almost hopping up and down with pleasure, 'the one that looks rather like Clement Attlee? I paid only ten shillings for that one—worth fully two pounds now, I dare say.'

"Lyndon Johnson is as different from Winston Churchill as the LBJ Ranch is from Chartwell, which is very different indeed. Yet there are odd echoes of Chartwell on the LBJ Ranch. Johnson is also a passionate pisciculturist, and he takes a personal interest in the care and feeding of the enormous catfish and black bass with which his four artificial ponds are stocked. He, too, loves gadgets and contraptions. He has rigged up a loud-speaking system, for example, which permits him to give orders at any time to anyone in the house or even in the swimming pool.

"But it was on a tour of the property, an exhausting experience no guest can hope to escape, that this reporter was first reminded of Chartwell. Again and again, Johnson drove his limousine at breathtaking speed across the rocky land to within easy smelling distance of a bunch of cattle, blowing the horn and shouting at the beasts to make them stand up. He would then behave precisely like Churchill with his goldfish—pointing out each animal in turn, occasionally comparing its appearance to that of some fellow politician, and telling his visitors just what he had paid for it and precisely what staggering profit he expected to realize. And whether Johnson is displaying his deer herd or a pumping system or even the graves of his ancestors, his visitors have the same feeling that visitors to Chartwell have—that they are expected, nay commanded, to exclaim and to admire."[2]

Lyndon on a tour of the Ranch in 1966: "We'll walk on up to the family graveyard now. These here are all live oaks and pecan, but the floods have mostly washed the pecans away. Live oaks' roots go out this way and the water runs over them. We wanted to plant one on the White House lawn. Each president, as you know, plants a tree—but we had to plant another type of tree. They felt the live oak wouldn't do well there.

"See this old fort over here? There's the commissary—that was the first building. This was the ranch headquarters. Over here is the watch tower. See the peep holes in it, on the commissary side? That's where they used to watch for the Indians. This here is the original rock where grandpa and grandma began. You can see the very place he located in the big Bible there.

"This was the concentration point for all of the cattle, thousands of cattle that the herders would eventually take to Abilene, Kansas.

"Here's the graveyard. My great-great-grandmother is buried in here, born in 1821. My grandfather and grandmother. My father and mother. My sister.

"I walk here nearly every morning. All these beautiful trees, so peaceful and quiet. I'm going to be buried there right next to my mother. There's my sister over there—see, they've left blank spaces. My youngest sister where her little stone is. My mother and father here, and then I'm next—my next sister and all the family will be buried in that little row. In 1955 when I had that heart attack, I thought I'd be joining them sooner than I wanted.

"I like these big trees here. It's a good place to walk and to rest.

"When I come here and stay two or three days it's a breath of fresh air; it's new strength. I go away ready to challenge the world. Sometimes when I come back here I think that I just might stay—because there's no other place, no Virgin Islands, no Miami coastline, no boat trips across the Atlantic that can do for me what this soil, this land, this water, this people, and what these hills, these surroundings can do. They represent memories of half a century and they provide the stimulation and inspiration that nothing else can provide."

SO LITTLE TIME

Before his inaugural on January 20, 1965, Lyndon delivered his State of the Union message to Congress. That came at a few minutes after nine on the evening of January 4. In it he outlined what he had in mind when he spoke of the Great Society; it was quite a lot.

The speech was a great success interrupted by applause, cheers, and even some stamping of feet. After all, many of the 68 Democrats in the Senate, compared to 32 Republicans, and the 295 Democrats in the House, compared to 140 Republicans, would have been back in Keokuk or Omaha had it not been for Lyndon's landslide. The applause became particularly enthusiastic when he mentioned what *Newsweek* called "that nagging little war in Vietnam." He said, "Our goal is peace in southeast Asia. That will come only when aggressors leave their neighbors in peace.

"What is at stake is the cause of freedom and in that cause America will never be found wanting."

Who but people like Wayne Morse and Ernest Gruening could disagree with that? None did, and even Fulbright, the chairman of the Senate Foreign Relations Committee, joined in the applause.

Cheers were also abundant when Johnson said that he was going to set up a Department of Housing and Urban Development to carry out his ambitious plans for rebuilding American cities. And education would be aided, yes, by the federal government, from preschool days through college. And, smiling on Lady Bird, who smiled back, he said that America was going to be beautified, "more large and small parks, more seashores and open spaces than have been created during any other period in our national history."

And more and more. Wouldn't it all cost money? Perhaps, but on the other hand, as he announced a few days later, he was going to *save* money by prohibiting all government departments from buying any new filing cabinets. He was, he said, going to eliminate *waste*, making the word itself sound slightly obscene, and he turned off lights in the White House, didn't he?

The country was, its president said, "Free and restless, growing and full of hope." Which seemed indeed to be so. And just in case anybody was thinking of doing anything counterproductive, like relaxing, he continued to send messages to Congress almost daily before he was inaugurated—the education bill, the health bill, the foreign aid bill, the bill to broaden our immigration laws, the arms control bill, and many many others.

The most important of these, in Johnson's mind, was the education bill, which included provisions for a Head Start program and a total of several billion dollars for schools, school libraries, scholarship loans, and university extension programs.

Hubert H. Humphrey: "Johnson was—to put it frankly, he was a nut on education. He felt that education was the greatest thing that he could give to the people; he just believed in it, just like some people believe in miracle cures."

George E. Reedy: "Johnson had an abnormal, superstitious respect for education. I believe he even thought it would cure chilblain."

The primary and secondary education bill, the first of a total of sixty education bills, passed the House on March 26 and the Senate on April 9, and was signed into law the following day in the old schoolhouse in Johnson City where he had started school himself at the age of four.

The inauguration came and went in a whirl of parties and galas, bands and color guards, celebrities and baton twirlers and Secret Service men. Like most of our national rites, it had its moments of high solemnity and then elements which at best could be called frivolous, like the lady from Fort Worth who arrived at one of the inaugural balls wearing a tiara that lighted up and spelled T-E-X-A-S.

Lyndon, by his own admission, enjoyed every minute of it and at times it seemed as if he danced with everybody. At one ball he changed partners nine times in thirteen minutes. He paid especial attention to the wives of congressmen and senators who might be useful to him in making the Great Society possible and also danced with a lot of Texas ladies at the last stop, the Sheraton-Hilton.

When finally he bid them all good night, he said that it had been a great day and a great night. Then he added, and one was either moved by it or laughed at it, "Don't stay up late. We're on our way to the Great Society."

Wilbur J. Cohen: "Now I'm going to tell you a very important story. It's one of the most important I know about Johnson. At the end of January 1965, shortly after he'd been inaugurated, Johnson called a meeting of the so-called congressional liaison officers of the various departments.

"He came in and sat down with us for what we thought would be five or ten minutes to wish us good luck, but he stayed for at least an hour, maybe an hour and a half.

"During that time he talked extemporaneously, and what he said was a three-hour credit course in American political history. He said, 'Look, I've just been elected and right now we'll have a honeymoon with Congress. With the additional congressmen that have been elected, I'll have a good chance to get my program through. Of course, for that I have to depend on you, the twenty or thirty people who are in this room.

"'But after I make my recommendations, I'm going to start to lose the power and authority I have because that's what happened to President Woodrow Wilson, to President Roosevelt and to Truman and to Kennedy.' He said, 'Every day that I'm in office and every day that I push my program, I'll be losing part of my ability to be influential, because that's in the nature of what the president does. He uses up his capital. Something is going to come up, either something like the Vietnam War or something else where I will begin to lose all that I have now.

"'So I want you guys to get off your asses and do everything possible to get everything in my program passed as soon as possible, before the aura and the halo that surround me disappear.

"'Don't waste a second. Get going *right now*. Larry, Wilbur—just remember I want this program through fast, and by fast I mean six months, not a year.'

"Of course, I don't mean to imply that if things had gone right, he wouldn't have run again. But to my mind what he was saying was that he had to put everything on the line, and if that meant I've got only one full term, that's fine. At least I'll get my program through. I would rather use up everything in one term than be cautious and play around and run for a second.

"And I think he had a correct historical evaluation, much better than Wilson, who was a great historian, and certainly better than Kennedy, who was cautious because he thought Goldwater would run against him in 1964 and that he'd beat him and *then* he could do what he wanted and get his program enacted.

"Johnson—here was this country bumpkin who had, like Truman, a more correct evaluation of the historical forces affecting the president than almost anybody else."

Willard Wirtz: "I remember in a cabinet meeting that year John Gardner was talking along, very conversationally, and he came to some item or other, I've forgotten about what, and he said, all of sudden, 'Of course, Mr. President, you know we can't do that.'

"And Lyndon Johnson leaped out of his chair and leaped halfway across the table and he pointed his finger at John and said, 'Mr. Secretary, don't ever say that.' And then he started around that room, just looking everybody in the eye, and pointing his finger at everybody at the table. He said, 'There is nothing this country can't do. Remember that.'

"Well, now, he believed that. And domestically he was doggone close, very doggone close. My gosh, when you think of what happened in 1965, you turn around two centuries. Just take civil rights and women, to mention two—he turned the whole country around."

Hugh Sidey: "During 1965 in particular I think Johnson would zero in on a congressman or a senator and get what he wanted, a good deal. I would be amazed at some of the devices he would use. He would lie, beg, cheat, steal a little, threaten, intimidate. But he never lost sight of that ultimate goal, his idea of the Great Society."

There was never any question in Lyndon's mind about where he would start. He would begin with Medicare, a national health program.

Three days after his State of the Union message, he asked the Eighty-ninth Congress to enact such a bill. At the same time he issued a statement in which he said:

> . . . I am proposing that every person over sixty-five years of age be spared the darkness of sickness without hope. I am asking that every person, under Social Security during his working lifetime contribute a modest amount, so that his basic health services can be financed. It will help meet the costs of hospital bills without in any way interfering with the freedom to choose their doctor or to choose their hospital.

Nothing much new there. Roosevelt had suggested something like that, but he hadn't absolutely insisted, perhaps because he had his mind on how the voters would react to a third term. Truman had made a similar suggestion, but he hadn't done much more, realizing that it would never get through Congress. Then, too, both Roosevelt and Truman were aware of the political strength of the American Medical Association, which had spent most of its energies and many millions of dollars fighting all governmental attempts to improve public health: compulsory innoculation against diphtheria, for instance, public venereal disease clinics for another, free centers for diagnosing cancer for a third. The AMA claimed that such measures and dozens· of others would "interfere with the sacred relationship between doctor and patient." Besides, said the AMA, government intervention would mean "socialized medicine," which remained undefined, though it sounded like something malignant.

And the AMA had always won. It had won in 1963 when Jack Kennedy had tried to get a similar bill passed and failed by four votes in the Senate.

So there was Lyndon with his landslide Eighty-ninth Congress willing to go along with anything the Chief wanted—except maybe Medicare. The real hurdle in the past had always been the House Ways and Means Committee, which could either vote the bill out or keep it bottled up in committee. The chairman was one Wilbur Mills of Arkansas. Mills had always been against Medicare, as were the majority of the members of his committee. But 1964 was a year in which, contrary to all predictions, Lyndon carried Arkansas. Wilbur Mills could read the election returns as well as anybody.

Mills announced that he was no longer opposed to Medicare, which was called the King-Anderson bill, and after Lyndon's message of January 7, said that he hoped to have the bill out of his committee and onto the floor of the House by March. Nevertheless, Lyndon, Lawrence O'Brien, who had been Kennedy's chief congressional liaison and was now Lyndon's, and Wilbur Cohen were afraid that despite Mills' change of heart, the majority of his committee would not go along with him. One member of the committee, John Byrnes, a Republican from Wisconsin, had introduced his own substitute for Medicare, one that stressed "voluntary" health insurance for the elderly; it had, it was said, been prepared with the help of an insurance company and one Gerald

R. Ford, then House minority leader. The AMA had a bill of its own introduced, professing something called Eldercare. It was considered nonsensical, and one congressman suggested an alternative bill to be called Doctorcare. It would be financed by a 2 percent federal tax on applesauce.

On March 9 Wilbur Cohen, at the invitation of Wilbur Mills, appeared before the committee to explain the various health plans. When Cohen finished his description of the Byrnes' bill, Mills turned to his colleague and said, "You know, John, I like that part of your bill about taking care of doctor bills as well as hospital expenses."

Cohen: "It was a brilliant political maneuver. Mills explained that he meant the Byrnes bill not as a substitute for King-Anderson but as an addition. He was passing the Republicans' own bill right back to them. He went on to say that he now thought of Medicare as a kind of three-layer cake—hospitalization for people over sixty-five being taken care of as planned in the original bill, a program for the health needs of the poor (not provided in the original bill), and that part of the Byrnes bill providing for the payment of doctors.

"Byrnes just sat there open-mouthed."

The next morning Cohen outlined the new bill before the Ways and Means Committee and estimated that a $500 million increase in the budget would take care of 80 percent of all the doctor bills involved after the patient had paid the first fifty dollars himself.

At the end of Cohen's presentation Mills said, "O.K. It sounds fine to me," after which Cohen rushed to the White House.

Cohen: "I wasn't sure about the additional $500 million, but Johnson said that would present no problem. Then he said something I thought was strange. He said, 'I'm going to run and get my brother.' Whereupon he told me a story about a man who wanted to work for the railroad as a switchman, and they were giving him an intelligence test. They said, 'What would you do if you saw a train coming from the east at sixty miles an hour and you turned around and saw a train coming from the west at sixty miles an hour,' and the man said, 'I'd run and get my brother.' Why would he get his brother? He said, 'My brother's never seen a train wreck.' At which point Lyndon said, 'If that expanded bill gets through that committee, I'll run and get my brother.'

"Then he repeated not to worry about the additional $500 million and told me to watch out for trains."

On the morning of March 26, after the committee had voted out the bill, Lyndon called a televised meeting with congressional leaders of both houses to discuss it. He described the various provisions and explained how the plan would work, after which he called on Wilbur Mills, giving him full credit for his committee's part in developing the historic bill.

Finally, Lyndon turned to Senator Harry Byrd, the chairman of the Senate Committee on Finance and a steadfast opponent of most of the twentieth century. Byrd could, and, unless prevented would, postpone hearings on the bill for an indefinite period.

Lyndon had no intention of letting that happen. Beaming, and in full view of a nationwide television audience, he said, "Senator Byrd, would you care to make an observation?"

Byrd, who seemed to shrink in size a little, said, "There is no observation I can make now, because the bill hasn't come before the Senate. Naturally, I'm not familiar with it. All I can say is that I will see that adequate and thorough hearings are held."

Lyndon, still smiling: "And you have nothing that you know of that would prevent that coming about in reasonable time—there is not anything ahead of it in the committee?"

Byrd, smaller still: "Nothing in the committee now."

Lyndon: "So when the House acts and it is referred to the Senate Finance Committee, you will arrange for prompt hearings and thorough hearings?"

Byrd, in a voice that was nearly inaudible: "Yes."

After which Lyndon thanked them all heartily. Carl Albert later observed that while most of those present that morning were familiar with "the Johnson treatment," that was surely the first time it had been seen on national television.

Did Lyndon leave it there? He did not. He was on the phone with every doubtful member of the House. The bill passed by a vote of 313 to 115 on April 8.

It was a great triumph, but did the president rest? He did not. "Now, Larry, now, Wilbur, get off your asses and get . . . and get me Senator . . . and Senator . . . and Senator . . ."

Mike Monroney: "I'd been down to look at one of the new planes that were coming off the line in Marietta, Georgia—Lockheed down there. We were coming back into Washington feeling no pain at all, and got in, and they said, 'They want you on the floor right away.' So I went to the floor and, lo and behold, they were getting all ready for a roll call on Medicare.

"I was sitting there, getting ready to vote, and my vote in the past had been against Medicare because my senior senator, Bob Kerr, had waged the leading fight against it. So lo and behold, we started the roll call vote and I got a call from the White House in the cloakroom, and I went there and he said, 'Mike, I'm short one vote on Medicare. Are you going to be the one that'll block this?'

"I said, 'Well, I don't know. I've voted against it before and I've supported my senior senator on the thing. I'm just having a hard time making up my mind. I believe in Medicare. I want it, but I want a program that we'll have a consensus on.'

"He said, 'Well, your vote is going to be the deciding vote, and I sure do need it.'

"I said, 'Well, I don't know Mr. President, what I'll do.'

"I came back and sat down as it got nearer and nearer my name on the roll call. Finally I voted for Medicare, and my vote was the one vote that was changed from before—to be for it. I'm always glad that I did. I think it's a great thing."

The day the bill passed the Senate, July 9, was, Lyndon said, "a great day for America."

The conference report was adopted, and on July 30, the president flew to Independence, Missouri; he signed the bill in the presence of Harry S Truman, who was eighty-one and who, Johnson said, had been the father of Medicare. Then he gave Truman and Mrs. Truman the first two Medicare cards.

After that the president called together the leaders of the AMA. There was the threat of a nationwide boycott of Medicare; it was rumored that 95 percent of the country's doctors would take part in it. Many of the doctors who came to the White House had protest in mind, but before they had time to say a word, Lyndon had launched into the subject of patriotism. He spoke of how fond he had always been of his "old family doctor" who had served so faithfully during his father's long illness, and later, during his mother's. He said that his respect for doctors was, he was sure, shared by most Americans. Medicine was, he said, a noble profession, the noblest profession of all. He said that he was certain the doctors of the United States would cooperate with a law that had been passed by the Congress of the United States and that would serve millions of Americans. Doctors were, he always knew, primarily interested in *service*. He said he was grateful for their exchanging views with him, thanks very much, very, very much.

Not surprisingly, to Lyndon anyway, the AMA announced that the predicted boycott would not come off. Within a short while 95 percent of the doctors of the United States were *supporting* Medicare.

And then *Lyndon's* phone started to ring. The callers all seemed to have southern accents, and they all said they were friends of Lyndon's. And the message was always the same. To get federal funds for Medicare, hospitals would, according to Title VI of the Civil Rights Act of 1964, have to desegregate. "And they won't, Lyndon. You know that. Do you want to be responsible for closing the St. Francis Hospital in Biloxi, Mississippi? That's what will happen if you put this thing into effect. They're not going to change their ways overnight. You know that as well as I do. Doctors won't treat the coloreds, and the nurses won't treat them." And so on.

Harry McPherson: "It was a painful time. Whatever he decided, thousands of people, either the elderly or the blacks, might have been deprived of hospitalization. It was an excruciating decision to make, but he made it. Comply. And they did."

A footnote to the story: In January 1968, after John Gardner resigned as secretary of HEW, Lyndon said to John P. Roche, a special White House consultant, "Does Wilbur Cohen look to you like a Jewish tailor from Brooklyn?" Roche said that he supposed, if one wished, one could describe Cohen that way, and Lyndon said, "Well, I don't care what he looks like; I'm going to make him secretary of HEW."

This he did, in spite of the fact that the White House was getting more than a thousand telegrams a day, all worded exactly the same, "Please do not appoint Wilbur J. Cohen secretary of HEW. It is my opinion that he is an enemy of American medicine."

THE COMMITMENT

If 1965 was a watershed year for much of the Great Society legislation, it was likewise so far as the American commitment in Vietnam was concerned. Two major and, it turned out, irrevocable decisions were made by Lyndon: in February, with no objections at all among his top advisers, he ordered a start to systematic bombing of North Vietnam; and in late July, with a single dissent, that of George Ball, undersecretary of state, the commitment of American ground troops began on a major scale.

After that there was no longer any turning back. America was committed; it was our war. And who made the commitment?

Lyndon: "Now there are many, many people who can recommend and advise, and a few of them consent, but there is only one who has been chosen by the American people to decide."[1]

Clark Clifford: "His senior advisers felt we were headed correctly in Vietnam. The legislative branch of the government agreed. It was rare to find a voice that counseled caution or advised that we not do it. The support for our involvement there was really overwhelming.

"Later some people believed, or chose to believe, or pretended for whatever reason to believe, that it was Lyndon Johnson's war or that at the very least he had out of intended evil expanded it.

"Whatever the hows or whys or wherefores of what happened before, there were, I think, very few experts on Southeast Asia who did not believe that the United States in 1965 should send in troops, that there was simply no alternative. And this, of course, is exactly where President Johnson's situation differed from those of Presidents Eisenhower and Kennedy.

"There are many people, again, who find this a Machiavellian decision, one plotted long beforehand in a Machiavellian way; I do not. Nor do I think it was a conspiracy or anything like it when the first troop commitment was made and found to be insufficient."

George W. Ball: "To some extent Johnson used me, calling me his devil's advocate. Rusk took the position from the beginning that the president was as much entitled to my views as his, and we had a strongly, diametrically conflicting position.

"Rusk, McNamara, Mac Bundy—we would have a session that would go on all afternoon, and in the course of it I would say, 'Mr. President, I think you're getting very bad advice. I think what Bob is saying and what Dean is saying is completely wrong.' Rostow took a position very early on and spent a good deal of time defending it, and most of us would agree that he was a terrible influence on the president. He played to Johnson's weaker side, always creating an image of Johnson standing against the forces of evil. He used to tell him how Lincoln was abused by everybody when he was at a certain stage of the Civil War, and 'this is the position you are in, Mr. President.' He spent a good deal of time creating a kind of fantasy for the president."

Edwin S. Weisl, Sr.: "George Ball was one of the opponents of the war from the beginning. Several times he appeared before the National Security Council and was urged by President Johnson to state his point of view opposing the war in Vietnam and to keep stating it and keep arguing it and keep having a dialogue on it."

J. Russell Wiggins: "He said that in spite of any differences, Ball was loyal and faithful and effective. He didn't agree with Ball and he had in some quarters a reputation for being a man who didn't tolerate dissent or opposition around him. Nothing could have disproven this more. He remained on the most friendly personal terms with Ball."

On the night of August 29, 1964, two days after his fifty-sixth birthday and the close of the Democratic National Convention, Lyndon had presided over a birthday celebration in Stonewall attended by neighbors, the Humphreys, reporters, and, of course, the Secret Service. Two tons of barbequed beef plus various other Texas dainties were served, and in the inevitable speech Lyndon said, as he would say many times during the campaign—it was part of a basic speech—"I have had advice to load our planes with bombs and to drop them on certain areas, but I think that would enlarge and escalate the war and result in our committing a good many American boys to fighting a war that I think ought to be fought by the boys of Asia to help protect their own land."[2]

The "advice" that Lyndon mentioned so casually was from the Joint Chiefs and General William Childs Westmoreland, "Westy," the general who in January would become commander of the American ground forces in South Vietnam, replacing General Paul D. Harkins. But by February 1965, the "advice" that six months before had been supported only by the military now received the endorsement of civilian personnel as well—as for example, Ambassador Maxwell Taylor, close friend of the Kennedys', particularly Bobby and Ethel. Taylor recommended bombing North Vietnam; so did the Kennedy-Johnson cabinet. So did Dean Acheson, that austere and revered man who had kept Harry Truman in line; so did those two awesome brothers who seldom disagreed, the Bundys of Boston, MacGeorge and William Putnam. Mac Bundy was special assistant to the president on national security affairs, as he had been during the Kennedy years; William Putnam Bundy was then assistant secretary of state for Far Eastern affairs. Lyndon, who could and sometimes did imitate both with devastating precision, was impressed by their lineage and their academic credentials— Groton, Harvard, and Yale. Lyndon's old friend Abe Fortas was and remained a dedicated hawk—bombing, troop commitments, whatever was necessary. What's more, most members of Congress would and did go along.

But Lyndon deliberately held back. During the 1964 campaign he certainly had no intention of making the liberals, who were nervous, though not yet "nervous nellies," any more apprehensive. Let Barry talk about "bombing," maybe even atomic bombing; Lyndon would and did talk about "peace," and he sincerely believed he could and would achieve it, in spite of the fact that in the spring of that year Westmoreland had told Bob McNamara that the war was going to be a long, costly affair.

By the time the '64 election was over and Lyndon was once again able to turn his full attention to other matters, new events in Vietnam had made a reassessment of the situation there necessary. North Vietnam, which seemed to consider a reunification of its country under communism worth almost any effort, had begun to send organized battalions of trained soldiers down the so-called Ho Chi Minh Trail, which ran along the eastern border of Laos. Not only did the presence of these "career military" alter the situation decidedly for the worse, but on top of that the Vietcong—Communist guerrilla forces in the South—had managed to train their own young men into a body to be reckoned with. What this meant, Lyndon was informed, was that all hopes of successfully combating this new enemy with the usual somewhat desultory South Vietnamese forces aided by their American "advisers," even though these latter numbered almost twenty thousand by now, were dim.

To put it bluntly, Lyndon was told the Vietcong were, at this juncture, winning the war. No matter, his advisers said, that he had told the American electorate barely weeks before that he would not "take reckless action which might risk the lives of millions and engulf much of Asia and certainly threaten the peace of the entire world." No matter that he had promised not "to send American boys nine or ten thousand miles away from home to do what Asian boys ought to be doing to protect themselves." Something drastic would have to be done. If the American people protested that they had been hoodwinked, lied to, deceived—and many would say just that—wasn't that better than losing the war?

On the morning of February 6 the Vietcong, armed with hand grenades and mortars, attacked the "advisers'" barracks at Pleiku in South Vietnam and a helicopter base four miles away. Eight men were killed; a ninth died later. More than a hundred were injured, and vast amounts of matériel were destroyed. It was not quite Pearl Harbor; it did, however, unite Lyndon's staff.[3] Mac Bundy called from Saigon where he was on a mission for the president to find out exactly what his colleagues in Washington were thinking about. What else was necessary? How long?

That afternoon Mac Bundy again called the White House Situation Room from Saigon. Cy Vance, who was then deputy secretary of defense, answered the phone. Bundy told him that he, General Westmoreland, and Ambassador Taylor had agreed that bombing should now begin.

The president called a meeting of the National Security Council for 7:45 that evening. The decision to start bombing received the unanimous support of everyone present, including Ball, who said, "We are all in accord that action must be taken. We do need to decide how we shall handle the air strikes publicly. We must make it clear that the North Vietnamese and the Vietcong are the same. We are retaliating against North Vietnam because Hanoi directs the Vietcong, supplies arms, and infiltrates men."[4]

The only immediate dissent came from Mike Mansfield, who said that the bombing might be getting us into a war with China and might bring Moscow and Peking together. But, according to Lyndon, "He proposed no alternative."

The proposed targets were army barracks connected with North Vietnam's infiltration southward. The bombing was to be a joint U.S.-South Vietnamese operation. Lyndon later wrote how seriously they all considered the possible consequences.

"'We have kept our gun over the mantle . . . for a long time now,' I said. 'And what was the result? They are killing our men while they sleep in the night. I can't ask our American soldiers out there to continue to fight with one hand tied behind their backs.'

"I thought that perhaps a sudden and effective air strike would convince the leaders in Hanoi that we were serious in our purpose and also that the North could not count on continued immunity if they persisted in aggression in the South."[5]

But one air strike is never enough, and, to be sure, when Mac Bundy and his team got back from Vietnam he recommended continuous bombing. Bundy arrived at the White

House at 11:00 P.M. February 7 with a thoroughly pessimistic report. Lyndon read it before going to sleep. The report bluntly said that the situation in Vietnam was deteriorating and that defeat appeared inevitable unless a new course of action were embarked upon. It reiterated that South Vietnam was without question America's responsibility; moreover, it would remain so for an indefinite time to come, until Ho and his Vietcong were defeated.

Parts of the report had been prepared with, among other members of the party, John McNaughton, assistant secretary of defense for internal security affairs, and it said that the bombing would be costly in terms of men and of planes, which Lyndon could not and did not deny.

On February 10 the Vietcong attacked an American barracks in Qui Nhon; seven Vietnamese and twenty-three Americans were killed. After that Lyndon, again with the approval of all of his advisers, ordered Operation Rolling Thunder, sustained bombing of the North, into execution.

George Aiken: "On the day the administration decided to carry on the bombing of North Vietnam some of us advised very strongly against it. We said it wouldn't stop the infiltration; it wouldn't bring the war to an earlier end, that the North Vietnamese would react the same as other people, including ourselves, if we started bombing them."

Morse and Gruening were no longer the only senators publicly criticizing what was happening in Vietnam; in addition to Aiken, they were joined by Frank Church of Idaho and George McGovern of South Dakota. Other senators, including Gene McCarthy, were visibly unhappy, but silent for the moment.

And, of course, the Vietcong were not bombed into submission; to the contrary, as the bombing went on they seemed more resilient than ever, and there were clearly more of them than before. The South Vietnamese soldiers continued to display their usual lack of enthusiasm for battle, and their government continued to be corrupt and unstable.

Lyndon kept calling congressmen and senators, particularly liberals, to the White House to demonstrate what restraint he was exercising. He was, he would assure them, no Curtis LeMay. LeMay earlier that year had retired as chief of staff of the air force, but before doing so he had advised a State Department official how to end the mess in Vietnam. All you had to do was drop some nuclear bombs on the Chinese mainland, "nuking the Chinks." Even more restrained generals, Lyndon sometimes said, knew only two words—*bomb* and *spend*. He, Lyndon, personally approved of every bombing target; not an outhouse could be bombed without his personal approval, and he was *restrained*.

For once, however, the "treatment" failed to work. Criticism did not recede; it swelled.

Even his speech at Johns Hopkins on April 7, in which he outlined his billion-dollar program for the Mekong Delta, "to provide food and water and power on a scale to dwarf even our own TVA," seemed to satisfy no one.

In April, according to *The Pentagon Papers*, the president had approved a troop increase of eighteen to twenty thousand men and had authorized "a change of mission" for the marines. There was to be no more talk of "advisers." In April and May the marines thereby suffered some two hundred fatalities while performing missions that should, should they not, have been performed by Asian boys.

By mid-July it was clear, yet again, that something more had to be done, something more drastic.

George E. Reedy: "I think that period was the most anguished I ever saw. He wanted to do anything, anything rather than send more troops."

John Sparkman: "Not long before the first escalation, in the summer of 1965, he had a group of us down there in the morning. He was going to have a news conference at eleven. He had to make a decision before that time. And if I ever saw a man literally torn to pieces, it was he that morning.

"He asked each one—he went around the fifteen or twenty of us who were there, and said, 'What would you advise?' And practically everybody said, 'I'd put more troops in there. I'd put whatever is necessary to hold them back.'

"It was the unanimous opinion of those men."

On July 28 Lyndon announced at his press conference and to a nationwide television audience that he would send an additional force of fifty thousand men—"combat support troops," they were called—to South Vietnam; more, he said in a masterly understatement, would probably be needed later.

He did not say that he already had agreed to an eventual total of a hundred thousand. By the end of 1965 there were 184,314 American men in Vietnam and, as we now know, that was only the beginning.

Some years later William Putnam Bundy was asked by a reporter for the BBC to explain what had happened.

Bundy said that he had expected Johnson would ask for congressional action, but instead the president had "opted for not presenting the course to Congress."

Bundy was asked if he considered that honest.

William Bundy: "Well, it depends on your view. It was certainly in my judgment at least as honest as many things that Franklin Roosevelt did in 1941. The trouble was that this turned out badly, and therefore looks much worse in history."

Well, there you are, I guess; there we all were and are, I guess.

Looking back on the sixties one remembers the youth—Norman Podhoretz called them "the youngs"—marching, carrying signs that were sometimes obscene, shouting, "Hey, hey, LBJ," and the rest of it. But most Americans are not marchers and do not go around carrying signs, obscene or otherwise.

What many of us seem to have forgotten—or perhaps don't wish to remember—is that from 1965, when the substantial increase in ground troops and bombing took place, and for some time following, not only were Congress and the majority of Johnson's senior advisers in agreement with the policy we were pursuing, so were the vast majority of the American people and the press. The big question was whether he was doing enough. Shouldn't we bomb them back to the Stone Age?

Bill Moyers: "Samuel Lubell [a conductor of public opinion polls] reported in 1965 that our policy there was supported by three out of four college students in New York

State. Free and Cantril [Lloyd A. Free and Hadley Cantril, *The Political Beliefs of Americans*, 1967] discovered in the same year that it was the young who most favored stepping up the war. The age group which provided the original escalation with its strongest support has also provided the most articulate and belligerent opponents to the war. The phenomenon President Johnson faced, of course, is that most Americans are both hawk and dove, a situation which has made the incongruities of public opinion all the more deceiving. . . . Sixty percent of the people in one poll expressed opposition to bombing large cities in North Vietnam, but 61 percent said they were for bombing industrial plants and factories. Three out of five, in other words, were for bombing, but they were not for bombing cities. At first blush, this seems to be inconsistent, but what it meant . . . was that Americans wanted the war to end as soon as possible, even if escalation was the way to do it. This explains why the president's standing in the polls increased sharply after he ordered a bombing pause in late 1965 and after he ordered the resumption of bombing when the pause did not produce negotiations."[6]

Gallup polls showed in March 1965 that when asked, *Should we continue present efforts or pull out?*, 66 percent of those polled said we should continue; 19 percent said we should pull out, and 15 percent had no opinion.

In March 1966, when asked, *Do you approve of the way Johnson is handling the Vietnamese situation?*, 50 percent approved; 33 percent did not, and 17 percent had no opinion.

As late as December 1967 Harris polls revealed that the public was continuing its hard line on the Vietnam war. On December 23, 1967, Harris reported "the prevailing mood in America today toward the Vietnam conflict is to intensify military pressure within limits and see the war through." Those limits were bombing airfields, supply lines in China, and using atomic ground weapons. Moreover, one out of four American adults—more than twenty-eight million voting-age citizens—favored going beyond these limits.

In other words, at the end of 1967 more Americans favored using atomic weapons than de-escalation. Memory is indeed a gentleman.

But back in 1965 most Americans were still unaware of Haiphong Harbor and the DMZ. Lyndon, however, was not unaware of the need for wide support, and that would be all the more likely if certain men of special prominence made known their approval of his present course of action. No one's endorsement was more to be desired than that of former President Dwight Eisenhower, so Lyndon was naturally delighted when Ike's former secretary of the treasury, Robert B. Anderson, whose economic advice had stood him in such good stead when he first took over as president, suggested that Lyndon and Ike get together.

On February 17, just a week after the decision to begin bombing the North, the two men met. As Lyndon described the meeting:

"We talked for about four hours, first in the Cabinet Room and later over lunch. . . . In his judgment, our air strikes against the North could not prevent the North Vietnamese from infiltrating men and supplies into the South if they wished to bear the cost of that effort. But the strikes could discourage the North Vietnamese. . . .

"Eisenhower saw merit in the idea suggested by General Wheeler of putting an American division into Vietnam just south of the demilitarized zone to help protect the

South, but he did not favor any large deployment at that time. Later in our talk he said that we could not let the Indochina peninsula fall. . . .

"He assured me of his full and complete support for any course of action I decided was necessary."[7]

Johnson was equally pleased by Harry Truman's expression of confidence, also by the endorsement of fellow Democrat Averell Harriman and of notable Republicans such as Henry Cabot Lodge, Nelson Rockefeller, Thomas E. Dewey, and even a young student at Phillips Exeter named Dwight David Eisenhower II.

But in 1965 most people, certainly Lyndon, were hoping along with D. David's grandfather that the North Vietnamese would soon be discouraged and retire.

Carroll Kilpatrick: "I think Johnson was doing what almost any president at the time might have done. I think Kennedy would have done about what Johnson did. I think we all at that time thought a little show of force and Ho Chi Minh would back down and that would do it. The feeling that we'd made a commitment, and that we didn't want another Cuba, was very widespread.

"You remember it was called 'the McNamara War.' And McNamara said he was proud to have it called 'the McNamara War.' But later he changed his attitude."

Max Frankel: "I think that going into the bombing period in early '65 there was nobody high in the administration who did not feel that within four or five months the enemy would be at the bargaining table.

"They thought they could achieve it by the threat of the American military machine coming in. I have no doubt in my own mind that the allegedly worse hawks among them would never have paid the price that they ultimately did if they had realized what was involved in the beginning. And I would count Lyndon Johnson among them."

Probably no expression of support so surprised Lyndon as did a letter he received shortly after Congress convened in 1966:

[Undated[8]]

Dear Mr. President,

Reading the newspapers and their columnists and listening to my colleagues in Congress (including myself) on what to do and what not to do in Vietnam must become somewhat discouraging at times.

I was thinking of you and your responsibilities while I was reading Bruce. Catton's book *Never Call Retreat*.

I thought it might give you some comfort to look again at another president, Abraham Lincoln, and some of the identical problems and situations that he faced that you are now meeting. I refer you to pages 56–63 and 371–381 of the Catton book. You see on page 381 that he became so discouraged in the late spring of 1864 that he wrote a memorandum saying he was expecting to lose the election.

Of course the situation improved a few months later but it does show how terribly distressed even he must have been at times.

Actually it is clear that the division within the North was much greater during various periods of time in that war though I recognize that there are not exact parallels and you face problems and situations that he did not have to meet.

In closing let me say how impressed I have been with the most recent efforts to find a peaceful solution to Vietnam. Our position within the United States and around the world has improved immeasurably as we face the difficult decisions of this year.

Respectfully,
Bob Kennedy

THE FROG FARM

As is surely apparent by now, Lyndon was a man of contradictions, *all* contradictions, it often seemed. He was, as we know, greatly gifted for understanding the needs of America and for meeting many of them, but in foreign affairs he was at best uncertain. And he was consistently ill-advised by people like Walt Whitman Rostow, who used a lot of big words to say very little.

Hubert H. Humphrey: "The one thing that he never felt comfortable with was the academic community; he felt that he wasn't accepted by them, and he wasn't. And yet he was the best friend they ever had in the White House for education. The liberals always had trouble accepting him, and this was from the beginning, long before the war in Vietnam became a real issue. He would say, 'I've got their legislation passed, bills that haven't been passed for decades, and they *still* won't accept me.'

"He would say, 'I don't understand it. I don't have the right eau de cologne for them.'

"The Johnson that people saw in the Rose Garden and on television was a very different Johnson than the real Johnson. He felt he had to be presidential and puritanical in the White House, but he was a cowboy at heart, personally and physically.

"He had to have people around him. Very much so. He was like a plant reaching out for water. Like a tree. And his whole demeanor was one great big long reach. If you weren't there, he'd just reach a little further to get you. And if he couldn't get you physically, he'd pick up the phone and get you. If he couldn't get you that way, he'd send an airplane and get you. He'd get you.

"Except for the 'Beautiful People'—these were the people who had no love for Johnson and no respect for him. And he knew it. He tried desperately on the one hand to gain it, and on the other hand he was angry. Georgetown to him was the center of a political conspiracy against him and his administration."

John Dodds: "Why did a man like Walt Whitman Rostow have the position and the power that he did in the Johnson administration? The reason is very simple. Walt Rostow, to people who don't know intellectuals, is the ultimate intellectual, and I think that's what he was to Johnson. What Walt said, Johnson believed. A man with all those degrees must know what he was talking about."

On the other hand, according to Marianne Means: "He liked to put them on, the so-called intellectuals. He always used to call canapes 'ore-doves,' and he did it deliberately.

It amused him, to see who would react and who wouldn't and how they would react. I think it was a device for sorting out the phonies. If people can be put off because of the pronunciation of a word instead of the content of what he was saying, then he had no use for them."

John P. Roche: "He put people down in ways that I thought were despicable. He did take people swimming bare-assed in the pool, and the kind of people he loved to do it with were characters like the great stone face, John Gardner. He dropped people like that on their aristocratic asses. And what it meant, stripped down, it meant, 'I got that great intellectual John Gardner in my pool swimming around bare-assed naked.'"

Peter Benchley: "Oh, I heard him say many times to Harry McPherson, for instance, who's from Texas and not from New York, after McPherson had expressed an opinion with which Johnson didn't agree, 'Well, all my New York intellectuals think the same way.' He was not patient with the liberals, the intellectuals so-called. And I think he had every reason to be impatient; they had been completely unreasonable toward him."

Harry McPherson: "Georgetown was the State Department, the foreign service officers. It was the Stevensonites and the Kennedyites and the *New York Times* and the *Washington Post* people, who disliked him.

"I used to fight against the word *insecure* about Johnson, but I think it's true that he was, profoundly so."

George E. Reedy: "Johnson always attributed his difficulty with the intellectual community solely to snobbery. There was an element of that, no question about it. But Johnson had as many troubles with intellectuals who had never got near Harvard or Yale or the Ivy League as those who had.

"I once arranged a meeting between him and Walter Prescott Webb, rather an extended meeting. I still remember Walter Webb, the great western historian, coming out of that meeting. He was mad. He said, 'George, that man asked me to write a speech on foreign affairs. I don't know anything about foreign affairs. My field of specialization is the West. Doesn't that man know what I do?'

"This was one of his problems. Johnson really didn't know what intellectuals did, and he assumed that if you brought in an intellectual that he was supposed to give you material to put in speeches. I really think he thought of intellectuals and what they did in the same sense that in the old days you'd teach your daughter to play 'Chopsticks' on the piano. Then on Sunday, when the priest came in, you would open up the curtains and dust off all the furniture in the living room—you kept it closed the other six days of the week—and your daughter would sit down and play 'Chopsticks.' It was sort of an accomplishment.

"I think he thought of education solely as a means of preparing someone for a job, and that if a man didn't study something that prepared him directly for a job, that is, other than teaching that particular skill, that then it became a sort of public relations thing. You see, he understood what engineers did; he understood what physicists did. But he had a great difficulty with historians, with philosophers, with sociologists."

Edwin S. Weisl, Sr.: "That so-called intellectual group, he always felt they'd never accept him. I don't know why he cared so much about them because, after all, it's just like old Mark Twain's story about the fellow who bought the frog farm—they made so much noise he thought the place was full of frogs, and when he bought it, he found there were only two frogs in the whole pond."

Walter Jenkins: "I don't think he ever felt inferior to anybody in native intelligence and ability. I think he did feel a shortcoming in language and finesse which you might get at Harvard and Yale. And he had a great sense of not knowing as much about music and art and being well read. Those subjects, some of them, were not featured quite as much at Southwest Texas State College."

Wilbur J. Cohen: "There was an inability of Johnson and the intellectuals to discuss the same problems in the same terms. And I think that Johnson made a very serious mistake in trying to get to the intellectuals through people like Eric F. Goldman."

John Dodds: "Eric Goldman, during his brief stay in the White House, was, I believe, largely confined to the East Wing, but when Johnson did see him, which was not often, he would say, 'That there is Bird's intellectual. He is a real in-tel-lec-shul. And he belongs to Bird. He just knows the answer to everything. Everything.'"

Eric Goldman, who was a professor of history at Princeton and the author of several popular histories, as well as being something of a television personality, was a special consultant to the president from shortly after the Kennedy assassination until the fall of 1966, after which time he wrote a kind of "insider's" book about Johnson's White House, *The Tragedy of Lyndon Johnson*. In his book Goldman states that in February 1965 Bess Abell, then White House social secretary, suggested that in the spring "something cultural" ought to be done. Something reminiscent of the Kennedy days when people like André Malraux and Pablo Casals seemed always to be showing up. Goldman eventually decided on a "White House Festival of the Arts," and after he received the approval of, among others, both the president and Lady Bird, he invited "major figures" in each of seven categories—painting, sculpture, music (serious and jazz), literature, photography, cinema, and the dance—to attend. Of the writers invited, at first only two said no. Edmund Wilson declined. E.B. White in his familiar graceful manner wrote, "Of course I'd do anything for the White House but, believe me, you don't want me. I've tried reading from my essays and for some reason . . . I just can't do it." [1]

Shortly before the hurriedly created festival, Goldman received a letter from Robert Lowell, the country's best-known and most respected living poet. Lowell had at first accepted the invitation but changed his mind. The letter, addressed to the president, said in part:

> Although I am very enthusiastic about most of your domestic legislation and intentions, I nevertheless can only follow our present foreign policy with the greatest dismay and distrust. . . . We are in danger of imperceptibly becoming an explosive and suddenly chauvinistic nation, and may even be drifting on our way to the last nuclear ruin. I know it is hard for the responsible man to act; it is also painful for the private and irresolute man to dare criticism. At this distinguished, delicate and perhaps determining moment, I feel I am serving you and our country best by not taking part in the White House Festival of Arts.
>
> Respectfully yours,
> Robert Lowell

The story of Lowell's withdrawal, not unexpectedly, was on the front page of the *New York Times* the next morning. Three others who declined to attend were Robert S. Brustein, about to become dean of the Yale Drama School; Alexander Calder, the sculptor, and Paul Strand, photographer.

What followed can generally be described as a shambles.

On Monday May 14, 1965, Mark Van Doren, then seventy-one and surely one of the gentlest men who ever lived, opened the festival, reading a statement defending Lowell and at the same time expressing appreciation for the hospitality of the president and the First Lady and for their encouragement of the festival.

John Hersey read from his classic, *Hiroshima*, rather than from his novels. *Hiroshima*, after all, was a warning, and a brilliant one, of what happens when nations are at war. Hersey prefaced his reading by saying, "I read these passages in behalf of the great number of citizens who have become alarmed in recent weeks by the sight of fire begetting fire. Let these words be a reminder. The step from one degree of violence to the next is imperceptibly taken and cannot easily be taken back. . . . Wars have a way of getting out of hand."[2]

There was not much laughter that day. One of the few lighthearted moments was when Phyllis McGinley read her poem *In Praise of Diversity* and, according to Goldman, added a new verse:

> And while the pot of culture's
> bubblesome
> Praise poets even when
> they're troublesome.[3]

We need not, I think, deal at length with the man who at the moment appeared to be the star of the festival, one Dwight Macdonald, who had been many things and was at that moment film critic for *Esquire* magazine. Macdonald had at first not been invited to the festival and signed a petition saying that those who had been invited should, like Lowell, not attend; when *his* invitation to the festival arrived, he decided, after all, to attend. During the day he drew up and circulated a petition saying, "We should like to make it clear that in accepting the president's kind invitation to attend the White House Arts Festival, we do not mean either to repudiate the courageous position taken by Robert Lowell, or to endorse the administration's foreign policy. We quite share Mr. Lowell's dismay at our country's recent actions in Vietnam and the Dominican Republic."[4]

A reporter asked Macdonald if he did not feel it was somewhat odd that he had, without an invitation to the festival, advised people who did have an invitation to decline, and then, when he received an invitation, accepted. The reporter said, "Now, having accepted, you use the invitation to tell your host what you think of him and try to turn his party into a mass meeting. If it is all so loathsome, why didn't you just stay away?"

Macdonald, a man grand of manner when he chose, said, "I am here because of an assignment to write an article about the festival."

Macdonald did write a piece, which, not surprisingly, was critical of the festival. It appeared in the *New York Review of Books*, one of the editors of which was Elizabeth Hardwick, then the wife of Robert Lowell.

No, Lyndon never made it with the intellectuals.

McPherson: "It never seemed to satisfy him that he was smarter and tougher and harder working and had more power than anybody else. That never seemed to give him the sense that Harry Truman had of being established within himself. Johnson, to use one of his favorite expressions, was always 'an hour late and a dollar short.'"

HYPERBOLE AND THE DOMINICAN REPUBLIC

Max Frankel: "Johnson was fundamentally dishonest in presenting the facts about what was happening in the Dominican Republic to the American people—pouring troops in there and telling ridiculous stories about fifteen hundred heads rolling around in the streets and so on. Whatever the credibility gap ultimately became, the combination of opposition to the policy and the horror at the government's handling arJ explanation of the event is probably where it was born."

On Saturday, April 24, 1965, Lyndon and Bird went to Norfolk, Virginia, to attend the Azalea Festival. Luci had been named queen of the festival. Lyndon placed the crown on her head, said a few innocuous words about daughters, then flew to Camp David where he hoped to spend the rest of Saturday and Sunday resting. Alas, that was not to be. Within the hour he got word that there was once again trouble in the Caribbean; this time in the Dominican Republic.

For quite some time it was not altogether clear who was revolting against what. Trujillo, who had despotically ruled the country for more than thirty years, had been assassinated in 1961. Juan Bosch, an anti-Communist liberal, had been elected president in 1962. Lyndon had attended his inauguration as a representative of President Kennedy, but had not been much taken with Bosch, an idealist, a poet, a short-story writer and philosopher, a maker of good speeches about freedom and the dignity of man, but with no program for a country that desperately needed one. After only seven months Bosch had then been ousted by a military coup.

After his overthrow, Bosch fled to Puerto Rico; President Kennedy, who had hoped to make the Dominican Republic "a showcase for democracy," thus showing up the Communist government of Fidel Castro, immediately, many thought much too hastily, cut off all American aid. This was at a time when the price of sugar was already alarmingly low, and the economy of the country was dependent on sugar.

In April 1965 the government was headed by Donald Reid Cabral, a civilian generally considered a moderate, but a man hated by the Bosch followers, by those to the left of Bosch, and by the far right. The Dominican Republic is a small country in which there are big hatreds.

An uprising of some kind was expected for May or June. Intelligence sources indicated that at least four different ones were being planned at the same time, and the U.S. ambassador, W. Tapley Bennett, a career diplomat whose first embassy was Santo Domingo, was back in the States discussing what should or should not be done when one or another of them occurred. As a rule Bennett did not pay much attention to the politics of the Dominican Republic, though he loved the cocktail parties, balls, and receptions. There were times when he seemed never to take off his white tie and tails.

On Sunday, April 25, a supporter of Bosch's moved into the presidential palace, and air force planes attacked the palace. Nobody seemed to know whose side they were on.

From the beginning it was clear that Communists and supporters of Fidel Castro were involved—how many no one knew. But so were a great many citizens who were not otherwise occupied, youths, adventurers, the bored, and chronically unemployed. Many people in the Dominican Republic were chronically unemployed. Still, there was talk in Santo Domingo and in Washington that the Dominican Republic was in the process of becoming "another Cuba," and no American president could allow that.

On April 28 Bennett, who by that time was back in Santo Domingo, sent a cable to Washington saying that "the country team [meaning all the important American officials in Santo Domingo] was unanimous that the time had come to land the marines." American lives were in danger, the cable added.

Bennett also forwarded a request from Colonel Pedro Bartholomew Benoit, a supporter of the ousted government, a "loyalist," saying that American troops were needed.

Benoit's appeal arrived in Washington on the morning of April 28. The request was granted; *no one* disagreed. The intervention started at once with the dispatch of four hundred marines, but in a country where the streets were clogged with thousands of rebels and nonrebels (who could tell them apart?), four hundred would clearly not be enough.

John Bartlow Martin, who had been John Kennedy's ambassador to the Dominican Republic, was brought to Washington from his home in Connecticut on the morning of April 30; the Eighty-second Airborne Division had started landing before dawn.

Martin: "Nobody was really sure what the hell they were going to do when they got there. That was what the meeting was about, you see. At one point Secretary Rusk reminded the president that it was a serious matter to start shooting up a capital city with American troops. And I said, 'That's the last thing we want to have happen, Mr. President.' And he said, 'No, it isn't. The last thing we want to have happen is a Communist takeover in that country.'

"He turned to McNamara and Wheeler and said, 'What would we have to have to take that island?' apparently not realizing that there were two countries on that island.[1] Because we were only really concerned with one. And they conferred briefly and said, I believe, that it would take two divisions.

"Then we went on talking, and the president wanted me to go down there and try to establish contact with the rebels.

"I was sent because Bennett didn't know the rebels, the Boschistas, and I did. Johnson wanted me to establish contact with them and try to help get a cease-fire. I'm probably making his instructions sound a little more clear than they really were that day. I was to go down and do what I could.

"I remember as we left the Cabinet Room I asked Bundy, 'How much time do you think we've got before they start shooting—taking the place, you know?' And he said, 'You might have forty-eight hours, but I doubt it.'

"The heat came from this crisis atmosphere, this feeling that if we don't do something within forty-eight hours we're going to shoot the place up. My purpose in going down there was to prevent a hell of a lot of Dominicans getting killed by United States troops. Because this seemed to me clearly the way the government was heading.

"The president ran the Dominican intervention like a desk officer in the State Department. I mean, I talked to him at least once a day, and sometimes I talked to him three times a day. He didn't stand back. I think that might account for his intemperate utterances on television. He lost his perspective on the thing."

On the evening of April 28 from the television theater at the White House Lyndon announced that he had just had a meeting with congressional leaders "on the serious situation in the Dominican Republic." He had told them it was necessary to send troops to protect American lives. The members of Congress had agreed. He added that four hundred marines had already landed; there had been no incidents.

In a broadcast on April 30 Lyndon said that there were "signs that people outside the Dominican Republic are seeking to gain control." He also pledged the support of the United States for the team from the Organization of American States that was then on its way to Santo Domingo to arrange for a cease-fire.

"The American nations cannot, must not, and will not permit the establishment of another Communist government in the Western Hemisphere. . . .

". . . Our beloved President John Kennedy less than a week before his death . . . told us, 'We in this hemisphere must . . . use every resource at our command to prevent the establishment of another Cuba in this hemisphere.' "

Martin: "The president did not rule out reinstalling Bosch as president of the Dominican Republic. He didn't say he'd go for it. He just didn't rule it out. He said 'Everything is open. All the options are open. Just go explore everything and see what you can get.' So this is what I did. And it was after talking to Bosch very late one night that I called the president and told him that I was going to meet Bosch again the next morning. And the next morning, Abe Fortas called me. I think he was with Johnson when he called.

"And he had this series of things we wanted Bosch to say. I believe that he and Johnson had cooked up these things. The main thing, of course, that they wanted him to say was that the United States had saved the country from a Communist takeover. I told Fortas I didn't think there was a chance in the world that he'd do this. Fortas said, 'Well, try it anyway. The president wants you to try it.' So I did, and, of course, Bosch just laughed.

"Bosch isn't stupid. He's a lot of things, but he isn't stupid."

*　　*　　*

Robert Hardesty: "He used to say about the crisis in the Dominican Republic, 'Bob, I remember very little about that period. The reason is, it happened so fast. When you're in the presidency, and when you've got a major decision to make, you just put everything out of your mind and focus on that decision like a laser beam and when the decision is finally made you just put everything else out of your mind because there's another one right behind it and then you've got to focus in on that.'"

That is no doubt true and may in part explain why Lyndon reported a few things about that hectic period wrongly; for instance that Bennett's cable asking for troops said that if they were not sent, "American blood will run in the streets." Sometimes hyperbole and lying are not easily distinguishable.

Johnson said that some innocent people had been murdered and beheaded—fifteen hundred of them, he said. Innocent people *were* killed, but no one has ever determined how many. There were no severed heads.

Lyndon remembered that once Bennett had called him while the embassy was under attack. Bennett "was talking to us from under a desk while bullets were going through his windows." Bennett said later that his office had never been attacked and that he had never talked to the president or anyone else from beneath his desk.

There is little question but that John F. Kennedy or any other American president might in 1965 have sent troops into the Dominican Republic under the circumstances that then prevailed, but Kennedy certainly would have acted with more finesse, not necessarily more forthrightly—more deftly, shall we say—and he might have sent fewer troops. At one point there were twenty-two thousand. True, there is said to be safety in numbers, and indeed only two American civilian casualties were suffered—two American reporters shot, in error, by the marines.

Henry Ashmore: "I had been down there and knew something about the situation. I think I can understand what Johnson did. He had the sad example before him of the Bay of Pigs, where they should either have stayed out or gone in but not done what they did, which was to go in halfway.

"I think he was determined not to repeat that error, but I think he overreacted to the point where he damned near sank the island under the weight of the American expeditionary force."

J. William Fulbright: "What astounded me about the Dominican Republic was that the first excuse given was that we were there to save American lives. The next was to prevent another Cuba. But when they asked Admiral Raborn [Raborn became director of the CIA on April 28] how many Communists they had identified as participating in the revolt, I think he said three.

"That made us look kind of silly, the whole idea that we were stopping a Communist takeover. Later they tried to identify more."

Martin: "Our policy seemed more erratic than it was. During the first few days, in a situation so chaotic and confused, it would be surprising if we had been able to lay out a policy neatly. But in fact, on two fundamental points, our policy did settle early and went unchanged; to protect United States lives and to prevent a Castro/Communist takeover.

"I have no doubt whatsoever that there was a real danger of a Communist takeover in the Dominican Republic."

Lyndon was able to start pulling the troops out after the OAS under the direction of its secretary-general, José A. Mora of Costa Rica, for the first time in its history, made use of a peace-keeping team in Santo Domingo. Lyndon was very grateful, perhaps excessively so. He told reporters, "That José Mora . . . did such a wonderful job, he can have anything I've got. He can have my little daughter Luci. Why, I'd even tongue him myself." [2]

Free elections were held in June 1966; Juan Bosch, who had said he was not a candidate, decided that he was a candidate after all, but was defeated by a former president, Joaquim Balaguer, who had been in New York at the time of the revolution, thus not having to take a side and make enemies. The election, observed by members from eighteen nations, was called by the OAS "an outstanding act of democratic purity."

OVERCOMING

Lyndon, who always insisted that he was unlucky, while almost all evidence proved the contrary, was, shall we say, *fortunate* with his 1965 Voting Rights Act. That was a year when a great many white Americans, including, it turned out, most members of the House and Senate, felt guilty.

On January 2 the Reverend Martin Luther King, Jr., began a voting rights drive for Negroes. In a speech before a Negro rally in Selma, Alabama, King said that an attempt would be made to convince Governor George Wallace and the Alabama legislature of the justice of the Negro cause. Failing that, King said, "We shall seek to arouse the federal government by marching by the thousands to the places of registration. We are not asking, we are demanding the right to vote."

The speech was made in a city with a Negro population of fifteen thousand, less than 1 percent of whom were registered voters, and it attracted worldwide attention. Dr. King had recently been to Oslo to accept the Nobel Peace Prize for 1964. Before that, as a kind of bon voyage gift, J. Edgar Hoover had called him "the most notorious liar in America." Dr. King had criticized some southern agents of the FBI for not being too diligent in investigating violations of civil rights.

On his arrival in Selma, King had walked up to the desk of the Hotel Albert and signed the register. A white woman stood on a chair and, watching this indignity, shouted, "Get him, get him, get him." A twenty-six-year-old gas station attendant who was a member of a small segregationist group, the National States Rights Party, obliged by hitting King in the head and kicking him in the groin. He was fined $100 and got sixty days in jail, and Dr. King got his room, $5.75 a night. No Negro had stayed there since the hotel had been built by slave labor to resemble the doge's palace in Venice.

Dr. King did not know it, but Lyndon's acting attorney general, Nicholas Katzenbach, was nearly finished—with the help of members of his staff at the Justice Department—

drawing up a voting rights bill that would meet the strict demands of the president and, he hoped, get passed by Congress. And, to be sure, have the support of leaders of the civil rights movement and most Americans.

The sheriff of Dallas County, Alabama, of which Selma was the county seat, was a fat, jowly man who had surrounded himself with deputies, "squirrel shooters," who, like the sheriff—his name was James Clark—did not like Negroes, particularly when they were also advocates of civil rights. Clark called them "the lowest form of humanity."

In 1964 when some Negroes had tried to register to vote at the Dallas County Courthouse, Sheriff Clark attempted to make them stand in line at the back door. When they refused, he and the "squirrel shooters" took a hundred or more to the county jail, assisting their way to police cars with cattle prods, night sticks, and punches in various susceptible parts of the body.

In 1965, soon after Dr. King's speech, when four hundred Negroes came to the courthouse to try to register, Sheriff Clark said he would slap them in jail if they did not go away, and he arrested sixty-six, chasing the woman who was chairman of the drive half a block down the street before he shoved her into a police car.

Some of this was seen on television screens across the nation, among them those in the White House. Lyndon seldom missed the evening news, and 1965 was a year when he insisted that Bird take a look at what was going on in Alabama, particularly on March 7, a Sunday.

Roger Wilkins: "In the late winter of 1965, SCLC [Southern Christian Leadership Conference] began a campaign in Selma, Alabama, that went on for five or six weeks, sputtered along, and appeared to be going nowhere, as many of the SCLC campaigns had appeared to be going nowhere.

"Finally, one day in early March, the campaigners marched over to the Edmund Pettus Bridge and were met by the Alabama State Police and by the Dallas-Alabama County Sheriff's Department. Some of the law enforcement officers were mounted on horses. I don't now recall whether the marchers were told to stop,[1] but my recollection is that they were not. My recollection is that the law enforcement officers simply formed up a line and shot tear gas into the crowd, rode horses into the crowd, swung their sticks, and generally stopped the march with an overwhelming display of force that was captured by television cameras and shocked and stunned the consciousness of the United States. Suddenly a campaign which had threatened to be a disaster for the civil rights movement had caught fire."

Seventeen Negroes were injured seriously enough to require hospitalization; one of them was young John Lewis, chairman of the Student Nonviolent Coordinating Committee.

On March 9, Lyndon issued a statement: "I am certain Americans everywhere join in deploring the brutality with which a number of Negro citizens of Alabama were treated when they sought to dramatize their deep and sincere interest in obtaining the right to vote."

That same day he sent LeRoy Collins, head of the Community Relations Service, as his personal representative to Selma.

On March 9, King and fifteen hundred other Negroes and whites started once again to march from Selma to Montgomery, Alabama, a distance of about fifty-four miles. This time the marchers were met just outside Selma, where state troopers were standing shoulder to shoulder to stop them. The marchers, following an agreement worked out between Collins and King to turn back at the first sign of resistance, did so. But that night three white Unitarian ministers who had participated were attacked by four white men in the streets of Selma. One of them, the Reverend James J. Reeb of Boston, was taken, unconscious, to a Birmingham hospital, where he died two days later.

That week the death of Reeb was mourned in cities and towns all over the country—as was what was happening in Alabama generally.

And Lyndon seemed to be doing nothing. Angry supporters of the civil rights movement began picketing the White House and sitting in on federal installations in Washington and all over the country. Those at the White House carried signs saying, among other, less polite, things, LBJ—Just You Wait. See What Happens in '68. A few demonstrators joined a group of tourists in the White House, then disengaged themselves from the tourists and staged a White House sit-in.

Most civil rights supporters wanted Lyndon to send federal troops to Selma to protect the rights of the marchers. That he had no intention of doing. He was sure that such a move would jeopardize the voting rights bill in Congress, and very likely defeat it.

Wilkins: "Meanwhile, it became clear that the president was pretty annoyed. He was having civil rights people in. They were urging him to take action, and he was saying, 'How can you turn on me? Look at what I've said. Look at the positions I've taken.' And they were saying, 'But the problem is now—today. What are you going to do about this issue?'"

On March 13, Governor George Wallace inadvertently came to the rescue. Lyndon met with him in the Oval Office at noon. Wallace, as expected, complained that malcontents, many of them trained, he said, in Moscow or New York, were preventing the maintenance of law and order in Alabama. Lyndon said that it seemed to him the contrary was true. A number of American citizens were demanding their rights and being prevented from attaining them by people like Sheriff Clark and, he was too courteous to add—this was, after all, a prime example of "the treatment"—George Wallace.

Lyndon: "We sat together in the Oval Office. I kept my eyes directly on the governor's face the entire time. I saw a nervous, aggressive man; a rough, shrewd politician who had managed to touch the deepest pride as well as prejudice among his people.

"It was to his pride as an Alabama patriot that I appealed when I asked the governor to assure me that he would let the marchers proceed in peace and would provide adequate troops to ensure the right of peaceful assembly."

Then came the question of who was going to protect the rights of the marchers. Wallace said, as Lyndon had known he would, that the sacred state of Alabama had to do that. The president agreed with enthusiasm.

Lyndon said that, on the other hand, should Alabama not protect the rights of the marchers, then he would send in federal troops to do so; as a matter of fact, he added casually, he had seven hundred of them "on alert." Wallace smiled, though not with the exuberance that he had displayed when they began their three-hour meeting.

The meeting ended, according to Lyndon, "on a note of cordiality." But Attorney General Katzenbach, who was present, remembers that the exchange had a somewhat different flavor.

Nicholas Katzenbach: "He [Wallace] was . . . trying to tell the president that it was his responsibility to turn off those demonstrations. President Johnson's response was, 'You know, George, you can turn those off in a minute.' He said, 'Why don'tcha just desegregate all your schools?' He said, 'You and I go out there in front of those television cameras right now, and you announce you've decided to desegregate every school in Alabama.' Wallace said, 'Oh, Mr. President, I can't do that, you know. The schools have got school boards; they're locally run. I haven't got the political power to do that.' Johnson said, *'Don't you shit me, George Wallace.'"*[2]

At 3:45 that afternoon the president, accompanied by Katzenbach, met with the press and faced the television cameras in the Rose Garden. He discussed what had happened in Selma; he said that it must not happen again and that all the power of the federal government would be used to enforce the right of the people in Selma and everywhere else in the United States to demonstrate peacefully. He said further that George Wallace had assured him that the law would be upheld in Alabama.

Horace Busby: "After Wallace left and the press conference was over, Johnson came down the hall to my office, and gave me a draft of a proposed message to Congress prepared by the staff of the Justice Department. I read it and said, 'Mr. President, I'm not a lawyer, but this is just junk. You can't use this. It's the same old stuff about how the federal government can't do anything about what's going on in Selma.'

"He kind of laughed, then he picked up the phone and called Katzenbach and said, 'Nick, Buzz says your draft is just junk.' Nick said he hadn't read it but would read it.

"After about forty-five minutes, Johnson came down to my office again, and he said, 'Katzenbach said you're right. He said it's even worse than you said. You know what that means? It means you're going to have to sit down there and write the message.'

"I had a copy of the Constitution there. I was reading the Fifteenth Amendment, and I realized that what I had always thought, what I believe most people, not just states' rights people, felt—namely that there was a constitutional prohibition preventing the federal government from interfering with what states did in elections—was not true. The Fifteenth Amendment clearly said that the states *can not* keep people from voting. And that Congress could pass laws preventing it. That was a whole new perception to me.

"So I started writing. It came out rapidly. I had about two pages of it written, and Johnson came back in and started reading over my shoulder. For years we'd argued about that. I'd told him time and again that you can't write with somebody watching over your shoulder.

"But he picked up the first two pages, and I could see that he was excited, and as I wrote he kept coming back."

The message, which was sent to the Hill on Monday, began:

In this same month ninety-five years ago—on March 30, 1870—the Constitution of the United States was amended for the fifteenth time to guarantee that no citizen of our land should be denied the right to vote because of race or color. The Fifteenth Amendment of our Constitution today is being systematically and willfully circumvented in certain state and local jurisdictions of our nation.

On Sunday at five in the afternoon Lyndon met with Senators Dirksen, Mansfield, and Tom Kuchel, the liberal Republican from California, as well as Speaker John McCormack and Representatives Carl Albert, Hale Boggs, and William McCulloch, a Republican from Ohio who was a strong advocate of civil rights.

Lyndon, who had already made up his mind what *he* wanted to do, asked the gathering whether or not he should ask for a voting rights act in person or have it delivered by messenger. Ev Dirksen thought a personal appeal might be misinterpreted as displaying panic, and Mike Mansfield, cautious as always, said the message should simply be sent to the Hill. Fortunately for Lyndon, who had every intention of doing the opposite, McCormack disagreed, and so did Carl Albert. By the time the meeting ended, the verdict was unanimous. The president should speak before both houses of Congress and, of course, a nationwide television audience.

Later that evening Lyndon put Dick Goodwin to work on the speech, outlining what he wanted to say, and, as usual, they kept rewriting it right up until the time they left for the Capitol. It was too long—all of Lyndon's speeches were too long. Nevertheless, it was one of the most important and eloquent speeches ever delivered by an American president. It was the one in which Lyndon Johnson, Texas accent and all, said:

> What happened in Selma is part of a larger movement which reaches into every section and state of America. It is the effort of American Negroes to secure for themselves the full blessing of American life.
>
> Their cause must be our cause, too. Because it is not just Negroes, but really it is all of us who must overcome the crippling legacy of bigotry and injustice.
>
> And we shall overcome.

When he finished it seemed that the cheers and the shouting and the applause and the not quite unanimous standing ovation would never end. Dick Goodwin had done it once again, he whom Lyndon called "one of the smartest men I ever met."[3]

On March 17, Wednesday, Frank M. Johnson, Jr., the federal district judge in Montgomery, upheld the right of the demonstrators to stage their march from Selma to Montgomery. Lyndon immediately enjoined George Wallace and all other country and state officials from interfering with the march and ordered that the marchers be protected. The next day Wallace appeared before a meeting of both houses of the state legislature to attack Judge Johnson as a man "who prostitutes our law." And he repeated his charge that many of the marchers were "Communist-trained." But that was old stuff. What was new was that that same day, Thursday, George sent a telegram to Lyndon. The president immediately called in the media in order to read the telegram to them. It said that to protect the marchers would require 6,171 men, 489 vehicles, and 15 buses, and the telegram added, the state of Alabama only had 300 state troopers and maybe 150 other officers, clearly not enough. The governor asked that the federal government "provide sufficient federal authority" to protect the marchers. The president said that there were not nearly enough federal "civilian personnel" to do what the governor asked. The governor did, however, have 10,000 Alabama National Guardsmen, quite enough to handle the assignment. However, "If he is unable or unwilling to call up the guard and to maintain law and order in Alabama, I will call the guard up and give them all the support that may be required."

Everything was going exactly as Lyndon had planned, and the final piece fell into place the next day. Lyndon was in receipt of still another telegram from George. This one avowed that the state of which he was governor could not afford to "bear the burden" of getting the guard to protect the marchers. To which the president replied:

"Because the court order must be obeyed and the rights of all American citizens must be protected I intend to meet your request by providing federal assistance to provide normal police functions. I am calling into federal service selected units of the Alabama National Guard and also will have available police units from the regular army to help you meet your state responsibilities. These forces should be adequate to assure the rights of American citizens pursuant to a federal court order to walk peaceably and safely without injury or loss of life from Selma to Montgomery, Alabama."

The march began at Browns Chapel Methodist Church in Selma the next afternoon at 12:47. There were now thirty-two hundred participants, and in the car that preceded them, helping protect them, rode Major John Cloud of the Alabama State Police, he who only two weeks before had commanded the forces that, with tear gas and billy clubs, had stopped the marchers at the Edmund Pettus Bridge.

On the twenty-fifth, Thursday, the marchers, now twenty-five thousand strong, reached Montgomery. Dr. King said, "We are on the move now—no wave of racism can stop us." That night, Mrs. Viola Luizzo, a white woman from Detroit who was driving from Selma to Montgomery to pick up a carload of marchers, was shot to death. Mrs. Luizzo was the mother of five.

The next day at 12:40 P.M. Lyndon appeared on television with J. Edgar Hoover at his side. Four men, he announced, members of the Ku Klux Klan, had been arrested by the FBI and would be tried for violating the civil rights of Mrs. Luizzo. (Murder is not a federal crime unless committed on federal property.) Lyndon praised the FBI and its director and denounced the Klan.

He said, "My father fought them many long years ago in Texas and I have fought them all my life because I believe them to threaten the peace of every community where they exist."

One reason for the quick arrest, which Lyndon did not mention, was that of the four men, one was an FBI informant.

Getting the voting rights act passed by Congress was not as easy as outsmarting old George, but Lyndon got busy doing what he did best.

Paul H. Douglas: "No one could have worked more vigorously for Negro voting rights than he, and I'm proud to say our progressive group in both the House and the Senate forgot old sores and wounds and turned around and helped him without questioning his motives."

James Farmer: "In that period I was sitting there in his office talking with him. He was on the telephone part of the time. I suspect part of that was to impress me with what he was doing. That's legitimate, too! But he was on the phone on the bill and was cracking the whip. He was cajoling; he was threatening, everything else—whatever tactic was required with that certain individual, he was using."

Sam Shaffer: "The southerners went through their usual paces in the filibuster. I remember calling Harry Byrd off the floor to tell him about something, and I said, 'Senator, are you going to participate in this filibuster?' He said, 'Yes, I'll have to do my part, but you know you can't stop this bill. We can't deny the Negroes a basic constitutional right to vote.'"

Majority leader Mansfield three times was unsuccessful in getting consent for limiting debate. Then on May 21, joined by Ev Dirksen, whose ears were once again attuned to the sound of Johnsonian praise, he filed a cloture petition. Cloture was invoked on May 25, and the bill was passed in the Senate by a vote of seventy-seven to nineteen the following day. It passed the House on July 9, and on August 6 before the signing, in a speech in the Rotunda before a statue of Lincoln, Lyndon said, "This good Congress, the Eighty-ninth Congress, acted swiftly in passing this act. I intend to act with equal dispatch in enforcing this act. Tomorrow at 1:00 P.M. the attorney general has been directed to file a lawsuit challenging the constitutionality of the poll tax in the state of Mississippi. This will begin the legal process which, I confidently believe, will very soon prohibit any state from requiring the payment of money in order to exercise the right to vote."

THE RIOTS

On August 11, only four days after the new voting rights law went into effect, rioting broke out, not in Harlem, where there had been rioting and looting the summer before, not in the South, where violence was expected, but in a section of Los Angeles known locally as Watts. Some people said Watts wasn't even a ghetto; neither was it exactly Beverly Hills; the houses were small, more like rabbit warrens really, and there were the inevitable rats, the empty bottles, the garbage everywhere, the filth, the stench. The area had the smell of defeat. The population was 95 percent Negro.

That particular early August had been very hot and very long. Each day seemed eternal, and then there were the nights. Night and day the streets were crowded with the jobless young and the jobless who were not so young. It was evening, 7:45 P.M., and a highway patrolman, white, stopped a car driven by a young Negro. The patrolman later said he suspected the young man of being drunk. The Negro resisted; the patrolman tried to force him into the patrol car; a crowd gathered, and bottles were thrown. Then the violence began to spread and to escalate; it continued throughout the night and for several days and nights thereafter. Stores were broken into and looted, and there were shouts of "Kill! Kill!"

Four days later thirty-four people had been killed; property damage from fire, looting, and other willful destruction was estimated at $40 million. The damage to the civil rights movement could not be calculated.

Ramsey Clark: "I think the whole nation was surprised; we just simply hadn't seen the warnings. We had looked at the civil rights problem as basically a southern problem, but we were approaching a year when half the blacks of the nation would be out of the South, and in fact the civil rights problems of the urban ghettos exceeded any that we were dealing with in the South."

On the evening of August 15, from Austin, the president issued a statement deploring the riots, adding, "But it is not enough simply to decry disorder. We must also strike at the unjust conditions from which disorder largely flows. . . . We must not let anger drown understanding if domestic peace is ever to rest on its only sure foundation—the faith of all our people that they share, in opportunity and in obligation, the promise of American life."

Joseph A. Califano: "You can't say Watts worked out well, but at least it didn't go beyond Watts, and from the president's point of view, he hung in and issued, when you look back on it, what was a remarkable statement in the context of those days. If you can recall what the climate was like in the wake of those riots, it was a very gutsy thing to do."

Lyndon: "As I have said, time and time again, aimless violence finds fertile ground among men imprisoned by the shadowed walls of hatred, coming of age in the poverty of slums, facing their future without education or skills and with little hope of rewarding work. These ills, too, we are working to wipe out."

Clark: "Mr. Johnson got along personally with the civil rights leaders. He listened with the greatest concern and open-mindedness all through '64, '65, '66, and '67. He wanted desperately, really, to learn and find out."

But even Lyndon recognized that those two old reliables, Whitney Young, Jr., and Roy Wilkins, were both a long way from the ghettos. Something was clearly wrong. Legislation was not enough. What was it *really* like living in a ghetto?

In the summer of 1966, there were again riots, this time in cities as far separated as New York, Chicago, Cleveland, Los Angeles, San Francisco, Atlanta, Detroit (a mere rehearsal for what would happen in 1967), Dayton, and Oakland.

Sherwin Markman: "The ghetto business started in December of 1966. The president one day called a meeting with the staff on a Saturday afternoon somewhere between Christmas and New Year's. He said something to the effect that, 'I want to know what's happening in the ghettos. I get all these reports from the bureaucracy and the experts. If I could, I'd go myself, but I can't. The next best thing is to have some of you fellows go out there and live in the ghettos and then report directly to me and tell me what's happening and any observations or ideas you have.'

"I was the only guy that took that suggestion up. I decided I'd go ahead and do it, and I started out."

A few weeks later Markman, accompanied by Ken Vallis, who had himself grown up in a ghetto and was then working for the Office of Economic Opportunity in Washington, went to Chicago.

Markman: "We lived in the South Side ghetto. We talked to many people of all kinds, went into people's homes, walked the streets at night. We went into block meetings of

Negroes. We talked to some extreme militants. It was a great eye-opener to me, and I wrote a report when I came back.

"The president liked short reports, but I just couldn't keep this one short. It finally ended up being a seven-page, single-spaced report which I sent in with a great deal of trepidation to the president, thinking I'd catch all kinds of hell. But amazingly enough, he was just enthralled with it.

"I wrote about the conditions that you find. I described how the ghetto schools, even the best schools, were so inadequate. And, of course, the rat problem. I think my report had something to do with the rat bill and with the fact that there was $250 million in additional monies for the summer of 1967.

"But after I sent in the report to the president, the next thing I knew, I started hearing from people like Jake Jacobsen and George Christian and Marvin Watson and others that the president not only liked the report but was carrying it around with him and reading it aloud in its entirety to various people he'd trap into listening to it.

"I know of one occasion months later, maybe a year later, and we were in the Cabinet Room. He had a bunch of congressmen in there, and he read that whole report, all seven pages, *aloud.*"

The report said in part:

> Besides living in obvious poverty which I saw—the rat- and roach-infested, atrociously high-priced ($120 per month) apartment hovels, the loitering on the streets, garbage on the ground, the poor and torn clothing—the people of these ghettos also live with a deep-felt bitterness. It was expressed to me in many forms, but it always came out as a belief that the ghetto Negro lives in a world which is severed from ours.

A drive to make Chicago "an open city" began on July 10, 1966, when Dr. Martin Luther King spoke to a rally in Soldier's Field; the audience of almost forty thousand was largely Negro. Dr. King himself was living with his family in a Chicago slum apartment. Dr. King's list of demands largely had to do with more decent housing and open housing in Chicago. After that there were demonstrations, Negroes carrying signs that said End Apartheid in Real Estate. Whites gathered and threw bottles and rocks at the marchers, shouting various obscenities. The whites carried signs saying things like King Would Look Good with a Knife in His Back. Indeed Dr. King was struck with a knife but continued marching.

Roger Wilkins: "When the Chicago riots came in July 1966, the president told Nick Katzenbach to send me out.

"That first night we went up to Dr. King's ghetto apartment. I had not had a high regard for Dr. King up until then. I thought he was kind of a showman. I'd seen all his worst sides. But I gained a respect for him that night that I will carry throughout my life.

"It was a real ghetto apartment, no question about it. We walked up the stairs to the third floor, and we could barely get in the apartment. It was jammed full of people. They were kids, gang kids. It was about one o'clock in the morning. There were forty, fifty, sixty people. Human bodies generate heat and other things, and this was Chicago in the summertime. Very hot. The apartment wasn't air-conditioned. There was no fan. It was not a pleasant place to be.

"In the middle of this, here is this Nobel Prize laureate, sitting on the floor, having a dialogue with semiarticulate gang kids. He was holding a seminar in nonviolence, trying to convince these kids that rioting was destructive; that the way to change a society was to approach it with love of yourself and of mankind and dignity in your own heart.

"For hours this went on; and there were no photographers there, no newspaper men. There was no glory in it. He also kept two assistant attorney generals of the United States waiting for hours while he did this. And when we did talk to him, it was four o'clock in the morning. We had to walk through the bedroom—it was a railroad flat—to get to the kitchen. His children were sleeping in the bedroom.

"He got Mrs. King up, and she gave us coffee. We sat and we talked. He was a great man, a great man!"

The violence in Detroit, where a third of the population was Negro, began early in the morning of July 23, 1967; earlier that month there had been riots and looting in other cities, in particular, Newark.

In Detroit the immediate cause of the rioting began early when the police raided an after-hours bar and arrested seventy-three Negroes and the bartender. A crowd gathered immediately, and the rumor spread that the cops had kicked a woman and beaten a man. That was enough.

Looting soon began, and hundreds of fires were set. At times it looked as if the entire city was in flames. Naturally, any discussion on civil rights now began with the question, "What do you want to do, reward them for rioting and looting?"

Harry McPherson: "That whole afternoon and evening in Detroit was a most trying one. We had Cy Vance and Warren Christopher in Detroit. There was no one in whom the president had more confidence in more situations than Cy, and he is an immensely talented and cool-headed man. The whole issue for hours was whether the governor and the mayor of Detroit would request troops. We were determined not to send them until they did.

"It was clear that sending troops into Detroit was an extraordinary measure. They hadn't been sent into any place since the wartime riots in Detroit in 1943."

Before dawn on July 24 Governor George Romney, who was then regarded seriously as a Republican presidential candidate, admitted that the Detroit police and the Michigan National Guard could not handle the situation. A few hours later, on orders from the president, nearly five thousand airborne troops were on their way to Selfridge Field, thirty miles from Detroit.

Wilkins: "I got to work Monday morning, and I got a call almost immediately from the attorney general, from Ramsey. He said, 'Come over right away.' John Doar, who was then assistant attorney general in charge of civil rights, and Warren Christopher, deputy attorney general, were already there.

"Ramsey said, 'We had a bad night in Detroit. We've been in touch with the governor. He wants troops. The president wants to have a meeting right away.'

"Romney had asked for troops, but he had been unwilling to declare that it was out of control, which was a statutory prerequisite. I also got the feeling that Romney was jockeying for position with the newspapers.

"The president came into the Cabinet Room. He assembled all of the information that the people in the room could give him, and decided on a course of action and the personnel to carry it out. He made it crystal clear that although he was dispatching troops to Detroit, he was putting a civilian, Cy Vance, in control. And he wanted this objective to be accomplished with the minimum, absolutely minimum amount of force. He didn't want loaded guns; and he didn't want bayonets. He was carrying out a terribly difficult decision, and he did it with compassion and humaneness."

Later that evening Lyndon went on television to justify to the electorate why he had decided to use troops in an American city.

McPherson: "Three or four times in the remarks the president said, 'I've been asked to do this by the governor and by the mayor because they cannot maintain order in Detroit.'

"It occurred to me that this was excessive and that it would come back to haunt us."

Indeed it did. Editorials in newspapers across the country accused Lyndon of playing politics with the lives of the people in Detroit.

Wilkins: "The private performance that day was magnificent; the public performance was terrible, which was part of the sadness of Lyndon Johnson. Because I think that a lot of the private things were much, much better than he was ever able to project to the country."

Thirty-seven Negroes and three whites were killed in Detroit between July 23 and July 30, and more than two thousand injured. Over five thousand homes had been destroyed. Almost fifteen hundred fires had been set. Damage was estimated at $350 million, maybe more. There had been more than five thousand arrests.

Walter Reuther summed it up for the press:

"We can take very little comfort and it does us no good to be the first city in America to achieve integrated looting."

Later in the summer of 1967 there were riots in many more cities, including Spanish Harlem, and the new head of the Student Nonviolent Coordinating Committee, who was neither a student nor nonviolent, made speeches advocating more militant methods by Negroes. He told listeners in Cambridge, Maryland, "You better go get yourselves some guns. The only thing honkies respect is guns." That was H. Rap Brown.

The Black Panthers were getting a lot of publicity. Eldridge Cleaver said that the United States was in the middle of a civil war in which neutrality was impossible. He told audiences, "If you're not part of the solution, you're part of the problem."

True, 175,000 more Negroes had registered to vote in Alabama, Georgia, Louisiana, South Carolina, and Mississippi, thanks to the 1965 Voting Rights Act. And true, Lyndon had appointed Thurgood Marshall to the Supreme Court, the first black man ever to hold that position. But as Walter Reuther said: "We have left some Americans behind. They are the 'have-nots' of America. Ugly economic facts feed their frustrations and their sense of hopelessness, which makes them strike out. If you expect them to act as part of our society, you are kidding yourselves."

USING UP CAPITAL

Tom Wicker: "They are rolling the bills out of Congress these days the way Detroit turns supersleek, souped-up autos off the assembly line. . . . The list of achievements is so long that it reads better than the legislative achievements of most two-term presidents, and some of the bills—on medical care, education, voting rights, and presidential disability, to pick a handful—are of such weight as to cause one to go all the way back to Woodrow Wilson's first year to find a congressional session of equal importance."[1]

That was in August 1965 and it had been quite a summer, unlike any in congressional memory. Of course the elementary and secondary education bills had been passed back in April, but such important measures as the excise tax reduction bill, the Medicare bill, the voting rights bill, and the housing and urban development bill, had been passed during the months when Congress was traditionally going through its summer doldrums. This year Congress hadn't had time for doldrums, not to mention vacations, hardly even a long weekend at the shore. The palest people in Washington that summer were members of Congress and their staffs.

Of course, to those who had been around awhile, and particularly to those who had worked for the Chief for any length of time, this was only par for the course.

People, of course, joined and left the presidential team—in that first year after the election alone, there were five cabinet changes, plus in July the replacement of George Reedy as press secretary by Bill Moyers, who, in turn, had been White House chief of staff following Walter Jenkins's resignation the preceding fall—but what is remarkable, given the demanding nature of their boss, is how many stayed. And not only that, but how good and competent a group they were, in the eyes of most observers.

Or no, maybe not so remarkable as that.

Max Frankel: "Johnson's staff were all first rate in that they were reflections of him and ultimately acquired his trust and confidence to the degree that they could try to budge him and manipulate him and to bring opposite views to his attention. They were slaves in the sense that they had to be available at ridiculous hours, from early morning until past midnight, and they worked themselves silly.

"But people like Califano and McPherson and George Christian[2] and Busby and Watson and so on I think served him extremely well. It's silly, I think, in terms of White House staff, to talk about the ideal or the right man. The first requirement is that he fit with the president."

John P. Roche: "I always thought his staff was first class. Joe Califano used to tell Johnson when he thought he was wrong. He would start a shouting match with him. And Harry McPherson also used to lay into Johnson. I mean he really used to sock it to him."

Robert Fleming: "When I first joined Johnson's staff, Lady Bird gave me some advice. We were down at the Ranch, and she said, 'He'll tell you to do things and some of them you won't want to do. If you don't think they're right, don't do them. You probably won't bring it up again, but he'll remember and will ask you. Then you're going to have to face him—that you decided not to do it.

"'If that makes him angry, and you see that he's angry, walk out on him. Leave the room because he will fire you. He doesn't want to fire you. Then you have a problem of what he can do about that. Walk out of the room and call me and tell me what the problem is and I'll see what I can do.' I said, 'Magnificent! Thank you very much!'

"That was on a Thursday—the first week I was there. Saturday morning he said: 'I want you to stay with me all day long, listen to my phone calls, sit in on my meetings, read what I read—get a flavor of what my problems are.' So from nine until three o'clock this went on. Then he said, 'Let's get something to eat.' We started over to the house, and on the way he stopped and said, 'You know, some things about me are hard to get used to because I tell you to do all sorts of things. But there are some of them I tell you to do that you won't think you ought to do.' He stopped and stared at me and said, 'Have you heard this before?' I said, 'Yes, sir, but I cannot possibly understand how you could know I heard it before?' He said, 'Well, the other morning I was putting on my necktie, looking out to see what the weather was like and I saw that Bird had you out for a walk and you didn't have a coat on. I figured something she wanted to say was important enough that she didn't think to ask you if you were going to get cold. So I tried to figure out what she'd tell you. And I think this maybe was it.'

"I said it was."

Harry Middleton: "It appeared to be impossible to fire Peter Benchley. This was long before Benchley became America's richest and best-known novelist.[3] Peter would come in late, take a long lunch, would play squash at the Y, would take a guitar lesson and come back after lunch and practice the guitar. I could hear him from my office strumming on the guitar.

"In any case, in April or May of '67 or '68, Peter had gone to a dinner party in Georgetown and Joe Califano called Peter at the party in Washington and said, 'You have to hurry back to the White House and finish this speech.' Peter said, 'No, no, no. I'm at a dinner party.' Califano said, 'I don't care if you're at a dinner party. You've got to get back to the White House and do this assignment.' But Benchley did not come back. Califano next morning went to the president and said, 'This is what happened.' And the president said, 'Well, fire him.' Califano came to Benchley and said, 'The president wants you fired,' and Benchley said back, 'Well, if the president wants me fired, the president will have to fire me.'

"Califano, with some reluctance, went back to the president and said, 'Mr. President, he won't leave.' And the president said, 'Look. I read in the *Washington Post* that you're the second most powerful man in Washington. I read in the *Washington Post* that you run the White House. I keep reading in the *Washington Post* that you're the most important man in Washington. Now do you mean to tell me that the most powerful man in Washington, the man who has more power, I read in the *Washington Post*, than the State Department can't fire a speech writer?' And Califano said, 'No, he won't leave.' So the president said, 'Well, have Harry McPherson do it.' And I guess all accounts agree on this, that Harry McPherson tried to do it and Peter Benchley gave him the same answer, 'If the president wants me to be fired, then the president has to fire me.'

"Well, eventually President Johnson was not about to take, to use his hyperbole, the power of the leader of the free world to fire a mere speech writer, and since Harry McPherson and Joe Califano wouldn't do it, Peter Benchley never got fired, and he stayed until the end of the administration."

Wilbur J. Cohen: "In 1965 the *Washington Post* talked to me and a few other people and asked, 'What are your future plans?' Without much thinking I said, 'Well, I'm a professor at the University of Michigan, and I hope to go back shortly and resume my professional status.' Couple other people said that. I picked up the Saturday morning issue, read it, and didn't think anything of it.

"My wife and I went to a cocktail party that afternoon, and when I got there, they said, 'President Johnson just called you.' He must have called my home first, and the operator said I'd just gone there. He'd called back. Sure enough, in about ten minutes, President Johnson calls.

" 'Wilbur?'

" 'Yes, Mr. President?'

" 'What is this I read in the paper that you're thinking of leaving me—the most extraordinary thing I ever heard of!'

" 'Mr. President, I didn't have anything in particular in mind.'

" 'I could afford to lose Mrs. Johnson better than I can afford losing you under the present conditions.'

" 'I'm not really planning to leave.'

" 'Okay. I want to make an arrangement with you—that you will not leave the administration without talking to me ahead of time.'

"I always remember this exaggeration, the ultimate exaggeration for him in the sense that Mrs. Johnson was the most valuable asset he had. But as I've said, he was given to hyperbole."

Or, as Bill Moyers put it, "Hyperbole was to Lyndon Johnson what oxygen is to life."

In any case, the staff worked long hours that summer of 1956, and right into the fall, proposing Great Society legislation.

On Sunday, October 3, the hectic summer over, Lyndon flew to New York to sign the immigration bill at the foot of the Statue of Liberty in New York Harbor. He had personally selected the spot without considering that while he would arrive by helicopter, everyone else—half the cabinet, numerous senators and representatives, Governor Rockefeller, Mayor Wagner, mayoral candidates John Lindsay and Abraham Beame, UN Ambassador Arthur Goldberg, and numerous other dignitaries—would be coming by ferry with the tourists. Never mind. The sun shone, the stars and stripes fluttered in the breeze, "America the Beautiful" was sung. Lyndon handed out pens, and the great stone lady hovered approvingly over it all.

On Monday, still in New York, Lyndon went to the thirty-fifth floor of the Waldorf Towers to talk privately with Pope Paul VI, who was there to address the United Nations

General Assembly. Back in Washington on Tuesday, however, Lyndon eluded the press and quietly slipped off to Andrews Air Force Base for a secret meeting with former President Dwight Eisenhower. How, Lyndon asked Ike, did a president deal with a serious illness?

On the Labor Day weekend Lyndon had in fact suffered a gall bladder attack, and after X rays his doctors had recommended surgery. With his passion for secrecy about his illnesses, Lyndon had allowed not so much as a hint of the problem to reach the press. Ike, however, managed to convince him that candor would be to his advantage. Thus later that day Lyndon, savoring the shock value of his surprise announcement, called Vice-President Humphrey into his office and calmly handed him a copy of the statement he was about to give to the press. Hubert was, though only momentarily, speechless. Lyndon reminded him that in the event of his own incapacity he, Hubert, would be in charge, and he couldn't resist a word or two on just what he would expect Hubert to do in that event.

Next, Johnson notified the press that there would be a cabinet meeting at 4:45 that afternoon, no reasons given. Only at the conclusion of that meeting did Lyndon finally summon the press. Still in the Cabinet Room, seated alone at the end of the long, highly polished table, he ended the suspense by reading in measured tones the opinions and decisions of his doctors. "I will therefore enter Bethesda Naval Hospital Thursday night for surgery Friday," he concluded. "The doctors expect there will be minimal time during which I will not be conducting business as usual."

Then, as if to prove that this impending event was nothing the nation need concern itself with unduly, Lyndon embarked on a two-day schedule of whirlwind activity visible as much as possible to press and photographers.

The operation started before seven the morning of October 8, with ten doctors and three Secret Service men (appropriately gowned and masked) in attendance. Two hours and fifteen minutes later the surgeons had removed Lyndon's gall bladder, complete with stone, plus a kidney stone found in the ureter. By noon the president was conscious, reported to be "on the road to recovery" and able once again "to make decisions."

Before he left Bethesda, Lyndon received a group of reporters, and in the course of describing his good health, he lifted his sport shirt to show them the foot-long incision that did, indeed, appear to be healing nicely. The photographers had a field day with that one, and there are people around the world today who remember little else about Lyndon Johnson except that he was the president who showed everyone everywhere his gall bladder scar. Later Lyndon explained the action by saying that he was trying to dispel a rumor that he was really in the hospital for cancer.[4]

Redmon: "I don't know anyone else who would open up and show his gall bladder scar. There has been a great deal of writing about this, analyzing it, psychoanalyzing it.

"I don't think there's anything to analyze. He just didn't mind. I think his mother was so crazy about him and he was so enchanted with himself that he thought everything about himself was enchanting to everybody, including his gall bladder scar."

*　　*　　*

Lyndon's prediction that he would quickly use up his presidential capital began to prove itself true even as the first year wound down. Gradually there began to appear chinks in the wall.

There was, for example, the matter of financing the Great Society. Whatever else it was or wasn't, the Great Society was *expensive*, and the money would have to come from somewhere. By the fall of 1965, it became clear that either one cut elsewhere—and every congressman hovered protectively over whatever federal project his district had—or one risked a very real inflation.

Wilbur Mills: "If you look at the spending performance you notice that September 1965 jumped precipitously over the level of September 1964, and it even went up sharply over that of August 1965. Add to that an additional $30 billion or more that was being spent in Asia, and you have the makings of a very serious inflationary crunch.

"I don't know that he realized it. I don't know that any of us realized it just at that time. But he was getting advice from Gardner Ackley and others that 1966 would not be a good year."

But Congress did not wait for 1966 to indicate that enough was enough. It rebelled that October against the District of Columbia home rule bill. The bill had long been advocated by the publisher of the *Washington Post*, Phil Graham, and after his death in 1963, by his wife and successor, Katharine. It was a liberal bill pure and simple, providing self-government for the populace of Washington, the majority of whom were black. Naturally, the southern congressmen were all against it.

Katharine Graham: "The president was very, very good about it, and kept trying to pass it. I think he really just felt that the bill was right.

"He called me up and said, 'What the hell are you all doing? Why aren't you out there asking everybody where they are and where their vote is and why they aren't working on this legislation? You know what they're doing—they're taking three-day weekends and in the end Dick Russell is going to screw them because he's smarter than they are.'"

Dick Russell did just that and the bill was defeated.

Only two days later another pet project met rejection, this time in the House, where a bill appropriating funds for rent subsidies for low-income families was defeated 185 to 162, even though the House had passed the original bill authorizing the program back in June.

That was the difference between June and October.

Still, taken as a whole, the Eighty-ninth Congress had, indeed, proved "fabulous," as Lyndon had said. Of the 115 legislative recommendations Lyndon sent to the Hill between January and October, he had later that year signed 90 into law. It was an extraordinary performance; whether or not it was also exemplary remained to be seen.

Wilbur J. Cohen: "I think he tried to do too much and worked too hard at it with too many small things mixed in with the large. The average person was unable to comprehend it all; it was too big; too much for him to swallow all at once.

"I think his major problem was that he was not able to persuade the American people that all this needed to be done. And yet he knew it had to be done."

WOMEN

During his postpresidential days, Lyndon was fond of reminiscing about all the things and people his administration should have done more about and for. Harry Middleton remembers one occasion in October of 1971 when he accompanied Lyndon to Abilene for the dedication of a new wing of the Eisenhower Library. Jewel Malechek, wife of the foreman of the Johnson Ranch, was also along. After the dedication, they were going to visit Harry Truman in Independence.

On the long drive to the Salina airport, Lyndon began lamenting the fact that the Johnson White House hadn't done enough for women. What he had in mind was not just women's rights, though he was for those too, but economic opportunity. Day-care centers, for instance. Why hadn't his administration set up more of them? Of course, he'd only had five years, but then five years is a very long time, really, and if only he'd worked harder, been more *aware* of the inequalities of the treatment of women. . . . He worried the subject all the way to the airport.

Lyndon liked women—liked them sexually, personally, professionally. At times he ranted at them, raved at them, screamed and shouted at them, but he did that to men as well. That was Johnson's way of equal treatment. And women responded to him on many levels.

Coates Redmon: "I first met him when he was still vice-president. I hadn't expected what I found, which was just a most attractive man. John Wayne plus. Big and tan and all-American, tough and sort of charming and beautifully dressed, which I had never expected."

Betty Furness: "One thing you've got to remember about Lyndon Johnson is that he *looked* like a president. He didn't look like somebody who was just walking around. He had enormous presence. In the first place, he was an enormous man. I think he was larger—physically larger—than most people think. It took my breath away to walk through the door of the office to meet this man."

Redmon: "He really enjoyed women and he needed them. He was very female-oriented. He would talk about his mother; he was crazy about Lady Bird. And he fell very easily into relationships with other women."

Many of these relationships were platonic; of those liaisons that were not, most were casual; several were long term. During the Senate years when Lady Bird was out of town—occasionally even when she wasn't—he would take someone—often one of his secretaries—to a social affair and introduce her around: "Wantcha t'meet mah girl."

There were always many women on his staff, attractive women. There was the story, no doubt apocryphal but widely circulated, about a girl on the White House staff who came back from a stay at the Ranch and said, "I have to get transferred out of here. There were no locks on the bedroom doors down there at the Ranch, which surprised me, but I wasn't too worried with all the Secret Service agents around. Then in the middle of the night I felt the presence of someone in my room. I was about to scream, when I heard a familiar voice say, 'Move over, honey; this is *yore* president.'"

Most of Lyndon's liaisons—not, of course, a word he was likely himself to have used—were with women whom he knew in other capacities as well, often with whom he had a real relationship, but occasionally an alternative situation presented itself. People who know, who were, presumably, there, tell of how at the 1960 convention in Los Angeles Lyndon, while standing in a reception line at the Biltmore, reached out to shake the hand of an attractive young lady only to find a room key left in his hand. Without batting an eyelash, Lyndon quietly slipped the key into his pocket and turned to the next well-wisher.

Later that day the same young lady was lounging in her room when there was a knock at the door and the sound of a key in the lock. The presidential candidate from Texas strode in. "Here ah am, honey," he said, and then, well, you know. Afterwards they slept for maybe half an hour, a no doubt much-needed rest on Lyndon's part, and then Lyndon woke, dressed, and, looking down at the drowsy young lady, held out his hand and said, "Ah want to thank you for yore help to mah campaign," and left.

Yet had you asked Lyndon if he were faithful to Lady Bird, he probably would have answered yes. And probably in his eyes he was. He was never in doubt about her importance to him, practically, professionally, emotionally.

Lenny Giovannitti: "He was devoted to her and loved her and wanted her to be there, and yet he exploited her because, after all, in the end—'It doesn't matter, all those little things I've done, excursions I've had. You're my anchor. You're the woman I want, I care about.'"

But he was also a powerful politician and, as his associate Erv Duggan said, "Like many politicians the love of applause and the search for sexual satisfaction are related. It's an ego hunger, and I think Lyndon was constantly looking for reassurance.

"The fact is, I think Lyndon was a notorious wolf. I think one of his insecurities was a sexual insecurity. He had been told that he was ugly enough times that he believed it. So he was a flirt, but I think he also loved women and had a high regard for them."

Mollie Parnis: "You were always aware that he was aware that you were a woman. He made you feel protected in his presence."

Wilbur J. Cohen: "Johnson had a lot of animal energy, and he had an attraction for women. He was attracted to intelligent and beautiful women like Mathilde Krim. My idea is, hell, there's nothing wrong with that. I think people misunderstood. I think he loved Mrs. Johnson, he had a lot of respect for her, but he also was a man."

Despite all the others, he remained devoted to Lady Bird, depended on her, sought her advice and was in love with her till the very end of his life.

Mary Margaret Valenti: "I think obviously there must have been a tremendously strong bond between him and his mother, and that always affects how a man feels about women, and his own feelings about his wife as a woman of great intelligence and character, and the qualities that he valued most. I think he did care, and he was sensitive to women. I never saw him put down a woman intellectually."

Elizabeth Goldschmidt: "I think Johnson was always seeking substitute father figures, and, to some extent, substitute mother figures. Helen Douglas and I have often discussed our relationship to Johnson, because I think it was different for us as women than for some others. We really had a maternal feeling for him, a protective feeling, and Helen said that's the way she felt, too—that when she disagreed with him, as she strongly did on Vietnam, she felt sorry that he was mistaken. Many people who were very bitter toward Johnson during those years could not really understand how people like Helen, Tex, and myself could be so tolerant of him. It was really sort of a familial affection.

"I think he felt toward Helen and toward me very much the same—this protective loyalty to old friends."

Harry McPherson: "Johnson does very well with women. At the time even when his polls were going down generally in the country, he maintained through most of that period a majority of support among women. Part of it, I think, is because he is a big man and conveys a sense of manliness. Some women, I suppose, find him gauche and with too many warts, too self-centered and all that, particularly highly involved, highly educated women who are deeply concerned with policy issues. But women qua women find him an attractive man."

Luci said her father was the least sexist of men—one of his favorite sayings being, "The greatest untapped natural resource in the United States today is woman power."

In 1961 Kennedy had appointed a commission on the status of women to study the problems concerning the advancement of women particularly in government, and to prepare a report. After all, he had a campaign promise to fulfill.

The commission set up seven task forces of people knowledgeable in the fields of education, civil and political rights, and federal and private employment. At the end of the study they submitted a report in which they recommended the formation of two groups: one an interdepartmental committee on the status of women, the other a citizens' advisory council on the status of women. Upon the report's submission, the group was terminated and the report duly filed. After he took office, Johnson appointed these two groups.

Maurine Neuberger: "In the summer of '63 I said to President Kennedy, 'I'm interested in your reelection and I'd like to see you give attention to *women*. You've won them over anyhow, personally, but if you could just show that you were interested in women,' and so on.

"I went to every Senate office, that is, somebody on my staff did,[1] and said, 'The president says he's willing to appoint women, but he doesn't know who they are or where they are. And you must have had women volunteers and women in your state who've helped you. Will you give me a list?' You know, those lists came in, reams of them. . . . And you know, we never heard a word from it. I reactivated it for Johnson."

Goldschmidt: "Kennedy had been very poor on the subject of women. It was a constant source of complaint with Mrs. Roosevelt and women leaders in the party that he hadn't appointed more women. So rather early in his administration Johnson made a big point of seeking out women; appointing women to high places. It may have been intuition with him, that this was another place where he could make a political pitch that would distinguish him from Kennedy."

*   *   *

At a cabinet meeting in January 1964, Lyndon announced his intention to appoint fifty additional women to government posts and said, "The day is over when top jobs are reserved for men."

Lindy Boggs: "When six weeks had passed by and there were only twenty, he wondered what on earth was going wrong. Thank goodness for the impatience of Lyndon Johnson."

Isabelle Shelton: "When he announced he was going to name fifty, he appointed sort of a three-woman task force.

"Lady Bird Johnson, Liz Carpenter, and Simone Poulain[2] were a fearsomely efficient trio, all in the White House at the same time. Jackie had beautified the White House and Lady Bird took on the country. If Lyndon Johnson had served another term I'm sure she would have beautified the world. She was really the early conscience of the new wave of conservation in this country."[3]

At the first annual presentation of the Eleanor Roosevelt Awards at the Women's National Press Club on March 4, 1964, Lyndon announced the names of the first ten women and said, "I would like at this time to make a policy announcement. I am unabashedly in favor of women. I'm insisting that women play a larger role in this government's plans and progress."

One early appointment was Betty Furness, a onetime movie star who was also nationally known for opening and closing the door of a Westinghouse refrigerator. She replaced Esther Peterson as special assistant to the president for consumer affairs.

Furness: "I was taken to the Oval Office. Lyndon sat me down on the couch and he had a rocking chair opposite me. He leaned forward and talked to me at some length about how he felt about consumers, and what he wanted me to do. He spoke marvelously. And I thought, 'I'm going to remember every single word he's saying because he's saying it so clearly.' Of course, I got out of the office and remembered nothing because I was so dumbstruck.

"I do remember one thing he said word for word. When I said I was pleased and wanted to do what he wanted me to do, he said, 'Betty, I want you to go out and tell the consumer that his government cares about him. And I want you to come back and tell me what's on his mind. . . .'

"Then this really adorable bear of a man shook my hand and walked me to the door."

Ms. Furness's last sentence illustrates one of the hazards of appearing regularly on television.

There were many other appointments as well.

John Bartlow Martin: "I don't think the Tariff Commission had ever had a woman. A vacancy occurred, and we went to the list of former winners of the Federal Women's Award and we found in there the name of Penelope Thunberg, who was an economist in international finance for the CIA. It was a magnificent appointment.

"Another woman who was very good was Anne Rivlin, who was an economist over at Brookings.[4] She went from Brookings into the HEW top strata while John Gardner was there. Then when an assistant secretary vacancy occurred she moved up into that."

Katie Louchheim: "Among the career women he gave several women presidential appointments. One was Ruth Van Cleve, who was in Interior, who was one of the first people the Republicans kicked out of her job—she was appointed head of the territories in the Pacific."

Then there was the Income Maintenance Commission—the so-called Heineman Commission for Welfare Reform. According to Wilbur Cohen, "When I went to him to get him to appoint the members of the commission, he said, 'I don't like the members you've got. Let's appoint some others.' And he suggested Barbara Jordan.

"Here's the president of the United States who says, 'Here's this terrific black woman coming up in the Texas legislature. Let's get her on the commission.' And that's how she got her first national recognition."[5]

All in all, he appointed twenty-seven women to high-level positions, and there might have been more, but many women, because of various family and other obligations, would not accept, a situation Lyndon just couldn't understand.

Martin: "It is very difficult to recruit women for a variety of reasons. One is that very few women gain sufficient professional visibility so that they're known even to other women. Secondly, those that do become known tend to have obligations which keep them from being as mobile as is necessary."

Elizabeth Rowe: "At the time of Churchill's funeral when he was sick in bed with the flu, the president sent for me and I went in and he was stretched out on his bed. He offered me the job of district commissioner, which is very flattering. He said that I was a real Washingtonian and loved my city, that I could do the job. I should do something for the city and I should do something for him. I told him I couldn't. I said that as chairman of the Planning Commission I felt myself stretched to do that job and to be a good wife and mother, and I just couldn't take on anything more. He was most persuasive, but I was firm. I just knew I couldn't do it.

"There was a dinner, I believe at the Statler, called the Candlelight Dinner. He spoke at it and he spoke about getting women in government. He said, 'But my big trouble is when I find somebody that's just perfect for the job, she turns me down.' I was right below him at the table right below the head table. I can still feel myself getting red. He didn't say who it was, but he looked right at me.

"I had let him down."

Johnson found it much easier to work with women than most presidents, including those women who were not in appointed government positions. Women like Mary Lasker, Mathilde Krim, and Florence Mahoney were very interested in health matters. Mrs. Krim, an Israeli, is a doctor on the staff of Sloan-Kettering Institute for Cancer Research. She was appointed to the Mental Retardation Committee. Mrs. Lasker and Mrs. Mahoney were both on the advisory committees of the National Institute of Health. Mrs. Lasker was also a leading supporter of Lady Bird's beautification program. And, along with Lady Bird, they had a good deal of influence with Lyndon.

Cohen: "If you really want to find out how things got done in the Johnson administration, you've got to find out from those four women. Because when other things couldn't be done and when I couldn't get something done, I worked through these four women. I was more successful in working through them than I was with the White House staff."

Mary Keyserling: "The years of his administration, those four and a half years after I was appointed in 1964 to head the Women's Bureau, was a time of unprecedented progress in the lives of women. I think women have realized more gains in many ways during this period than at any comparable period in our history.

"In 1963 an equal pay act had been passed by Congress so that people who do work of equal skill, equal effort, and equal responsibility would be compensated equally. This was the beginning. We were moving into a period of commitment to equality of opportunity for *people*. I think that this commitment was the core of Johnson's administration.

"Then another very important national gain was to take place in October of 1967. This relates to Executive Order 11246 with respect to sex discrimination. For some years it had been possible for a supervisor in government in posting a job vacancy to indicate that a man was wanted for the job, or a woman. The commission felt strongly that all jobs should be opened to people on the basis of qualification and that sex is relevant to job performance in so few cases. Because this was so clearly a problem in government service, limited job opportunities for women, the council strongly recommended that appointments be based on qualification throughout the federal service.

"In the field of civil and political rights legislation—in one year that we kept records there were nearly four hundred improvements in the state civil and political laws as they related to women. We had a few states that prohibited the service of women on state juries—that's gone.

"The work of the Women's Bureau has concentrated on advancing the position of the woman wage earner.

"In all this work we have had the strongest support of President Johnson."

Louchheim: "I had evidence of his prowomen feeling early on, when I first knew President and Mrs. Johnson and his respect for her opinion.

"He had rather amusingly said on occasions in which I was present how there wouldn't have been any point for him at home to have voted nay, because he would have been outvoted three to one by two daughters and his wife. And he used to joke about it a little, but I think it was a serious conviction on his part. He believed that women had a great contribution to make."

But Lyndon was certainly not unmindful of the fact that women also voted.

5

The Creek Is Rising

MORE GUNS AND LESS BUTTER

Nineteen sixty-six began euphorically. The Eighty-ninth Congress was back, ready once again, was it not, to pass anything and everything Lyndon asked for, "the laundry list," the works. The Great Society—Greater, Greatest Society.

In his State of the Union message the president said, "This nation is mighty enough, its society is healthy enough, its people are strong enough, to pursue our goals in the rest of the world [meaning Vietnam] while still building a Great Society here at home." As was said: guns *and* butter.

A Harris poll published on January 9 was most encouraging. "When Congress reconvenes this week, it will be riding the crest of the highest public approval registered in modern times. Fully 71 percent of the American electorate gives a favorable rating to the job done by Congress in 1965. This compares with only 35 percent who felt that way two years ago, shortly after the death of President John F. Kennedy.

"The reason for the increase is the widespread almost uniform praise that now abounds in the country for the legislative program adopted after President Johnson took [office]. Medical care for the aged, considered by the public the most important to them personally is now backed by 82 percent. Federal aid to education, judged the second most important piece of legislation, is supported by 90 percent. Cutting excise taxes, third in the list of popular priorities, is looked on favorably by 92 percent. And the voting rights bill, ranked number four by the public, is now supported by 95 percent.

"It is evident that many of last year's most controversial measures have been accepted and even become popular. . . . In fact, Congress has impressed the people so much that it is more popular than the president—four points higher than the chief executive's last recorded positive rating of 67 percent."

Lyndon frequently read that poll aloud to anyone who could not escape, leaving out the paragraph comparing his popularity and that of Congress, unless, of course, he was reading the poll to a member of Congress.

Of course there was going to be another civil rights act that year. This was to be the one Lyndon had been working up to all along. It would prohibit discrimination in housing, integrate classrooms, and end discrimination on juries. The "open housing" was the crucial part—there was to be no real discrimination in "the sale, rental and financing" of real estate. The bill was dispatched to Congress on April 26, confidently, even exuberantly. There would be no trouble at all in the House, and when it went to the Senate, he and Hubert would talk to old Ev, and old Ev would eventually come along as before.

But this time things did not work out as planned. It was an election year, and members of Congress had been back home, among the voters, and the voters, it appeared, were not friendly to open housing. Watts had unnerved them; it had angered some and frightened others. And now there was to be a law that would make it possible for *them* to move into *our* neighborhood. In spite of negative feelings, the bill passed the House on August 9, but it ran into trouble in the Senate right away.

Dirksen felt Congress should go slower than in 1965 and let the country absorb what had already been passed. As for open housing, "I am against the federal government stepping into what is essentially a private agreement between two people, the seller and the buyer," he said. And no amount of stroking or persuasion would cause him to change his mind, not even a ninety-minute session at the White House. And without Ev a cloture vote was impossible, as indeed it proved to be. The bill was withdrawn on September 19 after two cloture votes failed by ten-vote margins.

At the same time, Lyndon was busy dealing with another bill, one concerning crime.

John P. Roche: "Just after the idiot D.C. crime bill was passed by Congress in 1966, a bill that would have warmed the heart of Genghis Khan, the question was whether the president should veto it. I pointed out that the thing was unconstitutional. Harry McPherson prepared a veto message, but Johnson had another statement which in effect said, 'I don't like it, but I'll sign it.' And people were telling him to sign it. 'Let the courts do the dirty work. Why do you have to get on the hook for this? Everybody's against crime.' And so on. 'Down with crime!'

"And days passed, nine days, and if he didn't sign it in ten days it would become a law without his signature. We were all trying to figure out what he was going to do, and about two o'clock in the morning the White House phone in my house rang. It was a goddamned phone that went off in three bursts of clarions, bwurp, bwurp, bwurp. So my daughter heard this phone ringing and she got up and went in and somebody at the other end said, 'The president wants to speak to your father.' So she got me out of bed. And he said, 'I vetoed it.' I said, 'That's great, Mr. President.' He said, 'I vetoed it and you have destroyed me.' BANG. Down went the phone. I went back to my wife—still half asleep and said, 'The president says that I just destroyed him.' Next morning I found out that he got McPherson and Joe Califano on the phone—same message, same bang."

On October 5 at the White House before a group of Negroes running that fall for elective office, Lyndon made a very successful speech—perhaps his most successful—unrehearsed, and off-the-record. The subject was, or so Lyndon said, power, although it ranged over many areas, and it was Lyndon speaking, pure Lyndon.

He said: "You cannot find one minority group in this nation that hasn't been oppressed at some time or another. You cannot find one minority group that overcame its oppression at any time by means of violence. . . . Now that's history and that's a fact. You cannot find one minority group that wasn't able to ultimately overcome its oppression by the ballots, by learning to use its power, P-O-W-E-R, capital, at the polls, P-O-L-L-S."

He went on to tell them:

"Just a year ago . . . I signed into law one of the landmark bills of this generation, this century. That was the Voting Rights Act of 1965. The purpose of that was to make every voter registrar in the United States color blind, and it is working. A year ago . . . there were 112,000 Negro citizens registered to vote in the state of Alabama—112,000. Today there are more than 250,000. One year.

"Last year there were 35,000 Negroes that were registered to vote in Mississippi. Tonight that figure has more than quadrupled. . . .

"If enough of these backlash candidates are elected to Congress many national programs that mean everything to your people are going to be in deep trouble. Most of these national candidates are not just interested in putting the Negro down; they're interested in plunging a dagger into the heart of all the social welfare legislation. . . .

"When I came in in January [1964] I said, 'I want a poverty program and I want $800 million. That's more than Roosevelt had on PWA or WPA—all those lumped together. He'd turn over in his grave if he thought we could get that much—but I got the $800 million. The next year, I got $1 billion 500 million. Next year, I asked for $1 billion 750 million, up $250 million.

"Now I would like to have doubled it or tripled it or quadrupled it, but I just can't honestly say that I am going to hold back anything from the boys in the rice paddies in order to do it here, and I'm trying to do both at the same time. If you try and put two kids through college at the same time, you've got a man-sized job. Now when you're trying to fight in Vietnam and take everything they need and then do everything we need here at home, you've got a problem."

That was it. You could not have guns and butter after all. And guns won, as they usually do. Roosevelt had the same problem, and he solved it the same way. More guns, no more New Deal. But Franklin was fighting a *popular* war.

Johnson ended the speech to the Negro candidates by saying, "We haven't gone near as far as we're going to go in the next two years of my office if the good Lord is willing and the creeks don't rise."

That fall Lyndon attended a conference in Manila with the leaders of South Vietnam, Australia, and New Zealand. He decided to use the occasion to visit several other countries as well.

On October 17 he left for a seventeen-day trip during which he made twenty-seven speeches, beginning with remarks at Dulles Airport and resuming in Hawaii, Pago Pago, New Zealand, and Australia.

Lyndon never traveled light; he invaded Asia with a large staff and a planeload of busts—of himself.

James Symington: "You can't fault a man for wanting to give mementos and gestures of his friendship. But what he wanted to take with him was, I don't remember the exact figure, something like two hundred busts of himself. Some of them were white marblish in appearance and others were bronze-looking. It is, I think, unusual for a man to want to give a bust of himself in his lifetime, although it's difficult for him to give it any other time. But to make a mass-production gesture really boggles the mind.

"When we got to Manila, he wanted busts and other gifts to go to all the heads of state, and all of it done in one evening. I got a big cart and spent about an hour trundling through the hotel with these boxes of gifts, knocking on all the doors, getting rather curious looks, and explaining that I was chief of protocol with my little cart.

"Today there are heads of state all over Asia who are trying to decide what to do with the president's bust. But not just heads of state, because that would have been only a dozen or less. As I say, we had hundreds of them, so many, many people—cabinet ministers and all kinds of functionaries—received one. The president would say, 'I want a white one.' 'I want a bronze one.' 'I don't want the bronze one—I want the white one.' And you never had the one he wanted and you had to go back and get it. And: 'Damnit! Can't anyone do anything right?'"

Lyndon spoke at Los Banos in the Philippines, at the battle site at Corregidor; then he went to Vietnam and spoke to American troops at Cam Ramh Bay, spoke in Bangkok, at Kuala Lumpur in Malaysia, at a dinner for President and Mrs. Park in Seoul.

Lyndon: "After we landed in Korea we had to drive to the capital and every step of the sixteen miles people were packed ten and twenty deep. I never saw so much humanity in all of my years. It was as if I'd been running around looking for it. Advertising for it. They took us to a hill and we looked out on kind of a bowl setting—just as far as the eye could see little brown people were packed as close as you could pack sardines. It was a glorious sight to see—really something for a politician to witness. Finally, I was just so pleased with the reception that I leaned over to little President Park and I said, 'Mr. President, how many people do you reckon are here today?' And the interpreter translated my comment to him and they talked for a while and then the president walked down and got a hold of his general, his aide with all the braid and medals on and he talked to him a little bit. Then he went down and got a hold of the chief of police and they talked a little bit and it took about five minutes and it was holding up the introduction and everything and I wished to God I'd never asked the question. But finally they all came back and the president made a long speech and I stood there nodding and not understanding a word. Then the interpreter started, he said, 'Mr. President of the United States, the president of Korea say you ask him how many people here. He talk to the chief of police and the best estimate they got is about two million. The president, him say he really sorry, but that's all the people he got. . . .'"[1]

Hugh Sidey: "We came down below Seoul. We were up on a mountain, and it was the damndest scene I've ever seen. I've never seen so many people. We landed in a helicopter on top of that mountain, and they were like ants coming across the rice paddies on the dikes. Streams of humanity, crowded, just massed on the mountain. You could see them for miles either way.

"Johnson, whenever he saw a crowd that size, was in heaven. Sure as hell, what he saw for them was a Texas scene. You know, we'll build a dam down here, grow a little corn, put highways in—all that. Here was the vision, the old Johnson vision. Whenever he summed up what he wanted for the people, wherever he was, he'd say, 'We gotta give them a nice house with a rug on the floor and a little music playing in the background.'

"That was the symbol. That's what he wanted for the Koreans."

Not surprisingly, when Lyndon returned to Washington at Dulles Airport on November 2 he was hoarse.

But not all the talking, nor the junketing, nor the administering of "the treatment" in its various forms, could hide the evidence of erosion. There were signs of it everywhere, some of them small, some not so.

Before the year was over, Lyndon's special assistant and press secretary, Bill Moyers, under financial pressure, resigned.

Roche: "The day Moyers announced his resignation Senator Kennedy called up and invited him to lunch. Kennedy took him to the Sans Souci. In they walked, and there was a cameraman and, bang! The *Washington Star* had this front-page picture of Moyers and Bob Kennedy at the Sans Souci. Johnson just went right up the wall. Jesus Christ! It was such a setup too. You've got to hand it to Bobby. That was a beauty. Of course, after that nothing would ever convince Johnson that Moyers really hadn't been on the Kennedy payroll for years and years."

Johnson never forgave him. Moyers was one of the few people Johnson was never reconciled with who very much wanted to be reconciled. But of all Lyndon's surrogate sons, none was quite so golden, quite so admired, quite so bright and willing, as Billy Don—and the resignation came as a great shock to him. Only Walter Jenkins was missed so much.

Then there was the episode with the airline machinists. It could have been avoided. And Lyndon should have known better.

George E. Reedy: "The big airlines' machinist strike had been going on and on. I had a sinking feeling in the pit of my stomach, 'My God, I'll bet he's going to call the union negotiators into the White House.' And late that afternoon after trying to get hold of somebody in the White House I got the official announcement that he had called them into the White House, which I knew was going to be a disaster. And it was, sure enough. They agreed on a contract on Friday. There was a huge dramatic dash to the nearby TV station so he could announce very grandiloquently that they had settled. The machinists voted on Saturday, and as anybody that knew anything about labor organizations would know, they voted the contract down. And he left looking awfully silly."

Richard Neustadt: "The president mismanaged it in working out a deal with Meany before the mechanics had had a chance to turn down the board report. We'd assumed they'd vote down the first report. In union democracy, it's a tradition they have, especially this union. The White House got committed to the board's report and to a deal with the AFL-CIO—Meany was supposed to influence the nation, and he couldn't."

Reedy: "I regard that as a very significant turning point in his career as president, because after that nothing went right. I don't think that the airline strike made things go wrong, but I think that the forces that led to it were indicative of the sort of forces that were causing him trouble."

At the end of September when Lyndon had announced that he was going to see Thieu at a conference in Manila in late October, Nixon in a newspaper column said, "From diplomats in Tokyo to members of the president's own party in Washington, the question is being posed . . . Is this a quest for peace or a quest for votes?"

No matter what that trip was in quest of . . . it failed. Midterm elections are almost never encouraging to whoever is in power, and the 1966 elections emphatically were not. The Republicans gained three new senators and forty-seven seats in the House. And already the Great Society was being diminished. More than $5 billion in federal programs were either canceled or put off into the indefinite future. And the air strikes against the Hanoi area increased.

T.R.B. in the *New Republic* wrote, "The administration is in trouble. It seems to be coming apart. . . . The country loathes the war, but it also loathes the idea of not winning it." It was not long before the country, large sections of the populace, loathed the war more than the idea of not winning it.

On October 19 Senator George Aiken from Vermont suggested that the United States declare that "we have won the war in the sense that our armed forces are in control of the field and no potential enemy is in a position to establish authority in South Vietnam."

Leonard Marks: "I went to see the president one day not too long after Aiken spoke. I said that maybe Aiken was right, maybe we should say that we had won the war and pull out.

"In our long association I have seen him angry, though seldom at me, but that day he was as angry as I have ever seen him, and he didn't speak to me for some time after that. I was then director of the U.S. Information Agency.

"After the presidency, when he had returned to the Ranch, one day I said to him, 'Mr. President, why did you get so angry at me that time when I said that maybe we should do what George Aiken said?' He thought a moment, and then he smiled and said, 'Because I was afraid you and Aiken might be right.'"

It had begun. Guns *and* butter were giving way to more guns and *less* butter, much less butter, many more guns. The creek was rising.

THE WAR

It was a war unlike any other. Johnson's experience with war—no matter how often he referred to his "Pacific tour" and displayed his Silver Star—was clearly less than Kennedy's had been, enormously less than Eisenhower's, and less even than Truman's (Harry had, after all, served as a captain of field artillery in France during World War I). The president did not know what to make of this war. None of the major Western powers had joined him as an ally. The "front line" had a disconcerting way of shifting daily, almost hourly. And at home Congress, perhaps because it had not been given the option of declaring the war, refused to unite behind it.

The "opposition" senators, who had by the end of 1965 expanded from Morse and

Gruening to include not only Frank Church of Idaho and George McGovern of South Dakota, but also Eugene McCarthy of Minnesota, Gaylord Nelson of Wisconsin, Stephen Young of Ohio, Joseph Clark of Pennsylvania, Vance Hartke of Indiana, and J. William Fulbright of Arkansas, kept protesting that the president was not working hard enough to find a practical avenue for negotiations. And this in spite of the fact that back in April of 1965, at Johns Hopkins University in Baltimore Lyndon had said he was ready for "discussion or negotiations with the governments concerned, in large groups or in small ones, in the reaffirmation of old agreements or their strengthening with new ones. We have stated this position to friend and foe alike."

In fact, Lyndon said then, producing his *pièce de resistance*, the United States was ready for "unconditional discussions."

What "unconditional discussions" meant was not entirely clear. What it did not mean, of course, was a seat for the Vietcong insurgents at the negotiating table. The South Vietnamese government was adamant about that—they were not about to recognize the existence of either the Vietcong or its political counterpart, the National Liberation Front (NLF).

Spokesmen for the South Vietnamese government were Premier Nguyen Cao Ky and General Nguyen Van Thieu, final successors to the string of leaders who had followed Diem, and their joint position of leadership (after June of 1965) was one of the few consistent facts of the next decade. Ky, who possessed the impressive title of vice air marshall, had served with the French against the Algerian nationalists. He was known as "the cowboy" because of his habit of wearing a pearl-handled revolver strapped at his side. After he became premier, he discarded the revolver but kept his mustache, which made him look somewhat more mature than his actual thirty-five years. He had been, and remained, an admirer of Hitler's.

General Nguyen Van Thieu had come to power at the invitation of the South Vietnamese generals who had formed what was called a National Leadership Committee. Thieu and Ky had many things in common—among them a thirst for blood, spilling it carelessly and incessantly.

The day after the Johns Hopkins speech North Vietnam had announced its peace conditions. The war would end, it said, with the withdrawal of U.S. troops and the end of foreign bases in Vietnam, with the recognition of the National Liberation Front and with the reunification of Vietnam without interference from foreign powers.

Well that, for the time being, was that.

One senator who had advocated from the beginning recognition of the NLF, which after all effectively controlled a major part of the country, was Wayne Morse.

Hubert H. Humphrey: "They had a strange relationship. Wayne would constantly implant his foot right in Johnson's groin and yet a few days later they would be bosom buddies. They were both kind of rough-and-tumble brawlers in a way."

Early in 1966 Morse had submitted an amendment to repeal the Tonkin Gulf resolution of August 1964. Although many senators clearly would have desired just that, most were wary of the political uncertainties of too blatant a confrontation with the president. So when the vote was called on March 2, the amendment lost ninety-five to five. Among the no votes was J. William Fulbright.

Erv S. Duggan: "On the war in Vietnam Johnson forgave Morse because Morse was consistent. Morse had voted against the Tonkin Gulf resolution. But Fulbright—he considered him a turncoat."

Humphrey: "He would mention Fulbright's attacks and Church's attacks and Mike Mansfield's attacks. But every Thursday Morse would get up in the Senate and say he was going to impeach Johnson over the weekend. And Johnson would still call him up and ask him to come over to the White House. He never mentioned his attacks.

"Because he knew that after Wayne's attack on Thursdays, and this went on for months, years, Wayne would be back the next Monday and give a rip-roaring speech on the Senate floor about Johnson's great domestic programs.

"Then it would come Thursday again, and Wayne would want to impeach him again."

On March 3, the day after the defeat of the amendment to repeal the Tonkin Gulf resolution, Secretary of Defense McNamara ordered another 30,000 troops to Vietnam. The total of American "combat support troops" had now reached 235,000.

The bombing, in the meantime, continued. Begun in retaliation, it was continued in hopes of turning the tide. Lyndon still personally oversaw the selection of targets. There had been a six-day pause in May of 1964 to attempt to answer the critics who kept saying that it was the bombing that kept Ho from responding to peace feelers. It was halted again on Christmas Eve, 1965, and did not resume until January 31, 1966. In the interim Lyndon asked Congress for $12.8 billion more for the war it had never declared.

Charles Roberts: "When he cut back the bombing of North Vietnam it didn't come as a total surprise because by this time he was under so much pressure, especially from within his own party. There were so many people saying, 'We've got to try something else. We've got to do something different.' But I must say I never heard *him* say, 'I think we've got to try something else.'"

Also in that interim period J. William Fulbright began a series of hearings before the Senate Foreign Relations Committee, of which he was, of course, chairman, into the basis for and conduct of the war. The hearings, which were held in the caucus room of the Old Senate Office Building, were televised across the country. It was an unprecedented appeal to the people to deny support to their president.

One of the things that some senators on the Foreign Relations Committee wanted to look into was the construction scandal in Vietnam and the involvement in it of Brown and Root, Lyndon's old Texas friends.

During all of Lyndon's years in the Senate, his old friends George and Herman Brown had been prospering. To be sure, their ties with Lyndon were only a part of a spiderweb of ties with other Texas politicians, but Lyndon was the center of that web.

While Lyndon was busy in the Senate, the Brown and Root company had been equally busy with contracts to build bases in Spain and France, as well as on Guam and other islands in the Pacific that later found extensive use during Vietnam. Frequently the company's habit of revising cost estimates upward came into sharp conflict with General Accounting Office evaluations, but the navy always rose to their defense. In 1961 the secretary of the navy was John B. Connally.[1]

In the later fifties when the question had arisen where to put the proposed NASA space center, Florida, which since the Cape Canaveral Space Center was already there would have appeared the obvious place, was rejected in favor of a swampy stretch of Houston suburb. Lyndon, chairman of the Space Council, had heartily approved, just as he had approved Brown and Root's selection as primary contractor, but in fact Brown and Root had ample support from fellow Houstonian and congressman Representative Albert Thomas. Thomas was chairman of the House Appropriations subcommittee that approved the NASA budget, and he, like other local and national politicians from that part of Texas, held his job at the sufferance of the Brown brothers and a very few influential oil men.

But Brown and Root's involvement in the Vietnam construction scandal of the midsixties brought Lyndon a great deal of criticism. In 1962, the Defense Department announced a crash program to provide South Vietnam with the airfields, roads, harbors, and barracks necessary to its defense. The price tag, Congress was informed, would be a cool $1.2 billion, partly because the pressures of time did not allow the work to be accomplished by the military, which would normally have been the case, but called for bringing in private business under the largest contract of its kind ever awarded. Four companies in all were involved—Brown and Root, two companies previously partners of Brown and Root's, and a fourth company closely associated with it in Texas. The conglomerate—RMK-BRJ, as it was known—was clearly a family affair.

Just how large a part the then more or less powerless vice-president played in Brown and Root and Friends' selection is not clear. Perhaps very little. On the other hand, he is not known to have protested when RMK-BRJ paid their Vietnamese work force a fraction of what they paid their American, or objected to the after-hours antics of those same Americans, which included drinking heavily, abusing the villagers, and riding their Hondas up the steps of the Buddhist temples.

Finally, in spite of his lectures on the economy, Lyndon is not known even to have flinched when the losses due to waste and mismanagement and outright theft climbed into the hundreds of millions. What was the taxpayers' loss was clearly Texas's gain. As James Conaway points out in *The Texans*, "Two and a half billion dollars flowed into the state's defense industry in 1966 alone. Chemical companies sold more than $10 million worth of defoliants; there was rubber and petrochemicals, and an order for $186 million worth of aircraft fuel was placed with Texans that December. Brown and Root's revenues for 1966 were 57 percent higher than the previous year, before the crash program began."[2]

Just when Johnson might have felt buoyed by the resounding defeat of the Tonkin Gulf repeal in the Senate, new events in Vietnam sent his spirits plummeting. The unpredictable Ky suddenly removed from command of the First Corps of the South Vietnamese army General Nguyen Chanh Thi, the favorite of the Buddhist faction. Riots broke out all over the country, Ky was denounced, and anti-American slogans were chanted in the streets of Hué, Danang, and Saigon itself. American correspondents sent home reports of these events, and many Americans began to write their senators and congressmen to ask why we were sending our boys to fight and die in so unappreciative a country. What, they asked, was their president thinking of?

By May the senators in opposition to the war, known as the peace bloc, had increased to almost a third of the membership. Senator Fulbright continued to hold hearings in the Foreign Relations Committee, and Wayne Morse continued his harangues on impeachment. The president, frustrated at the continuing lack of response to his Christmas Eve bombing halt, doubly frustrated at being caught in the middle at home between the continued pressures of the hawks and the incessant criticism of the doves, struck back at the peace bloc and its followers in a speech at a Democratic party dinner in Chicago on May 17. The choice of language in the speech was unfortunate, and was to have repercussions far beyond any the president—or his speech writers—could have predicted.

After reiterating America's determination to meet her commitments, Lyndon said:

"Let those though who speak and write about Vietnam say clearly what other policy they would pursue. . . .

"After thirty-seven long days [of the bombing halt], while our men in uniform waited and while our planes were grounded on my orders, while our ambassadors went from nation to nation, we finally were forced to the conclusion that the time had not yet arrived when the government of North Vietnam was willing or could even be persuaded to sit down at a peace table and try to reason these problems out. Therefore our arguments need to be more persuasive, and our determinations need to be more convincing and more compelling than they have been.

"All I can say to you tonight is that the road ahead is going to be difficult. There will be some 'nervous nellies' and some who will become frustrated and bothered and break ranks under the strain, and some will turn on their leaders, and on their country, and on our own fighting men. There will be times of trial and tension in the days ahead that will exact the best that is in all of us."

Roberts: "'Nervous nellies' was an ad lib. He was losing that audience. They'd had a lot to drink, a long evening of entertainment. Finally the president came on, and he was reading his set speech, which was written like it was to be carved in stone, you know, a very dull speech. He threw out a couple of audience response questions to his audience, which required them to shout back yes or no. And then he got wound up a little further and he called his critics nervous nellies.

"While we were flying out there, he laid out to some of us on the plane what he considered his options to be in Vietnam, and I wrote them down. I think I got them verbatim, and to me it was much clearer than anything he had said in any of his speeches. This was in May 1966.

"He said, 'I've got four alternatives. The first one is to escalate. We could completely demolish them [meaning North Vietnam]. We could have a million men there so fast it would make your head swim. We've got the men, the machines, the armor to flatten them, but there's not 10 percent of the country that would support that kind of a war, and we've got to think about what the rest of the world would say. So that's out.'

"And he went on: 'The second alternative is to tuck tail.' And here he wrote the word *tuck* on a memo pad in front of him. 'We could tuck our tails between our legs and run for cover. That would just whet the enemy's appetite for greater aggression and more territory, and solve nothing.'

"Then he went on: 'The third alternative is the enclave idea, recommended by some experts like George Kennan'—he pronounced it Keenan—'and General [James] Gavin.

Well, that's like a jackass hunkering up in a hailstorm. We could stay there the rest of our lives. It would be expensive and prove nothing.'

"'The fourth alternative,' he finally concluded, 'is what we're doing: pressure with restraint, making this aggression so expensive to the enemy that he will sooner or later learn that we mean to stay there until those people are free. This is costly. But when you consider that since the end of World War II, from Greece to Vietnam, we've suffered a hundred and sixty thousand casualties, what we're fighting for now is worth the cost.'"

Harry McPherson: "The big problem he had was trying to rally support just so far. What he was trying to bring off in the American public was something like a semisatisfactory sexual experience. It's like necking—a hard neck, you know, but no going to bed. He knew that the only way really to win the war was to invade North Vietnam. There wasn't any other way. But if you did invade, you'd risk an awful big war with China and Russia, so you couldn't. You had to try to get the American people behind a half war. It was terribly hard to do.

"I think his impatience with this situation drove him to say things like 'nervous nellies.' I think that single phrase probably hurt him as badly as anything in his whole presidency, because it was about that time that large numbers of people—suburban families with college-age kids and that sort of thing—were getting to be troubled about the war. And the war was changing from a war fought by professionals. Jack Kennedy made us think it was all to be done by people with green berets on, but instead it was taking hundreds of thousands of draftees.

"He wanted to get his domestic program through and not make people feel that he was going to run a major land war in Asia. In the midst of all this he comes along and calls them nervous nellies. It was terrible. And yet I can appreciate his bind. What the hell *do* you say? How *do* you half lead a country in a war?"

On May 21, four days after his Chicago speech, Lyndon ordered American troops to Thailand to prevent Communist infiltration there. In June he ordered the bombing of the oil installations of Haiphong and Hanoi. That same month the Gallup poll revealed his popularity at 46 percent, which was then considered low. You had to go back to Harry Truman to equal it.

Secretary McNamara was suggesting that the president ask Congress to let him call up 235,000 men in the National Guard and the reserves. By June 1966 there would be 600,000 young Americans in uniform. And, oh yes, lest Lyndon forget, he would have to ask Congress for more money, quite a bit more.

George Ball was already wondering aloud whether we could win in Vietnam, although he went along, and Dean Rusk, that dependable country boy, said and repeated that if the Communists got any notion that we would abandon the democracy lovers in South Vietnam, the Communists would never "stay their hand." Lyndon agreed.

By October, when Lyndon personally visited the troops in Vietnam, there were about 400,000 there; and 6,664 of them were dead.

THE OTHER WAR

Hugh Sidey: "When he first visited the Mekong Valley as vice-president, he envisioned power lines and orderly farm fields. He stood in Korea below Seoul on the hill named Lyndon B. Johnson and dreamed the same way. In his office, at the end of a long, tiring discussion about the fighting in Vietnam, Johnson's aides saw light come into his eyes as he began to talk about the success of the new rice seed in India and how it meant more prosperity and security for all of Asia. . . . Johnson dispatched agriculture and economic experts to South Vietnam with far more joy than he did more troops. He asked for reports on improving the hog marketing, on dampening inflation, curtailing the black market, diversifying small farms, and all the other topics that he knew about.

"He may never have been more ecstatic over Vietnam than when he made his Johns Hopkins speech in April of 1965 and pledged a billion-dollar scheme for the development of Southeast Asia. It rang of New Deal oratory, referring to the Mekong River development as if it were the Tennessee Valley."[1]

Lyndon had said:

. . . We often say how impressive power is. But I do not find it impressive at all. The guns and the bombs, the rockets and the warships, are all symbols of human failure. They are necessary symbols. They protect what we cherish. But they are witness to human folly.

A dam built across a great river is impressive.

In the countryside where I was born, and where I live, I have seen the night illuminated and the kitchens warmed, and the homes heated, where once the cheerless night and the ceaseless cold held sway. And all this happened because electricity came to our area along the humming wires of the REA. Electrification of the countryside—yes, that too, is impressive.

A rich harvest in a hungry land is impressive. The sight of healthy children is impressive. These—not mighty arms—are the achievements which the American nation believes to be impressive.

In February 1966 Lyndon went to Honolulu to discuss with South Vietnam's Premier Ky and General Thieu ways to attain peace and to improve the economy, health and education of the Vietnamese. At the conclusion of the conference a joint statement was issued called the Declaration of Honolulu. "We must establish and maintain a stable, viable economy and build a better material life for our people—a true democracy for our land," the South Vietnamese government stated. In turn the United States declared its admiration of and support for a country where the people "build even while they fight."

Also at the Honolulu conference General Thieu and Marshall Ky issued a high-sounding pledge promising that very shortly, any day now, they would get to a constitution and present it to their people for study and debate, after which the happy South Vietnamese would enthusiastically and almost unanimously endorse it in a referendum. Thieu and Ky ended their proclamation:

"To those future citizens of a free democratic South Vietnam now fighting with the Vietcong, we take this occasion to say, 'Come and join in this national revolutionary adventure: come safely to join us through the Open Arms program.'"

Like so much else in the Vietnam war, one does not know whether to laugh or cry. Both, perhaps.

When Lyndon got back to Los Angeles, he told reporters, "I looked across the table at those brave and determined young men, Thieu and Ky. I thought also of the young Vietnamese soldiers, province chiefs, teachers and student leaders, who are really part of this new generation.

"They know and we know that this revolutionary transformation cannot wait until the guns grow silent and until the terrorism stops."

After the Honolulu conference Lyndon, as promised, sent agricultural and economic experts to Vietnam.

Robert Komer: "He felt that there should be this positive dimension on the war to build rather than destroy, which he called 'the other war.' When he first called me into his office and out of the blue said, 'I want you to take charge of the other war in Vietnam,' my first question was, 'Mr. President, what's the other war?'

"He had from the beginning this idea. He was constantly breaking out of the confines of Vietnam as a war—and seeing it as a problem of winning hearts and minds. That was something he understood. He was quite conscious from the very beginning that he had to do something about winning the allegiance of the Vietnamese.

"Lyndon had envisioned 'the other war' as largely being sort of a building of TVA and REA. He got some rural electrification guys out there and I discovered them down in one of the provinces. Two guys were trying to put up poles and a little diesel generator. I said, 'For Chrissakes, fellows, how are you coming along?'

"'Well,' they said, 'we think we can get a village, which is two or three little hamlets, wired in about four months.' I said, 'At that rate, it will be in the year 3,000 before we have rural electrification in Vietnam.' 'Well,' they said, 'it's a pretty slow process.' But Johnson loved REA.

"I tended to see pacification in a rather narrower and more immediate sense. I was a big one for roads and for bringing in the green revolution—the improved rice strains— from Los Spanos in the Philippines. But I also tried to provide the rule of law and order and police protection to the people."[2]

Pacification was enthusiastically endorsed not only by Lyndon, but, in the beginning, by a great many dedicated men on Ivy League faculties and at places where organized thinking went on, like the Hudson Institute and the Rand Corporation. Who could disagree with America's farsighted benevolence, our willingness to share the benefits of the Great Society, ours and Lyndon's?

George W. Ball: "Johnson could become almost poetic about what he wanted to achieve in Vietnam after the war."

Erv S. Duggan: "I think Johnson felt that after the war, this country could turn Vietnam, especially the Mekong Delta, into the Promised Land—the greatest country in the world. He had a terrific vision, although you could say it was quaint and naïve. He wanted a Marshall Plan for Vietnam."

Arthur ("Tex") Goldschmidt: "One of the things I discussed with Lyndon was the Mekong program. It was an exciting idea—bring the four countries together (Laos, Cambodia, Thailand, and Vietnam) for the development of the river. I remember he said, 'It's a great thing when people of such different cultures can get together on power.'"

Bill Moyers: "I think he wrongly thought that the same assumptions prevailed there that prevailed here. He'd say, 'My God, I've offered Ho Chi Minh $100 million to build a Mekong Valley. If that'd been George Meany he'd have snapped at it!'"

Robert Komer: "LBJ had no particular grasp of foreign cultures. He felt no particular need to delve into what made Vietnamese Vietnamese—as opposed to Americans or Greeks or Chinese. He was a people man, and he thought people everywhere were the same.

"He saw the Vietnamese farmer as being like the Texas farmer or the Oklahoma farmer. 'We're going to provide them with rural electricity. We're going to provide them with roads and water, and we're going to improve the rice crop.'"

Meanwhile, "pacification"—defined in Webster's Third as "the art or process of achieving or restoring peace; elimination of disturbance; tranquilization; subdual"—continued.

For a time benevolent Americans arrived in countless Vietnamese villages almost daily to explain to villagers, who were largely concerned with the rice crop, that democracy was better than communism, that we democrats grew larger-grained rice, more nutritious too. The villagers would usually nod, smile, and go till their rice fields. The village would be reported as pacified, and large and expensive and handsome charts would be sent to headquarters in Saigon and in Washington reporting enormous successes. The only trouble was that almost invariably after dark those sneaks, the Vietcong, would come into the same villages and demonstrate, often not by gentle means, the superiority of communism, and the villagers, who needed their sleep, would nod and smile and go back to sleep. Sometimes the Vietcong would have to kill a few villagers to make their point, and after a time, profiting from their lesson, the generous Americans had to do that, too.

The violence increased as violence always does. And the constitution took forever to write, perhaps because the hearts and minds of brave young Thieu and Ky were not quite in it. And the dams somehow never got built. The Mekong Delta is essentially the same now as it was before the war began, for that matter as it was a thousand years ago.

THE DOWNWARD SPIRAL

When Lyndon delivered his 1967 State of the Union message at 9:30 P.M. before a joint session of the Ninetieth Congress, assembled for the first time, he faced more Republicans than he ever had before, as well as a great many more conservative Democrats. He spoke for an hour and fifteen minutes, considerably longer than the previous year, and to less applause. Described in some detail were the statutes of his war on poverty but without his earlier enthusiasm, and he allotted, as one southern Democrat gleefully pointed out, only forty-five words out of several thousand to civil rights.

If the speech had any one focus, it was on the "all-out effort to combat crime." Lyndon planned, he said, to recommend the Safe Streets and Crime Control Act of 1967 to the Ninetieth Congress, with the federal government bearing the brunt of the cost. "Our country's laws must be respected," he said. "Order must be maintained." That drew considerable applause.

Vietnam came in for its share, of course, and in that regard he quoted Thomas Jefferson: "It is the melancholy law of human societies to be compelled sometimes to choose a great evil in order to ward off a greater." The parallels were obvious, but he drew them anyway. "We have chosen to fight a limited war in Vietnam in an attempt to prevent a larger war," etc., etc., etc.

Earlier that same day U Thant had voiced his disagreement with the American hard-line approach. "There will be no move toward peace so long as the bombing of North Vietnam is going on," the secretary-general said, and contested the theory that Vietnam was strategically vital to anyone but the Vietnamese.

Lyndon did not, of course, refer to U Thant's views.

One other thing Lyndon had promised, with Chief Justice Earl Warren nodding approval, was a crackdown on wiretapping. "We should outlaw all wiretapping—public and private," Lyndon said, "wherever and whenever it occurs, except when the security of this nation itself is at stake—and only then with the strictest governmental safeguards."

The FBI had considerably increased its reliance on wiretapping in recent years, especially during Bobby Kennedy's reign as attorney general. Kennedy had pressed for new legislation to permit increased usage of electronic surveillance. But after Kennedy left office wiretapping had come into public disfavor.

In May of 1966 Sheldon Cohen, commissioner of internal revenue, had sent a two-and-a-half-page memorandum on the subject to the president's office. The memo explored the federal statute concerning wiretapping, just what was and what was not legal and under what circumstances—in the opinion of the commissioner of internal revenue—and concluded defensively, "In short the Service is simply not wiretapping wrongly in the eyes of the law or of reasonable people."

Lyndon's reply was a blunt scribble: "Sheldon—stop it all at once—and this is final—no microphones, taps, or any other hidden devices legal or illegal if you are going to work for me. Lyndon."

During 1965 and 1966 the wiretap issue became further complicated when it began to be rumored that the FBI possessed certain tapes of goings-on in hotel rooms occupied by Martin Luther King in which King's voice, among other more or less incriminating sounds, was heard. The bureau had, it was said, supplied copies of these tapes to the president who—depending on whom you spoke to—was (a) shocked; (b) titillated; (c) bored.

Harry McPherson: "The FBI reports and tape recordings on King were not at the request of the president. The president's views about bugging were so extreme that he despised the existence of the reports and yet, like all of us, was impressed by what they revealed.

"Johnson didn't believe that the end justified *any* means; he did believe it justified quite a few means. But he had a curious degree of reserve and feelings of delicacy.

"He was probably as genuinely edgy about invasions of privacy as any public figure has ever been. He despised wiretapping, bugging, that sort of thing. Getting the goods on anybody by that means—by overhearing, eavesdropping—was anathema to him. He just hated it."[1]

Lyndon was never really a friend of Hoover's, in spite of the fact that the Johnsons had lived across the street from J. Edgar on Thirtieth Place for several years. Every president since Coolidge, probably, recognized that just as Hoover had been there when he came, Hoover would still be there when he left. And he knew, of course, *everything*, about everything.

Lyndon's real friend at the bureau was not Hoover, but a man named Cartha ("Deke") DeLoach, whom he had known since Senate days. DeLoach became assistant director in December 1965, at which point he took on the responsibility for all the investigative activities of the bureau. Lyndon, who always wanted everybody within instant reach, had a direct line installed between DeLoach's bedroom and the White House. Lyndon used DeLoach to acquire information on a myriad of subjects—it was so *handy*, and besides, he was on someone else's payroll.[2]

And Lyndon did find the FBI extremely useful. At their fingertips was all that information he needed to check out possible presidential appointments. He would, not infrequently, call the bureau from Air Force One just before taking off for Texas and ask that so-and-so, or possibly a whole list of so-and-so's, be checked out and the results be waiting for him at the Ranch on his arrival. "Air Force One Specials" they were called.

Jack Valenti: "I never knew of any use of the FBI in a way that I would find unethical. Unhappily though, what we think of as unethical today seemed to be perfectly all right then. For example, name checks, people who would come to receptions at the White House—the president was worried that he would have his picture taken some day with a guy at a reception and it would turn out that he was under indictment for perjury or murder or something because you don't know everyone that comes to the White House.

"Next were full field checks on people who were going to get jobs with the government; they went into great detail about that. I know of no time, to my certain knowledge, that the president ever ordered a check on somebody who was a political enemy that he was going 'to get.' I know, I've read in the papers that Johnson bugged Goldwater. If he did, I don't know how he got the information on what the bug produced in that campaign because again, I saw 90 percent, I guess, of everything that came by.

"During the '64 convention I was with him constantly, and I never heard anybody mention that there was a bug on Bobby Kennedy or a bug on Dr. King.[3] The bug was put on King during the Kennedy administration because of alleged Communist connections. That's what the bug was all about. Taps for national security didn't seem wrong then. It seems terribly wrong now."

Another use the president apparently made of the FBI was to "investigate" persons opposed to his Vietnam policies, although how extensive such investigation ever was is a matter of some disagreement. Lyndon suspected, at least at the beginning of the antiwar movement, that it was, must be, Communist-inspired. He was particularly sensitive to the volume of opposition mail he was receiving. He was frustrated by accounts of "teach-ins" in various of the country's institutions of higher learning, and he was especially annoyed by the antiwar demonstrations that seemed to be popping up not only along the eastern seaboard where they were, perhaps, to be expected, but all over the country. But his staff insists that he was always, always mindful of the First Amendment rights of the dissenters.

Will Sparks: "One day I said to Mr. Johnson, 'Mr. President, we know many incidences of where these demonstrations originated, and how they were financed. Why don't we just pick one and put down one, two, three, what the facts are, and let the public know that this goes on?'

"That's the only time I saw him really mad at me. He turned around and walked across the room, and he said to me, 'If I did that, Joe McCarthy would come right back out of his grave and we'd have that all over again. Don't you *ever* suggest anything like that to me again.'"

Obviously Vietnam was never far from the president's mind in 1967, and although the 1966 elections had brought a few new faces into Congress, it was already clear that that was not going to help. The peace bloc was, if anything, refortified, as evidenced by the protest that erupted after Lyndon ordered new air strikes on Hanoi on January 15. Only military targets, the president assured the country, and not the civilian population had been bombed. But when Hanoi issued an extensive casualty report, including, it said, many innocent citizens, children also, he was forced to admit that yes, it was possible that some civilians might have been hit and, yes, even killed.

Those were the hazards of war, even an undeclared one.

Then as if January had not already been bad enough, the one day that should have been triumphant ended tragically.

On January 27, Lyndon joined Dean Rusk, Arthur Goldberg, British Ambassador Sir Patrick Dean, the ambassador from the Soviet Union, Anatoly F. Dobrynin, and representatives from fifty-seven other countries in the East Room of the White House for the signing of the Treaty on Principles Governing the Activities of States in the Exploration and Use of Outer Space including the Moon and Other Celestial Bodies. The document, more familiarly known as the treaty barring nuclear weapons in outer space, was also signed amid similar ceremony in London and Moscow.

All of the principals spoke, and Goldberg delivered a message from U Thant as well. It was a momentous occasion—one of the three most significant accomplishments of his career, Lyndon later told Lady Bird.[4] Unfortunately, the exhilaration was to be short-lived.

Lyndon: "A little more than two hours later I was upstairs in the family quarters of the Executive Mansion where Mrs. Johnson and I were giving a reception in honor of retiring Secretary of Commerce John T. Connor and his wife. While John was proposing a toast, I was handed a folded note. It was from Jim Jones, my appointments secretary, and it read:

> Mr. President: James Webb just reported that the first Apollo crew was under test at Cape Kennedy and a fire broke out in the capsule and all three were killed. He does not know whether it was the primary or backup crew, but believes it was the primary crew of Grissom, White, and Chaffee.

"The shock hit me like a physical blow. I heard the applause for Connor's toast die down, and a silence began to settle over the room. Our guests were all looking at me. 'I have a sad announcement to make,' I said, and read the note aloud. There was a stir in the stillness of the room and the happy atmosphere changed to one of stunned grief. I managed a brief farewell to the Connors and left for the Oval Office."[5]

Lyndon was to comment many times on the eerie juxtaposition of events that day: the most tragic accident of the space program coupled with the most far-reaching international space treaty.

On February 8 Lyndon announced a four-day cease-fire in Vietnam to cover the Tet holiday period, as well as the period during which Lyndon's first letter to Ho Chi Minh would be received and might be considered. The United States, Lyndon said, was ready to talk unconditionally. His critics at home, on the other hand, said it was all a ploy to give him an excuse, when no immediate response from the other side emerged, to do what he did five days and eighteen hours later—further escalate the war by ordering the American command in Thailand to bomb Hanoi from Thai bases.

Then, amid further outcry, on March 6 Lyndon sent a special message to Congress asking for an increase in the monthly quota of draftees.

In March Lyndon appointed Ellsworth Bunker to succeed Henry Cabot Lodge as ambassador to Vietnam and then abruptly decided to accompany his new minister to his post—as far as Guam, anyway. There he could introduce him and his new deputy, Eugene M. Locke, to the Vietnamese leaders and at the same time review with "his generals" the present state of the war.

The conference, which began March 19, was not, from the beginning, a cheerful one. Much of the conversation revolved around inflation, black-marketeering, and corruption—all of which were rampant in South Vietnam at that time—and there was also the matter of inadequate security from South Vietnamese troops for the "revolutionary development teams" whose "pacification" of the hamlets and villages was so frequently interrupted by Vietcong guerrillas.

Gloomily, Lyndon turned to "Westy," but his analysis of the military situation was no more optimistic.

William C. Westmoreland: "I provided the group with a frank review of the military situation, including my assessment of the advantage the enemy gained from pauses in the bombing of North Vietnam. Concluding my remarks, I said that if the Vietcong organization failed to disintegrate, which I saw as unlikely, and we were unable to find a way to halt North Vietnamese infiltration, the war could go on indefinitely. As I sat down, my audience was painfully silent. On the faces of many of the Washington officials, who had obviously been hoping for some optimistic assessment, were looks of shock."[6]

April 1967 marked a death in Germany and a near death in Greece. Konrad Adenauer, former chancellor of West Germany, whom Lyndon had entertained at the Ranch on the weekend of the Bay of Pigs invasion in Cuba, died, and Lyndon flew to Bonn to attend the funeral. He made use of the opportunity to confer with European leaders, in particular Charles de Gaulle, whom he had missed seeing at Churchill's funeral two years before when his throat condition did not allow him to attend.

Lyndon had hardly returned from Germany when he was faced with the imminent death of another leader.

John Kenneth Galbraith: "Word came on the television one night that Andreas Papandreou was going to be shot by the Greek junta the next day—or in the very near future. He'd been in jail for some time. Andreas had been at Harvard, Minnesota, and Berkeley. He was a very good economist, one of the most brilliant academic politicians that ever existed. Everybody liked him. And everybody that evening who knew Andreas and had heard this called up wanting to know what could be done. Most economists knew that I knew Johnson and that we had a certain rapport, but they didn't know that we had broken apart on the Vietnam issue.

"I explained this difficulty to everyone who called, but finally about eleven o'clock, I guess, I said to Kitty, 'If they shoot Andreas tomorrow and I haven't done anything about it, that will really be bad.' So I called up Joe Califano at the White House. I said, 'Look, Joe, the president hasn't any reason to like what I've said lately on the Vietnam war, but this is something that's really troubling a lot of people who are his supporters and his friends.' I told him what the situation was. And Joe said, 'Let's see if we can get it all down on a half page of paper. The president hasn't gone to bed yet. He's entertaining some people over at the mansion.'

"So we did. One of the greatest features of Johnson was that he never went to bed. He worked pretty much around the clock, you know. So Joe and I worked this out, and I said to Kitty, 'This is all I can do, let's go to bed.' Then about two o'clock the telephone rang in her room, and she came in to tell me that it was Nick Katzenbach on the wire. Nick was chuckling, and calling me up to relieve my feelings with a message that he had just got from Johnson, which was, and I quote this exactly: 'Call up Ken Galbraith and tell him that I've told those Greek bastards to lay off that sonofabitch, whoever he is.'"

"And to complete the story, somebody then gave the story to *Newsweek*. *Newsweek* called up the next day to ask for confirmation. So I called up Joe, and said, 'Look, I think this reflects great credit on the president. I'm going to confirm it.' Then about a month or two later I was coming through Paris. Andreas had been released from jail and from the country, and I was coming through Paris and ran headlong into Andreas, who was in the company of Irene Pappas, and we went down to have a drink and he told me what happened. He was in a motel that had been made into a jail outside of Athens. Some American got permission to come and see him. As he was leaving, the American said, 'By the way—how are you fixed for reading matter?' and handed him *Newsweek* and there was the story—his first discovery that he wasn't going to be killed. He was very pleased to read it."

Before the spring was out yet another development of considerable consequence had taken place in regard to Vietnam. Lyndon decided to send General Creighton Abrams to Saigon to serve as deputy commander to Westmoreland. It would be Abrams's job to oversee the activities of the South Vietnamese military forces who had not, under Marshall Ky and General Thieu, proved themselves as effective as desired. And it was important that they be strengthened, because Westy, with Lyndon's backing, had in mind turning over more and more of the war effort to the South Vietnamese command.

It would be known as "Vietnamization."

WORD FROM HO

Direct communication between our government and Ho's was nonexistent, and Lyndon, it seemed, planned to keep it that way. He listened more and more, often somewhat desperately, to those superhawks Walt Rostow and Abe Fortas. And late in 1966 and early in 1967 Robert McNamara and Clark Clifford, to whom the president also listened, seemed still to have no doubts at all about the justice of American actions in Vietnam.

We are less certain about whom Ho was listening to. But in late 1966 and early 1967 three Americans, the first non-pacifist Americans ever, were allowed to go to Hanoi.

The first was Harrison Salisbury, who had been the head of the Moscow bureau of the *New York Times* from 1949 to 1954; he won the Pulitzer Prize in 1955 for a series of articles on the Soviet Union; in 1964 he became assistant managing editor of the *Times*. In December 1966, after trying for eighteen months, Salisbury was granted permission to go to Hanoi. He left immediately. On Christmas Day the *Times* printed his first of several dispatches from North Vietnam: "Contrary to the impression given by United States communiqués, on-the-spot inspection indicates that American bombing has been inflicting considerable civilian casualties in Hanoi and its environs for some time past."

Naturally, the Salisbury articles caused a great deal of controversy, and a great many half-hearted hawks became doves. But according to *Newsweek*, Salisbury's dispatches read "to American eyes . . . like the line from Tass or Hsinsha," and Clifton Daniel, then managing editor of the *Times*, who was technically Salisbury's boss, nonetheless said that Salisbury's reports and a North Vietnamese pamphlet were the same because, "they both come from the same source—the North Vietnamese government."

Harrison Salisbury: "When I came to North Vietnam I had a rather long—about a four-hour—conversation with North Vietnamese Premier Pham Van Dong, who was also a leader of the National Liberation Front of South Vietnam.

"I use the word conversation specifically because it was not entirely a newspaper interview. It was back and forth about American policy, some things on record, some things off the record. And some things were clearly said to me to bring back to Washington, having to do with negotiations.

"When I came back almost the first thing I did was to have a private meeting with Dean Rusk and Bill Bundy, who was then his chief assistant for Vietnamese affairs.

"It was not a very satisfactory meeting, I must say, because Rusk, whom I've known for years, wanted to use the meeting to argue American policy with me and I was not interested in arguing American policy at all. Bill, who I didn't know except casually, immediately recognized the significance of what I had to say.

"The essence of it was that there was a way to get around the deadlock in negotiations, which at that time revolved around the insistence of Hanoi that they would not talk until military operations were halted in Vietnam.

"Well, this was important, and I felt I had done my duty by giving it to Rusk. Others, such as Scotty[1] and other people who were in on this thing, felt that this was something that the president should know about, and in normal circumstances, it certainly would have been. Somebody in the White House—we never knew exactly who—put it up to Bill Moyers and, and Bill said, 'No way. Just absolutely no way. He doesn't want to talk to Salisbury or anybody like Salisbury. . . .'

"Bill Fulbright had gotten hold of me and asked me if I would come down and testify before the Senate Foreign Relations Committee on what I had seen. I said certainly I would. I had not known Fulbright before. I went down, and I must say that it was a good hearing—intelligent questions, very little flak; I thought it was quite businesslike, with the single exception of Fulbright himself. He kept asking me very sarcastic questions, in which he wanted to sort of share a sarcastic and sneering view of the present administration which I didn't feel it was my position to do. I was quite embarrassed by Fulbright, but not by anyone else.

"Directly after I had been in Hanoi, even as I left there, the same plane that I went out on, there arrived Harry Ashmore and Bill Baggs."

Harry Ashmore had been for many years executive editor of the *Arkansas Gazette* and had won many prizes for his editorials; in 1959 he had become director of the Center for the Study of Democratic Institutions in Santa Barbara, California. William E. Baggs was the editor of the *Miami News* and a member of the board of the center. Ashmore and Baggs spent nine days in Hanoi and two hours with Ho.

Harry Ashmore: "Ho's English was very good, but it was necessary to conduct the interview in Vietnamese because nobody else on the Vietnamese side had any English. Some had French, but none had English except Ho. So we were translated into Vietnamese, and then he was translated from Vietnamese into English. But he kept getting irritated with the interpreter and correcting him and making English asides to us, so it was quite an open and frank conversation and went on at great length. There was no question that he knew that we were going right straight back to the State Department, and he was talking through us to them.

"We brought back from Ho Chi Minh the basic proposition that they would not hold a meeting as long as the bombing continued, but they would discuss the terms of a meeting in some fashion on the assumption that if there was agreement the bombing would stop, that beyond that anything was open for discussion. The basic proposition as we reported it from their standpoint was that the separation of the country could continue for quite a long time as far as the North was concerned. They would insist that the NLF, which at that time was literally doing most of the fighting—there were some North Vietnamese troops in then but not too many—had to be recognized and had to be part of some kind of coalition government. Beyond that, they were fairly flexible as to how long the American withdrawal would take, et cetera.

"We had this long secret session in Washington [with State Department officials], and the upshot of it was that they said that they were very grateful and they would be in touch.

"After a month had passed and nothing had happened, I was beginning to wonder what the hell was going on. Fulbright saw Lyndon, either at the White House or some social event, and they had a little talk. Fulbright said, 'Lyndon, what did you think of what Ashmore and Baggs had to say about Ho Chi Minh and Vietnam?' Lyndon said, 'Well, I haven't seen them.' Fulbright said, 'You haven't seen them?' 'No,' he said, 'they talked to some fellows over there at the State Department. I haven't seen them. You know, Bill, I can't see everybody that goes over there and talks to Ho Chi Minh.'

"But then the next day, or shortly thereafter, he called Fulbright—Johnson did, he apparently had been thinking about it—and he said, 'Bill, I've asked the State Department to get those fellows back in here. I want you to be satisfied that they're being heard in the right places, so they're going to be in here Friday, and they're going to meet over there Saturday morning with Katzenbach and everybody. They're going to see the Pentagon people, and I want you to go along. I want you to be there so you'll be satisfied that it's all open and aboveboard.'

"This led to one of the most extraordinary confrontations I ever took part in. We got to Washington, Baggs and I, had dinner with Fulbright on Friday night, and on Saturday morning we went to Katzenbach's office. While we were waiting outside, Rusk passed a couple of times but didn't recognize us, couldn't seem to see us, and he never came to any of these meetings. Rusk never talked to us, nor did Johnson. There was somebody there from the White House who was a fairly junior fellow, just sort of sitting back in the corner. But there was Katzenbach, Harriman, Bundy, and then the senior professional people from Bundy's department, the Vietnam experts—there must have been five or six of those—and Fulbright sitting over here, and Baggs and me in the middle.

"So Fulbright unloaded. He came in shooting. This was when the situation was very bitter. He told them that he thought this meeting was a bunch of shit. What the hell were we wasting his time and our time and anybody else's time talking? 'All you guys,' he said, 'are committed to a military settlement. You don't want to negotiate; you're not going to negotiate. You're bombing that little piss-ant country up there, and you think you can blow them up. You've been doing this all the time. It's a bunch of crap about wanting to negotiate.' Well, you could feel the tension going up until hell wouldn't have it. Katzenbach was flushing and finally assured the senator that he at least wanted to negotiate a settlement.

"Anyway we had this conversation, at the end of which Harriman said, 'Now I have personal orders from the president that you can see anybody else you want to see. He suggested that McNamara you might want to see, he's over at the Pentagon now.'

"We went over to see McNamara and had a private audience with him that must have run about an hour, in which he told us that he had always been against the bombing in the North; never thought it was tactically, strategically sound. That it was a political matter, really, to placate the generals and the admirals, and that he had opposed it and he had supported the bombing pause we'd had before, and thought the bombing was a mistake. But they kept hollering about infiltration and one thing and another. That was the burden of that conversation, a right surprising one.

"Then we were asked to come back to the State Department, and we did, and met with Bill Bundy, who had a draft letter he wanted us to sign to Ho Chi Minh. It was a very conciliatory letter, one that I'm sure would have led to some further contact. The final version, which was mailed by me on Sunday afternoon, February 5, noted that a full report had been made 'to appropriate officials of the United States government on our recent conversation with you in Hanoi,' reiterated various State Department views which 'we believe are already known to you,' and concluded with the following personal observations:

> Speaking now wholly for ourselves, we believe the essential condition for productive talks is an arrangement under which neither side stands to gain military advantage during the period of negotiation. To achieve this end it may be that preliminary secret discussions would be helpful to determine the outline of a possible peaceful settlement.
>
> As we see it, these are practical considerations that have nothing to do with questions of "face." There is no doubt in our minds that the American government genuinely seeks peace. As private citizens our sole concern is in facilitating a discussion that will bring all matters at issue to official consideration. It is in this sense that we convey these comments, and invite any reply you may wish to make, which of course we would report to our government in complete discretion.

"It went out, I thought, in good faith. Fulbright knew all about it, which I then began to feel was some sort of insurance that was necessary. I was beginning to distrust people somewhat.

"We found out later, when Ho Chi Minh released a copy, that at the time our letter was going forward, one was going forward from the White House signed by Lyndon, a very hard-line letter which, if anything, escalated the proposition that we had made about bombing and infiltration. One that was, under the circumstances, designed to be rejected. I think that's the only way you could read it. It meant that they—Johnson— didn't want to talk for whatever reason. When we found this out we really were outraged, because here we had written this damned thing in the State Department and we had sent it in all good faith on behalf of the State Department. We were not told, if they knew, that the White House was sending a letter which undermined what our letter said; something that canceled out any possibility for conversation."

Lyndon's letter read, in part, as follows:

In the past two weeks, I have noted public statements by representatives of your government suggesting that you would be prepared to enter into direct bilateral talks with representatives of the U.S. government, provided that we ceased "unconditionally" and permanently our bombing operations against your country and all military actions against it. In the last day, serious and responsible parties have assured us indirectly that this is in fact your proposal.

Let me frankly state that I see two great difficulties with this proposal. In view of your public position, such action on our part would inevitably produce worldwide speculation that discussions were under way and would impair the privacy and secrecy of those discussions. Secondly, there would inevitably be grave concern on our part whether your government would make use of such action by us to improve its military position.

With these problems in mind, I am prepared to move even further towards an ending of hostilities than your government has proposed in either public statements or through private diplomatic channels. I am prepared to order a cessation of bombing against your country and the stopping of further augmentation of U.S. forces in South Vietnam as soon as I am assured that infiltration into South Vietnam by land and by sea has stopped. These acts of restraint on both sides would, I believe, make it possible for us to conduct serious and private discussions leading toward an early peace. . . .

If you are able to accept this proposal I see no reason why it could not take effect at the end of the New Year, or Tet, holidays. The proposal I have made would be greatly strengthened if your military authorities and those of the government of South Vietnam could promptly negotiate an extension of the Tet truce.

On February 15, 1967, Ho replied, in part:

In your message, you suggested direct talks between the Democratic Republic of Vietnam and the United States. If the government of the United States really wants such talks, it must first unconditionally halt the bombing as well as all other acts of war against the Democratic Republic of Vietnam. . . .

The Vietnamese people will never yield to force nor agree to talks under the menace of bombs.

Our cause is entirely just. It is our hope that the government of the United States acts with reason.

In September 1967 Ashmore "decided that the time had come to publish the account of the two letters—that is, ours and the president's letter to Ho. We did, and that created a great flap for about twenty-four hours, which led to Bundy issuing a white paper from the State Department in which he neither confirmed nor denied the fact of the two letters but suggested that Baggs and I were some kind of egomaniacs who were hurt because we had tried to settle the war and failed."

William Putnam Bundy: "Mr. Ashmore yields to an understandable feeling that his own channel was the center of the stage. It was not; it was a very, very small part of the picture."

Bundy denied that there was any substantive difference between the Ashmore-Baggs letter to Ho and that signed by the president. Ashmore disagreed. He said that the tone of his and Baggs's was "conciliatory" and the tone of the president's "harsh."

Of course the only interpretation of "tone" that really mattered was Ho's. And Ho was silent.

THE FRIEND OF ISRAEL

It was part of the Lyndon legend that Franklin Roosevelt some time in the late 1930s sent a friend and adviser, Judge Rosenman, on a special trip to New York to tell what was then referred to as "the New York Jewish community" to keep an eye on Lyndon B. Johnson, this New Deal congressman from, of all places, Texas.

Edwin Weisl, Jr.: "Our family relationship with President Johnson arose over thirty years ago through my father's[1] relationship with President Roosevelt's personal adviser and assistant.

"Roosevelt, it is well known, took a liking to Johnson and wanted to make sure that he got a broader acquaintance with people throughout the country, and he asked Hopkins to put Johnson in touch with someone in New York who could introduce him around, and Hopkins picked my father.

"Johnson got to know him, used to come up frequently and stay at our house or our apartment in New York, and we involved ourselves in many ways throughout his career, with helping him in his campaigns, helping him get newspaper support in Texas, and became very friendly with Johnson. We worked on his preparedness committee at one point, and in his campaign for the presidency in '60, and then in '64, we of course were very active."

Isaiah Kenan:[2] "One of Johnson's first statements concerning Israel was when he said to an Israeli diplomat shortly after the assassination of Kennedy, 'You have lost a very great friend, but you have found a better one.' And I would say that everything he did as president supported that statement."

Lyndon was particularly close to Ephraim ("Eppy") Evron, then second man in the Israeli delegation in Washington.

Harry McPherson: "Eppy is five foot three with a quintessential Jewish face, a long, skinny hooked nose and pointed ears, a quite elegant dresser, and one of the most marvelous people I have ever known.

"I think Eppy felt what I've always felt, that some place in Lyndon Johnson's blood there are a great many Jewish corpuscles. He really reminds me of a six-foot-three-inch slightly corny Texas version of a rabbi or a diamond merchant on Forty-seventh Street. He is just as likely to spill out all his woes, his vanity, his joy as the most gesticulating Jew. He has the kind of hot nature that one associates with Jews. He is not afraid of making a fool of himself—as Martin Buber describes—the kind of divine foolishness."

Ephraim ("Eppy") Evron: "Johnson's feeling about Israel came out very early in the crisis of 1957 when he was majority leader. When at that time President Eisenhower and Secretary of State Dulles wanted to force us to withdraw from Sinai, they threatened us with economic sanctions. Johnson persuaded Senator William Knowland of California, who was then minority leader, to come with him to the White House and tell the president that it just wouldn't do."

Lyndon, and Sam Rayburn too, were very much opposed to the Eisenhower Doctrine, which was clearly designed to placate the Arabs early in 1957, and Lyndon in the Senate managed to defuse some of the sanctions John Foster Dulles wanted to impose on Israel.

In the decade that followed both the Israelis and the Arab nations were hurriedly rearming, and by the spring of 1967 it was apparent that something serious was going to happen in the Middle East; it was a question of who would attack whom first and where and when. Colonel Gamal Abdel Nasser, then the leader of Egypt, had been seriously wooed in an exchange of friendly letters between him and Kennedy, but Johnson when he became president was notably cool. Colonel Nasser then, not unexpectedly, had turned to Russia for the affection—and the armaments—he craved. On May 14 the colonel mobilized his forces and on the sixteenth asked that the United Nations take its peace-keeping corps out of the Gaza Strip. U Thant, secretary general of the UN, with what most people thought was unseemly haste, agreed.

On May 17 Lyndon cabled Prime Minister Levi Eshkol: "I AM SURE YOU WILL UNDERSTAND THAT I CANNOT ACCEPT ANY RESPONSIBILITIES ON BEHALF OF THE UNITED STATES FOR SITUATIONS WHICH ARISE AS THE RESULT OF ACTIONS ON WHICH WE ARE NOT CONSULTED." In plain English that meant, "Take it easy."

The next day the UN troops withdrew from the strip. Egyptian troops took over. U Thant, who had been widely criticized for allowing the removal of the UN forces, started to Cairo to see Colonel Nasser. On the twenty-second Lyndon sent a cable to Kosygin urging the Russians to keep calm. He also sent a message to Nasser saying that he understood "the pride and aspirations of your people" but to avoid hostilities.

Too late. Before the letter was delivered, and before U Thant arrived in Cairo, Colonel Nasser announced that Egypt was closing the Gulf of Aqaba, thereby cutting off Israeli access to the Indian Ocean. "The Israeli flag will no longer pass the Gulf of Aqaba; our sovereignty over the gulf is indisputable. If Israel threatens us with war, we will reply thus: 'Go ahead, then.'"

Abe Feinberg: "During all that crucial time, he was in constant touch with me and with Levi Eshkol.

"At the time the Egyptians were threatening to close off the Straits of Tiran, which was where all the oil from Iran came in. I said to him that if and when that happened, Israel would be economically castrated. He got in touch with Eshkol after Nasser closed off the territory and asked him to hold off for forty-eight hours. Eshkol agreed.

"Then the forty-eight hours stretched into almost ten days, and Johnson was negotiating, or trying to negotiate."

John P. Roche: "On the Middle East I was involved in the presentation of the first statement the president gave on it, which was May 23, 1967, as I recall—before the war but after the Straits of Tiran had been closed. He called me up in the middle of the night and asked me to come in. Of course, his purpose at this time was to try to keep the Israelis from attacking and try to bring some pressure on Nasser to open the straits, and at the same time make it clear that he was not going to support the Arabs, that we were going to support Israel if it came to a crunch.

"The State Department had prepared a draft for him which was the most incredible document. It was a completely 'on the one hand,' and 'on the other hand' thing. It didn't cut any ice at all. It didn't have one declarative sentence in it as to what we were going to do.

"I worked until about two or three o'clock in the morning on May 23, using some quite tough operational language regarding the fact that the closing of the Straits of Tiran had been a violation of international law and norms and so forth. I called Walt Rostow and I read it to him, and Walt said, 'That sounds fine to me, but mark it for the president.' So I did mark it in the margin. I said to the president, 'I've checked it with Walt Rostow. Here it is, and it's what I think should go.'

"The next day there was tremendous pressure brought on Johnson to get him to come out for Israel. Jewish pressure groups in this country were lined up all the way from Washington to California, and Johnson engaged in one of his malicious little games. The various Jewish groups would call him, and what he did was he'd fish out the State Department draft and read it to them and say, 'Well, how do you feel about that? They think this is the kind of thing I ought to say. How does it sound to you?'

"So boom! The phones are ringing. The Israeli ambassador Avraham Harmon is over in Humphrey's office with Eppy Evron, who is practically in tears. So Humphrey calls me up, and he says, 'What do you know about this?' It was very embarrassing, because I happened to know that what I had written the night before had already gone on speech cards, and he was going on television. He'd approved it, signed it, everything else. But I couldn't say this to Humphrey. I mean, Johnson once said about ways of getting information around Washington: 'Telephone, telegraph, or tell Hubert!'

"All day Johnson went on doing this. I called Rostow. I said, 'For God's sake, what is he doing?' Walt said, 'Oh, he's just getting a little therapy for all this pressure they put on.'"

Lyndon read his televised message from the Fish Room at 6:10 that evening. He said, in part, ". . . the purported closing of the Gulf of Aqaba to Israeli shipping has brought a new and grave dimension to the crisis [in the Middle East]. The United States considers the gulf to be an international waterway and feels that a blockade is illegal and potentially disastrous to the cause of peace. The right of free, innocent passage of the international waterway is a vital interest of the international community."

He then called on the United Nations to act decisively and quickly in the matter. "I have been in close contact and will be in the days ahead with Ambassador Goldberg at the United Nations, where we are pursuing the matter with great vigor, and hope the Security Council can act effectively."

On May 26, Abba Eban, Israel's foreign minister, arrived in Washington to see the president. Lyndon made no commitments. He said, "I want to see that little blue and white Israeli flag sailing down the Straits of Tiran." The straits were, he repeated, an international waterway. But he could not ask his country directly to come to the aid of Israel; that would entail going to Congress and mean debate, perhaps lengthy, perhaps unpleasant debate.

The best thing, the president felt, and Eban could not disagree, was for the United States to be above it all, to avoid at all costs a direct confrontation with the Soviet Union.

Roche: "That night I was working and around nine thirty or ten o'clock the phone rang and he said, 'Come on down.' I went down. Walt Rostow was there, and the president had some of that poisonous low-cal Dr. Pepper, and I had a cup of coffee. He told a little bit about his visit with Eban. You know he was a great mimic, Johnson was. He did a takeoff on Eban, and he said, 'What do you think they're going to do?' We sat around and talked about what we thought the Israelis were going to do. Somebody, I forgot who it was, said, 'They'll wait.' It wasn't Walt. I said, 'I think they'll hit them.' He [Johnson] said, 'Yes, they're going to hit. There's nothing we can do about it.'

"I've seen in several places that the Israelis made him a commitment that they would not act until he had been able to go with his proposals to New York to the UN. They never flatly said that. Eban had hedged around and gave semi-semi, demi-quasi commitments, but never flatly made a total commitment."

Feinberg: "Finally, on the night of June 4 we had a Democratic rally in New York, and Johnson was the main speaker. I had gotten word that afternoon, and I went up to where he was sitting. I remember Mary Lasker was on one side and Mathilde Krim, who was then a professor at the Weizmann Institute, was on the other. And I whispered to him, on the side where Mrs. Krim was sitting. I said, 'Mr. President, it can't be held any longer. It's going to be within the next twenty-four hours.'

"Well, he made a speech that night that absolutely brought the house down, completely extemporaneous. About Israel and about its survival.

"Then, get this, in walked Bobby Kennedy with Steve Smith and his whole retinue. It was like the old gangsters used to travel with a crowd, you know. And Bobby resented the fact that Johnson had been so impressive, and Bobby said to me, 'I want you to get the leaders together in your apartment tomorrow.'

"And I said, 'Bobby, the president of the United States is running this operation.' He said, 'Well, I could go over your head and get them myself.'

"I said, 'And you can also go fuck yourself. I'm going to listen to the president of the United States and not to you.'"

Walt Rostow almost never brought bad news to Lyndon; on the subject of Vietnam, for instance, he was eternally optimistic. The light he saw at the end of the tunnel was always blazingly bright and had been since 1963, brighter every day.

But Rostow was awakened on the morning of June 5, 1967 at 2:50, Washington time, with the news that Israel was at war with Egypt. Just how it had started was not clear. No matter. It was trouble, big trouble possibly if the Soviet Union got restive. When he called the president at 4:30, Walt was already in the Situation Room, in the basement of the White House.

By seven it was clear that the Israelis had attacked Egypt and knocked out most of her air force. Ground fighting was also under way, and the Israelis' armored corps was winning decisively. At 7:57 McNamara called Lyndon to tell him that the hot line, installed in 1963 to provide instant communication between Soviet and American leaders, had been activated. Lyndon made considerable use of it that day and in the days that followed.

From the beginning there had been no doubt in Washington about which side would win the war. General Wheeler thought it would take the Israelis three or four days. Richard Helms, then director of the CIA agreed—unless, of course, Russia got into the fracas. But Russia was in no mood for intervention.

The UN Security Council called for a cease-fire on June 9. Egypt, whose ground forces had been driven from the Sinai Peninsula, accepted immediately. So did Israel. Syria, who had joined in the conflict, hesitated for twenty-four hours, by which time she had lost the Golan Heights. King Hussein of Jordan had thrown his support to Egypt, and his army had been routed by the Israelis, who had also captured tanks and guns by the hundreds.

It had been a total victory, the Gulf of Aqaba was reopened, and this time Israel had no intention of withdrawing from the territory she had occupied.

On June 10, just when a complete cease-fire seemed at hand, Kosygin called Johnson on the hot line and announced that unless Israel "unconditionally" halted operations at once, the Soviet Union would be forced to take action—*military* action. Where, Lyndon asked his advisers assembled in the Situation Room, was the Sixth Fleet at that moment? The Sixth Fleet, he was informed, was approximately 300 miles, or 10 to 12 hours, west of the Syrian coast, well out of its prescribed 100-mile limit.

"I told McNamara to issue orders at once to change the course and cut the restriction to fifty miles. . . . We all knew the Russians would get the message as soon as the monitors observed the change in the fleet's pattern. That message, which no translator would need to interpret to the Kremlin leadership, was that the United States was prepared to resist Soviet intrusion in the Middle East. . . .

"My last message to Chairman Kosygin went over the hot line just before noon. I pointed out that military action in the Middle East was apparently ending. I expressed my hope that the efforts of both our countries in the time ahead would be devoted to achieving lasting peace throughout the world."[3]

McPherson: "We couldn't say what we had said on the hot line about the necessity for Russia to keep its mitts off the Middle East.

"I once pleaded with the president to let me authorize Eppy to spill the beans. I saw that memo the other night. It's in the middle of a long memorandum to him about a conversation with Eppy and it's 'no, no, no' on the sides. Couldn't do it.

"But Eppy went to various places, Miami, Los Angeles, everywhere. He spoke to large collections of Jews, and he would simply say, 'I can't tell you anything about the facts, but let me tell you, I'm minister of Israel, and Lyndon Johnson saved Israel.

"Finally, he prevailed upon Eshkol to say that. And Eshkol did say it. Lyndon Johnson soon became the most popular man in Israel."

OLD FRIENDS

Abe Fortas and Lyndon had known each other since they were young New Dealers. In 1937, the year Lyndon was first elected to Congress, Fortas came to Washington in answer to an invitation from William O. Douglas, who had been one of his teachers at the Yale Law School and was then the chairman of the Securities and Exchange Commission. He made Fortas assistant director of the public utilities division of the SEC.

Fortas was born in Memphis, the youngest of five children of a Jewish cabinetmaker; he received a B.A. degree from Southwestern College in Memphis, an LL.B. from Yale in 1933, and spent four years on the faculty there, the youngest member ever. He was, of course, Phi Beta Kappa, and, the most prestigious position of all, editor of the *Yale Law Journal*.

Carolyn Fortas, Abe's wife, also attended the Yale Law School; she graduated second in her class. The Fortases lived in a beautiful red brick house in Georgetown. They drove or were driven in a Rolls Royce. They collected antiques and paintings, served gourmet meals with fine imported wines, and Abe, a man of wide intellectual curiosity, with an accent more of the Charles River than the Memphis side of the Mason-Dixon line, was a violinist, played in many string quartets, and was good enough for Isaac Stern to have called him a "consummate amateur." Mrs. Fortas, who smoked expensive cigars, was also a first-rate tax lawyer. They entertained often. Pablo Casals was a frequent guest.

Before Lyndon put the finger on him for the Supreme Court, Fortas was making $200,000 a year as a member of the firm of Arnold, Fortas, and Porter.

Paul A. Porter: "I was sitting in this very room [his Washington law office] when Goldberg went to the United Nations. President Johnson was in Springfield for Adlai Stevenson's funeral. He called Abe from Air Force One and said, 'I am arriving, and I'm going to announce your appointment to the Supreme Court.'

"And Abe said, 'God Almighty, Mr. President, you can't do that. I have got to talk to you about it.' Johnson said, 'All right. You can talk to me.'

"So then Abe talked to me about it and said he didn't want to do it. He wrote a long, handwritten letter to the president and Mrs. Johnson, and Abe being Abe, he never kept a copy. I got a playback of that. The president read the letter aloud to the family at the dinner table, in which Abe gave his reasons for declining this great honor, and there were copious tears wept.

"Well, we were in this room here working on a jurisdictional statement for the Supreme Court, and Abe gets a telephone call to come over to the White House for this press conference. Abe said, 'Look, you don't suppose he is going to lean on me some more about this.' I said, 'Oh, I think you are off the hook from what I have heard.'

"Well, I have a television in here, so I turned on the set—while I was working on this brief—to this press conference. The president announced he was sending fifty thousand boys to Vietnam, appointing John Chancellor to direct the USIA, and naming Abe Fortas to the Supreme Court."

Marianne Means: "He and Johnson got in this elevator, and Fortas was still saying no. So Johnson said, 'Now I want you to sit in the front row at the press conference.' And Fortas says, 'Why?' or something like that, and he says, 'Well, you know, I'm sending all these boys to Vietnam, and they're giving their life for their country and you can do no less. If your president asks you to do something for your country, can you run out on him?' Here the elevator doors open and Fortas is stuck with a decision already made.

"Under the mesmerizing effect of the president, Fortas marches in, takes his place, and is announced."

Porter: "Mrs. Fortas—Carol—was very upset. The president had called her during the afternoon and she wouldn't take the call.

"He apparently called the Fortas household that night. Abe has told me this story. Abe said he never heard anybody talk to the president like Carol did."

The confirmation of Fortas's appointment to the Court came on August 11; in the hearings before the Senate Judiciary Committee Fortas was widely praised.

That was in 1965. On June 13, 1968, Earl Warren, who was seventy-seven, outraged conservative Republicans yet again by submitting his resignation to the president. The president said, regretfully, that he would accept it as soon as a successor was named.

Sam Houston Johnson: "Lyndon decided to name his old friend Abe Fortas as chief justice, and he announced that he was going to appoint an even older friend, Homer Thornberry, an associate justice to take Fortas's seat.

"I thought it would have been better if Lyndon had submitted the names separately; then when Fortas got approved, he should have sent in Thornberry's name.

"But he didn't, and the Republicans were just waiting."

Waiting they were. First, they would dispose of Fortas. Fortas was a "crony." A crony is a presidential adviser you don't like.

The fact that Supreme Court justices and presidents conferred came as a surprise only to those who are ignorant of American history. They all did. Felix Frankfurter when he was a justice of the Supreme Court, for instance, consulted with Franklin Roosevelt frequently. Nobody called him a crony.

Everybody knew that Fortas had advised his friend Lyndon on the 1957 Civil Rights Act, and on the acts of 1960, 1964, 1965, *and* 1968. That did not go down well with southern senators like Sam Ervin of North Carolina. Ervin was not yet the American folk hero he was to become as a result of the Watergate hearings; he was then considered just another southern conservative.

Sam Ervin was a member of the Senate Judiciary Committee, which had to pass on Fortas's appointment before it could get on the floor. So was James Eastland, who in

1966 had been elected to his fifth term in the Senate by a Mississippi landslide. He did not like Justice Fortas's record on the bench or off. Neither did Strom Thurmond of South Carolina, also a member of the committee.

Fortas had been one of the five justices who in June 1966 were responsible for the infamous *Miranda* decision, which ruled that anyone arrested as a suspect for a crime had to be informed by the police of his constitutional rights, including the right to retain a lawyer. Police said that the ruling *encouraged* crime, that *Miranda* was nothing more than mollycoddling prisoners.

Thurmond, shouting at Fortas, 'Aren't you after the truth? What difference does it make if there is a lawyer present or not? What difference does it make if you're after the truth?'

Abe Fortas: "The difference is really nothing more than what is written in the Constitution."

Larry Temple: "As far as the Fortas appointment was concerned, most of us thought we were in pretty good shape. Not the president. From the very outset his whole mode of operation was one of crisis. He said, 'We're going to be in trouble on this.'

"He did not know, he never knew the charges that were going to be made, the low level the opposition to Fortas would reach, but he was always a man who could smell trouble.

"One of the things I remember quite vividly is that he said, 'We've got to get this thing through, and we've got to get it through early because if it drags out we're going to get beat. Dirksen will leave us.'

"I must confess that in the beginning I thought this was just nonsensical; I didn't believe it at all.

"We fed some information to Senator Dirksen approving the nomination, and he made several speeches backing Fortas. Somebody said, 'He's committed on record. He has made a speech on the floor of the Senate several times—and has stated publicly to the press that he's for the nomination.'

"The president said, 'Just take my word for it. I know him. I know that Senate. If they let this thing drag out very long, we're going to get beat.'

"I recall that the president would get very, very irritated and very, very frustrated at the fact that we couldn't get the hearings before the Judiciary committee set and concluded, and the report out of the Senate Judiciary committee as fast as he wanted to. Senator Eastland was one source of holding it up. Sam Ervin was one source of holding it up."

James Jones: "We kept telling him that we had the count, we had the votes, and he kept saying, 'You gotta move. You gotta button this down. We're losing. We're going to get beat. Griffin's going to take over.'"

Senator Robert P. Griffin of Michigan was another vigorous opponent of the Fortas nomination. Griffin voted, to put it gently, always with the conservatives. He was not possessed of a creative mind, but he was persistent and consistent—which in legislative matters is often more important.

One day in September Griffin announced that he had "turned up something that will kill the appointment." What he had turned up was that Fortas had accepted $15,000 from the American University Law School for teaching a nine-week course in what his former law partner, Paul Porter, described as "a summer seminar in which Fortas went into this whole new area of poverty law, law and public policy, law and psychiatry, teaching methods."

Porter had raised $30,000 from five friends who were businessmen. He had given the money to American University, and half of it had been paid to Fortas. The "conflict of interest" involved was that one of the businessmen *might* someday have a case before the Supreme Court. Not much, but in the late summer of 1968, with a lame-duck president in the White House and Richard Nixon in the wings, it was enough.

There were other odds and ends. Fortas had ruled that a movie having something or other to do with transvestites was not "obscene." The film was screened in the Capitol basement and looked at by several scholarly senators who were severely shocked. Add to the list of indictments that Fortas was soft on hard-core pornography.

And, though this was whispered rather than shouted, he was a Jew; there was a number you could call in Arlington, Virginia, where a recording made by the American Nazi party said that he was "a red-leaning Jew."

Harry McPherson: "There was no question there was a lot of anti-Semitism in the whole struggle. One southern senator, whom I shall not name, said to another, 'You're not going to vote for that Jew to be chief justice, are you?'"

Temple: "In any event the president was right as it turned out, and he called the shots exactly correctly because our support did start to deteriorate.

"On the American University thing, even our most ardent supporters were upset.

"And just as the president had predicted, and which I had not believed until it happened, Senator Dirksen ultimately announced that because of the information that had been revealed at the hearings and during the course of the consideration of the nomination, that he would not be able to support Justice Fortas."

In September the Judiciary Committee did recommend the nomination by a vote of eleven to six. But then Robert Griffin began a filibuster against the nomination, which was taken up by others of Fortas's opponents. In October the administration, it turned out mistakenly, asked for a vote on cloture. The vote was forty-five to forty-three, fourteen short of the two-thirds necessary. At this point Abe Fortas asked that his name be withdrawn, and it was.

The following May *Life* magazine printed an article saying that Fortas, while still a justice, had first accepted, then returned a $20,000 fee from the family foundation of Lewis Wolfson, who was having trouble with Abe's old home, the Securities and Exchange Commission. Later Wolfson was sent to prison for nine months for selling unregistered stocks.

In a letter to *Life* Abe Fortas stated that when he was a member of the Supreme Court he did not "participate in any of Mr. Wolfson's business or legal affairs."

Nevertheless, on May 15, he resigned his seat. Nearly ten years later, on January 23, 1977, a young investigative reporter named Bob Woodward uncovered a tape made secretly by Wolfson in 1970 which indicated that Abe's letter to *Life* was not exactly accurate. Abe had in fact advised Wolfson after he got on the Court; at one point he promised to intervene directly with the SEC, although he did not. After Wolfson's indictment and imprisonment he asked that Fortas arrange for a presidential pardon, which Abe also did not do.

When confronted with a transcript, Abe Fortas said, according to Woodward, that it could be correct.

Two final matters. Abe at this writing still practices law in a very handsome office in Georgetown; he has a very good and very profitable practice. He still plays the violin well, and the Fortases still serve gourmet meals and the very best wines. I don't know about the Rolls Royce.

Lyndon Johnson did not, according to all available evidence, know either about the American University connection or about Lewis Wolfson.

THE DISSENT

> Lyndon Johnson told the Nation
> Have no fear of escalation,
> I am trying everyone to please.
> And though it isn't really war,
> We're sending 50,000 more
> To help save Vietnam from Vietnamese.
> —Tom Paxton

On April 25, 1967, George McGovern said on the floor of the Senate:

"We seem bent upon saving the Vietnamese from Ho Chi Minh, even if we have to kill them and demolish their country to do it. . . . I do not intend to remain silent in the face of what I regard as a policy of madness which, sooner or later, will envelop my son and American youth by the millions for years to come."

Vietnam was our longest, costliest, and, as it went on, our least popular war; it was also the least understood. And the more attempts were made to explain it, the more puzzling it became.

Not that that was true in the beginning. Then it was enough that it was against communism, and as we have seen there were those dominoes that Dwight D. Eisenhower and John F. Kennedy had nightmares about.

But even in the beginning it seemed that if Johnson were to expand and enlarge Kennedy's domestic program, one must likewise expect him—"Let us continue"—to enlarge and expand the Kennedy foreign policy, which was imperialistic, as befitted a man whose favorite author, Lord John Buchan, was forever writing about the glories of young men going out to die gallantly for their empire.

John Kenneth Galbraith: "I spoke, privately and publicly, against what we were doing in Vietnam—oh, I'd say since 1961 after I first read the report from Maxwell Taylor and Walt Rostow after they'd been over there for Kennedy and had come back saying that if South Vietnam was to be saved, American troops would be necessary.

"As the Vietnam thing got worse, I made a good many speeches on it. To me, in some ways, the bitterest single feature of the Vietnam War was my breaking off relations with Johnson.

"During this time Kitty and I had had fairly constant access to the White House. I'd been very closely associated with him developing the poverty program, and I was on the supervising committee for the poverty program. My defection on Vietnam was something, had I been in his position, I would have felt very angry about.

"I hated it. I hated every minute of having to do it. And I know a lot of other people felt the same way.

"But I must say I never lost my respect for Lyndon Johnson."

Ernest Gruening: "My first attack was in October of 1963 when I criticized Jack Kennedy for sending so-called advisers down there, who were not advisers at all.

"The reason they were called advisers is that the Geneva Accords, which we'd agreed to support, forbade the introduction of any troops. So this was the first deception.

"On March 10, 1964, I made a speech entitled 'The United States Should Get Out of Vietnam.' It was a full-length speech, and it was the first statement made by anybody in public life. Being an old newspaperman, I knew it was news, and I fully expected to see it on the front pages of the *New York Times* and the *Post* the next morning. But not a line.

"But the interesting thing was that the wire services did summarize it and send it out to small papers throughout the country, with the result that I was deluged with letters, 404 by actual count, of which, believe it or not, all but 4 were favoring my position. They were very respectable letters, from deans of colleges and retired military men and ministers and so forth and said, 'Fine,' 'This is right,' and 'You're giving us something that we ought to know.' So that encouraged me to go on.

"Of course, you know, in retrospect, the whole thing is incredible. Why should we have gone down there? Well, the reason is that we were in the grip of an obsession. That obsession was that communism, China and Russia, were a monolithic combination determined to Bolshevize the world and that we had to stop them and that if we didn't stop them in Southeast Asia this would spread."

Edward Folliard: "In late July 1965 over lunch in the family dining room of the White House, Johnson said that he had talked often with former President Eisenhower about the war in Vietnam and that Ike had told him that it would be a tragic mistake for the United States to back down and allow the Communists to achieve a victory in Southeast Asia. He talked scornfully about those who were attacking him for the buildup of American forces over there, calling them belly-achers. He also had words of scorn for one of his advisers, a member of the Joint Chiefs of Staff, saying, 'He would like to bomb Peking tomorrow!'

"That same year, Mr. Johnson granted me an interview in the small room outside his White House office. He said he was distressed and perplexed by the failure of North Vietnam to understand the motives of the United States in Southeast Asia. He said it pained him to know that he was being pictured in Hanoi as a wheeler-dealer, a sort of emperor who wanted to conquer that Communist-ruled country when his true goal was the opposite of conquest.

"He said what he really wanted to do was to stop spending money on bullets and put a billion dollars into making life better in Southeast Asia, North Vietnam included."

Max Frankel: "By late '66 and early '67, the White House felt beleaguered within this country. They felt themselves on the defensive on it all, and from the president on down. The president set much of this tone, overcompensating. If the charge was that this was our client, or our puppet state, then he became extravagant in his claims of 'all the democracy that's at work out there.' And you know, 'After all, when did we last have an honest election in Boston?' he would say, looking at Bob Kennedy over his shoulder, and so on. If the reports were that the war isn't going too well, then, 'How the hell can you say that? We got their power plants last night. They can't last another six months.' This kind of talk.

"I don't think he ever fully believed those things himself. But he felt that the opposition at home was undermining the war effort; and that the whole ploy of bullying and threatening North Vietnam into negotiations was being undercut here; and that it was his duty single-handedly somehow to try to balance the noises coming out of this country."

George W. Ball: "Remembering the ugly McCarthy era, Lyndon Johnson feared a savage right-wing charge that the United States had abandoned Vietnam to a Communist fate. More than once he said to me: 'Don't worry about the hippies and the students and the Commies; they'll raise a lot of hell but can't do real damage. The terrible beast we have to fear is the right wing; if they ever get the idea I am selling out Vietnam, they'll do horrible things to the country, and we'll be forced to escalate the war beyond anything you've ever thought about."[1]

Harry McPherson: "Johnson's constant, unending fear was *always* the right, never the left. He didn't understand the left, the new left. That represented a true generation gap. 'But what in the world do they want?' he constantly was asking.

"But even so the new left, even during the height of the protests and all the rest of it, never really worried him. He thought his real trouble with Vietnam was with the right, that they would accuse his administration of not doing *enough* to win the war, that his whole administration was communistic. Sounds unrealistic now, but it was plenty realistic at the time—and from a great many points of view besides his."

By 1967 Lyndon was sure that the Communists were spending God alone knew how much money in the United States to finance the dissent and he asked Richard Helms, then head of the CIA and a regular at the Tuesday lunches, to investigate. Helms did so and told the president that there was no evidence that the dissenters were getting money from foreign sources. Hugh Sidey, then the White House correspondent for the presidency, says that at one point in 1967 Johnson shook that gigantic finger in Helms's face and said, "I simply don't understand why it is that you can't find out about that foreign money."

There were nervous nellies, of course; there were dissenters, discontents, long hairs, intellectual crazies and domestic Communists all over the place, including the hoodlums in and around Lafayette Park who kept shouting, "Hey, hey, LBJ, how many kids did you kill today?"

"Don't they know they're American?" he used to ask in frustration—often in despair.

Bill Moyers: "There were demonstrations over in Lafayette Park, and he went over to the window and came back shaking his head and said, 'They're making a terrible mistake. You know, they're attacking the country. I tell you, Moyers, you have been luckier than most people. When you die, there may be four or five hundred people who know you and will remember you. But when the ordinary John Q. Citizen dies, maybe twenty-five or thirty neighbors in the town where he lives and maybe fifty or sixty relatives, but even they will have vague memories. The only thing the guy has that gives him immortality other than his belief—he may be an atheist—is his citizenship as an American.' He said, 'He's part of an ongoing enterprise that was here before him and, God willing, it will be here after him. When he says, I am Joe Blow, that passes maybe on a tombstone for a while, but if you go to those graves down in central Texas you have to rub real hard to get the dust off them, and even then you can't see them.' He said, 'You know *that* even passes. They take your name away in the end. But,' he said, 'if you say I am an American, you're saying I'm as immortal as this Republic.' He said, 'For them to attack this country is to attack the immortality of most of the bastards who make up this country.'"

George E. Reedy: "Their life-style was totally different from his life-style as a young man. When he was a young man, as soon as you graduated from college you were very careful to comb your hair right and tie your tie right, get a pressed shirt, pressed suit, and you'd start making the rounds looking for a job which you'd get pretty quick. The long hair bothered him, the careless, sloppy clothing, the blue jeans. He'd look around the White House and he'd see a lot of young people that looked exactly like his ideal of what young persons should look like. And so to him that was the real American youth. I don't know where he thought people outside came from—probably Mars or Neptune or something like that."

Elizabeth Goldschmidt: "He said, 'I don't understand who these young people are that are opposed to the war. I never meet any of those young people. The young people that my daughters bring around are not like that. I just can't believe it.'

"I think that he truly did not understand the extent of the opposition to that war. I think it just didn't reach him."

Virginia Foster Durr: "The horror of the dichotomy in his presidency—all the people who were for him on the civil rights issue were against him, mostly, on the war issue. Not all, you know, but there was a great division there.

"And it was this division in his support, this dichotomy, that made his presidency so difficult. Mary Rather went to work for him the last year, and she had worked for him on the Hill for years. She was saying that the bliss, the joy, the fun, the good humor, the pleasantry of working for Lyndon on the Hill when he was a congressman or a senator, and then being in the White House that last year or two when he was being torn apart— she said it was an absolute horror. She just hated every minute of it. She just couldn't wait to get out of the White House, because he was just being torn so terribly."

Luci: "I could hear it from my bedroom. I'd wake up in the morning with it—'Hey, hey, LBJ, how many kids did you kill today?' And my husband was one of those boys. And that baby sleeping next to me was his only child. Lyndon Johnson's only grandchild. I'll never forget walking into my father's room at eleven o'clock some nights when he'd be watching the eleven o'clock news. We'd just go and sit with him. He really seemed to like to have your companionship if you never said a word. Boy, you'd better know when not to say a word.

"He never said anything and he never needed to, if you knew him, but he had looks that were like laser beams. And he'd be looking at the TV set and they'd be giving reports on fatalities that day and it was as if you were looking at a man who had a knife thrust into the pit of his stomach and turned over and over and over and over. He just physically looked like he was in agony.

"And one night, I'll never forget—he was eating dinner about midnight. I think the news had just gone off. And I walked in and I said, 'Daddy, I love you.' And I went over and sat down, and he was reading, and you could see tears just coming to his eyes and subsiding and coming and subsiding. I sat there for thirty minutes, and he never acknowledged my presence. And he was just torn up and caught up in it and so consumed by it at that time. It was a very painful sight—for a man who loved company, needed, wanted, thrived off people so much."

Ramsey Clark: "He came from flag country, and when he came to Vietnam it was 'My country right or wrong'—my loyalty to these United States, in their cause—whatever it might be, it's got to be right. World War I, World War II—that patriotism overwhelmed his sense of equality, dominated it.

"When you look at all the talk about body count—when you look at his terrible suffering, you know he's gone over the situation maybe three or four o'clock in the morning to see how many planes were lost. But I never sensed any concern for the other side. How many did the Vietnamese lose? How many people were killed in the village? How many South Vietnamese, how many North Vietnamese, how many Vietcong? It was *our* lives, *our* country; and they didn't figure, those people."

Wilbur J. Cohen: "The dissent—the disagreement, the argument, the questions about Vietnam spread even to his 'family,' his cabinet, the members of his most intimate circle.

"One day in a cabinet meeting we were having in the White House the president said, 'Does anybody have any questions?' Which he hadn't really done before. There was silence. He said, 'Does anyone have anything to bring up?'

"So I said, 'Yes, I have, Mr. President.' There was a deathly silence among all the cabinet. Here was the most junior guy opening up.[2] I said, 'My fourteen-year-old son and a lot of young men were over at my house the other night, and they asked me, 'Why are we in Vietnam?' I discussed it but my answer was not satisfactory to all these young boys who might have to serve. If you were asked that question, Mr. President, how would you answer it?'

"I could see Dean Rusk and McNamara thinking, 'Oh, Christ. What in hell caused Wilbur to ask that?' Anyway, the president took half an hour to answer, and the answer didn't make any sense whatsoever. I can't remember the words now, but it was very shocking to me. If he had given that answer publicly, he would just have been laughed out of court.

"Several of us subsequently talked with him again, saying that the answers weren't good enough. And the president arranged for us to see Dean Rusk and we had a long meeting with him and about four other cabinet officers. But Rusk wasn't any more persuasive than the president was.

"I think this was part of the problem—that Rusk and the president, whatever their reasons for being in Vietnam, and however they rationalized it for themselves, were not able publicly to rationalize it in a competent way. And I think this was a very unfortunate factor in the way they reacted to the outside world."

> Well, come on all you big strong men,
> Uncle Sam needs your help again,
> He's got himself in a terrible jam,
> Way down yonder in Vietnam,
> So put down your books and pick up a gun,
> We're going to have a whole lot of fun.
>   And it's one, two, three, what're we
>   fightin' for,
>   Don't ask me I don't give a damn,
>   Next stop is Vietnam.
>   And it's five, six, seven, open up
>   the pearly gates,
>   Well, there ain't no time to wonder wny,
>   Whoopee, we're all gonna die.
>   —Joe McDonald

IMPERFECT ALTERNATIVES

Shortly after the "Glassboro Summit" of June 1967 between Lyndon and Soviet Premier Kosygin, when it looked for a brief moment as if real progress had been made in improving relations between the United States and Russia, Secretary of Defense McNamara, Undersecretary of State Katzenbach, and General Wheeler flew to Vietnam for a five-day survey of the war. On their return McNamara met privately with the president. The defense secretary had little good to say about the prospects.

"There appears to be no attractive course of action," McNamara had already advised the president in May. "The probabilities are that Hanoi has decided not to negotiate until the American electorate has been heard in November 1968. Continuation of our present moderate policy, while avoiding a larger war, will not change Hanoi's mind. . . . So we must choose among imperfect alternatives."[1]

So Lyndon was half expecting a gloomy report from his defense secretary, but he was not expecting him to criticize General Westmoreland, which McNamara did, and vehemently. The president, for his part, stoutly defended "his" general. What's more, he said, everyone knew that McNamara had gone "to see the war," and everyone would want to know what, exactly, McNamara "saw." He, Lyndon, had enough troubles without mutiny from within, so would the secretary please prepare a statement for the press declaring how well everything was going—politically, economically and, yes, even militarily, in South Vietnam?

McNamara prepared the statement. Still, if the domino theory could be said to apply within Lyndon's own inner circle, it might be said that the first domino fell that day.

But silently. The Washington rumor mill caught puffs of smoke here and there, but no fire could be discerned. Vice-President Humphrey met regularly with the president and his closest advisers—Rusk, McNamara, Rostow, and Helms—and, said he, never heard the defense secretary put forward a dissenting view. Publicly everything was very, very correct.

But as 1967 wore on doubts about the war were rising everywhere. It was so *inconclusive*. And although one could argue a case for the public never being told the truth in any war, still the extent of distortion of the facts in this war appeared to be all out of proportion. There was that CIA guy in the U.S. embassy in Saigon with the unlikely name of Sam Adams who had, almost by chance, discovered extraordinary discrepancies between our publicized reports of Vietcong desertions and casualties and the bulletins put out by the Vietcong. It seemed that if one was to believe our reports, there could hardly be any Vietcong left at all, and yet clearly that was not the case. It was obvious to anyone who watched the seven o'clock news on television that the one thing there was no shortage of in South Vietnam was Vietcong.

And speaking of the seven o'clock news, that was another disturbing factor. How could the American people be expected to back a war that they saw pictured in its bloodiest form every evening on their television screens, and when they heard so much more of death, maiming, venereal disease, drug addiction, and corruption than they did acts of valor or battles bravely won?

And then there were those antiwar demonstrators who seemed never to tire of demonstrating, and whose protests had begun to seem less and less *noisy*, and more and more *reasonable*.

On September 3 South Vietnam held national elections under the constitution that its leaders had, miraculously, completed the previous spring. To no one's surprise General Nguyen Van Thieu was elected president and Marshall Nguyen Cao Ky, vice-president. Hubert was sent to represent the United States at the inauguration.

In his autobiography, *The Education of a Public Man*, Humphrey describes how he was "educated" about Vietnam on that trip, how reporters warned him not to believe the official reports that he would be shown, warned him that our policy was failing. The extent of the Americanization of the country came home to him. "We had taken over the economy, we had taken over the fighting, we had taken over South Vietnam. It had brought jobs and prosperity (at great cost to other facets of society, of course). Even Thieu's inaugural address had been largely written by our embassy." [2]

Humphrey describes how he tried to explain to Thieu that public opinion in the United States was shifting and that the people were not going to be willing to continue to support the war as it was presently being carried out.

"Thieu listened, delicately holding a cigarette, its smoke drifting up and away from him. He broke the pose to flick the ash from his cigarette in a manner that suggested that he was also flicking away what I had said.

"Then he spoke: 'No, you will be here for a long time.'" [3]

In November General Westmoreland returned to Washington to consult with the president. On the sixteenth a *New York Times* headline read: "WAR GAINS CALLED VERY

ENCOURAGING BY WESTMORELAND." A subheadline, however, was more indicative of the actual state of affairs: "General Asserts He Wants Promised Reinforcements As Soon As Possible."

On November 22 the *Times* headline ran: "WAR OF ATTRITION CALLED EFFECTIVE BY WESTMORELAND," and the accompanying story read:

"He and Bunker foresee a reduction in U.S. role if progress continues. Their conclusion is that the United States and their allies are steadily wearing down the enemy at present level of force and supply on both sides, and their assumption is that the Soviet Union, China, and the rest of the Communist world will not provide the additional weapons and men necessary to restore the military balance that is now going against Hanoi and the Vietcong."

Six days later Lyndon announced that the Secretary of Defense Robert McNamara would be leaving the cabinet to become the president of the International Bank. McNamara, who earlier that month had written a second memorandum titled "Outlook If Present Course of Action Is Continued," did not as yet have a successor.

In the middle of December Prime Minister Harold Holt of Australia was drowned, and Lyndon, who had made up his mind not to go to Texas for Christmas anyway, decided to attend the funeral and then, perhaps, should prospects look favorable, make a few stops on the way back. William Bundy and Walt Rostow accompanied him.

James Cross: "We went to Australia, stopping in Honolulu and in Pago Pago and in American Samoa. As we arrived at Canberra just a little after daylight, the president came in the cockpit. He said, 'Cross, we'll leave here in about thirty-six hours. You make some plans to go maybe up to Vietnam. Maybe we'll go to Thailand. And we might want to go by and see the pope. We might want to stop off and see Ayub Khan. But now don't go telling anybody.'"

The president descended from the plane at approximately 4:30 A.M. to be greeted by Richard G. Baron Casey, governor general of Australia, John McEwen, prime minister, and other unnamed and no doubt sleepy welcomers. McEwen thanked him for the "tremendous tribute you pay to our colleague Harold Holt, your friend," and Lyndon responded, "My country and I have lost a friend; the world has lost a very great man."

The next day the president, Bundy, and Rostow met with McEwen and other Australian ministers. The talk was principally of Vietnam, and at the end of it the Australian government, without much enthusiasm, restated its commitment to the United States position. Over lunch they met with President Park of Korea, and during what was described as a "working dinner," Lyndon discussed the current state of affairs in Vietnam with President Thieu, who just happened to have come down for the memorial service for Holt himself. After that meeting a joint statement was issued which reiterated all the usual points about South Vietnam's policy of reconciliation and Thieu's personal willingness to discuss "relevant matters" with the NLF as long as it was understood that by talking with it the government did not in any way recognize its existence.

Hugh Sidey: "Johnson wouldn't announce where he was going next. So ostensibly after he left Australia the president of the United States disappeared into the skies of Asia."

Cross: "We finally took off from Canberra, went to Melbourne, waited there about four hours while the president went through the memorial ceremony. Then we took off from Melbourne and went to Darwin, stayed there an hour or so for fuel, and went from Darwin to Khorat, Thailand, where the president spoke to some of the American combat pilots and crewmen there."

Considering that it was 5:30 A.M. when Lyndon delivered a speech of some twenty minutes or so, the pilots and crewmen were remarkably receptive. Lyndon dispensed a lot of Christmas cheer and warm praise. He could not, he said, give any assurance that the way ahead would be easier.

From Thailand, Cross piloted the plane, to no one's great surprise, to Vietnam itself, Cam Ranh Bay, where Lyndon dispensed more cheer to the troops and a number of medals to such notables as General William Westmoreland, General Creighton W. Abrams, Ambassador Ellsworth Bunker, Deputy Ambassador Eugene Locke, and Deputy for Pacification Robert Komer.

Cross: "We went from Cam Ranh to Karachi and visited with Ayub Khan for a while. In the meantime, I was trying to lay plans as best I could to try to get fuel and ground communications, as well as ground transportation, so we could go into Rome without tipping our hand that we were going. The president was concerned about a Communist demonstration in Rome. But we went, and we made it. We landed at Rome and he saw the Pope, and we slipped out of there, and the Communists never realized we were there."

Sidey: "Johnson took an exercise bicycle along—he had it bolted to the floor of the plane. And he kept denying that he was going to Rome, sitting on that bicycle, saying, 'I ain't going to Rome. I don't know what you're talking about.' Only Johnson could conceive that on Christmas Eve [actually December 23] he would drop in unannounced on the Pope. It was at the height of Vietnam, of course, and he figured that a big plea for peace right on the Vatican steps would be great.

"But he wouldn't tell the embassy; Freddy Reinhardt, the ambassador, found out about it secretly. Johnson didn't want to visit the Italian government, but the Pope wouldn't let him in unless he did.[4] Finally, Johnson admits we're going to see the Pope. Six American helicopters are flown up, we load in, we go around, we're circling over St. Peter's Square on Christmas Eve with all the clatter and dripping oil and the pigeons are flying off and thousands of people are down there for the Pope's blessing.

"We land in the Vatican garden, wreck the goddamn garden,[5] and go into the Pope's library. The Pope gives Johnson a fourteenth-century oil painting—lovely, you know, and then Johnson says, 'Luci wanted me to give you this.' And they come in with a big package wrapped in brown wrapping paper and it's got a big hemp rope tied on it. And the Pope is a dainty guy, and he tries to undo it and can't, and Johnson says, 'Your Holiness, let me help you,' and reaches into his pocket and pulls out a big jackknife. He flicks open the blade, rips the package, excelsior springs out all over the Oriental rugs and everything else. The press is over in the corner, and by this time we are in a state of shock. And the Pope—you have to remember he was a little guy—reaches in and pulls it out, and he's nose to nose with Johnson who says, 'She thought you'd want it as a Christmas present.'

"And Johnson gives him one of those large plastic busts of himself."

Following the exchange of gifts, Lyndon and the Pope had a little talk. Lyndon asked the Pope to intercede on the behalf of the American prisoners of war in North Vietnam. Afterwards Lyndon allowed as to how His Holiness had reminded him that "an honorable settlement of the painful and threatening dispute is still possible." Mutual restraint was what was needed, the Pope said, and Lyndon agreed.

The next day, safely back in Washington for Christmas Eve, Lyndon summed up his round-the-world-in-four-and-a-half-days odyssey for his fellow Americans. He contrasted Christmastime in Vietnam with the same in Rome, and he spoke of the brave young men who would spend Christmas in the rice paddies and the foxholes. It was, all things considered, a somber message, and the man who delivered it seemed startlingly changed from the one who, on Christmas Eve 1963, just four years before, had taken the press on a romping tour of the Ranch and then handed out presents to all.

"WHAT SHALL I DO?"

Hubert H. Humphrey: "He told me immediately after the 1964 election, I think it was the day after, when Muriel and I were at the Ranch, that he wasn't going to run for reelection, but I just didn't take him seriously.

"And I don't doubt that he ran it in and out of his mind a hundred, maybe a thousand times. He liked to test every idea, especially one as important as that, on everybody within hearing distance. And he always had a lot of people within hearing distance."

Lady Bird: "We must have discussed it hundreds of times, and the discussions began at the very beginning."

Willard Deason: "He always had this premonition about dying. I believe both his father and his grandfather died in their early sixties,[1] and he thought that would happen to him, which, of course, it did.

"But he didn't want anything like that to happen while he was president."

Lyndon: "I never saw Woodrow Wilson's picture in the Red Room of the White House, never looked at it that I didn't think that it might happen to me, that I would end another term in bed with a stroke and that the decisions of government would be taken care of by other people and that was wrong. I didn't want that to happen.

"I have been beset by health problems all my life, and while when I finished the presidency I think I was in as good health as I ever was, I had in 1955 been treated for a serious, almost fatal heart attack. My mind was always on that.

"I did not ever want this country to have a president who couldn't be a president for physical or whatever reasons."

Henry Gonzalez: "He told me to my face that the reason he didn't run again was that several doctors had told him he wouldn't last another term. Now when the doctors tell you that you won't last another term, it's not honest to seek four years. That's the way he felt."

Lady Bird: "I had hoped from the beginning that he would leave after his first full term, when he would have accomplished as much as he could, and there would still be time—I hoped—for a quiet life together."

William Lawrence: "It was less than eighteen months after the 1964 landslide that I began to wonder inwardly if LBJ would be a candidate for reelection. . . .

"My suspicions were aroused first in the fall and winter of 1965 when LBJ was confined to the Bethesda Naval Hospital with a combination gallbladder and kidney stone operation. At first he snapped back quickly, but then he relapsed. His staff, including press secretary Bill Moyers, openly admitted his pain, his fatigue, his need for a long rest and rehabilitation.

"Such talk of pain, of tiredness, of a need for rest would not have been unusual or unexpected in the ordinary patient. But now we were talking about LBJ, who, up to then, had been depicted as a kind of superman, who, disregarding the massive heart attack that had almost killed him ten years earlier, now thrived on work, work, work and no sleep in the White House. LBJ and his staff had made the president at least ten feet tall, but now they seemed to be talking about an ordinary mortal. . . .

"Then, in June, 1966, right after the California gubernatorial primary election, I came back to the White House with some direct questions for Moyers.

"'Has the president ever told or intimated to the staff that he might not be a candidate for reelection in 1968?' I wanted to know.

"Moyers replied indirectly, saying there had been nothing that positive, but that the president in moments of tiredness or frustration had been heard to cry out, as every president has cried out, that he would be happy indeed when his term of office ended and he would be rid of frustrations, problems, and so many critics.

"'Do you think the president will be a candidate for reelection?' I asked.

"Moyers was then closer to LBJ than any person with the exception of Lady Bird Johnson, and his answer therefore astounded me.

"'I wouldn't bet you a nickel either way,' said Moyers."[2]

Moyers: "I don't think I realized that he wasn't going to run again until after I left the White House on the fifteenth of February of 1967. I began to see signs from afar.

"Even so, it eluded me that he would voluntarily give it up. I saw the signs, but I didn't believe them."

Jake Pickle: "Around Labor Day in '67 he was trying to make his decision, whether he should or shouldn't run. He called me from the White House, and he said, 'Are you going to be in Austin on Saturday?' I said, 'Yes, I think so.' He said, 'Well, now, I'm going to ask John Connally to come up; I've got some things I want to talk about, and I want just you two there.'

"So my wife and I drove up, and sure enough there was John Connally and his wife. This was at the Ranch. And the president said, 'Well, come on.' And we left the ladies there, and the three of us got in the car, and we drove all over the Ranch, from one end of it to another and back and forth. We'd drive, and we'd stop up on a hillside and cut the motor, and just hop out. And explore: Should he run, why shouldn't he run, what was best for him, what was best for his family, what was best for the country, what was best for his party?

"After four or five hours of riding all over the Ranch, we finally came in.

"Lady Bird said, 'What did you decide? Have you decided?'

"The president said, 'All right, you've been talking about this for a long time, so we'll make this decision right now and make you happy.' And he said, 'I've decided that I won't run for reelection.'

"We parted company with a sworn pledge not to say anything about it. Now whether in his own mind that was an absolute, final decision or not, I don't know. He may have weakened his resolve at times later when some of the people in the Democratic party challenged him and literally tried to run him out of the party or the race. I think he got his back arched and was getting close to changing his mind once or twice."

James H. Rowe, Jr.: "A lot of people said that when they saw Johnson during the six months before his withdrawal speech, he kept saying, 'I'm not going to take any more of this. A man doesn't have to take this kind of thing.' But all of us who had known him for years had gone through this talk many times, many, and we didn't pay any attention to it."

James Gaither: "When we were down at the Ranch in December, we recommended in the legislative program holding back a couple of major proposals for the campaign, such as the child health act, which was a major program to bring comprehensive health services to mothers and their children through covering all poor children through the first year of life and then going ultimately to school age. And he said in front of Joe Califano and Larry Temple and Matt Nimetz and me that he might not be running, and he was going to present the whole proposal—the whole legislative program—in the State of the Union and in his messages and forget about all this talk of holding things.

"A little later on that day he took us for a tour of the new wing that he had just built for Mrs. Johnson, and said, 'Now that we may be coming down here to live full time, she has got to have more space.'"

Other family events had occurred during 1967 that had their own subtle influences on Lyndon's decision-making process. In June Luci, who had married Patrick Nugent the previous summer, gave birth to a son named for his father and maternal grandfather, Patrick Lyndon. Lyn, as he was known, quickly became a prime object of the president's affection and attention, and the prospect of being able to spend more time, from the few years he felt were left to him, with his grandson was a tempting one.

Dr. James Cain: "He had very few things that he could relax with. He had two or three things that I think were outstanding. Luci's baby, for instance. He could play with the baby and lose himself in this. He could take one of the dogs and play with the dog and lose himself in that. He could get on the telephone and call Dale Malechek, his ranch foreman, and talk with him for an hour or so, almost going to sleep while in the chair, when he was under the greatest of strain, talking about the bull in the east section or about some of the things they were planning. But these were relaxations that he needed very, very much."

Then in December Lynda married Marine Captain Charles Robb in an elegant White House ceremony. Captain Robb was under orders to go to Vietnam in March.

Lady Bird: "We drove back to the Ranch [on January 4, 1968], with John and Nellie, through pea-soup fog. After dinner we went back to Lyndon's bedroom—the four of us— and talked without interruption for nearly three hours. John said, 'You ought to run only if you look forward to being president again—only if you *want* to do it.' I think he meant Lyndon ought to run if he could find an element of joy in the work, but he ought not to run if the frustrations, the pain, the backbreaking work made him dread it. 'You also ought not to run just to keep somebody else from being president.'"[3]

Lyndon reiterated his primary concerns—his health, the possibility that if he stayed in office, it might fall on him to make a crucial decision involving nuclear power, the attitude of the soldiers in Vietnam. Would they see withdrawal as desertion?

George Christian: "Buzz [Horace Busby] and I were both advocates of his stepping down. Most of the others were arguing the other way. But Buzz and I felt that Johnson had become a lightning rod for everything people in the country wanted to jump on. We felt he probably could be reelected, but it wouldn't be worth having if he did it. It would be a hollow victory.

"We argued that point with him over and over, and, basically, he agreed with it. There was a time to go, and this was the time."

Lyndon spent much of the morning of January 17 going over what was generally agreed to be the eleventh draft of the State of the Union message he was to deliver that night. He also studied the draft of a statement—drawn up for him by George Christian— announcing that he would not run for reelection.

Lady Bird: "The announcement was not to be included in the text of the State of the Union message. If Lyndon decided to make it, the statement would come at the end, beginning with a line something like this: 'And now I want to speak to you about a personal matter . . .' He keeps looking from one to the other of us—those close to him— for an answer. But . . . there is nobody who can decide but him. . . .

"It was about 6:30 P.M. He was rushed. Standing in the door between the big Oval Office and his little one, he said, 'Well, what do you think? What shall I do?'

"I looked at him with that helpless feeling and said: 'Luci hopes you won't run. She wants you for herself and for Lyn and all of us. She does not want to give you up. Lynda hopes you *will* run. She told me so this afternoon, with a sort of terrible earnestness, because her husband is going to war and she thinks there will be a better chance of getting him back alive and the war settled if you are president. Me—I don't know. I have said it all before. I can't tell you what to do.'"[4]

The one person who seemed to be strongly recommending that Lyndon make his announcement that night was John Connally, primarily because the speech would be, of course, before the joint session of Congress, which would lend a certain dramatic effect. John, who had done some acting in his youth, was always conscious of theatrical potential.

Lyndon began that night by saying, "I was thinking as I was walking down the aisle tonight of what Sam Rayburn told me many years ago. The Congress always extends a warm welcome to the president—as he comes in."

He spoke of Vietnam, saying that since his last State of the Union message, "the enemy has been defeated in battle after battle." He said that the South Vietnamese had had democratic elections, all commendably successful. He added that although many victories had been and were continuing to be won, the enemy continued to pour men and matériel into battle in the hope that "America's will to persevere can be broken."

The enemy, he said, was wrong. "America will persevere. Aggression will never prevail.

"But our goal is peace—and peace at the earliest possible moment."

Then he spoke, at much greater length and more persuasively, about the fact that unemployment was too high, and he had some specific suggestions for decreasing it. He spoke of more money for model cities, of Medicare and Medicaid, of child health, and of all the great things he had had in mind for his Great Society, indeed still had in mind.

"I shall," he said, "also urge the Congress to act on other vital pending bills—especially the civil rights measures—fair jury trials, protection of federal rights, enforcement of equal employment opportunity, and fair housing.

"The unfinished work of the first session must be completed—the higher education act, the juvenile delinquency act, conservation measures to save the redwoods of California [he looked at Bird as he said that], and to preserve the wonders of our scenic rivers, the highway beautification act—and all the other measures for a cleaner and for a better, and for a more beautiful America."

True, there were problems, he acknowledged, but, "If there ever was a nation that was capable of solving its problems, it is this nation.

"If ever there were a time to know the pride and the excitement and the hope of being an American, it is this time.

"So this, my friends, is the State of Our Union, seeking, building, tested many times in this past year—and always equal to the test.

"Thank you and good night."

Lyndon: "That night before the television, I got to the last page and I reached in my pocket. I don't think I would have used it, but just to see if it was there. I don't know what I would have done if it had been. I don't think I would have done it then. But it wasn't there, and I didn't have to confront the problem.

"I went back to Mrs. Johnson and said, 'Why'd you have to keep that announcement?' And she said, 'I gave it back to you.' And I said, 'No, you didn't,' and we both looked through my pockets and then went on, and there it was by the telephone table."

Christian: "Later that evening, thinking maybe he had decided not to withdraw at all, I asked why. He said, 'I thought about it, but when I got over there I got to thinking about laying out this big program before Congress and telling Congress, 'This is the program I want done and, by the way, I'm not running for reelection.' So I just decided it was kind of strange and didn't do it.'

"Later he said, and this may be true, that he had given it to Mrs. Johnson and put it on her dressing table, and he said he later forgot to put it in his pocket.

"Myself, I think he decided *before* he went to the Hill that night that the occasion wasn't the time to do it. He had made up his mind beforehand. He always did."

Horace Busby: "If Lyndon had wanted to make a statement about the withdrawal that night, he would have done it. He certainly wouldn't have forgotten it. In his entire life I doubt that Lyndon Johnson ever forgot anything that he wanted to remember."

TÊT

Everybody—with the possible exception of the grunts who were doing the fighting—knew that something was up. In the early fall of 1967, U.S. Intelligence came up with the unsettling report that the North Vietnamese were planning a major offensive. The big question was when it would be. No one expected it to take place during Tet, the lunar new year Vietnamese holiday season, a kind of combination Christmas, New Year's and Easter in both the South and the North. But by the beginning of 1968 there were more and more indications that that was exactly when it would happen.

General Westmoreland made appropriate preparations. Previously planned unit movements were canceled or changed. Mobile reserve units were strategically positioned to be available where needed. Leaves were canceled. U.S. leaves, that is—the South Vietnamese were not about to lose their happy holidays, certainly not when there were all those Americans to fill in for them.

On January 22, Westmoreland reported to Lyndon that the enemy was showing "a very unusual sense of urgency." They apparently were hoping this campaign would be "decisive," perhaps in the same way Dienbienphu had been fourteen years earlier. Vietcong headquarters were even going so far as to predict "final victory"; in any case it appeared that the Communists would throw everything they had into this attack, in the hope of gaining victories that could be exploited for political purposes.

On the twenty-fourth Ambassador Bunker sent a cable to Lyndon asking that the bombing halt that had already been announced for the Tet truce be canceled in those areas of North Vietnam where the buildup for an offensive was going on. The announcement of the cancellation was to have been released on the twenty-ninth, but it wasn't. Everybody was too busy celebrating. The press office in Saigon was closed, and President Thieu had gone off to the Mekong to celebrate the holidays with his family. But then almost nobody, including the Americans, was not caught up in the holiday spirit—especially, in their own fashion, the North Vietnamese.

On January 31, in the middle of Tet, the Communists attacked 5 of South Vietnam's 6 largest cities, 36 of its 44 provincial capitals, and roughly a quarter of its 242 district capitals. And in Saigon itself a special Vietcong suicide squad blew a hole in the wall of the American embassy compound and managed to enter the grounds before they were stopped and killed.

Earle Wheeler: "A substantial number of the South Vietnamese units were at only half strength because they had returned to their homes on leave for the Tet holidays. The propaganda put out by the enemy, the captured POWs, defectors, and captured documents made very clear what the enemy objectives were: to fragment and destroy the South Vietnamese armed forces; to instigate uprisings in the major population areas against the government, and to destroy our logistic base and our command and control system. And they had actually made a very sizable attack against Tan Son Nhut Air Base where our command headquarters was located.

"The American embassy in Saigon was infiltrated by nineteen specially trained Vietcong; it was the least important part of the offensive, but certainly had the greatest impact on American thinking. Five American military men were killed by the Vietcong who were soon wiped out by American paratroopers who landed on the embassy roof. But dislodging the enemy from the other major cities and military posts the Vietcong occupied took somewhat longer. They still occupied a number of towns a month later. And they were in charge of the sacred city of Hué from January 31 until February 24, by which time the city that many considered the most beautiful in Southeast Asia was almost completely destroyed, and thousands of civilians were murdered and buried in a mass grave."

One of the minor incidents of the war that moved millions was only indirectly connected with Tet. It was a photograph, published in almost every newspaper in the world, showing a South Vietnamese brigadier general firing a bullet into the head of an unarmed prisoner. There are things that no one alive at that time will ever forget; that is one of them.[1]

But who was defeated? As usual, Ho took one view, Westy and the rest of the brass and the then more powerful men of the administration took the other. For the first time it seemed that a great majority of Americans agreed not with Westmoreland but with that man with a pointed beard, that Communist who had, or so we Americans had always been told, an unblemished record as a liar.

Clark Clifford: "Tet had a very substantial impact on me as it had on others. As I recall it was said in 1967 that we could see 'light at the end of the tunnel.' General Westmoreland indicated that he thought it entirely possible that we could begin to bring American boys home in 1968. Tet changed all that. The fact that the enemy could mount a simultaneous offensive against so many cities, towns, and hamlets at one time and that the effect of such an offensive, even though blunted militarily, could result in our military asking for an additional number of troops, amounting to over two hundred thousand, changed the complexion entirely.

"After Tet, I assure you, there was no suggestion that we could see any 'light at the end of the tunnel,' nor was there any thought of sending any American boys home. The whole thrust was exactly the reverse."

Yes, sir. The Battle of the Bulge all over again; how fortunate were it true, but it wasn't.

Robert Komer: "We genuinely had believed we were winning. Of course, we completely undermined the president's position, because when Tet turned out the way it did, it was in stark contrast to what the president had been telling the nation. The difference between November—hey, we're finally winning—and the next thing you know the U.S. embassy in Saigon is under attack—well, that robbed me of all my credibility and that of everybody else, especially the president."

Harry McPherson: "It was the feeling on the part of vast numbers of Americans that, particularly after Westmoreland and Bunker had come back in the fall of the year before and said that things were really just looking good; that after all that and after a tremendous commitment for three years—air power, five hundred and fifty thousand men and all the rest of it—that this crowd was still able to mount a major offensive that smashed into all kinds of cities and secure hamlets, that they were able to hold Hué for a long time while the marines encircled them, that they were able to get into Saigon and terrorize the population.

"The terrible quality of the war in Vietnam came home to people. It appeared that these guys didn't want to quit at all and were never going to quit; that our crowd was as caught off guard as ever."

On February 21 Johnson sent Wheeler to Saigon for consultations with Bunker and Westmoreland.

Wheeler: "People were far calmer in Saigon than they were in Washington. Tet had a tremendous effect on the American public . . . on the leadership of Congress . . . on President Johnson, and it had a major effect on the incoming secretary of defense, Mr. Clifford.[2] And it is my view that Clark began to reassess his position and moved to higher ground."

General Wheeler returned from Saigon on the morning of February 28 and reported to the president and a group of his senior advisers over breakfast at the White House.[3] He asked, essentially, for 206,000 more troops.[4]

For the first time his request fell on less than sympathetic ears. Although Johnson appointed a committee, headed by Clark Clifford and including Wheeler, McNamara, Rusk, Helms, and Maxwell Taylor, to examine alternatives, he never himself considered that 206,000 more young Americans was one of those alternatives. A week later Lyndon met again with his advisers. "I made it clear that I did not favor this proposal. . . . The fact was that I had firmly decided against sending anything approaching 206,000 additional men to Vietnam."[5]

John P. Roche: "Johnson hadn't under any circumstances considered 206,000 men. Wheeler figured this Tet offensive was going to be his handle for getting the shopping list okayed."

Harry McPherson: "It was about, I guess, in the last part of February that I began to talk to Clifford on occasion and with a sense of astonishment discovered that he had some real doubts about matters in Vietnam and our policy. I had some colossal ones. I talked to a number of guys who had been in the civilian side of things in Vietnam and I had spent two weeks out there and had gotten a sense of this, how dense an affair it was, how many strands were running through it, and how unsusceptible it was to the ordinary treatment of major power commitment—military and political and economic. And so I was a dove, I suppose, in that very unsatisfactory classification.

"On the other hand, John Roche, an extremely intelligent bird, was for commitment. And he believed he was right. And Dean Rusk is not a simpleton as Arthur Schlesinger and others have done their best to make him appear; he has a good mind and a sophisticated mind. Mac Bundy had been for the war and was still for the war at this time. Dean Acheson the same. So there was an argument, at least."

Clifford: "In the middle of March, the president made two speeches.[6] And they were really hard-nosed speeches, stern, facing up to the commitment that we had made, very determined speeches—in effect they were something of a restatement of our intention to seek and achieve military victory in Vietnam. I was deeply concerned about them. By the time those two speeches were made, I had the strongest feeling that we ought to be moving in the other direction.

"I recall making the statement that what the president should do was make a speech about peace. I now knew after what I'd gone through the preceding twenty-seven days that if we were going after military victory we were headed down a road that had no end."

McPherson: "Johnson's reaction to Clifford's doubting was terrible. He did mind it—of course he did. I would have minded it. When you've spent as much time laboring with this thing as he had, when so much that was in you was invested in this, when it had seemed the only decision to make, and when the judgment of history on his administration was riding on this, as it clearly was, no matter what else he did—on whether it had been right to escalate in Vietnam—having a young English-major lawyer sitting back sniping from the sidelines is an uncomfortable and an unwanted thing.

"The idea of opening this yawning issue, this chasm under your feet—imagine! Christ, you put five hundred and fifty thousand Americans out there; you've lost twenty-five thousand of them dead! What if it's wrong? What if we've made an error? All the conventional wisdom at the time was that we were right. And looking back on it, maybe it's one of those weird situations where in 1965 probably if you had thrown every conceivable calculation into a computer it would have come out saying, 'Go.'"

General Wheeler again visited Saigon on March 24, returning on March 26 with General Creighton Abrams, who was Westmoreland's deputy commander in Vietnam.

George W. Ball: "He [Johnson] called a meeting of the so-called senior advisers . . . We heard two briefings, and they were very discouraging about the effect of the Tet offensive, and what it had done to set the whole cause back in Vietnam. . . . The next day the group met. They were considering a request from Westmoreland for . . . more troops. . . . Secretary Clifford was there and he was limiting the response to a much smaller number, and he was beginning to develop grave doubts about the whole thing. . . .

"McGeorge Bundy led off saying that the group had met and that he had something he wanted to tell the president which he thought he would never say to him, that he now agreed with George Ball and this was the general sentiment of the group. And we went around, and it wasn't unanimous by any means, but there was strong advice to the president: 'Look, this thing is hopeless, you'd better begin to de-escalate and get out.' And this was the first time he'd ever heard anything of this kind. . . . I think he was very shocked. . . . He really couldn't believe it. Here were people like Dean Acheson and Douglas Dillon, people of that kind, who had been pretty stalwart up until then."[7]

Lyndon: "I don't think I was surprised at the direction in which their thinking was going. I think their recommendations were agreed to with a sense of relief. I didn't accept it all. I may have conveyed shock, although I tried to avoid leaving that impression."

McPherson: "I think by this time he had pretty much yielded to the Clifford view, the new Clifford view. For a long time they were struggling in him, I think. On the one hand he wanted, by God, to stand up and fight these guys out there and to fight those here who didn't want to fight those out there; on the other, he was getting depressed by the possibility of making it in Vietnam and of keeping the country with him long enough to make it."

THE CONTENDERS

In the beginning almost nobody, including Gene McCarthy himself, took his candidacy for the Democratic nomination for president very seriously. Nobody really wanted him; most of those who wanted to dump Lyndon wanted Bobby Kennedy, but Bobby kept repeating, good Democrat that he was, that he was not a candidate, not against a man of his own party who was the incumbent. Bobby had always been a party man, a machine man; his reputation as a lifetime liberal crusader came only during the last years of his life, the last twenty months largely.

And what kind of a liberal was McCarthy, the man from Watkins, Minnesota? He had first been elected to Congress in 1948 where he had a lackluster record; the truth was Congress bored him as the Senate, to which he was elected in 1958, would one day also bore him. Even some of those who supported him for the presidency thought he would soon become bored with that, too. In both the House and the Senate his legislative and attendance record were meager, and a great many people felt that he favored far too many special interests that as a true liberal, if he was a true liberal, he should have fought.

McCarthy, while not a first-rate poet himself, read and appreciated first-rate poetry, and to the amazement of Lady Bird he went to art galleries and looked at and appreciated art that Lyndon hadn't ever heard about, never did hear, and didn't want to. And he had been for an investigation of the CIA as early as 1965; he had criticized the sale of American arms to the underdeveloped nations and had called for "a national debate" on the issue of bombing North Vietnam.

Later Humphrey said he wasn't a bit surprised when in the fall or early winter of 1967 Gene said that he thought he would run for the presidency. Hubert told him that it was unlikely he could defeat the incumbent, any incumbent, and McCarthy said that he didn't expect to win. In essence, he said he wanted to get out of the Senate and he felt strongly about the war, so he might as well go out and get in a few primaries.

On November 30, 1967, at a little after ten in the morning, McCarthy entered the Senate caucus room and announced to the waiting press that he intended to enter the Democratic primaries in Wisconsin, Oregon, and Nebraska. He said he would make up his mind about the primaries in Massachusetts and New Hampshire during the next two weeks.

He spoke of the war and his opposition to it; he spoke of its cost both in human and monetary terms, and he concluded his statement by saying:

"I am not—as I'm sure I will be charged—for peace at any price, but for an honorable, rational, and political solution to this war."

For those who believed that Lyndon must go, that Lyndon's war must end, McCarthy's announcement was a great moment. At last there was someone behind whom those who detested the war, and who had worn out a lot of shoe leather and lung power protesting it, could rally.

When McCarthy was asked if he didn't think he was committing a case of political suicide, Gene said, "I don't think it will be a case of suicide. It might be an execution."[1]

But what about his organization? It was already being said that he didn't have one and being a nonorganizational man himself probably never would have, which proved to be the case.

Eugene McCarthy: "It will be pretty much a volunteer army."

And so it was. The boys had short hair, reasonably so anyway, and were always properly, even conservatively dressed. The girls no less so. If there was a hippie among them during the crucial campaign that preceded the March 11 primary in New Hampshire neither he or she was visible. These clean, almost overly polite young people, nearly ten thousand of them—"the children's crusade" it was called—went from door to door asking for support for Gene.

McCarthy finally chose or had chosen for him a campaign manager, Blair Clark, a gentle man who was a writer and editor and had been a classmate of Kennedy's at Harvard. Clark was not considered a very organized man.

What matter? As Gene himself said, "Organization is not that important in this kind of campaign. I plan to run because the issues are more important than the person."

Everybody thought that New Hampshire would be a fiasco. True, Gene had made an occasional eloquent and seemingly persuasive speech. In Manchester, for instance, considered, because of its newspaper, a center of blue-collar reaction and hawkishness, those who listened heard him say:

> The Democratic party in 1964 promised "no wider war." Yet the war is getting wider every month. Only a few months ago we were told that 65 percent of the population was secure. Now we know that even the American embassy is not secure.

The speech, though, was delivered in a monotone. Remembering Gene's dazzling effectiveness at the 1960 convention Joe Rauh said, "Maybe he's the kind of guy who can do it only once."

But then came primary day, and while McCarthy did not exactly win, he gained 42.2 percent of the popular vote. Lyndon got 49.4 percent, but McCarthy got twenty of the twenty-four convention delegates. It was an astounding result. In addition, fifty-five hundred Republicans had voted for him by writing in his name.

In his triumph McCarthy was ebullient. "If we come to Chicago with this strength," he told his young supporters, "there'll be no riots or demonstrations, but a victory celebration."

The cheers were deafening. At midnight Bobby Kennedy called to congratulate him. Publicly the president had nothing to say on the matter, but that day he did issue a statement praising the Senate for passing the Civil Rights Act of 1968. "I hope this bill will soon be before me for signing into law. I salute those who this day acted to bring that time—and a more perfect union—closer to hand."

Bobby had been approached many times by different people, one of whom was Allard Lowenstein, who in the summer of 1967 had launched a Dump Lyndon campaign. According to George McGovern, Bobby had turned down the offer. But feelings have been known to change, especially in politics.

George McGovern: "A number of dissident Democrats came to see me during the summer and the fall of 1967 and pleaded with me to become a candidate. I asked them to go see Bob Kennedy. They said they had already been there and he had grappled with them and turned it down—which didn't surprise me because I had been talking to Bob Kennedy as early as 1966 about running for president. I thought he should do it. I felt that it was going to be difficult to turn the president around on Vietnam and that Bob Kennedy was the only person who had the national stature, the name, the money, and the organizational power to do it.

"But when he turned them down Allard Lowenstein and others came to me on several different occasions with a fervent plea that I run.

"I asked Lowenstein to consider the fact that I was running for reelection in the Senate and that it might cost me my seat. I felt that none of us had a chance of winning the nomination but I thought the effort was worthwhile. So I suggested they pick a senator who was not up for election. Just off the top of my head I said, 'How about Gene McCarthy?'

"When they went to see McCarthy, he surprised both them and me by readily agreeing. This was in the fall of '67.

"A few days later I was talking to Arthur Schlesinger and I told him that I thought Gene was going to go. Within hours Bob Kennedy was on the phone in great distress, great anxiety, because I think he had wanted to keep his own options open through the fall and winter and watch the thing develop.

"My own guess is that Bob had intended all along to run if it looked like the dissension and disaffection in the country would continue to mount. He really wanted to announce before the New Hampshire primary results were in—ten days or two weeks before. I was one of those who tried to convince him that this would be unfair to McCarthy. I said, 'If you announce, you are going to split the dissenting vote in New Hampshire and a lot of people are going to write in your name. Then the McCarthy people are going to very legitimately say that you destroyed their day of glory.'"

But Lyndon, with his keen political instinct, had known it all along. Night after night, he would shake his head and say, "That little runt will get in. The runt's going to run. I don't care what he says now."

Lyndon: "I must admit that the results of the New Hampshire primary surprised me. I was not expecting a landslide. I had not spent a single day campaigning in New Hampshire, and my name was not even on the ballot.[2] And the fact that I received more votes, as a write-in candidate, than Senator McCarthy—49.5 percent as against 42.4 percent—seems to have been overlooked or forgotten. Still, I think most people were surprised that Senator McCarthy rolled up the vote he did.

"I was much less surprised when Bobby Kennedy announced his candidacy four days later. I had been expecting it."[3]

Sometime just before or after the New Hampshire primary Bobby offered to make a deal with Lyndon—that is, Bobby didn't use the term "deal," but that was how others, Hubert included, saw it. Bobby and Ted Sorensen had come up with the idea of a Vietnam commission to examine the war; the commission would, of course, be headed by Bobby and would come to bear his name in much the same way that the Commission to Investigate the Assassination of President John F. Kennedy was known only as the Warren Commission. If Lyndon would agree to appoint such a commission with Bobby as chairman, Bobby would in turn devote all his attention to that project and *would not enter the primaries*.

Lyndon, of course, had no intention of tossing that particular publicity plum in Bobby's direction, and although he sent Clark Clifford to discuss the matter, the whole thing came to nothing.

Frederick Dutton: "When Bob went through that silly exercise of the Vietnam commission—my analysis was that Bob had already passed over Niagara Falls and could not have retreated from the primaries if he'd wanted to. He'd have looked ridiculous. He was committed from the morning after New Hampshire.

"He said he'd get out of the race if they'd do this or that—that was Bob, the politician, trying to have his cake and eat it, too. He was trying to get the war over with, which he felt very strongly about at that time, and have great influence, and yet not necessarily have to challenge the president."

David Burke: "I do remember thinking that it doesn't happen that way, that you don't go make a deal with Lyndon Johnson, you don't go make a deal on the Vietnam commission. I know those who were involved in it disagree and think that it was a good idea and should have been tried.

"It's harder and tougher than that. One man is president of the United States; another man wants to be president of the United States. Now if Robert Kennedy was looking for an out by getting some major concessions from Lyndon Johnson on Vietnam, which I viewed the commission thing to be, then I was somewhat happier that he was looking for the out. But it always occurred to me, just as a single guy, that Lyndon Johnson could smell that fifty miles away and he would not acquiesce to anything like that. Why the hell should he?"

After New Hampshire Bobby said he would reassess his position and on March 16 he announced his candidacy in the caucus room of the old Senate Office Building where Jack had made the same announcement eight years earlier. His audience gave him a standing, cheering ovation.

By the end of March, he had visited sixteen states. His campaign was like that of a movie star; like that of his brother in 1960. People, old and young, grabbed at him, tried to tear buttons off his jackets, reached for locks of his hair. He was not much of a speaker. He never quite got over being nervous. His hands habitually trembled; his voice sometimes shook, and his prose, though written by masters, came out jerkily. Nevertheless, he was effective.

Then, on March 31, came like a bombshell the news a few had anticipated, many had hoped for, and none—in the general confusion and mixed emotions—quite believed.

MARCH 31, 1968

There are certain days, not many, that Americans remember, remember where they were, what they thought, what they said and did. For those of my generation the list would include Pearl Harbor, the death of Franklin Roosevelt, the dropping of the bomb on Hiroshima, V-E and V-J Days, both Kennedy assassinations, the assassination of Martin Luther King, and then this one, at the end of March 1968.

For the president and First Lady that day began at seven. Lyndon, who usually could and did sleep anywhere at any time, had spent a restless night. Lady Bird remembers that he had tossed and turned and even moaned a few times.

Lynda, who had been in California to say good-bye to Chuck Robb, who was on his way to Vietnam, was due to arrive at the White House shortly after seven.

Lady Bird: "I wanted to be right there at the door with open arms to meet her, but I begged Lyndon not to get up. 'No, I want to,' he insisted. So the operator called us in what seemed the gray early morning and both of us were downstairs at the entrance to the Diplomatic Reception Room at seven when she stepped out of the car. She looked like a ghost—pale, tall, and drooping. We both hugged her and then we all went upstairs. I took her into her room, helped get her clothes off, and put her to bed. She'd had a sedative on the plane, slept a little, not much—and it was, I think, partly emotion and partly the sedative that made her look so detached, like a wraith from another world. . . .

"When I went back into Lyndon's room, his face was sagging and there was such pain in his eyes as I had not seen since his mother died. But he didn't have time for grief. Today was a crescendo of a day. At nine in the evening, Lyndon was to make his talk to the nation about the war. The speech was not yet firm. There were still revisions to be made and people to see."[1]

Horace Busby: "I went back to the White House on Sunday, early. Johnson came into the sitting room, sat down next to me, and said something about how there were always personal things to be taken into account in a decision like this, as major as this one, but he said that what really bothered him was whether, after withdrawing, he could make his decisions effective. I told him that with his own supposed political ambitions removed, he would be even more effective. And he agreed, seemed to agree anyway, but said that he wanted a new draft of the withdrawal, emphasizing the fact that his interest was in unifying the country.

"By the time Lyndon got back from church, I had finished it. By then he had already talked to Humphrey, who couldn't believe that Johnson would say it, and I must say, I wasn't too sure myself. I was convinced I was right, that it was absolutely the thing to do, but I couldn't be sure that some damn fool wouldn't get to him and propose that he wait a while or not do it at all."

Hubert H. Humphrey: "The president came by unexpectedly on his way home from church. Muriel and I were getting ready to go to Mexico City. The president indicated that he wanted to be alone with me, although Jim Jones may have come into the den. The president told me I had better listen to the speech that night. I had read the speech—what I thought was the whole of it—including the part about halting the bombing and so on. I said I thought it was a very good speech, one of his better ones, and would be very convincing to the people. He said it wouldn't; that most people wouldn't believe a word he said, including Ho Chi Minh. He said that that alone would be a waste of time. Then he showed me what he said would probably be the ending."

James Jones: "When Humphrey got to the withdrawal part of the speech, he got white as a sheet. He was just stunned. He said, 'Mr. President, are you really going to do this?' He said that he was almost certain that he would but that there was a possibility that he wouldn't. 'As of now,' he said, 'I am almost certainly going to. Now you stand by in Mexico City where the White House operators will know where you'll be. I'll have Jim call you just before the speech tonight and tell you which it will be.' In the meantime the president said not to tell anyone, not even Muriel."

Busby: "When Johnson got back from seeing Humphrey, he said, 'Buzz, there isn't anybody on my side. Hubert, Luci, they all say I'm wrong.' I told him, 'Look, I've already said that you've got to march to your own step.' But at the time I noticed that he was calling people all over the country, and that meant that he wasn't just going to announce the bombing halt. He'd made up his mind that he was going to say what he called 'the second peroration.' But I wasn't positive. With him when were you ever positive?"

Arthur Krim: "Mathilde and I were guests at the White House that weekend. He'd told us as far back as, I guess, the late fall or early winter of 1965 that he wouldn't run again.

"But since I was in charge of raising money for the Democratic party during all that period, I can't help saying that I never believed it, and neither did Mathilde."

Lyndon: "Horace Busby was waiting for me in the Treaty Room in the White House when I returned. I worked with him putting the final touches on the speech. I wanted to say precisely what was in my heart and I believed that the nation—except for a dozen or so individuals—would be shocked and surprised."

Late in 1967 Tom Wicker had written in the *New York Times*:

"It is as likely that Johnson will get out of the White House and go back to Texas as it is that Dean Rusk will turn dove, Dick Nixon will stop running, or J. Edgar Hoover will retire."

And in his February 17 column in the *Chicago Daily News*, Carl Rowan, former head of the U.S. Information Service and Lyndon's former ambassador to Finland, had written that the odds of Lyndon's not running again "can't be better than a million to one."

Lady Bird: "Sometime during the afternoon—the time is very hazy on this day—I think it was around three o'clock, Lyndon went to his office, and I talked to Lynda and Luci. Both of them were emotional, crying and distraught. 'What does this do to the servicemen? They will think—"What have I been sent out here for?—Was it all wrong?—Can I believe in what I've been fighting for?"' Lynda and Luci seemed to feel that Lyndon has been the champion of the soldiers, and that his getting out would be a blow to them. Lynda said, with an edge of bitterness, 'Chuck will hear of this on his way to Vietnam.'"[2]

Later that afternoon, Lady Bird told Lyndon of their daughters' fears. He looked at her somewhat "distantly," as she recalled, and replied that the matter had, of course, been checked out with General Westmoreland, a more objective authority than Luci or Lynda, and the general had told him that whether or not he, Lyndon, was president was not one of the prime concerns of the men in Vietnam.

Harry McPherson: "He came into the office where I was working late in the afternoon; I had been reading the speech again, and I knew he had, too. He said to me, 'What do you think? Is it a good speech? I said that I thought it was excellent, one of his best.

"Then he wanted to know if I thought it would accomplish what he had in mind as far as the North Vietnamese were concerned. Would it bring the North Vietnamese to the peace table and cause them to talk? I said I wasn't so sure; that I thought the chances were about fifty-fifty.

"Finally, he said he had an ending of his own to add to mine, and I told him I wasn't surprised. He asked if I had any idea what he'd say. I said I thought I did and he wanted to know what I thought of it.

"I said something like, 'I'm very, very sorry, Mr. President.'

"He sort of smiled, and said, using his most Texas accent. 'Well, so long, pardner,' and he left."

What is not mentioned in the diary or indeed in *The Vantage Point*, which gives rather a full account of the activities of the day, is that shortly after he returned from seeing Hubert, Lyndon dropped briefly into Marvin Watson's office where he met with Terry Sanford, the former governor of North Carolina, who had just agreed to manage Lyndon's campaign for reelection; Jim Rowe, who was also working on the supposedly forthcoming campaign; John Bailey, chairman of the Democratic campaign; and Larry O'Brien, who was still postmaster general, to discuss what to do about what was certain to happen in Wisconsin. Lyndon was going to lose and lose big.

Lyndon congratulated and thanked Sanford, whose first meeting this was, and said that in his speech that night he would announce a partial bombing halt. He said nothing at all about the strategy that should be followed in the campaign that was presumed to be forthcoming. It was felt that violence would ensue; that the president's appearances would have to be limited to carefully selected sites. But that despite the coming probable loss to Gene McCarthy, he could still, although with difficulty, win the nomination and possibly even the election.

John P. Roche: "After spending all day at the White House Terry Sanford left for the airport still under the impression that he was the campaign manager.

"Not only that, I had already put an LBJ '68 bumper sticker on my car and I was wearing an LBJ '68 button. We were left with fifteen thousand of the goddamn things."

James H. Rowe, Jr.: "I was in the White House most of the day, but as I was leaving, Marvin Watson, who had been in and out of the meeting, said, 'Where are you going to be tonight?' I said, 'I'm going to be home. I want to listen to the president's speech. Why?'

"'Well,' Marvin said, 'the president might want to talk to you.'"

Clark Clifford: "I don't know what time it was, early evening, I guess. He told me he wanted to see me in his bedroom, and I went in and and he handed me the last two or three paragraphs of the speech, announcing his withdrawal, and said, 'I'd like you to read them.'

"I read them and you could have knocked my eyes off with a stick. I said, 'You've made up your mind?' He said, 'I've made up my mind. I'm actually going to do it.'

"I said, 'You're sure you've thought it out?' He said, 'I've thought out every phase.' That was about it except that I said I'd have to tell Mrs. Clifford. I didn't want her to hear it on television. So I walked out, and I remember Mrs. Clifford and Mrs. Rostow were there sitting on the sofa together.

"They were sitting there at the west end of the hall and I went up and told them. They both looked like they had seen a ghost. Neither of them could believe it. They were absolutely and completely destroyed."

Larry Temple: "He asked me to call all the cabinet members and a few others at the start of his speech. None of them knew what was coming. I had a very hard time getting them on the phone. The White House operator would find them and they'd say, 'Tell him I'll call back. I'm watching the president on TV,' and I'd say, 'That's why I want to talk to him,' whoever it was. I talked to all of the members of the cabinet except Dean Rusk."

Dean Rusk, who seemed always to be flying over the Pacific at crucial moments, was on his way to a previously scheduled meeting of the Vietnam War allies at Wellington, New Zealand. Jim Jones talked to him on the plane and after he told him said, 'Mr. Secretary, over.' Rusk's only response was 'Yes, Jim, over.' That was all.

Temple: "There was not one of them that knew. And the comments that each of them made show you—well, something about the men involved.

"Stewart Udall said, 'Oh, is that all? Well, thanks for calling me.' Willard Wirtz was pretty much the same way. Of course they were both Kennedy people. That made a difference.

"On the other hand, a man like Wilbur Cohen, who was a Johnson person, said, 'My God! Surely not. Tell him I love him, and I'm for him whatever he does.'"

A great many people were called just before the speech by various members of the White House staff and told of Johnson's decision, people like Larry O'Brien, Henry Fowler, Dick Russell, Robert McNamara, Orville Freeman, Abe Fortas, Carl Albert, George Meany, Mike Mansfield, Ramsey Clark, Jake Jacobsen, and Jake and Beryle Pickle. Beryle Pickle reported that her husband wept when he heard the news.

Humphrey wept when he heard the final words of the speech on a radio in the American embassy in Mexico City. But beneath the tears he had to know that whatever might happen in the forthcoming primaries, he, Hubert, had the best chance for the brass ring he had so often reached for in the past. McCarthy and Bobby Kennedy might do well enough in the primaries with the kids and the disenchanted, but when it came to the machines that ran the party, he, Hubert, would predominate. And so long as he supported "the great adventure in Vietnam," Lyndon would support him. Surely. Wouldn't he?

Just before 9:00 P.M. millions of persons across the country flicked on their television sets to hear the president. Seated at his desk, flanked by flags of his country and his office, Lyndon began:

"Tonight I want to speak to you of peace in Vietnam and Southeast Asia."

First he reviewed the outcome of the Tet offensive. It did not, he pointed out, "collapse the elected government of South Vietnam or shatter its army—as the Communists had hoped." Nor would that happen if the Communists were to mount such an offensive again soon. But if they did so, he said, new casualties would result on both sides.

"And the war would go on. There is no need for this to be so."

Lyndon went on to renew his offer to stop the bombardment of North Vietnam and to ask that talks begin promptly.

"I am taking the first step to de-escalate the conflict. We are reducing—substantially reducing—the present level of hostilities. And we are doing so unilaterally, and at once.

"Tonight, I have ordered our aircraft and our naval vessels to make no attacks on North Vietnam, except in the area north of the demilitarized zone where the continuing enemy buildup directly threatens allied forward positions and where the movements of their troops and supplies are clearly related to that threat.

"The area in which we are stopping our attacks includes almost 90 percent of North Vietnam's population, and most of its territory. . . . Whether a complete bombing halt becomes possible in the future will be determined by events."

Lyndon went on to declare that the United States was ready to send representatives "to any forum, at any time, to discuss the means of bringing this ugly war to an end," and named Ambassador Averell Harriman as his personal representative at such talks. "I call upon President Ho Chi Minh," he said, "to respond positively and favorably to this new step toward peace."

Lyndon went on to discuss at length the continued role South Vietnamese forces must play in the conflict, how some 13,500 more American "support troops" would be needed during the next five months, and how his proposed tax surcharge must be enacted to reduce the deficit that the war had brought about in the nation's economy.

Then at exactly 9:35, as planned, the president said:

"Fifty-two months and ten days ago, in a moment of tragedy and trauma, the duties of this office fell upon me. I asked then for your help and God's, that we might continue America on its course, binding up our wounds, healing our history, moving forward in unity, to clear the American agenda and to keep the American commitment for all our people.

"United we have kept that commitment. United we have enlarged that commitment.

"What we won when all our people were united just must not be lost in suspicion, distrust, selfishness, and politics among any of our people.

"Believing this as I do, I have concluded that I should not permit the presidency to become involved in the partisan divisions that are developing in this political year.

"With America's sons in the fields faraway, with America's future under challenge right here at home, with our hopes and the world's hopes for peace in the balance every day, I do not believe that I should devote an hour or a day of my time to my personal partisan causes or to any duties other than the awesome duties of this office—the presidency of your country.

"Accordingly, I shall not seek, and I will not accept the nomination of my party, for another term as your president.

"But let men everywhere know, however, that a strong, a confident, and a vigilant America stands ready tonight to seek an honorable peace—and stands ready to defend an honored cause—whatever the price, whatever the burden, whatever the sacrifice that duty may require.

"Thank you for listening.

"Good night and God bless all of you."

Charles Maguire: "Before he read the final passage I remember he did pause. I remember him lifting his head, opening his mouth; he uttered the first four or five words of the final section, and I don't really remember anything else. I know I didn't follow it in my reading copy as I was supposed to have. I remember a large exhalation of breath from Colonel Albright [of the Signal Corps]. I remember Mrs. Johnson smiling in a rather unusual way."

Robert Fleming: "When he finished the two-page peroration saying he wouldn't run again, and the camera went off, Mrs. Johnson and the two girls were sitting there, and one of the girls was crying; the other was sniffling. They stood up, he stood up, and Mrs. Johnson went over and threw her arms around him and said, 'Nobly done, darling.'"

Busby: "Watching him you could see he was clearly exhausted. When he was making the speech his hands trembled, and some people say they saw tears in his eyes. I wasn't sure he'd say it until he actually did."

"I don't think there were any regrets later. That is the invention of the so-called psychohistorians. Nor any bitterness. Nor any feeling—well, of course, you always have moments, everybody does, of regrets over something as major as that. But if you ask me, if he had to do it all over again, in my opinion anyway, he'd have done it 'all over again.'"

Everyone who saw the president that night after the speech described him as looking "relieved" or "relaxed."

He went to bed and he went to sleep at once, getting up the next morning at 7:30, as usual. Larry O'Brien thought he had never looked better. Not in recent months anyway.

O'Brien: "I talked to him about it and he said he had been seeking peace and as far as he was concerned he had explored every avenue. He put the rest of it in poker terms. He said, 'I put my last chips on the table, and that's all I've got left to assure the American people, telling them that I'm not going to seek reelection. I am trying to restore their confidence in me.'

"But then he said, and I'll never forget it, 'But I don't think that's enough. I don't think even forgoing the presidency will be enough. But that's the last chip I've got, and I put it on the table.'"

"MR. PRESIDENT, MARTIN LUTHER KING HAS BEEN SHOT"

On April 4, 1968, Lyndon flew to New York and attended the investiture of Terence James Cooke as archbishop of New York. Then he went to the United Nations where he discussed with Secretary U Thant and United States Ambassador Arthur Goldberg the meaning of Hanoi's agreement the day before to confer with U.S. officials preliminary to holding peace talks. Were Goldberg and U Thant as encouraged by that news as the president?

They were, and when Lyndon got back to the White House, he was feeling optimistic.

Later that evening he and his staff were scheduled to fly to Hawaii for a meeting with American officials stationed in Saigon.

Then at 7:30 Tom Johnson handed him a slip of paper on which he had written, "Mr. President, Martin Luther King has been shot."

King had been in Memphis to lend support to a strike of the city's thirteen hundred garbage men, most of them Negroes. There had been criticism of him for staying in the Holiday Inn, lush and largely white; so he moved to the Lorraine Motel in the Negro section of Memphis. Just before dinner that evening he was leaning over a second-story balcony talking to associates on the ground below. A sniper in a shabby rooming house across the street fired a single shot that struck Dr. King in the neck, severing his spinal cord. He died shortly after arriving at St. Joseph Hospital.

King's death set off the greatest wave of violence in the history of the civil rights movement. Within minutes after the announcement rioting and looting began in cities all over the country. A few minutes after nine, Lyndon went on national television to express his, Mrs. Johnson's, and the nation's grief at King's death. By that time fires were burning all over Washington. They were to number 711 in all before the terrible night was over. Nationwide, the destruction was monumental. By the time it was over there had been looting, rioting, and fires in 125 cities in 28 states. Forty-five people were killed; all but five were Negroes. More than half were in Washington.

The next morning, Lyndon proclaimed the following Sunday as a day of national mourning for Dr. King. That morning, too, he met with ten Negro leaders.

Bayard Rustin: "President Johnson first of all wanted to express to us his deep shock at what had happened and pledged to us on the other hand that he was going to continue the fight, that the loss of Dr. King should not mean that in any way the government was going to let up; that he would put all the force of government to work to find out who it was who had done this heinous act, and that in the meantime he wanted us to reassure the community that these things would be done. And he hoped that we would help the community go through in a peaceful manner—what was a terrible shock for the community.

"I think it was exactly what he should have done, and although things didn't seem very cool, the very fact that we were there I think helped."

Two months before, Lyndon had sent Congress yet another message on civil rights, asking once more for a bill that would include "fair housing." On March 4, after three previous failures, the Senate had voted cloture. Ev had once again proved himself adaptable; he had changed his mind and decided that he could, after all, support a fair housing act provided, of course, he be allowed to make a few changes. His support would depend, he said, "on how all-inclusive you make it, on what you excluded. For instance, if it did not apply to an individual. I have a house, and you want to buy it, and I don't want to sell it to you. That's one situation. When it's handled with brokers and agents—they operate under a license of the state. It's a different picture."

Ev was up for reelection that year. Negroes had done a lot for him in 1962; in 1968 black leaders might again see their way to supporting their friend Ev, and there were a lot of blacks in Chicago. In addition, Dirksen was head of the Republican platform committee, and if he came out publicly against open housing, it might not only cost him votes, it would cost many of his more liberal Republican colleagues votes. It might split the party, and, remembering 1964, Ev thought things over.

Finally, with the help of his son-in-law, Senator Howard Baker of Tennessee, Ev Dirksen announced at a press conference, "I think we have a very substantial area of agreement. That's why I say to you, there will be a bill."

In introducing the new bill, which did not substantially differ from that submitted two years earlier by the administration, Ev said that the only people who do not change their minds are either in cemeteries or insane asylums.

Ev did not bring quite as many Republicans along with him as he had hoped; still there were enough.

Robert C. Weaver: "We got it through the Senate largely through the efforts of Fritz Mondale.[1] He was just a newcomer and probably had about twenty-eight black constituents, so it wasn't politically inspired. It was just what he believed in.

"So we got it through the Senate but then we couldn't get it out of the House.

"After the president indicated that he wasn't going to run again, he didn't have much leverage, certainly not as much as he would have liked to have. We were getting nowhere in the House when Martin Luther King was assassinated. Within forty-eight hours after that the bill passed. He just put everything aside. This is it. This is the time. And he knew how to take advantage of whatever cards he had."

The bill passed the House six days after Dr. King's death. The vote was 250 to 171. The next day, April 11, Lyndon signed the Civil Rights Act of 1968, which he dedicated to Martin Luther, King, Jr., in the East Room of the White House.

Not everything in the field of civil rights, however, worked out quite so fortunately in 1968. The Kerner Commission, headed by Otto Kerner, governor of Illinois, and ten other persons of eminence, including Mayor John Lindsay of New York, had been at work for seven months studying the causes for the riots that by then seemed a regular summer occurrence. The commission reported that there was no evidence anywhere of any conspiracy. It also concluded that the United States was "moving toward two societies, one white, one black—separate and unequal." The movement apart, the report continued, could be reversed by adequate action. It was estimated that the "adequate action" would cost $30 billion, just to begin. Lyndon, who at first had hailed the report as "one of the most thorough and exhaustive studies ever made," wondered where the additional $30 billion was going to come from. Congress was already demanding that the original poverty budget of $30 billion be cut by at least $6 billion.

Besides, he didn't believe that the United States was split into two societies. "We seem on the move—I refuse to accept a diagnosis of deep racism. I can't ignore the progress we have made in the decade to write equality on our books of law."

Roger Wilkins: "Mr. Johnson need not have balked at the acceptance of the Kerner Commission's report. It was perfectly in line with his actions as president and with the accomplishments of his administration. I think probably, maybe the word racism, white racism, frightened him. He didn't want to go down in history as the president who had pointed his finger at his own people. This I think is understandable.

"I really got so mad at him. After all, he had appointed that commission with great fanfare; they just couldn't wait to have the commission's picture in the paper in the White House in the Cabinet Room and all of that. The commission report was issued and zilch! Just silence."

Ramsey Clark: "The Kerner report came to the president at a time that the financial burdens of the federal government were the most difficult that they had been at any time or were later during President Johnson's administration.

"There seemed to be a real risk that cutbacks would have to be made in domestic programs that had been labors of love for him—education and poverty and things like that. And here this report came and said, 'But we've got to do many, many times more. We've got to spend billions.'"

And then there was the Poor People's Campaign, which had been planned for Washington before King's death; it was carried on by King's successor, the Reverend Ralph W. Abernathy. Early in May, nine caravans of poor people arrived in Washington. They were mostly Negroes, but there were also Indians, Mexican-Americans, and Puerto Ricans. Other caravans continued to arrive until nearly the end of June.

Their intent was to construct a shanty town and remain there until Congress met their demands. Many of them built their shanties out of plywood and canvas in West Potomac Park, two and a half miles from the Capitol, a mile from the White House. It was called Resurrection City, U.S.A. And it was not a thing of beauty.

Clark: "Resurrection City appalled Johnson. He loved Washington. It represented everything good that he believed in—physical beauty, grace in government, heroic monuments, human dignity. To see these pitiful poor people with their ugliness and misery sprawled on the monument grounds really hurt him, deeply hurt him. I think he was quite courageous in controlling himself and letting us proceed as we did.

"But you can't avoid the truth. And the truth is that we have poor people. It's awfully ugly, and you just can't hope to confine them in the ghettos and never think about them. And what the American people really said was, 'We don't want to see it. We don't want to know about it. If it has got to exist, keep it out of our sight.'"

Harry McPherson: "I suggested that he see Abernathy and Mrs. King, have them in for breakfast on Sunday, and talk to them, and tell them some of the things we had done and some of the things we planned to do. But apparently he didn't think much of that idea and in any event, Ramsey had already made a deal with Abernathy, I believe, in which they would march up to the Capitol and go off limits up there and be arrested, which was what they needed as a symbolic act to close it down.

"The final wiping out of Resurrection City was done without serious incident. It was as much a political quagmire as it was a physical one. The leadership soon slipped out of Abernathy's hands. He was treated as a man of no consequence by other Negroes there."

By the end of June, the poor were out of sight if not out of mind. A lame-duck president in the White House was not going to get much legislation through Congress. Not this session, and surely not more civil rights legislation. Look at the debris those people left in West Potomac Park.

THE PEACE TALKS

He had shocked the nation with his announcement that he would not seek reelection. Wouldn't that show everyone—the dissenters, the picketers at 1600 Pennsylvania Avenue—that his intentions for a peaceful settlement of the war were serious?

Hadn't he tried? There had been bombing pauses—fourteen so far—in an attempt to get Ho to the table. They had all been unsuccessful. Hadn't he made several trips to the Pacific to view the situation firsthand? The substantial bombing halt begun March 31 with Lyndon's withdrawal speech continued, despite the conflicting advice of various of his advisers.

Abe Fortas: "I think I heard all of the proposals that were made about how if we cease the bombing Chou would talk to Sam, and Sam would talk to Ho Ho Ho and Ho Ho Ho would talk to so-and-so, and something good would happen. Candidly, as I told Johnson and the assembled group at the time—different words on many occasions—they all sounded to me like horseshit. And they were. Horseshit!"

George Aiken: "The leaders of the North Vietnamese government had acquired such animosity for President Johnson that I predicted they'd never sit down at a table and sign any agreement with him. I held that the war would simply have to phase out, informally almost, and I might say that Ambassador Lodge also held that position while he was in Vietnam."

There were others, like Senator J. William Fulbright who had told the Senate on April 2 that he did not believe the halt would move Hanoi in the direction of peace talks. Averell Harriman said, "If I had to bet whether there would be a favorable response to the March 31 speech I would have said the reply would be negative. But it did start the talks."

In the meantime Harry Ashmore and Bill Baggs had gone back to Hanoi where they were the guests of Hoang Tung, the editor of the party newspaper *Nham Dan*. The three had been talking for several days about the prospects for peace talks when to their mutual surprise came word of Lyndon's withdrawal.

Harry Ashmore: "So we were there when the bombing stopped. They took us out of the hotel and put us in a special villa, and we only saw Hoang Tung. He clearly was going back and talking to his principals. We were urging them to take the speech seriously. Although the bombing halt was not quite what Johnson had said it was—they were still bombing a hell of a lot farther north than the line that had been announced[1] and there were all kinds of odd spot-bomb drops around town, some of which we could even hear—we kept saying, 'You've got to take this seriously. For a fellow like Lyndon Johnson to announce that he's not going to stand for reelection, this is an act of political self-immolation. This is like one of your monks setting himself on fire. You can't ignore this; it has to be taken seriously. You should respond, by all means.'

"I don't know whether we had any effect on their final decisions or not. They blew hot and cold for two or three days; finally we were given an *aide-mémoire* in which they accepted the proposition that they would meet and proposed Phnom Penh, Cambodia, as the meeting site."

Lyndon received word that North Vietnam had agreed to establish contacts preliminary to peace talks with the United States on April 3. Three-quarters of the message was the usual anti-American line, but the last sentence was something new:

> However, on its part, the DRV [Democratic Republic of Vietnam] government declares its readiness to send its representatives to make contact with U.S. representatives to decide with the U.S. side the unconditional cessation of bombing and all other war acts against the DRV so that talks could begin.[2]

That same evening a return message was sent to Hanoi via the American embassy in Vientiane, Laos. The United States had, the message read, studied the North Vietnamese statement and would accept their proposal. Averell Harriman would be available to meet at any time with their designated representative. April 8 in Geneva was suggested, or any other reasonable alternative as to time and place.

Hanoi responded five days later. Yes, their ambassadors would meet with ours. In Phnom Penh. Lyndon met with his advisers at Camp David, and another message was forwarded for immediate delivery to Hanoi. The United States had no diplomatic representation in Cambodia, North Vietnam was reminded. Could not a neutral capital be agreed upon? Vientiane, perhaps? Rangoon? Djakarta? New Delhi?

On April 11 came Hanoi's answer—Warsaw. But Warsaw, openly pro-Hanoi, was not exactly the State Department's idea of a neutral capital. New suggestions were sent. Colombo? Kabul? Katmandu? Kuala Lumpur? Rawalpindi? Tokyo? Or, since Hanoi seemed to prefer Europe, perhaps Brussels, Helsinki, Rome or Vienna? The answer came back—Warsaw.

By coincidence, the same day that Lyndon first heard from Hanoi, he had his last encounter with Bobby Kennedy. The president had, in his March 31 speech, agreed to meet with and brief all the major candidates, and Bobby was the first to take him up on the offer. He and Ted Sorensen met with the president, Walt Rostow, and Charles Murphy for more than an hour in the Cabinet Room.[3]

The meeting was amicable on the surface, almost friendly. Lyndon told Bobby that despite reports to the contrary, he doubted that they would be very far apart if they sat at the same table. He had removed himself as a candidate for reelection, he said, so that no one could say that what he was doing was self-interested.

Bobby praised the March 31 speech and the "unselfish" and "courageous" position the president had taken. Discussion of the current military situation in Vietnam followed. "People try to divide us," Lyndon said, "and we both suffer from it. . . . I feel no bitterness or vindictiveness. I want everybody to get together to find a way to stop the killing."

Toward the end Bobby asked about the political situation. "Where do I stand in the campaign? Are you opposed to my effort and will you marshal forces against me?"

"I want to keep the presidency out of this campaign," Lyndon said. "I'm not that pure, but I am that scared. The situation of the country is critical. I will try to run this office so as to have as much support and as few problems as possible."

He held no enmity toward him, Lyndon told Bobby. Of course he felt closer to Hubert—Hubert had been everything a president could ask for in a vice-president. Being a vice-president was hard; he knew that well. Being majority leader—that was the best job he'd ever had. Bobby's brother John had always treated him well as vice-president, and he had always tried to support President Kennedy.

Warming to his subject, Lyndon continued expansively. He had never wanted to be president, he said; he had been "counting the days to the end of his term ever since the beginning." Also, he had always thought of it as the "Kennedy-Johnson administration"—he, Lyndon, had just been carrying on a family matter. He had never fired a Kennedy appointee, and the country would have been better off, he said nodding at Sorensen, if you, Ted, had stayed. He had done his best to carry on President Kennedy's policies and programs, and he liked to think that every day Bobby's brother looked down at him and approved and agreed that yes, he had kept the faith.

"You are a brave and dedicated man," Bobby said. The two never met again.

Also in April Lyndon announced the resignation of Arthur Goldberg as ambassador to the United Nations and his replacement by the former assistant secretary of state who had warned Lyndon against his Vietnam policy from the beginning—George Ball.

And on the twenty-sixth of the month occurred in New York City the largest antiwar demonstration yet. Several hundred thousand people, many of them no longer young, marched through the streets carrying placards and chanting slogans, and an estimated eighty-nine thousand gathered for the rally in the Sheep Meadow. A *partial* bombing halt, said the peaceniks, was not enough; neither was *talk* of peace negotiations. STOP THE BOMBING! they chanted. PEACE NOW! PEACE NOW!

Then at ten o'clock on the morning of May 3, Lyndon called a news conference in the East Room. He began:

"Good morning, ladies and gentlemen. I was informed about one o'clock this morning that Hanoi was prepared to meet in Paris on May tenth, or several days thereafter. . . . I have sent a message informing Hanoi that the date of May tenth and the site of Paris are acceptable to the United States."

Lyndon was, of course, sharing the headlines that spring with the Democratic presidential hopefuls. On April 27 Vice-President Humphrey had announced his candidacy, and Lyndon had in turn announced that he would, of course, support Hubert. There were those who said such endorsement was not to Humphrey's benefit, but they didn't say it publicly. Not yet.

On May 29 Eugene McCarthy won the Oregon primary with 45 percent of the vote to Robert Kennedy's 39 percent. But on June 4 Robert Kennedy won both the South Dakota and the California primaries. The latter was close, and Kennedy was in Los Angeles that night celebrating victory when he was shot in the kitchen of the Ambassador Hotel by a Jordanian immigrant, Sirhan Bishara Sirhan.

Lady Bird: "It was a short night. The phone jarred me awake from a deep sleep. Lyndon was saying tersely, 'Will you come in here?' . . . . The hands of the clock stood at 4:20.

"He was propped up against the pillows, looking as though he had never been asleep, and all of the TV sets were turned on. He was listening intently, and I realized at once that something serious was happening. I am not sure whether I heard it first from the TV set or from Lyndon. Senator Kennedy had been shot. . . .

"The whole terrible event had taken place under the eye of the television cameras, and we saw, over and over, the film of the shooting itself and heard the light crack of the gun. We saw Senator Kennedy lying on the floor, a pool of blood under his head. . . . It couldn't be true. We must have dreamed it. It had all happened before."[4]

Lyndon had been informed of the shooting at 3:30 A.M. by Walt Rostow, the first person notified by the men on duty in the Situation Room in the basement of the White House. Before morning he had talked three times with Attorney General Ramsey Clark, twice with Secret Service Director Jim Rowley, with Defense Secretary Clark Clifford and, of course, with J. Edgar Hoover. He ordered Rowley to provide Secret Service protection to all the candidates and their families; if there weren't enough Secret Service to go around, the FBI was to help, or the marines.

Harry McPherson: "Johnson was terribly agitated after Kennedy's shooting. The day before Kennedy died he would listen to the account from the Ambassador Hotel over and over. He had floods of information coming in from the Justice Department and other places about Kennedy's condition. I don't know—he must have been filled with a hundred competing emotions."

That evening shortly after 10:00 P.M., while the Senator's life still hung in balance,

Lyndon went on nationwide television to speak of his shock and dismay at the shooting. He told his listeners that "we cannot, we just must not, tolerate the sway of violent men among us. We must not permit men who are filled with hatred, and careless of innocent lives, to dominate our streets and fill our homes with fear."

Lady Bird: "It was a little past 1:00 A.M. when we heard the three rings that signal Lyndon's elevator, and he came in with Joe Califano and Harry McPherson, Larry Temple, Jim Jones, and George Christian. They all sat down for dinner while Lynda and I sat with them in our robes. Dinner was interrupted by constant telephone calls. The conversation was about how to get through the gun bill, the chances for crime legislation, and then a report from the Secret Service that Senator Kennedy was sinking and it would be a matter of hours."[5]

The next day Lyndon issued Proclamation 3853 announcing that Sunday, June 9, would be observed as a national day of mourning for Senator Robert F. Kennedy, and that from then until interment the flag should be flown at half-mast.

Early that summer Lyndon sent to Congress a special message proposing a constitutional amendment to lower the voting age to eighteen. Of special relevance to the potential voters concerned was the line, "The age of eighteen, far more than the age of twenty-one, has been and is the age of maturity in America—and never more than now."

Few voters of any age were happy about the bill Lyndon signed the next day putting into effect the 10 percent income tax surcharge that he had been pressing for since early 1967 and had managed to mention in almost every major speech since then. Prophesying doom in the form of exorbitant prices, unparalleled interest rates, and dangerous budget and balance-of-payment deficits if the bill were not enacted, Lyndon would remind his listeners that a family of four with a yearly income of less than $5,000 would not be affected. That, however, did little to make the bill more palatable. Most of us, even then, made more than that, and we were duly resentful.

Besides, it was a war tax, clear and simple. When are war taxes ever popular?

Once he had his surcharge, however, Lyndon was glad to forget about it and turn to more popular legislation such as the nuclear nonproliferation treaty. In the middle of June he had gone to the United Nations to attend that body's formal endorsement of the agreement, and on July 1 he and the representatives of more than fifty-five other countries signed the treaty in the East Room of the White House. As with the limited test ban treaty and the outer space treaty, also concluded during his presidency, signings took place simultaneously in London and Moscow.[6]

There were few pluses that summer. Precious few.

The American delegation at the Paris peace talks of 1968 was headed by Averell Harriman. Cyrus Vance was second in command; Lieutenant General Andrew J. Goodpaster, Philip Habib from the Saigon embassy, and William Jorden, Far East specialist on the National Security Council were the other members. Xuan Thuy and Ha Van Lao represented North Vietnam. South Vietnam refused to attend.

Preliminary discussions stalled almost immediately over what shape table the real talks, once they got under way, should take place around, and which side should speak first.

In the meantime, conventions were approaching, political speeches abounding, and Vietnam was, of course, *the* issue. Lyndon declined to take an active part; he was too busy reading the latest cables, trying desperately to get the peace he had promised in lieu of his own reelection.

Hubert H. Humphrey: "I remember what he said to me. 'Hubert, anybody can get a headline, and you can get a headline by some proposal that you make that's different from what this administration's pursuing, but I can get you peace. And if we get peace, you have won the election!' Well, that was pretty hard, you know, to resist and I knew he was struggling for peace. Averell Harriman and Cyrus Vance were in Paris, two of our best people, and I had to be very careful that I didn't say anything during that critical period that would jeopardize their efforts, that would show a break in the administration."[7]

In Paris, though, the talks dragged on. What, the U.S. team would ask the Hanoi delegation, would North Vietnam actually *do* if the bombing came to a complete halt? And Hanoi would never say. Stop the bombing *first*, they would answer, and then we'll discuss what we might or might not do.

In mid-July Lyndon flew to Honolulu—his sixth and last trip to the Pacific during his administration. He and General Creighton Abrams, who had replaced Westmoreland, met with President Thieu and leading members of the South Vietnamese government who still refused to send a delegation to Paris. How could they, they asked, when the Hanoi government insisted that the NLF also be represented? That argument went back to 1964, but in 1968 it seemed somehow to matter less.

Lyndon and Thieu also discussed the possible withdrawal of American troops. But the South Vietnamese clearly still lacked leadership in their army and their supplies were inadequate.

Clark Clifford: "The goal of the Saigon government had become utterly antithetical to the goal of the United States. One, the Saigon government did not want the war to end. Number two, they did not want the Americans to pull out. Number three, they did not want to make any settlement of any kind with Hanoi or with the Vietcong or the NLF. They preferred it the way they were. With 540,000 American troops they were in no danger whatsoever, and if we stayed there long enough ultimately perhaps we could exhaust Hanoi and then maybe they wouldn't have to make any settlement at all.

"In addition, when you've got 540,000 troops in a country and thousands of civilians, it's just as though you had a golden pump running, and were pumping the money in there and they certainly all liked that fine."

So the Paris talks droned along, accomplishing little, and August—convention month—arrived. In Miami the Republicans nominated Richard Nixon, again, for their candidate, and Nixon selected Spiro Agnew, governor of Maryland, to share the ticket.

And in Chicago the Democrats prepared for the worst.

A CHANGE IN CAST

The nightmare that was the 1968 Democratic National Convention occurred in Chicago from August 25 to 30. Antiwar groups, most of them long-haired kids, demonstrated outside the convention hall. Mayor Richard Daley, determined, among other less noble reasons, to forestall the possibility of another incident like Kennedy's assassination in California, had federal troops airlifted into the city and activated the National Guard. For extra protection, the convention hall was surrounded with barbed wire, which reminded many people of Nazi Germany.

Throughout the convention the sights and sounds of the demonstrators, often obscene, were seen and heard on television sets all over the world. But so were the scarcely peaceful words, also often obscene, and the brutal actions of the Chicago police. Before the convention ended they even invaded downtown hotels and beat up demonstrators and more than a few bystanders; it was not a pretty sight. Altogether, it was as if the democratic processes in the country had totally come asunder.

Larry Temple: "The convention coincided with Johnson's birthday,[1] and there were a great many people who wanted to do something to celebrate. The president's friends thought that even those who had opposed him within the Democratic party would want to pay tribute to him as a man who had done a lot for the party.

"Lyndon Johnson was not prepared to conclude that there was any place in the United States that he had to decline to go out of fear. But because of the unruliness of the crowd within and without the hall where the convention was being held, I think he decided that, despite the fact that a lot of people were urging him to come, it would be better not to."

John Bartlow Martin: "I was at the convention and the Johnson presence there was overwhelming. There were a few of us dissidents. But Johnson had control. He was trying to get a plank that would justify his Vietnam policy and get his candidate Humphrey nominated, on the theory that Humphrey would not break with him during the campaign."

Charles Bartlett: "It's my impression that he would have accepted a draft movement at the 1968 convention, that he always found it hard to believe that in the end the party wouldn't come back to him. I don't think he had the feeling that Hubert Humphrey would be a strong candidate or a strong president, and I do have the feeling that Lyndon Johnson sort of believed that the party in its wisdom would say, 'Let's keep what we've got.'"

Max Frankel: "George Christian said, 'I think he would have liked to have been asked to come back.' Marvin Watson and others were running around the convention trying to concoct this, but George said, 'I think if he had been asked he would have gloried in the ability to say no.'"

Bartlett: "The labor people were very strong obviously, and they had determined that they were going to nominate Hubert Humphrey. But the question of whether Mayor Daley would not have liked to nominate Johnson is an interesting one. I know that he had given some encouragement to Bobby. I know that he had very gloomy thoughts about Vietnam and thought that Johnson ought to cut his losses and get out. He certainly was interested in Teddy Kennedy and suggested to the Kennedy people that he would like Teddy as the nominee instead of Hubert Humphrey.

"I've always thought that what Daley had in mind was to get Teddy committed to some degree and bring him out and have him available and then somehow get Lyndon Johnson in as the nominee and Teddy as the vice-president.

On Wednesday evening the balloting began, and by 11:47 with Pennsylvania's vote, to no one's great surprise, Humphrey received the nomination. Lyndon called from Texas to congratulate him. Senator Edmund S. Muskie of Maine was selected by Humphrey as his vice-presidential candidate. Teddy, it was said, had been asked several times, but indicated he was not interested.

Hubert H. Humphrey: "Most of my people felt that Johnson would be more of a liability than an asset. I think they were dead wrong.

"I know a lot of people say that he didn't help me as much as he should, but I never went right to him and said, 'Mr. President I need you—I want you to speak for me—I want you to get out there and help me. You've got to do it.'

"And when we did ask him, at the end of the campaign, he moved heaven and earth. He delivered the crowds; he raised money. He did a helluva lot more than some of the people who were criticizing him."

The subject of speeches, however, became a sore point. Johnson was said to have become enraged with some of the speeches Humphrey was delivering on Vietnam. Negotiations were under way in Paris when on September 30 Humphrey spoke at Salt Lake City:

> As president I would stop the bombing of North Vietnam as an acceptable risk for peace because I believe it could lead to success in the negotiations and thereby shorten the war. . . .
>
> Now if the government of North Vietnam were to show bad faith, I would reserve the right to resume the war.

He added that he would call for an immediate cease-fire, with international supervision, followed by supervised withdrawal of all foreign forces from South Vietnam.

Actually, Hubert had called Lyndon before making the speech to inform him of its contents and assure him that it was not meant to be a major departure in policy. It was, however, widely interpreted to be just that—a refutation of Lyndon's Vietnam policy— and various of Humphrey's aides were delighted.

Harry McPherson: "There were people who, of course, were telling Humphrey that he had to dissociate himself from Johnson, from the administration. I thought they were right insofar as they were talking about helping Humphrey become visibly an independent man. I thought they were wrong insofar as they thought Humphrey could dissociate himself from policies that he had supported for, lo, so many years. If he had done that, Humphrey would have conveyed the feeling of a wishy-washy, flip-flopping, and insubstantial man. That's the impression he did convey, unfortunately.

"The thing that really racked Johnson up was Vietnam and Humphrey's attempts to go both ways. The Salt Lake City speech didn't seem to say that one would stop the bombing independently of any action on the other side, but at Kansas City Humphrey said, 'I would stop the bombing *period.*' Johnson got furious with that."

John Bartlow Martin: "I think Johnson hurt Humphrey very badly. I told Humphrey that I thought he had to get hold of the president, and tell the president that he was going to have to renounce Ky and Thieu and run against them, and, to that extent, break with the president on Vietnam. And I told him I thought it was his only chance. And he said he'd do it, tell him, 'I'm sorry, Mr. President, I can't support your policy in Vietnam all out any longer', and we arranged an appointment with Johnson for the next day at the White House.

"So the next day we went over to the EOB to find out how Humphrey's appointment was going with LBJ. And there wasn't any appointment. Somebody on the Johnson staff said that since it had been leaked to the press that Humphrey was going to see Johnson today to talk about Vietnam, the president was canceling the appointment."

The question of where the presidential candidates stood on the question of a complete bombing halt was of no small relevance to what was going on in Paris. The U.S. position there had crystallized around three guarantees. First, "prompt and serious" talks would have to follow, and by "serious" the American delegation meant talks involving the South Vietnamese government whom Hanoi had throughout the summer referred to as "puppets" and "lackeys" and with whom they had been saying they would never sit down to talk. Second, the demilitarized zone between North and South Vietnam would have to remain inviolate—all traffic down the Ho Chi Minh trail would have to cease. And third, the Vietcong in South Vietnam would have to refrain from attacking major cities such as Saigon, Danang, and Hué.

The North Vietnam position remained the same. These were "conditions," and they would have no "conditions." The United States must stop the bombing "unconditionally."

But during the second week in October a break in the stalemate seemed possible. The North Vietnamese privately asked our delegation in Paris "if we would stop the rest of the bombing if we had a clear answer concerning South Vietnam's participation in the next stage of talks." The message was relayed to Washington and from there to Bunker and Abrams in Saigon.

Lyndon: "We were ready to set an early date for total cessation of armed attacks against the North. We planned to suggest that 'serious talks' begin the day after the bombing halt and would insist that representatives of the Republic of Vietnam had to take part. . . .

"The next day Bunker discussed the entire situation with Thieu. He reported that the South Vietnamese leader was ready to go along."[2]

But no sooner did real progress appear to have been made than objections came—first from Hanoi, and then, when those had been painstakingly ironed out, from Saigon.

Lyndon: "I believe South Vietnam's failure to move with us on the bombing halt announcement and to send a delegation promptly to Paris had at least as much to do with American domestic politics as with Saigon politics. Thieu and Vice-President Ky and their colleagues had become convinced . . . that Mr. Nixon would win the presidential election. . . . They had been urged to delay going to the Paris meetings and promised they would get a better deal from a Nixon administration than from Humphrey. I had no reason to think that Republican candidate Nixon was himself involved in this maneuvering, but a few individuals active in his campaign were."[3]

Primary among those "few individuals" was Anna Chennault, the Chinese-born widow of American General Claire Chennault, the Flying Tiger hero of World War II. Madame Chennault, a very rich lady who was exceedingly fond of Richard Nixon, did not want a bombing halt, feeling, no doubt correctly, that such a halt late in the campaign would help elect Hubert Humphrey.

Lyndon knew that Chennault was in frequent touch with the Thieu government in Saigon; the good madame, who had been assigned a special code name—"Little Flower"—by her Saigon contacts, was under special FBI surveillance.

Clark Clifford: "As we began to make progress in Paris, the Saigon government was kept posted all the time. A statement was even prepared for release in Saigon and release in Washington, exactly the same wording, announcing the day that the bombing was to stop and that the substantive talks were to begin and that the Saigon government was to have a representative there.

"The president was to announce this very important development on the evening of October 31 when suddenly out of a clear sky the Saigon government says no.

"They were the hope. The Saigon government could end the killing in Vietnam and here it was dragging its feet. And all the time American boys were dying."

Averell Harriman: "This was a great shock to Johnson. Someone was sending information to them, 'Don't do anything before election.' They were advised by their friends, including Madame Chennault, that if we did have peace, Humphrey would be elected."

Up until the evening of October 31 when Lyndon was to appear on television, meetings and phone calls continued in a desperate attempt to get the South Vietnamese to change their minds. When a little after 7:00—Lyndon was to begin his address at 8:00—word came from Bunker that Thieu was still asking for changes, most of his advisers decided to go ahead with the original agreement.

Lyndon spoke from the White House. He discussed the progress of the Paris talks, and then said: "I have now ordered that all air, naval and artillery bombardment of North Vietnam cease as of 8:00 A.M. Washington time, Friday morning."

He ended by saying:

"I do not know who will be inaugurated as the thirty-seventh president of the United States next January. But I do know that . . . I shall do everything in my power to move us toward the peace that the new president—as well as this president and, I believe, every other American—so deeply and urgently desires."

Five days later the ballots were cast and Richard Nixon was elected.

SO LITTLE I HAVE DONE, SO MUCH I HAVE YET TO DO

At his last news conference at the National Press Club on January 17, 1969, Lyndon said:

"I don't think my administration has done enough in hardly any field. I tell this story every day, but it is very true. Some of you have heard it two or three times already today.

"It is reputed that Prime Minister Churchill, at the end of World War II, was called upon by a group of temperance ladies, and a little lady in tennis shoes, the chairman of the group, said, 'Mr. Prime Minister, we want to tell you—' They had come to complain about his drinking habits and said: 'We want to tell you that we are reliably informed that if all of the alcohol you have consumed during World War II, if it were emptied in this room, it would come up to about here.'

"And the Prime Minister looked at the floor and then at the ceiling and he said: 'Well, my dear little lady, so little have I done, so much I have yet to do.'"

The fact that he was leaving office hadn't slowed Lyndon down one bit.

Lady Bird: "It was a windup time and he just thought of all those things he wanted to get done and he made lists and did them and he really did count the days even more carefully then because there were less of them."[1]

James Jones: "He wanted to keep on the pressure to get his programs passed. He kept telling us, you gotta move; you gotta button it down now; we're losing time; we're going to get beat. We really didn't have any kind of slowdown until the very end."

It had been a good Christmas, even if the peace talks were somewhat stalled, for two long-awaited events finally happened that December.

One such was the release of the eighty-two man crew of the U.S. Intelligence ship *Pueblo*, which had been seized in international waters (though the seizers had vociferously claimed otherwise) by the North Koreans on January 23 of that year. Involved negotiations for their release had gone on for eleven months, both in and out of the United Nations.

At the time Lyndon had responded by ordering air power into South Korea as a precautionary gesture, and the North Koreans, in their turn, had announced that the crew of the *Pueblo* would be put on trial and, if found guilty, punished as criminals. The threat had, not surprisingly, caused considerable uproar across the country. There were even some members of Congress, dovish on Vietnam, who saw the North Korean challenge as an outright act of war.

Lyndon's final decision was to do as little as possible. Patience. Let the force of the waves subside. Wait for the calm. Take the matter to the UN Security Council and let it be aired before the world. Encourage your friends—maybe even some not known to be your friends—to put pressure on the North Koreans to cooperate.

Those were slow avenues to justice, but they paid off. The proposed trial was never held. Negotiations got under way at Panmunjom. Finally, eleven long months after their capture, and in the last month of Lyndon's administration, the crew members of the *Pueblo* were released and allowed to return home. Home for Christmas.

Almost as heartening was the event, two days after Christmas, when the three men in the Apollo spacecraft, which had just circled the moon, splashed safely down into the Pacific. The space program to get a man on the moon that Lyndon, in his role as head of the Space Council, had advised President Kennedy to embark upon back in 1961 was now only a few steps away from its consummation.

When the astronauts came to the White House on January 9, Frank Borman told Lyndon that they had a picture of the Ranch that they felt sure the president would want. Then they handed him a photograph of the earth taken when the Apollo was circling the moon.

January was, it sometimes seemed, one continuous farewell party. Lyndon was going out in style. And among the gala events was a lavish party in New York at the Pierre Hotel on January 13 given by Brooke Astor. Fortunately for both Lyndon and Lady Bird, the next day's State of the Union address was not scheduled until 9:00 P.M.

Luci: "The night of daddy's last State of the Union speech, it got to be just about thirty minutes before the speech was going to go on and we were literally on our way out the door and daddy says, 'Where's Lyn?' And I said, 'Daddy, Lyn's gone to bed.' It was nine o'clock at night. And mother said, 'He's in bed of course.' Lynda Bird chimed in too, 'Of course, Lyn's in bed.'

"'Well, my father said, 'Isn't he going to go to the State of the Union speech?' And I said, 'No, sir, nobody mentioned anything about it.' My mother said, 'That's the most ludicrous thing I've ever heard of in my whole life. An eighteen-month-old baby doesn't belong at a State of the Union speech.'

"And my father looked over at her with that very direct and forceful look and he said, 'Bird, I'd just love to have you at the State of the Union speech, and I'd just love for you to take your daughters if you choose to, and that includes all those other relatives that you invited, if you want to, and even some of those dear close friends. But it's my State of the Union speech and it's my last one and the only person I'm inviting is Patrick Lyndon. If any of the rest of you want to come, that's just fine, but I'm only inviting him.'

"So I went and got Lyn dressed. Lynda Bird and mother were just appalled, and the whole way up to the Hill they kept trying to get me to leave Lyn in the car and get some friend to come over and take care of him, or even miss it myself, but for heaven's sake, *not* take Lyn to the State of the Union speech. But my father had told me that the only person that he was inviting was Lyn and I was for sure going to take him. And I did. I brought his bottle. We sat up in the gallery and Lyn behaved impeccably."

Lyndon spoke that evening in a soft, never abrasive tone of voice, so much so that when he finished, no one for a moment seemed to realize that the speech was over. When they did, there were cheers from both Democrats and Republicans, and as he walked back down the aisle, dozens of hands grabbed for his. Many members of Congress were misty-eyed, and the press reported that Lady Bird wept. She denied it. She was laughing, she said, at Patrick Lyndon Nugent, who at eighteen months was without doubt the youngest listener ever to be present at a State of the Union message. "He might not remember it," his grandfather had remarked, "but I would."

There were, at the last cabinet meeting, many speeches, mostly sentimental, and Lady Bird came in to say good-bye. "It has been a high excitement to have been associated with people like you," Lyndon said, "a great adventure. I have loved it, every hour of it, and I have learned a lot, I think.

". . . I am just so proud of you, every one, and so glad my country has had your services and I have had you as friends. Several words I have cut out of my vocabulary. Among them are 'last' and 'good-bye.' So I will look forward to seeing you all."

All that remained now, besides the daily flow of business, were the personal things.

Most presidents spend their last night in the White House quietly. The Johnsons, typically, gave one last party—this one for the White House staff and their families.

Larry Temple: "They had a little orchestra up there, a little marine four- or five-piece band. I remember the only sad thing was when they struck up 'Hello, Dolly' and everybody on the staff sang the 'Hello, Lyndon' song that brought lots of tears to lots of eyes."

Lyndon said: "There is nothing that I would change, as I look back, of any consequence that I have done. You say, 'He sure is a hardheaded stubborn devil.' Well, that is the way I saw it and that is the way I see it now. But I have had the privilege of doing so many things that the average fellow can't do at all."[2]

The morning of January 20 was cold and gray and overcast. Lyndon was awakened at seven by his military valets. Usually only one was on duty at a time, but on this the last morning, they were both there. He spent some minutes looking through some last documents. Then he and Lady Bird had breakfast together by the window facing toward the Jefferson Memorial.

Wilbur J. Cohen: "We were still fooling with ideas on the morning of January twentieth. I was in touch with the White House to see if the president still wanted to issue a statement in favor of more scholarship aid for students in college. No, he didn't. But we had a lot of things going, and finally Jim Gaither called me about 10:30 and said, 'I can't get to the president any more. It's all over.'"

About 10:30 the Nixons arrived and not long afterward they all drove to the Capitol. And then it was all over. At 12:15 Richard Nixon was sworn in as thirty-seventh president of the United States.

Lyndon: "President Nixon said to me, 'How did you feel when you weren't president anymore?' And I said, 'I don't know whether you'll understand this now or not, but you certainly will later. I sat there on that platform and waited for you to stand up and raise your right hand and take the oath of office, and I think the most pleasant words that I ever—that ever came into my ears were 'So help me God' that you repeated after that oath. Because at that time I no longer had the fear that I was the man that could make the mistake of involving the world in war, that I was no longer the man that would have to carry the terrifying responsibility of protecting the lives of this country and maybe the entire world, unleashing the horrors of some of our great power if I felt that that was required."

After the inaugural there was a luncheon at the Cliffords, and from there the Johnson party, including Lyn and the Robbs' new baby daughter Lucinda, went directly to the airport where they were greeted by a huge crowd of people who had come to say good-bye.

Temple: "It was a very moving ceremony at the airport—a great outpouring of his friends, his cabinet, key congressional leaders, the whole thing.

"Here a Republican president had just been sworn in, the parade was still going on, and one of the people at the airport was George Bush![3] I told him, 'George, I don't know what you're out here for, but I think it's a very kind gesture.' And he said, 'Well, he's my president, and he is leaving town; and I didn't want him to leave this town without my being out here and paying my respects to him.'"

The plane landed at Bergstrom Air Base rather than in Austin where the students would no doubt have demonstrated. At Bergstrom the crowd of five thousand was very enthusiastic. A sign above the base operations building said, WELCOME HOME, MR. PRESIDENT AND FAMILY, and the Longhorn band played "The Eyes of Texas" and "Ruffles and Flourishes." Lyndon did not lose the opportunity to address the crowd, saying that he hoped people would be understanding of Nixon, and added, "Whether we are Democrats or Republicans, Texans or New Yorkers, we love our country."

The applause was thunderous, no dissenters anywhere.

Lyndon pressed some flesh; then bidding good-bye to Luci, who, with Lyn, was going to their home in Austin, he and Lady Bird, Lynda, and Lucinda got on the Jetstar and flew to the Ranch.

Lady Bird: "We got to the Ranch just as dark was falling. There around the hangar were about five hundred local folks, some who had known Lyndon all his life and his father before him. Lyndon invited everybody into the hangar and made them a long and glowing talk about how glad he was to be home."

Lyndon: "The weather was mild and warm at the Ranch. After we changed into comfortable clothes, Lady Bird and I walked around the yard together. In the carport behind the house the luggage was piled in a giant mound. For the first time in five years there were no aides to carry the bags inside. Lady Bird looked at the scene and began to laugh. 'The coach has turned back into a pumpkin,' she said, 'and the mice have all run away.'"[4]

6

The Winter of LBJ

FLAWS IN A DIAMOND

Katharine Graham: "Both his faults and his virtues were on a very big scale. I think his purposes were high, and he was a flamboyant, extraordinary, and fascinating personality.

"I also think it's terribly sad that his own personality got in the way so much. I've often had to sit there when he was talking and hold on to my chair to keep from doing something I knew in my head would have done no good.

"I kept thinking I could tell him how to get along with people because with just a little difference it would have really worked."

Lyndon: "People don't understand one thing about me, that is, that the one thing I want to do is my job. Some are always writing that I'm a back-room operator. They say I'm sensitive. How would you like your little daughter to read that you are a 'back-room operator,' a 'wirepuller' or a 'clever man'? People don't understand."[1]

Even Rebekah felt the press gave the wrong impression of Lyndon. In writing to her son on March 22, 1958 she said:

> The article in *Time* is basically good. It tells of your strength, accomplishments, consecration to service, high abilities, and outstanding qualities, but in the effort to picture you as one who has frailties and faults as well as virtues, the writer descends to exaggeration and superficiality. The line, "Lyndon Johnson would rather be caught dead than in a suit that cost less than $200," is as injurious as untrue. I think that remark gives a completely false idea of you. I didn't like the intimation that you are quite a dictator. Perhaps tho', darling, I am attaching too much importance to unfortunate and untrue remarks. A flaw in a diamond stands out while the blemish on a pebble is unnoticed.

Lyndon's temper was one flaw that seldom went unnoticed.

Peter Benchley: "Of course everybody had heard about his temper, but I only saw an example of it once. That concerned Haywood Smith, the military aide. Haywood was walking with the president toward the helicopter in Texas. I guess there must have been a number of helicopters out there. The president started toward one, and Haywood said, 'Mr. President, that's your helicopter over there.' And the president said, 'They're all mine, Haywood.' Now he said this in nobody's company except the company of Haywood Smith, and the next morning the whole story was in the *Washington Post*.

"Of course there was no doubt about how the story had got out, and Haywood walked into the White House Mess looking as though his whole family had just been killed in an airplane crash and he had just been demoted to private first class. He sat down. He was ashen, and he said that he had gotten it up one side and down the other.

"I have never seen a man who looked quite the way he looked."

Gerald Siegel: "He was sometimes a mean sonofabitch. He was petulant. He was capable of childish temper tantrums. You can't describe them in any other way. A very ambitious man, very sensitive to how easily you could get off course. A little penny on the track could derail the monstrous train, and he didn't want anybody putting pennies on his track.

"But if anyone really made a cropper of a mistake, he was compassionate. It was the small mistakes he was intolerant of. I think he realized that if you really made a cropper, there was damn little he could do to make you feel worse.

"What you had was a man who had never quite learned to control this tremendous power within him. This, for lack of a better word, temper, emotion, the well of desire and ambition, aspiration, just flowed out of him like an explosive force. Whenever it was frustrated, he behaved like a youngster with a temper tantrum, turned on us, lashed out without restraint.

"Not always. I've seen him on important things when he was more restrained than Job himself. But on the lesser things, as I said, he would erupt like a volcano." [2]

Jack Valenti: "He was loving, warm, and kind, but he was a mean bully when he wanted to be and he could humiliate you, both publicly and privately. He would castigate you for being one millimeter off in what you were doing. I don't understand it, and never will. But Johnson's kind of like life itself—you take the sunsets and sunrises, but you also take the avalanches, floods and plagues.

"Sometimes I thought he was too tough on some of his associates in the White House, and I would tell him so. He would respond in one of two ways—if he was in a pretty good mood he would say, 'Oh, well, maybe you're right, maybe I was'—or he would say, 'You let me be the judge . . .' and his eyes would narrow to slits, and the force would then gather in the room, and you would know you were treading on dangerous territory.

"Johnson could be a tiger if there was any scandal, any mishandling of the public business by a man while he was working at the White House. He would have cut your balls off."

Robert Kintner: "He never picked on me because I would have just walked out. But he did pick on the Joe Califanos, the Bill Moyers, the Walt Rostows. Walt almost had a heart attack every time he buzzed around. He was a fearful character—Johnson. Inside. But on the outside, he had a tendency when he bawled people out very unduly, he would later try to make it up—he'd do nice things.

"He used to bawl the hell out of Juanita Roberts. But a friend of mine, Leonard Marks, told me that in the last month before he died, instead of bawling her out, he used to get up and hold her chair and do the kind of things that Johnson never did in his life. I had the feeling he thought he was about to meet his Maker and he had sort of a fundamentalist, Church of Christ kind of religion."

Juanita Roberts: "Of course, I've known him since he and Mrs. Johnson got married and worked for him in many places and many times, including the White House; I was there with him from the beginning until the end. He was always exacting—by which I mean he always knew what he wanted and he would tell you in detail, being sure you understood it. And when he was certain that you did, he wanted it done exactly as he had described it—and quickly, on the double."

Ashton Gonella: "It was sort of a challenge to keep up with what he expected of you. He expected perfection. I don't think either one of them [Lyndon and Lady Bird] had much tolerance for mistakes."

Larry Temple: "You know the president insisted that if you went to the bathroom or decided to scratch your nose or something you had to let the White House operator know what you were doing. Just in case he ever needed you he wanted to know where everybody was all the time."

Coates Redmon: "If you were having lunch—no matter what restaurant it was—the waiter would come with a message there was a telephone call. It would always be the president wanting to know what you were doing, what you were eating—'Now have you salted and peppered it?' etc. He always insisted, even though the telephone operator at the White House dailed the number, that you were at the Sans Souci where all the Georgetown crowd ate lunch, and he would add, 'Well, you enjoy your lunch—but hurry back—I need you.'"

William Jorden: "He was an inveterate user of Alexander Graham Bell's instrument and it didn't take very much to prompt him to pick up; so if he read something in the paper, or if he read something in the briefing memos or staff papers, etc., that interested him he'd get on the phone and call the guy involved and say, 'What the hell are they doing to us here?' and 'What does this mean,' etc. And he didn't just *pick* up the telephone; he *grabbed* the telephone. Secretaries say that he just grabbed the phone away from them while they were talking, cut off their conversation and dialed *his* number. And they would just be in tears. I think it was the thing that almost did him in, trying to look at three television stations at once and trying to talk over two or three telephones at the same time."

Robert C. Weaver: "I think he would have called Jesus Christ on the telephone if he had a number for Him, at any time. We had all these little white phones leading directly from the White House and he would call at any hour, any time. And very often he would call you at home about something and he would be in the office and he'd have the stuff in front of him and you wouldn't but you'd be expected to know about it."

John P. Roche: "He used that horn on the desk, that microphone for his phone, so that by the time it came out of my phone, it sounded like a riot on Fourteenth Street as heard through the subway tunnel at Forty-second. I couldn't understand half of what he was saying. I'd just hold the phone out at arm's length and every so often say, 'Yes, sir,' and let it go at that, because he was just talking. So many people, again, have misunderstood him, it seems to me. They thought he was screaming at them; in fact he was screaming at the universe, and they were just witnesses to it."

Erv S. Duggan: "Johnson loved to call people early in the morning because it was a way of being in control. Getting one up. 'Here I am up with the chickens; and you're groggy in bed. What's the matter with you?'"

Horace Busby: "Once I came to meet him at the National Airport. I don't remember just when it was or whether he was arriving or taking off. But I do remember that I found him at a place where there were three public telephones and he said, 'Horace, don't try to use any of those three phones. I've got a long-distance call in progress on all three!'

"Then I noticed that the receivers were off all three hooks and you could hear the voices of the operators trying to complete all three calls."

Yolanda Boozer: "He would sometimes come into the office and say something like, 'Well, I see we're putting on a few pounds, aren't we?' Which meant that you'd better go on a diet. He had a way of planting seeds in your mind. Or if you hadn't had your hair done, he would come in to the office and say, 'Well, it's getting a little windy out there, isn't it?'

"He was adamant about your not having a run in your stocking. He could see it a mile away. I'd be so nervous every time I'd start to walk away from him. I knew I would get the complete up-and-down look. I mean *scrutiny*. And if you had even a little bit of a run, you'd better change those stockings. It was best always to have an extra pair in your drawer."

Thomas G. Corcoran: "Lyndon was a very high-powered bird. And every once in a while he would be nastier than hell to one of his subordinates. He was never nasty to me because I was papa. And he was never nasty to Jim Rowe. But one day when he was feeling real mean he miserably bawled out a subordinate and Jim resigned. And sent him a letter telling him that he was an arrogant sonofabitch."

James H. Rowe, Jr.: "When he was maddest, he just talked in a soft, gentle voice. When he used that voice, you knew he was madder than at any other time. He and I have had a number of explosions over the years. Quite a number."

Sherwin J. Markham: "He was mercurial. A great one for both overpraising and overcriticizing, depending on his mood and what the impetus has been on the instant. I mean, he could, at one moment, tell you you're the greatest thing that ever came down the pike; and then, in the next instant, say you're the most idiotic, stupid sonofabitch that's ever been around."

Will Sparks: "There was one occasion in the Oval Office where he was in the middle of telling a funny story to me and Bob Hardesty and several others of his staff when one of his several telephones buzzed. He stopped the story, took the phone, and proceeded to give whoever it was one of the worst tongue-lashings I've ever heard in my life. 'Goddamn sonofabitch, you can't even find your ass with both hands.' He went through all of that. That guy on the other end of the phone must have been on the verge of a heart attack to be talked to like that by the president of the United States. And having done all that, he slammed down the phone, shoved the drawer in his desk closed, and said, 'Well, now as I was saying . . .'"

Henry Gonzalez: "He'd be in the helicopter, and he'd chew the devil out of the marine sergeant because the air-conditioning wasn't on or something. He was suffocating and he'd chew him out. Five hours later he'd be saying, 'Sergeant, I understand that your wife is very sick. Now what are you doing around here? Here's some money. Now you go over there and stay with her until she gets well. Don't worry about anything.' A man of that kind is not one man; he's many men."

Abe Feinberg: "He had a great capacity to be penitent after he had his emotional orgasm. He could suddenly turn around and skin you alive if you were working for him, if he didn't like what you were doing. Then in the next minute, he'd put his arms around you.

"Only once did he get angry at me. It was at the end of a rather long meeting about Israel. He said, 'You know, I've invited President Nasser to the White House.'

"And I told him that yes, I had heard about it, because there had been some publicity in the papers about it, and I told him, 'I wish you would remind him that keeping open the Straits of Tiran is even more important than the Straits of Sharm Al Sheik, because Israel can keep those open—they're right off her own territory. But in order to keep the Straits of Tiran open, she'd have to attack Yemen, southern Yemen, and other countries.'

"Then this cloud came over his eyes. When I saw that cloud, I realized that I'd made the mistake of reminding him that he may have overlooked a point in geography. Now, I've seen him angry at other people, with all the yelling and the shouting, but this time I saw his eyes become opaque, literally, as they sometimes did if he was very, very angry and didn't express it. And all he said to me in this very soft voice was, 'How would you like to be president of the United States?'"

Robert M. Jackson: "I remember one thing that greatly impressed me way back when we were young and poor. He had what I thought was a peculiar attitude toward money. His idea of money was to buy something for somebody with it. I remember one time just before Mother's Day when I told him I was going downtown to get my mother's present. He thought that was a wonderful idea and so he went with me. But instead of just buying a present for his mother, he bought things for the mothers of many people that he knew from Texas. And I knew he couldn't afford it. That was characteristic of him."

Tom Johnson: "In 1967 when I first started working for him I rode the bus to work because we had two children—my job paid $7,500 a year—and we could hardly make living expenses. And one morning about 7:30 he started looking for me over some kind of crisis and he called my house twice. My wife, Edwina, said I was on the bus. When I got to my office around 9:00 they told me I had better get over to the mansion, that I was in big trouble. When I got there Lyndon said, 'Well, do you also bring a *brown paper bag?*' And I said, 'What do you mean, sir?' He said, 'I've been trying to get you for the last hour and a half and Edwina tells me you are on a bus so I also figure you must bring your lunch in a brown paper bag.' I said, 'Well, you know we have only one car and I hate to have Edwina drive me down here every day. The bus just works out. I'm sorry.' And the next morning, even though he had just about eliminated all the White House cars, he assigned me a car and a driver and also gave me an annual $7,000 increase in pay."

Joseph A. Califano: "He expressed gratitude in a variety of ways. Sometimes you'd get a note and if he thought you were real good he'd write something very extravagant. When he went on that long trip to the Far East, I was the only senior staff member that was going to be left at the White House. The morning he left he just poured gifts on. He gave me an electric toothbrush and a razor. He gave me some pearls for my wife. And lots of praise also because he knew I was going to have a murderous two weeks, and that since he was going to be exactly twelve hours off kilter I'd be talking to him on the telephone at all hours.

"It was very nice to receive gifts from him, but sometimes he didn't realize what problems he was causing you. My kids were over at the White House one night and he gave us a beagle. You don't know what it is to get a dog at nine o'clock on a Sunday night in Washington."

Ramsey Clark: "Johnson was a compulsive giver. He just wanted to give something always. I don't think I have ever gone by that he didn't wind up giving me something. It might even be something he'd given me before. I think I've got four or five copies of *My Hope for America*.

"You could laugh about some of it, because a lot of it was kind of junky stuff, but the point was, he wanted to give people something—he really did."

Patrick Nugent: "He was always in the habit of giving people something or other whether it was a pocketknife or a cigarette lighter, and it always had his name on it. Depending upon whom the recipient happened to be, he'd pull something out of his pocket and say, 'Here, I want you to keep this as a memento of your visit to the Ranch; but for God's sake don't embarrass me by leaving it in a whorehouse someplace."

Robert Livingston: "He loved presents. He was mad about presents, both to give and receive. He was very generous, but he was—and I don't want to say like a child, but he loved getting something. He just loved presents."

Lynda: "He didn't want gifts that were practical. He would want a flashy new belt—or a super shirt or a great-looking tux. You know, he didn't want something that was just going to keep him warm, cover his feet—and he would make derogatory remarks about it. 'Give those old blue socks to such and such.' And he would tease us about things we gave him or didn't give him. I remember once I went to England before Chuck and I were engaged, and when I came back I brought back these big wide ties, very mod for daddy, and he said, 'Thank you very much but I think that Chuck ought to have them.' And Chuck got them. Made my feelings hurt. He didn't accept gifts as well as he should. But I was not going to be the first one to tell him."

Jake Jacobsen: "One time on one of our trips to the Ranch we were driving around, and somebody had just acquired another piece of land down there, and on it was living a family just as poor as church mice. There were about six of them living in the same room—just a miserable situation, not untypical of country living in Texas. He drove by and looked at that place, didn't say anything, came back. The next thing he said, 'Jake, you'd better get hold of our architect in Austin and have him design a couple of extra rooms for that house. Don't say anything about it.'"

Father Wunibald Schneider: "At Christmas time he would have loads of presents for all the Latins there at the Ranch and he would especially invite them for the Christmas party.

"He encouraged them to go to school and get a good education. He would be very,

very concerned about them. There was a little black boy—the son of one of the hands working the Ranch—he had something wrong with his leg. His leg was in a cast. Johnson was so affectionate. He would take this little boy in his arms and say, 'Give me a kiss.'"

Harry McPherson: "There was one time when I was working in the Senate with him, pushing him to take up an immigration bill which would allow about sixty thousand people to come in from Eastern Europe. It would have been a big change in the immigration laws. And I kept pushing, pushing. And finally one day he came out of his office and said, 'What are we going to do today?' And I said, 'Senator, you've just got to take up this immigration bill.' He turned around and said, 'You've got a little Jew in you, don't you? That curly hair. You've got some Jew in you, don't you?'

"But he was wide open in the older way when it was all right to tell all the ethnic stories and use all the dialects and all that. But he did have a much sharper feeling for groups who had had a hard time, blacks and Chicanos, especially anybody who had ever served him."

Ramsey Clark: "He wanted to get a Latin-American on the bench. There had never been a Spanish-American as a federal judge in the history of the country. And we finally found a fellow named Rinaldo Garza from Brownsville, Texas. Johnson did get him on the court, and he's still there, and I think he has been a very good judge.

"Anyway, before Garza got the job—the decision had been made that day but it wasn't official, Garza and I went up to Washington for a final interview and Johnson put on a performance. It was one of the rarest things I've ever seen him do; he got so emotional. There were things that had happened that made him very distrustful of judges; it had to do with the '48 election. But he started talking to Garza and he just oozed open and said, 'I want you to be the greatest judge that ever lived. When you walk down the streets of Brownsville, the most miserable little Mexican children will look up as if it was the second coming of Jesus Christ Himself. 'There's Justice Garza! There's Justice Garza!' And oh, my God—Rinaldo was crying, he was so touched. I was touched, too. It was a magnificent thing. And of course Garza was so shaky when he came out of that interview it took him five years before he could do a mean thing."

Jack Valenti: "He was not the most sophisticated man in the sense of personal habits. I mean, he'd scratch his ass or pick his nose, or go to the bathroom, and while he was taking a leak he'd just never stop talking. He was full of these things that we may call coarse manners, or that somebody else might call vulgar. If it were not the president they might be called 'earthy.' He was a very earthy man."

Coates Redmon: "I don't remember what year it was, but one day Hayes, my husband, came home laughing himself sick, saying 'You wouldn't believe what I saw.' He explained that he had said to Bill Moyers, 'Gee. I never get to see the president when he's doing these outrageous things everyone tells me about. And the next time he does one, I want to be in on it. I'm working for the man and I want to see this.'

"So one day Bill telephoned him to come quick to the president's bedroom. I think Lynda Bird was in there, and Mrs. Johnson, and Marie Fehmer was taking dictation. The president was lying on his side in his bed and facing the group. There was a nurse on the other side, the three television sets were all going, and he was going snap, snap, snap. He's batting dictation to Marie, he's switching the channels, he's yelling at Bill—and I think there were others there, someone from one of the networks and another from the White House staff—and he's yelling at them too. And everybody in this fairly large group was acting normal as all get out. And Hayes said that he started to walk around a little, because he couldn't figure out what the nurse was doing there. Bill said, 'Can't you see?' Hayes said, 'No, I can't see anything.' But little by little it *was* getting apparent, and Bill whispered to him, 'Well, you wanted a good one, you got a good one—he's having an enema.'"

Monk Willis: "In many ways he was sometimes a crude man. I've been with him when he decided he wanted his back rubbed, and he didn't care how many women were around. He'd just take off all his clothes and lie down on the bed and say, 'Rub my back.' The queen of England could have been there. He didn't give a damn. He wasn't doing anything that was immoral. He was just doing what comes natural."

Sam Shaffer: "There was a great streak of coarseness in Johnson. The redeeming factor in the coarseness is that it was—these expressions—so skillful. He once took me around his Ranch. There was a magnificent cattle fence there and he said, 'Look at that fence— just as straight as an Indian goes to shit.'

"Later he took me to the family burial plot. Grass doesn't grow green in the Hill section of Texas, but it was green here, a very carefully tended little graveyard. There was his father's headstone, a few other relatives were buried there—and he said, 'Sam, this is where I'm going to be buried.' And then the next thing I know, and so help me God, this is a true story, he's got his fly open and he's urinating a stream as if it came from a horse, and all the while he continues talking to me."

Walter Jenkins: "I just think he had no false sense of modesty. I don't think it ever occurred to him that some people would be offended when he talked to somebody in his underwear or while sitting on the john. He felt that the human body was a thing of nature that was to be treated as such."

Tex Goldschmidt: "I once had four solid hours with him, talking about all kinds of things relating to the United Nations, and at one point he went into the bathroom and in order to hear what he was saying I followed. And I stood at the bathroom door while he took a crap, then shaved and showered all the while continuing his conversation as though what he was doing was the most normal thing in the world."

William W. Heath: "The first time he was back at the Ranch after becoming president he told me this story. He said, 'You know, as a small boy I learned a habit from my father. At night the last thing he would do before he'd go to bed, he'd go out on the front porch—the moon and stars were shining—and he would urinate off the front porch and commune with nature. And so I developed that habit when I was at the Ranch.'

"He said that it was a pleasant feeling to be out in the countryside with nobody anywhere near and look at the moon and the stars, and he said that when he got back to the Ranch from Washington, he planned to continue that. 'But,' he said, 'the first night I got home, and it got to be about the time I decided to go to bed, and I kept thinking about the Secret Service men—you can't enjoy a thing like that with a couple of those standing there watching you.

"'So I sort of waited till I thought I could give them the slip, and I eased out on the front porch, and I started, and right in the middle this big floodlight hit me. And you know, when you're startled in the middle of this, you get it over with quickly. I turned to these Secret Service fellows, and I remonstrated with them, and they said, "Mr. President, we cannot permit you to come out here in the dark alone; there might be somebody lurking out here who would shoot you. You just simply can't do this."

"'I knew they were right, so I didn't say any more to them. But the next night I really gave them the slip. I told one of them to go do something, and the other to do something else, and I thought I had time to rush out on the porch again. And damn, if they didn't do it again! Threw that light on me. I just decided to give it up.'

"He said, 'The small pleasures of life you have to give up.'"

Richard Bolling: "He was a crude bastard. Mr. Rayburn wasn't crude. Man-talk was all right with Rayburn but if there was a lady anywhere near—that was a classic separation of the two. I wouldn't say Johnson was vulgar—he was barnyard. Vulgar sort of implies something else to me. I think he was just damn crude—always scratching his crotch and picking his nose in mixed company.

"Now I don't think Lyndon's language was as bad as Nixon's. I don't think Lyndon would call anybody a motherfucker, for example. That would shock *him*.

"I'll never forget another time. He had some injury—hernia or something—and even with the girls present in his office he pulled his pants down to show it.

"And he'd sit at his front-row desk in the Senate—he was a great bone scratcher—and it wouldn't matter if there was a woman there—he'd pull up his huge scrotum while talking. We men used to be a bit embarrassed by this.

"There was just this earthy, coarse streak in him. Incidentally, President Truman wasn't earthy, but he could be quite scatological. Johnson's jokes often would be sexual. I never heard Truman utter a sexual joke but I did hear him make many scatological remarks. Once someone asked him what his philosophy of life was. I'll never forget his answer: 'Never kick a fresh turd around on a hot day.' But on sexual matters Truman was very prim. But Johnson was different. Let me give you an example. After being asked what he thought of Jerry Ford he said—and I got this from Bill Theis, who headed the Senate staff of the UPI—'Ford's economics is the worst thing that's happened to this country since pantyhose ruined finger-fucking.'"

Hubert H. Humphrey: "When you listen to Nixon's tapes, you see that he was uncomfortable with profanity; it was his way of trying to show he was a tough guy. But with Johnson it was just part of him, part of the language, part of the music. Those were the black keys of the piano he played. It wasn't discordant or out of joint at all. It just flowed along. He was apt to be talking to a preacher and using the same language. And the only time he ever became a phony was when he tried to be too pure."

Lois Roberts: "To me there was something appealing about the man's very vulgarity because it was somehow so American. It was not the phoniness of what I call middle-America. It was the real, vulgar, low-class American. And he didn't change when he was president. He went right on, didn't try to clean up his language."

Charles Boatner: "If it was an off-color joke he would not tell it in front of Mary

Margaret. He would not tell it in front of any of the girls. He would not tell it in front of Bird. There were certain old expressions that the Washington press corps tried to hang on him, but I have heard my grandfather, who was one of the first cattle-brand inspectors of the state of Texas, say, 'That sonofabitch hasn't got sense enough to pour piss out of a boot.' The idea that those expressions were just Johnson's is wrong, you know. 'Let's get down to the nut gut,' that's an expression on every ranch."

Wright Patman: "I'll tell you one thing for sure. Lyndon didn't ever say a word that his pappy didn't say—and worse. Sam Ealy was a country man, and he talked like a country man. He was just like Lyndon in another way—when he wanted to talk to you, he got right up to you, nose to nose, and sometimes he'd grab hold of you just the way Lyndon used to."

Humphrey: "Mr. Johnson always said—of a lot of people—'I've got his pecker in my pocket.' That's one expression. Another was, 'I want a guy to be 150 percent loyal, kiss my ass in Macy's window and stand up and say, "Boy, wasn't that sweet!"' Every man in that kind of political position really wants that. He seldom expresses it so colorfully, or as directly, as Mr. Johnson does."

John Dodds: "His speech was filled with country rhythms, country similes, metaphors that came from people who are born on the land and live on the land. He would say, 'It was raining as hard as a cat pissing on a flat rock.' When he was majority leader he was asked why he hadn't replied to a speech by Vice-President Nixon and he said, 'I may not know much, but I do know the difference between chicken shit and chicken salad.'"

William C. Westmoreland: "Not long after my return from Saigon, President Johnson told Kitsy that he understood that Quarters 1, the chief of staff's residence at Fort Meyer, has a spectacular view of the federal city. When, he asked, was Kitsy going to invite him to a little family dinner? . . .

"Kitsy finally concluded that a little family dinner might be construed to mean the president and Mrs. Johnson, their daughter Lynda (Luci was away), and because of the president's high regard for Bus Wheeler, the chairman of the Joint Chiefs, and Mrs. Wheeler. She invited them for the evening of October 8, 1968. . . . The view from Quarters 1 was much as the president had pictured it, and the dinner proved a success, particularly when it came to a dessert that was, apparently, a presidential favorite: rum pie.

"The president, having finished his pie, noted that General Wheeler had eaten only a few bites of his.

"'Buzz,' the president whispered, getting the chairman's attention . . .

"'Yes, Mr. President,' General Wheeler responded.

"'Are you through with your pie?'

"'Yes, Mr. President.'

"'May I have it?'

"'Yes, Mr. President.'

"Whereupon the President, under the eaglelike gaze of Mrs. Johnson, ate what remained of General Wheeler's pie."[3]

George Christian: "He'd be talking, and maybe he'd reach over and get somebody else's butter. I remember on the press plane coming back from Australia to Manila for the Manila conference in 1966, the prime minister of New Zealand and his wife flew with him up there. . . . And they were all having breakfast in the cabin of the plane with some of the press around, and he just absentmindedly reached over and ate a piece of bacon off the plate of the prime minister's wife.

"And the press got on to it and blew it up, almost made an international incident out of it.

"It was just him. If somebody would be sitting on his right and eating ice cream—he was on a diet half the time and craved sweets—all of a sudden he'd just reach over and get a spoon of ice cream. Like some kid.

"He loved just plain canned green peas, and if they put them in a bowl by his place with a lot of the juice, because he liked the pot liquor, sometimes he would pick up the bowl and eat the peas that way. He would have a plate in front of him and would bring the bowl over to where he could eat. And that kind of surprised and shocked some people the first time they saw it.

"The press sometimes seized on these idiosyncrasies because he was different. He could be the most urbane, intellectual man, and yet he could be a Hill Country rancher with all the rough edges. He could switch it on and switch it off.

"Several times he told me, 'I'm cooped up in this place, and I don't have a minute of my own. I'm beset with problems. They don't bring me anything unless it can go either way, and I have to decide it.' And he said, 'By God, I'm going to do what I want to do. If I want to drink a glass of whiskey, I'm going to drink a glass of whiskey. And if I want to have bad manners, I'm going to have bad manners. I've got to have some freedom to do what I want to do.'"

William S. White: "Curiously enough I think one of the reasons he didn't go down better politically was that his faults were highly masculine faults and that our society is becoming increasingly less masculine; that there's a certain femininity about our society that he didn't fit into. I'm not speaking in crude terms of sexual aberration, because he was in a sense a kind of American Henry VIII. I mean to say, if he wanted to belch at the table, he belched at the table, and so on. His shortcomings were not the polite, pleasant little shortcomings, but the big ones—high temper, of course, too driving a personality, both of others and himself, too much of a perfectionist by far. But in short, when they made him they never made a little man, they made a very big one—with equivalent faults.

"But I have never known him to pick on a small person in a small situation. At least he chose his adversaries of equivalent size and I think that's a pretty good epitaph for him."

THE PRIVATE CITIZEN

To no one's surprise the retirement did not begin well. During the first weeks Lyndon, as always, made the most of his displeasures, liberally sharing them with anyone who was within hearing distance. As we know by now he was never one to suffer in silence.

Thank God it didn't last long.

Elizabeth Goldschmidt: "We went to the Ranch—it was the Easter following his departure from Washington. Bird urged us to come, I think because she was trying desperately to find a way to pull Johnson out of what was clearly a depression. And he absolutely refused to discuss anything that was less than twenty-five years old.

"We talked about things from our youth, and he remembered so-and-so. But nothing relating to the presidency.

"Bird was obviously frantic about his state of mind, and at dinner she said, in her bright chipper way, 'Let's go look at some movies from our days in the White House.' And Johnson said, 'Oh, they don't want to see that old stuff. That's all past and done with.' She said, 'No, I think they'd like it,' and we said okay. So we went up to the hangar that they'd made into a little auditorium and the projectionist said, 'What year should we take?' She said brightly, 'Oh, let's take the last year.' And he promptly went to sleep; he refused to look."

Then—nobody seems to remember exactly where or when or why—the gloom ended, and he started doing all the things he had never had time for.

Lady Bird: "You know, Lyndon rushed all his life. From the time we got married in '34 until he left Washington in '69, he was always in a rush. These last years, there were no pressing demands. We were sort of living on our own time."[1]

Lyndon: "One of the things I enjoyed most was being able to go to bed after the ten o'clock news at night and sleep until daylight the next morning. I don't remember ever having an experience like that in the five years I was in the White House."[2]

Luci: "I was very, very worried. I thought thirty-five years in public service and this is going to be like putting him in a tomb. But he discovered play. That was a word that was not in his vocabulary. He didn't understand it. And he discovered his grandchildren and it was a delightful time."

Lady Bird: "He had a lot of little sentimental journeys which he enjoyed tremendously, such as the one to see Congressman Ewing Thomasson, aged about ninety, who had served with him in the House of Representatives. And he had time to go to a football game nearly every Saturday during the fall season."

Further, his sense of humor had come back.

John Dodds: "One day, during the postpresidency he and Doris Kearns[2] were out in the boat. It was a magic afternoon—the sky was blue, the water was blue, the boat was magnificent—and they were roaring along, and he turned to her and said, 'I sure do miss the Middle East!'"

Frank Erwin: "All the stuff about his being pessimistic and bitter that has been printed—that's just absolute bullshit. He seemed very contented. He seemed content to let history deal with his presidency at a distance, to let the record stand for itself. He knew he had a problem with his heart and because of some other physical disabilities that he had, he spent time getting his affairs in order. He sold a lot of his holdings, made a gift to the federal government of some land around his home. And he tried to get things in order for what was inevitable."

Tom Johnson: "I felt an obligation or a sense of loyalty and went back with him. I expected him to be very unhappy. I felt for him—a man who had been a leader of the free world, in public life for more than thirty years, was going to have a helluva transition.

"But it was not as difficult as I expected. What he did was go to work. He went to work on the Ranch. He started running that Ranch the way he had run the presidency— involved in every piece of it. Then he became chief executive officer of the Texas Broadcasting Company. And it wasn't only television. It was Muzak and Photo Processing and Capitol Cable, and everything else.

"He became his own ranch foreman. Dale Malechek reported to him; Jesse Kellam of the TV station reported to him. He became chief of staff of his office staff, and I reported to him on that.

"He was very involved with Frank Erwin on the building of the library—choosing the location—choosing the architect.

"And then, of course, the memoirs—he would spend hours recording and more hours editing them.

"At times I found him depressed, but that was because the pain was such a constant problem. He was suffering from angina, and he chewed on those nitroglycerine pills occasionally. He knew he wasn't in good health."

Abe Feinberg: "And driving the car. He never should have driven the car. The doctor had told him not to drive. But he did.

"And he took up smoking again; he smoked like a fiend."

Robert Hardesty: "Johnson was just having a hell of a good time. He'd take us down to Acapulco, and to quarterhorse races over in Fredericksburg. He'd go up to New York to see Krim, McNamara, and Henry Ford, and go partying. He had fits of depression, of course, but he was enjoying himself and doing things he wanted to do, for the first time."

Nixon and Johnson had parted on cordial terms and the new president took some pains to keep his predecessor informed on matters of state, especially the progress, or lack of it, on Vietnam. Every week a briefing would arrive by plane from Washington. Occasionally Nixon would dispatch a cabinet member or similar luminary to fill Johnson in personally. When Henry Kissinger came to call, it was obvious that Johnson had not entirely abandoned his way with people's names.

Coates Redmon: "In December 1969 I ran into Henry Kissinger in Cambridge, and he said, 'Oh, Coates, I vant to tell you something *mar-ve-lous*. I've just been down to the LBJ Ranch. I vas called down to give him a foreign policy briefing, and I vent, and, Coates, he's crazy!'

"I said, 'Johnson's crazy like a fox. He knows what he's doing.' Henry said, 'No, Coates, he's crazy.' I said, 'In what way is he crazy?'

"And he said, 'Vell, first I got down there, and he called me "Dr. Kee-sing-er." Kee- sing-er! Like I vas the prime minister of Germany. He thought I was Kee-sing-er!' I said, 'No, he didn't, Henry, he was putting you on.' And he said, 'No, Coates, he thought I vas Kee-sing-er. And then he got me all mixed up and called me Dr. Schles-ing-er. He didn't know who I was—he vas all mixed up. Then he vent up to a picnic table and he said, "Henry, do you know vat that is?" And I felt I should say, "No, sir," because I knew how crazy he vas. So I said I didn't know vat it vas, and he said, "That is a *picnic table*, Henry."

"I said, 'He's putting you on, Henry!' 'No, Coates, he's crazy.'"

In his book, *Before the Fall*, William Safire relates a similar story.

William Safire: "On his first trip to the Pedernales to brief LBJ, Kissinger was given a tour that led him to believe the former president had him confused with West Germany Chancellor Kurt Kiesinger. 'This was Comanche territory,' LBJ told him. 'You know, you Germans were great Indian fighters.' Passing some picnic tables, LBJ pointed out that he had them installed along the roadside instead of hot dog stands, 'because you Germans love picnics.' Referring to his instructions to his secretary of state, he said, 'Ah tol' Dean Rusk—"Git on yo' horse!" That means "high priority," professor!' Kissinger was especially shaken by President Johnson's habit of calling him 'Professor Schlesinger.'

"'Lady Bird Johnson drove me back to the air strip,' Henry recounted, 'and she asked me how I thought President Johnson seemed these days. I mumbled something about "serenity in retirement" and she almost drove off the road. I suppose flattery has to be related to reality, however vaguely.'"[3]

Yolanda Boozer: "You would have thought that not being president any longer and not having the responsibilities of the nation, that he would relax. But he was just driven by this energy—'I've got to go out and see about my pipe. It's not working right.'

"He was an early riser, we all know that, so around eight thirty or nine he would go *back* to bed, get comfortable, and read his newspapers. And so that was the time he would sometimes call me in and do some of the work with the mail.

"He would work from his bedroom. Usually Mrs. Johnson was having coffee with him in the morning when I would arrive and he would be in his bed reading the newspapers. Then, in a matter of thirty minutes, he would be in the office ready to go on his rounds and see about his irrigation and his cattle. By then he would have talked to Dale a number of times. I'm sure he would start contacting Dale Malechek about six in the morning!

"He really loved the Ranch and that was the reason he didn't want to accept any invitations to go anywhere. He just didn't want to leave. He and Mrs. Johnson would get invitations to go spend a weekend down in Florida—go on a yacht. He'd always come back and say, 'Oh, I had a good time, but what did I miss?' 'How are my pumps?' 'How is the water?' 'How is the south pasture?' 'What is Dale doing about this bull or that bull?' It was always the Ranch."

Dale Malechek: "He became one of us. He was into the irrigation project and he carried the irrigation pipes and helped us work cows. He helped us there for about a year. I thought the pipes were damn heavy for what he'd been through. That was neither here nor there; he wanted to get out there and show us that he could. And he did.

"I never worked for a harder man in my life, but he was the best. If you did the work, he'd stand behind you and if you didn't you had hell to pay."

James Jones: "We visited there one time and his ranch foreman Dale Malechek said, 'Gee, I hope he runs again for president. There I was at six in the morning milking the cows—somebody had given him some dairy cows, it was a new operation—and lo and behold, there's the president standing there in his pajamas and his house shoes saying, "How are the dairy cows? Do the fences need to be fixed?"'"

* * *

One of Lyndon's retirement projects begun while he was still president, the building of a model nursing home in Austin.

Larry Temple: "In late '68, not long before the election, he called me and he said, 'Goddamn it, Larry, there are a lot of old people in this country who aren't getting the proper care. They keep telling me that everybody is doing as good a job as they can. It's a goddamn lie. They're not. Everybody's not doing it, and those that are doing it are doing it because they can make money out of it.'

"'We treat old people like we treat animals,' he said. 'Just put them in a cage somewhere until they die.'"

Lyndon had told Temple he wanted to do something in Austin that would be a model for taking care of old people all over the country, and that Temple should call Frank Erwin, who was then chairman of the board of regents at the University of Texas in Austin. Erwin said the university could contribute some money to the project, and Lyndon said that HEW had a few spare millions that could be used as a pilot program where old people would have, according to Temple, "what was for lack of a better description—a combination apartment and hospital."

Temple: "Frank Erwin said that he would suggest that we name it for the president's mother, 'the Rebekah Baines Johnson Home.'

"I wrote a memo to the president about that. And he said, 'Goddamn you, Frank's got no judgment, no sense. Why should you tie my poor mother into that and tie me into that? Somebody will catch this. The *New York Times* will write it up that I was spending a bunch of federal money for a memorial to my mother. You tell Frank that we're going to do the project, but tell him to forget that he ever mentioned my mother in connection with it.'

"We got to working on it but we weren't able to finish it by the time he went out of office. Then when the Nixon people came in, they started to leak stories that there was going to be an investigation of HEW and the nursing home. Jack Anderson had something in his column about it, and when it got really hot there were some people who said we ought to give up the whole thing.

"The president said, 'Hell, no. We're going to forget all about those attacks. That's the reason these things don't get done because somebody puts on a little heat. If all of you are afraid and want to cut and run, you just do it. Transfer it to me. I'll be the nonprofit organization that gets it built.'

"He went to Nixon in 1971 or 1972 and said, 'Somebody is screwing with my program. I haven't asked for much, but this is something that I started, something that's good, that's worthwhile, and I won't benefit from it except for the enjoyment of seeing something worthwhile done. You tell your folks there isn't any stealing; nobody's getting anything out of this except old folks.

"This was direct to Nixon. And it got the dogs called off.

"After it was completed, we got the Catholic diocese as sponsor and they helped put up some of the money and we were going to name it the bishop somebody rest home.

"So somebody sent Johnson a memo, and he called me on the phone and said, 'Larry, what are they doing to me? You and Frank Erwin promised me that they would name it after my mother. All these years I have relied upon that, that it would be named for my mother.' I said, 'Mr. President, I thought you didn't want it named after your mother.' He said, 'Where did you get a silly idea like that? Why sure, I want it named after my mother. It would be a great honor to have it named after her. You promised me it would be named after my mother, and I counted on it, and now they aren't going to.'

"Anyway if you look out there on the freeway you'll see a series of lights. That's the Rebekah Baines Johnson Nursing Home."

Then there were the trips to Acapulco every February. Lyndon and Lady Bird and the people they brought with them or who flew in from New York and Washington and Texas stayed in an elegant villa owned by former Mexican President, Miguel Aléman. The Johnsons flew in family, friends, air-conditioners as well as a cook, liquor, food, and bottled water. Nobody needed to fear Montezuma's revenge during that month in the sun. Arthur Krim sent down the latest movies for evening viewing, and Lyndon invariably went to sleep during the showings.

Mary Hardesty: "When he was in Acapulco there were always people coming and going, including what we called the 'Beautiful People'—like the Laurence Rockefellers and Mollie Parnis—but on this one visit there were just six of us at the breakfast table, and we didn't get up from the table until lunch time.

"He was in rare form that day, stories, imitations, things he remembered—his youth, the presidency, his years in the Senate. Just everything, and all of it was so fascinating that we didn't realize any time at all had passed, and Mrs. Johnson finally said something about if we were going to have lunch . . . and we looked at our watches and couldn't believe it.

"People were always invited with no more than twenty-four hours notice. He called it 'keeping my options open.' I suppose some people were upset, but you could never remain upset for long because he was so amusing. If he was sad and depressed then, it was not apparent to those of us who were around him."

Mollie Parnis: "Some people would call it selfish, and I suppose it would have been selfish if he'd thought about it. But if he wanted to sit on the beach in the morning, we all sat on the beach in the morning because it never occurred to him that that wasn't what everybody would want to do."

Robert Livingston: "I remember the first trip my mother, Mollie Parnis, ever made to Acapulco. He had just finished his book. He would sit and read, passage by passage, aloud. She said later, 'I thought I was going out of my mind.' She said he would say, 'What do you think of this?' And you had to sit there and he would read and read, and then he'd say, 'And now I'm going to tell you what I said to George Ball . . .'"

Although Lyndon considered himself totally out of politics and refused to give interviews to reporters—which fed the rumors that he was massively depressed—on April 7, 1970, in Washington he sat down to a five-hour lunch with reporters and editors from the *Washington Post*.[4] In March he had gotten angina and been hospitalized in San Antonio, and according to Richard Harwood, "He came in . . . looking less tall, less bulky than I had remembered him. His hair was almost completely white, and was growing long in the back."

Haynes Johnson: "He was somewhat subdued when he came into the room. . . . He was on a diet of 850 calories a day, he said, and was getting back his strength gradually. There had been quite a bit of pain this time."

Harwood: "As he talked . . . he seemed to take on another appearance: The pallor and signs of sickness went away and all of a sudden you were sitting with a vigorous, commanding, strong man whose mind was so clear, so well organized, so quick that you suddenly became aware of the power of that personality, of the ability to dominate and persuade and overwhelm. . . . What came through above all was not his 'complexity' but the simplicity of his passions and loves and hates and singleness of his mind and mental processes. People were loyal or disloyal; brave or cowardly; constant or inconstant; petty or grand; they loved their country or they were sunshine patriots. The war had obviously left him baffled about the attitudes of his country and had hurt him because it obscured the great works of the Great Society, a cause in which he still believed."

When the entire afternoon passed and he did not return, Lady Bird sent over an anxious note, which was delivered by a maid, asking him to please come rest.

Haynes Johnson: "LBJ said, 'I want you to know, no matter how we differ about things, I feel I am at the table of friends, and I want to thank you for letting me come and visit with you.' He got up and left after shaking hands with each person present."

Harwood: "There were some bitter-end Johnson critics around that table, but they didn't have the heart or desire to sock it to him. They sat there, drinking it all in, and when it was over some had tears in their eyes and they all stood up and gave him their applause."

Haynes Johnson: "We thought we might never see his likes again. And perhaps we were right."[5]

In that summer of 1970 the birthplace was officially transferred to the National Park Service. Lyndon was very proud of the birthplace home and since it was so near the Ranch he couldn't resist any opportunity to conduct a personal tour or to sell some copies of his memoirs. He'd ride over in his convertible, with the top down, waving to people. "You all come on in." And he would take them on a tour pointing out "that was my crib," and "that's my mother's this and my mother's that," and according to Yolanda Boozer, whenever she couldn't find him for a meeting, she would call the birthplace and sure enough someone would say, "He's been here all morning," or "He's just leaving; he's been here for two hours, and we've done a booming business selling books."

Boozer: "I soon became aware that one of my duties was selling *The Vantage Point* at the birthplace, and every day I would have to give him an account of how many copies were sold. He would stop at the birthplace himself and shake hands with people and say, 'Aren't ya gonna buy one of my books?' . . . 'Now if you do I'll sign it right here—give me a pen!' And he'd start signing—and before we knew it there was a crowd and a line of people."

Into the Lyndon Baines Johnson Library and the establishment of the Lyndon Baines Johnson School of Public Affairs on the campus of the University of Texas at Austin went Lyndon's hopes for posterity. "It's all here," he said at the dedication of the library in May 1971, "the story of our time—with the bark off. There is no record of a mistake, nothing critical, ugly or unpleasant that is not included in the files here. We have papers from my four years of public service in one place for friend and foe to judge, to approve or disapprove." There were, too, his hopes for giving his fellow Texans the kind of intellectual opportunities then seemingly only enjoyed by Harvard intellectuals and their ilk. The library is the national respository of every slip of paper, every document having to do with Lyndon's long public life; Lyndon himself said there were thirty-one million of them, there are now several million more. The building, known locally as the mausoleum, is architecturally forbidding, certainly uninspired from the outside. Inside the documents are backed with handsome red folders, five stories of them encased in glass.

Dedication day, May 22, 1971, was a typical May day in Texas, alternating clear and threatening, very windy. The spray from the outdoor fountain, which normally shoots up into the air fifty to sixty feet, became uncontrollable when the wind gauge failed to operate, resulting in a number of distinguished and disgruntled guests getting their feet wet, among them Humphrey, Muskie, Goldwater, Dillon, and members of the Johnson cabinet.

Senator Philip Hart of Michigan summed it up by saying, "I never thought I'd come to Austin, Texas, and know half the people I saw."

According to Monk Willis, for Lyndon "that was the greatest day in the world. He was in hog-heaven that day. He had them all there—Goldwater and all the bunch. Nixon came . . ."

Yes, Nixon came, but so did the demonstrators, some two thousand strong, sixty Vietnam veterans in the vanguard. They were not allowed too close—the whole area was blocked off by the Secret Service—but their chants "No more war" and "Johnson's war" could at times be heard with a kind of Greek chorus effect to Nixon's speech, accepting the library for the country.

The library had a helicopter landing pad on its roof, and Lyndon would often fly there from the Ranch. Someone pointed out that while Lyndon Johnson was not exiled royalty, he tended to live like one.

As with the birthplace, he was avidly interested in the numbers of tourists visiting the library, and he would seize at opportunities to get people to the library.

Harry Middleton: "One day at a football game at the stadium, which is just across the street from the library, Johnson said, 'Ask the announcer to announce over the public address system that after the game people should come to the library for some cool water and to go to the can.'"

Harry didn't think much of the suggestion—the library had all of one public water fountain, and one public bathroom for each sex—though Lyndon would probably get a few books sold and be able to show off a few memorabilia before the riot started.

But even without football game attendances, the library prospered. By its fifth anniversary, attendance had passed the three million mark—averaging more than two thousand visitors a day. Not a bad memorial at that.

*　　*　　*

Warren Woodward: "His craggy face was kind and mellow in those days. His hair was long; it swept back and curled on the ends like that of an elder statesman in the Andy Jackson vein. The lines in his face were deep, but in all, Lyndon Johnson appeared less strange than in those horrendous days at the end of his term. Outside the gaze of the public eye, he aged gracefully."[6]

"But he aged quickly, too."

Woodward accompanied Lyndon in the spring of 1972 to Tennessee for Buford Ellington's funeral, after which Lyndon and Bird went on to Charlottesville to visit Lynda and her family. There Lyndon suffered another heart attack.

Ted Gittinger: "There is a persistent story that Lyndon at Charlottesville in '72 got up from bed and said, 'Bird, I'm goin' home to die—you can come if you want to,' or words to that effect. It was a typical Lyndon remark; Sam Ealy had said almost exactly the same thing when he was dying."

Leo Janos: "Convinced he was dying,[7] he browbeat Lady Bird and his doctors into allowing him to fly home to Texas. So, late in the night of his third day of intensive care, a desperately sick LBJ was rushed to the airport and ferried back to Brooke Army Medical Center in San Antonio. The departure was so sudden that the Charlottesville hospital director, hearing a rumor that Johnson might try to leave, rushed to the hospital only to find LBJ's empty wheelchair in the parking lot.

"Miraculously he survived, but the remaining seven months of his life became a sad and pain-wracked ordeal. 'I'm hurting real bad,' he confided to friends. The chest pains hit him nearly every afternoon—a series of sharp, jolting pains that left him scared and breathless. A portable oxygen tank stood next to his bed and Johnson periodically interrupted what he was doing to lie down and put on the mask to gulp air."[8]

Despite the pain Lyndon had hoped, said he had hoped, anyway, to attend the 1972 Democratic convention in July in Miami Beach, "if only to stand up and take a bow." But Larry O'Brien, among others, sent word that his attendance would be unwise. There would be demonstrations and possibly violence. Lyndon had wanted Ed Muskie as the presidential candidate, but when it turned out to be his persistent critic, Senator George McGovern, Johnson loyally said he would support him.

Lyndon had followed the convention on television. What he saw and heard depressed him. It was not the party he had known and supported his whole life through. True, there were some of the old familiar faces, comforting to behold, but who in heaven's name were all these others—the long hairs, the gays; what was gay?—and these odd movie stars?

Still, in his role as elder statesman, Lyndon was not above dispensing advice to presidential candidates. McGovern listened but seemed not to have heard.

Liz Carpenter: "I was in the plane with McGovern, flying into Texas, and we got Johnson on the phone and he said, 'I would quit attacking Nixon on Vietnam. Everybody knows that it's behind us. But,' he said, 'I would go after him on the Big Rich.' He said, 'The Republicans always sell you out to Wall Street and this is the worst bunch of all.'

"It was the most critical thing I ever heard Johnson say about Nixon. And McGovern hung up the telephone and did exactly what he was planning to do, which was to go on about the war."

Nevertheless, McGovern did make a little-known pilgrimage to the Ranch.[9]

George McGovern: "We arrived there about 10:30 in the morning, and visited with him and Lady Bird under a big live oak tree.

"He started off by asking me if I got his telegram congratulating me on the nomination and I told him I had and appreciated it. He said, 'Well, I want you to know, I'm for you. I know there are people around here saying that they think they can please me by opposing George McGovern, but,' he said, 'they're not talking for me. I'm for you. I've always supported the Democratic nominee and I'm going to support you.' And he made that point in a dozen different ways.

"Then he said, 'Now on the war. I think you're crazy as hell, and you think I'm crazy as hell; so let's just not talk about that. Let's talk about America and about this election.' And then he proceeded to tell me what he thought I needed to do to correct certain suspicions about me in the minds of the American people. He said, 'I would tell the people of this country that America has been good to me. That when I was a poor boy growing up in South Dakota, my father and mother had no money but they did give me the opportunity to go to school. That my state had given me the opportunity to serve in the House and Senate of the United States. That I was proud and privileged to serve the country in wartime as a bomber pilot in World War II and that I wanted to serve the nation as president.'

"He said, 'Tell 'em some of the homespun, down-to-earth background of yours. It doesn't hurt to let people know you're proud of this country.' I thought it was very good advice and I wish I'd done more of it.

"Along about one thirty, as we were finishing lunch, I could tell he was in some physical pain. So I asked him how he was feeling and he said, 'Well, every day I start out pretty well, but then by afternoon these damn pains start bothering me, and at four o'clock, I'm pretty well through. I go lay down.' So we stayed maybe another hour, and he stayed with us till we left. He struck me as a man who really knew he had something terribly wrong with him, although he didn't seem to be distressed about it."

It is impossible to believe that Lyndon Johnson felt any enthusiasm for Richard Nixon, who had defeated Lyndon's old friend Helen Gahagan Douglas in a campaign of monumental ugliness and who Mr. Sam thought was the worst man he had ever served with. But he did nothing for McGovern except write one letter to a local weekly newspaper endorsing him. Not that McGovern wanted him to do more.

Thomas G. Corcoran: "He thought McGovern was the most inept politician, inept presidential candidate anyway, in all of history."

Those who heard Lyndon's remarks, always private, about McGovern, said they were often the same as what he had said about King Olaf of Norway after a state dinner, "He is the dumbest king I have ever met. I didn't know they made kings that dumb.

"I didn't know they *made* presidential candidates that dumb."

Lyndon was not at all surprised in November, when, despite the whiff of Watergate, Nixon won the election; he did express amazement—quite often—that a Democratic candidate could carry only *one* state. Even in 1936 Alf Landon of Kansas, who was a Republican, for Christ's sake, had carried *two*.

To be sure, Lyndon's weakness grew every day. But he did use his waning energies for speaking out about what he still cared for, had always cared for. He was always a man who knew what his priorities were.

He accepted an invitation to speak on September 16, 1972, at the seventy-fifth anniversary of the Scott and White Clinic in Temple, Texas. And he immediately got in touch with Horace Busby.

Horace Busby: "He called me in Washington and asked if I would come down and work with him on what he wanted to say. 'I would like to get some things off my chest,' he explained.

"When I arrived at the Ranch, he almost seemed to be waiting at the door. I was hardly inside before he picked up a favorite cap and headed outside, saying, 'Come on, we need to take a long ride.'

"The ride continued through the morning and into early afternoon. Reluctantly, it appeared, he said he had to return to the house. 'If I don't get my oxygen and my sleep,' he explained, 'I begin to feel it in my chest.' At his request, I followed him on into the bedroom. He changed into pajamas, spent a few minutes adjusting the oxygen controls, and finally slipped under the covers. Holding the oxygen mask in one hand, he began 'dictating' what he wanted to say, gesturing as he did so with the other hand.

"'This country isn't over the hill,' he said, 'We aren't on the skids. This is a just country. It's a beautiful country. All this moaning and complaining isn't true, isn't right and it isn't leadership.'

"When I sat down at the typewriter, I knew I had received two messages that morning—one was Lyndon Johnson's message about the country, the other was a distinct message about himself. The message about himself composed the first lines of the text of the speech.

"'With the coming of September each year, we are reminded, as the song says, that the days are dwindling down to a precious few. By the calendar, we know that soon the green leaves of summer will begin to brown; the chill winds of winter will begin to blow and—before we are ready for the end to come—the year will be gone.'

"When we were alone in the office he read the first lines aloud for still another time.

"'That's just right,' he said. 'That's just the way I wanted it.'" [10]

Despite a growing feebleness and the almost unending pain, when his old friend and admirer Isabelle Shelton of the *Washington Star* visited him on September 22, she found "a man of rare tranquillity presiding over his ranch on the Pedernales.

"On that night, former Democratic governor John Connally, once a Johnson protégé, was giving a party at his nearby ranch for President Nixon and the Texas Democrats who had 'switched' for the year.

"Johnson alluded during the evening at his home, to the 'nice party I hear John and

Nellie are givin' tonight.' In the same breath he talked about the visit several weeks earlier from George McGovern.

"The former president talked in gentleness about the campaign, dropping remarks in with after-dinner reminiscences about past events as if it all had happened a long time ago.

"While the humor and memory and charm were there, the passion was gone.

"Still the expansive host, Johnson once again had swept up his visitors for a twilight tour of the acres of Texas country bearing the LBJ brand. He didn't drive the car anymore. Mrs. Malechek was at the wheel, and the former president and Lady Bird were squeezed in beside her.

"Otherwise, little seemed changed. He was still in command, as the car rode the familiar, sprawling spread, pursuing deer that leaped out of the headlights' glare." [11]

Then in October 1972 the final negotiations for the sale of the TV station were completed.

Leonard Marks: "He kept pressuring that he wanted to sell the TV station, and I kept urging him not to do it. He asked me what it was worth, and I told him. It was a very desirable property and I'm sure that there were clients of ours who would be willing to buy it. He said, 'No, don't you do anything about it. I have to make up my mind.' Then one day he called me and told me that he had been in discussion with the L.A. *Times* [the *Times-Mirror*]. He personally handled this. He told me that the president of the L.A. *Times* and his lawyer were coming to Austin. So I went to Austin and we spent a couple of days on negotiations. He handled it masterfully. God—if he hadn't been president, he'd have been the biggest tycoon this world has ever seen. He'd have rivaled the head of the largest corporation. He'd have made the largest fortune.

"He didn't look good that October. He was suffering, you could tell. He was speaking at a slower pace. We were worried because he stayed up too late, but you weren't going to tell him that."

On December 31, Lyndon called Horace Busby again and, among other things, talked about his plans for the coming year.

Busby: "He wanted, he said, 'to get really active this year.'

"'After the inauguration,' he explained, 'we'll have four years behind us and I think I can speak up a little more. I've got some programs up there that are kicking around and I'd like to go more places and see more people again.'

"While he did not always take kindly to inquiries about his health, I ventured a question anyway, asking how he had been feeling.

"'Just fair,' he replied, 'I'm trying to get in better shape so the doctors will let me go to Mexico next month and rest up in the sun. But it's not good.'" [12]

Lyndon never went to Mexico. He did, however, during those few weeks left before he died, attend three funerals.

Lady Bird: "He was very upset by going to funerals, but he made himself go. I kept telling him sometimes that he didn't have to go, but he really felt that he should. And each one was a particularly harrowing experience. One was the memorial service for

Hale Boggs, who had disappeared and no doubt died months before. That, as I recall, was probably in December.

"Another was in a way the most tragic of all. A whole busload of young school children were going to some church affair in south Austin. They were killed and they had a mass funeral service and a mass burial. He went to that, and that's one that I felt sure he could skip."

But Johnson had a special closeness to the people in south Austin where the busload of children were killed. Horace Busby talks about how Austin's proud old family elite in the north "resented him politically and were contemptuous of him socially . . . but across the river, in the modest homes of south Austin where the 'little people' lived, he always had the votes.

"'These people,' he said, with sudden intensity, 'are my people. When nobody else was with me, they stood by me. When they hurt, I hurt. Nothing,' he repeated the word twice more, 'is ever going to keep me away from them in times like they're going through.'"[13]

Lady Bird: "The third funeral was President Truman's of course. Those three, each one a very real, harrowing emotional experience in their different ways."

Erwin: "Just a couple of weeks before he died, he invited me to bring my two boys out to the Ranch. He insisted on going around with us, helping select the horses, etc.

"He'd made peace with himself and pretty much got everything done. He'd gotten his book written; the library was operating; he'd gotten his fiscal affairs in order and sold the television station. He'd gone over it very intelligently. He balanced his gifts of his land against the profit of the television station. He itemized his taxes. I mean, he was on top of everything."

Marks: "About two weeks before his death I came down to Austin to a meeting of the Lyndon Baines Johnson Library. Frank Stanton was along. We were going back in Frank's plane. LBJ said he wouldn't drive out to the airport with us, which he customarily did. . . . The helicopter was going to pick him up and take him to the Ranch. It was about two weeks before his death. LBJ took me aside and led me out toward the hall, and he says, 'You know, I want to thank you so much for all you've done for me and the family. Over the years, you've been so loyal and so faithful and so good. Frequently, we take these things for granted and we never say what we mean. I just want you to know I'm very grateful.' Gave me the shivers and I said, 'Why are you telling me this? You've got a long way to travel.' He said, 'No, I used to feel that way, but I don't anymore.' It was his way of saying good-bye. And he did it with a couple of other people, I since learned."

Lyndon Baines Johnson died at 3:50 P.M. on January 22, 1973. A few minutes before his death he called the Ranch switchboard from his bedroom. He asked for Mike Howard, one of the Secret Service men. Howard was momentarily unavailable, but the switchboard operator reached two other agents, Ed Newland and Harry Harris. They rushed to the bedroom with a portable oxygen unit. Lyndon was lying on the floor beside the bed and appeared to be dead. They tried to revive him, Newland with mouth-to-mouth resuscitation. He was unsuccessful; when Howard reached the bedroom at 3:55 and tried external heart massage, that, too, was unsuccessful.

At 4:05 Mrs. Johnson was reached in a car near the library, and as soon as possible she took a helicopter from the library to San Antonio. At 4:19 the body was placed aboard a family plane, a Beech King Air, and flown to the Brooke Army Medical Center, where the president was pronounced dead. Mrs. Johnson arrived at 4:49; later she returned to the apartment above the television station in Austin, where she spent the night. In the *Washington Post* Haynes Johnson wrote: "Perhaps the most poignant aspect of Lyndon Johnson's death is that this most public man, who was in his element when surrounded by cheering crowds, died alone, calling for help. His wife, who had stood by him in every crisis and on whom he relied so much, was away. His daughters, grandchildren, cronies, and friends whom he loved to regale with his inimitable stories, were absent." [14]

The day and night after his death, he lay in state at the library where about twenty thousand people filed past the flag-draped casket. People were still arriving the next morning when the body was removed and flown to Washington and taken from the airport to the Capitol rotunda.

Harry Provence: "The citizens of Washington lined up early along Constitution Avenue to await in the crisp sunlight the arrival for the last time of the man whose 'reach for greatness' had affected them for most of their lifetime.

"At 2:20 P.M. the funeral coach from Andrews Air Force Base met the horse-drawn caisson at Sixteenth and K streets beside the White House where LBJ labored for five years and more. The military units and the limousines bearing family and officials swung in line. The long march to the Capitol drummed up the avenue with a beat become all too familiar to spectators and to TV viewers in the past decade.

"Some eighteen thousand military men walked ahead of the caisson as it was pulled by seven white geldings. There was the mournful sound of muffled drums as the uniformed troops marched at 120 paces a minute.

"Behind the caisson was the riderless horse, Black Jack, boots and spurs reversed in the stirrups, denoting a fallen leader." [15]

James Blundell: "My wife and I went to the Capitol where he was lying in state. We got there about one in the morning. It was the coldest night of the winter. The line was toward the back of the Supreme Court. My wife said, 'It's going to take a long time, but it's all right.' But it was cold. I just watched that crowd. I guess 60 percent were black. I listened to the conversations. One black woman, with a little girl, said, 'People don't know it, but he did more for us than anybody, any president, ever did.' They were aware. That was his epitaph as far as I was concerned."

Dorothy McCardle: "Leonard Marks had just come down from the Hill. He said that Mrs. Johnson had said that the thing Lyndon hated most was to be by himself. So we all decided to keep watch beside his casket."

The next morning the casket was moved to the National City Christian Church at eight o'clock. The pastor, Dr. G.R. Davis, conducted the service.

Leontyne Price, at her request, sang "Take My Hand, Precious Lord," and "Onward Christian Soldiers."

Nancy Dickerson: "The day of the funeral was perfect—cold but brilliantly sunny. Lady Bird was dignified, proud, and splendid. President Nixon led the official mourners, and members of the establishment, including some of the hypocrites who had maligned him in life, were there in full force. In death they could not tarnish the moment which belonged to those loyalists who had stood by him through the years and knew how hard he had tried, especially on Vietnam. The day belonged to those who understood that although victory had eluded him and events had proved him wrong, he had given more than they could ask of themselves. . . . No man could have tried harder. It was for these people, and not for the Washington establishment, that the first line of the eulogy was intended.

"Marvin Watson, the Johnson friend and aide who also came from the Texas Hill Country, stood up and defiantly began, 'He was ours and we loved him beyond all telling of it.'" [16]

Bob Ray Sanders: "To me Lyndon Johnson was the greatest President that ever sat in Washington or Philadelphia. I am the first to admit that my feelings are very selfish and very personal.

"You see, I can remember not being admitted in downtown movie houses in my hometown, Fort Worth, Texas.

"I can remember riding on the back of the bus, and then riding a yellow bus to school each day because some people in this part of the country felt I wasn't good enough to go to school with white children—even those who lived near me.

"I can remember not being allowed in Fort Worth cafeterias unless, of course, I was going there to wash dishes or clean up.

"I can remember the 'white' and 'colored' signs over water fountains and on rest room doors in department stores.

"I can remember thinking as I started to college that I probably would not be able to get a job in Texas because of that plague called discrimination.

"But then, I, too, can remember watching on television—I think it was July 2, 1964, as that far-reaching civil rights bill was signed into law by the president, Lyndon Johnson. Moments before I had almost cried as the president stood before the world and told why such legislation was needed—I knew he was right because I was standing in line with the rest of the needy.

"I also remember that moving State of the Union address, when the president borrowed the slogan from the civil rights movement and declared '*we* shall overcome . . .' And I felt he was right, and I still hoped that he was right.

"And I remember one day while in Austin working on a story about the soon-to-open Lyndon Baines Johnson Library that the former president came over and chatted, not about anything in particular, but he did mention that the library was going to be something for future generations to enjoy.

"I don't care what anybody else says. When it comes to presidents, to me, the man with the horn-rimmed glasses and beautiful southern accent was my 'main man.'" [17]

The body was returned to Austin late on the afternoon of the twenty-fifth and was taken in a motorcade to the Ranch, where before several hundred people Father

Wunibald Schneider, the priest at the little church in Stonewall, gave the eulogy. He quoted from Lyndon Johnson's favorite book in the Bible, Ecclesiastes: "Mourn but a little for the dead for they are at rest." John B. Connally contributed: "Along this stream and under these trees he loved he will now rest. He first saw light here. He last felt life here. May he now find peace here."

Bill Porterfield: "The matriarch of the Johnson clan was Aunt Jessie Hermine Johnson Hatcher, at eighty-eight the ninth and last surviving child of Grandfather Sam Ealy Johnson, Sr. Now there was never any question about Aunt Jessie's attendance at the graveside services. The doughty old girl would be there to see her Lyndon off. The prayer was that she would not catch her death of cold.

"The twenty-one-cannon salute fell short by two. A howitzer misfired twice. . . .

"Aunt Jessie Hatcher, two weeks to the day . . . caught a cold and it went into pneumonia. They buried her in the same cemetery."[18]

The Rev. Dr. Billy Graham was also at the graveside; he, too, spoke of Lyndon Johnson's love of the Hill Country, and he quoted John Donne on death: "It comes equally to us all and makes us all equal when it comes."

Luci: "I remember a black man hobbled up. He was ninety-two years old. I tried to comfort him by telling him my father loved him and his people, 'Ma'am, you don't have to tell me he loved me. He showed he loved me. A tree would have had to fall over me to keep me from being here today.'"

THE FAREWELL ADDRESS

Roger Wilkins was not at the funeral, but he remembers very well the last time he saw Lyndon Johnson, at an evening party in New York in the fall of 1971 at Molly Parnis's.

Roger Wilkins: "We'd been told that Lyndon Johnson would be there and he was. His back was to us, and he was standing there telling a story, and his hair had turned white, but he was still huge, and you could see his head bobbing, telling a story to a star-studded audience. Mrs. Johnson was standing there and Walter Cronkite and Barbara Walters and David Frost.

"So Parnis goes and grabs his arm as he's talking, and you know, he didn't want to be interrupted for nothing, right? So he kind of shakes her off, but she's persistent. He finishes the story and then turns toward me and he has this funny look like, 'Who is this I'm about to meet?' on his big huge face of his. All of a sudden his face goes into a kind of puzzle and he says, 'I know, I know you.'

"I said, 'You should know me, Mr. President. You made me.' He said, 'Little Roger!'[1] I was smoking a cigarette, and at that point he gives me a bear hug, just grabs me like that. Well, he was so big, you know, and I didn't want to burn him with my cigarette; so he's got me bending backwards.

"And while he's holding me, he starts telling all those assembled celebrities what a great man I am and he goes on about that. 'Oh, this man went out into the dangerous places during the sixties, and we couldn't have gotten through the sixties without him and he did this and he did that and he's one of the great public servants of our time.' It was bullshit, but I loved it.

"So then he and I moved to the side, and I found myself saying, 'Mr. President, when you were president you said that you wanted to finish the job that Lincoln had begun, and I'm puzzled. Just because Richard Nixon is president doesn't mean that you don't have one of the two most powerful voices in this country. That's a voice we desperately need now and I don't see why you're not speaking up. I really don't. The country needs you and needs you to speak out on those things and I wish you would,' and he said, 'Do you really think so?' I said, 'Oh, yes sir, I surely do. People respect you and your voice is really needed.' And so he said, 'Well, what should I do?' And I said, 'Talk to somebody,' and he said, 'Like who?' And I said, 'I guess the black guy you like best is Uncle Roy.' I said, 'Hell, why don't you have him down to the Ranch?' And he said, 'You know, I was going to have this celebration for the library and maybe that's a good time to do that. I think I will.'

"I said, 'Mr. President, it would be a great thing if you did.'

"So then I was off talking to another group later in the party and I looked across the room or something and he was off by himself, leaning against the piano, just all by himself, looking at me, and I smiled at him and he smiled at me, a very gentle, sweet smile. He just waved at me and smiled. That was the last time I saw him.

"And then, before he died, he made that marvelous speech."

Shortly after the library was dedicated in May 1971, it was decided, largely by Lyndon himself, that there would be a series of symposia, national figures as well as local, meeting to debate various public issues. Education, for instance. What had been done for it during the administration of the man who wanted to be known as "the education president?" And what was its status three years after he had left the White House? The second—again it was largely Lyndon's idea—was to be on civil rights.

Harry Middleton: "The symposium on education was in January 1972 and was very good. We started planning the civil rights symposium almost immediately. That was to be in December that same year.

"It was to open on Monday, December 11, and the night before the president was to have a reception at his home, at the Ranch.

"But that Sunday turned out to be a bitterly cold day. So cold and icy was it that we got word that the plane carrying many of the participants from Washington couldn't land at the Austin airport, and they would have to come here by bus. So it just looked as if everything was getting off in a shambles.

"We had a suite for the Warrens and a suite for the Humphreys, but because of the late hours the bellboys weren't on and everybody was carrying luggage.

"We tried to get everybody going early the next morning, which was hard because it had been a late night the night before, and then we got word that the president couldn't get in from the Ranch, it was so icy. I was just heartsick at that. But then we got word that he was coming anyway, that he was at the wheel himself, that he got impatient with whoever was driving this snowmobile, and he took over and drove it. At any rate, he did appear, just at the magic moment, and he was there all that day, and we had a reception in the library that night and he seemed to be in very good form."

Lady Bird: "Lyndon had been quite sick the night before and up most of the night. The doctor came at six o'clock in the morning. I was determined that he wasn't going to attend that symposium, and the doctor insisted that he absolutely, positively could not go—but he went.

"I now realize it was all right that he went, because he knew what he was spending and had a right to decide how he wanted to spend it."

Who would have thought, though, that it would ever get that cold and icy in Austin, Texas? Elspeth Rostow, chairman of the planning committee for the symposium, remembered:

"On Sunday, it got colder and icier, and the Secret Service called saying they thought I should know that the plane containing Chief Justice Warren, Senator and Mrs. Humphrey, etc., was experiencing brake difficulty over San Antonio. So they bused participants from San Antonio to Austin, which gave Earl Warren a good opener. He said he expected to come here to discuss civil rights but not actually be bused in order to do it. The next morning I couldn't get out. I was supposed to introduce Humphrey in the morning. I missed that. The symposium had started when I got there—about noon. LBJ was wearing boots and enjoying every minute of it. He looked at me and said, 'Well, I drove here seventy miles and in my condition. The first thing I asked, "Where is Mrs. Rostow?" They said, "Mr. President, she hasn't been able to make it." "How far away does she live?" "Four miles, I guess, Mr. President!"' And he enjoyed this immensely."

Hugh Sidey: "The strain took its toll. For Johnson . . . the night was filled with pain and restlessness. His doctors suggested, pleaded, ordered him to give up his scheduled address the next day. He ignored them. He put on his dark-blue presidential suit and those flawlessly polished oxfords and came back the next morning."[2]

Middleton: "We were scheduled to begin at nine o'clock. The president showed up, much to our surprise. He didn't look very good. I told him that if he wanted to, he didn't have to go out in front, that we had a closed circuit television monitor in the back, and he could go watch it on closed circuit. So he did that. Mrs. Johnson came, and she spent part of her time out in the audience and part of it with him."

Sidey: "The men and women who carried the civil rights banner for two decades had assembled. There were some new faces among them, but the focus was on men like Hubert Humphrey, Roy Wilkins, Clarence Mitchell and former Chief Justice Earl Warren. They showed up with more wrinkles than they used to have, more gray hair, and a lot more discouragement. From the beginnings of the two-day meeting it was plain that civil rights no longer had a clear national leader. Nor could anyone perceive any sympathy for the cause in the White House."[3]

Some of the newer faces in the symposium included Patricia Roberts Harris, Vernon E. Jordan, Jr., Reynaldo G. Garza, Barbara Jordan, Julian Bond, Henry Gonzalez. And some others with different ideas.

Middleton: "There were people in the audience who were making demands for equal time. Tom Johnson and I met with them. I said, 'We've got this thing all set up. It's going to be a terrible intrusion if we try to open it up for you, but I'll make a request of the chairman, and I'll abide by whatever he says.' So I got Burke Marshall to come down, and I told him about it, and he said, 'Well, I don't think we ought to do it. But I think in fairness to the president we ought to let him know that they've planned a demonstration if we don't.'

"So I went back to where the president was watching on closed-circuit television. Then I began to be aware of the fact that he was not well at all. It just took all the courage that I could muster to tell him, because this was such a happy occasion for him. I said, 'Mr. President, I hate to tell you this, but you've got to make a decision. I wish I could make it for you, but I can't.' And I told him what was happening, and that Burke Marshall was just totally against doing this, but that if we didn't do it, it might turn the whole thing into a shambles.

"The president said, 'Well, ask Burke to come in here for a moment.' So I went to the platform and got Burke. And the president said, 'Burke, I'm not really afraid of that demonstration. I've seen lots of them. I just don't want anybody to think that they haven't had a chance to speak. We're talking about equal rights, and I think that you and I would not really want people to leave here thinking that they were not going to get their chance to say something. So I think we ought to give them some time.'

"Marshall went back out, and at an appropriate time, he said, 'There is a group here that has asked for special time because they feel the position they want to make has not been made, and it is President Johnson's wish that their presentation be made.'

"Then it went back to normal and then it came time for the president to speak. He had slipped in and was sitting on a front seat.

"And I don't suppose that anybody who saw him come up will ever forget it. He was very slow on those steps. He had a good speech to make—he went further in this speech than he had ever gone before. He began slowly; he warmed up to it."

At one point Lyndon took a nitroglycerin pill out of his pocket and popped it into his mouth, the first time, and the last, that he did that in public. He talked in a low but steady voice for about twenty minutes. Among the things he said were:

I didn't want this symposium to spend two days talking about what we have done. The progress has been much too small; we haven't done nearly enough. I'm kind of ashamed of myself that I had six years and couldn't do more. . . . So let no one delude himself that his work is done . . . as I see it, the black problem is not one of just regions or states or cities or neighborhoods. It is a problem, a concern, and responsibility of this whole nation. Moreover, and we cannot obscure this blunt fact, the black problem remains what it has always been, the simple problem of being black in a white society. That is the problem which our efforts have not addressed.

To be black, I believe, to one who is black or brown, is to be proud, is to be worthy, is to be honorable. But to be black in a white society is not to stand on level and equal ground. While the races may stand side by side, whites stand on history's mountain and blacks stand in history's hollow. We must overcome unequal history before we overcome unequal opportunity. . . .

This is precisely the work which we must continue. This is the whole important part of this meeting. Not what we have done, what we can do. So little have we done. So much we must do. . . .

It's time we get down to the business of trying to stand black and white on level ground. . . .

We know there's injustice. We know there's intolerance. We know there's discrimination and hate and suspicion. And we know there's division among us. But there is a larger truth. We have proved that great progress is possible. We know how much still remains to be done. And if our efforts continue and if our will is strong and if our hearts are right and if courage remains our constant companion, then, my fellow Americans, I am confident we shall overcome.

Sidey: "When he was done he acknowledged the applause and stepped off the stage to take a seat in the auditorium. Then squabbling broke out among the black factions."[4]

The more radical of the blacks present wanted the symposium to express their views, particularly their views of the Nixon administration. The Reverend Kendall Smith of the National Council of Churches in New York, and Roy Innes, chairman of the Congress of Racial Equality, had composed a statement, which Smith then delivered: "Racism under the administration of Richard Nixon has increased. This gathering of great Americans must not leave Austin without an organized, ongoing structure dedicated to reconvening and to combatting injustice in America, as was done by your Administration. . . .

"To adjourn today makes this symposium no more than an empty ritual honoring one man. . . . For this symposium not to expand and deal with a new definition of equality is to refuse the sun of a new day. We demand the extension of today's agenda."

Middleton: "The President bounded back up the steps then, and by this time it was the old LBJ of vintage times, and he put on this splendid performance that everybody remembers. Totally impromptu. Totally impromptu! The formal speech had ended; now it was just Lyndon Johnson from the courthouse square."

Sidey: "The fatigue of the night before seemed to drop away, the old adrenaline machine pumping back into action. Going to the microphone with his hands molding the air, he delivered one of his sermons on brotherhood and reason, flavoring it with one of those marvelous stories about a backwoods judge and the town drunk, reminiscences of when he arrived in Hoover's Washington and the bonus marchers were driven down Pennsylvania Avenue."[5]

Lyndon: "Now I want you to go back all of you, and counsel together—the way Burke Marshall used to in the Kennedy days and later in the Johnson days—in that soft, kind way. Just cool and push off wrath, indulge, tolerate, and finally come out with a program with objectives, with organization. . . . Let's try to get our folks reasoning together and reasoning with the Congress, with the cabinet! Reason with the leadership and with the president. There's not a thing in the world wrong—as a matter of fact, there's everything right—about a group saying, 'Mr. President, we would like you to set aside an hour to let us talk.' And you don't need to start off by saying he's terrible, because he doesn't think he's terrible. Start talking about how you believe that he wants to do what's right and how you believe *this* is right, and you'll be surprised how many who want to do what's right will try to help you. . . .

"While I can't provide much go-go at this period of my life, I can provide a lot of hope and dream and encouragement, and I'll sell a few wormy calves now and then and contribute.

"Let's watch what's been done and see that it's preserved, but let's say we have just begun, and let's go on. Until every boy and girl born into this land, whatever state, whatever color, can stand on the same level ground, our job will not be done!"

Sidey: "People came to the stage and crowded around him as he tried to leave. They were all reaching for a bit of the old magic. But nobody got so much of it as Mr. Youngblood, a thin, aging black who used to wait on tables in Austin's ancient Driskill Hotel, where Johnson sweated out election night returns. The former president and the former waiter stood there for a few seconds gripping hands, and if any questions lingered about what Lyndon Johnson had tried to do for his country, they were answered right then."[6]

That was mid-December, and before January was over he was dead. But as Lady Bird said, he was right to have gone. He belonged there that day. He did know what he was spending, and afterwards, if you could have asked, you knew he would have said that he had no regrets.

ACKNOWLEDGMENTS

I owe a debt that can only be acknowledged, never paid, to Nancy Sorel, who arrived more than two years ago as a highly recommended and superbly qualified researcher; she very quickly became an editor and writer as well. Nancy, a former teacher of the English language at, among other places, the New School, is herself a published writer, the author of a book called *Word People*. She was a true collaborator on this book. It could never have been finished without her. It was only finished because of her.

Elisabeth A. Jakab arrived at G. P. Putnam's in May 1979 and was confronted with a huge suitcase full of most of an early draft of this manuscript, spent the next four months editing it, clarifying it, shaping it. Elisabeth arrived at my glass house in Brewster, New York, the Wednesday after Labor Day and she worked here four days a week every week save one until mid-December. She then returned to the Putnam offices in New York and continued to work on the manuscript until at last it went to the copy editor and the printer. I have worked with many editors; Elisabeth is the most diligent, the most helpful, the most intelligent, the most good-humored. Above all, the most skilled.

David W. Elliott, author of the novels *Listen to the Silence* and *Pieces of Night* and researcher for *Plain Speaking*, has been of enormous help in countless ways during the five years it has taken to create *Lyndon*.

Carol Hanley came in the summer of 1978 to type the manuscript; she very shortly became a researcher and writer with an extraordinary memory for details. I attribute the latter at least in part to the fact that she has eight children, all of them at home. She always knew where everything was and where what was missing should be. Carol also worked in the glass house, which bulged a little at times. She is still here, making sure that no detail is overlooked, no question unanswered.

My thanks, too, to Peter Israel, himself a writer and editor, who took much time off from corporate duties to see this book through its final editing; and to Edward C. Chase, who encouraged me to undertake the book and made it possible.

I am also grateful, as I have said, to Lady Bird Johnson, who patiently answered all my questions, which many times must have seemed naïve and impertinent. Lynda Robb and Luci Nugent were also generous with their time and memories.

Two Texas historians, Gary Gallagher, now a member of The Lyndon Baines Johnson Library staff, and Ted Gittinger, who are also both writers, were skilled researchers in Austin. Mike Gillette, chief of acquisitions and the oral history programs, was particularly helpful and generous with his time.

Of course the Lyndon Baines Johnson Library, with its more than thirty million documents, was basic to this book. During my fifty-eight visits there I consulted 276 oral histories of which I have made generous use. I consulted many more but made no use of them. Many persons taped before Lyndon's death apparently thought he would get up the morning the interview was transcribed and rush to the library to read it. At an earlier time he might have, but by the time most of the early interviews were done his energies had dwindled, though I doubt that his curiosity had. I am indebted to the oral historians T. Harri Baker, Dr. Joseph B. Frantz, Michael Gillette, Stephen Goodell, David G. McComb, and Paige Mulhollan. Harry Middleton, director of the library, gave me valued help. So did Philip Scott and James Wadsworth of the audio-visual archives. And Claudia Anderson, Yolanda Boozer, John Fawcett (now with the Library of Congress), Linda Hanson, Tina Lawson, and Nancy Smith all helped me many times in many ways.

Konrad Kelley and John Tiff were helpful with their own collection of oral histories and memories at the Lyndon B. Johnson National Historic Site in Johnson City.

I made use of the Franklin Roosevelt Library in Hyde Park, New York, and Nancy Sorel found a great many useful oral histories at the John F. Kennedy Library, which was then in temporary headquarters in Waltham, Massachusetts. William Johnson of the staff there was particularly helpful and patient.

The Texas collection in the Seth Richardson Room at the University of Texas at Austin was useful, and while I did not visit the familiar and loved Truman Library in Independence during the preparation of *Lyndon*, I consulted with its skilled staff by telephone many times. There were other libraries as well to mention. The staff of the public library in Danbury was especially forbearing when there were as many as half a dozen telephone calls a day. Also forbearing were the staffs of the libraries in White Plains, Katonah, and Greenburgh, New York.

Rae Sammis started what became a file of more than twelve thousand cards on *Lyndon*. Isabelle Bates rapidly typed large parts of the early drafts of this book. Nancy Perlman of G. P. Putnam's Sons tirelessly organized the typing and the retyping and the retyping. Coates Redmon, who became a friend, remembered things nobody else did and told me things nobody else could. Bill Broyles, editor of *Texas Monthly* and a friend, published much valued material, and past and current issues of the *Texas Observer* were always helpful.

ABBREVIATIONS

AAA—Agricultural Adjustment Act/Administration
ADA—Americans for Democratic Action
CCC—Civilian Conservation Corps
DRV—Democratic Republic of Vietnam
EEO—(President's Commission on) Equal Employment Opportunity
FCC—Federal Communications Commission
FEPC—Fair Employment Practices Commission
HEW—(Department of) Health, Education and Welfare
LCRA—Lower Colorado River Authority
NAACP—National Association for the Advancement of Colored People
NLF—National Liberation Front
NRA—National Recovery Act
NSC—National Security Council
NYA—National Youth Administration
OAS—Organization of American States
OEO—Office of Equal Opportunity
OPA—Office of Price Administration
PWA—Public Works Administration
REA—Rural Electrification Administration
RFC—Reconstruction Finance Corporation
SCLC—Southern Christian Leadership Conference
TVA—Tennessee Valley Authority
UAW—United Automobile Workers
USIA—United States Information Agency
WPA—Works Progress Administration

CONGRESSIONAL TERMINOLOGY

Administration bill—A bill that originates with the president.
Bring a bill to the floor—After a bill has been voted out of committee, it may be "brought to the floor" of the House or Senate for debate.
Caucus—A gathering of party members to make decisions on policy and/or elect party leaders.
Cloture—To set a time limit on debate, thereby preventing a filibuster.
Conference committee—A joint committee from the House and Senate who meet to produce a compromise bill from bills that have passed both houses but in different forms.

H.R. 0000—A bill that originates in the House of Representatives.

Majority/minority leader—The elected leader of the majority/minority party in either house. It can happen that a party in the majority in one house will be in the minority in the other.

Pairing—When a member of either house cannot be present at a particular vote or otherwise prefers to abstain from voting, he may find another member prepared to vote for the opposite side of the bill and the two may "pair," thereby offsetting each other.

President pro tem of the Senate—The senator who presides over the Senate in the vice-president's absence.

Quorum—The minimum number of members that must be present in order for a vote to be valid. A "quorum call" takes place when some member suggests the "absence of a quorum" in the chamber, and bells are rung to notify members to return to the chamber.

Recommital—To refer proposed legislation back to the committee that first considered it.

Reconsideration—To take up again a bill previously acted upon.

Refer to committee—To send a bill or matter to a particular committee for consideration.

Report out of committee—To submit to the full House or Senate the results of the committee's findings and its vote.

Roll call vote—Reading aloud the names of the members in order to record the individual votes.

Rule 22—In the Senate, that rule which allowed unlimited time for debate on a measure—in other words, a filibuster.

S. 0000—A bill that originates in the Senate.

Speaker of the House—The presiding officer of the House of Representatives

Sponsor a bill—To propose or urge the passage of a particular bill. A bill may be "sponsored" by several congressmen.

Table a motion or bill—To postpone consideration of a particular motion or bill.

Veto—After a bill has passed both houses, it is sent to the president, who can either sign it into law or "veto" it, thus preventing or delaying it from becoming a law. A bill that has been vetoed may still become law if two-thirds of the Senate votes to "override the veto."

Vote present—To record one's presence at a roll call vote without voting either for or against the bill in question.

Whip—The assistant to the majority or minority leader who enforces party discipline and ensures attendance at crucial votes.

VOICES IN *LYNDON*

Unless otherwise specified, quotes of Lyndon's that appear in this book come from various radio and television interviews throughout his political career. Many of the quotes used here were never broadcast.

BESS ABELL. Daughter of former Senator Earl Clements of Kentucky; Mrs. Johnson's social secretary.

GARDNER ACKLEY. Chairman of President's Council of Economic Advisers, 1964–68; ambassador to Italy, 1968–69.

GEORGE AIKEN. Republican senator from Vermont, 1941–75.

ROBERT S. ALLEN. Originator with Drew Pearson of "Washington Merry-Go-Round" column, 1932–42; after World War II, during which Allen served with General George Patton, he began a daily syndicated column "Inside Washington," 1949– .

STEWART ALSOP. Syndicated columnist with his brother Joseph; contributor to *Newsweek; Saturday Evening Post.*

CLINTON P. ANDERSON. Democratic senator from New Mexico, 1949–73; chairman of Aeronautical and Space Sciences Committee, 1963–73.

JACK ANDERSON. Reporter for the "Washington Merry-Go-Round" column from 1947; partner, 1965– ; owner, 1969– .

HARRY ASHMORE. Newspaperman; editor of Arkansas *Gazette,* 1948–59; senior fellow, Center for the Study of Democratic Institutions, 1959–, president, 1969–74.

TOINETTE BACHELDER. Secretarial assistant, White House, beginning in Franklin Roosevelt's presidency through Lyndon's presidency.

BOBBY BAKER. Secretary to the Senate majority, 1955–63.

LEONARD BAKER. Journalist; author; reporter for the *St. Louis Globe Democrat* and *Newsday;* Washington correspondent, 1958– .

GEORGE W. BALL. Undersecretary of state, 1961–66; ambassador to UN, 1968.

MALCOLM BARDWELL. San Antonio businessman; secretary to Congressman Maury Maverick in the 1930s.

CHARLES BARTLETT. Washington correspondent for the *Chattanooga Times*, 1946–63; columnist for the *Chicago Sun-Times*, 1963–75, *Chicago Daily News*, 1975– .

SUSAN BARTLETT (MRS. ROBERT BARTLETT). Wife of delegate to Congress from Alaska.

JACK BELL. Chief political writer, head Senate staff, AP; author.

PETER BENCHLEY. Presidential speech writer, 1967–69, who has since gained some fame as well as fortune as the author of among other novels, one about sharks called *Jaws*.

MONROE BILLINGTON. Historian, author; chairman of the history department at New Mexico State University.

SHERMAN BIRDWELL. Classmate of Lyndon's at Southwest Texas State Teachers College; worked with Lyndon on the NYA.

KENNETH BIRKHEAD. Assistant to the Senate majority whip, 1953–55; finance director, Democratic National Committee, 1957–59; assistant to the secretary of agriculture for congressional liaison, 1961–66.

JAMES BLUNDELL. Early Texas associate, active in 1941, 1960, and 1964 campaigns.

CHARLES BOATNER. The *Fort Worth Star Telegram* city editor, 1947–61; special assistant to the vice-president, 1961–63; assistant to the secretary and director of press information, Department of Interior, 1964–70.

HALE BOGGS. Democratic congressman from Louisiana, 1941–72; chairman of Joint Economic Subcommittee on Foreign Economic Policy, 1957–72.

LINDY BOGGS. Co-chairman of the Ladybird Special, 1964; Democratic congresswoman, Louisiana, 1973– ; succeeded her husband on his death in a plane crash in 1973.

RICHARD BOLLING. Democratic Congressman from Missouri, 1949– ; chairman, Joint Economic Committee.

HYMAN BOOKBINDER. Special assistant to the secretary of commerce during the Kennedy administration.

YOLANDA BOOZER. Member of Lyndon's Senate, presidential, and postpresidential staffs; presently executive secretary of Lyndon B. Johnson Foundation.

CHESTER BOWLES. Diplomat, author; Ambassador to India, 1951–53 and 1963–69; Democratic congressman from Connecticut, 1958–60; undersecretary of state, 1961–62.

BENJAMIN C. BRADLEE. Journalist; reporter for Newsweek, 1953–61; bureau chief, 1961–65; managing editor, the *Washington Post*, 1965–68; executive editor, 1968– .

BILLY LEE BRAMMER. Member of senatorial staff, 1955–59; author of the brilliant political novel *The Gay Place* in which the protagonist, Fenstemaker, sounded suspiciously like Lyndon.

HENRY BRANDON. Journalist and editor, the *Sunday Times* of London.

H. S. ("HANK") BROWN. Texas AFL leader.

HAROLD BROWN. Director of defense research and engineering for the Department of Defense, 1961–65; secretary of air force, 1965–69; president, California Institute of

Technology at Pasadena, 1969–77; secretary of defense with the Carter administration, 1977– .

RUSSELL MORTON BROWN. Lawyer and friend from early Washington days.

MCGEORGE BUNDY. Dean of the Faculty of Arts and Sciences at Harvard, 1953–61; Special assistant to the president for National Security Affairs 1961–66; president, Ford Foundation 1966–79; professor of history, New York University, 1979– .

WILLIAM PUTNAM BUNDY. Assistant secretary of defense for international security affairs, 1963–64; assistant secretary of state for Far Eastern affairs, 1964–69; editor, *Foreign Affairs*, 1972– .

SIMON BURG. Johnson family friend.

DAVID BURKE. A close associate of the Kennedy family.

HORACE BUSBY. Johnson friend and adviser for twenty-five years; secretary to the cabinet and special assistant to the president during part of the presidential years.

JAMES CAIN. Personal physician to President Johnson, 1946–73.

JOSEPH A. CALIFANO. Deputy secretary of defense, 1964–65; special assistant to the president, 1965–69; secretary of HEW, 1977–79.

ELIZABETH ("LIZ") CARPENTER. Staff director and press secretary to Mrs. Lyndon B. Johnson, 1963–68; presently assistant secretary of education for public affairs.

LESLIE CARPENTER. *San Antonio News* Washington bureau chief; executive assistant during vice-presidency; husband of Liz Carpenter.

CLIFF CARTER. Political associate and friend.

MARGARET CARTER (MRS. JACK CARTER). Early campaign worker; delegate to Democratic state convention (Texas) in 1956.

DOUGLASS CATER. Washington editor of *Reporter* magazine, 1950–63; special assistant to the president, 1964–68; presently senior fellow, Aspen Institute for Humanistic Studies.

ANTHONY CELEBREEZE. Secretary of HEW, 1962–65; judge, Sixth Circuit Court of Appeals, 1965– .

GEORGE CHRISTIAN. Press secretary to Texas governors Price Daniel, 1957–63; and John Connally, 1963–66; Special assistant to the president, May–December 1966; White House press secretary, 1967–69.

BETHINE CHURCH (MRS. FRANK CHURCH). A political professional in her own right; she is daughter of Idaho governor Chase Clark.

FRANK CHURCH. Democratic senator from Idaho, 1957– .

EDWARD CLARK. Lawyer and banker, Johnson family friend and adviser; ambassador to Australia, 1965–68.

KENNETH B. CLARK. Educator; psychologist; consultant on personnel, Department of State, 1961–68; director of HARYOU—Harlem Youth Opportunities Unlimited, Inc. distinguished professor emeritus of psychology at City College, City University of New York.

TOM C. CLARK. Associate justice, U.S. Supreme Court, 1949–67.

W. RAMSEY CLARK. Lawyer; assistant attorney general, 1961–65; deputy attorney general, 1965–67; attorney general, 1967–69.

LUCIUS D. CLAY. Commander in chief, U.S. forces in Europe and military governor, U.S. zone, Germany, 1947–49; President Kennedy's personal representative in Berlin, 1961–62.

HARLAN CLEVELAND. Assistant secretary of state for international affairs, 1961–65; ambassador to NATO, 1965–69.

CLARK CLIFFORD. Lawyer; close adviser to Presidents Truman, Kennedy, Johnson, and Carter; chairman, Foreign Intelligence Advisory Board, 1963–68; secretary of defense, 1968–1969.

WILBUR J. COHEN. Assistant secretary of HEW, 1965–68; secretary of HEW, 1968–69.

JOHN B. CONNALLY. Secretary to Congressman Johnson, 1938–41; campaign manager, 1948; election adviser, 1956, 1960; secretary of the navy, 1961; governor of Texas, 1963–69; secretary of the treasury, 1971–72; frequent presidential candidate.

THOMAS G. CORCORAN ("TOMMY THE CORK"). Lawyer; Washington counsel during the thirties and adviser to Roosevelt and Johnson; friend from congressional days.

NORMAN COUSINS. Author; educator; editor of the *Saturday Review* 1942–71, 1973–77; his most recent book is *Anatomy of an Illness.*

BEN CRIDER. Childhood and family friend.

WILLIAM CROCKETT. An assistant secretary of state for administration. He accompanied LBJ on overseas trips during the vice-presidency.

WALTER CRONKITE. CBS–TV correspondent, 1950– .

JAMES CROSS. Pilot of Air Force One.

LLOYD CUTLER. Lawyer; adviser on Cuban prisoner exchange; executive director, National Commission on the Causes and Prevention of Violence, 1968–69; presently counsel to President Carter.

PRICE DANIEL. Democratic senator from Texas, 1953–56; governor of Texas, 1956–63.

JONATHAN DANIELS. Author; editor, the *News and Observer*, Raleigh, North Carolina, 1948–70; administrative assistant to President Roosevelt, 1943–45.

BILL DAVIDSON. Writer. Member of staff of *Yank* magazine during World War II. Contributing editor of *Look* magazine, *TV Guide, Panorama.*

SID DAVIS. Journalist. White House correspondent, Westinghouse Broadcasting Company, 1959–68; chief, Washington news bureau, 1968–77; director, NBC news, Washington, 1977– .

WILLARD DEASON. Lawyer; college classmate, NYA associate, and personal friend; appointed to Interstate Commerce Commission in 1965.

T. KELLIS DIBRELL. San Antonio lawyer; former FBI agent and supporter of Coke Stevenson in 1948.

NANCY HANSCHMAN DICKERSON. News correspondent: CBS, 1960–63; NBC, 1963–70; nationally syndicated Washington news analyst, 1971– .

CHARLES DIGGS. Democratic congressman from Michigan, 1955– .

C. DOUGLAS DILLON. Ambassador to France, 1953–57; undersecretary of state, 1959–61; secretary of the treasury, 1961–65. Wall Street banker and son of a Wall Street banker at the very center of what Richard H. Rovere called "The American Establishment."

EVERETT ("EV") M. DIRKSEN. Republican senator from Illinois, 1951–69; Senate minority leader, 1959–69.

MICHAEL V. DISALLE. Governor of Ohio, 1959–63.

JOHN DODDS. Editorial executive at Holt, Rinehart and Winston; G. P. Putnam's Sons; Simon and Schuster.

HELEN GAHAGAN DOUGLAS (MRS. MELVYN DOUGLAS). Actress, opera singer; Democratic congresswoman from California, Seventy-ninth to Eighty-first congresses. Defeated for Senate by Richard M. Nixon in 1950.

PAUL H. DOUGLAS. Democratic senator from Illinois, 1949–67; chairman of Joint Economic Committee, 1959–67; leader of Senate liberals.

WILLIAM O. DOUGLAS. Associate justice, U.S. Supreme Court, 1939–75.

ERV S. DUGGAN. Author; aide and speech writer to President Johnson, 1966–68.

ANGIER BIDDLE DUKE. Chief of protocol, White House and Department of State, 1961–65; U.S. ambassador to Spain, 1965–68; ambassador to Denmark, 1968–69.

ROBIN DUKE (MRS. ANGIER BIDDLE DUKE).

RALPH DUNGAN. Assistant to President Kennedy, 1961–63; special assistant to President Johnson, 1963–64; ambassador to Chile, 1964–67.

CLIFFORD DURR. Alabama lawyer; member of RFC during Roosevelt's presidency; member of FCC, 1941–48; prominent civil liberties leader.

VIRGINIA FOSTER DURR (MRS. CLIFFORD DURR). Friend from congressional years; civil rights advocate; sister-in-law of Supreme Court Justice Hugo Black.

FREDERICK G. DUTTON. Special assistant to President Kennedy, 1961; assistant secretary of state for congressional relations, 1962–64; deputy national chairman, Citizens for Kennedy and Johnson, 1960.

BENNO ECKERT. Childhood friend.

HELMER ECKERT. Childhood friend.

ROBERT C. ECKHARDT. Democratic congressman from Texas, 1967– .

INDIA EDWARDS. Vice-chairman of the Democratic Committee; chairman of the women's division.

ALLEN J. ELLENDER. Democratic senator from Louisiana, 1937–72.

BUFORD ELLINGTON. Governor of Tennessee 1959–63, 1967–72; director of Office of Emergency Planning, 1965–66.

FRANK ERWIN. Powerful Texas conservative and former regent of the University of Texas. Friend of both Johnson and John Connally, he frequently acted as buffer between them.

EPHRAIM EVRON. Israeli minister to U.S., 1965–68; ambassador to U.S., January 1979– .

JAMES FARMER. Founder and national director of Congress of Racial Equality (CORE), 1961–66; president, Center for Community Action in Education, 1965– .

CREEKMORE FATH. Austin lawyer. Political adversary of Johnson.

JOHN HENRY FAULK. Author of *Fear on Trial*; a Texan who, until he was felled by the blacklist, was a radio entertainer and storyteller for CBS.

TRUMAN FAWCETT. Childhood friend; later Johnson City druggist.

ABE FEINBERG. Chairman of executive committee, American Trust Company; president, Development Corporation for Israel.

MYER FELDMAN. Lawyer; Deputy special counsel to the president, 1961–64; counsel to the president, 1964–65.

O. C. FISHER. Democratic Congressman from Texas, 1943–74.

ROBERT H. FLEMING. Journalist; chief of the Washington bureau of ABC, 1961–65; deputy press secretary, 1966–68; assistant director of USIA, 1968–69; staff, House of Representatives, 1969– .

EDWARD FOLLIARD. Journalist; White House correspondent for the *Washington Post*.

SAM FORE. Publisher, Floresville, Texas, *Journal*; friend and supporter from congressional years.

MICHAEL FORRESTAL. Lawyer; senior member, White House national security staff, 1962–65.

ABE FORTAS. Washington lawyer; associate justice, U.S. Supreme Court, 1965–69.

MAX FRANKEL. Journalist; chief Washington correspondent for the *New York Times*, 1968–73; Sunday editor, 1973–76; editorial pages editor, 1977– .

ORVILLE FREEMAN. Governor of Minnesota, 1955–61; secretary of agriculture, 1961–69.

LAWRENCE FUCHS. Associate of Eleanor Roosevelt; faculty, Brandeis University 1951–, dean of faculty, 1960–61; Peace Corps director, the Philippines, 1961–63.

J. WILLIAM FULBRIGHT. Democratic senator from Arkansas, 1945–75; chairman of Foreign Relations Committee, 1959–75.

GORDON FULCHER. Publisher, *Atlanta Citizen's Journal*; formerly managing editor of the *Austin American*.

BETTY FURNESS (MRS. LESLIE MIDGELEY). Broadcast journalist, consumer adviser, actress; special assistant to the president for consumer affairs, 1967–69; chairman of President's Committee on Consumer Interests, 1967–69; executive secretary, Consumer Advisory Council, 1967–69.

JAMES GAITHER. Lawyer; White House aide, 1966–68.

JOHN KENNETH GALBRAITH. Economist, educator, and author; administrator, OPA, 1941–43; professor of economics, Harvard, 1949–75; ambassador to India, 1961–63; chairman, ADA, 1967– .

DR. HECTOR GARCIA. Founder, American G.I. Forum; special ambassador to the inauguration of the president of the Republic of Venezuela, 1964; U.S. representative to Twenty-second General Assembly, UN.

JOHN GARDNER. Writer, educator. Chairman, president's task force on education, 1964, White House Conference on Education, 1965; secretary of HEW, 1965–68; chairman, Urban Coalition, 1968–70, Common Cause, 1970–77.

ELIZABETH GATOV. Founder of the citizen's lobby, Common Cause; treasurer of U.S., 1961–62. Democratic national committeewoman from California, 1956–65.

SIM GIDEON. Lawyer; general manager of the Lower Colorado River Authority.

MICHAEL GILLETTE. Chief of acquisitions and oral history programs at Lyndon Baines Johnson Library.

LENNY GIOVANNITTI. Writer; director, producer, NBC news, 1962–70; producer and writer of many NBC-TV documentaries including "The Hill Country; Lyndon Johnson's Texas," 1966.

TED GITTINGER. Texas historian; faculty, University of Texas at Austin, researcher, oral history department, Lyndon Baines Johnson Library.

STELLA GLIDDEN. Johnson family friend; editor, the *Johnson City Record Courier*; postmistress of Johnson City.

ARTHUR E. ("TEX") GOLDSCHMIDT. Director of power division, department of the interior, 1942–49; director for technical assistance, UN, 1950–67; U.S. representative to the UN Economic and Social Council, 1967–69; friend from congressional years.

ELIZABETH GOLDSCHMIDT (MRS. ARTHUR GOLDSCHMIDT). Member of Kennedy Task Force on Health and Social Security Legislation, 1960–61; vice-president, Crusade Against Poverty, 1965–66; member of Citizens Advisory Council on Status of Women, 1965–68.

ERNEST GOLDSTEIN. Lawyer; professor of law, University of Texas, 1955–65; counsel, Coudert Frères, Paris, 1966–67, partner, 1969– ; special assistant to the president, 1967–69.

BARRY GOLDWATER. Republican senator from Arizona, 1953–65, 1969– ; Republican nominee for president in 1964.

ASHTON GONELLA. Member of Senate staff; later personal secretary to Lady Bird Johnson.

HENRY GONZALEZ. Democratic congressman from Texas, 1961–79.

ANDREW J. GOODPASTER. U.S. Army officer; assistant to chairman, joint chiefs of staff, 1962–66; director, joint staff, 1966–67; commandant, National War College, 1967–68; member of U.S. delegation to Paris peace talks on Vietnam, 1968; deputy commander, U.S. forces in Vietnam, 1968–69; supreme allied commander in Europe, 1969–74 ; commandant, West Point 1977– .

HELENE LINDOW GORDON. School friend of Luci's; joined Lady Bird's staff during postpresidency.

ALBERT GORE. Democratic congressman from Tennessee, 1939–53; senator, 1953–71.

CALLAN GRAHAM. Former member FBI; supporter of Coke Stevenson in the 1948 Senate race.

KATHARINE GRAHAM. Newspaper executive; president of the Washington Post Company, 1963–73; chairman of the board, 1973– .

PHILIP GRAHAM. Publisher of the *Washington Post*, 1948–63; political adviser.

ELINOR GREEN. Retired foreign service officer who has served, among other places, in Paris, Vietnam, Ottawa, and Switzerland.

H. M. GREENE. Professor, Southwest Texas State Teachers College.

ERNEST GRUENING. Democratic senator from Alaska, 1959–69; early critic of Vietnam policies.

LLOYD HACKLER. Assistant press secretary, 1966–69; associate director, Information Service, Veterans' Administration.

JAMES C. HAGERTY. Press secretary to President Eisenhower, 1953–61; vice president, ABC, 1961–75.

WALTER G. HALL. Galveston banker; Texas liberal.

LLOYD HAND. Lawyer; senatorial staff, 1957–61; White House chief of protocol, 1965–66.

D. B. HARDEMAN. Longtime associate of Sam Rayburn's.

MARY HARDESTY (MRS. ROBERT HARDESTY). Associate during postpresidential years.

ROBERT HARDESTY. LBJ's speech writer, collaborated on *The Vantage Point*.

RAYMOND HARE. Career diplomat. Served as ambassador to Saudi Arabia, Lebanon, Egypt, and Turkey, among others. Assistant secretary for Near Eastern and South Asian affairs, Department of State, 1965–66. President, Middle East Institute, Washington, 1966–69; chairman, 1969–76.

W. AVERELL HARRIMAN. Ambassador to Russia, 1943–46, and Great Britain, 1946; secretary of commerce, 1946–48; governor of New York, 1955–58. Assistant secretary of state for Far Eastern Affairs, 1961–63; ambassador-at-large, 1961, 1965–68; undersecretary of state for political affairs, 1963–65; presidential representative to Paris peace talks with North Vietnam, 1968–69.

OREN HARRIS. Democratic congressman from Arkansas, 1941–66; U.S. district judge, western and eastern districts, Arkansas.

PATRICIA ROBERTS HARRIS. Lawyer, educator; professor of law, Howard University, 1963–65, 1967–69; U.S. ambassador to Luxemburg, 1965–67; secretary of HUD, 1977–79; presently secretary of health and social services, succeeding Joseph A. Califano.

GILBERT HARRISON. Editor in chief, the *New Republic*; 1954–74.

RICHARD HARWOOD. Journalist; associated with the *Washington Post* since 1961; deputy managing editor from 1976.

WILLIAM W. HEATH. Austin lawyer, active in state politics; U.S. ambassador to Sweden, 1967.

ROGER HILSMAN. Director, Bureau of Intelligence and Research, Department of State, 1961–63; assistant secretary of state for Far Eastern affairs, 1963–64; professor of government, Columbia University, 1964– .

HENRY HIRSCHBERG. Lawyer; best man at Johnson's wedding.

ANNA ROSENBERG HOFFMAN. Congressional liaison under Roosevelt.

LUTHER HOLCOMB. Protestant clergyman; chairman, Texas Advisory Commission on Civil Rights; member, National Advisory Commission on Community Relations and the Equal Employment Opportunity Commission, 1965– .

JERRY HOLLEMAN. Labor leader; assistant secretary of labor under Kennedy.

WELLY K. HOPKINS. Lawyer; general counsel, United Mine Workers of America, 1940–66; counsel, trustees, UNMWA, Welfare and Retirement Fund, 1966– .

BETTY HUGHES (MRS. RICHARD HUGHES).

RICHARD HUGHES. Governor of New Jersey, 1961–70; chief justice, New Jersey Supreme Court, 1973–.

SARAH HUGHES. Judge, U.S. district court, Northern District of Texas, 1961– .

RALPH HUITT. Political scientist; professor of political science, University of Wisconsin, 1959–65; assistant secretary for legislation, Department of HEW, 1965–69; executive director, National Association of State Universities and Land Grant Colleges, Washington, 1970– .

HUBERT H. HUMPHREY. Democratic senator from Minnesota, 1949–64 and 1971–78; vice-president, 1965–69; candidate for president, 1968.

CHET HUNTLEY. News commentator, NBC, 1955–70.

ROBERT M. JACKSON. Editor, the *Corpus Christi Caller*; in early Washington days, a clerk for Texas Congressman R. E. Thomason.

JAKE JACOBSEN. Old friend; special counsel to the president, 1965–67.

MICHAEL JANEWAY. Editor, *The Atlantic*, 1966–70, managing editor, 1970–76, executive editor, 1976–77; editor, the *Boston Globe Sunday Magazine* section, 1977– .

LEO JANOS. Member of Johnson's presidential staff; Houston correspondent for *Time* magazine, 1969– .

LEON JAWORSKI. Lawyer; special assistant attorney general, 1962–65; director, Watergate Special Prosecution Force, 1973–74; special counsel, House Committee on Standards of Official Conduct, 1977– .

WALTER JENKINS. Trusted friend and chief assistant from early congressional years. During presidency, White House special assistant, 1963–64.

ALFRED E. ("BOODY") JOHNSON. Lyndon's roommate at San Marcos.

EDWINA JOHNSON (MRS. TOM JOHNSON). Friend of the family.

HAYNES JOHNSON. Journalist; associated with the *Washington Star*, 1957–69; the *Washington Post* from 1969, managing editor from 1973.

W. THOMAS JOHNSON. White House fellow, 1965–66; deputy press secretary, 1967; special assistant to the president, 1968; executive staff, Texas Broadcasting Corporation, 1969–73; executive editor, publisher, *Dallas Times Herald*, 1973–77; president and chief operating officer of the *Los Angeles Times*, 1977– .

JAMES JONES. Special assistant to the president, 1965–69; Democratic congressman from Oklahoma, 1973– .

LUTHER E. JONES, JR. Houston debate student of Johnson's; assistant on Congressman Richard Kleberg's staff.

WILLIAM J. JORDEN. Diplomat; *New York Times* foreign correspondent, 1952–58, Washington bureau, 1958–61; deputy assistant secretary of state for public affairs, 1965–66; senior member, staff, National Security Council, 1966–68; member, U.S. delegation to Paris peace talks on Vietnam, 1968–69; postpresidential assistant, 1969–72; ambassador to Panama, 1974– .

NICHOLAS DEB. KATZENBACH. Lawyer. Professor of law, University of Chicago law school, 1956–60; U.S. deputy attorney general, 1962–64; acting attorney general, 1964–65; attorney general, 1965–66; undersecretary of state, 1966–69.

CARROLL KEACH. Campaign staff, 1937, 1941; later editor, the *Robstown Record*.

JOSEPH KEENAN. Chicago labor leader; secretary, International Brotherhood of Electrical Workers; member, President's Advisory Committee on Labor-Management Policy.

JESSE KELLAM. College classmate; NYA associate, director after 1937; general manager of KTBC and KTBC-TV; on the board of regents of University of Texas at Austin.

ISAIAH KENAN. Israel's chief lobbyist in Washington for many years.

ROBERT KENNEDY. Attorney general, 1961–64; senator from New York, 1965–68.

ROGER KENT. California lawyer; chairman of California Democratic Coordinating Committee.

LEON H. KEYSERLING. Economist, lawyer; administrator, U.S. Housing Authority, 1937–42; Council of Economic Advisers: vice-chairman, 1946–50; chairman, 1950–53; congressional consultant, 1953– .

MARY D. KEYSERLING (MRS. LEON H. KEYSERLING). Economist; director, Women's Bureau, Department of Labor, 1964–69; chairman, D.C. Commission on the Status of Women, 1973–76.

CARROLL KILPATRICK. Journalist; White House correspondent, the *Washington Post.*

ROBERT E. KINTNER. First came to Washington in 1934 as correspondent for the *New York Herald Tribune.* Friend from congressional days when syndicated with Joseph Alsop; later president of ABC, 1949–56, and NBC, 1958–65; special assistant to the president, 1966–67; secretary to the cabinet.

ROBERT KOMER. Senior staff member, NSC, 1961–65; deputy special assistant to the president for national security affairs, 1965–66; special assistant to the president, 1966–67; deputy to commander, USMACV for Cords, 1967–68; ambassador to Turkey, October 1968–April 1969; adviser to secretary of defense for Nato affairs, 1977– .

ARTHUR KRIM. Lawyer; president, United Artists, 1951–69; chairman of the board, 1969–78; special consultant to the president, 1968–69; chairman, President's Club, 1962–68; chairman, Democratic Advisory Council to Elected Officials, 1973– .

ARTHUR KROCK. Newspaperman and author; chief, Washington bureau, the *New York Times,* 1953–67.

THEODORE KUPFERMAN. Democratic congressman from New York, 1965–69; New York Supreme Court justice, 1969–71; associate justice, appellate division, 1971– .

MARY LASKER. New York social leader and pioneer supporter of medical research; chairman of National Health Education Committee.

GENE LATIMER. Houston debate student of Johnson's; assistant on Congressman Richard Kleberg's staff.

WILLIAM H. LAWRENCE. Journalist; White House reporter, the *New York Times;* national affairs editor, ABC News, 1961–72.

RAY E. LEE. Newspaperman; editor on the *American Statesman;* associated with Johnson during early campaigns.

KITTY CLYDE LEONARD. Childhood friend.

DAVID LILIENTHAL. Director, TVA, 1933–41, chairman, 1941–46; chairman of Atomic Energy Commission, 1946–50; chief executive officer, Development and Resources Corporation, 1955– ; cochairman of Joint Postwar Development Group, Vietnam, 1967–70; author.

GOULD LINCOLN. Journalist and editor, the *Washington Star.*

OTTO LINDIG. Childhood friend.

PETER LISAGOR. Washington correspondent for the *Chicago Daily News*, 1950–59; chief of the Washington bureau 1959–76.

ROBERT LIVINGSTON. New York City human rights commissioner; theatrical and television producer; motion picture executive, Warner Brothers, 1958–72; publisher, *More* magazine, 1975–76; son of Mollie Parnis.

FRANK LLOYD. Lawyer in Alice, Texas.

KATHRYN DEADRICH LONEY. Lyndon's first schoolteacher.

STUART LONG. Austin newspaperman; member of the Texas Democratic Executive Committee, 1948.

KATIE LOUCHHEIM. Vice-chairman, Democratic National Committee, 1956–60; deputy assistant secretary of state for community advisory services, 1963–66; deputy assistant secretary of state for educational and cultural affairs, 1966–68; U.S. board member of UNESCO, 1968–69.

HERSCHEL LOVELESS. Governor of Iowa, 1957–60; national chairman, Farmers for Kennedy-Johnson.

DOROTHY MCCARDLE. Newspaper columnist, the *Washington Post*.

JOHN W. MCCORMACK. Democratic congressman from Massachusetts, 1928–71; Speaker of the House, 1962–71.

DAVID MCDONALD. President, United Steelworkers of America, 1953–65.

GALE MCGEE. Democratic senator from Wyoming, 1959–77; permanent representative to the U.S. mission to the OAS, 1977– .

GEORGE MCGOVERN. Democratic congressman from South Dakota, 1957–61; senator, 1963– ; Democratic presidential nominee, 1972.

ROSE MCKEE. Washington correspondent for UPI; Johnson appointed her director of information for the Department of Commerce.

ROBERT S. MCNAMARA. President, Ford Motor Company, 1960–61; secretary of defense, 1961–68; president of the World Bank, 1968– .

HARRY MCPHERSON. Lawyer, counsel for Senate Democratic policy committee, 1956–63; assistant secretary of state for education and cultural affairs, 1964–65; special assistant to the president, 1965–66; special counsel to the president, 1966–69.

WILLIAM B. MACOMBER, JR. Assistant secretary of state for congressional relations, 1957–62; ambassador to Jordan, 1961–64; assistant administrator, AID, 1964–67; assistant secretary for congressional relations, Department of State, 1967–69; deputy undersecretary of state for administration, 1969–73; ambassador to Turkey, 1973–77; president Metropolitan Museum of Art, 1978– .

WARREN G. MAGNUSON. Democratic congressman from Washington, 1937–44; senator, 1944– ; friend from early congressional days.

CHARLES MAGUIRE. White House fellow, 1965–66; speech writer; secretary to the cabinet, 1967–68.

DALE MALECHEK. Ranch foreman, LBJ Ranch.

MIKE MANATOS. Administrative assistant to the president, 1961–69; congressional liaison with the Senate.

THOMAS C. MANN. Assistant secretary of state for Inter-American Affairs, 1964; undersecretary of state for economic affairs, 1965–66.

MARYA MANNES. Writer; author of *More in Anger, Message from a Stranger*, and *They*, among other works.

STANLEY MARCUS. Associated with Neiman-Marcus from 1926; president, 1950–72; chairman of the board, 1972–75; chairman of the executive committee, 1975–77. Author of *Minding the Store* and *Quest for the Best*.

SHERWIN J. MARKMAN. Assistant to the president, 1966–68; congressional liaison.

LEONARD H. MARKS. Washington lawyer, attorney for KTBC and KTBC-TV interests; director of USIA, 1965–68.

BURKE MARSHALL. Assistant attorney general for civil rights, 1961–65; chairman of National Advisory Committee on Selective Service.

THURGOOD MARSHALL. U.S. circuit judge, Second Circuit Court of Appeals, 1961–65; solicitor general, 1965–67; associate justice, U.S. Supreme Court, 1967– .

JOHN BARTLOW MARTIN. Ambassador to Dominican Republic, 1962–64; author; biographer of Adlai Stevenson.

JOE MASHMAN. Helicopter pilot; flew the Johnson City Windmill in 1948.

MARGARET MAYER. Journalist; Washington correspondent for the *Dallas Times Herald*.

MARIANNE MEANS. Political columnist; Washington bureau correspondent, Hearst headline service, 1959–61, White House correspondent, 1961–65; political columnist, King Features syndicate, 1965– .

GEORGE MEANY. President of AFL-CIO, 1955–79.

HARRY MIDDLETON. Staff assistant to the president, 1967–69; collaborator on *The Vantage Point*; director of the Lyndon Baines Johnson Library, 1970– .

VIRGINIA ("SKOOTER") MILLER (MRS. DALE MILLER). Family friend.

WILBUR MILLS. Democratic congressman from Arkansas, 1939–75; chairman of the Ways and Means Committee, 1957–74.

NEWTON MINOW. Lawyer; special assistant to Adlai Stevenson in 1952 and 1956 presidential campaigns; chairman of FCC, 1961–63.

CLARENCE MITCHELL. Washington director of the NAACP, 1950– ; U.S. representative to the 7th special session, 30th UN general assembly, 1975– .

MIKE MONRONEY. Democratic congressman from Oklahoma, 1939–51; senator, 1951–69. Friend from congressional years.

BOOTH MOONEY. Author; senatorial speech writer and assistant, 1953–58.

BILL D. MOYERS. Senatorial and vice-presidential staffs from 1954 (intermittent); assistant and deputy director of the Peace Corps, 1961–64; special assistant to the president, 1963–67; press secretary, 1965–67; publisher, *Newsday*, 1967–70; editor-in-chief, Bill Moyers' Journal, 1970–76 ; 1978– .

JAMES NASH. Austin businessman (oil and banking).

ROBERT R. NATHAN. Economist; member, National Planning Committee, American Veterans Committee; national chairman, ADA, 1957–59; economic consultant to many foreign governments; board of economic advisers for *Time* magazine, 1973– .

RICHARD E. NEUSTADT. Political scientist, educator; professor of government, Columbia, 1954–64, Harvard, 1965– ; special consultant to the president, 1961–66;

special consultant to the State Department, 1962–69; director, Bureau of the Budget, 1961–70.

DOROTHY NICHOLS. Member of staff (intermittent), 1939–64; first woman staff member.

A. H. NOLLE. Dean at Southwest Texas State Teachers College during Lyndon's student years there.

ROBERT NOTTI. Democratic campaign organizer, 1960.

LAWRENCE F. O'BRIEN. Special assistant to the president for congressional relations, 1961–65; postmaster general, 1965–68; chairman, Democratic National Committee, 1968–69, 1970–72; commissioner, National Basketball Association, 1975–.

KENNETH P. O'DONNELL. Political right hand and personal friend to John F. Kennedy; appointments secretary, 1961–64.

JACQUELINE ("JACKIE") KENNEDY ONASSIS. Wife of President John F. Kennedy; First Lady, 1960–63.

DOROTHY PALMIE. Member of congressional staff.

MOLLIE PARNIS. Dress designer.

GEORGE PARR. Longtime political strongman in south Texas; the Duke of Duval County.

J. R. PARTEN. Texas oil man, liberal, consistent defender of human rights; board of regents, University of Texas, 1935–55; director, chairman of The Fund for the Republic, Inc., 1953–75.

WRIGHT PATMAN. Served with Sam Ealy Johnson in Texas legislature; Democratic representative from Texas, 1929–76; chairman of Banking and Currency Committee, 1963–75.

JOE PAYNE. Childhood friend.

DREW PEARSON. Syndicated columnist.

CARL L. PHINNEY. Lawyer; Texas National Guard, 1925–61, commanding general, 1953–61. Brother of Robert.

ROBERT PHINNEY. Director, District Nine, WPA, Austin, 1935–40; postmaster, Austin, 1947–52; district director, IRS, Austin, 1952– .

JAKE PICKLE. Congressman from Texas, 1963– ; family friend.

DEVRIES PIERSON. Congressional liaison; special counsel to the president.

PAUL A. PORTER. Lawyer; New Deal administrator; member and chairman of FCC, 1944; for many years law partner of Abe Fortas.

BILL PORTERFIELD. Journalist; author; reporter for the *Houston Chronicle*; graduate, as was Lyndon, of Southwest Texas State Teachers College.

HARRY PROVENCE. Editor, the Waco *Tribune–Herald*.

RICHARD S. ("CACTUS") PRYOR. Entertainer; Austin radio and TV personality.

DAN QUILL. San Antonio postmaster; early Texas friend.

A. PHILIP RANDOLPH. Organizer, Brotherhood of Sleeping Car Porters, 1925; president emeritus, 1968; vice-president, AFL-CIO, 1957– .

MARY RATHER. Friend; secretary after 1941; she had previously worked for Alvin Wirtz.

JOSEPH L. RAUH, JR. Lawyer; Washington counsel, UAW, 1951–63, 1966– ;

general counsel, 1963–66; chairman of Americans for Democratic Action, 1955–57; vice chairman, chairman, District of Columbia Democratic Committee, 1952–67; general counsel, Leadership Conference on Civil Rights, 1964– .

BENJAMIN H. READ. Special assistant to the secretary of state and executive secretary to the Department of State, 1963–69; director, Woodrow Wilson International Center for Scholars, Smithsonian Institution, 1969–73.

EMMETTE S. REDFORD. Childhood friend; appointee to numerous wartime and postwar governmental positions; professor of government and public affairs at the University of Texas at Austin, 1970– .

COATES REDMON. Peace Corps official, 1963–67; speech writer for Rosalyn Carter, 1977–78; book reviewer of the *Washington Post*.

GEORGE E. REEDY. Educator, author, lecturer; congressional correspondent for UPI before and after World War II; staff consultant for Senate Armed Services Preparedness Subcommittee; staff director, Democratic Policy Committee, 1953–60; special assistant to the vice-president, 1961–63; White House press secretary, March 1964–July 1965; special consultant to the president, 1968–69; dean of the College of Journalism, Marquette University, 1972– .

ELLIOT RICHARDSON. Government official; assistant to Senator Leverett Saltonstall, 1953–54; lieutenant governor of Massachusetts, 1965–67, attorney general, 1967–69; secretary of HEW, 1970–73; secretary of defense, January–May 1973; attorney general, May–October 1973; ambassador to Great Britain, 1975.

CHALMERS ROBERTS. Journalist, author; chief diplomatic correspondent, the *Washington Post*, 1953–71; columnist, 1971– .

CHARLES ROBERTS. Contributing editor, White House correspondent for *Newsweek*.

JUANITA ROBERTS. Long time friend and personal secretary through the White House years.

LOIS ROBERTS (MRS. CHALMERS ROBERTS).

RAY ROBERTS. Friend and associate from NYA days; congressman from Texas, 1962– .

JOHN P. ROCHE. Educator; national chairman of ADA, 1962–65; special consultant to the president, 1966–68; professor of politics, Brandeis University, 1956–73; professor of civilization and foreign affairs, Fletcher School of Law and Diplomacy, 1973– ; nationally syndicated columnist 1968– .

NELSON ROCKEFELLER. Governor of New York, 1959–73; vice-president of the United States, 1974–76.

ELSPETH ROSTOW (MRS. WALT W. ROSTOW). Dean, LBJ School of Public Affairs, University of Texas at Austin.

EUGENE DEBS ROSTOW. Dean, Yale Law School, 1955–65; professor of law and public affairs, 1964–; undersecretary of state for political affairs, 1966–69; president, Atlantic Treaty Association, 1973–76.

WALT WHITMAN ROSTOW. Professor of economic history at MIT, 1950–60; chairman of Policy Planning Council of the Department of State, 1961–66; special assistant to the president for national security affairs, 1966–69; presently professer of economics and history at the University of Texas in Austin.

FENNER ROTH. Deputy area director, Economic Development Administration, Department of Commerce.

PAYNE ROUNDTREE. Childhood friend.

RICHARD H. ROVERE. Author and journalist; staff writer, the *New Yorker*, 1944–79.

ELIZABETH ROWE (MRS. JAMES H. ROWE). Friend from congressional days; executive secretary, Washington bureau of the ILO, 1943–49; chairman of National Capital Planning Commission, 1961–68.

JAMES H. ROWE, JR. Lawyer; friend and adviser from congressional years; staff member of several New Deal agencies; secretary and assistant to president Roosevelt, 1938–41; assistant attorney general, 1941–43; counsel to the Democratic Policy Committee, 1956.

DEAN RUSK. Educator; state department, 1946–51; president of Rockefeller Foundation, 1952–60; secretary of state, 1961–69; professor of international law, University of Georgia, 1970– .

BAYARD RUSTIN. Civil rights leader; race relations director, Fellowship of Reconciliation, 1941–53; special assistant to Dr. Martin Luther King, 1955–60; president, A. Philip Randolph Institute, 1966– .

WILLIAM SAFIRE. Journalist; author; special assistant to President Nixon, 1969–73; columnist, *New York Times*, 1973– .

HARRISON SALISBURY. Newspaperman; Moscow correspondent, the *New York Times*, 1949–54; New York staff, 1954–63; assistant managing editor, 1964–72; associate editor, 1972– ; editor, Op-Ed page, 1970–73; author.

LEVERETT SALTONSTALL. Republican senator from Massachusetts, 1944–67.

BOB RAY SANDERS. Station manager of radio station KERA-FM in Dallas.

HAROLD BAREFOOT SANDERS, JR. Dallas lawyer; assistant deputy attorney general, 1965–66; assistant attorney general, 1966–67; legislative counsel to the president, 1967–69. Democratic nominee for the House, 1958; for the Senate, 1972; defeated both times.

RICHARD M. SCAMMON. Director, Elections Research Center, Governmental Affairs Institute, 1955–61, 1965– ; director, Bureau of the Census, 1961–65; member, OAS electoral mission to the Dominican Republic, 1966.

RAY C. SCHERER. NBC White House correspondent, 1952–69, London correspondent, 1969–73, Washington correspondent, 1973–75.

ARTHUR M. SCHLESINGER, JR. Historian; professor of history at Harvard, 1954–61; special assistant to the president, 1961–64; professor of humanities, City University of New York, 1966– .

REV. ARTHUR WUNIBALD SCHNEIDER. Pastor, St. Francis Xavier Church (Roman Catholic), Stonewall, Texas.

SAM SHAFFER. Journalist; on the staff of *Newsweek* magazine, 1945–75, much of the time in Washington.

JOHN SHARON. Democratic party campaign organizer, 1956, 1960; presidential adviser on foreign affairs.

ISABELLE SHELTON. Journalist, the *Washington Star*.

ALLAN SHIVERS. Governor of Texas, 1949–57; president, U.S. Chamber of Commerce, 1967.

HUGH SIDEY. Correspondent, *Time* magazine, 1958– ; columnist, "The Presidency," 1966– ; chief of Washington bureau, 1969– ; author.

GERALD SIEGAL. Washington lawyer; counsel to the Democratic Policy Committee, 1956–60; vice-president, former counsel, the *Washington Post*. Currently chief counsel of the Senate Rules Committee.

BYRON SKELTON. Judge. U.S. Court of Claims, Washington, 1966–77; senior federal judge, 1977– ; prominent Texas Democrat.

JOHN SKUCE. Director of research, Congressional Quarterly, Inc., news research agency, Washington.

THEODORE C. SORENSEN. Lawyer; assistant to Senator John F. Kennedy, 1953–61; special counsel to the president, 1961–64; author.

CHARLES SPALDING. Friend and campaign aide of John F. Kennedy.

JOHN SPARKMAN. Democratic congressman, 1937–47, and senator from Alabama, 1947–79. Democratic nominee for vice-president, 1952.

WILL SPARKS. Staff assistant to the president; writer.

ADRIAN SPEARS. U.S. district judge, Western District of Texas, 1961–62; chief judge, 1962– ; prominent Texas Democrat.

JOHN C. STENNIS. Democratic senator from Mississippi, 1947– ; chairman of Select Commission on Standards and Conduct, 1965–75; chairman of Armed Services Committee, 1969– .

O. B. SUMMY. Childhood friend.

JOHN L. SWEENEY. Federal cochairman of Appalachian Regional Commission, 1965–67; assistant secretary for public affairs, Department of Transportation, 1967.

JAMES SYMINGTON. Washington lawyer; executive director, President's Committee on Juvenile Delinquency and Youth Crimes, 1965–66; chief of protocol, 1966–67; congressman from Missouri, 1969– .

HERMAN TALMADGE. Governor of Georgia, 1948–55; Democratic senator from Georgia, 1957– .

HOBART TAYLOR, JR. Lawyer; executive vice-chairman, President's Committee on Equal Employment Opportunity, 1961–65; special assistant to the vice-president, 1963; associate counsel to the president, 1964–65; director, Export-Import Bank, 1965–68.

HOBART TAYLOR, SR. Houston businessman and civic leader; early Johnson supporter.

WILLIE DAY TAYLOR. Johnson family friend and member of the press staff, 1965–68.

LARRY E. TEMPLE. Lawyer; special counsel to the president, 1967–69.

J. WILLIAM THEIS. Newspaperman; Washington correspondent, International News Service, 1942–58; chief, Senate staff of UPI, 1958–68; bureau chief, Hearst newspapers, Washington, 1968–76.

CLARK W. THOMPSON. Democratic congressman from Texas, 1933–35; 1947–67.

HOMER THORNBERRY. Close family friend; Democratic congressman from Texas, 1949–63; U.S. district judge, Texas Western District, 1963–65; U.S. judge, Court of Appeals, Fifth Judicial Circuit, 1965– .

JOHN TOWER. Republican senator from Texas, 1961– .

STERLING TUCKER. Executive director, Urban League, Washington, D.C., 1956; chairman, D.C. City Council.

GRACE TULLY. Secretary to President Roosevelt from the 1930s; later on the Johnson senatorial staff.

STEWART UDALL. Democratic congressman from Arizona, 1955–61; secretary of the interior, 1961–69; writer, syndicated column, "Udall on the Environment," 1970– .

JACK VALENTI. Special assistant to the president, 1963–66; president, Motion Picture Association of America, 1966– ; director, American Film Institute.

MARY MARGARET WILEY VALENTI (MRS. JACK VALENTI). Johnson's secretary primarily during the Senate period.

CARL VINSON. Democratic congressman from Georgia, 1914–65; chairman of Naval Affairs Committee, 1931–49; chairman of Armed Services Committee, 1949–53, 1955–65.

ROBERT WALDRON. Assistant to Congressman Homer Thornberry; now a leading Washington designer.

GEORGE WALLACE. Governor of Alabama, 1963–66, 1971– ; independent candidate for president, 1968; Democratic primary candidate, 1972 (until accident), 1976.

PAUL WARNKE. General counsel, Defense Department, 1966–67; assistant secretary for international security affairs, 1967–69; chief negotiator, SALT, 1977– .

EARL WARREN. Chief Justice of the United States, 1953–69; chairman of the Special Commission to Investigate the Assassination of President Kennedy.

GEORGE L. P. WEAVER. Assistant secretary of labor for international affairs.

ROBERT C. WEAVER. Administrator, Housing and Home Finance Agency, 1961–66; secretary, Department of Housing and Urban Development, 1966–68; president, Bernard M. Baruch College, 1969–70; distinguished professor of urban affairs, Hunter College, 1970– .

TERRELL MAVERICK WEBB. Widow of both Congressman Maury Maverick and Walter Prescott Webb, eminent historian.

HELEN WEINBERG. History teacher at Sam Houston High School when Johnson was debate coach.

EDWIN WEISL, JR. Lawyer; assistant special counsel, Senate Preparedness Investigating Committee, 1957–58; assistant attorney general in charge of land and natural resources, 1965–67; in charge of civil division, 1967–69.

EDWIN WEISL, SR. Lawyer, friend, and political adviser; national Democratic committeeman; chief counsel, Senate Preparedness Investigating Committee.

WILLIAM C. WESTMORELAND. Commander, U.S. Military Assistance Command, Vietnam, 1964–68; army chief of staff, 1968–72.

EARLE G. WHEELER. Army chief of staff, 1962–64; chairman of Joint Chiefs of Staff, 1964–70.

JUNE WHITE (MRS. W. S. WHITE). Former correspondent for the *Boston Herald*.

WILLIAM S. WHITE. Journalist, author; Washington staff, the *New York Times*, 1945–58; nationally syndicated political columnist, 1958– .

JAMES RUSSELL WIGGINS. Editorial staff, the *Washington Post*, 1947–68; ambassador to the UN, 1968–69; editor, publisher, the Ellsworth (Maine) *American*, 1969– .

CLAUDE C. WILD, SR. Congressional campaign manager, 1937.

ROGER WILKINS. Columnist; special assistant, foreign aid director, state department, 1962–66; director, community relations service, Department of Commerce, 1964–66; assistant attorney general, 1966–69; progress director, Ford Foundation, 1969–72; editorial page staff, *Washington Post*, 1972–74; editorial board, *New York Times*, 1974–79; editorial board, *The Nation*, 1980– .

ROY WILKINS. NAACP executive positions, 1931–77, director, 1965–77.

MONK WILLIS. Family friend in east Texas; administrative assistant to Congressman Ray Roberts; Texas political figure.

GLEN WILSON. Member of senatorial staff.

JAMES W. WILSON. Lawyer; member of senatorial staff.

ALVIN WIRTZ. Prominent Texas lawyer and state senator; Lyndon's early political mentor.

WILLARD WIRTZ. Secretary of labor, 1962–69.

HARRIS WOFFORD. Special assistant to President Kennedy, 1961–62; director, Ethiopian program, Peace Corps, 1962–64; associate director, Peace Corps, 1964–66; president, College at Old Westbury, State University of New York, 1966–70; president, Bryn Mawr College, 1970– .

LEONARD WOODCOCK. International vice-president, UAW, 1955–70; president, 1970–77; chief of mission, U.S. Liaison Office, Peking, 1977– .

WARREN WOODWARD. Joined Senate staff with Horace Busby in 1949; close friend of Johnson's from that point on.

FRANCIS EUGENE (GENE) WORLEY. Democratic congressman from Texas, 1941–50; associate judge, U.S. Court of Customs and Patent Appeals, 1950–59; chief judge, 1959–72; senior judge, 1972– .

ZEPHYR WRIGHT. Johnson family cook.

RALPH YARBOROUGH. Democratic senator from Texas, 1957–71.

ANDREW YOUNG. Executive director, Southern Christian Leadership Conference, 1964–70; Democratic congressman from Georgia, 1973–77; U.S. ambassador to the UN, 1977–79.

WHITNEY YOUNG, JR. Executive director, National Urban League, 1961–71.

RUFUS YOUNGBLOOD. Secret service officer since 1951; assigned to Vice-President Johnson in 1961, accompanied him on trips abroad, was with him in Dallas on November 22, 1963, and served him as his "special man" during the presidency.

ALBERT ZACK. Labor union official; director of public relations, AFL–CIO, 1957– .

H. A. ("TONY") ZIEGLER. NYA district director, Fort Worth, during Lyndon's days.

Family

LYNDON BAINES JOHNSON. 36th president of the United States.

SAM EALY JOHNSON, JR. Lyndon's father.

REBEKAH BAINES JOHNSON. Lyndon's mother.

CLAUDIA ("LADY BIRD") TAYLOR JOHNSON. Lyndon's wife.

LYNDA BIRD JOHNSON ROBB. Elder Johnson daughter.

LUCI BAINES JOHNSON NUGENT. Younger Johnson daughter.

SAM HOUSTON JOHNSON. Lyndon's brother.

ANTONIO TAYLOR. Lady Bird's brother.

AUNT JESSIE HATCHER. Sam Ealy's sister, Lyndon's aunt.

AVA JOHNSON COX. Lyndon's first cousin.

ELAINE FISCHESSER. Lady Bird's cousin.

PATRICK NUGENT. Luci's former husband.

NOTES

A Stormy Arrival

1. Rebekah wrote two accounts of Lyndon's birth and childhood. The first, a Christmas gift for him when he was majority leader, is an unpublished booklet referred to here as the "Christmas gift account," and is on file at the Lyndon Baines Johnson Library in Austin. The second is briefer and appears as part of a more comprehensive study of the Johnson and Baines families as a whole. Titled A *Family Album*, it was edited after Rebekah's death by John S. Moursund and published in 1963 by McGraw-Hill.
2. The Austin newspapers of the time report that there was a storm the night of Lyndon Johnson's birth, and the Pedernales was indeed over its bank. But the storm was by no means unusual for the Hill Country.
3. From *Texas Heartland, A Hill Country Year*. Texas A and M University Press, 1975.
4. Tom, who never married, drowned in the Brazos River in 1877 at age thirty-nine.
5. The Johnson homestead was referred to interchangeably as a farm and a ranch. In Texas a ranch is a very expansive sort of place and is more socially desirable than a farm, even a farm that is making you rich while the ranchers are going broke. Either a ranch or a farm may be called a "place." A rancher who calls his ranch a "place" is being modest; a farmer who calls his "place" a "ranch" is lying.

6. A *Family Album*, pp. 22–23.
7. Ibid., p. 30.
8. Ibid.
9. Ibid.
10. Ibid., p. 29.
11. Ibid.
12. Ibid., p. 30.
13. From the Christmas gift account.
14. Ibid.
15. Lyndon, probably about three, and baby Rebekah.
16. From the Christmas gift account.
17. Ibid.
18. From a speech Lyndon gave at the White House Conference on Natural Beauty in May 1965.

Rebekah

1. A *Family Album*, p. 30.
2. Ibid., p. 28.
3. From an interview Rose McKee of UPI had with Rebekah.
4. Ibid.
5. The *Washington Post Sunday Book Review*, June 6, 1976.
6. The *Record-Courier* was the local newspaper of which Stella Glidden was editor for many years. She confirms Rebekah's activities as journalist, both for her paper

and others. According to her, Sam Ealy took the paper, a folio, as part payment on some real estate and owned it for a short time, probably less than six months, during which time she wrote all the copy for the inside pages.

7. The two letters that follow are clearly from the San Marcos period.

8. But Lyndon wrote more than just letters from San Marcos. In the Mother's Day issue of the campus paper, the *College Star*, he wrote a lengthy editorial tribute to motherhood, filled with such adulations as "all vocabularies fail when we attempt to describe Mother's traits" and "the splendid characters who have proven the most potent and vital force for good in the world." Rebekah must have been pleased.

9. Rebekah wrote to a friend from San Marcos where the family lived during the period that several of the children (after Lyndon) were in college there: "Sam pines for Johnson City and speaks of it as if it were a regular Paradise. The others of us are not so carried away with its charms. We may go back there to live, but I certainly do not look forward to the prospect."

Running, Running, Running

1. From the Christmas gift account.
2. The country school at Stonewall. The Johnson City school had eleven grades.
3. Rebekah's mother, who was living with them at the time.

Sam Ealy

1. *My Brother Lyndon*, p. 47.
2. Ibid., pp. 30–31.
3. In 1956 under what instigation remains unclear, a cross was burned by the entrance to the Johnson Ranch. Lady Bird remembers seeing the blackened outline after the fact.
4. As recorded in *Lyndon Baines Johnson: The Formative Years*, by William C.

Poole, Emmie Craddock, and David E. Conrad, pp. 40–41.
5. Ibid., p. 42.

Three Churches and A Courthouse

1. From the Christmas gift account.
2. Stewart Alsop, *The Center*, p. 60.

San Marcos

1. From a postpresidential speech at San Marcos.
2. From an interview with Robert E. McKay, May 21, 1965, prepared for but never printed by *Look* magazine.
3. The San Marcos is one of several streams in the area which derive from artesian wells of very constant temperature.
4. Jim Ferguson called him "the Grand Gizzard."
5. As quoted by Lyndon's friend Willard Deason and recorded in Pool, Craddock, and Conrad's *Lyndon Baines Johnson: The Formative Years*, p. 96.
6. The Black Stars was a secret society comprised mostly of football heroes; Lyndon and several others organized the White Stars in competition.
7. The editors of *The Formative Years* refute Nichols's assertion about the lengthy stories in the *Star* that spring.

How Do You Do, Mr. Johnson?

1. As we know it was not after college but during college; however, it was easier to say *after* college.
2. The boy's name was Juan Gonzales, but I have found no other record of him.
3. A takeoff on a song sung by a famed vaudeville team of the time named Billy Jones and Ernie Hare; as I recall, the record was in almost every American home that had a phonograph; it was not possible to avoid it.

4. This speech is pure Lyndon, unhampered by ghosts; true, difficult to follow sometimes, but the intent is clear enough, and it is refreshing.
5. Lyndon's salary in Cotulla as principal was $1,135 a year. As Dorothy Nichols says, "Nearly $95 a month wasn't bad in those days."

Speaking for Pat Neff

1. Or so he told Robert E. McKay in 1965. Records at Pearsall indicate he was originally hired as a public speaking teacher at $50 per month; as that would appear to be only a part-time position, a subsequent agreement may account for the considerable disparity in job description and salary.
2. Lyndon told McKay $260, but records at Sam Houston High, then at 1304 Capitol, show that his basic salary was $160 a month (for a ten-month term); Uncle George, after all, made only $238 a month, good pay for the time—especially for a teacher.
3. "Resolved: That a substitute for trial by jury should be adopted."
4. All quotes of Lyndon's in this chapter are from the Robert E. McKay interview.
5. From an interview with Helen Weinberg, Houston, August 14, 1964, as it appears in Pool, Craddock, and Conrad's *The Formative Years*, p. 159.

Mr. Dick

1. From a reminiscence of Russell Morton Brown, who turned much of his memories of these times into an unpublished novel.

"It Was Announced Today"

1. Civilian Conservation Corps.
2. At that time Blanco County, where Johnson City was located, was in the Fourteenth Congressional District; by 1937 when Johnson first ran for Congress it was in the Tenth District.
3. The word *maverick* is an eponym coined from Maury's grandfather Sam, who never branded his cattle; loose calves not part of a herd were thereby dubbed "mavericks."
4. Huey Long was assassinated that same year by a young doctor in Louisiana—at least that is the official version. There is still considerable controversy about the matter in the state, almost as much as that connected nationally with the death of John F. Kennedy. Many people in Louisiana and throughout the country were delighted that day—and who's to say that Roosevelt himself was not secretly pleased—but as Lyndon often said, "There weren't many poor folks among them. They knew who and what Huey was."

"On the Way"

1. Williams's grandfather, also something of an idealist, freed a thousand slaves during the Civil War. By the time the war ended he had lost everything.
2. Monroe Billington discusses the matter in detail in his article, "Lyndon B. Johnson and Blacks: The Early Years," from the *Journal of Negro History*, January 1977, pp. 26–42.
3. This chapter section has been very much helped by an unpublished thesis for a master of arts degree at Texas Tech University. The thesis is by Deborah Lynn Self and is titled "The National Youth Administration in Texas, 1935–39."
4. Lyndon later gave other versions of this episode, differing in detail. Documents available so far seem to support this one as do the accounts of those who knew Lyndon at the time.
5. In his autobiography, *Let the Glory Out* (New York: Viking, 1972), former Senator Albert Gore of Tennessee wrote: "In 1937 when asked in a public opinion poll, 'If there were only two political parties in this country—one for conservatives and one for liberals—which would you join?' Sixty-one percent of southerners replied 'liberals' as

compared with 47 percent of New Englanders, 51 percent of Middle Westerners, 50 percent in the Plains states, 51 percent in the Rocky Mountains, and 54 percent of Far Westerners." (Pp. 117–18.)

6. The Roosevelt plan for the Supreme Court.

7. In July 1937, S. 1392 was enthusiastically "returned to the Judiciary Committee" by the Senate, seventy to twenty-one, from which it never emerged; it was Roosevelt's first major defeat in that body since he became president.

However, Willis Van Devanter, the most conservative of the justices, soon resigned, and in August Roosevelt appointed Hugo L. Black, fifty-one, of Alabama to Van Devanter's seat on the court, the first of nine appointments to the nine-man court.

By 1942 there were still only nine members of the U.S. Supreme Court, but only one, Chief Justice Owen J. Roberts, was not a Roosevelt appointee.

8. Robert E. Kintner, then a Washington newspaperman, a correspondent for the *New York Herald-Tribune*, remembers not the conversation but Johnson's account of it when he first met Lyndon on the train to Fort Worth.

9. From Trohan's reminiscences, *Political Animals* (New York: Doubleday, 1975), p. 352.

Remaking America

1. Chairman of the House Naval Affairs Committee.

2. Washington was much more lovable in those days. I once actually got invited to Harold Ickes's house, where Virginia Foster Durr, who looked like the winner of a campus beauty contest, was one of the guests. I loved them all. Their sleeves were all rolled up for remaking the world.

And it did seem everybody knew everybody else—everybody *worth* knowing, anyway. No one knew any Republicans. But we all adored the Roosevelts, especially Eleanor, and once she said, "Why don't you come to dinner on Tuesday?" I think it was forty-eight hours before I realized she meant at the *White House.*

3. Michael Janeway notes in his thesis *Lyndon Johnson and the Rise of Conservatism in Texas* that later Milo Perkins said of Johnson: "He was the first man in Congress to go to bat for the Negro farmer."

4. Maury Maverick was defeated in 1938 after serving two terms in Congress.

5. Rural Electrification Administration.

6. Then Roosevelt's appointments secretary.

Roosevelt's Boy

1. In Michael Janeway's thesis, *Lyndon Johnson and the Rise of Conservatism in Texas*, he writes, "From 1937 on, an anti-poll tax or anti-lynching bill was approved on the floor of the House of Representatives on the average of once every two years. Johnson either voted against or was paired against every one of them after he came to Congress. He had always said that he favored a Constitutional amendment abolishing the poll tax. This did not smack of federal 'force,' while it appealed to poor white voters who liked the poll tax even less than the politically organized Negro voters of Texas cities."

2. *The Johnson Eclipse*, etc., pp. 200–01.

3. "Profile of a President," Leslie Carpenter, the *Dallas Times-Herald*, February 9, 1964.

4. J. Russell Wiggins, former editor of the *Washington Post* and Lyndon's appointee as U.S. ambassador to the United Nations: "In the days before investigative reporting, so-called, a rule was that you never quoted anybody after he'd had two drinks or what he said after nine o'clock at night."

5. Vol. 2, pp. 693–94.

6. Lyndon himself claimed to have raised $60,000, but his estimates of campaign expenditures, his own in particular, were always notoriously low.

7. Instead of the estimated loss the Democrats did indeed gain five seats in the House that

year. And, of course, Franklin Roosevelt won his third term.

The Defeat

1. Vol. 3, p. 526.
2. For most of the material about Pappy's early life I am indebted to Frank Goodwyn's *Lone-Star Land*.
3. The lyrics to this last have fortunately been preserved:

   > A mother is a mother
   > Wherever you find her
   > Be she a Queen
   > Or an organ grinder.

4. By Texas law if a vacancy occurs while ·Congress is in session, a special election must be held within ninety days; in this case, before July 8.
5. On April 21, 1836, Sam Houston and his troops surprised and defeated a much larger contingent of Mexican troops under Santa Ana on the San Jacinto River. The battlefield, on the shores of the Houston Ship Channel, has a monument that is shaped like the Washington Monument except that it is fifteen feet higher. It has a single star at its base. April 21 is a big day in Texas; strong men weep.
6. Just the year before Lloyd Stark, then governor of Missouri, told Harry Truman, then a U.S. Senator, that people in Missouri were urging him to run against Truman, but that he would under no circumstances do it. Harry waited until Stark left his office, then turned to his secretary and said, "That son of a bitch is going to run against me!" And he was right.

   Harry was never taken in by the con man; Lyndon almost invariably was.
7. Joe Belden, using essentially the same methods as George Gallup, began his polling of Texans during the 1940 presidential campaign while he was still a student at the University of Texas. Belden polls were usually very accurate.
8. One issue virtually ignored in this campaign was that of the poll tax. O'Daniel had opposed it vigorously in his 1938 gubernatorial campaign, but it had since receded in importance and apparently no candidate felt it was worth making an issue of in 1941.
9. Although Speaker Rayburn had openly announced his support of Johnson, his district went for O'Daniel.

Pearl Harbor—Before and After

1. It was the first time I had heard him speak formally. I found him hopelessly corny and his accent painful; corn, of course, was not uncommon in those days.
2. Also, what Lyndon did not mention, was that at the time a southerner was likely to be more effective than a New Englander.
3. The use of Hull had, as Mr. White says, already been cleared by Roosevelt; I doubt that Hull's name was suggested to Sam Rayburn or that the secretary of state's letter arrived only ten minutes before the debate closed. But I have been unable to discover any proof to the contrary, and drama is drama.

Pacific Journey

1. Prell, Hatch, Bench, and Greer were the pilots.
2. J. B. Lippincott, Philadelphia and New York, 1964.
3. Martin Caidin and Edward Hymoff, *The Mission*, p. 79.
4. Ibid., p. 119.
5. Ibid., p. 123.
6. Ibid., p. 125.
7. Ibid., p. 126.
8. The alert reader will find certain similarities between the official communiqués in a popular war like this one and those in an unpopular war like Vietnam.
9. *The Mission*, pp. 128–29.
10. The copilot with Greer was Australian Flight Sergeant G. A. McMullin.
11. *The Mission*, pp. 155–56.
12. Ibid., p. 158.
13. Ibid., pp. 166–67.

The Home Front

1. Although Lyndon never chaired the watchdog-type subcommittee he had in mind, he did head two subcommittees of the House Naval Affairs Committee during the war. The first, formed to oversee the Navy's procurement program and general warfare management, was rather meagerly budgeted funds on the premise that that would keep its activities within bounds. Johnson merely circumvented that difficulty by borrowing naval reserve officers from the Navy Department to staff his extensive investigations.

    The second subcommittee was formed in May 1945 when five members of the Naval Affairs Committee were selected by chairman Carl Vinson to make a tour of Europe, ostensibly to check on surplus Navy property and at the same time give the congressmen a firsthand view of the conditions in postwar Europe. The trip included stops in London, Paris, Rheims (where they met General Eisenhower), Bremen, Marseilles, Naples, Rome (where they met Pope Pius XXII), Oran, Casablanca, Rabat, Cannes, Nice, Monte Carlo, and Munich, more or less in that order. They also went to Dachau, a day Lyndon seldom mentioned again because, according to Lady Bird, "He just couldn't talk about it."

"KTBC"

1. Others besides Connally, Pickle, and Phinney included Jesse Kellam, Sherman Birdwell, Walter Jenkins, Willard Deason, Ed Clark, and Merrill Connally. Only the last did not continue an active relationship with Lyndon.
2. Valenti appeared on Susskind's *Open End* on January 14, 1976.

The Geriatric Problem of 1948

1. Several Texas newspapers at the time said the Sikorsky was loaned to Lyndon by Wesley W. West, a Houston oil man, one of the richest and most reactionary—the same West who had inherited the KTBC purchase option from his father and passed it along to Austin businessman E. G. Kingsbery. It was also said that although the Texas aircraft companies did not lend him planes, they poured a good deal of money into his campaign—not surprising considering his advocacy of the world's largest air force. None of these allegations was ever proved. Naturally, in 1948, as always, Brown and Root money was readily available to Lyndon.
2. Many years later Truman reminded me that one should, on the twenty-sixth of July, wet or dry, sow turnips. No further explanation was ever volunteered.

The Duke of Duval and Alice

1. Later Lyndon, who in retrospect found much of the campaign amusing, would frequently tell the story of the two Mexican boys.

    "What's the matter, Pablo? You look sad."

    "I am sad, Pedro. My father came to Alice last week, and he didn't come to see me."

    "Pablo, your father has been dead for seven years."

    "I know, but he came back to Alice last week to vote for Lyndon Johnson, and he didn't come to see me."
2. They were later joined by a third person, Jim Gardner.
3. By H. Gordon Frost and John H. Jenkins, 1968, p. 277.

The Law is the Law

1. Approximately a week had passed since Judge Davidson's hearing in Fort Worth.
2. Each Supreme Court justice, in addition to sitting on the bench in Washington, is also responsible for a federal court district. Hugo Black's district included Texas; the court was in New Orleans.
3. On October 7 the U.S. Court of Appeals, meeting a week earlier than was originally intended, ruled in an extended opinion (170 F. 2s108) and cited Supreme Court precedents to the effect that the Constitution provides that each house of Congress judge the qualifications of its own members:

   We are of the opinion . . . that there is here no case for interference by a federal court . . . in a senatorial primary; that the injunction ought not to have been granted; and that the motion to dismiss ought now to be sustained.

   Finally, on January 31, 1949, the Supreme Court declined to review the decision of the Fifth Circuit Court of Appeals (336 U.S. 904).
4. President Truman was at least fond of Lyndon; Justice Black reportedly was not.

Treading Lightly

1. Although Russell was no doubt the strongest voice on the committee, he was, technically speaking, second in command; the chairman was Millard Tydings of Maryland. Russell became chairman in 1951.
2. From his thesis *Lyndon Johnson and the Rise of Conservatism in Texas.*
3. "Lyndon B. Johnson and Blacks: The Early Years," *Journal of Negro History* (January 1977).
4. General Harry Vaughan was President Truman's military aide; he had served with the president in Battery D during World War I. He was also Truman's most criticized associate, there being the matter of six Deepfreezes he was said to have accepted.
5. From his paper "The Leland Olds Controversy," 1973.
6. Old Harry, never one to be bested if he could help it, promptly appointed Olds to two other posts—one, as the only full-time member of the Water Resources Policy Commission, and the other as a member of the interior's New York and New England Interagency Committee—neither of which required Senate confirmation.
7. Janeway, op. cit.

Getting Ahead

1. Alfred Steinberg, *Sam Johnson's Boy*, p. 325.
2. *LBJ: An Irreverent Chronicle*, p. 18. The conversation occurred in 1953 shortly after Mooney started working for Lyndon.

Minority Leader

1. McFarland hadn't been much of a leader or, for that matter, much of a senator; Lyndon called him "Booby" McFarland.
2. Taft was discovered to have terminal cancer shortly after the session opened. By July he was dead.
3. Janeway, op. cit.
4. For this quote and other material in this chapter the author is indebted to Rowland Evans and Robert Novak, *Lyndon B. Johnson: The Exercise of Power*, chapter 4.

Summer of '54

1. Maury Maverick, Jr., the son of the congressman, who died on June 8 of that year.
2. The Johnson television station, KTBC-TV, was the only one in Austin.

Joseph Raymond McCarthy

1. Hiss was an adviser in the State Department from 1936–47. He was a member of the American delegation to the Yalta conference in February 1945 and later that year presided at the UN organizing meeting in San Francisco.
2. The party had long since stopped issuing cards to its members, and it seems unlikely that if by chance one had an outdated one, he or she would carry it around, especially to work in the State Department.
3. The three Democratic members—Symington of Missouri, Jackson of Washington, and McClellan of Arkansas—boycotted the committee completely between July of '53 and January of '54. Republican members included Mundt of South Dakota, Dirksen of Illinois, Potter of Michigan, and later at the hearings, Dworshak of Idaho.

Majority Leader

1. As George E. Reedy pointed out, "The majority leader of the Senate has no authority really. The rules, the customs, the traditions of the Senate only give him one advantage over any other senator, and that is, if two senators stand up simultaneously and seek recognition and he is one of them, the chair will always recognize the majority leader."
2. *LBJ: An Irreverent Chronicle*, pp. 49–50.
3. Much as they disliked the numbers of housing units involved, the Republicans were basically in favor of the bill.

The Long Shadows

1. The 1952 Immigration and Nationality Act, popularly known as the McCarran-Walter Act, removed racial bars to immi-gration, but also barred the admission of Communists and other "subversives."
2. Well, mostly—until after the presidency anyway.
3. All politicians exaggerate, southwestern politicians in particular. But Texas politicians exaggerate absolutely, and Congressman Pickle is no exception. The hall in Whitney held about a thousand people, and even the most enthusiastic newspaper observer found that no more than fifteen hundred people attended the rally.

   Not unimpressive, though, considering that the town of Whitney then had a population of fewer than fourteen hundred people.
4. Rowe's law partner.

The Southern Manifesto

1. The House vote was 209 to 203.
2. In 1949 Truman vetoed the Kerr bill, which would have done away with federal price control over natural gas.
3. *Let the Glory Out*, p. 102.
4. Earle Clements paid heavily for his loyalty; in November he lost his seat to Republican Thruston Morton, and as his daughter Bess Clements Abell says, he knew that his vote for the disability amendment was the cause, but he did not regret it. Mrs. Abell became Lady Bird's social secretary in the White House.
5. At the strong urging of his attorney general, Herbert Brownell, a reluctant Eisenhower had formulated a civil rights bill, rather strong for its time and geared toward attracting Negro votes to the Republican cause, which it did.

Adlai Again

1. From a letter to John Erickson, September 30, 1955. *Speak, Mr. Speaker*, p. 280.
2. From a letter to Carrell V. Head, September 8, 1955. Ibid.
3. *LBJ: An Irreverent Chronicle*, pp. 116–17.

4. This incident was described to Hubert J. Muller by Harry Ashmore and is included in his *Adlai Stevenson: A Study in Values*, pp. 175–76.
5. A lot about Lyndon's being a "true son of the Hill Country" and how he loved the people and that the love they felt for him had turned into something I'm afraid "Big John" referred to as "an unquenchable flame of trust."
6. *LBJ: An Irreverent Chronicle*, p. 120.
7. Kennedy must have forgotten that Franklin Roosevelt ran for the vice-presidency in 1920 with James M. Cox on the Democratic ticket that was defeated by Warren Harding and Calvin Coolidge. The loss did not exactly "bury" Roosevelt.

A First Step

1. Shivers appointed an archconservative, W. A. Blakely, interim senator. The special election for Daniel's Senate seat was won by Ralph Yarborough, whom Daniel had defeated for the governorship. Nothing incestuous about Texas politics.
2. Lyndon's response to Israel and the Middle East is discussed in detail in "The Friend of Israel."
3. O'Mahoney was the sole sponsor of the amendment in its original form; Kefauver and Church came in later as the amendment was revised.
4. "Letter to Washington," *New Yorker* (August 31, 1957).

One Big Happy Family

1. "It's One Big Happy Family," by Maxine Cheshire, *Washington Post* (January 3, 1956).
2. From a memorandum dated April 21, 1956.

Sputnik and Other Matters

1. Muskie was perhaps fortunate that his Senate career overlapped so briefly with Lyndon's; Paul Douglas, the only professional economist in the Senate, tried for four terms to get on the Senate Finance Committee and only succeeded after Lyndon became vice-president.
2. *Look* magazine (August 18, 1959).

"In Those Days at Least You Knew"

1. The bill, S. 499, featured an antibombing provision, provided for the extension of the Civil Rights Commission, granted subpoena powers to the Justice Department in investigations of voting rights infractions, and established a Federal Community Relations Service.
2. But even this was watered down from the original provision to allow such referees to be appointed only after the Justice Department had sued and obtained a federal court order that would require the registration of persons so discriminated against.
3. *Civil Rights*, vol. 1, 1960–66, was used extensively in the preparation of this chapter.

Arthur and Modred

1. Kennedy carried Wisconsin with 56 percent of the vote to Hubert's 43.5 percent. But the vote was viewed as inconclusive because Kennedy did best in the heavily Catholic industrial areas where many Republican Catholics crossed over to vote for him. Humphrey did not consider himself "badly beaten," although he was often called "the third senator from Wisconsin." He did, however, realize that West Vir-

ginia, where Republican crossovers were not permitted, would be his last chance.

2. This was, of course, prior to her visit with Lyndon in Washington that spring.

3. *Pulling No Punches*, p. 227.

4. 1960 Senate voting participation scores showed Kennedy scoring 35 percent, Humphrey 49 percent, Symington 58 percent, and Johnson 95 percent.

5. *LBJ: An Irreverent Chronicle*, p. 122.

6. Ibid., p. 127.

7. Krock's memory fails him here. The lines are correct, but they refer not to an incident between Arthur and Modred, but to one between Modred and Lancelot in the "Guinivere" section of the poem. Modred has climbed to the top of the garden wall to spy on the Queen, hoping to catch her in some scandalous behavior, when he is caught in the act by Lancelot chancing by. Lancelot, says Tennyson, "pluck'd him by the heel,/ And cast him as a worm upon the way." It was this "small violence done" that rankled with Modred from that point on. To Krock's credit, the sand castle story is at least as charming.

  8. Michael V. DiSalle, then governor of Ohio, says in his book *Second Choice* that "along the way he [Stevenson] had given Kennedy his word that he would not be a candidate."

"The Word in Los Angeles Is . . ."

1. Arthur M. Schlesinger, Jr., in *Robert Kennedy and His Times* says that Bobby, Joe Rauh, and Walter Reuther, among others, felt that when, once in Los Angeles, such "expected Johnson supporters" as Hubert Humphrey and Eugene McCarthy declared for Stevenson, it was a strong indication that the Stevenson drive was "a Johnson front organized to prevent a Kennedy nomination on the first ballot." Why these two strongly liberal Minnesotans should have been expected to support Johnson over Stevenson he does not say.

2. A Minneapolis businessman and close friend of Humphrey's.

3. Who hit whom depends on who tells the story. Evans and Novak report that it was Rauh who hit O'Connor after O'Connor tried to block Rauh's entry into the room. Rauh's reason for his visit was in exact opposition to Lyndon's; i.e., to persuade Humphrey to declare for Kennedy and thus put himself in line for the second spot.

4. A progressive disease brought about by atrophy of the adrenocortical glands. It was once fatal, but is now successfully treated, although not cured, by cortisone.

5. Lyndon also held a press conference on the fifth to announce his candidacy. He replied to a reporter's question on the matter that to the best of his knowledge all candidates of the Democratic party enjoyed good health.

6. *Pulling No Punches*, p. 229.

7. They were equally outraged that the Johnson forces—John B. Connally in particular—should see fit to revive the ghost of Joe Kennedy's fraternization with Neville Chamberlain and support of his appeasement policies before World War II. In the last day or two before the balloting, Johnson himself, desperate, took up the refrain.

8. From the memorandum Graham put together after the convention concerning the part he played in the events there. The memorandum was among papers given to the author by Katherine Graham.

9. From the memorandum.

Wednesday Night

1. Truman declined to come to the convention because he said it was already "fixed" for Kennedy.

2. Manatos misremembers here; New Jersey gave all its forty votes to favorite son, Governor Robert Meyner. Probably it was Kansas, which did pass, that Manatos is referring to.

3. The final ballot count was Kennedy, 806; Johnson, 409; Symington, 86; Stevenson, 79½; all others combined, 140½.

And Thursday Morning

1. Of that list Sorensen elaborates further in his book *Kennedy:* "I had submitted to the Senator and brother Bob several weeks earlier, as had many others, a list of potential vice-presidential nominees. On my list 22 names were reduced to 15 and then to six. . . . Those ruled out on my list were too liberal, too conservative, too inarticulate, too offensive to some groups in the party, too much like Kennedy in strengths and weaknesses or too young. . . . I placed at the top of my list, as did many others, the name of one man who had none of these disqualifications and many qualifications: Lyndon B. Johnson." (Pp. 162–63.)
2. In a memorandum he wrote two months after the convention, Arthur Krock reports that Kennedy personally encountered Symington in a hotel corridor that night after the nomination and said to him, "You are my first available choice for the vice-president." Of course, Kennedy could have met with Clifford and then run into Symington by chance, although there is no other evidence that Kennedy went to any hotel that night. He did go back to the apartment on North Rossemere Boulevard, and presumably the private room Clifford speaks of was there.
3. From *David Dubinsky: A Life with Labor*, p. 292.
4. All the quotes by Phil Graham in this chapter are from the memorandum.
5. Of course the way Phil Graham, Walter Jenkins, and Lady Bird remember these events is in direct contrast to what Bobby Kennedy told Arthur M. Schlesinger, Jr., as reported in *Robert Kennedy and His Times*. Apparently Bobby told Schlesinger that he did see Johnson, had a long conversation with him alone, tried to extricate his brother from the commitment, was met with tears on Lyndon's part, and gave up the attempt. Sam Rayburn does not even figure in Bobby's account to Schlesinger.
6. It was probably during this conversation that Bobby is reported to have said to Rayburn that perhaps, rather than be vice-president, Lyndon might prefer to be Democratic national chairman, and Rayburn is reported to have given Bobby a long look and answered, "Shit!"

From Boston to Austin

1. The visit to Hyannis Port, Lyndon's first meeting with Kennedy since the convention, was brief. Most of the scheduling was done in Washington during the rump session.
2. It is illegal to accept campaign contributions in a public building.
3. The parade was canceled because of the rain.
4. Hale and O'Brien were tackle and running back respectively on the Texas Christian football team.
5. Thruston Morton.

A Joyless Victory

1. The *New York Times* reported that both men killed two deer, Lyndon shooting one through the heart from a distance of six hundred yards—"The best shot I have ever seen," Kennedy is reported to have said.
2. According to Arthur M. Schlesinger, Jr., in *A Thousand Days*, p. 153.

Keeping Lyndon Happy

1. Kennedy's remark was widely reported.
2. In June 1961, the Johnsons bought The Elms, Perle Mesta's lovely hilltop home on Fifty-second Street, N.W. It was modeled after a French chateau. Some of its walls and floors had been imported directly from ancient castles in France, and many pieces of furniture, which were included in the purchase, were duplicates of French originals.

The Man with No Shirt

1. From a letter to Philip Graham.
2. Of course, while Lyndon's formal education ended at San Marcos, Galbraith did go on to the University of California at Berkeley, where he was awarded a Ph.D. in 1934, after which he taught economics at Harvard and Princeton.
3. *The Ambassador's Journal*, p. 123.

Americans in Berlin

1. Lyndon, in a National Security Council meeting July 13, favored even more drastic moves including an increase of $5 billion to the defense budget and standby wage and price controls.
2. D. B. Hardeman's account of the story as Lyndon retold it to him.
3. Brandt did not forget being reprimanded by Lyndon. As he says in his autobiography, *Encounters and Insights*, published in Germany in 1977, of this visit, "On a Saturday evening, he had to get shoes from a store which had been closed because he liked mine so much. Since his feet were two different sizes, he needed two pairs. On Sunday, we had to get a collection of electric shavers as presents for friends. Later that same evening, the director of a manufacturing company came to the Berlin Hilton to take an order for a considerable number of small ashtrays. . . . Johnson's disarming explanation: 'They look like a dollar and cost me only twenty-five cents.'"
4. Other reports indicated it was more like three hundred thousand.

August in Ankara

1. Komer was then White House special assistant for noncommitted nations and advised the president on disarmament policy.

2. From October 1968 until April 1969 Komer was ambassador to Turkey, appointed, of course, by President Lyndon B. Johnson.

The 101st Senator

1. *Wheeling and Dealing* by Bobby Baker and Larry L. King (New York, W. W. Norton, 1978).
2. Perhaps I should add that, having been raised in a family in which a number of uncles were insurance men, it never struck me as strange that commissions were split and that when loads of money were involved, like two $100,000 life insurance policies, various grateful uncles gave the insuree a little present. A bottle of whiskey was not uncommon; a case of whiskey, except for rot-gut stuff, was rare, a Magnavox stereo even more so. But I was young at the time; Marshalltown, Iowa, was not Washington, D.C.; and the 1930s were not the 1960s.

Dumping Lyndon

1. Mrs. Lincoln, Kennedy's personal secretary, published *Kennedy and Johnson* (New York: Holt, Rinehart and Winston, 1968).

November 22, 1963

1. Ralph Yarborough, a liberal Democrat, became senior senator from Texas after John Tower, Republican, was elected to Johnson's old seat. John Connally, elected governor the previous November, was then still a Democrat.
2. *Twenty Years in the Secret Service*, pp. 112–13.
3. As dictated to Lyndon's secretary, Marie Fehmer, on the flight back to Washington.
4. *A White House Diary*, pp. 4–5.

The Flight Back

1. 2:47 Dallas time. What happened in Dallas had taken place in three hours' time.
2. *The Death of a President, November 20–November 25, 1963* (New York: Harper and Row, 1967).

The Long Weekend

1. Accounts of it vary widely. In the Manchester book, Lyndon is quoted by Mrs. Lincoln as saying he wanted "his girls" in her office by 9:30 that morning. That, according to Manchester, was Bobby's memory as well. (In *Robert Kennedy and His Times*, Arthur M. Schlesinger, Jr., mentions no such encounter.)

There was understandably a certain amount of general confusion that morning, as well as some tardy communication, which led to a misunderstanding. Although recordings from Air Force One the previous day indicate General Clifton reporting that Lyndon told him he planned to work out of the EOB for the time being, on the helicopter trip from Andrews the night before, McNamara, Ball and Bundy had agreed that, for the sake of the national image, the president should move into the Oval Office as quickly as possible and had impressed this fact on Lyndon. Bundy remembers Lyndon having doubts that this was the right thing to do. Later, Bundy suggested to Lyndon that the Oval Office might be ready the next day.

The following morning Bundy went very early to the White House and spoke with Robert Kennedy and Mrs. Lincoln. When they expressed the need for more time, Bundy went to Lyndon's office in the EOB and left the following message in the care of his secretary, Mildred Stegall:

November 23, 1963
8:05 A.M.

When you and I talked last night about when the President's office in the West Wing would be ready, I thought possibly it would be immediately. However, I find they are working on President Kennedy's papers and his personal belongings, and my suggestion would be that—if you could work here in the Executive Office Building today and tomorrow, everything will be ready and clear by Monday morning.

I am arranging an office in the Executive Office Building for Mrs. Lincoln to handle Mr. Kennedy's personal effects, if that is all right with you.

Unfortunately, Lyndon, accompanied by Bill Moyers, did not stop by his office in the EOB before going to the Oval Office, so he did not see Bundy's message. He too, of course, encountered Bobby Kennedy and Mrs. Lincoln, to both of whom he expressed his condolences. There apparently was some discussion of timing, at which point Bobby Kennedy and Mrs. Lincoln, perhaps because they had already gone into the matter with Bundy an hour before, perhaps because they were distraught, took offense. Bill Moyers, who was present, said that Lyndon was not at all rude, but, on the contrary, told Mrs. Lincoln when he saw her packing up things, "You don't have to do that—you just take your time."

In any case, Bundy was under the impression that an amicable arrangement had been agreed upon by all the parties concerned that the new president would move into the Oval Office after the funeral. And Lyndon himself came away with the impression that there were absolutely no hard feelings about the matter at the time. The later reports of his "insensitive" behavior consequently came as a good deal of a surprise.

2. *A White House Diary*, p. 7.
3. Also present besides the cabinet members themselves were White House press secretary Pierre Salinger, special counsel Ted Sorensen, and Jack Valenti.

4. Bobby had first not planned to attend, but was persuaded to by Mac Bundy. Lyndon suggested that the assembled cabinet members wait for Bobby's arrival; Bobby later interpreted this as Lyndon making a point of his tardiness.
5. These included Dean Rusk, secretary of state, C. Douglas Dillon, secretary of the treasury, Robert McNamara, secretary of defense, Robert F. Kennedy, attorney general, John A. Grounouski, postmaster general, Stewart Udall, secretary of the interior, Orville Freeman, secretary of agriculture, Luther Hodges, secretary of commerce, W. Willard Wirtz, secretary of labor, and Anthony Celebreeze, secretary of health, education, and welfare.
6. From William Lawrence's autobiography, *Six Presidents, Too Many Wars,* p. 268.
7. *A White House Diary,* pp. 8–9.
8. *Reporter* magazine (December 1963).
9. Meetings with chiefs of state, their consorts, and chiefs of government continued for several days. Prince Philip of Great Britain paid a call; others included prime ministers Ikeda of Japan, Pearson of Canada, and Inonu of Turkey, and presidents Luebke of Germany, and Macapagal of the Philippines.
10. Mrs. Kennedy and the children moved out of the White House on December 6, but Caroline's kindergarten class continued to occupy the top floor until the Christmas recess.

Building Bridges

1. Not quite final; a few more finishing touches were added later that morning by several people.
2. Among the ninety members of the Business Council, a liaison group between business and government, Johnson talked to in the Fish Room were Henry Ford II, Frederick Kappell, chairman of AT&T, and Roger Blough of U.S. Steel.

The Warren Commission

1. Dulles and McCloy were the two appointees requested by Bobby Kennedy. McCloy was a Wall Street lawyer, naturally, Harvard graduate, president of the World Bank, renowned member of the War Department during World War II, and adviser, too, mostly on foreign affairs, to Truman and Kennedy and later Lyndon, former military governor and high commissioner for Germany, and former chairman of the Chase Manhattan Bank. At that moment, he was chairman of the Ford Foundation.
2. P. 121.
3. Ibid.
4. Ibid., p. 120.

First Lady

1. "LBJ's Rambunctious Retirement," *Harper's Weekly,* January 24, 1975.

End of the First 100 Days

1. A week later the president accepted Sorensen's resignation as special counsel to the president. He and Brook Hays, a special assistant, were the first of the Kennedy aides to go, and one by one after that most of the others resigned. Sorensen was probably the one man close to Kennedy personally whose departure Lyndon truly regretted.

The War on Poverty

1. From a letter to Harry Middleton, director of the Lyndon Baines Johnson Library.
2. *The Vantage Point,* p. 72.

3. Ibid., p. 75.
4. From a speech, "Community Action and the Social Programs of the 1960s," delivered at the Lyndon Baines Johnson Library symposium "Toward New Human Rights," November 12–16, 1976.
5. *The Education of a Public Man*, pp. 411–12.
6. Peter Joseph, *Good Times*, p. 239.

The Courtship of Ev Dirksen

1. *The Vantage Point*, p. 157.

Unveiling The Great Society

1. Lyndon had asked for twenty; apparently that was his compromise.
2. Other reports have it that Valenti edited Goodwin's first version heavily and that only after Moyers persuaded Lyndon to read the original did Goodwin's prose win.

The Inheritance

1. Briefing no. 3.
2. On May 8, 1963, about ten thousand Buddhists in Hué marched in protest against the regime of Diem, a Catholic, whose government was increasingly dominated by his brother Nhu and by Madame Nhu, a lady of formidable temperament and appearance. Such demonstrations were forbidden by Diem's government, which also did not approve of the many Buddhists who were burning themselves to death in public. Madame Nhu called them "monk barbeque shows."
3. Remarks of Bobby Kennedy's in this chapter are taken from a series of interviews conducted in the spring of 1964 by John Bartlow Martin.
4. Sir Robert Thompson, head of the British Advisory Mission to Vietnam, 1961–65.

5. *Many Reasons Why: The American Involvement in Vietnam*, by Michael Charlton and Anthony Moncrieff (New York: Hill and Wang, 1978), p. 82.

Tonkin

1. A good deal of this chapter is possible only because of the detailed chronology and detective work done by Eugene F. Windchy for his exemplary book, *Tonkin Gulf: A documentary of the incidents in the Tonkin Gulf on August 2 and August 4, 1964 and their consequences* (New York: Doubleday, 1971).
2. Advisers who met regularly with the president on Tuesdays for lunch and to discuss foreign policy. Original participants included Dean Rusk, Robert McNamara, and McGeorge Bundy; later General Earle Wheeler, Richard Helms, and Walt Rostow also attended. Press secretaries Bill Moyers and George Christian also took part.
3. *The Education of a Public Man*, p. 352.
4. General Earle G. Wheeler had become chairman of the Joint Chiefs only a few weeks before, in July.
5. *Tonkin Gulf*, p. 212.
6. Ibid., p. 215.

To Run or Not to Run

1. July 29, 1964.
2. Mutual dislike was not the only reason for dropping Bobby. The week before the Democratic convention a Harris poll showed that 33 percent of the Democrats in the South would bolt the ticket if Bobby were on it; only 4 percent would bolt if Humphrey were on it. Surveys showed that Bobby was not popular with the business community either.
3. *Time* magazine, which just that week had run a highly critical article about Lady Bird.
4. The thirty-five previous presidents, that is.

A Lovely Campaign

1. In four days the Lady Bird Special made sixty-seven stops, traveled 1,682 miles, and Mrs. Johnson made forty-seven speeches.
2. He was referring to the 1964 Civil Rights Act.
3. The senator was Joseph Weldon Bailey, and the state he didn't name was Mississippi. Bailey, who served as a senator from Texas, was born and educated in Mississippi.
4. Which is to say that they played on the racial issue and never raised the real issues. This excerpt was taken from a tape recording of the actual speech delivered in New Orleans on October 9 and differs somewhat from the official version in the presidential papers, which quotes from the prepared text from which Johnson frequently digressed.
5. Actually, two other newspapers, the *Chicago Tribune* and the *Cincinnati Enquirer* had had the story but decided against printing it.

   The original leak was said to have come from the Washington police department to members of the Republican National Committee. Others said the leak had come from the FBI. Many felt then and still feel that Jenkins was entrapped by Goldwater people.

   Moyers many years later wrote in *Newsweek*, "I had never thought that what happened to Walter Jenkins was a conspiracy of anything more than bone-crushing work and too little rest. Goldwater himself had refused to make a serious issue of it in the campaign."
6. The statement read: "My heart is aching today for someone who has reached the end point of exhaustion in dedicated service to his country. Walter Jenkins has been carrying incredible hours and burdens since President Kennedy's assassination. He is now receiving the medical attention which he needs. I know our family and all of his friends—and I hope all others—pray for his recovery. I know that the love of his wife and six fine children and his profound religious faith will sustain him through this period of anguish."
7. The ad, which was created by the New York firm of Doyle, Dane, Bernbach, showed a small girl audibly counting the petals she is plucking from a daisy. Then the screen faded to a countdown in what is clearly an atomic testing site. Finally, the screen dissolved into a mushroom cloud. Neither Goldwater nor the Republican party was mentioned.
8. It seems unlikely that Rebekah would allow Lyndon to go to the Texas House of Representatives in his bare feet, but on the last night of the campaign—what the heck. A little political license here is not only allowed; it is called for.

A Good Place to Walk

1. Built in 1890 by a German farmer, the house and several hundred acres of land had been purchased by Lyndon's Aunt Frank and Uncle Clarence Martin in 1912. Their family lived there for forty years, until the Johnsons acquired it.
2. From "Lyndon Johnson: How Does He Do It?" by Stewart Alsop, *The Saturday Evening Post*, January 24, 1959.

The Commitment

1. "Two Threats to World Peace" speech at Omaha, June 30, 1966, on the occasion of the sending of the five millionth ton of grain to India.
2. Lyndon conveniently ignored the fact that although he may be refusing to drop bombs "on certain areas," he was already dropping them on certain other areas, namely North Vietnamese naval bases and oil storage tanks, as a result of the Tonkin incident.
3. Dean Rusk was in Florida that day recovering from influenza—when he heard the

news he called his undersecretary collect; Ball happened to be at the White House with Lyndon, who told the operator, according to Henry D. Graff, "George will take it, but charge it to the State Department, not the White House." *The Tuesday Cabinet*, p. 59.
4. *The Vantage Point*, p. 124.
5. Ibid., p. 125.
6. From an article, "One Thing We Have Learned," by Bill Moyers for *Foreign Affairs* 46, no. 4 (July 1968).
7. *The Vantage Point*, pp. 130–31.
8. According to Arthur M. Schlesinger, Jr., in *Robert Kennedy and His Times*, the letter must have been written in January 1966; Lyndon, in a reply written by Jack Valenti and dated January 27, said that he knew exactly how Lincoln felt. Lincoln had told a friend that all the responsibilities of the administration "belong to that unhappy wretch called Abraham Lincoln."

The Frog Farm

1. Eric Goldman, *The Tragedy of Lyndon Johnson*, p. 423.
2. Ibid., pp. 465–66.
3. Ibid., p. 469.
4. Ibid., p. 471.

Hyperbole and the Dominican Republic

1. The other country on the island of Hispaniola is Haiti.
2. Frank Cormier, *LBJ: The Way He Was*, p. 190.

Overcoming

1. They were not.
2. *My Soul Is Rested*, by Howell Raines (New

York: G. P. Putnam's Sons, 1972), p. 339.
3. Alas, their relationship was not to endure; Goodwin resigned in September and became one of the more vocal critics of what was going on in Vietnam.

Using Up Capital

1. *New York Times*, August 10, 1965.
2. George Christian became press secretary after Moyers resigned in December 1966.
3. After he wrote *Jaws*, that is.
4. On January 17, 1968, at a National Press Club news conference, his last as president, Lyndon gave yet another explanation of his action: "I did show my scar, but it was only after a question from Sarah McClendon [Texas correspondent]. She jumped up behind the weeds out there on the golf course—maybe it wasn't the golf course, but it was a grassy area, I remember, near the Bethesda Hospital—and she said, 'Mr. President, you have been in office almost two years and what do you have to show for it?' And I get blamed for giving her the truth."

Women

1. Maurine Neuberger served as senator from Oregon from 1960 to 1966.
2. Simone Poulain was with the press office.
3. From a booklet entitled "Women in Public Life. Report of a Conference, November 9–11, 1975," Lyndon B. Johnson School of Public Affairs, University of Texas at Austin, 1976.
4. The prestigious Washington institution.
5. Barbara Jordan later became a congresswoman from Houston, Texas, and was on the House Judiciary Committee that investigated the Watergate affair.

More Guns and Less Butter

1. From the South Lawn remarks, September 13, 1968.

The War

1. Connally's association with Brown and Root went back to 1946 when, at their instigation, the Capitol National Bank of Austin lent him the $25,000 he needed for his share in KVET. Ideologically, the Browns were much closer to Connally than they were to Johnson.
2. Pp. 112–13.

The Other War

1. *A Very Personal Presidency*, p. 209.
2. Komer was an early advocate of pacification and in January 1966 was asked to take charge of the program. He was forever issuing optimistic reports about the plan's success. The reports, issued in Washington, were seldom backed up by observers in South Vietnam. And Komer soon decided that troops should be used to carry out the program.

    In May 1967, Johnson asked General Westmoreland to take the program over and he made Komer Westmoreland's assistant, though Komer was largely responsible for what happened. The program was now known as the Civil Operations and Revolutionary Development Support (CORDS), and its goal was not so much "pacification," a word never very satisfactorily defined anyway, as it was to relocate those Vietnamese (some said there were as many as two million of them) who were not under military control. When villagers would not or could not be moved, their villages were burned, sometimes the villagers as well. Though Komer, of course, did not burn anything himself, he was known to grunts (enlisted infantrymen) and combat officers as "Blowtorch."

The Downward Spiral

1. The question of whether or not Johnson resorted to taping conversations in the White House arose after the Watergate hearings when members of the Nixon staff said that on moving into the White House they had had to dismantle a complicated taping system left behind by Johnson. Clearly a certain amount of taping was done. Harry Middleton, director of the Lyndon Baines Johnson Library in Austin, affirmed that the library has in its possession eight cardboard cartons in which Johnson's tapes are preserved; the cartons are sealed and cannot, by instruction, be opened for fifty years.

    However, according to syndicated columnist Marianne Means in her column on November 3, 1974, "one extremely sensitive and explosive tape" remains in the custody of Walt Rostow.

    The tapes at the library are said to be mostly of telephone conversations, some transcribed by hand and some recorded by Dictaphone. According to Richard Vauter, public information director of the GSA, in an article from the July 17, 1973, *Washington Star*, "a limited number of recordings of meetings in 1968 in the Cabinet Room, mostly concerning national security affairs," are included as well.

    Also quoted in the *Star* article was Joseph A. Califano, who said that Johnson could record telephone calls in the Oval Office but had to turn the recorder on by hand, as opposed to the Nixon system, which was automatic. George Christian told the *Star* reporter that "the White House had the capability to record almost anything—meetings, telephone conversations, or what have you," but agreed with Califano that the system was not automatic.

    Miss Means also wrote in her column that "Johnson aides insisted that Johnson recorded only isolated conversations principally in the foreign policy area." The eight cartons, she said, "would not be adequate to store five years of steady or even frequent recordings."

2. According to William Sullivan, former assistant to Hoover, in his book *The Bureau: My Thirty Years in Hoover's FBI*, written with Bill Brown, Lyndon went one step further during the presidency and with DeLoach's help transferred secretarial personnel on his staff—Mildred Stegall for one—to the FBI payroll, although such personnel never actually did work for the FBI. Mrs. Stegall confirms that report.
3. Perhaps not a "bug," but according to Sullivan, again at Johnson's request the FBI did have a "surveillance team" on Robert Kennedy at the 1964 convention, a "continuation" of the one it already had on Dr. Martin Luther King.
4. The other two were the August 1941 extension of the draft and the Civil Rights Act of 1957.
5. *The Vantage Point*, p. 270.
6. *A Soldier Reports*, p. 214.

Word From Ho

1. James ("Scotty") Reston, a longtime Washington reporter and columnist for the *Times*.

The Friend of Israel

1. Edwin Weisl, Sr., was a lawyer for the Hearst Corporation, among many others.
2. Kenan was Israel's chief lobbyist in Washington for many years.
3. *The Vantage Point*, pp. 302–03.

The Dissent

1. *Diplomacy for a Crowded World*, p. 64.
2. Wilbur Cohen was appointed secretary of HEW early in 1968.

Imperfect Alternatives

1. *The Vantage Point*, p. 369.
2. *The Education of a Public Man*, p. 348.
3. Ibid., pp. 348–49.
4. The plane landed at a remote airfield and the president met with leaders of the Italian government at a prearranged country rendezvous.
5. There was actually a small landing pad there.

"What Shall I Do?"

1. Sam Ealy died before his sixty-first birthday; on the other hand, Lyndon's paternal grandfather lived until he was seventy-seven. Grandfather Baines died when he was sixty.
2. *Six Presidents, Too Many Wars*, pp. 270–71.
3. *A White House Diary*, pp. 611–12.
4. Ibid., pp. 616–17.

Tet

1. The man with the gun was Brigadier General Nguyen Ngoc Loan, chief of South Vietnam's National Police, now living in the United States.
2. Clark Clifford replaced Secretary of Defense McNamara on March 1, 1968.
3. Also present were Vice-President Humphrey, Secretaries Rusk and McNamara, Secretary of Defense designate Clifford, General Taylor, Deputy Secretary of Defense Paul Nitze, CIA Director Helms, Walt Rostow, George Christian, Tom Johnson.
4. The number varied between 205,000 and 206,000.
5. *The Vantage Point*, p. 402.

6. The two speeches referred to are remarks to delegates to the National Farmers Union Convention in Minneapolis on March 18, 1968, and remarks at the Conference on Foreign Policy for Leaders of National Nongovernmental Organizations on March 19, 1968, at the Department of State, Washington, D.C.
7. *Many Reasons Why*, pp. 131–32.

The Contenders

1. When McCarthy arrived in Chicago for the Democratic convention on August 25, 1968, almost twenty thousand people were waiting for him. He said, "Quite a few people have shown up for the execution."
2. While his name was not on the ballot, and he had not campaigned, the printed ballots that were available for the voters were quite professional. It was not your usual write-in. There were three parts to be filled out; one part—which was forwarded to the White House—entitled the voter to a picture of Lady Bird and Lyndon by return mail.
3. *The Vantage Point*, pp. 537–38.

March 31, 1968

1. *A White House Diary*, p. 642.
2. *A White House Diary*, p. 644.

"Mr. President, Martin Luther King Has Been Shot"

1. Walter F. Mondale succeeded to Humphrey's Senate seat when Humphrey became vice-president.

The Peace Talks

1. Actually no "line" was announced in the speech. It clearly read that the bombing would stop "except in the area north of the demilitarized zone where the continued enemy buildup directly threatens allied forward positions and where the movements of their troops and supplies are clearly related to that threat."
2. *The Vantage Point*, p. 495.
3. Notes were taken and are recorded in *The Vantage Point*, pp. 539–42.
4. *A White House Diary*, pp. 679–80.
5. Ibid., p. 682.
6. The Treaty was ratified by the Senate the following March.
7. From *Bill Moyers' Journal*—"Hubert Horatio Humphrey: A Conversation," WNET-TV, April 11, 1976.

A Change in Cast

1. According to Humphrey, Lyndon had arranged it so himself.
2. *The Vantage Point*, pp. 515–16.
3. Ibid., pp. 517–18.

So Little I Have Done, So Much I Have Yet to Do

1. *The Journey*.
2. From the Briefing no. 2.
3. A fellow Texan via Connecticut, among other things.
4. *The Vantage Point*, p. 568.

Flaws in a Diamond

1. *Time* magazine, March 17, 1958.
2. Johnson was not the first president to have a hot temper. Consider this description from Patrick Anderson's book, *Men Around the President*:

> An unwelcome report of some baseless criticism or some unfinished labor or some blemished performance could ignite an explosion almost fiercely physical. His voice would shout, his cheeks flame with rage, his arms wave threateningly. And I recall one of his oldest associates murmuring, after witnessing one such scene, "My God, how could you compute the amount of adrenaline expended in those thirty seconds? I don't know why long since he hasn't had a killer of a heart attack."

> Johnson in a rage? No— the "bland" Eisenhower as described by Emmett Hughes. One might also cite Evelyn Lincoln's description of Kennedy dressing down an innocent naval officer after *another* officer gave him a faulty weather report. Or Paul Fay's story of Kennedy berating a navy cook who served him fried instead of broiled chicken.

3. A *Soldier Reports*. pp. 383–84.

The Private Citizen

1. From *U.S. News & World Report*, December 24, 1973, "The LBJ Nobody Knew." An interview with Lady Bird Johnson, copyright © 1973 by U.S. News & World Report.
2. Doris Kearns, White House Fellow and author of *Lyndon Johnson and the American Dream*, was at the Ranch working on *The Vantage Point*.
3. From pp. 157 and 158.
4. After the lunch, at Ben Bradlee's request, Richard Harwood and Haynes Johnson each wrote down his impression of the afternoon, which Bradlee later combined into one memorandum. In later years Harwood and Johnson used some of the material in their book *Lyndon*.
5. Richard Harwood and Haynes Johnson, *Lyndon*, p. 168.
6. Pictures of Johnson published at the time of the convention showed his hair to be almost shoulder length.
   Robert Hardesty: "I had been in the hospital and since I got out, I had not had a haircut. My kids thought it looked great. But one day when I went out to see Johnson we were sitting by the pool and he said he thought I needed a haircut. I gave a smart-ass answer and said, 'Yes, Mr. President, but I don't want to look like those sonofabitches around Nixon—Haldeman, Ehrlichman—the whole bunch have short hair.' He nodded, and the next time I saw him his hair was growing over his collar."
7. In addition to his heart troubles, Johnson had severe stomach pains which were diagnosed as diverticulitis.
8. Leo Janos, "The Last Days of the President: LBJ in Retirement," *Atlantic* (July 1973).
9. The McGovern trip to the Ranch was a carefully kept secret; there is no record even at the Lyndon Baines Johnson Library of the exact date. It was between the twentieth of August and the first of September.
10. From Horace Busby's article "LBJ Toward the End: Getting Things in Order," *L. A. Times*, June 26, 1973.
11. *Washington Star*, September 1972.
12. Busby, op. cit.
13. Ibid.
14. From "Recollection," *Washington Post*, January 24, 1973.

15. "Thousands Fill Capital to Bid Lyndon Farewell," Waco *News-Tribune*, January 25, 1973.
16. Nancy Dickerson, *Among Those Present*, p. 156.
17. Newsroom's Tribute to LBJ, Channel Thirteen: "My Main Man," Dallas, January 23, 1973.
18. "Farewell to LBJ: A Hill Country Valediction," *Texas Monthly*, May 1973.

The Farewell Address

1. Little Roger, Roy's nephew, is six feet tall and weighs 180 pounds. Lyndon was six four and weighed 220.
2. Hugh Sidey, "One More Call to Reason Together: A Gathering at the Lyndon Baines Johnson Library, University of Texas." *Life* magazine, December 29, 1972.
3. Ibid.
4. Ibid.
5. Ibid.
6. Ibid.

BIBLIOGRAPHY

Books

Abels, Jules. *The Degeneration of Our Presidential Election.* New York: Macmillan, 1968.

Acheson, Dean. *Present at the Creation.* New York: W. W. Norton, 1969.

Alsop, Joseph, and Stewart Alsop. *The Reporter's Trade.* New York: Reynal, 1958.

Amrine, Michael. *This Awesome Challenge.* New York: G. P. Putnam's Sons, 1964.

Anderson, Clinton, with Milton Viorst. *Outsider in the Senate.* New York: World, 1970.

Anderson, Jack, and James Boyd. *Confessions of a Muckracker.* New York: Random House, 1979.

———, and Ronald W. McCarthy May. *The Man, The Senator, the "Ism."* Boston: Beacon, 1952.

Anderson, Patrick. *The President's Men: White House Assistants of FDR, HST, DDE, JFK, and LBJ.* New York: Doubleday, 1968.

Ashman, Charles. *Connally: The Adventures of Big Bad John.* New York: William Morrow, 1974.

Ashmore, Harry S., and William C. Baggs. *Mission to Hanoi.* New York: G. P. Putnam's Sons, 1968.

Austin, Anthony. *The President's War.* New York: J. B. Lippincott, 1971.

Bainbridge, John. *The Super-Americans.* New York: Doubleday, 1961.

Baker, Bobby, and Larry L. King. *Wheeling and Dealing.* New York: W. W. Norton, 1978.

Baker, Leonard. *The Johnson Eclipse.* New York: Macmillan, 1966.

Ball, George W. *Diplomacy for a Crowded World.* Boston: Little, Brown, 1976.

Barber, James David. *The Presidential Character.* Englewood Cliffs, N.J.: Prentice-Hall, 1972.

Bell, Jack. *The Johnson Treatment.* New York: Harper and Row, 1965.

Berman, Edgar, M.D. *Hubert.* New York: G. P. Putnam's Sons, 1979.

Bolling, Richard. *Power in the House*. New York: Capricorn, 1968.

Bradlee, Benjamin C. *Conversations with Kennedy*. New York: W. W. Norton, 1975.

Brammer, Billy Lee. *The Gay Place*. Boston: Houghton Mifflin, 1961.

Brandt, Willy. *Encounter and Insights*. Germany, 1977.

Bundy, William P., editor. *The World Economic Crisis*. New York: W. W. Norton, 1975.

Burns, James MacGregor, editor. *To Heal and to Build*. New York: McGraw-Hill, 1968.

————. *John Kennedy: A Political Profile*. New York: Harcourt, Brace, 1959.

Caidin, Martin, and Edward Hymoff. *The Mission*. New York: J. B. Lippincott, 1964.

Califano, Joseph A. *A Presidential Nation*. New York: W. W. Norton, 1975.

————. *The Student Revolution: A Global Confrontation*. New York: W. W. Norton, 1970.

Carpenter, Liz. *Ruffles and Flourishes*. New York: Doubleday, 1970.

————, editor. *LBJ: Images of a Vibrant Life*. Austin: Friends of the LBJ Library, 1973.

Cater, Douglass. *Power in Washington*. New York: Random House, 1964.

Chambers, William Nisbet. *The Democrats 1789–1964*. New York: Van Nostrand, 1964.

Chandler, David Leon. *The Natural Superiority of Southern Politicians: A Revisionist History*. New York: Doubleday, 1977.

Charlton, Michael, and Anthony Moncrieff. *Many Reasons Why*. New York: Hill and Wang, 1978.

Chennault, Anna. *The Education of Anna*. New York: Times Books, 1980.

Chester, Lewis, Godfrey Hodgson, and Bruce Page. *An American Melodrama*. New York: Viking, 1969.

Christian, George. *The President Steps Down*. New York: Macmillan, 1970.

Churchill, Randolph S., and Winston S. Churchill. *The Six Day War*. Boston: Houghton Mifflin, 1967.

Civil Rights—Volume 1: 1960–66. Edited by Lester A. Sobel. New York: Facts on File, 1967.

Civil Rights—Volume 2: 1967–68. Compiled by Steven D. Price. New York: Facts on File, 1973.

Cochran, Jacqueline. *The Stars at Noon*. Boston and Toronto: Little, Brown, 1954.

Cohen, Dan. *Undefeated*. Minneapolis: Lerner, 1978.

Conaway, James. *The Texans*. New York: Alfred A. Knopf, 1967.

Cook, Fred J. *The Nightmare Decade*. New York: Random House, 1971.

Cormier, Frank. *LBJ: The Way He Was*. Doubleday, 1977.

Cotton, Norris. *In the Senate*. New York: Dodd, Mead, 1978.

Crouse, Timothy. *The Boys on the Bus*. New York: Random House, 1972.

Davie, Michael. *LBJ: A Foreign Observer's Viewpoint*. New York: Duell, Sloan and Pearce, 1966.

Demaris, Ovid. *The Director*. New York: Harper and Row, 1975.

deToledano, Ralph. *RFK: The Man Who Would Be President*. New York: Signet, 1967.

Dickerson, Nancy. *Among Those Present*. New York: Random House, 1976.

DiSalle, Michael V. *Second Choice*. New York: Hawthorn, 1966.

Dolce, Philip C., and George H. Skau, editors. *Power and the Presidency*. New York: Charles Scribner's Sons, 1976.

Donovan, Robert J. *Eisenhower. The Inside Story*. New York: Harper and Brothers, 1956.

Douglas, Paul Howard. *In the Fullness of Time*. New York: Harcourt, Brace, Jovanovich, 1972.

Dubinsky, David, and A. H. Raskin. *David Dubinsky. A Life with Labor*. New York: Simon and Schuster, 1977.

Duke, Cordia Sloan, and Joe B. Frantz. *6,000 Miles of Fence*. Austin: University of Texas Press, 1961.

Dulaney, H. G., and Edward Hake Phillips, editors. *Speak, Mr. Speaker*. Bonham, Texas: Sam Rayburn Foundation, 1978.

Edwards, India. *Pulling No Punches*. New York: G. P. Putnam's Sons, 1977.

Eisenhower, Dwight D. *The White House Years. Mandate for Change*. New York: Doubleday, 1963.

Elizur, Yuval, and Eliahu Salpeter. *Who Rules Israel?* New York: Harper and Row, 1973.

Evans, Rowland, and Robert Novak. *Lyndon B. Johnson: The Exercise of Power*. New York: New American Library, 1966.

Faber, Doris. *The President's Mothers*. New York: St. Martin's Press, 1968.

Fairlie, Henry. *The Kennedy Promise*. New York: Doubleday, 1973.

Fall, Bernard B. *Street Without Joy: Indochina at War, 1946–54*, 4th edition. New York: Schocken, 1972.

Fay, Paul B. *The Pleasure of His Company*. New York: Harper and Row, 1966.

Fehrenbach, T. R. *Lone Star: A History of Texas and the Texans*. New York: Macmillan, 1968.

Ferber, Edna. *Giant*. New York: Doubleday, 1952.

The Final Assassinations Report. Report of the Select Committee on Assassinations. U.S. House of Representatives. Foreword by Tom Wicker. Special introduction by G. Robert Blakely. New York: Bantam, 1979.

Fitzgerald, Frances. *Fire in the Lake. The Vietnamese and the Americans in Vietnam*. Boston: Little, Brown, 1972.

Fox, Sylvan. *The Unanswered Questions about President Kennedy's Assassination*. New York: Award Books, 1965.

Frank, Gerald. *An American Death*. New York: Doubleday, 1972.

Frantz, Joe B. *Texas: A Bicentennial History*. New York: W. W. Norton, 1976.

––––––. *Thirty-seven Years of Public Service: The Honorable Lyndon B. Johnson*. Austin, Texas: Shoal Creek Publishing Co., 1974.

Fulbright, J. William. *Old Myths and New Realities and Other Commentaries*. New York: Random House, 1964.

––––––. *The Arrogance of Power*. New York: Random House, 1966.

————. *The Pentagon Propaganda Machine*. New York: Liveright, 1971.

Galbraith, John Kenneth. *Ambassador's Journal*. Boston: Houghton Mifflin, 1969.

————. *The New Industrial State*. New York: Houghton Mifflin, 1967.

Galloway, John, editor. *The Kennedys and Vietnam*. New York: Facts on File, 1971.

Garrow, David J. *Protest at Selma*. New Haven: Yale University Press, 1978.

Garson, Barbara. *Mac Bird*. New York: Grove, 1966.

Geyelin, Philip V. *Lyndon B. Johnson and the World*. New York and Washington: Praeger, 1966.

·Gold, Gerald, editor. *The Watergate Hearings*. New York: Viking, 1973.

Goldman, Eric F. *The Tragedy of Lyndon Johnson*. New York: Alfred A. Knopf, 1969.

Goldston, Robert. *The American Nightmare*. Indianapolis and New York: Bobbs-Merrill, 1973.

Goldwater, Barry. *The Conscience of a Conservative*. New York: Hillman, 1960.

Goodwyn, Frank. *Lone–Star Land—20th Century Texas in Perspective*. New York: Alfred A. Knopf, 1955.

Gore, Albert. *Let the Glory Out*. New York: Viking, 1972.

Goulden, Joseph C. *The Superlawyers*. New York: Weybright and Talley, 1971.

————. *Truth Is the First Casualty*. New York: Rand McNally, 1969.

Graff, Henry F. *The Tuesday Cabinet*. Englewood Cliffs, N.J.: Prentice-Hall, 1970.

Graves, John. *Hard Scrabble*. New York: Alfred A. Knopf, 1974.

Gunther, John. *Inside U.S.A.* Revised edition. New York: Harper and Row, 1951.

Halberstam, David. *The Unfinished Odyssey of Robert Kennedy*. New York: Random House, 1968.

————. *The Best and the Brightest*. New York: Random House, 1972.

————. *The Powers That Be*. New York: Alfred A. Knopf, 1979.

————. *Ho*. New York: Random House, 1971.

Haley, J. Evetts. *A Texan Looks at Lyndon*. Canyon, Texas: Palo Duro Press, 1964.

Harris, Richard. *A Sacred Trust*. New York: New American Library, 1966.

Harwood, Richard, and Haynes Johnson. *Lyndon*. New York: Praeger, 1973.

Hecht, Marie B. *Beyond the Presidency*. New York: Macmillan, 1976.

Herr, Michael. *Dispatches*. New York: Alfred A. Knopf, 1977.

Hilsman, Roger. *To Move a Nation*. New York: Doubleday, 1967.

Hoffer, Eric. *In Our Time*. New York: Harper and Row, 1976.

Hoopes, Townsend. *The Limits of Intervention*. New York: David McKay, 1969.

Howar, Barbara. *Laughing All the Way*. New York: Fawcett, 1973.

Humphrey, Hubert H. *The Education of a Public Man*. New York: Doubleday, 1976.

Hyman, Sidney. *The Politics of Concensus*. New York: Random House, 1968.

————. *The American President*. New York: Harper and Brothers, 1954.

Ickes, Harold. *Secret Diary*, 3 vols. New York: Simon and Schuster, 1953.

Jenkins, John H., and H. Gordon Frost. *"I'm Frank Hamer."* 1964.

Johnson, Lady Bird. *A White House Diary.* New York: Holt, Rinehart and Winston, 1970.

Johnson, Lyndon Baines. *My Hope for America.* New York: Random House, 1964.

———. *The Choices We Face.* New York: Bantam, 1969.

———. *The Vantage Point.* New York: Holt, Rinehart and Winston, 1971.

Johnson, Rebekah Baines. *A Family Album.* Edited by John S. Moursund. Introduction by President Lyndon Baines Johnson. New York: McGraw-Hill, 1965.

Johnson, Sam Houston. *My Brother Lyndon.* Edited by Enrique Hank Lopez. New York: Cowles, 1969.

Jordan, Terry G. *German Seed in Texas Soil.* Austin, Texas: University of Texas Press, 1975.

Joseph, Peter. *Good Times.* New York: William Morrow, 1974.

Kalb, Marvin, and Ellie Abel. *Roots of Involvement.* New York: W. W. Norton, 1971.

Kearns, Doris. *Lyndon Johnson and the American Dream.* New York: Harper and Row, 1955.

Key, Val Dimer Orlando, and Alexander Heard. *Southern Politics in State and Nation.* New York: Alfred A. Knopf, 1949.

Kinch, Sam, and Stuart Long. *Allan Shivers.* Austin, Texas: Shoal Creek Publishing Co., 1973.

Kissinger, Henry. *White House Years.* Boston: Little, Brown, 1979.

Koskoff, David E. *Joseph P. Kennedy.* Englewood Cliffs, N.J.: Prentice-Hall, 1974.

Krock, Arthur. *The Consent of the Governed and Other Deceits.* Boston: Little, Brown, 1971.

———. *Memoirs.* New York: Funk and Wagnalls, 1968.

Lash, Joseph P. *Eleanor and Franklin.* New York: W. W. Norton, 1971.

———. *Eleanor: The Years Alone.* Foreword by Franklin D. Roosevelt, Jr. New York: W. W. Norton, 1972.

Lasky, Victor. *It Didn't Start with Watergate.* New York: Dial, 1977.

Lawrence, William. *Six Presidents, Too Many Wars.* New York: Saturday Review Press, 1972.

Lea, Tom. *The King Ranch.* Boston: Little, Brown, 1957.

Leslie, Warren. *Dallas Public and Private.* New York: Avon, 1964.

Levin, Murray. *Political Hysteria in America.* New York: Basic Books, 1971.

Lincoln, Evelyn. *Kennedy and Johnson.* New York: Holt, Rinehart and Winston, 1968.

McCarthy, Abigail. *Private Faces, Public Places.* New York: Doubleday, 1972.

McKay, Seth Shepard. *Texas Politics, 1906–1944.* Lubbock, Texas: Texas Tech Press, 1952.

———. *W. Lee O'Daniel and Texas Politics, 1938–1942.* Lubbock, Texas: Texas Tech Press, 1947.

McMurtry, Larry. *In a Narrow Grave.* New York: Simon and Schuster, 1968.

McNamara, Robert S. *The Essence of Security.* New York: Harper and Row, 1968.

McPherson, Harry. *A Political Education.* Boston: Little, Brown, 1972.

Manchester, William. *The Glory and the Dream*. Boston: Little, Brown, 1973.

———. *The Death of a President*. New York: Harper and Row, 1967.

———. *American Caesar*. Boston: Little, Brown, 1978.

Marcus, Stanley. *Minding the Store*. New York: Signet, 1974.

Martin, John Bartlow. *Overtaken by Events*. New York: Doubleday, 1966.

———. *Adlai Stevenson and the World*. New York: Doubleday, 1977.

Memorial Services in the Congress of the United States and Tributes and Eulogy of Lyndon Baines Johnson. Compiled under the direction of the Joint Committee on Printing, U.S. Government Printing Office, Washington, D.C., 1973.

Miller, Merle. *Plain Speaking*. New York: G. P. Putnam's Sons, 1974.

Minor, Dale. *The Information War*. New York: Hawthorn, 1970.

Mooney, Booth. *LBJ: An Irreverent Chronicle*. New York: Thomas Y. Crowell, 1976.

———. *Roosevelt and Rayburn*. Philadelphia and New York: J. B. Lippincott, 1971.

———. *The Politicians: 1945–1960*. Philadelphia and New York: J. B. Lippincott, 1970.

Morris, Willie. *North Toward Home*. Boston: Houghton Mifflin, 1967.

Moursund, John S. *Texas Heartland, A Hill Country Year*. Texas A & M University Press, 1975.

Moyers, Bill. *Listening to America*. New York: Harper and Row, 1971.

Muller, Herbert J. *Adlai Stevenson*. New York: Harper and Row, 1967.

Nevin, David. *The Texans*. Bonanza Books, 1967.

Newfield, Jack. *Robert Kennedy*. New York: E. P. Dutton, 1969.

Nicholas, William. *The Bobby Kennedy Nobody Knows*. Greenwich, Conn.: Fawcett, 1967.

Nixon, Richard M. *RN: The Memoirs of Richard Nixon*. New York: Grosset and Dunlap, 1978.

Nizer, Louis. *Reflections Without Mirrors*. New York: Doubleday, 1978.

Oberdorfer, Don. *Tet*. New York: Doubleday, 1971.

O'Brien, Lawrence F. *No Final Victories*. New York: Doubleday, 1974.

O'Donnell, Kenneth P., and David F. Powers. *Johnny, We Hardly Knew Ye*. Boston: Little, Brown, 1970.

Official Warren Commission Report on the Assassination of President John F. Kennedy. New York: Doubleday, 1964.

O'Neill, William L. *Coming Apart*. Chicago: Quadrangle, 1971.

Parmet, Herbert S. *The Democrats*. New York: Macmillan, 1976.

Pearson, Drew. *Diaries: 1949–1959*. Edited by Tyler Abell. New York: Holt, Rinehart and Winston, 1974.

Peres, Shimon. *David's Sling*. New York: Random House, 1970.

Peters, Charles, and John Rothchild, editors. *Inside the System*. Introduction by Richard H. Rovere. New York: Praeger, 1973.

Pilat, Oliver. *Drew Pearson*. New York: Harper's Magazine Press, 1973.

Pool, William, Emmie Craddock, and David E. Conrad. *Lyndon Baines Johnson: The Formative Years*. San Marcos, Texas: Southwest Texas State College Press, 1965.

———. *A Historical Atlas of Texas*. Austin, Texas: Encino Press, 1975.

Porterfield, Bill. *LBJ Country*. New York: Doubleday, 1965.

Powers, Thomas. *The Man Who Kept the Secrets*. New York: Alfred A. Knopf, 1979.

Provence, Harry. *Lyndon B. Johnson*. New York: Paperback Library, 1964.

The Public Papers of the Presidents. Lyndon B. Johnson. Washington, D.C.: Office of the Federal Register National Archives and Records Service. General Services Administration.

Two Volumes 1963–64. Printed 1965. U.S. Govt. Printing Office.

Two Volumes 1965. Printed 1966. U.S. Govt. Printing Office.

Two Volumes 1966. Printed 1967. U.S. Govt. Printing Office.

Two Volumes 1967. Printed 1968. U.S. Govt. Printing Office.

Two Volumes 1968–69. Printed 1970. U.S. Govt. Printing Office.

Raines, Howell. *My Soul Is Rested*. New York: G. P. Putnam's Sons, 1977.

Rather, Dan, and Gary Paul Gates. *The Palace Guard*. New York: Harper and Row, 1974.

Reedy, George E. *The Twilight of the Presidency*. New York: World, 1970.

———. *The Presidency in Flux*. New York: Columbia University Press, 1973.

Report of the National Advisory Commission on Civil Disorders. Special introduction by Tom Wicker. New York: Bantam, 1968.

Reston, James. *Sketches in the Sand*. New York: Alfred A. Knopf, 1967.

Roberts, Chalmers M. *The Washington Post*. Boston: Houghton Mifflin, 1977.

———. *First Rough Draft*. New York: Praeger, 1973.

Roberts, Charles. *LBJ's Inner Circle*. New York: Delacorte, 1965.

Roche, John P. *Sentenced to Life*. New York: Macmillan, 1974.

Rossiter, Clinton. *The American Presidency*. New York: Harcourt, Brace and World, 1956.

Rostow, Walt Whitman. *Diffusion of Power*. New York: Macmillan, 1972.

Rovere, Richard Halworth. *Senator Joe McCarthy*. New York: Harcourt, Brace, 1959.

———. *Arrivals and Departures*. New York: Macmillan, 1976.

Rowe, Robert. *The Bobby Baker Story*. New York: Parallax, 1967.

Safire, William. *Before the Fall*. New York: Doubleday, 1975.

Sale, Kirkpatrick. *Power Shift*. New York: Random House, 1975.

Salinger, Pierre. *With Kennedy*. New York: Doubleday, 1966.

Salisbury, Harrison E. *Behind the Lines Hanoi*. New York: Harper and Row, 1967.

Schandler, Herbert Y. *The Unmaking of a President*. Princeton, N.J.: Princeton University Press, 1977.

Schell, Jonathan. *The Time of Illusion*. New York: Alfred A. Knopf, 1976.

Schlesinger, Arthur M., Jr. *Robert Kennedy and His Times*. Boston: Houghton Mifflin, 1978.

————. *A Thousand Days*. Boston: Houghton Mifflin, 1965.

————. *The Coming of Power. Critical Presidential Elections in American History*. Edited by Arthur M. Schlesinger, Jr. New York: Chelsea House, 1971.

————. *The Imperial Presidency*. Boston: Houghton Mifflin, 1973.

————. *The Coming of the New Deal*. Boston: Houghton Mifflin, 1959.

Sevareid, Eric. *Candidates, 1960*. Edited and with an introduction by Eric Sevareid. New York: Basic Books, 1959.

Shawcross, William. *Sideshow*. New York: Simon and Schuster, 1979.

Sheehan, Neil, Hedrick Smith, E. W. Kenworthy, and Fox Butterfield. *The Pentagon Papers*. Toronto and New York: Bantam, 1971.

Sherrill, Robert. *The Accidental President*. New York: Grossman, 1967.

————. *Gothic Politics in the Deep South*. New York: Grossman, 1968.

Sherwood, Robert E. *Roosevelt and Hopkins*. New York: Harper and Brothers, 1948.

Sidey, Hugh. *A Very Personal Presidency. Lyndon Johnson in the White House*. New York: Atheneum, 1968.

Singer, Kurt, and Jane Shirrod. *Lyndon Baines Johnson*. Minneapolis: T. S. Denison, 1964.

Smith, A. Robert. *The Tiger in the Senate*. New York: Doubleday, 1962.

Smith, Merriman. *Merriman Smith's Book of Presidents*. Edited by Timothy G. Smith. New York: W. W. Norton, 1972.

Sorensen, Theodore C. *Kennedy*. New York: Harper and Row, 1965.

Sparks, Will. *Who Talked to the President Last*. New York: W. W. Norton, 1971.

Steinberg, Alfred. *The Man from Missouri: The Life and Times of Harry S. Truman*. New York: G. P. Putnam's Sons, 1962.

————. *Sam Rayburn*. New York: Hawthorn, 1975.

————. *Sam Johnson's Boy*. New York: Macmillan, 1968.

Stern, Philip M., with the collaboration of Harold P. Green. *The Oppenheimer Case*. New York: Harper and Row, 1969.

Stone, I. F. *In a Time of Torment*. New York: Random House, 1967.

Stout, Richard T. *People*. New York: Harper and Row, 1970.

Sullivan, William C., with Bill Brown. *The Bureau: My Thirty Years in Hoover's FBI*. New York: W. W. Norton, 1979.

Sulzberger, C. L. *An Age of Mediocrity*. New York: Macmillan, 1973.

Talese, Gay. *The Kingdom and the Power*. New York: World, 1966.

Terkel, Studs. *Hard Times*. New York: Pantheon, 1970.

Texas Almanac, 1964–1965. Dallas: A. H. Belo Corporation, 1963.

Thomas, Helen. *Dateline: White House*. New York: Macmillan, 1975.

Thomas, Lately. *When Even Angels Wept*. New York: William Morrow, 1973.

Tindall, George Brown. *The Emergence of the New South, 1913–1945*. Louisiana State University, 1967.

Trewhitt, Henry L. *McNamara: His Ordeal in the Pentagon*. New York: Harper and Row, 1971.

Trohan, Walter. *Political Animals*. New York: Doubleday, 1975.

Tugwell, Rexford G. *Off Course—From Truman to Nixon*. New York: Praeger, 1971.

Ungar, Sanford J. *FBI. An Uncensored Look Behind the Walls*. Boston: Little, Brown, 1975.

Valenti, Jack. *A Very Human President*. New York: W. W. Norton, 1975.

Vanden Heuvel, William, and Milton Gwirtzman. *On His Own: Robert F. Kennedy 1964–1968*. New York: Doubleday, 1970.

Vogelgesang, Sandy. *The Long Dark Night of the Soul*. New York: Harper and Row, 1974.

Wakefield, Dan. *Supernation at Peace and War*. Boston: Little, Brown, 1968.

Walker, Stanley. *Texas*. New York: Viking, 1962.

Wattenberg, Ben J. *The Real America*. New York: Doubleday, 1974.

Webb, Walter Prescott. *An Honest Preface and Other Essays*. Boston: Houghton Mifflin, 1959.

Weintal, Edward, and Charles Bartlett. *Facing the Brink: An Intimate Study of Crisis Diplomacy*. New York: Charles Scribner's Sons, 1967.

West, J. B. *Upstairs at the White House*. New York: Coward, McCann & Geoghegan, 1973.

Westmoreland, William C. *A Soldier Reports*. New York: Doubleday, 1976.

The White House Transcripts. Introduction by R. W. Apple, Jr., of the *New York Times*. New York: Bantam, 1974.

White, J. Roy. *Limestone and Log: A Hill Country Sketchbook*. Austin, Texas: Encino Press, 1968.

White, Theodore H. *The Making of the President, 1960*. New York: Atheneum, 1961.

————. *The Making of the President, 1964*. New York: Atheneum, 1965.

————. *The Making of the President, 1968*. New York: Atheneum, 1969.

————. *The Making of the President, 1972*. New York: Atheneum, 1973.

————. *Breach of Faith: The Fall of Richard Nixon*. New York: Atheneum, 1975.

White, William S. *The Responsibles*. New York: Harper and Row, 1972.

————. *The Professional: Lyndon B. Johnson*. Boston: Houghton Mifflin, 1964.

White, W. L. *Queens Die Proudly*. New York: Harcourt, Brace, 1943.

Wicker, Tom. *On Press*. New York: Viking, 1978.

————. *JFK and LBJ: The Influence of Personality Upon Politics*. New York: William Morrow, 1968.

Wildavsky, Aaron. *The Revolt Against the Masses and Other Essays on Politics and Public Policy*. New York and London: Basic Books, 1971.

Windchy, Eugene G. *Tonkin Gulf*. New York: Doubleday, 1971.

Winter-Berger, Robert H. *The Washington Pay-Off*. Secaucus, New Jersey: Lyle Stuart, 1972.

————. *Report of the National Advisory Commission on Civil Disorders*. New York: Bantam, 1968.

Wise, David. *The Politics of Lying*. New York: Random House, 1973.

Witcover, Jules. *Eighty-five Days: The Last Campaign of Robert Kennedy*. New York: G. P. Putnam's Sons, 1969.

Wright, William. *The Washington Game*. New York: Saturday Review Press, 1974.

Wyden, Peter. *Bay of Pigs*. New York: Simon and Schuster, 1979.

Youngblood, Rufus W. *Twenty Years in the Secret Service*. New York: Simon and Schuster, 1973.

Newspapers

CHICAGO: *Chicago Tribune*

ENGLAND: *Manchester Guardian*

LOS ANGELES: *Los Angeles Times*

NEW YORK: *New York Times*; *Wall Street Journal*

TEXAS: Austin *American Statesman*; Bastrop *Advertiser*; *Blanco County News*; *Blanco County Record*; Brenham *Banner-Press*; *Burnet Bulletin*; *Caldwell News*; *Corpus Christi Press*; Dallas *News*; Dallas *Times-Herald*; Elgin *Courier*; Ennis *News*; Fort Worth *Star-Telegram*; Fredericksburg *Standard*; Granger *News*; Houston *Chronicle*; Houston *Post*; Johnson City *Record-Courier*; Luling *Signal*; San Angelo *Standard-Times*; San Antonio *News*; Shamrock *Texan*; *Taylor Daily Press*; Waco *Tribune-Herald*; Wichita Falls *Times*

WASHINGTON, D.C.: *Washington Post*; *Washington Star*

Magazines

Among the Friends of LBJ; *Atlantic*; *Commentary*; *Foreign Affairs*; *Harper's*; *Journal of Negro History*; *Life*; *Look*; *Nation*; *Newsweek*; *New Yorker*; *New York Times Magazine*; *Prologue*; *Reporter*; *Saturday Review*; *Texas Monthly*; *Texas Observer*; *Time*; *U.S. News & World Report*

TV and Movies—Broadcast

CBS News Special—"LBJ: Tragedy and Transition." Broadcast on May 2, 1970. Reporter: Walter Cronkite.

CBS News Special—"LBJ: Lyndon Johnson Talks Politics." Broadcast January 27, 1972. Reporter: Walter Cronkite.

CBS News Special—"Some Friends of President Johnson." Broadcast January 24, 1973. Reporter: Walter Cronkite.

NBC Broadcast—"The Hill Country." May 9, 1966. Reporter: Ray Scherer; executive producer: Fred Freed; producer: Len Giovannitti.

Newsroom's Tribute to LBJ, Channel Thirteen: "My Main Man," Dallas, January 23, 1973.

Bill Moyers' Journal—"Hubert Horatio Humphrey: A Conversation." WNET-TV, April 11, 1976.

"An Essay on Watergate." WNET-TV, October 31, 1973.
David Susskind, interview with Allard Lowenstein. Broadcast January 14, 1976.

Unbroadcast

Many hours of unbroadcast interviews—CBS News, Walter Cronkite, reporter.
Nine hours unbroadcast film from "The Hill Country." Ray Scherer, reporter.
Film—*The Journey of Lyndon Baines Johnson*. Executive Producer: Charles Guggenheim. Directed and produced by Bob Pierce. Property of The Lyndon B. Johnson Foundation.
Film—*Home Place*, made by the Navy White House Photographic Unit in 1968 of Lady Bird giving a tour of the Ranch house. LBJ appears briefly near the end to reminisce about growing up in the Hill Country.
Home movies. Personal films of the Johnson family.

Miscellaneous

T. Harry Williams. *Huey, Lyndon and Southern Radicalism*. Presidential address of the Organization of American Historians. Chicago, Illinois, 1963.
Leslie Carpenter. *Profile of a President*. Dallas Times Herald: February 9, 1964.
F. Edward Hebert. "I Went, I Saw, I Heard." A pamphlet published privately by J. E. McCarthy, New Orleans: circa 1945.

Briefings Nos. 1 through 5

The following meetings were held at the White House by Lyndon Johnson—all off the record. For clarity, they were numbered 1 through 5 and will be referred to as such in footnotes.
1. On September 26, 1968, with members of HEW.
2. (Undated.) With members of his cabinet in which he reiterates his position on Vietnam and his intentions with regard to the Paris peace talks. It also covers his telephone conversation with the three presidential candidates concerning his decision to halt the bombing.
3. On November 19, 1968, with columnists.
4. On October 10, 1968, with Robert C. Weaver, Department of HUD.
5. On September 29, 1966, with members of the Brookings Institution, Washington, D.C.

Correspondence

Voluminous correspondence between members of the Johnson family, ranging from 1929 through the 1950s.
Correspondence between Lyndon Johnson and John Kennedy from 1956 through 1963.

Correspondence to or from FDR from the Personal Papers File in the archives of the Franklin Delano Roosevelt Library in Hyde Park.

Letters from Carroll Kilpatrick to Phil Graham in 1961.

The writer corresponded, usually many times, with almost all those he interviewed. It seems unnecessary to repeat their names here.

Diaries

Lyndon Johnson's World War II Diary
The Vice-Presidential Diaries of Lyndon Johnson
The Presidential Diary of Lyndon Johnson

Memorandums

A memorandum written by Philip Graham, publisher of the *Washington Post*, on his role in the events of the 1960 Democratic National Convention in Los Angeles. The memorandum was furnished to the author by Katharine Graham.

Several lengthy memorandums which at the time written were classified "Eyes Only" to the president and have since been reclassified on a variety of subjects pertaining to foreign policy. They cover the entire span of his administration (November 1963–January 1969).

A memorandum requested by Benjamin C. Bradlee, at the time managing editor of the *Washington Post*, of *Post* reporters Richard Harwood and Haynes Johnson, who attended a Johnson off-the-record meeting with personnel of the *Post* on April 7, 1970. The memorandum was furnished to the author by Benjamin C. Bradlee.

George W. Ball kindly lent me copies of scores of memorandums he sent to the president and others questioning the wisdom of what we were doing in Vietnam during the years 1965 and 1966.

A memorandum to the president from Sherwin Markman dated February 1, 1967, concerning life in the Negro ghetto in the mid-1960s, based on his experience on Chicago's South Side.

Symposiums (Published and Unpublished)

The following symposiums were sponsored jointly by the Lyndon Baines Johnson Library and the School of Public Affairs at the University of Texas at Austin:

Educating a Nation: A Changing American Commitment. Kenneth W. Tolo, editor (January 24–25, 1972).

Equal Opportunity in the United States: A Symposium of Civil Rights. Robert C. Rooney, editor (December 11–12, 1972).

The American City: Realities and Possibilities. Kenneth W. Tolo, editor (October 8–9, 1973).

Beyond Today's Energy Crisis. Kenneth W. Tolo, editor (November 11–12, 1974).

The Arts: Years of Development, Time of Decision. Albert A. Blum, editor (September 29, 1975).

Women in Public Life: Report of a Conference. Beryl A. Radin and Hoyt H. Purvis, editors (November 9–11, 1975).

The Presidency and the Press. Hoyt H. Purvis, editor (April 23, 1976).

Toward New Human Rights: The Social Policies of the Kennedy and Johnson Administrations. David C. Warner, editor (November 12–16, 1976).

The President and the Congress. A Shifting Balance of Power (November 15–17, 1977).

Government and the Humanities (December 3–5, 1978).

The Business of the Nation and the Nation's Business; Toward a New Partnership (March 1–2, 1979).

Tapes

National Archives and Records Services Administration tapes:

Recordings of radio communications between Air Force One and the White House on November 22, 1963. Three tapes.

Edison Dictaphone recording of telephone conversation between Lyndon Johnson and Theodore C. Sorensen on June 3, 1963.

Lyndon Johnson rehearsing, March 31, 1968.

Presidential press conference, November 17, 1964.

Remarks to government class at San Marcos, Texas. Lyndon Johnson speaks to students at Southwest Texas University, April 27, 1970.

Lyndon Johnson's remarks to student senate at Southwest Texas University, San Marcos, Texas, April 27, 1970.

Lyndon Johnson's remarks to college officials in the president's office, San Marcos, April 27, 1970.

Lyndon Johnson and students of Southwest Texas University—questions and answers, April 27, 1970.

Lyndon B. Johnson Library Dedication Ceremony, May 22, 1971. Two tapes.

Lyndon Johnson's speech to the First National Congress of Black Professionals in Higher Education, April 5, 1972.

Remarks by Lyndon Johnson at Southwest Texas State University, San Marcos, Texas, November 4, 1972.

Interview with Joseph A. Califano on June 11, 1973. Two tapes.

Senator William Benton speech before the Lyndon B. Johnson School of Public Affairs and Lyndon Johnson's remarks, December 4, 1972. Two tapes.

Lyndon Baines Johnson Library tapes:

Recording made at the LBJ Ranch on November 17, 1977, "One More Story."

Recording made of a reunion held at the Library on the weekend of July 14 and 15, 1979, for former National Youth Administration staff.

Recording on the humor of Lyndon Johnson prepared by the Lyndon Baines Johnson Library audio-visual staff.

Recording of remarks of Lyndon Johnson's friends at Reagan House, Stonewall, Texas, August 26, 1974.

Miscellaneous tapes:

Recordings made by the author at parties, one at the home of Liz Carpenter in Washington, D.C., on March 1, 1976, the other at the home of Larry Temple in Austin on April 26, 1976.

Recording made in December 1963 by Liz Carpenter, at Leslie Carpenter's request, of her experience in Dallas, November 22, 1963.

Theses

"The National Youth Administration in Texas 1935–1939." Deborah Lynn Self. Master's thesis. Texas Technological College, 1974.

"The Texas Senatorial Election of 1941." James W. Parten, Jr. Master's thesis. Texas Technological College, 1941.

"Lyndon Johnson and the Rise of Conservatism in Texas." Michael Janeway. Master's thesis. Harvard University, 1962.

"The Leland Olds Controversy." Michael Gillette. Graduate Seminar paper. University of Texas at Austin, 1973.

"The Hero and the Anti-Hero." Mary Hardesty. Term paper. University of Texas at Austin, 1976.

Miscellaneous Unpublished Material Consulted

A national tribute to Lady Bird Johnson on the occasion of her sixty-fifth birthday. December 11, 1977, at the Lyndon Baines Johnson Library, Austin, Texas.

Chronology of Lyndon Johnson from birth on August 27, 1908, to day he left office—January 20, 1969.

Notes taken by Marie Fehmer, Johnson's personal secretary, on November 22, 1963.

Exclusive interview granted by Lyndon Johnson to Robert E. McKay on May 21, 1965, on education.

Lyndon Johnson's speech to the First National Congress of Black Professionals in Higher Education, April 5, 1972.

Lyndon Johnson and the art of biography. Paper given by T. Harry Williams at the 1977 AHA Convention in Dallas, Texas, December 29, 1977.

Public Opinion about President Johnson. His Policies and Programs. A report prepared for the White House by Lloyd Free, March 20, 1967.

The Christmas gift account. A typescript book prepared by Rebekah for Lyndon as a Christmas present in 1954, containing photographs, charts, etc., of the family history.

Portions were later compiled and published in *The Family Album*. (See Bibliography—Books.)

The voting record of Lyndon Johnson from the files of the Lyndon Baines Johnson Library.

White House South Lawn remarks by Lyndon Johnson. Unpublished and off the record, September 13, 1968.

Historic Research Study including historical base maps and historic structure report: Lyndon B. Johnson National Historic Site, Blanco and Gillespie counties, Texas. Historic data by Edwin C. Bearss.

Interviews by the Author

The Johnson Family

LADY BIRD JOHNSON: Interview 1. On May 26, 1975, at the Lyndon Baines Johnson Library.

Interview 2. On June 25, 1975, at the Lyndon Baines Johnson Library.

Interview 3. On June 28, 1976, at the library.

Interview 4. On June 30, 1976, at the Ranch in Stonewall, Texas.

Interview 5. On February 7, 1977, at the library.

Interview 6. On February 14, 1977, in a car driving around the Ranch, Stonewall, Texas.

Interview 7. On October 10, 1978, at the library.

LYNDA BAINES JOHNSON ROBB: At a party at her home in McLean, Virginia, which was recorded on June 23, 1975.

On March 26, 1976, also in her home in McLean, Virginia.

LUCI BIRD JOHNSON NUGENT: At two parties at her home, recorded on April 27, 1976, and September 16, 1976.

Interview 1. On April 27, 1976, at the library.

Interview 2. On November 9, 1977, at the library.

SAM HOUSTON JOHNSON: Six interviews at his apartment in the Alamo Hotel, Austin, Texas, during January, April, June, and September of 1976.

Interviews by the Author

Others

BESS ABELL
MONSIGNOR E. ROBERT ARTHUR of St.
  Patrick's Church, Washington, D.C.
BOBBY BAKER
GEORGE W. BALL
PETER BENCHLEY
JAMES BLUNDELL
LINDY BOGGS
RICHARD BOLLING
YOLANDA BOOZER
BENJAMIN C. BRADLEE
BILLY LEE BRAMMER
RUSSELL MORTON BROWN
McGEORGE BUNDY
HORACE BUSBY
JOSEPH A. CALIFANO
LIZ CARPENTER
GEORGE CHRISTIAN
JO ANN CHRISTIAN
BETHINE CHURCH
W. RAMSEY CLARK
CLARK CLIFFORD
BENJAMIN V. COHEN
WILBUR J. COHEN
JOHN B. CONNALLY
THOMAS G. CORCORAN
NORMAN COUSINS
WILLARD DEASON

JOHN DODDS
HELEN GAHAGAN DOUGLAS
ANGIER BIDDLE DUKE
ROBIN DUKE
BENNO ECKERT
HILMER ECKERT
ROBERT ECKHARDT
FRANK ERWIN
EPHRAIM EVRON
CREEKMORE FATH
JOHN HENRY FAULK
ABE FEINBERG
MYER FELDMAN
ROBERT H. FLEMING
ROBERT FRATKIN
J. WILLIAM FULBRIGHT
BETTY FURNESS
CATHERINE GALBRAITH
JOHN KENNETH GALBRAITH
STELLA GLIDDEN
ELIZABETH GOLDSCHMIDT
ARTHUR E. ("TEX") GOLDSCHMIDT
BARRY GOLDWATER
HENRY GONZALEZ
CALLAN GRAHAM
KATHARINE GRAHAM
ELINOR GREEN
LLOYD HACKLER

LLOYD HAND
D. B. HARDEMAN
MARY HARDESTY
ROBERT HARDESTY
HUBERT H. HUMPHREY
MURIEL HUMPHREY
WALTER JENKINS
ALFRED B. ("BOODY") JOHNSON
EDWINA JOHNSON
W. THOMAS JOHNSON
JAMES JONES
WILLIAM JORDEN
JESSE KELLAM
KONRAD KELLEY, JR.
ISAIAH KENAN
ROBERT E. KINTNER
ROBERT KOMER
ARTHUR KRIM
MARY LASKER
ROBERT LIVINGSTON
FRANK LLOYD
GEORGE MCGOVERN
HARRY MCPHERSON
LEONARD H. MARKS
MARGARET MAYER
MARIANNE MEANS
HARRY MIDDLETON
CLARENCE MITCHELL
BOOTH MOONEY
BILL D. MOYERS
JAMES NASH
DOROTHY NICHOLS
PHIL NICHOLS
LAWRENCE F. O'BRIEN
MOLLIE PARNIS
J. R. PARTEN
ESTHER PETERSON
HELEN PHINNEY
ROBERT PHINNEY
JAKE PICKLE
HARRY PROVENCE
AUDREY RAPOPORT
BERNARD RAPOPORT

MARY RATHER
JOSEPH L. RAUH, JR.
COATES REDMON
GEORGE E. REEDY
CHALMERS ROBERTS
JUANITA ROBERTS
LOIS ROBERTS
RAY ROBERTS
JOHN P. ROCHE
LORETTA ROSS
ELSPETH ROSTOW
WALT WHITMAN ROSTOW
RICHARD H. ROVERE
ELIZABETH ROWE
JAMES H. ROWE, JR.
DEAN RUSK
HARRISON SALISBURY
RAY C. SCHERER
SAM SHAFFER
ISABELLE SHELTON
HUGH SIDEY
GERALD SIEGAL
MILDRED SIEGAL
JOHN SKUCE
LIZ SMITH
TED SORENSEN
WILL SPARKS
HOBART TAYLOR, JR.
WILLIE DAY TAYLOR
LARRY E. TEMPLE
LOUANN TEMPLE
HOMER THORNBERRY
BARDYL TIRANE
JACK VALENTI
MARY MARGARET WILEY VALENTI
ROBERT WALDRON
LEW WASSERMAN
ROBERT C. WEAVER
TERRELL MAVERICK WEBB
ED WEIDENFELD
SHEILA WEIDENFELD
DR. DAVID WEISMAN
JAMES RUSSELL WIGGINS

ROGER WILKINS
MONK WILLIS
JAMES W. WILSON

WILLARD WIRTZ
ZEPHYR WRIGHT
RALPH YARBOROUGH

Interviews by Mr. Ted Gittinger, Researcher and Texas Historian

LADY BIRD JOHNSON on August 21, 1979.
SIMON BURG
ED CLARK
T. KELLIS DIBRELL

VINCENT HARRIS
DALE MALECHEK
JEWEL MALECHEK

Oral Histories from the Lyndon Baines Johnson Library, Austin, Texas

HENRY AARON
GEORGE AIKEN
ROBERT S. ALLEN
J. LINDSAY ALMOND, JR.
CLINTON P. ANDERSON
HARRY ASHMORE
WAYNE ASPINALL
TOINETTE BACHELDER
MALCOLM BARDWELL
CHARLES BARTLETT
ROBERT BARTLETT
SUSAN BARTLETT
LUCIUS BATTLE
LEO C. BEEBE
JOSEPH A. BEIRNE
DAVID BELL
HENRY BELLMON
PETER BENCHLEY
ROBERT L. BENNETT
BERYL ANN BENTSON (MRS. LLOYD
    BENTSON, JR.)
WILLIAM F. BILLINGS
KENNETH BIRKHEAD
DAVID BLACK
JAMES BLUNDELL
CHARLES BOATNER
HALE BOGGS
RUTH BOOKER
YOLANDA BOOZER
CHESTER BOWLES
EDMUND G. ("PAT") BROWN

H. S. ("HANK") BROWN
DR. HAROLD BROWN
OMAR BURLESON
DOROTHY VREDENBURGH BUSH
DR. JAMES CAIN
LIZ CARPENTER
HODDING CARTER, JR.
MARGARET CARTER
DOUGLASS CATER
ANTHONY CELEBREEZE
EMANUEL CELLER
GEORGE CHRISTIAN
FRANK CHURCH
NORMAN M. CLAPP
TOM CLARK
W. RAMSEY CLARK
CLARK CLIFFORD
WILBUR J. COHEN
ELLEN TAYLOR COOPER
WILLIAM COSTELLO
BEN CRIDER
WILLIAM CROCKETT
JOHN H. CROOKER
JAMES CROSS
JESSE CURRY
PRICE DANIEL
JONATHAN DANIELS
WILLARD DEASON
DR. MICHAEL E. DeBAKEY
CHARLES DIGGS
C. DOUGLAS DILLON

RIPLEY S. DILLON
EVERETT M. DIRKSEN
MICHAEL V. DiSALLE
HELEN GAHAGAN DOUGLAS
PAUL H. DOUGLAS
ERV S. DUGGAN
RALPH DUNGAN
RALPH DUNLAP
CLIFFORD DURR
VIRGINIA FOSTER DURR
FREDERICK G. DUTTON
ALLAN J. ELLENDER
BUFORD ELLINGTON
JAMES A. FARLEY
JAMES FARMER
THOMAS K. FINLETTER
O. C. FISCHER
ELAINE FISCHESSER
SAM FORE, JR.
MICHAEL FORRESTAL
ABE FORTAS
L. H. FOUNTAIN
HENRY FOWLER
MAX FRANKEL
ORVILLE FREEMAN
GORDON FULCHER
BETTY FURNESS
JAMES GAITHER
DR. HECTOR GARCIA
SIM GIDEON
ELIZABETH GOLDSCHMIDT
ERNEST GOLDSTEIN
ASHTON GONELLA
ANDREW J. GOODPASTER
HELENE LINDOW GORDON
LINCOLN GORDON
ELMER GRAHAM
KATHARINE GRAHAM
H. M. GREENE
ERNEST GRUENING
JAMES C. HAGERTY
WALTER G. HALL
ROBERT HARDESTY
AVERELL HARRIMAN

OREN HARRIS
PATRICIA ROBERTS HARRIS
JESSIE HATCHER
WILLIAM W. HEATH
CHARLES HERRING
LISTER HILL
ROGER HILSMAN
HENRY HIRSCHBERG
LUTHER HODGES
ANNA ROSENBERG HOFFMAN
LUTHER HOLCOMB
JERRY HOLLEMAN
WELLY K. HOPKINS
BETTY HUGHES
RICHARD HUGHES
SARAH HUGHES
HUBERT H. HUMPHREY
CHET HUNTLEY
HENRIETTE WYETH HURD
PETER HURD
FRANK IKARD
DANIEL INOUYE
ROBERT M. JACKSON
JAKE JACOBSEN
LEON JAWORSKI
WALTER JENKINS
LUTHER E. JONES, JR.
MARVIN JONES
NICHOLAS DE B. KATZENBACH
CARROLL KEACH
CLAUDE KELLAM
LEON H. KEYSERLING
MARY D. KEYSERLING
SAM E. KINCH
ARTHUR KROCK
MARY LASKER
GENE LATIMER
RAY E. LEE
ERICH LEINSDORF
DAVID LILIENTHAL
GOULD LINCOLN
OTTO LINDIG
FRANK LLOYD
EUGENE M. LOCKE

Stuart Long
J. C. Looney
Katie Louchheim
John W. McCormack
Ernest W. McFarland
Gale McGee
George McGovern
Charles McGuire
Harry McPherson
William B. Macomber, Jr.
John W. Macy
Lester Maddox
Warren G. Magnuson
Dale Malechek
Mike Manatos
Thomas C. Mann, Jr.
Stanley Marcus
Sherwin J. Markman
Leonard H. Marks
Burke Marshall
Thurgood Marshall
John Bartlow Martin
Ernest May
Timothy May
George Meany
Perle Mesta
Dale Miller
Emma Guffy Miller
Wilbur Mills
Newton Minow
Clarence Mitchell
Mike Monroney
R. H. Montgomery
Ralph Moreland
Thruston Morton
James M. Nabrit
Richard E. Neustadt
Dorothy Nichols
Matthew Nimetz
Jacqueline Kennedy Onassis
Dorothy Palmie
J. R. Parten
Wright Patman
Eugene Patterson

Harvey Payne
Drew Pearson
Joseph A. Pechman
Robert Phinney
DeVries Pierson
Paul A. Porter
Harry Provence
Richard S. ("Cactus") Pryor
Dan Quill
Mary Rather
Joseph L. Rauh, Jr.
Benjamin H. Read
Emmette S. Redford
George E. Reedy
Elliot Richardson
Chalmers Roberts
Charles Roberts
Ray Roberts
A. Willis Robertson
Nelson Rockefeller
Will Rogers
Mitchell Rogevin
Elspeth Rostow
Eugene V. Rostow
Fenner Roth
Payne Roundtree
Elizabeth Rowe
James H. Rowe, Jr.
Bayard Rustin
Leverett Saltonstall
Harold Barefoot Sanders
Josefa Baines Saunders
Richard M. Scammon
Arthur M. Schlesinger, Jr.
John Ben Shepperd
Whitney Shoemaker
Gerald Siegel
Byron Skelton
John Sparkman
Adrian Spears
Max Starke
John C. Stennis
Sam V. Stone
John L. Sweeney

JAMES SYMINGTON
HERMAN TALMADGE
ROBERT S. TAFT, JR.
ANTONIO J. TAYLOR
HOBART TAYLOR, JR.
HOBART TAYLOR, SR.
WILLIE DAY TAYLOR
LARRY E. TEMPLE
LENA THOMAS
R. E. THOMASON
CLARK W. THOMPSON
HOMER THORNBERRY
BASCOM TIMMONS
JOHN TOWER
STERLING TUCKER
GRACE TULLY
STEWART UDALL
JACK VALENTI
CARL VINSON
FRED M. VINSON, JR.
JERRY VOORHIS
LOUIS WALTER

PAUL C. WARNKE
EARL WARREN
GEORGE L. P. WEAVER
ROBERT C. WEAVER
TERRELL MAVERICK WEBB
EDWIN L. WEISL, JR.
EDWIN L. WEISL, SR.
EARLE G. WHEELER
JUNE WHITE
WILLIAM S. WHITE
JAMES RUSSELL WIGGINS
CLAUDE C. WILD, SR.
ROGER WILKINS
ROY WILKINS
EUGENE WILLIAMS
HELEN WILLIAMS
JAMES W. WILSON
EUGENE WORLEY
ANDREW YOUNG
WHITNEY YOUNG, JR.
SAM YORTY
H. A. ("TONY") ZIEGLER

Oral Histories from the Johnson City Project

SIMON BURG
BENNO ECKERT
STELLA GLIDDEN
KITTY CLYDE LEONARD
OTTO LINDIG

VIRGINIA ("SKOOTER") MILLER
JOE PAYNE
BETTY WEINHEIMER
TOM WEINHEIMER

Oral Histories from the John F. Kennedy Library

ELIE ABEL
CARL ALBERT
JOHN BADEAU
CHARLES BALDWIN
ROSS BARNETT
CHARLES BARTLETT
WILLIAM BAT
DAVID BELL
JACK BELL
BERNARD BEUTIN
JIM GRANT BOLLING

HYMAN BOOKBINDER
CHESTER BOWLES
DON BRADLEY
HENRY BRANDON
DAVID BURKE
JAMES M. BURNS
JOHN BURNS
JAMES B. CAREY
LUCIUS D. CLAY
WILLIAM CONNORS
MICHAEL DiSALLE

Margaret Dixon
William O. Douglas
Patrick Doyle
Philip Farley
James Farmer
Myer Feldman
Edward Folliard
Lawrence Fuchs
J. William Fulbright
Elizabeth Gatov
William Gaud
Albert Gore
Camille Gravel
Milton Gwirtzman
Raymond Hare
Gilbert Harrison
John F. Henning
Theodore Hesburgh
Barbara Ward Jackson
Joseph Keenan
Robert Kennedy
Roger Kent
Joseph Kraft
Arthur Krock
Theodore Kupferman
William Lawrence
Helen Lempart
Anthony Lewis
Gould Lincoln

Peter Lisagor
Katie Louchheim
John W. McCormack
David McDonald
George McGovern
James McShane
William B. Macomber, Jr.
Thurgood Marshall
Clarence Mitchell
Robert R. Nathan
Gaylord Nelson
Maurine Neuberger
Robert Notti
John Patterson
Thomas Pattison
William Proxmire
Benjamin H. Read
Arthur M. Schlesinger, Jr.
John Sharon
Hugh Sidey
George Smathers
Charles Spalding
James Symington
Stuart Symington
Robert C. Weaver
Fraser Wilkins
Donald Wilson
Albert Zack

Oral History from the Herbert Hoover Library

Lyndon Baines Johnson

Oral History from the Truman Library

Gould Lincoln

INDEX